Interactivity and the Future of the Human–Computer Interface

Pedro Isaias
Information Systems and Technology Management School, The University of New South Wales, Australia

Katherine Blashki
Victorian Institute of Technology, Australia

A volume in the Advances in Computational Intelligence and Robotics (ACIR) Book Series

Published in the United States of America by
  IGI Global
  Engineering Science Reference (an imprint of IGI Global)
  701 E. Chocolate Avenue
  Hershey PA, USA 17033
  Tel: 717-533-8845
  Fax: 717-533-8661
  E-mail: cust@igi-global.com
  Web site: http://www.igi-global.com

Library of Congress Cataloging-in-Publication Data

Names: Isaias, Pedro, editor. | Blashki, Kathy, 1961- editor.
Title: Interactivity and the future of the human-computer interface / Pedro
  Isaias and Katherine Blashki, editors.
Description: Hershey, PA : Engineering Science Reference, an imprint of IGI
  Global, 2020. | Includes bibliographical references and index. |
  Summary: "This book addresses the main issues of concern within
  interface culture and design with a particular emphasis on the design,
  development, and implementation of interfaces. It also explores the
  generational implications for design of human and technology
  interaction"-- Provided by publisher.
Identifiers: LCCN 2019042215 (print) | LCCN 2019042216 (ebook) | ISBN
  9781799826378 (hardcover) | ISBN 9781799826385 (paperback) | ISBN
  9781799826392 (ebook)
Subjects: LCSH: Human-computer interaction.
Classification: LCC QA76.9.H85 I5775 2020 (print) | LCC QA76.9.H85
  (ebook) | DDC 004.01/9--dc23
LC record available at https://lccn.loc.gov/2019042215
LC ebook record available at https://lccn.loc.gov/2019042216

This book is published in the IGI Global book series Advances in Computational Intelligence and Robotics (ACIR) (ISSN: 2327-0411; eISSN: 2327-042X)

British Cataloguing in Publication Data
A Cataloguing in Publication record for this book is available from the British Library.

For electronic access to this publication, please contact: eresources@igi-global.com.

Advances in Computational Intelligence and Robotics (ACIR) Book Series

Ivan Giannoccaro
University of Salento, Italy

ISSN:2327-0411
EISSN:2327-042X

Mission

While intelligence is traditionally a term applied to humans and human cognition, technology has progressed in such a way to allow for the development of intelligent systems able to simulate many human traits. With this new era of simulated and artificial intelligence, much research is needed in order to continue to advance the field and also to evaluate the ethical and societal concerns of the existence of artificial life and machine learning.

The **Advances in Computational Intelligence and Robotics (ACIR) Book Series** encourages scholarly discourse on all topics pertaining to evolutionary computing, artificial life, computational intelligence, machine learning, and robotics. ACIR presents the latest research being conducted on diverse topics in intelligence technologies with the goal of advancing knowledge and applications in this rapidly evolving field.

Coverage

- Computational Logic
- Artificial Life
- Robotics
- Cognitive Informatics
- Artificial Intelligence
- Computational Intelligence
- Agent technologies
- Pattern Recognition
- Synthetic Emotions
- Fuzzy Systems

IGI Global is currently accepting manuscripts for publication within this series. To submit a proposal for a volume in this series, please contact our Acquisition Editors at Acquisitions@igi-global.com or visit: http://www.igi-global.com/publish/.

Titles in this Series

For a list of additional titles in this series, please visit:
https://www.igi-global.com/book-series/advances-computational-intelligence-robotics/73674

Deep Learning Applications and Intelligent Decision Making in Egineering
Karthikrajan Senthilnathan (VIT University, India) Balamurugan Shanmugam (Quants IS & CS, India) Dinesh Goyal (Poornima Institute of Engineering and Technology, India) Iyswarya Annapoorani (VIT University, India) and Ravi Samikannu (Botswana International University of Science and Technology, Botswana)
Engineering Science Reference • © 2020 • 335pp • H/C (ISBN: 9781799821083) • US $245.00

Implementing Computational Intelligence Techniques for Security Systems Design
Yousif Abdullatif Albastaki (Ahlia University, Bahrain) and Wasan Awad (Ahlia University, Bahrain)
Information Science Reference • © 2020 • 270pp • H/C (ISBN: 9781799824183) • US $195.00

Managerial Challenges and Social Impacts of Virtual and Augmented Reality
Sandra Maria Correia Loureiro (Business Research Unit (BRU-IUL), Instituto Universitário de Lisboa (ISCTE-IUL), Lisboa, Portugal)
Engineering Science Reference • © 2020 • 318pp • H/C (ISBN: 9781799828747) • US $195.00

Innovations, Algorithms, and Applications in Cognitive Informatics and Natural Intelligence
Kwok Tai Chui (The Open University of Hong Kong, Hong Kong) Miltiadis D. Lytras (The American College of Greece, Greece) Ryan Wen Liu (Wuhan University of Technology, China) and Mingbo Zhao (Donghua University, China)
Engineering Science Reference • © 2020 • 403pp • H/C (ISBN: 9781799830382) • US $235.00

Avatar-Based Control, Estimation, Communications, and Development of Neuron Multi-Functional Technology Platforms
Vardan Mkrttchian (HHH University, Australia) Ekaterina Aleshina (Penza State University, Russia) and Leyla Gamidullaeva (Penza State University, Russia)
Engineering Science Reference • © 2020 • 355pp • H/C (ISBN: 9781799815815) • US $245.00

Handbook of Research on Fireworks Algorithms and Swarm Intelligence
Ying Tan (Peking University, China)
Engineering Science Reference • © 2020 • 400pp • H/C (ISBN: 9781799816591) • US $295.00

701 East Chocolate Avenue, Hershey, PA 17033, USA
Tel: 717-533-8845 x100 • Fax: 717-533-8661
E-Mail: cust@igi-global.com • www.igi-global.com

Editorial Advisory Board

Table of Contents

Section 3
Technical Advances

Detailed Table of Contents

Section 1
Participation and Accessibility

Chapter 1

Aline Bossi Pereira da Silva, School of Technology, University of Campinas, Brazil
Celmar Guimarães da Silva, School of Technology, University of Campinas, Brazil
Regina Lúcia de Oliveira Moraes, School of Technology, University of Campinas, Brazil

Accessibility evaluation of websites is normally done before its deployment, but there is a lack of accessibility maintenance after website evolution. This chapter hypothesizes that adopting a continuous website accessibility validation process could facilitate accessibility maintenance after each evolution. To this end, the authors adapted an accessibility evaluation tool to send periodical reports of accessibility faults to website managers. Weekly accessibility reports were sent to the website's managers and the number of accessibility faults was monitored. Besides, these managers answered questions about their awareness of the regulation and the faults found on their websites. The results suggested a notable lack of interest in regulatory compliance and a strong lack of sensitivity to disabled people's limitations.

Chapter 2

Maria Alciléia Alves Rocha, IFFluminense, Brazil
Gabriel de Almeida Souza Carneiro, IFFluminense, Brazil

Web content should suit both a general audience and visually-impaired individuals. Therefore, Web applications should be assessed against accessibility standards as Web Content Accessibility Guidelines (WCAG) and the Brazilian e-Government Accessibility Model (eMAG). This chapter presents MIAV's development process and the obtained results. The MIAV complies with the WCAG and eMAG, combining automated and user-opinion-based assessment approaches. First, a pilot test was run to fine-tune MIAV. Next, participants were asked to identify and report several accessibility issues on IFFluminense's Portal, Q-Academico, and Moodle. They then suggested enhancements for better browsing experience. AccessMonitor was run and tested the same Web pages to generate two indicators: the average accessibility index and the percentage of nonconformities by accessibility level. Results showed that none of the evaluated applications met all the accessibility criteria. These experiments allowed IFFluminense's IT degree students to raise an awareness of the significance of Web accessibility.

Chapter 3

Saulo Silva, University of Minho, Portugal
Mariana Carvalho, University of Minho, Portugal
Orlando Belo, University of Minho, Portugal

While interactive systems have the potential to increase human work performance, those systems are predisposed to usability problems. Different factors might contribute to these problems during the interaction process and as result, the decision-making process might be compromised. This work uses decision support system methods and tools to assist in the analysis of the usability of a university library website, measuring the constructs of effectiveness, efficiency, and learnability. The pilot study involved thirty-five subjects, and after collecting data, a multidimensional view of the data is created and discussed. Later, a What-if analysis is used to investigate the impact of different scenarios on system-use. The work has the potential to assist designers and system administrators at improving their systems.

Chapter 4

Vivian Varnava, University of Edinburgh, UK
Aurora Constantin, University of Edinburgh, UK
Cristina Adriana Alexandru, University of Edinburgh, UK

The use of technology-based interventions for ameliorating ASD core deficits has been growing in popularity. However, limited technologies are available that can help children with autism (aged 6 to 11) cope with changes, and these do not typically incorporate the methods used or recommended by practitioners. This project addressed this gap through the design, development and evaluation of a prototype app to support children with ASD overcome their difficulties with changes. The researchers report on preliminary work in developing this app, in which they decided not to involve children with ASD before getting some evidence that the app may be useful and suitable for them. Therefore, the design at this stage was informed by the research literature and design studies involving typically developing (TD) children, practitioners and researchers. The evaluation studies revealed that: 1) the app is easy to use; 2) the activities are perceived as fun and engaging; 3) the app may be suitable for children with ASD.

Section 2
Engagement, Immersion, and Agency

Chapter 5

Werner Walder Marin, Mackenzie Presbyterian University, Brazil
Pollyana Notargiacomo, Mackenzie Presbyterian University, Brazil

In the last decades the interest in creativity has grown. One of the questions that has risen from this interest is whether it is possible to aid the development of creativity. This chapter reviews a study on the possibility of developing a digital game with this. The game Luovus was created, utilizing previous research on the subject of creativity and digital games as learning aids. The game has been tested with a group of users and seems to be an effect on the player's self-perceived creative capabilities and society's impact on their creativity. This chapter will also cover studies and past experiments on the subject and how they can be of interest to future experiments.

Ehm Kannegieser, Fraunhofer IOSB, Germany
Daniel Atorf, Fraunhofer IOSB, Germany

Flow and immersion are states of extreme concentration on an activity. For serious games, that is games, which focus on achieving learning effects in players, high flow and immersion during gameplay can help to improve these learning effects. Both flow and immersion are currently only measured using questionnaires, which is both delayed and subjective. This work introduces a study, which aims to further the understanding of how flow and immersion are linked and to ease future work towards a new measurement method using physiological data.

Hao Wang, Department of Computer Science, National Chiao Tung University, Taiwan
Chien-Wen Ou Yang, Department of Computer Science, National Chiao Tung University, Taiwan
Chun-Tsai Sun, Department of Computer Science, National Chiao Tung University, Taiwan

In terms of digital media usage, immersion refers to user involvement in and focus on a single activity. However, the commonality of multi-tasking raises questions regarding whether one could enjoy immersion when using more than one media at the same time. Self-report questionnaires and eye trackers were used to measure the immersive experiences while playing video games and watching a television program at the same time. While we found evidence of immersion across the two activities while multitasking, some immersion dimensions were significantly weaker. However, we also noted that immersion experiences from multiple media might be cumulative. A possible explanation for our results is that the act of switching between two media compensated for any down time, users could abandon a less attractive medium and switch to the other, resulting in an impression of continuous immersion in the overall multitasking experience. On the other hand, keeping active awareness of other media beyond the current focus might be a primary cause of immersion degradation.

Hao Wang, Department of Computer Science, National Chiao Tung University, Taiwan
Wen-Wen Chen, Department of Computer Science, National Chiao Tung University, Taiwan
Chun-Tsai Sun, Department of Computer Science, National Chiao Tung University, Taiwan

To provide ideal learning environments for a wider audience, game designers must understand differences in how experienced and less experienced players learn new games. Using a sample of players with different experience levels, our goal is to understand learning processes for a simple real-time strategy game. Data from observations, post-game interviews, and eye movement recordings indicate that the majority of study participants relied on a trial-and-error approach, with more experienced gamers using a structured mental model involving feedback and expectations about making progress. Specifically, experienced gamers in the sample tended to use a top-down learning style emphasizing connections between goals and available actions, and to focus on the functions of game objects. There are also interfaces in which all experience levels of participants share the same opinion. For example, alarming voices/sound effects can catch their attention and be helpful while pop-ups are largely annoying.

Chapter 9

Mahima Maharjan, University of Tasmania, Australia
Soonja Yeom, University of Tasmania, Australia
Soo-Hyung Kim, Chonnam National University, South Korea
Si Fan, University of Tasmania, Australia

This article presents a study on emotions of students and their reactions towards learning and watching video clips with different personality traits, with the help of existing facial expression analyzing applications. To demonstrate this, the user's expressions are recorded as video while watching the movie trailer and doing the quiz. The results obtained are studied to find which emotion is most prevalent among the users in different situations. This study shows that students experience seemingly different emotions during the activity. This study explores the use of affective computing for further comprehension of student emotion in learning environments. While previous studies show that there is a positive correlation between emotion and academics, the current study demonstrated the existence of the inverse relation between them. In addition, the study of the facial analysis of movie trailer confirmed that different people have different ways of expressing the feeling. Results of the study will help to further clarify connection between various personality traits and emotions.

Chapter 10

Kenneth Chen, Drexel University, USA

Ever since MDA was publicized by Hunicke, Leblanc, and Zubek in 2004, it has become a building block for game developers and scholars. However, it has also incited several misconceptions that have spread among students and the gaming community. For example, players have overused the term "mechanics," to the point that it is virtually meaningless. On the other side, the terms "dynamics" and "aesthetics" have been comparatively neglected, despite their value. Building upon our experiences of teaching an undergraduate game design course, we argue that these misconceptions stem from the ways that consumers have misinterpreted the MDA framework. Game educators are not necessarily working with experienced designers: they are working with students who are often more passionate about playing games than making them. Thus, game educators need to target this misconception in order to shed light on preconceived biases.

Chapter 11

Arsineh Boodaghian Asl, Karlstad University, Sweden
Michel Gokan Khan, Karlstad University, Sweden

Participatory design is a technique which is being used by system designers to involve the end users and product owners throughout the design process. Even though utilizing this approach brings customers to the design process, implementing it requires a budget, a place, time, and other resources. This chapter demonstrates a model-based approach to facilitate the selection of interviews for each design phase such as listing elements for the interface, choosing location for components, making decision for the general look of the component, finally making the component interactable. Interface designers can use the model to choose different type of interview method for different design phases such as interface components, sketching, lo-fi prototyping and hi-fi prototyping, according to their resources. The research focus is on four different participatory design interview method, which are GUI-ii face-to-face, GUI-ii screen-sharing, GUI-ii Ozlab, and traditional face-to-face interview.

Chapter 12

    Mariana Michels Fontoura, Federal University of Technology - Paraná (UTFPR), Brazil
    Marília Abrahão Amaral, Federal University of Technology - Paraná (UTFPR), Brazil

The role of gender in the design of technologies has been a topic of growing importance in fields such as interaction design, HCI, and games. Understanding that technology development and usage practices emerge within the cultural processes, the authors propose in this chapter a discussion about the notions of traditional femininity, its relation to video games, as well as new approaches to female representation. It is also assessed the cultural understanding of gender, sex, and sexuality, as well as how these notions may influence the players experience. The issues discussed and briefly analyzed here point to a production and regulation of gender by technologies such as video games. Therefore, the goal is to assess how gender notions and relations influence the design and use of games in terms of visuals, narrative and sociability.

Chapter 13

    Haya Hasan AlKhatib, Prince Sultan University, Saudi Arabia
    Evi Indriasari Mansor, Prince Sultan University, Saudi Arabia
    Zainab Alsamel, Prince Sultan University, Saudi Arabia
    Joud Allam AlBarazi, Prince Sultan University, Saudi Arabia

This research aims to study the use of VR games to entertain players while teaching and improving the knowledge of Quran Tajweed for teenagers. Tajweed is an Islamic science that studies the correct recitation of the letters and words in the Qur'an. Teenagers between the ages of thirteen to eighteen were chosen for this research because it has been proven that learning at an early age ensures long-lasting knowledge, and in addition, teenagers are more capable of controlling and modifying their pronunciation. As teenagers nowadays are exposed to a variety of game technologies and their expectations and satisfaction levels are particularly high, a 3D VR game was introduced as an attractive modern solution. Viewed on HTC Vive, a 3D VR game prototype consisting of two levels was developed and evaluated by 20 teenage participants. The evaluation session resulted in a positive outcome with a few suggestions for future modifications.

Section 3
Technical Advances

Chapter 14

    Hafiz Muhammad Umair Munir, Department of Mechanical Engineering, Tokai University,
        Japan & Department of Mechatronics Engineering, National University of Sciences and
        Technology, Islamabad, Pakistan
    Waqar S. Qureshi, Department of Mechatronics Engineering, National University of
        Sciences and Technology, Islamabad, Pakistan & Robot Design and Development Lab,
        NUST College of Electrical and Mechanical Engineering, Rawalpindi, Pakistan

3D facial reconstruction is an emerging and interesting application in the field of computer graphics and computer vision. It is difficult and challenging to reconstruct the 3D facial model from a single photo because of arbitrary poses, non-uniform illumination, expressions, and occlusions. Detailed 3D facial models are difficult to reconstruct because every algorithm has some limitations related to profile view, fine detail, accuracy, and speed. The major problem is to develop 3D face with texture of large poses, wild faces, large training data, and occluded faces. Mostly algorithms use convolution neural networks and deep learning frameworks to create facial model. 3D face reconstruction algorithms used for application such as 3D printing, 3D VR games and facial recognition. Different issues, problems and their proposed solutions are discussed. Different facial dataset and facial 3DMM used for 3D face reconstructing from a single photo are explained. The recent state of art 3D facial reconstruction and 3D face learning methods developed in 2019 is briefly explained.

Analysis of multidimensional function properties is required for industrial applications. The solution of its problems is a challenge in economics, sociology, chemistry, biology, biochemistry, and other sciences. For example, the study of the potential energy surface (PES) of a free molecule is of fundamental importance in structural chemistry because it is necessary to determine the stable conformations of a molecule and the ways of interconversion between them. However, if the PES is a function of more than three rotational coordinates, the costs of its quantum-chemical calculation rapidly increases and the problem of its graphical visualization can be hardly solved for a large number of variables. This work describes how a specially developed multidimensional interpolation procedure can contribute to solve these problems. To visualize a five dimensional (5D) hypersurface, the authors applied a special coordinate system.

Preface

As our digital interactions disrupt and augment the means by which we negotiate our way through life, we are continually confronted with unprecedented opportunities to access and interact with knowledge and community. Our experiences with technologies are via interfaces of ever-increasing intelligence. These intelligent interfaces have proliferated in both numbers and function, transforming our interaction, engagement and agency with increasingly more organic and intuitive methods. Emerging technologies using artificial intelligence (AI) intuit human behaviours and gestures, and many researchers are working towards that with which humans are still struggling; understanding and responding to non-verbal communication.

Our escalating reliance on intelligent interfaces affords us the potential to fundamentally determine the ways in which we interact with each other, with our surroundings and with the technologies of the future. This transformation has already begun.

Does this digital revolution make us happier, more economically and politically stable, more inclusive, less violent? Even if we ensure that the applications we develop enable agency and increased autonomy, will such applications be available to everyone?

Significant technological developments also come with significant impact and compromise to the human condition. Much of the current technology available has required that humans adapt to the technology and have altered the ways in we work, play and communicate with each other. From the early days of research into human and machine interaction, the interface has been the focus of efforts to improve the ability of the machine to intuit the needs of the human user. Many of those innovative technologies that we embrace are developed to specifically imitate human behaviour and augment our activities.

Whilst we may be wowed by the ever-increasing sophistication of some of the latest developments in hardware and software we should be mindful of the need to remember that it is not the technology, but rather the ways in which it enables us to more meaningfully engage with the world around us, that is important.

This aggressive exploration, design and development of both immediate future and potential interactions readily encourage innovation and research.

As technology development accelerates at seemingly breakneck speed, many researchers express significant concerns for the challenges to human agency, resulting in significant impediments to our autonomy. Many citizens are fearful of the ways in which their usage and interactions with data might be exploited with the express purpose of monitoring the ways in which we choose to interact in order to exert power and control. Early childhood educators argue that the heavy reliance on technology for leisure and play activities may lead to serious deficits in cognitive and social skills. Social and political anxieties include the fear that as AI subsumes tasks previously undertaken by human labour, the resultant job loss will widen social and economic divides. Civil unrest abounds across the globe and many argue that the use of autonomous weapons, cybercrime and weaponized information create significant challenges to the well-being of society.

The apparent default setting for our society seems to be heading towards exploration and discovery rather than responding to societal needs.

Whilst technically-driven progression has the potential to impel innovation and discovery, specific end-user needs and requirements are often overlooked or completely disregarded in the pursuit of the new. With the increase in demand for intelligent technologies the human body becomes an instrument, a tool. In this future, we will wear devices, have them implanted into our bodies and allow them to monitor our every movement, feeling and gaze. Many HCI practitioners express concern for this imagined future.

2020 is a year in which we live in two worlds. Our physical reality and the digital world we inhabit through our devices. Many of us have friends all over the world with whom we share rich and meaningful relationships, yet we may not recognise them if we saw them in the street. These two worlds are currently very poorly integrated; in order to participate fully in one, we are compelled to ignore the other and thus our attention oscillates between the two. Whilst these devices provide us with access to significant amounts of information, they are remarkably inefficient at assisting us with important social and emotional aspects of being human, such as; expressing creativity, articulation of emotion and socially appropriate behaviours.

Current inputs are almost exclusively explicit; we need to type, swipe and speak to enable action. The future holds exciting possibilities for implicit inputs such as contextual surroundings, our emotional state and our behavioural and non-verbal cues.

Such interfaces and forms of interaction offer us a formidable alternative to current methods of interaction at the human-computer interface.

In addition to technical skills, those with human-centered skills, will have an important role as we plunge into the future. These are people who understand that intelligent interface technologies have the potential to profoundly transform our future in positive ways. We are ready for that future. Are you?

As ever-increasing intuition and intelligence denotes the development of interfaces, our authors utilise technological advances to illustrate the ways in which they hope to transform the ways in which humans interact with technology – from interaction to engagement. This transforms us from a passive, disempowered user to a user with agency and control.

In this collection of work from researchers around the globe, you will find research and applications utilising the latest developments in human-centered design, tools and techniques. As the reader will discover, the authors in this volume demonstrate ways in which we can use technology to enable greater creativity, community and inclusivity.

This volume, containing the work of HCI researchers and practitioners from around the globe, will have relevance for both the learner and the experienced professional. In this edited volume we hope to offer a breadth and depth of knowledge that will appeal to a diverse readership. Students in first-year undergraduate programs will gain insight into the breadth of the field and importantly, understand its importance to the ways in which we use technologies. The experienced HCI practitioner will find the specificity and depth they require for application in a wide-ranging variety of topics. Tertiary educators will find a variety of exemplars for use as case studies within the HCI classroom.

We have brought together a community of scholars for this edited volume, all of whom exploring a range of innovative methodologies, processes, technologies, tools and techniques for the design, development and support of interactivity between humans and machines.

The reader will readily discern the diversity, complexity and range of the research presented here, from developing neural networks to inspiring and supporting creativity. Much of this innovative research is already in use and has been adapted to current user populations across the globe. Other more challenging research and experimentation promises to pose some interesting conundrums for our future

We have so much to look forward to in the future of interactivity and the human-computer interface.

This volume of work is divided into three sections; Section One – Participation and Accessibility, Section Two – Immersion, Engagement and Agency and Section Three – Technical Advances. Each of these sections is further divided into individually authored chapters in which authors share their research experiences and explorations into Interactivity and the Human Computer Interface.

SECTION 1: PARTICIPATION AND ACCESSIBILITY

Accessibility requirements in the design and development of interaction are regarded by the HCI practitioner as aphoric, yet accessibility remains a significant problem in the design and development of interaction between humans and the technological systems they use to negotiate their way through work, educational and leisure activities. As the research of our contributing authors in this first section indicate, less than one percent 1% of developers take accessibility guidelines into account in their design and development. Whilst some countries, such as Brazil, have introduced legislation for enforcing inclusive practices in the development of websites, the authors in this section reveal that significant disparities remain between regulation and its implementation.

In Chapter 1, "Providing Continuous Web Accessibility Evaluation: A Case Study on the Evolution of Governmental Websites", the authors discuss a key aspect of designing for interaction. Accessibility, so often presumed, is regarded as a basic requirement of interface design. As the authors discover, many public websites require significant change to their "accessibility" if they are to provide a service that is inclusive of the needs and requirements of all users. The work of the authors reveals a considerable gap between the regulatory requirements for web accessibility in Brazil, and their subsequent implementation. From government websites we move to the education of website developers to improve the implementation of the same laws discussed in Chapter 1. The authors of Chapter 2, "An Inclusive Method to Support the Web Accessibility Assessment and Awareness-Raising: MIAV", focus on inclusive practices for students with disabilities. The authors present us with the dual issues of; the provision of accessibility on the learning platform for a cohort of students and the education of students learning to design and develop websites.

In Chapter 3, "What-If Analysis on the Evaluation of User Interface's Usability", the authors review one of the most important tools for education and research; a university library web site. Using industry standard guidelines (ISO/IEC 25066:2015), the authors offer an evaluation of the usability of a library website utilising multidimensional view and further propose the use of a data warehouse (DW) as a multidimensional data solution. The authors suggest that such a usability evaluation method has the potential to substantially improve results, by enabling the extraction of additional information from the data, thereby enriching the usability evaluation results.

The remaining research in this section offers the reader an example of the implementation of an application designed and developed for a specific user group. Chapter 4, "ChangeIt: Toward an App to Help Children With Autism Cope With Changes". In this chapter the authors discuss the benefits of technology-based interventions for ameliorating the social and communication difficulties confronting users, particularly children, on the Autism Spectrum. For users with ASD (Autism Spectrum Disorder) the lack of predictability and control associated with using technology presents challenges that may appear insurmountable. The authors offer an alternative, with an application that may assist users with ASD to improve communication skills using technology, yet without the customary distress they may have previously experienced.

SECTION 2: ENGAGEMENT, IMMERSION, AND AGENCY

This section explores the ways in which designers and developers have variously defined engagement, immersion or agency. Murray's work (1997) remains a definitive account of engagement, immersion and agency despite predating most of the technological advances discussed in this book. The authors in this section offer the reader insights into the ways in which each has battled with engagement, immersion or agency to enhance user experience.

The first chapter in this section, Chapter 5, "Creativity and Digital Games: A Study of Developing Creativity Through Digital Games", explores the creative capabilities of technology. The authors suggest that interacting with a digital game may have positive effects on the development of creativity. In addition, the authors propose the possibility that such interactions may also have an effect on the player's ability to self reflectively engage in an analysis of their own, and society's, impact on creativity.

Chapter 6, "A Study to Further Understand the Link Between Immersion and Flow", discusses the significance of these two seemingly polar opposites; immersion and flow. Whilst both are critical to successful learning, much of the available research argues that each creates an inverse response to the other. The authors argue that a correlation between the two is not only possible but also achievable.

In Chapter 7, "Measuring and Comparing Immersion in Digital Media Multitasking", the authors developed a study to address a similar issue. Focusing on the division of a user's attention between two or more media, the authors seek to understand the nature of immersion by posing a number of research questions that evaluate levels of immersion and participation.

In Chapter 8, "Play Teaches Learning? A Pilot Study on How Gaming Experience Influences New Game Learning", the authors argue that irrespective of the large body of research on the positive learning aspects of playing digital games, there is a dearth of work that seeks to understand the processes involved in learning a new game. As the authors suggest, given the number of new games entering the market and competing for user dollars, this becomes an important issue for game designers.

Chapter 9, "Affective Computing in E-Learning Modules: Comparative Analysis With Two Activities", focuses on the detection and recognition of emotional expression during the learning process. The authors discuss their use of video techniques to evaluate the emotional state of learners whilst interacting with learning material. In addition, the relationship between emotional intelligence (EI) and academic performance (AP) is examined and a significant positive association between them is discussed.

In Chapter 10, "The Fallacies of MDA for Novice Designers: Overusing Mechanics and Underusing Aesthetics", the authors discuss the vagaries of educating students' whom choose game development as a career. The authors argue, that as many of the students select game development as a career because of their passion and enthusiasm for games as their leisure activities, they approach their studies with preconceived misconceptions premised on their experience as consumers rather than creators. Students make design decisions premised on mechanics almost to the exclusion of aesthetic considerations. Game educators across the globe will readily recognise this as the hallmark of undergraduate game development students.

Arguing that designers of interfaces require a participatory design methodology whereby they can pick and choose their own hybrid versions of traditional techniques, the authors of Chapter 11, "Model-Based Interview Method Selection Approach in Participatory Design", present the reader with a mathematical model. This model will assist designers by enabling them to list their own parameters such as resources, design phases and interview methods. This will facilitate increased collaboration and engagement in the process of development by potential user groups.

In Chapter 12, "Femininities and Technologies: Gender Identities and Relations in Video Games", the authors discuss the ways in which normative gender roles, identities and relations shape the design of video games. In addition, the authors contend that perceptions of femininity are reinforced or subverted by games, as technological artefacts and are systematically affected by social, historical and cultural dynamics

With the remaining chapter in this section, we continue to focus on the social and cultural milieu in which we interact with digital games. Chapter 13, "A Study of Using VR Game in Teaching Tajweed for Teenagers", attempts to increase learning outcomes when learning Tajweed, rules for recitation of the Qur'an. As the learning of Tajweed is compulsory, the authors contend that the positive benefits of games-based learning could assist students with conceptual understanding and reinforcement of developing skills.

SECTION 3: TECHNICAL ADVANCES

The future of human interaction with intelligent interfaces is dependent upon a solid foundation of supporting infrastructure. As our encounters with intelligent interfaces continue to exponentially develop in both complexity and authenticity, the tools, networks and platforms upon which they are reliant, become crucial to our experience. The following authors contribute to this important groundwork.

In Chapter 14, "3D Single Image Face Reconstruction Approaches With Deep Neural Networks", the authors discuss the computational costs of obtaining an authentic 3D facial reconstruction. The authors offer an alternative to existing practices that rely on multiple images for input and focus on employing a single image using deep neural network architecture. Using this method, the authors suggest that the fine detail of facial form and structure, accuracy and low computational cost can be achieved.

Chapter 15, "Visualization and Minima Finding of Multidimensional Hypersurface", introduces us to multidimensional data visualisation as a method for extracting meaningful data within the chaos of seemingly limitless sources of information. As the authors argue, such a task is both complex and challenging however the resultant enhancements to human cognition enable discovery and exploration.

We hope that researchers, educators and practitioners of interactivity and HCI continue to seek opportunities to improve, enhance and support the relationships between humans and the technologies. As we move into the next decade we hope that the next generation work towards some of the challenging issues of 2020 such as; improving human collaboration across borders, develop policies and tools to ensure that digital transformation will be directed at developing our humanity and finally, transforming economic and political systems to enable humans to interact with technology in meaningful ways.

As editors we are cognisant of the privilege we have in offering the research of HCI practitioners from all over the globe in this comprehensive volume of both theoretical and applied research. We are confident that readers will find much in this volume that is both innovative and challenging. We look forward to inspiring the students of HCI, both present and potential, to explore interactivity and human-computer interaction: they are our researchers and practitioners of the Future.

The editors would like to acknowledge the help of all the people involved in this project and, more specifically, to the authors and reviewers that took part in the review process.

In addition, the editors would like to thank each of the authors for selecting this edited volume to share their research with the world. Each author contributed knowledge and time to assist in the development of this volume and without their expertise and support, this work would not have become a reality. The editors wish to acknowledge the invaluable contribution of the reviewers, each of whom contributed to improving the quality, coherence, and content of each chapter, each section, and the book as a whole.

The journey towards our future promises to be both challenging and exhilarating as we continue to evolve alongside the technologies that will assist, augment and support the communities in which we live, work and play.

Pedro Isaias

Katherine Blashki

Section 1
Participation and Accessibility

Chapter 1
Providing Continuous Web Accessibility Evaluation:
A Case Study on the Evolution of Governmental Websites

Aline Bossi Pereira da Silva
School of Technology, University of Campinas, Brazil

Celmar Guimarães da Silva
https://orcid.org/0000-0001-6112-892X
School of Technology, University of Campinas, Brazil

Regina Lúcia de Oliveira Moraes
https://orcid.org/0000-0003-0678-4777
School of Technology, University of Campinas, Brazil

ABSTRACT

Accessibility evaluation of websites is normally done before its deployment, but there is a lack of accessibility maintenance after website evolution. This chapter hypothesizes that adopting a continuous website accessibility validation process could facilitate accessibility maintenance after each evolution. To this end, the authors adapted an accessibility evaluation tool to send periodical reports of accessibility faults to website managers. Weekly accessibility reports were sent to the website's managers and the number of accessibility faults was monitored. Besides, these managers answered questions about their awareness of the regulation and the faults found on their websites. The results suggested a notable lack of interest in regulatory compliance and a strong lack of sensitivity to disabled people's limitations.

DOI: 10.4018/978-1-7998-2637-8.ch001

INTRODUCTION

Accessibility may be defined as all accessible space, building, furniture, urban equipment or element that can be reached, activated, used and experienced by anyone, including those with reduced mobility (ABNT, 2015). The term "accessible" refers to both physical and communication accessibility.

For Tanaka and Rocha (2011), accessibility on the web allows people with disabilities to assimilate web content, navigate, interact and even contribute to it. From Freire, Bittar, and Fortes (2008) technical point of view, web accessibility creates ways for all users to understand the content and interact with the website without technical restrictions.

According to Cunningham (2012), the main beneficiaries of web accessibility are people with vision, hearing or physical limitations. Regulatory compliance allows disabled people full access to websites, including those websites with complex content such as dynamic tables and menus.

The dissemination of the Brazilian government's information and services on the Internet influenced the decision to establish an accessibility regulation, contributing to the digital and social inclusion of citizens (Bach et al., 2009). Indeed, 23.9% of the Brazilian people have visual, auditory, motor or intellectual disabilities (IBGE, 2010). Besides, 6.7% of these people indicated that their respective disabilities are strong or impeditive. More precisely, they stated that they have permanent difficulty (or even cannot) seeing (even if wearing glasses), hearing (even if using a hearing aid), or walking or climbing steps; or they stated that they have some permanent mental or intellectual disability that limits their usual activities, such as working, going to school, playing, etc. (Botelho and Porciúnicula, 2018). Therefore, a significant part of these citizens may not access all information provided by non-accessible websites.

In Brazil, two laws define website accessibility as a mandatory requirement for public administration websites. They were introduced in 2000 (Laws no. 10,048 and 10,098) and they were regulated in 2004 (Decree no. 5,296). Despite these laws and regulations, after more than a decade, it is difficult to find acceptable accessibility compliance levels regarding Brazilian government's websites. Even when they have some accessibility certificate, they do not remain accessible over time.

Applying accessibility rules on websites can make web content available for all users, including people with a disability or temporary limitation. Currently, there are tools available for testing the adherence of websites to these rules. However, professionals responsible for website maintenance usually run these tests only once, at the end of the development process. Afterward, constant changes implemented daily by users tend to insert accessibility faults. After these changes, people responsible for maintaining the websites often do not revalidate their websites, using neither an expert's review nor specific tools. This lack of website evaluation process avoids meeting accessibility standards and may cause a regression in website quality.

Aware of this problem, the goal of this work is to test the hypothesis that adopting a continuous accessibility validation process will allow keeping them accessible, despite maintenance and modifications made throughout its existence. In order to test this hypothesis, the authors enhanced an accessibility evaluation tool for doing this kind of validation. This tool runs experiments that help to continually test the accessibility faults along with the website's maintenance phase.

Considering the experiments, the authors run tests in two samples, aiming to identify the faults inserted or corrected during website maintenance procedures. After that, the authors sent an email with a questionnaire to the focused website managers. The results show that feeding the website maintainers with data about accessibility tools was not enough for engaging them in a process of accessibility enhancement.

Therefore, the researchers concluded that there is a gap between the existence of accessibility laws and the real interest of governmental institutions in implementing them.

This work is organized as follows: the next section presents the main web accessibility concepts and related works; in sequence, the research methodology is presented, followed by the experiments' results and discussions; the final sections point out future research directions and conclude the work.

It is worth noting that this chapter is an extended version of a previous work of the authors (Silva, Silva, & Moraes, 2019).

BACKGROUND AND RELATED WORK

This section comprises two parts. The first one presents accessibility guidelines and evaluation. The second presents the web accessibility evaluation types and some tools available, summarizing works related to accessibility during website evolution.

Accessibility Guidelines and Evaluation

The Web Content Accessibility Guidelines - WCAG 2.0 were considered for the tests of this research. The Web Accessibility Initiative (WAI), a W3C research group, was responsible for creating the WCAG. According to Flor (2009), in May 1999, W3C published the WCAG 1.0, and in 2008, W3C updated the recommendations to WCAG 2.0. Therefore, it is indicated that web accessibility policies refer to WCAG 2.0. The latest version of the accessibility guidelines was released on July 5th, 2018 and it is called WCAG 2.1.

Aizpurua et al. (2009) indicate that the WAI group presented a WCAG 2.0 version to overcome some restrictions of the WCAG 1.0. Besides, version 2.0 also covered the new technologies that constitute the actual web. It is also more understandable and facilitates automatic testing.

About the organization, just like WCAG 1.0, the new version is organized into three levels called A, AA and AAA. Level A includes recommendations that are important for accessibility. AA level includes the best accessibility adaptations, and AAA level includes recommendations that, if met, will improve the accessibility of the evaluated project.

Tangarife and Mont'Alvão (2005) reported that the e-government accessibility model for the Brazilian government (e-MAG) is a recommendation to make accessibility fit the reality of Brazilian websites. According to the official document, the last version of the e-MAG guideline is 3.0. It is based on WCAG 2.0, and was launched in December 2008 considering the new research on web accessibility.

This version extends WCAG 2.0 by adding new success criteria, definitions to support them, guidelines to organize the additions, and a couple of additions to the conformance section.

Related to the accessibility evaluation, there are different ways to evaluate the accessibility of a website. Vu, Tuan and Phan (2012) highlighted the differences between automatic, semi-automatic and manual evaluation. The automatic evaluation considers the client-side and displays the non-conformity and suggestions to fix the faults. Semi-automatic tools require a personal intervention and accessibility knowledge as it is necessary to interpret the textual recommendation and to identify the items not included in the tool report.

Website accessibility monitoring can be done in different ways, either in real-time, regular intervals or in specific stages of website development. Fong and Meng (2009) stated that governmental websites represent not only a public image but also a reliable service platform for many users. The authors presented the best practices, models, tools and techniques for measuring, monitoring, and maximizing the efficiency and effectiveness of e-government services. They also created a web-based system to monitor the performance and state of public services in real-time, highlighting the phase of monitoring as an essential phase of the development life cycle of a web system.

There are several tools to validate website accessibility. DaSilva (Acessibilidade Brasil, 2017) was the first tool available to analyze the accessibility of Portuguese language websites. The recommendations considered by the tool are based on the principles of WCAG 1.0 and 2.0 (W3C) and the Brazilian recommendations (e-MAG), allowing the analysis of all website pages and indicating the non-conformity with the recommendations. The validator VaMoLà (VaMoLà Project, 2010) automatically verifies some accessibility requirements based on the recommendations of WCAG 2.0 and the requirements of Italian laws. Tanaguru (Océane Consulting, 2014) is a website accessibility assessment tool that tests the recommendations of WCAG 2.0, Section 508 (United States) and AccessiWeb. The AChecker tool (Inclusive Design Institute, 2011) checks individual HTML pages for compliance to accessibility standards. The tool supports the international recommendations WCAG 1.0 and 2.0, and regional recommendations such as BITV 1.0 (Germany), Section 508 (United States) and Stanca Act (Italy).

Accessibility and Website Evolution

The investigation of the accessibility during the evolution of websites and the study about the low adhesion to the accessibility regulations have been an important target pursued by several research projects.

Santana and Paula (2013) performed accessibility tests considering two samples. The first one is composed of a selection of 1,000 websites, which have been chosen in a ranking that classifies websites based on their quality (popular websites). The second sample is a random selection of 1,000 websites. Considering the random sample, 14.89% (around 148 websites) are accessible (i.e., compliant with the Web Content Accessibility Guidelines (WCAG) 2.0 guidelines); considering the sample with popular websites, only 4.34% (around 43 websites) are accessible. The authors conclude that the higher accessibility non-conformance in popular websites is due to their dynamic contents, given that constant changes can increase the number of accessibility faults.

İşeri, Uyar, and İlhan (2017) performed accessibility tests in websites of 38 higher education institutions of Cyprus Island. The analysis is related to compliance with the WCAG 2.0. Considering this sample, the authors conclude that none of the evaluated websites are error free and most of them do not achieve an acceptable web accessibility compliance level.

Menzi-Cetin et al. (2017) performed a study on usability with visually impaired students using university websites that inform them about the opportunities and events taking place on campus. According to the results, finding the final exam dates on the academic calendar posed major difficulties, and accessing the course schedule web page was the task that required the most time. The test results indicated the need for a search engine on each page, a text version for all pages, rearrangement of the web link sequences with tabs, and more information about visual resources. The studies concluded that not only accessibility can indicate a good experience for users, but usability is important as well, especially for people with disabilities.

Some works focus on governmental websites. Ferreira, Chauvel, and Ferreira (2007) presented an accessibility study based on the websites of Brazilian public organizations. According to the law, these websites must be compliant with the W3C accessibility rules (WCAG) and the Brazilian recommendations (e-MAG). The work evaluates the degree of adherence of these websites to those accessibility guidelines. The authors realized that the number of websites that comply with those guidelines decreased, which may happen due to the difficulty of keeping websites accessible when they are constantly updated.

Other countries have low rates of accessibility in governmental websites as well. Shah and Shakya (2007) presented a work that evaluated 27 Nepal governmental websites. They observed very low compliance with the recommendations as only 11.1% of the websites complies with the regulations. The authors concluded that Nepal, in 2006, needed to make an effort to improve the website accessibility.

Luján-Mora, Navarrete, and Peñafiel (2014) also addressed the lack of accessibility on governmental websites. They indicate that these sites are not always ready to provide services to people with disabilities. These authors evaluated the accessibility of a group of e-government websites from all South America countries and Spain. Based on the results obtained, they observed that all evaluated websites presented some accessibility problems.

Al-Soud and Nakata (2010) evaluated 30 Jordanian governmental websites in terms of accessibility, usability, transparency and agility. The results show low adherence to the accessibility rules and concluded that people involved in the project are not sufficiently aware of the accessibility guidelines (i.e. there is a lack of training).

Acosta, Acosta-Vargas and Luján-Mora (2018) evaluated the accessibility of e-Government interactive services offered by two official entities of the Latin America countries considering the WCAG 2.0. The Latin America countries considered are: Argentina, Bolivia, Brazil, Chile, Colombia, Costa Rica, Cuba, Dominican Republic, Ecuador, El Salvador, Guatemala, Guayana, Haiti, Honduras, Mexico, Nicaragua, Panama, Paraguay, Peru, Suriname, Uruguay and Venezuela. French Guiana has not been considered because it is a France territory. The results of this research show that none of the evaluated websites which offer e-government services meet an acceptable level of accessibility. Additionally, several recommendations are presented to correct all accessibility errors detected in the analyzed web page. These recommendations can be applied to websites worldwide to achieve universal access to eGovernment websites.

Freire, Russo and Fortes (2008) conducted an exploratory research that comprises the application of a questionnaire that covered the 27 Brazilian states. The authors suggested that the existence of accessibility faults in the website is due to the lack of professional training and information by those responsible for the website development and test. This is the same suggestion presented in the Santana and Paula (2013) study, which also pointed to the same reason, i.e. the lack of professional training. The authors concluded that between 85 up to 95% of the focused websites present accessibility faults.

RESEARCH METHODOLOGY

To define the research methodology, firstly, the authors visited the publication available in the literature and selected the ones that bring some background and work more closely related to the authors' goals. Works addressing accessibility and website evolution, accessibility evaluation, and tools and accessibility guidelines and standards were selected for a more detailed read. A summary of those works made up the Background and Related Work section of this work. The selected works brought some ideas to the experiment design, and showed us the prevalence of WCAG guidelines in both evaluation work and implementation by tools. They also gave us a list of potential tools that could be considered for adaptation, as they provide a good accessibility evaluation but they are not able to automatically and continuously evaluate the websites to check the guidelines compliance after evolution.

Based on the knowledge brought by the literature, our decision was to adapt a tool for the continuous system monitoring regarding the accessibility assessment based on WCAG. As mentioned before, there are some efficient tools for system monitoring by demand. The reuse of one of them for accessibility continuous assessment is more appropriate due to the complexity embedded in the accessibility checking. Developing a new tool from scratch would demand significant time beyond the risk of having a worse tool than the available ones. Moreover, this adaptation should include a feature to notify the websites' owner when accessibility rules are broken.

The next decision was related to the selection of the websites as well as the design of the experiments. The first criterion was to choose only governmental websites, because there is a national law (the decree no. 5,296) that requires these websites to comply with both WCAG and e-MAG guidelines. Therefore, those responsible for these websites should be more concerned with the guidelines compliance. As already discussed, the goal of this research is to test whether adopting a continuous accessibility validation process over time (i.e. considering website evolution) helps to maintain a website accessible. The second criterion, applied to the first sample, is to compose the first case study with governmental websites that had already undergone accessibility tests. This last criterion was not applied to the second sample; the second use case was thought to test many of governmental websites and the decision was to select the City Halls' websites of the State of São Paulo.

The experiment design for both use cases consisted of splitting the selected websites into two groups, a test group and a control group. In addition to the tests, questionnaires were applied. In the second use case, some participants received a phone call complementing the research.

The next sections present more details of these decisions: benchmarking the existing tools for our purposes (tool selection), the description of the selected tool adaptation, and the samples selection. The issues related to the experiments are presented in the Case Studies Section.

The Tool Selection

The main characteristic of the tool to be selected is its license type, which must be open source. For the development of this work, it was imperative the tool can be developed in a collaborative public manner; the source code should be available for studies; and modifications and redistribution of the software to anyone and for any purpose must be allowed. Table 1 shows a list of tools cited in related work that are open source license or free software or both.

Considering the tools presented, both VaMoLà (VaMoLà Project, 2010) and AChecker (Institute for Inclusive Design, 2011) fit the project requirements. VaMoLà considers the WCAG 2.0 recommendations and it is customized to Italian law. The AChecker tool can test universal recommendations (WCAG 1.0 and WCAG 2.0), enabling more global information testing reports.

Additionally, the AChecker tool suggests possible corrections to fix the accessibility faults found. This feature can be considered a support for the training process, minimizing the weaknesses highlighted by some authors (Al-Khalifa and Al-Khalifa, 2011 and Bailey and Pearson, 2010). Therefore, the AChecker tool was selected to be adapted as it fulfills the requirements of this work.

Table 1. Tool comparison

Tool	Guideline	Platform	License
DaSilva	WCAG 1.0 WCAG 2.0 e-MAG	Web	Free Software
VaMoLà	WCAG 2.0 Allegato	Web	Free Software and Open Source
Tanaguru	WCAG 2.0 Section 508 AccessiWeb	Web	Open Source
AChecker	WCAG 1.0 WCAG 2.0 Section 508 Stanca act BITV 1.0	Web	Free Software and Open Source

The Tool Adaptation

The process of adapting the AChecker tool to enable it to perform a continuous assessment involves changing the tool's database structure and source code. This section summarizes this process.

The implementation of website monitoring in AChecker periodically executes an accessibility evaluation and informs the evaluation outcomes for the professionals responsible for the website. The authors added to AChecker a "Monitor" tab that groups the continuous accessibility assessment features. Some screens of the tool are available in Appendix 1.

A user that wants to register a website for accessibility monitoring must provide the title and URL of the website that will be registered. In addition, he may define the address that will receive accessibility assessment notifications, the period between two consecutive assessments, and the guidelines to be considered in the evaluation that can be BITV 1.0 (Level 2), Section 508, Stanca Act, WCAG 1.0 (Level A, AA and AAA), WCAG 2.0 (Level A, AA and AAA).

The evaluation starts on the day registration was complete, and this date is used as the starting point for the other executions according to the configured period. In every evaluation, the tool stores the assessment results in the database. They can be accessed later through the tool and through a link sent in the email configured to receive information from the tests.

AChecker has a relational database structure managed by MySQL (version 5.6.23), a database management system which uses SQL statements. The tools' original database structure consists of 32 tables. The tables added to transform AChecker into a continuous assessment tool were: AC_monitor, AC_monitor_period, AC_monitor_result_errors, and AC_monitor_result. The AC_monitor_period table stores the configured periods between assessments. The AC_monitor table stores information about the evaluated website, accessibility assessment settings, options, and the period. The AC_monitor_result_errors table stores all information related to checking for failed guideline items. In addition, when an image inserted in the code has accessibility issues, its access address is also stored in this table. The AC_monitor_result table stores the total scan results. For each assessment, the tool inserts only one record in this table. This table stores information about the guideline and the website under evaluation. Potential errors and user actions to deal with an error are also stored in this table.

Concerning the programming structure, the original tool follows object-oriented programming development patterns. The tool adaptation added some classes responsible for maintaining the tracked website registrations, maintaining period records, and error checking and storing.

To create or edit a website record for monitoring, the authors added new pages to transform the AChecker tool into a continuous assessment tool. They enable users to create or edit a period using a form. A preview page gathers all the results that are stored in the system database related to the evaluations. Thus, users may see a rating history of each site at any time on the page. For automation of accessibility testing, the tool configures a "cron" task on the server.

The Samples Selection

As previously mentioned, the governmental websites were chosen because it is assumed that they must comply the Brazilian accessibility laws (under the decree no. 5,296), effective since December, 2004. For the first case study the chosen website are the ones that were previously evaluated by the Clareou website (Santos and Bastos, 2007), which classifies the websites based on their accessibility level. Therefore, 21 websites from the government category considered accessible by the Clareou website were selected to compose this first case study.

In the second case study we considered a larger number of governmental websites related to the City Hall's websites of the State of São Paulo. In this case, the authors run a previous evaluation of these websites with the support of the enhanced version of AChecker tool. This first evaluation intended to record the existent accessibility faults to compare to the evaluation results over time. The initial sample has 645 websites that were submitted to accessibility tests for 45 days.

CASE STUDIES

This section presents the experiments to validate the enhanced version of the AChecker tool as well as test our hypothesis that adopting a continuous accessibility validation process over time (i.e. considering website evolution) helps to maintain a website's accessibility.

Use Case 1: Experiments Using the First Sample

Although Clareou classified the 21 websites used in the first sample as free of accessibility faults, the researchers submitted them to a new test supported by the adapted AChecker tool. The goal of this preliminary test was to reinforce the quality of the website under the analysis of the AChecker tool, aiming to avoid discrepancies between the implementation of both tools which could impact the results. In addition, there was a lack of guarantee that the classification provided by the Clareou refers to the last version of the focused websites. This procedure showed appropriate since there were seven unavailable websites (some files were not found and errors were displayed) and two websites did not show accessibility failures. Those nine websites were removed from the test.

After capturing data from the remaining 12 websites, half of them (called Group 1) were selected to receive weekly emails informing the research context, the accessibility failures found and suggesting how to fix the corresponding faults.

Table 2. Initial and final failure analysis of Group 1 of first sample

	First week results	Last week results	Difference between total initial failures and total final failures	
Website 1	376	351	-25	-6.65%
Website 2	600	703	103	17.17%
Website 3	218	218	0	0.00%
Website 4	441	452	11	2.49%
Website 5	823	282	-541	-65.74%
Website 6	392	409	17	4.34%

The reason for choosing half of the sample was to create a control group of websites (called Group 2). It would help to verify if the awareness about the accessibility faults would influence the accessibility improvement, allowing a comparison between the awareness and the unawareness of the accessibility faults.

For 30 weeks, the experiments were performed checking 6 websites and registering the number of accessibility failures found in each week to each website for further analysis.

Use Case 1: Experiment Results

In the first sample, after testing websites from Group 1 (6 governmental websites) with the adapted AChecker tool, the results obtained were compared with the results of the training period (i.e. the period before the emails were sent to the website managers). Table 2 shows the comparative results between the total initial failures and total final failures of Group 1. It was observed that there was a decrease in the number of failures in 34% of the websites tested, no changes in 16% of them, and an increase in 50% of them (as summarized in Table 4). Observing the results in more detail, only one website presented a significant decrease of 65.74% in the accessibility failures. On the other hand, the highest increase was 17.17% in another website.

Still in the first sample, considering the websites in Group 2 (no email was sent to the managers of this sample) and the same test period (training and 30-weeks experiment period), it was observed that in 60% of the websites the accessibility failures decreased while there was an increase in 40% of them. It is important to highlight that, although the percentage of websites with a decrease in the number of failures is significantly higher than the websites of Group 1, only one website presented an expressive decrease while the others had a very small decrease. During the Group 2 testing, one website was unstable

Table 3. Initial and final failure analysis of Group 2 of first sample

	First week results	Last week results	Difference between total initial failures and total final failures	
Website 1	485	479	-6	-1.24%
Website 2	87	90	3	3.45%
Website 3	769	565	-204	-26.53%
Website 4	374	369	-5	-1.34%
Website 5	1001	1092	91	9.09%

Table 4. Comparison of failure results

	Group 1	Group 2
Decreased	34%	60%
Increased	16%	0%
Remained	50%	40%

and could not be tested. Table 3 shows the comparative results between the total initial failures and total final failures of Group 2, and Table 4 presents the results of each tested group.

Use Case 2: Experiments Using the Second Sample

The websites of this group (the City Halls' websites of the State of São Paulo) were submitted to a preliminary test to check their accessibility level. During the preliminary tests, the number of accessibility failures was recorded for each website in order to compare with the data captured during the 45-days test period. During this period, the adapted AChecker tool sent emails to the website managers to make them aware that the accessibility failures were found.

After the preliminary test period, the websites were grouped considering the size-based distribution of cities according to the last IBGE census, which considered that 88.3% of São Paulo cities are classified as small cities, 10.3% as medium cities and 1.4% as large and metropolis cities (IBGE, 2010). First, the 645 websites were divided into two groups (one of them the control group), and one of them was divided into 3 groups (the ones submitted to accessibility tests), summing up four groups. So, the tested groups were composed of 99 websites each, randomly selected, preserving the distribution previously mentioned (i.e. 88 small cities, 10 medium cities and 1 large city). The groups have no intersection, i.e., each website belongs to only one group.

On different dates, each group was set up to receive emails reporting the research context, the accessibility failures found by the AChecker tool and the suggestion to fix the corresponding faults. The emails were sent weekly for 30 weeks. After 30-weeks testing, all managers of the tested websites received a questionnaire. It highlighted the importance of accessibility and the main goal of the research (i.e., to investigate whether governmental websites take into consideration the WCAG 2.0 recommendations). It also invited them to answer a set of questions related to the awareness of this context and of the emails that were sent. This questionnaire is available in Appendix 1.

In addition to the questionnaire, as a complimentary evaluation, 2.5% of the tested websites of the second sample and 2.5% of untested websites were randomly selected to receive a direct contact (via phone) to understand the accessibility training level, as well as to invite them to participate in the research by answering the questionnaire.

Use Case 2: Experiment Results

After capturing the initial data (training period), the adapted AChecker started to send a weekly email to the website managers of the websites under test. The email reported the accessibility failures found, their severity and suggestions for corrections. Table 5 presents the results of each group. Note that the fourth group is the group of 321 websites that did not receive emails. It is possible to observe that the

Table 5. Comparative failure statistics

	Group 1	Group 2	Group 3	Group 4*
Decreased	44%	41%	47%	48%
Increased	38%	40%	43%	39%
Remained	18%	19%	10%	13%

* Group 4 is the Control Group, that received no email.

results are very similar, with a decreasing percentage varying from 41 up to 48%, an increasing percentage from 38 up to 43%, and 10 up to 19% remained stable. Based on these results, it was not possible to identify a significant difference among the groups, even considering the group that received no email.

After the experiment periods of each group, a questionnaire was sent by email to 297 website managers twice a week for 9 weeks. Amongst those, 2.5% of the websites that received the failures' notifications were randomly chosen and 2.5% of the websites that received no emails were directly contacted (by phone). The purpose of this contact was to raise the awareness of the website managers related to the research and accessibility issues. The results obtained in this stage were the following:

- 10% of the emails sent with the questionnaire attached were opened (30 emails)
- 1% of the emails sent were triggered (3 emails)
- 12.79% of the emails received requested removal of the mailing list (38 emails)
- 5.05% of the emails received answered the questionnaires (15 emails)
- 1.34% of the emails were answered after direct contact (phone) (4 emails).

The websites that received emails and phone calls (8 websites) presented the following results before the calls:

- 75% are interested but asked to forward the email to someone else (6 websites)
- 12.5% have no interest in the research (1 website)
- 12.5% had already received the questionnaire and reports (1 website).

The same websites after the phone call, when they were re-invited to answer the questionnaire by phone, returned the following:

- 25% answered the questionnaire after the call (2 websites)
- 75% did not respond to the questionnaire even after the call (6 websites).

Other eight websites that were untested (i.e. received no email) when directly contacted returned by phone the following results:

- 62.5% are interested in receiving the notifications and the questionnaire (5 websites)
- 37.5% have no interest in the research (3 websites).

Figure 1. The knowledge about Brazilian regulations

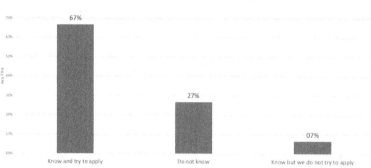

Figure 2. Sources of improvements

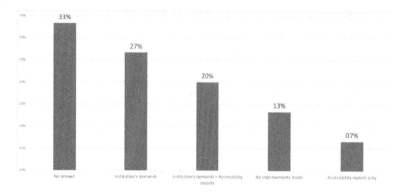

Figure 3. Reasons of remained accessibility faults

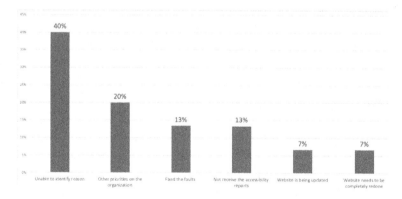

The emails with the questionnaire in attachment were sent to the website managers, and after the call, the results obtained are as follows:

- 25% answered the questionnaire after the call (2 websites)
- 75% did not answer the questionnaire even after the call (6 websites).

Figure 4. The usefulness of receiving the reports

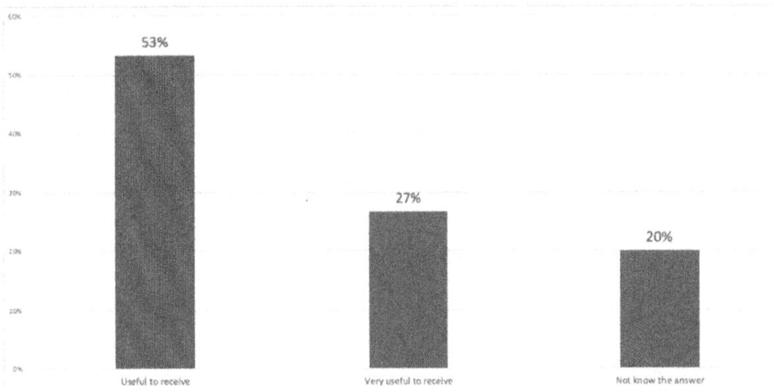

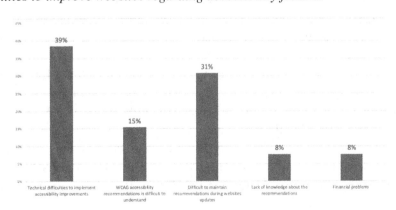

According to the received questionnaire answers (15 answers), the results indicate that 66.7% of the website managers are aware of the law and tried to apply it, only 26.7% have no knowledge about the laws and 6.6% are aware of the law but are unable to apply it. Figure 1 presents this result.

Considering the participants involved in the previous phase of the experiment, 60% regularly received the accessibility reports generated by the AChecker tool during the whole preliminary test period. Regarding the website improvements during the evaluated period (December 2016 to March 2017), 33% of respondents were unable to justify accessibility improvements made on their website; 26.7% said that the website improvements are due to other institution demands; 13% answered that no improvements were done; 20% stated that the website improvements were done to attend the institution demands and the faults reported by AChecker tool as well; and only 6.7% reported that the improvements were made considering only the report of failures sent by the AChecker tool. These results are presented in Figure 2.

When the managers were asked about the reason why the websites remained with accessibility faults, 40% of them were not able to identify the reason, 20% reported that there were other priorities in the organization, 13.3% answered that they did not receive the accessibility reports that were sent during the experiment period, 6.7% reported that the website was being updated, 6.7% admitted that the website needs to be completely redone and this task will be completed soon, and only 13.4% answered that they fixed the faults responsible by the failures. Figure 3 presents these results.

Figure 5. Difficulties to improve websites regarding accessibility failures

Figure 6. Relative reduction of accessibility failures of second sample

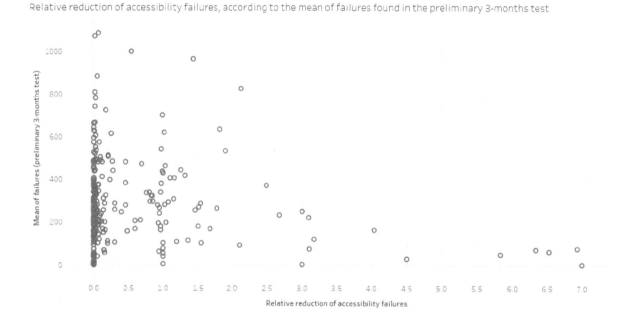

Regarding the usefulness of receiving the reports to make accessibility improvements, 80% of the participants thought it was useful to receive them and 20% of them did not know how to answer this question. These results are presented in Figure 4. Moreover, 86.7% of the respondents told us that they would like to continue receiving the accessibility reports.

When questioned about the difficulty of adopting accessibility rules, 38.5% of respondents indicated that there are technical difficulties in implementing accessibility improvements, followed by 30.8%, which reported that it was difficult to maintain recommendations during website updates. WCAG accessibility recommendations are difficult to understand to 15.4% of the respondents, 7.7% complained about financial problems, and 7.6% indicated a lack of knowledge about the recommendations. Figure 5 presents these results.

The failure data shown in Figures 6 and 7 provide an overview of what potentially happened during the monitoring period of the second sample. It also tries to identify if any effort to solve the accessibility issues was made during this period. In this case, the websites considered were the ones that receive notifications with accessibility recommendations to fix and presented an increase or reduction in the number of failures. Considered this sample, the data were normalized to the average of failures in the preliminary 3-months test.

In Figure 6, the value on the X-axis represents the multiplication factor to find the reduction of accessibility failures according to the failures found in the preliminary 3-months test (Y-axis). This graph shows an expressive number of websites clustered around multiplication factor 1. This fact indicates that the same amount of failures found in the preliminary test has been resolved. However, this information is not enough to conclude that failures were totally solved because other failures may have been inserted.

It is possible to observe that many websites have had almost no effort to fix the faults (points near multiplication factor 0). Besides, about 37 sites (out of 285) corrected more failures than the ones initially

Figure 7. Insertions and reductions of accessibility failures of second sample

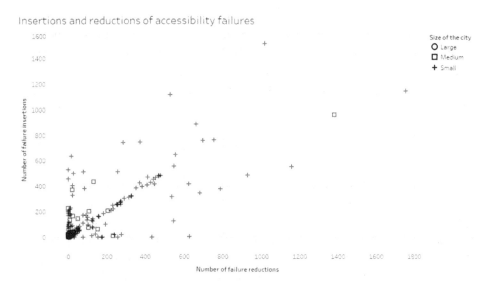

found (points over the value 1.0). Finally, some sites had few failures initially and it was corrected up to 7 times the total of failures initially found.

Figure 7 represents the absolute error reduction compared with the absolute error insertion. The diagonal concentration of dots represents websites that solved the same amount of failures that were found initially. Dots below the main diagonal indicate websites that reduced more failures than those that were found at the beginning of the experiment. On the other hand, dots above the main diagonal refer to the websites that reduced fewer failures than those found in the beginning.

This analysis unveiled the need of monitoring each failure of the websites instead of the number of failures only. Identifying, classifying and tracking each accessibility failure individually would help to measure its life-time, as well as the classes of failures in which managers focus their solving efforts.

FUTURE RESEARCH DIRECTIONS

This work evaluated governmental websites, which should be accessible due to accessibility laws. A possible future work is to assess non-governmental websites in order to identify the knowledge and interest of other areas in relation to the accessibility. In addition, it is possible to include the Brazilian recommendations (e-MAG) in the tool for a more comprehensive evaluation of the Brazilian scenario.

It is highly recommended the implementation of a translation package for the tool to allow Portuguese speakers to better understand the failure's description and their links with the recommendations. This suggestion is based on the questionnaire applied, in which one of the answers showed that 15.4% of respondents have considerable difficulty in understanding the WCAG accessibility recommendations.

CONCLUSION

The web is characterized as an important way of communication that promotes a quick movement of information without people having to move physically. But the lack of accessibility on websites makes it difficult for disabled people to navigate and interact with those websites and contribute to them. Accessibility barriers can appear on websites in all stages of their development and especially after their publication. In fact, daily changes and the insertion of contents by the users tend to add accessibility faults in the website. If these changes are not revalidated (e.g. with the support of accessibility tools), the website will be no longer compliant with accessibility standards.

The goal of this work was to test the hypothesis that adopting a continuous accessibility validation process in websites would allow keeping them accessible, despite maintenance and modifications made throughout its existence. The results of our experimental analysis provided strong evidences that this hypothesis is incorrect, at least in the context of Brazilian governmental websites.

This work evaluated two samples of Brazilian governmental websites. The first one consisted of 21 websites in the government category, presented by Clareou as compliant with its accessibility guidelines. The second sample considered 645 City Hall websites of the cities of São Paulo, Brazil, selected on IBGE Cidades (IBGE, 2010).

Analyzing the results of the evaluation enables to conclude that public Brazilian institutions still have a lack of interest in accessibility issues. This happens even after the regulation of Decree no. 5,296 in December 2004, which established a period of 12 months for public administration websites of public interest or government-funded institutions to comply with those recommendations. On the first and second samples, the evaluated websites had low adherence to accessibility standards. When website managers were notified of the problem by email describing the failures and solutions to fix them, it was observed no interest by the majority of the managers, even after 7 months of monitoring. Unfortunately, the effort to report the failures and guide the managers to fix the faults did not work, as the behavior of the notified websites manager and the ones that were not notified were quite similar.

Considering the institutions that were inquired by phone about the research, only 6.7% indicated that the improvements were made as a result of the indications in the report sent by the system. Another 20% reported that there was a lack of priority for these improvements over other tasks. The others considered helpful to receive the reports or advised that they wanted to continue receiving the accessibility reports. However, they did not put any effort to fix the faults.

In addition, it is concluded that there was difficulty in reaching responsible for the information of the institution on the Internet. In particular, the group of institutions that had direct contacts (telephone calls) could not even identify the person responsible for responding to the evaluation questionnaire.

Based on the results, it is possible to assume that the low adherence to the research was due to the lack of priority in the application of Decree no. 5296, which requires that the websites must be accessible. Besides, if an employee participates in the survey and informs that accessibility is not enforced as demanded in regulated laws, he would be admitting to being negligent in their functional responsibility. There was a noticeable lack of interest in the issue of accessibility on websites, even though this is a legal requirement on governmental websites.

REFERENCES

ABNT (Associação Brasileiras de Normas Técnicas). (2004). *ABNT NBR 9050: Acessibilidade a edificações, mobiliário, espaços e equipamentos urbanos.*

Acessibilidade Brasil. (2017). *DaSilva - Avaliador de Acessibilidade para Websites.* Retrieved from http://www.dasilva.org.br

Acosta, T., Acosta-Vargas, P., & Luján-Mora, S. (2018, April). Accessibility of eGovernment Services in Latin America. In *Proceedings of the 2018 International Conference on eDemocracy & eGovernment (ICEDEG)* (pp. 67-74). IEEE. 10.1109/ICEDEG.2018.8372332

Aizpurua, A., Arrue, M., Vigo, M., & Abascal, J. (2009). Transition of accessibility evaluation tools to new standards. In *Proceedings of the 2009 International Cross-Disciplinary Conference on Web Accessibility* (W4A) (pp. 36-44). ACM. 10.1145/1535654.1535662

Al-Khalifa, A. S., & Al-Khalifa, H. S. (2011). An educational tool for generating inaccessible page examples based on WCAG 2.0 failures. In *Proceedings of the International Cross-Disciplinary Conference on Web Accessibility* (p. 30). ACM. 10.1145/1969289.1969328

Al-Khalifa, H. S., Al-Kanhal, M., Al-Nafisah, H., Al-Soukaih, N., Al-Hussain, E., & Al-Onzi, M. (2011). A pilot study for evaluating Arabic websites using automated WCAG 2.0 evaluation tools. In *Proceedings of the 2011 International Conference on Innovations in Information Technology* (pp. 293-296). IEEE. 10.1109/INNOVATIONS.2011.5893835

Al-Soud, A. R., & Nakata, K. (2010). Evaluating e-government websites in Jordan: Accessibility, usability, transparency and responsiveness. In *Proceedings of the 2010 IEEE International Conference on Progress in Informatics and Computing* (Vol. 2, pp. 761-765). IEEE. 10.1109/PIC.2010.5688017

Bach, C. F., Ferreira, S. B. L., Silveira, D. S., & Nunes, R. R. (2009). Diretrizes de acessibilidade: uma abordagem comparativa entre WCAG e e-MAG. *Revista Eletrônica de Sistemas de Informação, 8*(1).

Bailey, C., & Pearson, E. (2010). An educational tool to support the accessibility evaluation process. In *Proceedings of the 2010 International Cross Disciplinary Conference on Web Accessibility (W4A)* (p. 12). ACM. 10.1145/1805986.1806003

Bailey, C., & Pearson, E. (2011). Development and trial of an educational tool to support the accessibility evaluation process. In *Proceedings of the International Cross-Disciplinary Conference on Web Accessibility* (p. 2). ACM. 10.1145/1969289.1969293

Botelho, L., & Porciúncula, K. (2018). Os desafios para a produção de indicadores sobre pessoa com deficiência - ontem, hoje e amanhã. [The challenges for producing indicators on people with disability - yesterday, today and tomorrow]. In Panorama nacional e internacional da produção de indicadores sociais: grupos populacionais específicos e uso do tempo [National and International Overview of Social Indicator Production: Specific Population Groups and Time Use]. IBGE, Brazilian Institute of Geography and Statistics. Retrieved from https://biblioteca.ibge.gov.br/visualizacao/livros/liv101562.pdf

Cunningham, K. (2012). *Accessibility Handbook: Making 508 Compliant Websites.* O'Reilly Media, Inc.

de Santana, V. F., & de Paula, R. A. (2013, May). Web accessibility snapshot: an effort to reveal coding guidelines conformance. In *Proceedings of the 10th International Cross-Disciplinary Conference on Web Accessibility* (p. 2). ACM. 10.1145/2461121.2461144

Ferreira, S. B. L. (2007). E-acessibilidade: tornando visível o invisível. *Revista Morpheus – Estudos Interdisciplinares em Memória Social, 6*(10).

Flor, C. S. (2012). Diagnóstico da acessibilidade dos principais museus virtuais disponíveis da internet [Master thesis]. Centro Tecnológico, Universidade Federal de Santa Catarina.

Fong, S., & Meng, H. S. (2009, November). A web-based performance monitoring system for e-government services. In *Proceedings of the 3rd International Conference on Theory and Practice of Electronic Governance* (pp. 74-82). ACM. 10.1145/1693042.1693058

Freire, A. P., Bittar, T. J., & Fortes, R. P. (2008). An approach based on metrics for monitoring web accessibility in Brazilian municipalities web sites. In *Proceedings of the 2008 ACM Symposium on Applied Computing* (pp. 2421-2425). ACM. 10.1145/1363686.1364259

Freire, A. P., Russo, C. M., & Fortes, R. P. (2008). A survey on the accessibility awareness of people involved in web development projects in Brazil. In *Proceedings of the 2008 International Cross-disciplinary Conference on Web Accessibility (W4A)* (pp. 87-96). ACM. 10.1145/1368044.1368064

IBGE (Instituto Brasileiro de Geografia e Estatística). (2010). *CENSO 2010*. Retrieved from http://www.censo2010.ibge.gov.br

Inclusive Design Institute. *AChecker*. Retrieved from https://achecker.ca/

İşeri, E. İ., Uyar, K., & İlhan, Ü. (2017). The accessibility of Cyprus Islands' higher education institution websites. *Procedia Computer Science, 120*, 967–974. doi:10.1016/j.procs.2017.11.333

Luján-Mora, S., Navarrete, R., & Peñafiel, M. (2014, April). Egovernment and web accessibility in South America. In *Proceedings of the 2014 First International Conference on eDemocracy & eGovernment (ICEDEG)* (pp. 77-82). IEEE. 10.1109/ICEDEG.2014.6819953

Menzi-Cetin, N., Alemdağ, E., Tüzün, H., & Yıldız, M. (2017). Evaluation of a university website's usability for visually impaired students. *Universal Access in the Information Society, 16*(1), 151–160. doi:10.100710209-015-0430-3

Santos, R., & Bastos, G. *Clareou*. Retrieved from http://clareou.com/

Shah, B. P., & Shakya, S. (2007, December). Evaluating the web accessibility of websites of the central government of Nepal. In *Proceedings of the 1st International Conference on Theory and Practice of Electronic Governance* (pp. 447-448). ACM. 10.1145/1328057.1328154

Silva, A. B. P., Silva, C. G., & Moraes, R. L. O. (2019). On the use of a continuous accessibility assessment process for dealing with website evolution. In *Proceedings of the International Conferences Interfaces and Human Computer Interaction 2019; Game and Entertainment Technologies 2019; and Computer Graphics, Visualization, Computer Vision and Image Processing 2019* (pp. 35-42). IADIS Press.

Tanaguru Project. (2017). *Tanaguru Monitor*. Retrieved from http://www.tanaguru.com/en/

Tanaka, E. H., & Da Rocha, H. V. (2011). Evaluation of web accessibility tools. In *Proceedings of the 10th Brazilian Symposium on Human Factors in Computing Systems and the 5th Latin American Conference on Human-Computer Interaction* (pp. 272-279). Brazilian Computer Society.

Tangarife, T., & Mont'Alvão, C. (2005, October). Estudo comparativo utilizando uma ferramenta de avaliação de acessibilidade para Web. In *Proceedings of the 2005 Latin American conference on Human-computer interaction* (pp. 313-318). ACM. 10.1145/1111360.1111394

VaMoLàProject. (2010). *VaMoLà Monitor*. Retrieved from http://sourceforge.net/projects/vamola-monitor/

VU., T.H., Tuan, D. T., & Phan, V. H. (2012). Checking and correcting the source code of web pages for accessibility. In *Proceedings of the 2012 IEEE RIVF International Conference on Computing & Communication Technologies, Research, Innovation, and Vision for the Future* (pp. 1-4). IEEE.

World Wide Web Consortium. (1999). *Web content accessibility guidelines (WCAG) 1.0*. Retrieved from http://www.w3.org/TR/WCAG10/

World Wide Web Consortium. (2008). *Web content accessibility guidelines (WCAG) 2.0*. Retrieved from http://www.w3.org/TR/WCAG20/

World Wide Web Consortium. (2018). *Web content accessibility guidelines (WCAG) 2.1*. Retrieved from http://www.w3.org/TR/WCAG21/

ADDITIONAL READING

Brazil. (2007). Portaria (Ordinance) MP no. 3/20107. Brazilian Ordinance that institutionalizes the e-Government Accessibility Model e-MAG within the scope of the Information and Computer Resource Management System – SISP. Retrieved from http://www.siga.arquivonacional.gov.br/index.php/legislacao-e-normas/legislacao-portarias/336-portaria-mp-n-3-de-7-de-maio-de-2007-e-mag

Brazil. (2009). Decree no. 6949. Brazilian Decree that promulgates the International Convention on the Rights of Persons with Disabilities and its Optional Protocol. Retrieved from http://www.planalto.gov.br/ccivil_03/_ato2007-2010/2009/decreto/d6949.htm

Brazil. (2014). e-MAG – Modelo de Acessibilidade em Governo Eletrônico (Accessibility Model in Electronic Government). Retrieved from http://emag.governoeletronico.gov.br

Brazil. (2015). Law no. 13146/2015. Brazilian Law on the Inclusion of Persons with Disabilities (Statute of Persons with Disabilities). Retrieved from http://www.planalto.gov.br/ccivil_03/_Ato2015-2018/2015/Lei/L13146.htm

IBGE, Brazilian Institute of Geography and Statistics. (2015). National Research of health 2013: life cycles Brazil and Major Regions. Retrieved from https://biblioteca.ibge.gov.br/index.php/biblioteca-catalogo?view=detalhes&id=294525

ISO/IEC. (2012). ISO/IEC 40500:2012. Information technology - W3C Web Content Accessibility Guidelines (WCAG) 2.0.

Kirchner, M. (2002). Evaluation, repair, and transformation of Web pages for Web content accessibility. Review of some available tools. In *Proceedings of the Fourth International Workshop on Web Site Evolution* (pp. 65-72). IEEE. 10.1109/WSE.2002.1134091

Kobayashi, A. M. R., Letizio, C. C., & Tanaka, E. H. (2011). Relationship between accessibility and software evolution. In *Proceedings of the 10th Brazilian Symposium on Human Factors in Computing Systems and the 5th Latin American Conference on Human-Computer Interaction* (pp. 298-302). Brazilian Computer Society.

Leporini, B., Paternò, F., & Scorcia, A. (2006). Flexible tool support for accessibility evaluation. *Interacting with Computers*, *18*(5), 869–890. doi:10.1016/j.intcom.2006.03.001

Moreno, L., Martínez, P., & Ruiz, B. (2008). Guiding accessibility issues in the design of websites. In *Proceedings of the 26th Annual ACM International Conference on Design of Communication* (pp. 65-72). ACM. 10.1145/1456536.1456550

Sassaki, R. K. (2003). *Vida Independente: história, movimento, liderança, conceito, filosofia e fundamentos* (pp. 12–16). São Paulo: RNR.

Stallman, R. (2009). Viewpoint: Why "open source" misses the point of free software. *Communications of the ACM*, *52*(6), 31–33. doi:10.1145/1516046.1516058

Story, M. F., Mueller, J. L., & Mace, R. L. (1998). *The universal design file: Designing for people of all ages and abilities*. Retrieved from https://eric.ed.gov/?id=ED460554

Vanderdonckt, J. (1999). Development milestones towards a tool for working with guidelines. *Interacting with Computers, 12*(2).

KEY TERMS AND DEFINITIONS

CSS: Technology for setting web page style.

E-MAG: E-Government accessibility model for the Brazilian government.

Free Software: Software that contains permission for anyone to use, copy and distribute, as purchased or modified, for free or at a cost. More specifically, there is a requirement that application source code is available.

HTML: Hypertext markup language; language for web page development.

Javascript: Script-based programming language that adds some dynamic features to the website.

Open Source: This concerns the source code of software which can be used and adapted for different purposes.

W3C: World Wide Web Consortium is an international community that organizes web development and recommendations.

WAI: Web Accessibility Initiative group responsible for forming WCAG accessibility guidelines.

WCAG: Web Content Accessibility Guidelines or web accessibility recommendations.

APPENDIX 1

Details and Screens of the Adapted Tool

The achecker tool can be started in three ways: entering the website URL to be evaluated, selecting and uploading the HTML file to be evaluated, or inserting the website HTML code to be evaluated in the application clipboard. From this, the tool starts the evaluation and informs, in the screen, the classification of the nonconformities found. These nonconformities may be known issues, likely issues, and potential issues.

For unauthenticated user system access, only the "Web Accessibility Checker" tab is available. It has three options for checking immediate accessibility without storing test information. The first evaluation option is performed through the website URL. Another option is the evaluation performed by uploading the HTML file that will be evaluated. The last evaluation option is performed by providing part of the HTML code to be evaluated.

To gain access to the advanced features of the tool, it is necessary to create a login authentication in the tool. The registration process requires filling out a form with the fields: login name, password, password confirmation, email, first and last name. After registration, a confirmation email is sent to the user and it is necessary to follow the procedure indicated in the email for the registered account to be enabled for use. The registration form is illustrated in Figure 6.

The "Monitor" tab was created to manage all the features that contribute to the operation of continuous accessibility verification. In this area, it is possible to create and edit the periods in which the verification may be repeated.

To register a website for accessibility monitoring, it is necessary to complete a form with the settings that will be repeated throughout the assessment. In the form, a user may inform the title of the website to be registered and its URL. Also, he may select the period in which the tests will be repeated, which

Figure 8. System access registration

Figure 9. Screen for creating a new monitoring record

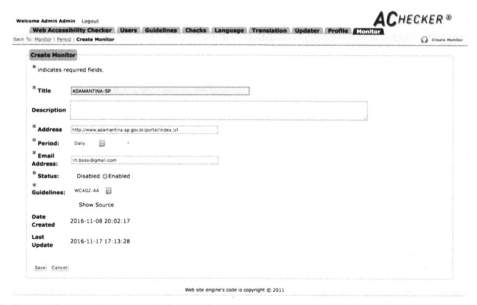

Figure 10. Screen to edit tracking

Figure 11. Screen for creating a period record

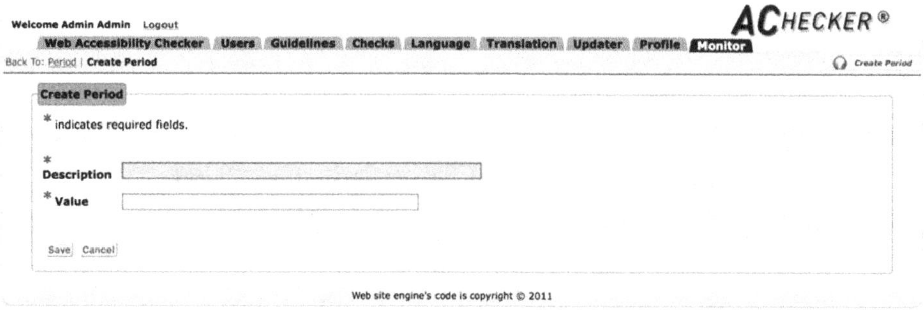

Figure 12. Registered period list

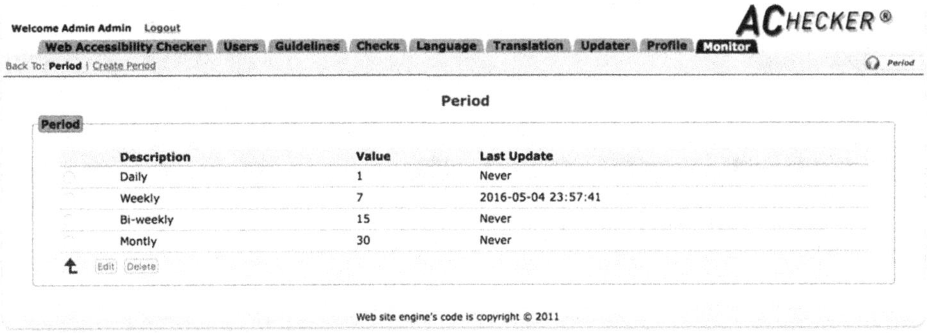

Description	Value	Last Update
Daily	1	Never
Weekly	7	2016-05-04 23:57:41
Bi-weekly	15	Never
Montly	30	Never

email will receive accessibility assessment notifications, and which guidelines will be tested. The user can enable or disable the evaluation through these forms. Figures 9 and 10 show the screens for creating or editing a website record.

The user may create or edit a period, i.e., he may define a period name and the number of days for the period. Figures 11 and 12 show the screens for creating a period record and listing the records already entered.

The system database stores test results of each automatic execution of an accessibility assessment. Therefore, a user can analyze the evaluation history of each evaluated website at any time in a table that gathers all the results of the evaluations. For its operation, the page receives id from the evaluated website and displays the tabulated data of the evaluations already performed. Figure 13 exemplifies this table.

Figure 13. Screen of assessment results obtained from daily website monitoring

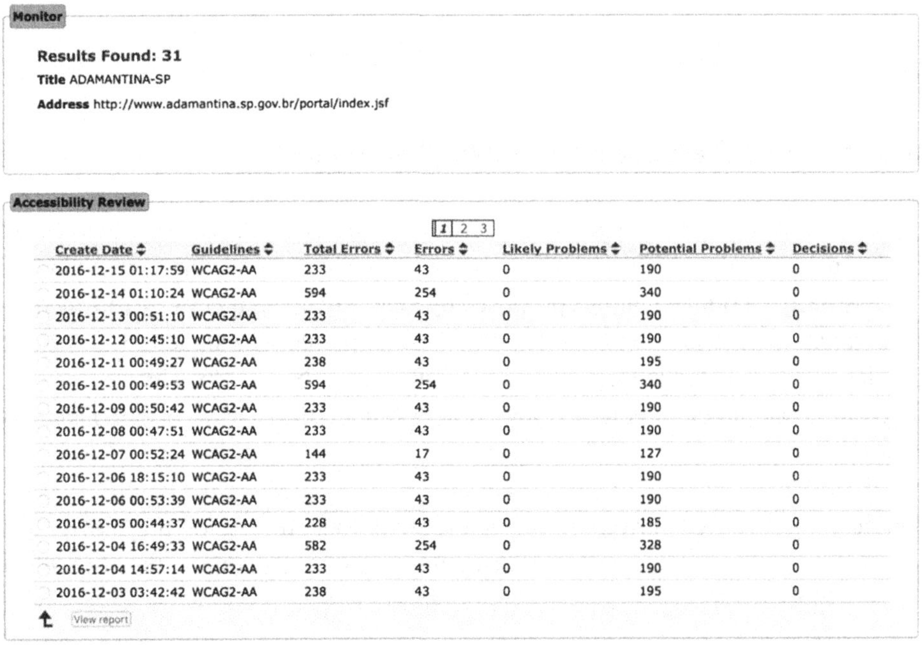

Create Date	Guidelines	Total Errors	Errors	Likely Problems	Potential Problems	Decisions
2016-12-15 01:17:59	WCAG2-AA	233	43	0	190	0
2016-12-14 01:10:24	WCAG2-AA	594	254	0	340	0
2016-12-13 00:51:10	WCAG2-AA	233	43	0	190	0
2016-12-12 00:45:10	WCAG2-AA	233	43	0	190	0
2016-12-11 00:49:27	WCAG2-AA	238	43	0	195	0
2016-12-10 00:49:53	WCAG2-AA	594	254	0	340	0
2016-12-09 00:50:42	WCAG2-AA	233	43	0	190	0
2016-12-08 00:47:51	WCAG2-AA	233	43	0	190	0
2016-12-07 00:52:24	WCAG2-AA	144	17	0	127	0
2016-12-06 18:15:10	WCAG2-AA	233	43	0	190	0
2016-12-06 00:53:39	WCAG2-AA	233	43	0	190	0
2016-12-05 00:44:37	WCAG2-AA	228	43	0	185	0
2016-12-04 16:49:33	WCAG2-AA	582	254	0	328	0
2016-12-04 14:57:14	WCAG2-AA	233	43	0	190	0
2016-12-03 03:42:42	WCAG2-AA	238	43	0	195	0

Figure 14. Accessibility report screen with suggestions for correcting accessibility failures

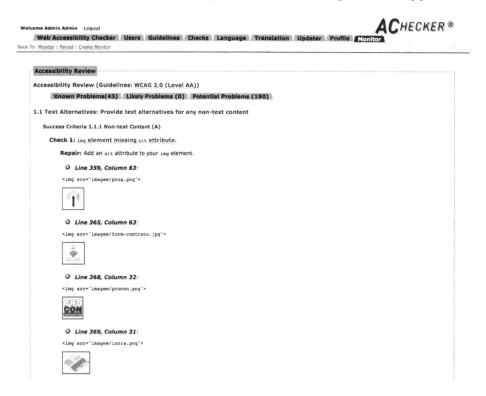

The user may select a record and request a report via the "View Report" button. The report retrieves the stored information and displays the exact evaluation result. The page responsible for generating the detailed report and an example result is represented in Figure 14.

APPENDIX 2

Questionnaire About the Second Sample (Translated)

This form is part of research under the master's degree of Aline Bossi Pereira da Silva, underway at the University of Campinas (UNICAMP). This research has as one of its main objectives to investigate if the WCAG 2.0 accessibility recommendations proposed by W3C are being met by government websites. In addition, the research seeks to identify the difficulties in complying with Federal Laws No. 10,048 and No. 10,098, which were regulated in December 2004 with Decree No. 5,296. This decree sets a deadline for public administration, public interest, or government-funded websites to be adequate to meet these recommendations.

As part of the research, we monitor Brazilian government websites for compliance with WCAG recommendations for a specified period of time and send periodic reports on the subject to the contact emails of these websites. You are currently receiving this form through one of these emails because we think it is important to receive your feedback regarding the monitoring and the possible impact it has had on your institution.

Thus, we have requested your relevant collaboration, answering the questions formulated below, so that we can better understand how this process may or may not have helped those responsible for meeting these recommendations. This is a short questionnaire that can be completed in about 10 minutes. Please note that in no time will your name or your organization's ID be disclosed, serving only for general statistical surveys.

1. How urgently does your institution consider it necessary to meet accessibility criteria on your site?
    a. Very urgent
    b. Urgent
    c. As urgent as other site-related tasks
    d. When possible, as there are other priorities
    e. Never
    f. I do not know how to answer

2. Has your institution been regularly receiving site accessibility reports generated by our system?
    a. Yes, but I had not noticed so far
    b. Yes
    c. Not
    d. I do not know how to answer

3. Regarding accessibility improvements made to your site from December 2016 to March 2017:
    No improvements made
        a. Improvements were made, resulting only from accessibility reports received
        b. Improvements were made, resulting only from other demands of the institution
        c. Improvements were made as a result of both accessibility reports received and other demands from the institution.
        d. I do not know how to answer

4. If accessibility improvements were not made from December 2016 to March 2017, please indicate the main reason:
    a. Failure to receive an accessibility report
    b. The disinterest of the institution
    c. Lack of priority for these improvements over other tasks.
    d. I do not know how to answer
    e. Other:

5. Regarding the usefulness of receiving these reports to make accessibility improvements, you (or the institution you represent):
    a. Considered that it was very helpful to receive them
    b. Found it helpful to receive them
    c. Considered that it was not helpful to receive them

    d.   Found it pointless to receive them

    e.   I do not know how to answer

6.   Regarding the continued receipt of these reports, you (or the institution you represent):

    a.   Would like to stop receiving these reports

    b.   Would like to continue receiving these reports

    c.   I do not know how to answer

7.   Federal Laws No. 10,048 and No. 10,098 were regulated in December 2004 with Decree No. 5,296, which establishes a deadline for the accessibility (sic) of all public administration websites, of public interest or funded by the Government. Are you aware of this law? Try to apply it?

    a.   We do not know.

    b.   We know but do not try to apply.

    c.   We know and try to apply.

8.   In your opinion, what is the biggest difficulty that website owners have for this adequacy? If accessibility improvements have not been made from December / 2016 to March / 2017, please indicate the main reason

    a.   Technical implementation difficulty

    b.   Difficulty understanding WCAG accessibility recommendations (https://www.w3.org/WAI/intro/wcag)

    c.   Difficulty maintaining recommendations during site upgrades

    d.   Other:

9.   Please report positive points about the report and its receipt:

10.   Please report negative points about the report and its receipt:

11.   Add any other comments that you think are relevant and that may contribute to this research.

Chapter 2
An Inclusive Method to Support the Web Accessibility Assessment and Awareness-Raising:
MIAV

Maria Alciléia Alves Rocha
IFFluminense, Brazil

Gabriel de Almeida Souza Carneiro
IFFluminense, Brazil

ABSTRACT

Web content should suit both a general audience and visually-impaired individuals. Therefore, Web applications should be assessed against accessibility standards as Web Content Accessibility Guidelines (WCAG) and the Brazilian e-Government Accessibility Model (eMAG). This chapter presents MIAV's development process and the obtained results. The MIAV complies with the WCAG and eMAG, combining automated and user-opinion-based assessment approaches. First, a pilot test was run to fine-tune MIAV. Next, participants were asked to identify and report several accessibility issues on IFFluminense's Portal, Q-Academico, and Moodle. They then suggested enhancements for better browsing experience. AccessMonitor was run and tested the same Web pages to generate two indicators: the average accessibility index and the percentage of nonconformities by accessibility level. Results showed that none of the evaluated applications met all the accessibility criteria. These experiments allowed IFFluminense's IT degree students to raise an awareness of the significance of Web accessibility.

DOI: 10.4018/978-1-7998-2637-8.ch002

1. INTRODUCTION

The development of accessible Web applications is paramount to include people with disabilities, especially in their education and vocational training. The Internet provides new educational features that people with disabilities can benefit from supported by assistive technologies. Assistive technologies aid the visually-impaired in carrying out activities independently (Sartoretto & Bersch, 2017).

According to the United Nations report, the world's population in 2019 was estimated to total 7.7 billion (UN, 2019). Over a billion people (or about 15% of the world's population) were estimated to be living with some form of disability (WHO, 2018). In Brazil, whose population was around 200.6 million, 6.2% of people have at least one of four forms of disabilities (intellectual, physical, auditory or visual) wherein visual impairment (3.6%) is the prevailing one (IBGE, 2015). Botelho and Porciúncula (2018) highlighted the proportion of people with disabilities in Brazil's population was 23.9%, according to the first release of 2010 Census, but both values are valid and investigate different dimensions of the disability phenomenon. The National Health Survey measured disability as impediments and the 2010 Census measured disability in the broad sense that may reflect problems in functions, body structures, and activities (Botelho & Porciúncula, 2018). Regardless, the amount of people who may face learning issues is expressive.

In the 1980s, the Brazilian Constitution guaranteed school attendance to disabled people, preferably, in regular schools. After that, the Brazilian Education Guidelines and Framework Law (LDB, in Portuguese) emphasized the need for specialized support services (Brazil, 1996). LDB enforces and promotes, under conditions of equality, the exercise of primary rights and freedoms aiming at their social inclusion and citizenship (Brazil, 2015). Also, Brazil enacted the United Nations Convention on the Rights of Persons with Disabilities (CRPD) in 2009 (Brazil, 2009). CRPD's Article III outlines accessibility as a general principle. Specifically on Web accessibility, the Brazilian Law for the Inclusion of Persons with Disabilities enforces that Web site accessibility is mandatory. This law aims to promote access to information and services made available throughout the Internet to people with disabilities, in accordance with the international practices and accessibility guidelines (Brazil, 2015).

IFFluminense is a Brazilian vocational education and training school, located in upstate Rio, which trains students to work as skilled IT technicians, Information Systems Bachelors and Computer Engineers. IFFluminense's support center for students with special educational needs (NAPNEE, in Portuguese) assists all attending visually-impaired students. In this context, two problems were observed. The first problem refers to the difficulties that IFFluminense's visually-impaired students experience when performing tasks on Q-Academico (Qualidata, 2017), Moodle (Moodle, 2017) and IFFluminense's Portal (Brazil, 2018). IFFluminense's Portal publishes news on academic activities. Q-Academico provides information about students' grades and attendances. Moodle provides educational content and assignments. The second problem refers to the difficulty experienced by IFFluminense's IT students to understand the significance of Web accessibility. Although they study the Brazilian Accessibility Law and international accessibility standards, they fail to follow accessibility recommendations they are taught when doing Web-development-related assignments in course. Carter and Markel (2001) already reported a similar problem when they estimated that one percent of Web developers take accessibility into account when designing Web pages. These facts demonstrate the need for actions to build an awareness of the significance of Web accessibility.

To enforce the inclusion of people with disabilities is crucial to: (i) develop an inclusive method so visually-impaired users actively evaluate the accessibility of Web software products; and (ii) make IT professionals aware of the significance of Web accessibility. To achieve these goals, Carneiro and Rocha (2019) introduced MIAV (Inclusive Method for Accessibility assessment by Visually-impaired users). The MIAV complies with WCAG (Web Content Accessibility Guidelines), version 2.0 (W3C, 2008) and Brazilian eMAG (e-Government Accessibility Model) guidelines (Brazil, 2014). Thus, MIAV enables the assessment of some accessibility criteria in an automated way using AccessMonitor (FCT, 2012) and in other ways based on user experience and the opinion of users when carrying out their assignments. The strategy to combine two accessibility assessment methods aims to reduce the effort and overcome AccessMonitor's limitations. In this way, MIAV enables visually-impaired users to actively participate in accessibility assessment. They can give their opinion based on their own experiences when perform the predefined evaluation guide tasks using the Web application. In addition, non-visually impaired users can develop empathy simulating visual impairment when perform the evaluation guide tasks.

This chapter presents MIAV's development process step by step and the obtained results. In this line, the main objectives of this work are: to evaluate the Web accessibility of IFFluminense's Portal, Q-Academico and Moodle from the user perspective, using MIAV; and to raise the awareness of IF-Fluminense's IT students of the significance of Web accessibility.

This chapter is divided into five sections. This introductory section states the problem and the research objectives. Section 2 defines accessibility and assessment criteria based on the Brazilian and international standards. It also summarizes problems and related studies on accessibility assessment. Section 3 describes the steps taken in developing MIAV to achieve said objectives, the tools used when assessing the accessibility criteria. Section 4 explains the MIAV use to assess accessibility of IFFluminense's Portal, Q-Academico and Moodle, characterizing its participants. It also presents the accessibility issues and levels, as well as suggestions for enhancements. In addition, remarks on the students' perceptions of the accessibility significance are reported. Finally, the conclusion summarizes the main findings, the limitations of this research and future works.

2. ACCESSIBILITY ASSESSMENT

This section summarizes the fundamental concepts and the technical literature about Web- application accessibility assessment, based on the study of literature, tools and international standards.

Fundamental Concepts and Standards

The ISO/IEC 25010 Standard defines a product quality model composed of eight characteristics. Each characteristic is related to a set of sub characteristics. The product quality model includes usability as "degree to which a product or system can be used by specified users to achieve specified goals with effectiveness, efficiency and satisfaction in a specified context of use" (ISO/IEC, 2011). According to ISO/IEC 25010 (ISO/IEC, 2011), accessibility is a sub characteristic of usability that means degree to which a product or system can be used by the largest number of people regardless of their physical characteristics or capabilities to achieve a specified goal in a particular context of use. Web accessibility means that everybody can access and use the Web regardless of having a disability (Moreno, 2008). On the other hand, lack of accessibility on the Web makes it difficult for people with one or more disabilities to browse the Web interact with other users or contribute to it (da Silva, da Silva & Moraes, 2019). In order to enhance accessibility, Web content should be delivered in accordance with the standards, such as the Brazilian eMAG and WCAG.

WCAG documents explain how to make Web content more accessible to people with disabilities. WCAG is developed in cooperation with individuals and organizations around the world, with a goal of providing a single shared standard for web content accessibility that meets the needs of individuals, organizations, and governments internationally (W3C, 2018). The WCAG 2.0 covers four principles: perceivable, operable, understandable and robust. These principles relate to 12 guidelines containing one or more success criteria, totaling around 60 criteria. ISO/IEC 40500: 2012 (ISO/IEC, 2012) standardized the WCAG 2.0. In June 2018, W3C published WCAG 2.1, extending WCAG 2.0 by adding one guideline and new success criteria, totaling 78 compliance criteria.

Each criterion is assessed against three levels of conformance. According toW3C (2018) Level A is the minimal level of conformance in which the Web page satisfies all the Level-A success criteria, or it provides a conforming alternate version. Level AA is an intermediate level that ensures accessibility for most users, since Web pages must meet all A and AA success criteria. Level AAA is the highest level, since Web pages satisfies all success criteria.

The Brazilian eMAG is a tailored version of the WCAG 2.0 guidelines for the accessibility assessment of Brazilian government's Web applications. Compliance with eMAG is mandatory in all virtual environments of the Brazilian government (Brazil, 2007). Brazilian eMAG contains sections on markup, behavior, content/information, presentation/design, multimedia and form. These sections list 45 accessibility recommendations.

Problems and Related Studies

Web application accessibility should be evaluated considering domain, accessibility criteria and evaluators' profile. Ahmi and Mohamad (2019) research results points at an increased rate of web accessibility literature over the years since 2001, which indicates a growing awareness of its importance and specific requirements. The technical literature shows that accessibility assessment is generally performed via tools, user experience and opinion or by checking standards compliance.

Considering the number of criteria and web pages to be evaluated, tools such as AccessMonitor (FCT, 2012) can provide quick insights on Web application accessibility. W3C (2016) list about 133 tools consisting of software or online services that help to determine if Web content meets the accessibility guidelines. The list includes AccessMonitor as dynamic logo that summarizes results based on samplings (W3C, 2016). According to Carneiro and Rocha (2019) an automatic evaluation method consists of algorithms that search the code of each Web page to highlight all nonconformities against the standards.

However, several situations require human assessment because these tools alone fail to properly evaluate some criteria. For instance, if the Alt attribute describes an image incorrectly, the tool approves it although visually-impaired individuals would identify this as a problem, since they consider the context in which an image appears (Carneiro & Rocha, 2019). Even the most effective mechanical testing methods and what appears to be well-written accessible HTML code cannot fully account for all potential accessibility issues (Bradbard & Peters, 2010). Thus, the true test of a Web application's accessibility is that undertaken by disabled users. In addition, evaluation methods that take into account users' opinion and experience ensure language clarity and opportunities to suggest significant enhancements on the evaluated applications (Carneiro & Rocha, 2019).

Empirical studies have examined Web applications for barriers to accessibility (da Silva, da Silva & Moraes, 2019; İşeri et al, 2017; Acosta-Vargas et al., 2016). These studies show that Web applications are not designed for accessibility. In addition, da Silva, da Silva and Moraes (2019) concluded that there is a gap between the enactment of accessibility Law and a real interest of Brazilian governmental institutions in implementing them. Oliveira, de Souza and Eler (2017) evaluated the main Web portals of 28 Brazilian federal agencies with ministry status and concluded that most of their Web portals fail to comply with the accessibility laws and standards.

The technical literature suggests university's Web sites are not accessible either. Out of the 11 samples involving Web sites of U.S. postsecondary institutions, 60 to 90 percent of the Web sites had some form of accessibility barrier (Bradbard & Peters, 2010). Fernández et al. (2010) presented a study on the accessibility on the 77 Spanish university's Web sites and they concluded these Web sites are not accessible by law. Espadinha et al. (2011) characterized the accessibility of all public Portuguese universities' homepages and the support services they offered to disabled students. The overall accessibility rate of the Web pages was not acceptable. Pereira et al. (2013) presented the results of the accessibility level of Websites and portals of Brazilian institutions in higher education. The analysis revealed that only 1.49 percent of XHTML (eXtensible Hypertext Markup Language) codes and 13.42 percent of CSS (Cascading Style Sheets) codes were classified as valid by the tools provided by W3C. Abu Shawar (2015) showed that accessibility errors of universities' Web sites in Jordan and the Arab region exceed the ones in England by 13 times, and 5 times respectively. Acosta-Vargas et al. (2016) proposed a study to assess the Web accessibility of 20 university Websites from all around the world. They conclude that most of the tested Web sites do not achieve an acceptable level of compliance to WCAG 2.0. Menzi-Çetin et al. (2017) evaluated the usability of a Turkish university Website asking five visually-impaired students to think aloud while performing eleven tasks involving their university's Web pages. Out of the eleven tasks, five tasks were not successfully completed by all students. İşeri et al. (2017) described the results of a study about the Web accessibility of the Cyprus Island's 38 higher-education institutional Web sites. This study also aimed to raise awareness among institute administrators and Web site developers about Web accessibility. The results showed that all the surveyed Web sites failed one or more of WCAG 2.0 guidelines. Acosta-Vargas, Acosta and Luján-Mora (2018) described accessibility problems in 348 main university Web sites in Latin America randomly selected. They used WAVE, a tool that performs a complete automatic analysis referring to WCAG 2.0 success criteria. Their results indicate that no Web site reached an acceptable accessibility level. A frequent problem was the lack of an alternative text for images.

Neither of the former papers specifically asked the visually-impaired to assess IFFluminense's Portal's and Moodle's and Q-Academico's accessibility. It motivates assessing these Web applications' accessibility using MIAV.

3. MIAV OVERVIEW

MIAV is a hybrid approach to assess Web pages' accessibility, so users evaluate certain accessibility criteria and AccessMonitor evaluates other accessibility criteria automatically. MIAV was designed so that the visually- impaired users could assess accessibility grounded on their experience and opinion when carrying out their activities. In addition, IT students can use MIAV to become aware of the Web accessibility significance when simulating total blindness.

Figure 1. MIAV's development process

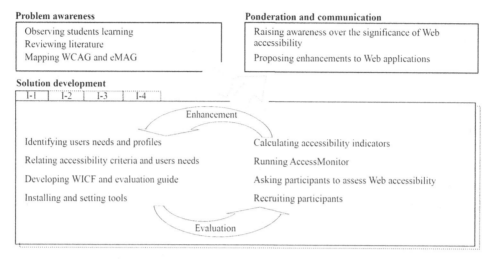

This section shows MIAV's development process. Also, it describes the evaluated accessibility criteria and the accessibility assessment tools related to MIAV's structure and tasks.

MIAV Development Process

Figure 1 outlines MIAV's development process.

The first phase refers to the problem perception by observing IFFluminense's students in learning activities. Visually-impaired students experience accessibility issues when browsing the Web. On the other hand, software development undergraduates ignore accessibility guidelines even after having studied the technical literature on accessibility and becoming familiar with the international standards for Web accessibility.

Developing a solution to those problems is an interactive, iterative and incremental process. This process is interactive because assessing accessibility requires user participation including visually-impaired users who can make suggestions for relevant enhancements. The process is iterative and incremental because subsequent cycles for evaluation and enhancement are essential. Each cycle refers to a moment in time when the Web application provides certain content, which generally varies over time. The evaluation and enhancement cycle was performed 4 times, iterations named I-1 and I-2 and I-3 and I-4. Specifically, this chapter summarizes I1 results and details results I2, I3 and I4.

The results of one or more cycles are analyzed aiming to improve the evaluated Web applications' accessibility, as well as the evaluation method. Implementing the enhancement suggestions may lead to a new evaluation and enhancement cycle. In addition, users should ponder on the importance of Web accessibility based on their own experience.

MIAV Structure and Tasks

To support accessibility assessment, the MIAV cycle covers 8 tasks - 4 for planning and 4 for evaluation. During the planning phase, the first task aims at screening user profiles and the main activities they

Table 1.eMAG and WCAG criteria evaluation techniques

eMag		WCAG 2.0	Techniques
Markup	1.1	4.1.1Parsing, 4.1.2 Name, Role, Value	AccessMonitor
	1.2	1.3.1Info and Relationships	
	1.3	1.3.1Info and Relationships, 2.4.10 Section Headings	
	1.4	1.3.2Meaningful Sequence, 2.4.3 Focus Order	
	1.5	2.4.1Bypass Blocks	
	1.6	1.3.1Info and Relationships	
	1.7		
	1.8	3.2.3 Consistent Navigation	Not evaluated
	1.9	3.2.5 Change on Request	AccessMonitor
Behavior	2.1	2.1.1 Keyboard, 2.1.2 No Keyboard Trap	AccessMonitor
	2.2		
	2.3	3.2.5 Change on Request	
	2.4		
	2.5	2.2.1 Timing is adjustable	
	2.6	2.3.1 Three Flashes or Below Threshold Not evaluated	Not evaluated
	2.7	2.2.2 Pause, Stop, Hide	AccessMonitor
Content/ information	3.1	3.1.1 Language of Page	
	3.2	3.1.2 Language of Parts	Q1
	3.3	2.4.2 Page is titled	AccessMonitor
	3.4	2.4.8 Location	Q2
	3.5	2.4.4 Link Purpose (in context), 2.4.9 Link Purpose (link only)	Q3
	3.6	1.1.1 Non-textual Content	AccessMonitor
	3.7		
	3.8		Q4
	3.9	1.3.1 Info and Relationships	AccessMonitor
	3.10		
	3.11	3.1.5 Reading Level	Q5
	3.12	3.1.3 Unusual Words, 3.1.4 Acronyms	Q6
Presentation/ design	4.1	1.4.3 Contrast (minimum)	AccessMonitor
	4.2	1.3.3 Sensory Characteristics, 1.4.1 Use of Color	Not evaluated
	4.3	1.4.4 Resize text	AccessMonitor
	4.4	2.4.7 Focus is visible	Q7
Multimedia	5.1	1.2.1 Audio-only and Video-only (Prerecorded), 1.2.2 Captions (Prerecorded), 1.2.6 Sign Language (Prerecorded), 1.2.8 Media Alternative (Prerecorded)	AccessMonitor
	5.2	1.2.1 Audio-only and Video-only (Prerecorded), 1.2.2 Captions (Prerecorded), 1.2.6 Sign Language (Prerecorded)	
	5.3	1.2.3 Audio Description or Media Alternative (Prerecorded), 1.2.5Audio Description (Prerecorded), 1.2.7 Extended Audio Description (Prerecorded)	Q8
	5.4	1.4.2 Audio Control	Q9
	5.5	2.2.2 Pause, Stop, Hide	Q10
Form	6.1	1.1.1 Non-textual content	Q11
	6.2	1.3.1 Info and Relationships	AccessMonitor
	6.3	2.4.3 Focus Order	Q12
	6.4	3.3.2 Labels or Instructions	AccessMonitor
	6.5		Q13
	6.6	3.3.1 Error Identification	Q14
	6.7	1.3.1Info and Relationships	AccessMonitor
	6.8	1.1.1 Non-textual content	

perform using Web applications. The second task aims to relate the main activities to WCAG and eMAG criteria. Table 1 aids to decide which accessibility criteria would be evaluated using AccessMonitor or user experience and opinion (questions Q1 to Q14). Depending on the activities performed by users, some criteria are not applicable and such could be disregarded.

Third task intents to prepare data collection tools such as written informed consent form (WICF) and evaluation guide, based on the user profiles and the main activities. The evaluation guide lists and details the tasks that participants had to accomplish in the accessibility assessment and a questionnaire, available in TXT format. The questionnaire includes open questions to evaluate Web application accessibility, the screen reader used and the guide itself. Accessibility- related questions are:

Q1. Did you notice a language change in the Web application's content?
Q2. Did the Web application report your location on site?
Q3. Did the Web application describe links clearly and succinctly?
Q4. Did the Web application make content available in accessible formats?
Q5. Did the Web application allow reading and understanding the information?
Q6. Did the Web application provide an explanation for the acronyms, abbreviations and unusual words?
Q7. Did the Web application evidence elements with focus, that is, was the selected element read?
Q8. Did the Web application offer an audio description for the videos?
Q9. Did the Web application provide an audio control for the sound?
Q10. Did the Web application allow you to pause, stop or hide the video, slideshow or animation available on the home page?
Q11. Did the Web application provide a text alternative for buttons?
Q12. Did the Web application establish a logical browsing order?
Q13. Did the Web application confirm the login form information was successfully submitted?
Q14. Did the Web application identify and describe the data entry errors?

Whenever needed, the fourth task aims to set up the tools to carry out the accessibility assessment. For instance, installing the NVDA (NVAccess, 2017) screen reader which visually- impaired user uses to browse textual content.

The evaluation phase begins by recruiting participants. Sighted or visually- impaired users receive WICF with an invitation to evaluate the Web application they use. Those who agree run the evaluation guide. Next, AccessMonitor run on the same pages evaluated by the users, to assess other criteria. For each Web page, AccessMonitor computes the accessibility index and the number of nonconformities by WCAG accessibility level (A, AA, or AAA). Because a Web application has several pages, MIAV covers the calculation of two new indicators based on the AccessMonitor results: the average accessibility index and the percentage of nonconformities by WCAG accessibility level (A, AA, or AAA). Finally, enhancement suggestions are listed for Web pages and assistive tools and evaluation guide itself grounded on the observations and results of the assessment.

4. USING MIAV FOR ACCESSIBILITY ASSESSMENT AND AWARENESS RAISING

This section presents the results of the iterations for accessibility assessment using MIAV. As the first iteration (I-1) was a pilot test, the results for a Web page's accessibility are not presented. The first iteration focused on improving the evaluation guide and the questionnaire. Indeed, this section describes the objectives of the other iterations (I-2 and I-3 and I-4), their participants, and the evaluated Web pages. Subsequently, it presents the evaluation results based on participants' opinion and the AccessMonitor tests. Finally, it lists participants' suggestions for enhancement and their perceptions on accessibility.

Study Procedures

First task consisted of a semi-structured interview with NAPNEE's coordinator to identify visually-impaired students' profiles and needs. During the interview, the coordinator reported that NAPNEE supports about 30 disabled students per year who five were visually-impaired in 2018. Three of them agreed to participate in the third iteration (I-3). Moreover, the NAPNEE coordinator highlighted that assignments involving images are difficult for the visually-impaired to perform. The coordinator also reported that NAPNEE provides for assistive tools such as NVDA. In addition, NAPNEE holds the duty to prepare specialized teaching materials for visually-impaired students.

Visually- impaired students reported being familiar with NVDA and being technology-skilled when performing routine and academic activities. They read news on IFFluminense's Portal at the computer; two participants reported doing it weekly. One participant reported who check their academic achievement in Q-Academico daily. Although no participant had used Moodle before, the researchers asked them to assess its accessibility because they might use it in the future (Carneiro & Rocha, 2019).

The researchers chose from Table 1 which accessibility criteria to evaluate for each Web application that visually- impaired students use. Figure 2 in part show evaluation guide tailored to address needs and activities that students reported. In particular, on IFFluminense's Portal, participants were asked to choose the news that drew their interests. After reading the news, they were asked to inform the news' URL (Uniform Resource Locator). The participants accessed a course with three activities on Moodle provided by IFFluminense, which allowed them to perform the accessibility assessment. Activity 1 aimed to find out if the visually-impaired students were able to access Moodle's content in the PDF format, which is often the case when made available by teachers. Activity 2 has an external link to evaluate the HTML content. Activity 3 aimed to investigate if students were able to assess Moodle's and its educational videos' accessibility, observing the audio shift between NVDA and video. At Q-Academico, students were asked to check their percentage of attendance on a course they attended and access their enrollment voucher in the PDF format, using their own access credentials.

The first iteration (I-1) aimed to identify enhancements on the evaluation guide and questionnaire. At the trial stage, after giving the "Web Accessibility: A Practical Approach" short course in July 2018, seven students were asked to assess a Web page's accessibility. Only one participant was visually-impaired. Based on the pilot-test results, the data collection tools were improved as follows: (i) the multiple-choice questions were replaced by open questions as Figure 2 because the screen reader made participants confused to choose their answers; (ii) the instructions in the evaluation guide were rephrased to become easier to understand.

Figure 2. Part of evaluation guide

Evaluation guide to assess IFFluminense Portal and Q-Academico accessibility
Directions: please follow the steps and answer the questions. When the NVDA read "your answer" type "Y" for Yes, "N" for No, "NA" for "Not Applicable" or "IDK" for "I do not know".

Step 1. You switch to the Web browser window by pressing ALT and TAB keys simultaneously and you access www.iff.edu.br
Step 2. On the homepage you look for and access the "Latest News" link.
Step 3. You choose a news your interest and access it.
Step 4. You select the news' URL(Uniform Resource Locator) using TAB key.
Step 5. You copy the news' URL by pressing CTRL and C keys simultaneously.
Step 6. You switch to the evaluation guide window by pressing ALT and TAB keys simultaneously.
Step 7. You look for question 7.1 and paste the URL by pressing CTRL and V keys simultaneously.
7.1 What the news' URL?
Step 8 You answer questions on IFFluminense's Portal accessibility.
8.1 Did the IFFluminense's Portal report your location on site? Your answer:
8.2 Did the IFFluminense's Portal describe links clearly and succinctly? Your answer:
8.3 Did the IFFluminense's Portal allow reading and understanding the information? Your answer:
8.4 Did the IFFluminense's Portal provide an explanation for the acronyms, abbreviations and unusual words? Your answer:
8.5 Did the IFFluminense's Portal evidence elements with focus, that is, was the selected element read? Your answer:
8.6 Did the IFFluminense's Portal allow you to pause, stop or hide the video, slideshow or animation available on the home page? Your answer:
8.7 Did the IFFluminense's Portal provide a text alternative for buttons? Your answer:
8.8 Did the IFFluminense's Portal establish a logical browsing order? Your answer:
8.9 What do you suggest to improve the accessibility of the IFFluminense's Portal?
Step 9. You switch to the Web browser window by pressing ALT and TAB keys simultaneously.
Step 10. You access the IFFluminense's Portal homepage.
Step 11. On the homepage you look for and access the "Academic System" link.
Step 12. You choose the "Student" link.
Step 13. You access Q-Academico using your credential and password.
Step 14. You choose a course and check their percentage of attendance.
Step 15. You save their enrollment voucher in the PDF format.
Step 16. You switch to the evaluation guide window by pressing ALT and TAB keys simultaneously.
Step 17. You look for question 17.1 and answer questions on Q-Academico accessibility.
17.1 Did the Q-Academico report your location on site? Your answer:
17.2 Did the Q-Academico describe links clearly and succinctly? Your answer:
17.3 Did the Q-Academico allow reading and understanding the information? Your answer:
17.4 Did the Q-Academico provide an explanation for the acronyms, abbreviations and unusual words? Your answer:
17.5 Did the Q-Academico evidence elements with focus, that is, was the selected element read? Your answer:
17.6 Did the Q-Academico provide a text alternative for buttons? Your answer:
17.7 Did the Q-Academico establish a logical browsing order? Your answer:
17.8 Did the Q-Academico confirm the login form information was successfully submitted? Your answer:
17.9 Did the Q-Academico identify and describe the data entry errors? Your answer:
17.10 What do you suggest to improve the accessibility of the Q-Academico?

The second iteration (I-2) took place in July 2018 and the fourth iteration (I-4) happened in July 2019, during human-computer interaction classes. These iterations aimed to assess the accessibility of IFFluminense's Portal, as well as to identify enhancements on the NVDA and the questionnaire. The procedures performed in those iterations also aimed to make participants aware of the importance of Web accessibility. In this case, the students' reactions during the experiment were observed and noted. At the end of the experiment, participants were asked to give their opinion on the significance of Web accessibility.

Regarding the third iteration (I-3), Carneiro and Rocha (2019) reported accessibility evaluation results for Q-Academico, Moodle and IFFluminense's Portal, based on the user experience and opinion of visually-impaired students. Three visually-impaired students (named P3-1, P3-2 and P3-3) individually assessed IFFluminense's Portal's, Q-academico's and Moodle's accessibility in August 2018. It took them two hours to complete the proposed activities in the evaluation guide and to answer the questionnaire.

In this research, participants were selected by convenience, including partially- or fully-blind IFFluminense's students. As not all participants are visually-impaired, the sighted participants were asked to turn off their computer monitor and put on headphones to have a blind-user experience. They were asked to complete the evaluation guide's activities and answer the questionnaire, available in TXT format,

Table 2. Participants' profiles

Iteration	Participants	Age	Gender	Visually-impaired	Course
I-2	P2-1	32	Male	No	Information Systems
	P2-2	24	Female	No	Information Systems
	P2-3	30	Male	No	Information Systems
	P2-4	20	Male	No	Information Systems
	P2-5	28	Male	No	Information Systems
	P2-6	21	Male	No	Information Systems
I-3	P3-1	26	Female	Yes	Geography
	P3-2	25	Female	Yes	Information Systems
	P3-3	23	Female	Yes	Computer technician
I-4	P4-1	25	Male	No	Information Systems
	P4-2	25	Female	No	Information Systems
	P4-3	22	Male	No	Information Systems
	P4-4	20	Female	No	Information Systems
	P4-5	22	Male	No	Information Systems
	P4-6	23	Male	No	Information Systems
	P4-7	23	Male	No	Information Systems

using the NVDA screen reader. Students were also given a printed list of basic NVDA and computer commands. A total of 16 students, aged between 20 and 32, participated in three iterations (I-2, I-3 and I-4), as presented in Table 2. Most participants (87.5%) are Information Systems undergraduate students, 62.5% are male and 37.5% female. Three participants are visually-impaired (18.8%).

Table 3 lists the Web pages participants evaluated. In third iteration (I-3), all participants accessed three Q-Academico and four Moodle Web pages, which require access credentials. In iterations I-3 and I-4, all participants accessed the main page and the latest news on IFFluminense's Portal. Participants P2-4 and P2-5 did not inform the page they accessed, which made it impossible to perform AccessMonitor tests. In the fourth iteration (I-4) the participants were grouped. One group was made up of P4-1 and P4-2. Another group with P4-3 and P4-4 and P4-5 and a third group consisted of P4-6 and P4-7. In this case, each participant used the NVDA screen reader to perform the evaluation, but they answered the questionnaire by group consensus. This strategy enabled participants to discuss their perceptions.

Results and Discussions

Tables 4 and 5 show the results for each accessibility assessment question from Table 1. Table 4 shows the participants' responses for the second and fourth iterations (I-2 and I4). Table 5 shows the participants' responses of third iteration (I-3). Blank cells (in tables 4 and 5) indicate the question is not applicable to that Web application. Participants were comfortable to answer some questions in detail, not following the evaluation guide's directions to type "Y" for Yes, "N" for No, "NA" for "Not Applicable" or "IDK" for "I do not know". In such cases, their answers were adjusted and highlighted (*). In situations where participants did not enter the answer, the cells were highlighted (-).

Table 3. Web pages

Iteration	Participants	Links
I-2	P2-1	http://portal1.iff.edu.br/nossos-campi/centro-de-referencia
	P2-2	http://portal1.iff.edu.br/nossos-campi/itaperuna/noticias/iff-itaperuna-prorroga-prazo-de-inscricao-de-salas-tematicas-e-prototipos-para-a-7a-semana-academica
	P2-3	http://portal1.iff.edu.br/nossos-campi/itaperuna/noticias/nae-itaperuna-divulga-lista-para-cadastro-de-carteirinha-de-transporte
	P2-4	Participant did not state
	P2-5	Participant did not state
	P2-6	http://portal1.iff.edu.br/reitoria/noticias/iff-divulga-a-1-a-convocacao-da-lista-de-espera-do-sisu-2018-2013-2-o-semestre
I-3	P3-1 until 3	https://academico.iff.edu.br/
	P3-1 until 3	http://ensino.centro.iff.edu.br/moodle/
	P3-1 until 3	http://portal1.iff.edu.br/
	P3-1 until 3	http://portal1.iff.edu.br/noticias/ultimas-noticias
	P3-1	http://portal1.iff.edu.br/nossos-campi/macae/noticias/resultado-preliminar-do-processo-seletivo-para-estagio-no-campus-macae
	P3-2	http://selecoes.iff.edu.br/estagio/macae/2018/processo_seletivo-1/comunicado
	P3-3	http://portal1.iff.edu.br/noticias/vencedores-de-concurso-em-parceria-com-a-cplp-receberao-premiacao-na-reditec-2018
I-4	P4-1 until 7	http://portal1.iff.edu.br/
	P4-1 until 7	http://portal1.iff.edu.br/noticias/ultimas-noticias
	P4-1	http://portal1.iff.edu.br/reitoria/noticias/diretoria-de-tecnologia-da-informacao-lanca-portal-de-eventos-do-iffluminense
	P4-2	
	P4-3	http://portal1.iff.edu.br/nossos-campi/campos-centro/noticias/redes-sociais-atrapalham-desenvolvimento-de-alunos-diz-pesquisa
	P4-4	
	P4-5	
	P4-6	http://portal1.iff.edu.br/nossos-campi/campos-centro/noticias/arraia-da-federa-vai-reunir-mais-uma-vez-a-comunidade-do-campus-campos-centro
	P4-7	

The uniform evaluation results for IFFluminense's Portal were compared in the three iterations. In the second and third iterations, 77.8% of participants these iterations (7 out of 9) reported that their location on the Web page was not informed (Q2). But this trend is reversed in the fourth iteration, which indicates an improvement in this criterion. Participants, in the last two iterations, stated that IFFluminense's Portal describes links clearly and succinctly (Q3). Most of the answers (9 out of 12) obtained in the three iterations indicate that IFFluminense's Portal did not provide an explanation for the acronyms, abbreviations and unusual words (Q6). Half of participants (6 out of 12) realized that focus was visible (Q7). 66.7% of participants in the second iteration (4 out of 6) reported that IFFluminense's Portal did not provide a text alternative for the buttons (Q11). However, this criterion showed an improvement in the two subsequent iterations, since 100.0% of participants in the fourth iteration found out a text alternative for the buttons. Another criterion remains negative: most of the participants, in the I-2 and I-4 iterations, stressed that IFFluminense's Portal did not establish a logical browsing order (Q12). Positively most participants (8

Table 4. Accessibility assessment results of I-2 and I-4

Questions	IFFluminense's Portal								
	I-2						I-4		
	P2.1	P2.2	P2.3	P2.4	P2.5	P2.6	P4.1 and P4.2	P4.3 and P4.4 and P4.6	P4.6 and P4.7
Q1									
Q2	Y	N	N	N	N	Y	Y	-	Y
Q3	Y	Y	N	N	Y	N	Y	-	Y
Q4									
Q5	N	Y	N	N	Y	Y	N	Y	Y
Q6	N	N	N	N	N	N	NA	N	Y
Q7	-	N	Y	Y	N	Y	Y	N	N
Q8									
Q9									
Q10	-	N	N	IDK	Y	-	NA	NA	N
Q11	N	N	N	Y	Y	N	Y	Y	Y
Q12	-	Y	N	N	N	N	N	N	Y
Q13									
Q14									

Table 5. Accessibility assessment results of I-3

Questions	IFFluminense's Portal			Q-Academico			Moodle		
	P3.1	P3.2	P3.3	P3.1	P3.2	P3.3	P3.1	P3.2	P3.3
Q1							NA*	N	N
Q2	N	N	N	N	Y	Y	N	Y	Y
Q3	Y	Y	Y*	Y	Y	Y	Y	Y	Y
Q4							Y	Y	Y
Q5	Y	Y	Y	Y	Y	N	Y	Y	Y
Q6	N	N	IDK*	NA*	N	Y*	NA*	N	Y
Q7	Y	N	Y	Y	Y	Y	Y	Y	Y
Q8							N	N	N
Q9							Y	N	Y
Q10	NA*	N*	NA*						
Q11	Y	Y	N	Y	Y	Y			
Q12	Y	Y	IDK*	Y	Y	Y			
Q13				Y	Y	Y	Y	Y	Y
Q14				N	Y	Y	N	Y	Y

Source: (Carneiro & Rocha, 2019)

out of 12) reported that IFFluminense Portal allows reading and understanding the information (Q5). Probably most participants did not notice the "multimedia gallery" section on the homepage bottom of IFFluminense Portal. As a result, evidences about Q10 are inconclusive, which requires improving the evaluation guide to explore this section in future evaluations.

On Q-Academico, Carneiro and Rocha (2019) reported all participants in the third iteration (I-3) answered "Y" for Q3, Q7, Q11, Q12 and Q13. Only P3.3 emphasized that the enrollment voucher had not been made available in an accessible format because it is presented as an image without any associated textual description. Although Q4 was not included in the evaluation guide, that accessibility barrier impacted Q5 answer. Answers on acronyms, abbreviations and unusual words (Q6) were controversial as participants disagreed with each other. 2 out of 3 participants stated that Q-Academico reported their location (Q2) and identified data entry errors (Q14).

As for Moodle, all participants carried out the three activities. According Carneiro and Rocha (2019) they all agreed that Moodle's links were presented in a clear and direct way (Q3); Web content was in an accessible format (Q4); Web content reading and understanding was ensured (Q5); and the selected elements were read and highlighted (Q7 and Q13). However, Moodle failed to signal a language change (Q1); to inform location (Q2); to provide an explanation for the acronyms, abbreviations and unusual words (Q6) and to identify data entry errors (Q14). Notably the audio description for videos on Moodle is problematic. They all reported that Moodle did not offer any audio description for the available videos (Q8). Q-Academico and Moodle were better evaluated than IFFluminense's Portal by the visually- impaired mainly regarding Q2 and Q7.

Other accessibility issues were observed when using the evaluation guide. For instance in step 13 (see Figure 2) Q-Academico's login page does not differentiate the entry fields for login and password, NVDA only informed "editing", which troubled proper access by blind users. During evaluations, participants reported NVDA limitation, meaning that the user always has to listen to all the Web page information from the top on the side menus to find the desired content, notably the links within a text. Consequently, when switching between the Web page and the evaluation guide, reading was repeated from the beginning of the Web page. A similar problem has also been reported by Menzi-Çetin et al. (2017) in whose study users found it unnecessary and annoying to hear the screen reader program read all the links repetitively every time a page was opened. This drawback made the accessibility assessment longer. When a participant used the copy and paste feature, NVDA did not report the content that was copied nor the paste action. This way, users cannot realize what they did. Similarly, in iteration I3 whose participants were visually- impaired, the participants who did not copy and paste the password "Aluno12." from the evaluation guide on Moodle were not able to access it. That happened because NVDA is not case sensitive for letter "A" and does not read the period "." in the password, although Moodle requires passwords to have capital letters and special characters. Also, Moodle requests confirming completion of each task. But because NVDA does not read the "Once submitted, you will not be able to change the answers for this attempt" message in the pop-up box, participants did not hear it. These problems are difficult to detect when blind users do not participate in the accessibility assessment.

In order to complete the accessibility evaluation, AccessMonitor automatically tested the remaining accessibility criteria in Table 1. AccessMonitor counts nonconformities and calculates the accessibility index for each evaluated Web page as described in FCT (2012). Based on these data, two indicators for each Web application were generated: (i) the average accessibility index and (ii) the percentage of nonconformities corresponding to each accessibility level.

Table 6. IFFluminense's Portal's nonconformities by accessibility level (%)

WCAG 2.0	AccessMonitor tests	Iteration (I-2)			Iteration (I-4)		
		A	AA	AAA	A	AA	AAA
1.1.1	Image alternative text	6.2			7.0		
1.1.1	Markup of image maps				6.2		
2.4.1, 4.1.2	Insertion of multimedia				5.8		
1.3.1, 2.4.10	Markup of header						
2.4.5, 2.4.4, 2.4.9, 4.1.2	Markup of links, menus and text links	5.8		25	5.8		25
2.4.1	Links to skip information blocks	12			12		
1.1.1, 1.3.1, 3.2.2, 3.3.2, 4.1.2	Markup of forms				2.1		
4.1.1	Standards W3C: (X) HTML + CSS						
1.3.1, 1.4.1, 1.4.4, 1.4.5, 1.4.9	Presentation/obsolete elements and attributes		3.5			3.5	
1.4.4	Use of absolute units					20	
2.4.2, 2.4.5, 2.4.8	Metadata						
3.1.1	Markup of page primary language						
1.4.3, 1.4.6, 1.4.8	Information contrast						
1.4.8	Text formatting			16			16
1.3.1	Data tables						
1.3.2	Layout tables						
2.1.1, 2.1.3	JavaScript use						

Table 6 shows the percentage of nonconformities obtained in second and fourth iterations (I-2 and I-4) for IFFluminense's Portal. Blank cells in Table 6 and Table 7 indicate that the assessed Web application passed the accessibility test.

Table 7 shows the percentage of nonconformities obtained in the third iteration (I-3) for IFFluminense's Portal, Q-Academico and Moodle. According Carneiro and Rocha (2019), items such as "markup of links, menus and text links" and "presentation/obsolete elements and attributes" are the most significant, since they impact all the evaluated applications.

Comparing iterations' results for IFFluminense's Portal, the percentage of Level A nonconformities (see respective columns A) increased from 17.6% (3 out of 17) the second iteration to 47.1% (8 out of 17) tested criteria in third iteration. In the fourth iteration these criteria improved by 35.3% (6 out of 17). Despite the raise in the accessibility level on IFFluminense's Portal, the accessibility barriers remained the same as follows: "Markup of links", "Menus and text links", "Use of absolute units", "Text formatting", "Links to skip information blocks" and "Image alternative text".

Conversely, in all iterations, issues related to metadata, information contrast, data tables and layout tables were not identified. Yet all assessed pages failed to achieve the WCAG compliance because Web applications had at least one nonconformity in level A, level AA or level AAA. These results demonstrate that none of the evaluated Web pages met the accessibility criteria when evaluated by users and AccessMonitor.

The average accessibility index for IFFluminense's Portal reflected the percentage of nonconformities obtained in iterations as expected. In the first iteration, the four assessed pages from IFFluminense's Portal

Table 7. Nonconformities by accessibility level (%) obtained in the third iteration

WCAG 2.0	AccessMonitor tests	IFFluminense's Portal			Q-Academico			Moodle		
		A	AA	AAA	A	AA	AAA	A	AA	AAA
1.1.1	Image alternative text	7.0			6.2			6.2		
1.1.1	Markup of image maps	6.2								
2.4.1, 4.1.2	Insertion of multimedia	5.9								
1.3.1, 2.4.10	Markup of header				5.9					5.6
2.4.5, 2.4.4, 2.4.9, 4.1.2	Markup of links, menus and text links	5.9		25.0	5.9	100.0				25.0
2.4.1	Links to skip information blocks	12.5			25.0					
1.1.1, 1.3.1, 3.2.2, 3.3.2, 4.1.2	Markup of forms	2.2			4.3					
4.1.1	Standards W3C: (X) HTML + CSS	12.5			12.5			12.5		
1.3.1, 1.4.1, 1.4.4, 1.4.5, 1.4.9	Presentation/obsolete elements and attributes	4.3			5.8	3.6		5.9	3.6	
1.4.4	Use of absolute units		20.0			40.0				
2.4.2, 2.4.5, 2.4.8	Metadata									
3.1.1	Markup of page primary language				25.0			25.0		
1.4.3, 1.4.6, 1.4.8	Information contrast									
1.4.8	Text formatting			25.0			16.7			
1.3.1	Data tables									
1.3.2	Layout tables									
2.1.1, 2.1.3	JavaScript use				20.0					

Source: (Carneiro & Rocha, 2019)

had an average index of 6.3. Next, the average index dropped to 5.6. In the fourth iteration, the average index rose to 5.9. The overall average was 5.9. The average index for the four pages from Moodle was 6.8. The three assessed pages from Q-Academico were assigned an average index of 4.3. The highest average index achieved by Moodle reveal an accessibility concern by Moodle's developers.

Suggestions for Enhancements

Regarding IFFluminense's Portal, Q-Academico and Moodle, when participants were asked how those Web applications could be improved, several suggestions were given. Three participants from the second iteration (P2-1 and P2-3 and P2-4) suggested link-related improvements. P2-4 reported that throughout the experience he listened to messages like: "ball, list containing 6 items, list containing 2 items, ball link Facebook, ball link Instagram". In third iteration, P3.3 reported that a lot of information is repeated on IFFluminense's Portal and on Moodle's pages. P3.2 and P3.3 suggested that Web pages' content be provided in a readable format for screen readers. Also, P3.1 suggested more shortcuts to facilitate information access. Two participants in the fourth iteration suggested that the on screen components be better described and using a logical navigation. Three others also suggested shortcuts to make navigation easier. Such enhancement proposals are compiled as follows:

- The enrollment voucher provided by Q-Academico should be compatible with screen readers (Q4 and Q5).
- The first link on Q-Academico and IFFluminense's Portal should lead users back to the homepage, and provide a shortcut key on the keyboard associated to that link.
- IFFluminense's Portal and Q-Academico should have shortcut commands to allow easy access to the main content (2.4.1 Links to skip information blocks).
- Non-textual content should have an equivalent textual description in all Web applications (1.1.1 Image alternative text).

As for enhancement suggestions for NVDA, in iterations I-2 and I-4, participants were unfamiliar with NVDA. Ten participants (76.9%) reported having had problem to understand the screen reader's voice. The reported reasons are the speed and unclear way words are pronounced. In the third iteration, no participant suggested any enhancements on NVDA.

As for the evaluation guide, all participants found it easy to follow the directions and to understand the questions. Because the guide aimed to evaluate three software products in a row, in the third iteration, more questions and directions were given, which caused participants to rate it as lengthy and tiresome. This issue is resolved by using MIAV to evaluate only one Web application at a time, as in iterations I2 and I4, whose participants did not complain about it. P4.1 and P4.2 reported that "the evaluation guide is very good. The problem is how difficult it is to carry out the evaluation without seeing".

Accessibility Awareness-Raising

In iterations I-2 and I-4, students in the Human-Computer Interaction course evaluated of IFFluminense's Portal's accessibility using MIAV simulating total blindness. These students had taken previous classes on Web development, software quality and accessibility standards such as WCAG and eMAG. Students were invited to volunteer and they signed a WICF containing instructions for the experiment. Out of the nineteen students in the course, six of them participated in the second iteration and seven in the fourth iteration. Six students did not participate.

Participants received a printed list with the shortcuts and NVDA commands. Also, participants were told to turn off their computer monitors, put on headphones and use NVDA to perform the tasks in the evaluation guide. The evaluation guide was already installed on the desktops in TXT format.

Participants' reactions during the experiment were carefully observed. At first, they were surprised, but agreed to participate in the challenge. One participant said: "I can't use the computer without seeing it!". The other participants agreed. When the challenge started they focused on listening carefully to the instructions and performed the tasks proposed in the evaluation guide. Often times, they were not able to understand the read instruction so they used the shortcuts of the form to restart reading.

Somewhere during the challenge the participants could not find out in which of the running application they were on, i. e. they did not know if they were on the Web browser, the Windows desktop or the evaluation guide file. The evaluation was then interrupted. They turned on their monitor just to place the reading cursor on the desired application. Noteworthy that this is not possible when the evaluators are visually-impaired. It took them about one hour to complete the tasks to assess IFFluminense's Portal's accessibility.

After completing the assignments, students were asked to report on their experience and the significance of Web accessibility. Their answers demonstrate that the blind browsing experience was vital for them realize the importance of accessibility. One student stated: "I had not realized that it was so difficult for the visually-impaired to access information. Now I understand how significant accessibility is". In addition, they were unanimous in realizing that Web accessibility is critical. The experience gave them a sense of empathy and responsibility.

5. CONCLUSION

The two main objectives of this work were achieved. On the accessibility assessment of IFFluminense's Portal, Q-Academico and Moodle, the results and discussion section shows respective accessibility issues and indicators. In addition, evaluation using MIAV pointed several suggestions for improving accessibility of these Web applications considering the combination of AccessMonitor results with user experience and opinion. Regarding the significance awareness of accessibility, the application of MIAV in iterations I-2 and I-4 enabled IFFluminense's Information Systems students to have a total blindness experience when browsing IFFluminense's Portal with the support of NVDA. This experience allowed students to become fully aware of the significance of Web accessibility and develop empathy with visually-impaired peers. Future studies may indicate whether this awareness have an effect on the development of more accessible Web pages.

The main contribution of this work is identification of accessibility issues and improvement suggestions for the evaluated Web applications. MIAV strongly contributed to identifying major accessibility issues on the assessed Web pages from the active participation of visually-impaired users. Developers of these software products can resolve their accessibility shortcomings to provide visually-impaired students with fully accessible content. Besides that, all the iterations also asked about evaluation guide and questionnaire to enhancement of the MIAV itself whose results showed that participants found it easy to understand and use. This finer assessment shows that MIAV outperforms automatic assessment tools. Other contribution is awareness-raising of IFFluminense's Information System students on the accessibility importance.

Consideration on threats to validity is essential to enable confidence in research results and assure the research quality (Mustafa, Labiche &Towey, 2019). Empirical studies must treat: internal validity, external validity, construct validity and conclusion validity (Ghazi et al., 2018).This research has some threats to validity that the researchers describe with respective mitigation actions.

Construct validity requires verifying that research measures what it intends to measure. To reduce this threat, the researchers defined accessibility evaluation guide and questionnaire based on the eMAG and WCAG standards, as well as the tasks commonly performed using evaluated Web applications. AccessMonitor was chosen because it had been used in independent research with similar purposes, such as Medina, Cagnin and Paiva (2015) and Marçal et al. (2015). In addition, the calculation of accessibility indicators considers the values obtained through AccessMonitor.

Internal validity refers to factors affecting research outcomes that researchers did not account. A threat is the bias in interpreting the findings due participants that might have misunderstood the accessibility evaluation guide and questionnaire. To minimize this threat, a pilot study was conducted in first iteration (I-1). During the pilot study, NVDA screen reader limitations led participants to inappropriately answer the questions. The researchers improve evaluation guide and questionnaire based on pilot study observations. In addition, the researchers highlighted answers diverging with evaluation guide in the results table using "*" and "-" to avoid misinterpretation.

External validity relates to generalization of research results to other contexts. A threat to the external validity of this study is the sample representativeness, mainly due to the reduced number of participants who evaluated each Web page. In addition, the most of participants had no visual impairment or experience with NVDA screen reader. The researchers asked sighted students to experience total blindness by turning off their computer's monitor and using NVDA. Despite the reduced number of participants being very small, Nielsen and Landauer (1993) argued that a single evaluator can identify one-third of usability problems, and three evaluators are enough to map out 70% of them. The researchers argue that asking more users to evaluate accessibility increases costs, but the benefits improving Web applications accessibility may not increase at the same proportion. This research results are applicable to improve the accessibility of the evaluated Web pages. Therefore, conclusions should not be generalized to other Web pages.

One threat to conclusion validity refers to the completeness of the data on which the research is based. The researchers recognize that only a fraction of the pages of each Web application was assessed because the Web pages are dynamic, which requires that MIAV be applied periodically to assess their current accessibility level. Kane et al. (2007) state that dynamics nature of Web applications and the accuracy of automated test tools can be considered limitations of the used method. To address this limitation, three evaluation iterations of the IFFluminense's Portal were performed at different times. Q-Academico and Moodle were not evaluated in the fourth iteration because IFFluminense has plans to replace them the latest versions.

Suggestions for future works are: (i) to report accessibility results and enhancement suggestions to IFFluminense IT department; (ii) to make MIAV compliant with WCAG 2.1; (iii) to use MIAV to assess the accessibility of Web applications in others areas such as banking, health care and government services; (iv) to analyze the impacts of periodic evaluations on the accessibility indices of the evaluated applications and the daily lives of the visually-impaired users who use them; and (v) to analyze the effect of students' awareness on the accessibility indices of the Web applications they develop. MIAV allows developing Information Systems degree students' empathy regarding challenges faced by the visually-impaired. These future professionals are expected to work hard to develop accessible Web applications.

ACKNOWLEDGMENT

The authors would like to thank the students who participated in this trial and NAPNEE's coordinator for participating in this research and IFFluminense for providing the required infrastructure for the tests. Especially, the researchers thank Marcos K. Pessanha for proofreading the English chapter.

REFERENCES

W3C, World Wide Web Consortium. (2008). Web content accessibility guidelines (WCAG), version 2.0. Retrieved from https://www.w3.org/Translations/WCAG20-pt-PT

W3C, World Wide Web Consortium. (2016). Web Accessibility Evaluation Tools List. Retrieved from https://www.w3.org/WAI/ER/tools

W3C, World Wide Web Consortium. (2018). Web Content Accessibility Guidelines (WCAG) 2.1. Retrieved from https://www.w3.org/TR/WCAG21/

Abu Shawar, B. (2015). Evaluating Web Accessibility of Educational websites. *International Journal of Emerging Technologies in Learning, 10*(4), 4–10. doi:10.3991/ijet.v10i4.4518

NV Access. (n.d.). About NVDA. Retrieved from https://www.nvaccess.org/

Acosta-Vargas, P., Acosta, T., & Luján-Mora, S. (2018). Challenges to assess accessibility in higher education websites: A comparative study of Latin America universities. *IEEE Access, 6*, 36500–36508. doi:10.1109/ACCESS.2018.2848978

Acosta-Vargas, P., Luján-Mora, S., & Salvador-Ullauri, L. (2016). Evaluation of the Web accessibility of higher-education websites. In *Proceedings of 15th International Conference on Information Technology Based Higher Education and Training* (pp. 1-6). Academic Press. 10.1109/ITHET.2016.7760703

Ahmi, A., & Mohamad, R. (2019). Bibliometric Analysis of Global Scientific Literature on Web Accessibility. *International Journal of Recent Technology and Engineering, 7*(6), 250–258.

Botelho, L., & Porciúncula, K. (2018). The challenges for producing indicators on people with disability: yesterday, today and tomorrow. In: *National and International Overview of Social Indicator Production: specific Population Groups and Time Use*. IBGE, Brazilian Institute of Geography and Statistics. Retrieved Sep 24, 2019, from https://biblioteca.ibge.gov.br/visualizacao/livros/liv101562.pdf

Bradbard, D. A., & Peters, C. (2010). Web accessibility theory and practice: An introduction for university faculty. *The Journal of Educators Online, 7*(1), 1–46. doi:10.9743/JEO.2010.1.1

Brazil. (1996). LDB Law of Directives and Bases of National Education, Brazil. Retrieved from www.planalto.gov.br/ccivil_03/LEIS/L9394.htm

Brazil. (2007). Brazilian Ordinance that institutionalizes the e-Government Accessibility Model eMAG within the scope of the Information and Computer Resource Management System – SISP, Brazil. Retrieved from http://www.normas.gov.br/materia/-/asset_publisher/NebW5rLVWyej/content/id/54991011

Brazil. (2009). Brazilian Decree that promulgates the International Convention on the Rights of Persons with Disabilities and its Optional Protocol, Brazil. Retrieved from http://www.planalto.gov.br/ccivil_03/_ato2007-2010/2009/decreto/d6949.htm

Brazil. (2014). eMAG - Accessibility Model in Electronic Government, Brazil. Retrieved from http://emag.governoeletronico.gov.br

Brazil. (2015). Brazilian Law on the Inclusion of Persons with Disabilities (Statute of Persons with Disabilities), Brazil. Retrieved from http://www.planalto.gov.br/ccivil_03/_Ato2015-2018/2015/Lei/L13146.htm

Brazil (2018). IFFluminense Portal. Retrieved July 2, 2018, from http://portal1.iff.edu.br

Carneiro, G. de A. S., & Rocha, M. A. A. (2019). MIAV: an inclusive method for accessibility assessment by visually impaired people. In *Proceedings of International Conference Interfaces and Human Computer Interaction 2019 (part of MCCSIS 2019)* (pp. 57-64). Academic Press. 10.33965/ihci2019_201906L008

Carter, J., & Markel, M. (2001). Web accessibility for people with disabilities: An introduction for Web developers. *IEEE Transactions on Professional Communication*, *44*(4), 225–233. doi:10.1109/47.968105

da Silva, A. B. P., da Silva, C. G., & Moraes, R. L. de O. (2019). On the Use of a Continuous Accessibility Assessment Process for Dealing with Website Evolution. In *Proceedings of International Conference Interfaces and Human Computer Interaction 2019 (part of MCCSIS 2019)* (pp. 57-64). Academic Press.

Espadinha, C., Pereira, L. M., da Silva, F. M., & Lopes, F. M. (2011). Accessibility of Portuguese Public Universities' sites. *Disability and Rehabilitation*, *33*(6), 475–485. doi:10.3109/09638288.2010.498554 PMID:20594034

FCT, Foundation for Science and Technology. (2013). AccessMonitor. ACCESS Unit of FCT, I.P. Portugal. Retrieved from http://www.acessibilidade.gov.pt/accessmonitor

Fernández, J. M., Roig, J., & Soler, V. (2010). Web Accessibility on Spanish Universities. In *Proceedings of 2nd International Conference on Evolving Internet* (pp. 215-219). IEEE.

Ghazi, A. N., Petersen, K., Reddy, S. S. V. R., & Nekkanti, H. (2018). Survey Research in Software Engineering: Problems and Mitigation Strategies. *IEEE Access*, *7*, 24703–24718. doi:10.1109/AC-CESS.2018.2881041

IBGE, Brazilian Institute of Geography and Statistics. (2015). National Health Survey (PNS) 2013: Life Cycles. Brazil and Major Regions. Retrieved from https://biblioteca.ibge.gov.br/visualizacao/livros/liv94522.pdf

İşeri, E. İ., Uyar, K., & İlhan, Ü. (2017). The accessibility of Cyprus Islands' higher education institution websites. *Procedia Computer Science*, *120*, 967–974. doi:10.1016/j.procs.2017.11.333

ISO/IEC. (2011). ISO/IEC 25010:2011. Systems and software engineering — Systems and software Quality Requirements and Evaluation (SQuaRE) — System and software quality models.

ISO/IEC. (2012). ISO/IEC 40500:2012. Information technology - W3C Web Content Accessibility Guidelines (WCAG) 2.0.

Kane, S. K., Shulman, J. A., Shockley, T. J., & Ladner, R. E. (2007, May). A Web accessibility report card for top international university Web sites. In *Proceedings of the 2007 international cross-disciplinary conference on Web accessibility (W4A)* (pp. 148-156). ACM. 10.1145/1243441.1243472

Marçal, B., Amante, M. J., Pinto, C., & Neto, L. (2015, December). Evaluation of the accessibility levels of the pages and bibliographic catalogs of the libraries of higher education institutions. In *Proceedings of the III International Conference for Inclusion (INCLUDiT)*. Academic Press.

Medina, J. L., Cagnin, M. I., & Paiva, D. M. B. (2015). Investigating accessibility on web-based maps. *Applied Computing Review*, *15*(2), 17–26. doi:10.1145/2815169.2815171

Menzi-Çetin, N., Alemdağ, E., Tüzün, H., & Merve, Y. M. (2017). Evaluation of a university website's usability for visually impaired Students. *Universal Access in the Information Society, 16*(1), 151-160.

Moodle. (2017). Moodle PTCE - Campus Campos Centro. Retrieved from http://ensino.centro.iff.edu. br/moodle/

Moreno, C. G. (2008). Web accessibility. In C. Calero, M. A. Moraga, & M. Piattini (Eds.), Handbook of Research on Web Information Systems Quality (pp. 163–180). Hershey, PA: IGI Global. doi:10.4018/978-1-59904-847-5.ch010

Mustafa, N., Labiche, Y., & Towey, D. (2019, July).Mitigating threats to validity in empirical software engineering: A traceability case study. In *Proceedings of the 2019 IEEE 43rd Annual Computer Software and Applications Conference (COMPSAC)* (Vol. 2, pp. 324-329). IEEE. 10.1109/COMPSAC.2019.10227

Nielsen, J., & Landauer, T. (1993). A mathematical model of the finding of usability problems. In *Proceedings of the INTERACT'93 and CHI'93 conference on Human factors in computing systems* (pp. 206-213). ACM. 10.1145/169059.169166

Oliveira, A., de Souza, E. M., & Eler, M. M. (2017, May). Accessibility model in electronic government: Evaluation of Brazilian web portals. In *Proceedings of the XIII Brazilian Symposium on Information Systems* (pp. 332-339). Academic Press. 10.5753bsi.2017.6060

Pereira, A. S., Machado, A. M. & Carneiro, T. C. J. (2013). Web Accessibility Evaluation on Brazilian Institutions in Higher Education. *Informacao & Sociedade - Estudos, 23*(3), 123-142.

Qualidata. (2017). Welcome to Q-AcademicoWeb. Retrieved from https://academico.iff.edu.br

Sartoretto, M., & Bersch, R. (2017). Assistive Technology and Education. Retrieved from http://www. assistiva.com.br/tassistiva.html

United Nations, Department of Economic and Social Affairs, Population Division. (2019). World Population Prospects 2019: Ten Key Findings. Retrieved from https://population.un.org/wpp/Publications/Files/WPP2019_10KeyFindings.pdf

WHO, World Health Organization. (2018). Disability and health: Key facts. Retrieved from https://www. who.int/en/news-room/fact-sheets/detail/disability-and-health

ADDITIONAL READING

Angélico, M. J., Silva, A., Teixeira, S. F., Maia, T., & Silva, A. M. (2020). Web Accessibility and Transparency for Accountability: The Portuguese Official Municipal websites. In Open Government: Concepts, Methodologies, Tools, and Applications (pp. 1579-1605). Hershey, PA: IGI Global.

Antkers, A., Miller, S., Galleher, S., Reid, B. E. & Schofield, B. (2018). Authorship and Accessibility in the Digital Age (September 11, 2018). Authors Alliance, Silicon Flatirons, and Berkeley Center for Law & Technology Roundtable Report, 2018. Retrieved from https://ssrn.com/abstract=3254959

Hilera, J. R., Otón, S., Timbi-Sisalima, C., Aguado-Delgado, J., Estrada-Martínez, F. J., & Amado-Salvatierra, H. R. (2018). Combining multiple Web accessibility evaluation reports using semantic Web technologies. In *Advances in Information Systems Development* (pp. 65–78). Springer. doi:10.1007/978-3-319-74817-7_5

Ismail, A., Kuppusamy, K. S., & Nengroo, A. S. (2018). Multi-tool accessibility assessment of government department websites: A case-study with JKGAD. *Disability and Rehabilitation. Assistive Technology*, *13*(6), 504–516. doi:10.1080/17483107.2017.1344883 PMID:28766367

Ramakrishnan, I. V., Ashok, V., & Billah, S. M. (2019). Alternative Nonvisual Web Browsing Techniques. In *Web Accessibility* (pp. 629–649). Springer. doi:10.1007/978-1-4471-7440-0_32

Silveira, B. C. A., Silva-de-Souza, T., & da Rocha, A. R. C. (2018, October). Software Accessibility for Visually Impaired People: a systematic mapping study. In *Proceedings of the 17th Brazilian Symposium on Software Quality* (pp. 190-199). ACM. 10.1145/3275245.3275266

Singh, S., Bhandari, A., & Pathak, N. (2018, April). Accessify: An ML Powered Application to Provide Accessible Images on Web Sites. In *Proceedings of the Internet of Accessible Things* (p. 29). ACM. 10.1145/3192714.3192830

Tsatsou, P. (2019). Digital inclusion of people with disabilities: A qualitative study of intra-disability diversity in the digital realm. *Behaviour & Information Technology*, 1–16. doi:10.1080/0144929X.2019.1636136

KEY TERMS AND DEFINITIONS

eMAG: The Brazilian e-Government Accessibility Model.

HTML: Hypertext Markup Language. Language used to write electronic documents, to be interpreted by browsers and screen readers.

IFFluminense: A Brazilian VET school in upstate Rio.

MIAV: An Inclusive Method for Accessibility Assessment by Visually-impaired users and awareness-raising that complies with WCAG and Brazilian eMAG guidelines. MIAV combines two techniques for accessibility assessment: an automated one and one based on users experience and opinion.

NAPNEE: IFFluminense's Support Center for Students with Special Educational Needs.

Q-Academico: A Web application through which teachers record course grades so that their students access them.

W3C: The World Wide Web Consortium (W3C) is an international consortium to develop protocols and guidelines that ensure long-term growth for the Web.

WCAG: The Web Content Accessibility Guidelines (WCAG) covers general principles of Web accessible design. ISO/IEC 40500: 2012 (ISO/IEC, 2012) standardized the WCAG.

Chapter 3
What–If Analysis on the Evaluation of User Interface Usability

Saulo Silva
https://orcid.org/0000-0002-0675-7173
University of Minho, Portugal

Mariana Carvalho
https://orcid.org/0000-0003-2190-4319
University of Minho, Portugal

Orlando Belo
https://orcid.org/0000-0003-2157-8891
University of Minho, Portugal

ABSTRACT

While interactive systems have the potential to increase human work performance, those systems are predisposed to usability problems. Different factors might contribute to these problems during the interaction process and as result, the decision-making process might be compromised. This work uses decision support system methods and tools to assist in the analysis of the usability of a university library website, measuring the constructs of effectiveness, efficiency, and learnability. The pilot study involved thirty-five subjects, and after collecting data, a multidimensional view of the data is created and discussed. Later, a What-if analysis is used to investigate the impact of different scenarios on system-use. The work has the potential to assist designers and system administrators at improving their systems.

DOI: 10.4018/978-1-7998-2637-8.ch003

INTRODUCTION

Currently, industrial society is experiencing transformations without precedents. Technological improvements shape how people work and live. For the working sector, transformations that might improve work processes are always on demand. As work is an inseparable part of the human life, transformations in work processes have the potential to impact how humans live. While part of this impact is positive, challenges always exist and must be addressed. For instance, the use of steam power to mechanise production was introduced in First Industrial Revolution, dated around 1760s, creating plenty of opportunities, such as improving production processes and creating new factories and cities (Xu et al., 2018). General challenges to be addressed were to create good work and living conditions in the newly created factories and cities, respectively. Second Industrial Revolution (dated around 1870s) intended to improve production by employing electric power generated from combustion engines, inaugurating the mass production era (Xu et al., 2018). General challenges during that event were related to continue improving professional and social life in dimensions ranging from economy and politics, to urbanisation and transportation. Automated production era is introduced during the Third Industrial Revolution (dated around 1960s), based on electronics and information technology (Xu et al., 2018). Examples of general challenges were related to improvement of several dimensions, such as social aspects of work, diversification in energy sources used in production, development of production, management and governance systems, amid others.

Fourth Industrial Revolution programmes, represented by initiatives such as Industrie 4.0 (also referred to as Industry 4.0) in Germany or Smart Factoring in USA, implies the evolution of industrial workforce, i.e., the use of new types of interactions between human operators and machines (Lorenz et al., 2015). Thanks to technologies such as Big Data Analytics (Russom, 2011), Information Systems (Stair & Reynolds, 2013) and Industrial Internet of Things (Rawat et al. 2017), a new set of applications are possible, bringing improvements in industrial areas such as maintenance, coordination among jobs, decision-making, among others. To achieve production growth, industries escalate the use of technology for employees. Even though, this phenomenon is not restricted to industrial sector, this introduction provides a "thermometer" of how technology use is escalating. Therefore, an increasing number of systems are becoming part of the modern person's routine, regardless of work position or salary.

Among the several types of today's existing computer systems, it is possible to highlight one type, those that human operators interact with, referred to as Interactive Systems (Benyon, 2014), pervasive in all sectors of modern society. The kind of interaction processes existing between humans and computers might range from directly manipulating system controls (e.g., configuring medical devices or pre-setting flight parameters in cockpit) to monitoring the system when it automatically changes between previously programmed configurations (e.g., monitoring assembling line equipment in industrial sector, monitoring the application of treatment by Radiation Medical equipment or monitoring Energy Plants' control panels). It is important to underline that for the interaction process to take place, those systems must provide interfaces to be used by humans, which in turn are designed for supporting their decision-making processes. The human interface is also referred to as User Interface (UI) or Man-Machine Interface, and according to (Benyon, 2014) is defined as the part of the system with which humans come into contact, physically, perceptually and conceptually. When such interfaces use sophisticated graphical support – Graphical User Interfaces (GUI) –, they provide graphical elements to control the system – e.g., buttons, screens, text boxes, or sliders. User interfaces seek to provide system representation to the user, exposing the processes behind the system under control. Users make use of the system to achieve an established goal with it, and if the UI has flaws or problems, the goal is unachieved. Some systems have critical functions, such as medical, energy and aeronautical systems, and in such cases, are referred to as critical interactive systems, or High Assurance (HA) systems. For those systems, problems in the UI design have the potential for causing losses of different nature, such as financial, environmental or social, which Leveson (2011) characterises as accidents.

To prevent such kind of problems, the development of user interfaces requires knowledge from different domains, such as Software Engineering, Ergonomics, Psychology, just to name a few. UI experts make use of information from those domains to perceive what are the aspects considered important for system use, and therefore how to provide the best solutions in terms of computer controls that suit human expectations, consequently averting gaps that could induce to interaction errors. Human Computer Interaction (HCI) research field gather human interaction designers, responsible for engineering UI observing human factors aspects from the previously referred domains, as well as employing various evaluation methods to ensure safe and effective operation of the interaction process. Usability evaluation is one of research areas in HCI, investigating how usage aspects might be impacted by software engineering and human factors related aspects. Usability research employ means for understanding how humans perceive the systems in terms of constructs, such as learnability, efficiency, or efficacy, as well as how to design systems that comply with those dimensions. Those are important aspects that we must consider when the goal is supporting human expectations and their related decision-making processes, a concept that when related with computers is referred to as decision support systems (DSS) by Fick and Sprague (2013). For some researchers, DSS represent a kind of interactive system that managers use for accessing business data, while for others DSS represent analytical models suited for decision-making processes. Regardless of the group and how they understand the concept, its importance is unquestionable, as it intercepts different fields of the modern world.

In this work, we focused in a particular UI: a university library website, which provides curated and catalogued information, and therefore are among the most essential resources for students and researchers. Producing a well-designed website is of major importance for universities and companies' system designers, seeking to support their strategic goals. Well-designed websites can be valuable tools for users, as it supports their decision-making processes, fulfilling their needs and expectations, assisting them in task accomplishment. Several criteria exist to define what a well-designed website is, such as reliability and security (Fernandez et al., 2011). However, from the user point of view, usability is an important aspect to consider (Djamasbi et al., 2010; Okhovati et al., 2017).

Our work was to find a way for evaluating the referred library website, considering the user reported data (ISO/IEC, 1998), differently from other ways of evaluating usability as considered in ISO/IEC 25066:2015, Common Industry Format (CIF) for Usability (ISO/IEC, 2016) (e.g., inspection-based evaluation, user behaviour observation-based evaluation). Okhovati et al., (2017) highlighted that end users expect the library website to be easy to use, efficient in performing a specific task and ensure their satisfaction when they use it. Therefore, all efforts that can be deployed for ensure the correctness and way of working of websites are important, not only in terms of automatic or manual evaluations, but especially considering human factors. This is why a multidimensional view of the usability evaluation has the potential to improve the analysis results. It allows for the extraction of additional information from the data, satisfying the role of DSS for those interested in providing a well-designed UI. By assisting in the control, analysis and visualisation, regarding companies and its processes it also has potential to improve how decision-makers and practitioners understand the new decision models and methods in information analysis, such as management information systems for Business and Information Systems fields.

As a multidimensional data solution, we propose the use of a Data Warehouse (DW), which evolves from the DSS according to Golfarelli and Rizzi (2009), providing a new computer environment for strategic information, obtained from pre-existing systems in companies. Additionally, it is proposed the application of a What-if analysis approach for enriching the usability evaluation results. Consequently, the contributions of this paper are as follows: to provide a literature review for themes such as DSS, What-If Analysis and Usability Evaluation, as well as to provide a clear understanding of how they are related. Our goal was to bring all those concepts without losing sight of its centrality for the evaluation of interactive computer system's interfaces, i.e., its importance on how they can be used for improving those interfaces. The remaining part of this paper is organised as follows: Section 2 provides related work about usability and DSS. Section 3 presents considerations about the experiment design and implementation of the multidimensional data view. Section 4 presents the usability analysis based on data collected from respondents from the investigation framework constructs, an instance of DSS analysis method using What-if Analysis, as well as considerations for future work. Finally, Section 5 offers some conclusions remarks.

RELATED WORK

According to Lee & Kozar (2012) there is lack of consensus for which dimensions to consider for evaluating poor website usability. Evidence exists that most evaluation studies of digital libraries are related with usability (Kous et al., 2018). Usability can be seen as a set of multiple constructs derived from various perspectives, such as effectiveness, efficiency, subjective pleasure, or memorability, with large focus on interface design (Jeng, 2006). Describing all the possible usability evaluation methods used in libraries websites is not within the scope of this work - for a more in-depth review about usability and its impact on digital libraries research see Jeng (2005), Xie (2006), or Chowdhury et al. (2006). The work of Lee & Kozar (2012) presents in-depth literature review about website usability, their theoretical models and constructs, as well as the relationships between them. Nielsen and Rubin are important actors in the history of usability research, as they begin the development of usability engineering techniques for computer software design applied to Web design in the early 1990s (Nielsen, 2003). About usability, they establish that "is a quality attribute that describes how easy user interfaces are to use" (Kous et al., 2018). The work of Bevan (1995) reveals positive correlation between usability and quality. Several definitions of usability and which characteristics are considered in the model have been proposed. In their critical analysis and proposal of taxonomy for usability, Alonso-Ríos et al. (2009) provide a list of how other experts consider usability constructs (Table 1). One of the most widely accepted conceptualisation for usability is provided by the chapter of Ergonomics of human-system interaction of the International Organization for Standardization (ISO), which is Standard ISO 9241-11. This document has a long history of contributions for building the basis of understanding and application of usability, which was meticulously described by Bevan et al. (2015). In this particular case, usability is considered as "the extent to which a product can be used by a specified user to achieve specified goals with effectiveness, efficiency and satisfaction in a specified context of use" (ISO/IEC, 1998). ISO 9241-11 considers the construct of Effectiveness as measurements related to the accuracy and completeness at which users achieve specific goals (e.g., accuracy could represent the number of errors while completing a certain task and deviations from regulations established for task completion, while efficacy could be measured by the number of sub-tasks completed within a task list). Additionally, ISO 9241-11 considers the Ef-

Table 1: Usability classifications (based on Alonso-Ríos et al., 2009).

Authors	Attributes
Nielsen (1993); Nielsen and Loranger (2006)	Learnability, efficiency, memorability, errors and satisfaction;
Preece, Benyon, Davies, Keller, & Rogers (1993)	Safety, effectiveness, efficiency, and enjoyableness;
Preece et al. (1994)	Learnability, throughput, flexibility, and attitude;
Quesenbery (2001, 2003, 2004)	Effectiveness, efficiency, engagement, error tolerance, and ease of learning;
Abran et al. (2003)	Effectiveness, efficiency, satisfaction, learnability and security;
Seffah, Donyaee, Kline, and Padda (2006), Lee & Kozar (2012)	Efficiency, effectiveness, productivity, satisfaction, learnability, safety, trustfulness, accessibility, universality, and usefulness.

ficiency construct as a measurement of the resources used to achieve effectiveness (e.g., in this list of measurements the authors can consider the measurements of material resources used to complete tasks, measurement of time resources to complete a task or even measurement of physical effort, such as mental effort required to complete that task). Finally, the standard considers the construct of Satisfaction as the measurement of discomfort while making use of the product (e.g., one can consider the measurements of the subjective level of experienced discomfort while making use of a product or developing a task, or also positive/negative comments during the use).

Since the constructs considered by ISO 9241-11 are the most widely applied to examine usability aspects, Joo (2010) proposed an experiment to study the correlation between effectiveness, efficiency, and satisfaction. By adopting an assessment model based on ISO 9241-11 to operationalise the research instrument, twelve students were recruited to assess a digital library system. When evaluating the final results of the assessment, the Pearson correlation coefficients (r) of all constructs was calculated, providing evidence of strong correlation between all the constructs ($r > 0.6$), with higher correlation between effectiveness and satisfaction ($r = 0.889$). Due to these findings, the authors decided to propose a different framework used as research instrument, in which the construct of satisfaction gave place to the construct of learnability as part of the research instrument. The Learnability construct is based on software engineering aspects, such as the usability model proposed by Nielsen (Nielsen, 1994), which refers to how easy it is for casual users to learn a system, or based on ISO/IEC 9126 (ISO/IEC, 2001) and ISO/IEC 25010:2011 (ISO/IEC, 2011), referring to the capability of a software product for enabling users to learn how to use it (learnability measurements could include time taken for first time users to achieve tasks with the product/system in different sessions using it, where decreasing time indicates

Table 2: Characteristics of the strategic information according to Ponniah (2011).

Characteristics	Description
Integrated	Must be a single, enterprise wide view.
Data Integrity	Information must be accurate and must conform to business rules.
Accessible	Easily accessible with intuitive access paths, and responsive for analysis.
Credible	Every business factor must have one and only one value.
Timely	Information must be available within the stipulated time frame.

Figure 1. A typical simulation model for what-if analysis

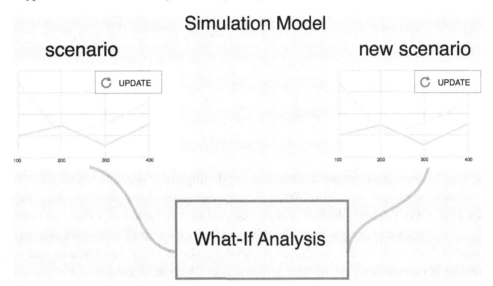

higher learnability rates). Additionally, Joo (2010) identifies several studies that consider learnability as a key attribute of the usability (Nielsen, 1994; Brinck, 2001; Guenther, 2003).

The increasing business competitiveness has led to the need of obtaining information that improves strategic planning capacity. Ponniah (2011) describes strategic information as those with added value, sharing characteristics (details in Table 2) such as integration, integrity, accessibility, credibility and that are timely. In order to achieve this, one possibility was to re-signify pre-existing data in the companies, obtaining multidimensional information from it that might assist in a decision-making process. DSS are then characterised by their mission to improve the decision-making process, by providing either interactive systems that managers can use to access data, or analytic models suited for the decision-making process. From the need to re-signify data, the concept of data warehouse (DW) emerged. Muntean and Târnăveanu (2012) highlights that a DW is defined as a special kind of a database, in which atomic data are gathered from several sources in a structured way for creating a multidimensional and oriented version of the corporative truths, which allows for precise initiatives to support decision making processes. There are several divergences about the best approach for defining DW architecture, in terms of quality, high performance or scalability. Ralph Kimball, for instance, supports the idea that each business area should freely implement its own databases, based on their requirements (Matouk & Owoc, 2012). Bill Inmon in contrast, supports a top-down approach, in which the databases are developed according to the DW final project, i.e., a central scheme working as a model for the departments to develop their own databases (Breslin, 2004).

The importance of usability is undeniable. It has the potential to increase user satisfaction, to improve efficiency and productivity and to decrease costs (Mazumder, 2012). Usually, the evaluation of usability involves activities such as collecting, analysing and critiquing usability data (Ivory and Hearst, 1999). The analysis is a crucial phase in this process due to the importance of interpreting data and analysing results. What-If analysis is a technique that can assist in this task. It assists the user in creating and running simulation models, considering complex relationships between business variables, also referred to

Figure 2. Goal-seek example (a) and results (b)

a)   b)

as scenarios, based on human information. Therefore, modelling a user interaction with a user interface is one of many advantages of the integration of What-If analysis simulation in usability evaluation processes.

Golfarelli, et al. (2006) defines What-If analysis as a method that allows for decision makers to create hypothetical scenarios and analyse possible effects in the behaviour of a complex system caused by changing variables' values. In other words, this technology allows beforehand assessment in business outcome as result of manipulating parameters and changing what can be considered as normal business behaviour, without endangering real business. This technology ends up being useful in testing and validating business hypotheses and a safer solution to address any doubt, like for instance, answer the What-If type question such as "What if a new strategy is pursued?" What-If analysis also assists to ensure that the subsequent decisions will have some success, by assisting the user in simulating the hypothetical scenarios and analyse the outcome. Moreover, it allows analysing different scenarios and perspectives of business, anticipating some possible solutions. The process of What-If analysis implements a simulation model (Figure 1). This model represents the real business model and can be composed by a set of scenarios based on historical data. The user is responsible to delineate the axis of analysis, the set of values for analysing and the set of values of the scenario, considering his/her goals. To perform the What-If analysis, an appropriate tool is required, which can perform the analysis to provide new (altered) scenario.

Goal seek is Microsoft Office Excel's (Excel, 2019) built-in What-If analysis tool, which helps the user to answer What-If type questions by showing what could be the effects of changing a cells' value in a specific scenario. In other words, it determines what value a user should enter in an input cell to get the desired result in a cell that contains a formula. Goal seek receives a formula cell, the desired value and the cell to change in order to achieve the target and performs all the need calculations giving the user the wanted value. A symbolic example of how goal seek works (Figure 2) is as follows. Considering a retail company and a basic model with the number of units sold (1500 units), retail price ($15) and discount (25%), a calculation formula is used to calculate the total revenue reveals $16,875.00. The main goal of this analysis is to discover how many units the retail company needs to sell to reach $25,000 of revenue (Figure 2a). In antecedence, however, is important to define the "Set cell", "To value" and "By changing cell" in the goal seek dialog box. The set cell is the revenue cell (represented by D5 cell), and the goal is to alter this cell to '$25,000', by changing the cell of the '1500' units sold (represented by D2). After Goal Seek is performed (Figure 2b), the tool (Excel) informs that the Goal Seek provides a solution: 2222 units need to be sold to achieve the target value.

The literature of What-If analysis provides some relevant references about its use in usability evaluation. For instance, Hearst and Landay (1999) surveys a state of the art of automation of user interface usability evaluation and suggest that the use of What-If analysis in an earlier development phase can assist in avoiding costly mistakes. A simulator referred to as Monte Carlo (Rubinstein and Kroese, 2016) employs a probabilistic simulator model that uses What-If analysis and is frequently used in usability evaluations. Arh and Jerman-Blazic (2007) proposed a complex decision-making solution for the evaluation of learning management systems, by studying and analysing usability, applicability and adequacy of learning management systems. These authors suggest making use of What-If analysis in the learning management systems evaluation and analysis phase. Eklund et al., (2008) implement a usability evaluation method for software development by making use of eXtreme Programming (Agile Methodology for Software Development). During the usability evaluation setup, the authors use What-If analysis to simulate several types of analysis. What-If analysis is also referred in other Human-Computer Interaction (HCI) literature, such as in aviation safety, where Rungta et al. (2013) presents a formal verification approach based on simulation and on model checking to guarantee the safety in human-machine systems. The models are created by making use of Brahms, which embeds What-if analysis and allows for modelling several components by making use of simulation; and in discrete event simulation models with virtual reality integration, Turner et al. (2016) uses What-If analysis in the experimentation and validation of the discrete event simulation model.

EXPERIMENT DESIGN

In this paper we show how we extended usability analysis by making use of a DW as a DSS, keeping the centrality of the interactive system's user interfaces analysis, this section is devoted to present the considerations about the design of the experiment, i.e., the research strategy to design the research instrument, gather the data from end users, deploy a DW, as well as use scenarios and What-If analysis to improve the usability analysis. The first subsection presents the information about user interfaces and usability analysis, as well as information about the research instrument. Information about the data collection in the experimental design is also provided. The second subsection presents information about the DW design created to support a multidimensional view of the research instrument, including the transition between the research instrument data to the fully deployed DW. Finally, the third and last subsection presents information about how to use scenarios and What-If analysis to improve the user interface under analysis. Limitations of this research are presented in the last subsection.

Gathering, Preparing and Storing Data

The word 'usability' refers to methods that improve ease-of-use during the design process. In general, the usability of a system has the potential to impact how users accomplish tasks in a system. To provide well-designed interactive systems, tools and methods are required for understanding the usability of user interfaces, as well as for improving them (Root and Draper, 1983). In this work, the authors adopted the usability evaluation model and associated evaluation survey tool proposed by Joo (2011), tailored to academic libraries websites. The authors decided to design the research instrument in the form of a research survey, which is used to obtain necessary data to analyse. The survey makes use of structured questionnaire, composed by a set of closed questions, as opposed to open-ended questions where the responder is free to provide his own answers. In this case, we used the Likert scale to transform order points into a linear scale (Babbie, 1999) and to address two groups of information, namely:

Table 3. Likert Scale defined for the research instrument (Babbie, 1999)

(1) I strongly disagree	(2) Disagree	(3) Slightly disagree	(4) I do not agree or disagree	(5) Slightly agree	(6) I agree	(7) I totally agree
(Do not answer at all to the required)	(Serves with failed the minimum required)	(Meets partially below the expectations)	(Neither agree or disagree)	(Meets partially above the expectations)	(Meets completely the expectations)	(Above the expectations)

1. Demographic information (filter questions), for exploring the characteristics of the different study groups.
2. Research questions information, also referred to as usability evaluation instrument, directly related with the usability evaluation model in the context of academic libraries, proposed by Joo (2011).

Typically, the scale rating ranges from 5, 7 and 9 points. We decided to use a 7 points scale (Table 3), starting with the alternative "I strongly disagree" (1 point), following additional six intervals, until the final interval designated "I totally agree" (7 points), respectively. The research survey was designed for collecting information in a monthly basis periodicity.

The process of data collection intended for evaluating the University of Minho's central library website. The research instrument was hosted in a specific computational platform for data gathering and treatment, where university's staff (including master and PhD students, as well as researchers) was invited to participate in the research. The research instrument that is proposed is composed by filter and specific questions. As part of the set of filter questions the authors' highlight investigated respondent characteristics such as gender, age, university status, level of computer skill and computer's use frequency of the respondent (detailed in Table 4). Respondents' profiles are also presented.

As for the specific questions, each respondent is requested to indicate his classification to six questions regarding each of the three research constructs (properties) investigated, namely effectiveness, efficiency and learnability. The questions are detailed in Table 5.

A number of thirty-five respondents ($n = 35$) participated in the experiment. All the answers were collect by making use of specific web platform. Worth noticing that although the amount of data collected represent small data volume for a DW, it represents a case study that fits the dynamics of a Web application, from where periodic data is collected, therefore increasing data volume.

A previous step before the DW design and implementation is related with the definition of the operational system, i.e., the database from where the data is selected. By this definition, the research instrument might be an operational system itself. For this research, the Data Base Management System (DBMS) adopted to host both operational system and DW databases was MySQL (MySQL, 2001).

Based on the collected data and the pre-established requisites for usability evaluation the authors decided to design a decision support data structure especially conceived for this usability case analysis. This structure includes all the analysis dimensions the authors considered to be the most relevant for the case, namely "Date", which is a temporal dimension, "Question", which supports the questions themselves, "Respondent", where the authors characterised in terms of frequency, skill, or gender, who answered the usability question, and "Property", which is the dimension that describes the property associated with a particular question. These four dimensions are materialised in four relational tables ("Date_Dim", "Question_Dim", "Respondent_Dim", and "Property_Dim") that jointly with a fifth table – a fact table

Table 4. Characteristics and profile of the respondents

Category name	Characteristic	Profile (%)
Gender	Female	20
	Male	80
	Prefer not to declare	-
Age	18-24	85.7
	25-30	5.7
	31-40	5.7
	41-50	-
	51-60	2.9
Status	Graduation/Master Student	94.3
	PhD Student	5.7
	Professor/Researcher	-
Level of computer skill	Intermediate level	14.3
	Advanced level	54.3
	Expert level	31.4
Use frequency	Daily or Almost Daily	100
	Once or Twice a Week	-
	Once or Twice a Month	-
	Once or Twice a Year	-

("Usability_Fact") – formed a relational star-schema (Figure 3), one of the most typical configuration for a data warehouse. The definition of the granularity level of the fact table is an important aspect in the design of the data warehouse, as it impacts directly its performance and analysis capacity. A very high level of granularity might reduce system performance, once it stores a higher number of registers. A very low level of granularity might affect the analysis, since the data are usually shortened. The proposed grain of the analysis is then the classification given by each of the respondents to the specific questions of the research instrument. The field "ScaleValues" in the fact table "Usability_Fact" is responsible for storing this specific information.

Obtaining the multidimensional data view of the collected data implies the extraction, transformation and loading the data received from the Web-based form into the data warehouse. To accomplish this task the authors have developed an ETL (extract-transform-load) process, represented in Figure 4.

This process is crucial. It needs to be carefully performed for ensuring the correct data gathering and storing into the data warehouse structures, and guaranteeing that the data can be used to identify new strategic information (e.g., tendencies) to improve the decision-making process. ETL operations are usually performed by a set of tools known as back-end tools, in reference to the tools used by the engineers in charge of maintenance and management operations of such kind of systems, as opposed to front-end tools, which managers and decision-makers make use for activities such as consulting reports, graphics and information using the DW system. According to Kimbal (1996), the main operations performed by the back-end tools are: 1) extraction of data from internal and external sources; 2) cleaning or normalisation of the extracted data; 3) loading data into the data warehouse; and 4) updating data (refresh).

Table 5. Constructs and measurement items from investigation framework, adapted from Joo (2011)

Constructs	Item
Effectiveness	1 - I can usually complete a search task using the University of Minho's Library website.
	2 - I am successful in general in finding academic resource(s) using the University of Minho's Library website.
	3 - Overall, the University of Minho's Library website is useful in helping me find information.
	4 - I usually achieve what I want using the University of Minho's Library website.
	5 - The resources I obtain from the University of Minho's Library website are usually useful.
	6 - University of Minho's Library website usually covers sufficient topics that I try to explore.
Efficiency	7 - It is easy to find the academic resources that I want on the University of Minho's Library website.
	8 - The University of Minho's Library website is easy to use in general.
	9 - I can complete a resource finding task quickly using the University of Minho's Library website.
	10 - The University of Minho's Library website is well designed to find what I want.
	11 - It is easy to perform searches on the University of Minho's Library website.
	12 - I get the results of searches quickly when using the University of Minho's Library website.
Learnability	13 - It was easy to learn to use the University of Minho's Library website.
	14 - The terminologies used on the University of Minho's Library website are easily understandable.
	15 - The University of Minho's Library website offers easy-to-understand menus.
	16 - The University of Minho's Library website has appropriate help functions.
	17 - The University of Minho's Library website provides well-organized help information for new users.
	18 - It does not take a great deal of effort for new users to become proficient with the University of Minho's Library website.

Figure 3. The usability star-schema of the data warehouse

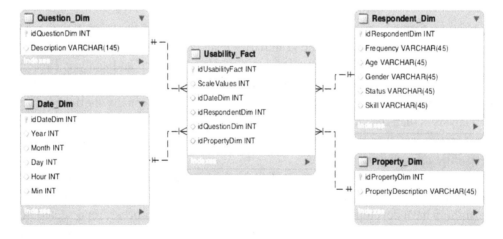

Figure 4. A general view of the ETL flow

Figure 5. The BPMN Model of the ETL Process

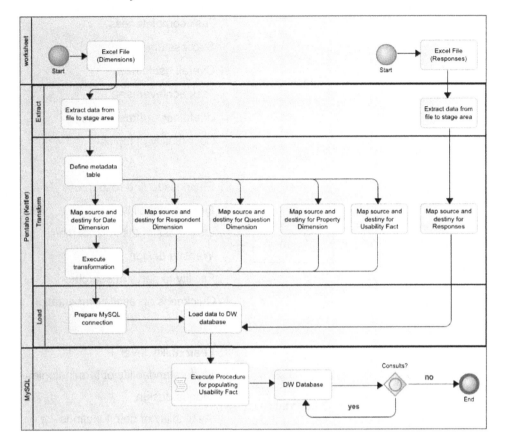

During the migration process, different types of needs might exist until the required result is achieved. Therefore, the utilisation of different back-end tools in different phases of the project is frequent. In this case, the authors choose to work with two, namely: Pentaho Data Integration (Pentaho, 2019), often referred to as Kettle, which is the Pentaho component in charge of ETL activities (Casters et al., 2010); and MySQL Workbench (MySQL Workbench, 2019), which is the database management tool available for MySQL. Figure 5 presents the BPMN (Business Process Model and Notation) model proposed to execute ETL operations.

This process was organised in two different parts. In the first part, the Kettle tool was used to normalise and load the data from the operational system into the data warehouse, namely to populate the dimensions tables and to create data mappings in a staging area, which was used to support all the transformation tasks integrated in the ETL process. In the second part, all the data consolidation tasks are performed, and the fact table is populated. This task is executed with the assistance of the back-end tool MySQL Workbench. Once that all the data from the dimensions, as well as from the retention area are in the DW database, a SQL procedure is used to populate the respondents answers for each question (fact), as well as to create the relations between the primary keys of the dimensions tables and the foreign keys from the fact table. MySQL Workbench tool is also used as front-end tool, i.e., for consulting the DW.

Figure 6. Usability evaluation model for this chapter

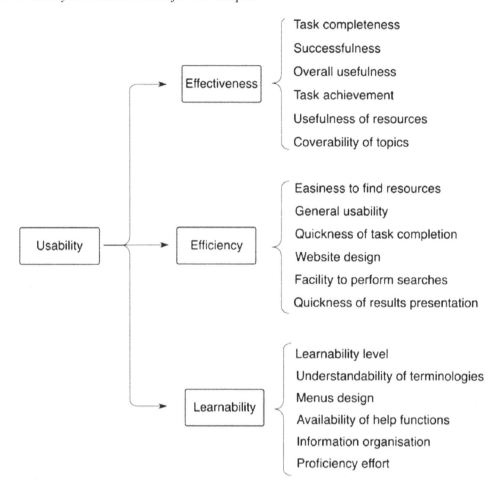

USABILITY ANALYSIS

The usability evaluation instrument is unsuitable for drawing conclusions about metrics from the respondents (e.g., task performance, session length, or average screen per visit) neither from the website (e.g., load time, retention rate or page load speed). Therefore, this section is dedicated to summarise the analysis results according to the respondents experience perception towards effectiveness, efficiency and learnability of a software artefact. This is a Human-centred approach, defined by ISO 9241-210 (ISO, 2010) and conceptualised as a way to "systems design and development that aims to make interactive systems more usable by focusing on the use of the system and applying human factors/ergonomics and usability knowledge and techniques".

Effectiveness

In this study, Effectiveness is measured by the questions 1-6 in the evaluation framework (Table 5). Level of success for finding resources is reported as "Neither agree or disagree". Overall perception of website's usefulness is reported as "Neither agree or disagree". Task achievement aims to measure the user perception about task completion by making use of the user interface. Nielsen highlights that the ability of user's to complete tasks is an important indicator of success rates. Users "Neither agree or disagree" on reporting task completion rate while using the website. Usefulness of resources investigates the perception of usefulness of the website. The literature frequently correlates lack of usefulness with low user adoption. Users reported, "Neither agree or disagree" on the measurement of the item. Coverage of topics is an important aspect for any university's library, since its main mission includes delivering a wider range of information for its selected and highly exigent public. End users reported they "Neither agree or disagree" that the university's library provides enough coverage.

Efficiency

Efficiency is measured by the questions 7-12 in the evaluation framework presented in Table 5. Easiness to find resources is one of the most important measurements in usability, frequently correlated with the quality design of products. On this topic, users reported the website "Meets partially above the expectations". End users report the general usability of the website as "Neither agree or disagree". About how quick users report achieving a certain goal with the website "Meets partially the expectations". This aspect is frequently correlated with efficiency in the literature. Website design measurement accounts for perception of (good) design of the website in question, and is indeed a difficult topic for the casual (i.e., non-designer) user to evaluate. Users accounted the website design "Meets partially the expectations". Users "Neither agree or disagree" on the facility to perform searches with the website. Users measure as "Meets partially above the expectations" the speed on results presentation for searches conducted with the website's search tool.

Learnability

Finally, Learnability is measured by the questions 13-18 in the evaluation framework presented in Table 5. User perception about the level of facility for learning the website, as well as the level of understanding for the terminologies used in the website are reported as "Neither agree or disagree". Menu design is an important topic to facilitate navigation in websites. Users reported that the website's menu design "Neither agree or disagree". As part of a good user experience with any user interface, good documentation should be provided for the user, such as user manuals, reference sheets, and help functions directly in the user interface. Uses reported that existing help functions in the website "Neither agree or disagree". Information organisation accounts for good help information design in the website. Users reported that help information design "Neither agree or disagree". An important aspect of usability might be considered as the level of effort necessary for a new user to become proficient with a product (e.g., websites). There is evidence that products that are easy to learn are frequently considered easy to use. End users reported that the effort necessary to become proficient with the website "Neither agree or disagree".

What-If Analysis

What-If analysis is a valuable method that can be useful to verify the outcome of three possible application scenarios. For instance, let's consider the representation for aggregated value of each construct, namely effectiveness, efficiency and learnability. After the DW implementation, those representations can assist the designer to understand the user perception for each construct. Therefore, the final evaluation given

Figure 7. Scenario manager for goal seek too

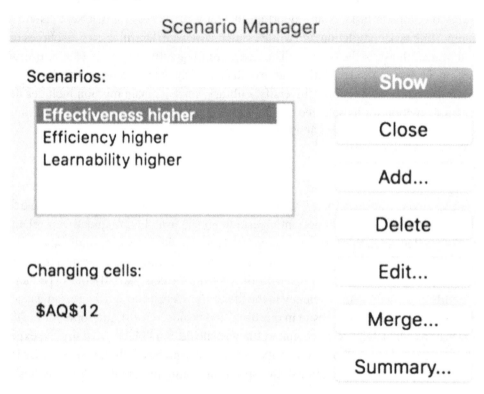

for the constructs is composed by the pair '[order point/representation]' in the linear scale, in which the order point is obtained by verifying the mode value of each construct, and the representation in the linear scale can be obtained by consulting the Likert Scale. Effectiveness and Efficiency constructs are scored 4.0, whereas its respective representation in the linear scale is "Neither agree or disagree" to the construct questions. Learnability construct is score 5.0, translating to "Meets partially the expectations" in the linear scale of the construct questions. Thus, the overall system final evaluation represents the value "I do not agree or disagree" in the linear scale. Using the previous rationale, the designer could hypothetically wonder how the system score behaves when one of the constructs is scored maximum classification, indicating final users "totally agrees" to the construct questions. Therefore, three applications scenarios are presented: i) effectiveness scores 7, ii) efficiency scores 7 and iii) learnability scores 7. Figure 7 depicts the scenario manager, a tool that works as an interface to the Goal Seek tool.

The outcome of the analysis, presented in Table 6, demonstrates the possible effect changes in all scenarios. In Scenario 1, due to the application of maximum score for the Effectiveness construct, the overall result presented is 5 ("Meets partially above the expectations"). In the application of maximum score for the Efficiency construct, described in Scenario 2, the overall result presented is 7 ("Above the expectations"). Last, when applying maximum score for the Learnability construct in Scenario 3, the overall result is 6, which, "Meets completely the expectations". Existing historical data can be used, when available, to run the simulation model against, determining a forecast considering how time aspects from the evaluations can impact the simulation outcome. Based on this overall outcome, a designer might

Table 6. Outcome of goal seek application

Scenario 1		Scenario 2		Scenario 3	
Effectiveness	7,0	Effectiveness	7,0	Effectiveness	6,0
Efficiency	5,0	Efficiency	7,0	Efficiency	6,0
Learnability	5,0	Learnability	6,0	Learnability	7,0
Result	5,0	Result	7,0	Result	6,0

justify his/her decisions to change policies or allocate resources to best suit the strategy of improving the website.

SOLUTIONS AND RECOMMENDATIONS

Effectiveness evaluation address problems such as task completion, which is positively correlated with software faults, mostly unidentified during testing phases. Considering task completion as effectiveness measurement means investigating whether the user is able to complete a task using the user interface. One of the aspects that impacts task completion in websites, which system designers need to be aware is related with menu design. Several user experience guidelines and heuristics exist to assist designers in providing the design that copes with user expectation, avoiding the user to premature and inexpertly end his/her navigation with the website, consequently his/her task.

Efficiency evaluation address problems such as amount of resources required completing tasks. This is indirectly correlated with software quality, once unnecessary functionality is costly not only in terms of implementation, but also in terms of maintaining. One of the aspects that might be considered as measurement of efficiency is website performance in the sense of time required to loading pages. Maximum productivity is only achieved with minimum time required for the users to receive the information they requested from the website's server (El-Aleem et al., 2005). Although there are also other aspects that affect website time loading related with server and networking, website design decisions that are important to achieve best efficiency can be also highlighted. This is the case of how graphics are used in the design, language/script technology, libraries, etc.

Learnability evaluation address problems such as the misuse of universal representations for software interfaces. When designers incorporate software API and frameworks in their development practice to create user interfaces that provide universal representation of icons, graphical controls (e.g., lists, buttons, data input widgets, etc.), they create the same interaction style from other systems, facilitating user adaptation towards new technology. They have the potential to improve learning rates, which might benefit several types of systems, especially those used infrequently (e.g., kiosks, vending machines, digital libraries, among others).

CONCLUSIONS AND FUTURE WORK

In this research, the authors presented a discussion on the topic of usability evaluation and analysis on User Interfaces of Interactive Systems that are expected to be useful for designers and administrators of website from a number of universities libraries, to assess the quality of their websites. During the work, the authors provided literature review for themes such as Usability Evaluation, DSS and What-If analysis. Usability evaluation is not a recent topic, however the topic has received renewed attention due to the challenge of establishing different constructs and measurements for an increasingly enlarging family of new products and services. To assist in this task, DSS play an important role. Even though not particularly discussing Quality of Software's regulations, the aim was to bring all those concepts without losing sight of its centrality for the quality assessment of interactive computer system's interfaces. The authors presented a case study, in which the central library website of the University of Minho is evaluated by a group of respondents for usability aspects. As result of the analysis, some design considerations regarding the investigated constructs are discussed. The authors also investigated how a research instrument, based on tree constructs, namely effectiveness, efficiency and learnability, can capture the perceived usability of those websites. The instrument makes use of different Usability evaluation constructs if comparing with ISO 9241-11, which also consider satisfaction as research construct.

The goals proposed in this research are achieved, providing evidence that the usability of a website can be verified in terms of effectiveness, efficiency and learnability. A structured methodology to create a multidimensional view of the data is presented, based on Data Warehouse. Evidence that DSS methods can be used for assisting in extending the usability analysis, performing additional analysis for verifying possible effects in hypothetical scenarios, analysing hypothetical system behaviour, based on What-if analysis is also provided. This has the potential for assisting system designers and administrators to maintain and improve their systems. Hereafter, the authors indicate the main limitations regarding the current research. The authors highlight the need to extend the end user participation to other university staff (e.g., library and department employees, etc.), which has the potential to cover a wide range of opinions regarding the usability aspects considered.

Another aspect to consider is the existence for methodological improvement regarding the research instrument. While translating linear scale to order points might provide a simplified method for the respondent to mark his/her answer for the proposed question, it provides the researcher a smaller universe of space of analysis. Including a non-response option (e.g., "no opinion") could provide an alternative for undecided respondents, therefore capturing more realistically user opinions. Automating the evaluation method would allow for improvements in the analysis, such as in user's task completion assessment, which can capture user's time tracking when measuring Effectiveness. Automatically restoring the respective point scale related to each measurement allows the presentation of order points to the interface designer.

One last aspect is related with the Quality in Use model, defined in ISO/IEC 25010 (ISO, 2011), which considers Effectiveness and Efficiency from ISO 9241-11, adding the construct of Freedom from Risk, either in economic, health and environmental terms. In this sense, possible negative outcomes when using the system (e.g., due to low effectiveness) in terms of Quality in Use model are not addressed by this research.

Future work in this research includes making use of other usability evaluation methods, as well as usability evaluation constructs, automating the process of analysis. Regarding the What-If analysis simulation, the authors can try to refine the presented scenarios, by trying other hypotheses and analysing the impact of changing construct 'values. Another possibility is to verify how the constructs classifications are distributed among the types of end user, also based on their status to the university, their level of computer skill of use frequency. New scenarios might include variations on those variables.

ACKNOWLEDGMENT

This work was supported by Conselho Nacional de Pesquisa (CNPq), COMPETE: POCI-01-0145-FEDER-007043, and FCT –Fundação para a Ciência e Tecnologia within the Project Scope: UID/CEC/00319/2019. We also want to thank Instituto Federal de Educação, Ciência e Tecnologia de Goiás (IFG).

REFERENCES

Abran, A., Khelifi, A., Suryn, W., & Seffah, A. (2003). Usability meanings and interpretations in ISO standards. *Software Quality Journal*, *11*(4), 325–338. doi:10.1023/A:1025869312943

Alonso-Ríos, D., Vázquez-García, A., Mosqueira-Rey, E., & Moret-Bonillo, V. (2009). Usability: A critical analysis and a taxonomy. *International Journal of Human-Computer Interaction*, *26*(1), 53–74. doi:10.1080/10447310903025552

Arh, T., & Jerman-Blazic, B. (2007). Application of Multi-Attribute Decision Making Approach to Learning Management Systems Evaluation. *JCP*, *2*(10), 28–37.

Babbie, E. (1999). *The basics of social research*. New York, NY: Wadsworth.

Benyon, D. (2014). Designing interactive systems: A comprehensive guide to HCI, UX and interaction design.

Bevan, N. (1995). Usability is quality of use. *Advances in human factors ergonomics*, *20*, 349-349.

Bevan, N., Carter, J., & Harker, S. (2015). ISO 9241-11 revised: What have we learnt about usability since 1998? In *Proceedings of the International Conference on Human-Computer Interaction* (pp. 143-151). Springer. 10.1007/978-3-319-20901-2_13

Breslin, M. (2004). Data warehousing battle of the giants. *Business Intelligence Journal*, *7*, 6–20.

Brinck, T. Gergle D. & S. Wood, D. (2001). Usability for the Web: designing Web sites that work. Elsevier.

Casters, M., Bouman, R., & Van Dongen, J. (2010). *Pentaho Kettle solutions: building open source ETL solutions with Pentaho Data Integration*. John Wiley & Sons.

Chowdhury, S., Landoni, M., & Gibb, F. (2006). Usability and impact of digital libraries: A review. *Online Information Review*, *30*(6), 656–680. doi:10.1108/14684520610716153

Djamasbi, S., Siegel, M., & Tullis, T. (2010). Generation Y, web design, and eye tracking. *International Journal of Human-Computer Studies*, *68*(5), 307–323. doi:10.1016/j.ijhcs.2009.12.006

Eklund, T., Tétard, F., Ståhl, P., Hirkman, P., & Back, B. (2008*)*. Usability evaluation of an XP product. In *Proceedings of the 19th Australasian Conference on Information Systems (ACIS)* (pp. 280-289). Academic Press.

El-Aleem, A. A., El-Wahed, W. F. A., Ismail, N. A., & Torkey, F. A. (2005). Efficiency Evaluation of E-Commerce Websites. In WEC (2) (pp. 20-23). Academic Press.

Fernandez, A., Insfran, E., & Abrahão, S. (2011). Usability evaluation methods for the web: A systematic mapping study. *Information and Software Technology*, *53*(8), 789–817. doi:10.1016/j.infsof.2011.02.007

G. Fick, & R. H. Sprague (Eds.). (2013). Decision Support Systems: Issues and Challenges. In *Proceedings of an International Task Force Meeting* (Vol. 11). Elsevier.

Golfarelli, M., & Rizzi, S. (2009). *Data warehouse design: Modern principles and methodologies*. New York: McGraw-Hill.

Golfarelli, M., Rizzi, S., & Proli, A. (2006). Designing what-if analysis: towards a methodology. In *Proceedings of the 9th ACM international workshop on Data warehousing and OLAP* (pp. 51-58). ACM. 10.1145/1183512.1183523

Guenther, K (2003). Assessing web site usability.

Hearst, M., & Landay, J. (1999). Improving the Early Phases of Web Site Design via Informal Design Tools and Automated Usability Assessment.

ISO. (2001). *Standard 9126: Software Engineering Product Quality*, parts 1, 2 and 3.

ISO. (2011). *IEC 25010: 2011. Systems and Software Engineering—Systems and Software Quality Requirements and Evaluation (SQuaRE)—System and Software Quality Models.*

ISO. (2016). *IEC 25066: 2016. Systems and software engineering — Systems and software Quality Requirements and Evaluation (SQuaRE) — Common Industry Format (CIF) for Usability — Evaluation Report.*

ISO/IEC (International Organization for Standardization). (1998). *Standard 9241: Ergonomic Requirements for Office Work with Visual Display Terminals (VDT)s, Part 11. Guidance on Usability*, Retrieved from https://www.iso.org/obp/ ui/#iso:std:iso:9241:-11:ed-1:v1:en

Ivory, M., & Hearst, M. (n.d.). Comparing performance and usability evaluation: new methods for automated usability assessment.

Jeng, J. (2005). What is usability in the context of the digital library and how can it be measured? *Information Technology and Libraries*, *24*(2), 3. doi:10.6017/ital.v24i2.3365

Jeng, J. (2006). Usability of the digital library: An evaluation model. *College & Research Libraries News*, *67*(2), 78.

Joo, S. (2010). How are usability elements efficiency, effectiveness, and satisfaction correlated with each other in the context of digital libraries? *Proceedings of the American Society for Information Science and Technology*, *47*(1), 1–2. doi:10.1002/meet.14504701323

Joo, S., Lin, S., & Lu, K. (2011). A usability evaluation model for academic library websites: Efficiency, effectiveness and learnability. *Journal of Library and Information Studies*, *9*(2), 11–26.

Kimball, R. (1996). *The data warehouse toolkit: practical techniques for building dimensional data warehouses* (Vol. 1). New York: John Wiley & Sons.

Kous, K., Pušnik, M., Heričko, M., & Polančič, G. (2018). Usability evaluation of a library website with different end user groups. *Journal of Librarianship and Information Science*.

Lee, Y., & Kozar, K. A. (2012). Understanding of Website Usability: Specifying and Measuring Constructs and Their Relationships. *Decision Support Systems*, *52*(2), 450–463. doi:10.1016/j.dss.2011.10.004

Leveson, N. (2011). *Engineering a safer world: Systems thinking applied to safety*. MIT press.

Lorenz, M., Rüßmann, M., Strack, R., Lueth, K. L., & Bolle, M. (2015). *Man and machine in industry 4.0: How will technology transform the industrial workforce through 2025*. *The Boston Consulting Group*.

Matouk, K., & Owoc, M. L. (2012). A survey of data warehouse architectures—Preliminary results. In *Proceedings of the 2012 Federated Conference on Computer Science and Information Systems (FedCSIS)* (pp. 1121-1126). IEEE.

Mazumder, F. K., & Das, U. K.Fourcan Karim Mazumder. (2014). Usability guidelines for usable user interface. *International Journal of Research in Engineering and Technology*, *3*(9), 79–82. doi:10.15623/ijret.2014.0309011

Microsoft. (2019). *Microsoft Excel*. Retrieved from https://products.office.com/pt-pt/excel?rtc=1

Muntean, M. I., & Târnăveanu, D. (2012). *A Multidimensional View Proposal of the Data Collected Through a Questionnaire*. *Database Systems Journal*, *3*(4), 33–46.

MySQL. (2019). *MySQL 8.0 Community Edition*. Retrieved from https://www.mysql.com/

MySQL Workbench. (2019). *MySQL Workbench 8.0*. Retrieved from https://www.mysql.com/products/workbench/

Nielsen, J. (1994). Usability inspection methods. In *Conference companion on Human factors in computing systems* (pp. 413–414). ACM.

Nielsen, J. (2003). Usability 101: Introduction to usability.

Nielsen, J., & Loranger, H. (2006). *Prioritizing web usability*. Berkeley, CA: New Riders Press.

Okhovati, M., Karami, F., & Khajouei, R. (2017). Exploring the usability of the central library websites of medical sciences universities. *Journal of Librarianship and Information Science*, *49*(3), 246–255. doi:10.1177/0961000616650932

Pentaho (2019). *Data Integration – Kettle*. Hitachi Vantara Community. Retrieved from https://community.hitachivantara.com/docs/DOC-1009855-data-integration-kettle

Ponniah, P. (2011). *Data warehousing fundamentals for IT professionals*. John Wiley & Sons.

Preece, J., Benyon, D., Davies, G., Keller, L., & Rogers, Y. (1993). *A guide to usability: Human factors in computing*. Reading, MA: Addison-Wesley.

Preece, J., Rogers, Y., Sharp, H., Benyon, D., Holland, S., & Carey, T. (1994). *Human-computer interaction*. Reading, MA: Addison-Wesley.

Quesenbery, W. (2001). What does usability mean: Looking beyond 'ease of use'. In *Proceedings of the 18th Annual Conference Society for Technical Communications*. Academic Press.

Quesenbery, W. (2003). Dimensions of usability: Opening the conversation, driving the process. In *Proceedings of the UPA 2003 Conference*. Academic Press.

Quesenbery, W. (2004). Balancing the 5Es: Usability. *Cutter IT Journal*, *17*(2), 4–11.

Rawat, D. B., Brecher, C., Song, H., & Jeschke, S. (2017). *Industrial Internet of Things: Cybermanufacturing Systems*. Springer.

Root, R. W., & Draper, S. (1983). Questionnaires as a software evaluation tool. In *Proceedings of the SIGCHI conference on Human Factors in Computing Systems* (pp. 83-87). ACM. 10.1145/800045.801586

Rubinstein, R. Y., & Kroese, D. P. (2016). *Simulation and the Monte Carlo method* (Vol. 10). John Wiley & Sons. doi:10.1002/9781118631980

Rungta, N., Brat, G., Clancey, W. J., Linde, C., Raimondi, F., Seah, C., & Shafto, M. (2013). Aviation safety: modeling and analyzing complex interactions between humans and automated systems. In *Proceedings of the 3rd international conference on application and theory of automation in command and control systems* (pp. 27-37). ACM. 10.1145/2494493.2494498

Russom, P. (2011). Big data analytics. *TDWI best practices report*, *19*(4), 1-34.

Seffah, A., Donyaee, M., Kline, R. B., & Padda, H. K. (2006). Usability measurement and metrics: A consolidated model. *Software Quality Journal*, *14*(2), 159–178. doi:10.100711219-006-7600-8

Stair, R., & Reynolds, G. (2013). *Principles of information systems*. Cengage Learning.

Turner, C. J., Hutabarat, W., Oyekan, J., & Tiwari, A. (2016). Discrete event simulation and virtual reality use in industry: New opportunities and future trends. *IEEE Transactions on Human-Machine Systems*, *46*(6), 882–894. doi:10.1109/THMS.2016.2596099

Xie, H. (2006). Evaluation of digital libraries: Criteria and problems from users' perspectives. *Library & Information Science Research*, *28*(3), 433–452. doi:10.1016/j.lisr.2006.06.002

Xu, M., David, J. M., & Kim, S. H. (2018). The fourth industrial revolution: opportunities and challenges. *International journal of financial research*, *9*(2), 90-95.

ADDITIONAL READING

Adler, P. S., Winograd, T. A., & Winograd, T. (Eds.). (1992). *Usability: Turning technologies into tools*. Oxford University Press on Demand.

Carroll, J. M. (Ed.). (2003). *HCI models, theories, and frameworks: Toward a multidisciplinary science.* Elsevier.

Issa, T., & Isaias, P. (2015). *Sustainable Design.* Springer London. doi:10.1007/978-1-4471-6753-2

Keefer, D. L., Kirkwood, C. W., & Corner, J. L. (2004). Perspective on Decision Analysis Applications, 1990–2001. *Decision Analysis*, *1*(1), 4–22. doi:10.1287/deca.1030.0004

Nielsen, J. (1994). *Usability engineering.* Elsevier.

KEY TERMS AND DEFINITIONS

Data Warehouse: Data repository that aggregates data from multiple sources.

Decision Support System: Set of techniques, tools and data to assist with analysis and decision-making.

Effectiveness: The degree to which some action is successful in producing a desired result and achieving success.

Efficiency: The state of achieving maximum productivity with minimum wasted effort or wasted expense.

Learnability: The quality of allowing users to easily become familiar with something.

Satisfaction: the measurement of discomfort while making use of the product.

Usability: the degree to which a specific piece of software can be used by specified users to achieve quantified objectives with effectiveness, efficiency and satisfaction in a use context.

What-If Analysis: Data simulation in which the goal is to explore and analyse the behaviour of a specific complex system, to test some given hypotheses.

Chapter 4

ChangeIt:
Toward an App to Help Children With Autism Cope With Changes

Vivian Varnava
University of Edinburgh, UK

Aurora Constantin
University of Edinburgh, UK

Cristina Adriana Alexandru
University of Edinburgh, UK

ABSTRACT

The use of technology-based interventions for ameliorating ASD core deficits has been growing in popularity. However, limited technologies are available that can help children with autism (aged 6 to 11) cope with changes, and these do not typically incorporate the methods used or recommended by practitioners. This project addressed this gap through the design, development and evaluation of a prototype app to support children with ASD overcome their difficulties with changes. The researchers report on preliminary work in developing this app, in which they decided not to involve children with ASD before getting some evidence that the app may be useful and suitable for them. Therefore, the design at this stage was informed by the research literature and design studies involving typically developing (TD) children, practitioners and researchers. The evaluation studies revealed that: 1) the app is easy to use; 2) the activities are perceived as fun and engaging; 3) the app may be suitable for children with ASD.

INTRODUCTION

Autism Spectrum Disorder (ASD) is a neurodevelopmental disorder characterized by deficits in social interaction and communication combined with repetitive patterns of behaviour and interests, including resistance to change (APA, 2013). In spite of progresses in early diagnosis and interventions, ASD is typically lifelong (Hourcade et al., 2012; Knapp, 2009), impacting both individuals with ASD and their

DOI: 10.4018/978-1-7998-2637-8.ch004

families. A person's employment, social and personal functioning, standard of living and quality of life are some of the domains which can be affected by autism. In turn, services and support for individuals with autism are also seriously impacted. For example, the total cost of supporting individuals with ASD in the UK is estimated to exceed £28 billion per year.

For individuals on the spectrum, the world seems frightening due to its unpredictability (Turner, 1999). For children with ASD, changes can be particularly challenging and even small ones, such as taking a different route to school, can cause distress (APA, 2013). The stereotypical reaction is to attempt to gain control and security by creating rigid rules. Many individuals with autism have obsessive desire for sameness and routine. Often, they create routines and rituals that they strictly follow and therefore they struggle to alter their routine when changes appear, both expected and unexpected.

The difficulties in tolerating changes, as well as the strict adherence to routines and sameness, have been associated with anxiety since the earliest descriptions of the autism (Kanner, 1943). Anxiety in children with ASD leads to negative life experiences (Farrugia and Hudson, 2006) and deficits in social skills (Bellini, 2004).

Researchers and practitioners clearly highlight a stringent need for more effective interventions targeting individuals with ASD (Parsons et al., 2009). The use of technology in interventions with people with ASD has become very popular. A variety of technologies such as mobile computing, virtual reality or robotics have been introduced to improve social communication skills and support practitioners' work (Grynszpan et. al, 2014, Morin et al. 2018). Recently, a call for new technological tools to help professionals and families was launched at the ITASD (Innovative Technology for Autism Spectrum Disorders), Paris, France (ITASD, 2014).

However, the current methods applied for supporting children with ASD cope with changes mentioned in the literature are either non-technological, or do not combine all the recommended methods including Activity Schedules, Social Stories™ or coping strategies typically used by the practitioners (e.g. counting). Our work is the first attempt to design a technology that can provide support to practitioners in applying all these methods with children with ASD in an easy, friendly and interactive way.

BACKGROUND

Individuals on the spectrum do not differ in terms of outer appearance from the typically developing individuals, but they show peculiarities in terms of social interaction, behaviour and communication. Children on the spectrum find it very difficult to develop social skills and they usually isolate themselves (APA, 2013). The relationships with others are limited or absent and they demonstrate deficiency to engage in activities with peers (Schopler & Mesibov, 2013). They may also have communication difficulties which can range from those involving non-verbal communication to language impairments (APA, 2013). In general, autistic people may struggle to initiate and sustain a conversation and language subtleties, such as verbal expressions or jokes, are not easily understood (Spence et. al., 2004). Many individuals with autism demonstrate repetitive patterns of behaviour and interests, such as stereotyped body movements, repetitive speech, continuous use of parts of objects (i.e. spinning the wheels of a toy car), rigid and atypical interests and strong attachment to routines (APA, 2013). As a result, if changes occur, they may cause challenging behaviours such as aggression, self-injurious behavior, tantrums, or non-compliance (APA, 2013).

The two primary methods used to help children with autism cope with change are Activity Schedules and Social Stories™. Activity Schedules are often used to help children with ASD cope with the challenges posed by various activities or behaviours during an individual task or throughout the day (Dettmer et al., 2000). Visual Activity Schedules promote independence and predictability, and help with the transition between activities (Banda et al., 2009). Using them, children with autism are encouraged to follow routine schedules. Introducing changes into the routine schedule, for example by using slightly different materials or paths walked, is also recommended so that children can develop adapting skills (Mesibov et al., 2005). The schedule should remain predictable, but details should vary so that the child learns to focus on the overall picture rather than the details.

Social Stories™ are also used to help children with ASD cope with changes. First introduced by Gray (2019) – they represent short stories describing certain situations, skills, contexts, or concepts which are following a set of ten criteria. One of the main aims of Social Stories™ is to improve children's social understanding. They have proved effective in increasing communication skills and social interaction, and at the same time decrease the inappropriate behaviours (Thiemann et al., 2001). Example stories could teach children about daily routines, such as getting dressed, or could prepare them for novel events, such as moving to a new house. Social Stories™ usually include images, which can be helpful for children to easier grasp the gist of the story (Dettmer et al., 2000).

MAIN FOCUS OF THE CHAPTER

Motivation

A series of technological applications have been developed to support practitioners in creating Visual Activity Schedules (Cramer et al., 2011) and Social Stories™ (Constantin, 2015). However, limited technologies are available that can help children with autism cope with changes, and these do not typically incorporate the methods used or recommended by practitioners. Tools previously developed focus on assisting children with ASD transition between activities in the school environment. Therefore, our research work explores how technology can be best designed to help children with autism cope with changes. The changes addressed in this project are divided into three categories: expected changes (e.g. a road trip), unexpected changes (e.g. a sudden event happening) and transition between activities (e.g. from one class to another). The researchers designed and developed an app called ChangeIt, which may enhance the work of practitioners in helping children with ASD cope with changes. The target age group was 6-11 because, according to Huitt and Hummel, 2003, at this age the children become much more logical and demonstrate a more sophisticated thinking. This chapter reports on preliminary work, in which the researchers decided not to involve children with ASD before getting some evidence that the app may be useful and suitable for them. Instead, the researchers involved typically developing (TD) children, as well as practitioners and researchers in ASD and Human-Computer Interaction (HCI) as proxies in the initial design and evaluation of the app. The results of the evaluation were very promising, suggesting that the app has potential in helping children with autism cope with changes. However, more studies for the app design and evaluation, involving children with ASD, are necessary until these results can be considered generalisable.

Figure 1. Methodology

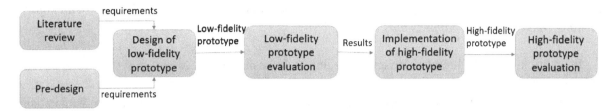

Methodology

The researchers used a User-Centered Design (UCD) framework, in which users were involved at every stage of the design process (Norman et al., 1986). However, despite children with autism being the end users of our proposed app, involving them in empirical studies can cause distress, and is moreover very time and resource consuming. Instead, the researchers involved TD children, as suggested by other reports (Frauenberger et al., 2012), because they could bring their age-related expertise in the initial design of technology. Also, they involved HCI experts with experience in usability, and ASD practitioners and experts, who could advise what is appropriate to help children with ASD cope with changes.

The project followed a methodology which is represented in Figure 1 and is detailed in the next sections.

SOLUTIONS AND RECOMMENDATIONS

Pre-Design

During the pre-design stage, the researchers conducted one-to-one semi-structured interviews with one ASD practitioner and two researchers on HCI/ASD (Table 1) with the aim of gathering their practical experience with helping children with ASD deal with changes.

The outcomes were intended to determine the changes that autistic children find difficult to cope with, determine the current procedures being used by the practitioners and identify any features that the app should include.

The qualitative data was analysed using Thematic Analysis (Braun & Clarke, 2006) with pre-established themes as follows: changes, current procedures and practices, and features the tool should include. After analyzing the data, the changes mentioned were divided into two categories: expected changes and unexpected changes. Specifically, E1 stated:

Table 1. Participants in the interviews

Participant	Position/Occupation	Areas of expertise
E1	Social Worker, Trainer in a centre with autistic individuals	Teaching individuals with autism
E2	HCI expert, Senior Laboratory Manager	HCI, developing games for children with autism
E3	Speech language therapist, worked with children with ASD for 30 years	Teaching children with autism and typical-developing children

It could be very difficult to cope with changes to a timetable and there are always changes in school ... It could be difficult to cope with a planned change and it could be very difficult to cope with an unpredictable change and that happens too.

In addition, from the literature review, changing and transitioning between activities was also considered as another category.

Based on the literature review and interviews, three main methods for helping children with autism cope with changes were identified: Visual Activity Schedules (Dettmer et al., 2000), Social Stories™ (Gray, 2019) and a list of 'coping strategies'. Visual schedules are used to prepare children with autism for changes in advance and all the participants highlighted how important this is. It can also help children transition between and within activities and E3 stated:

The most common one, the daily routine schedules that we use, it supports routines, understanding foreign routines and then planning for change...If there is a plan change they(teachers) show where the change is and they can explain what is going to happen.

Then, she also remarked that:

Changes are unpredictable where timetables are predictable.

and she added:

Perhaps a Social Story™ about how a child manages change...Social Stories™ are really, really helpful, I think, for explaining change and how to manage change.

Social Stories™ can be used to explain when and why something is happening and how the children should react. Therefore, the children can better understand the situation and prepare for a change. This method can be used to prepare children for both expected changes such as moving houses, but also unexpected changes, such as a fire alarm.

The third method that was identified during the interviews was coping strategies which the practitioners used to help children overcome difficulties after changes. Practitioners enumerated a series of such strategies, such as counting, listening to a song that the child likes or watching their favourite cartoons. Coping strategies are usually used to tackle challenging situations. For instance, parents of children with ASD employ coping strategies, such as avoidance strategies or social support seeking strategies, to cope with stress (Vernhet et al., 2018). However, there is no research on applying coping strategies to help children with ASD cope with the challenges created by changes, as far as the authors are aware.

The researchers decided that the app would include all of the above. This stage also involved a workshop using pens and paper with two TD children (Table 2) with the aim of identifying the reaction of children to undesirable changes and their strategies to coping with them. At the same time, the researchers could gather information with regards to what features the tool should contain and how it should be designed. The data were analysed using coding and axial coding as described in Saldana (2013). Both children showed disappointment when they had to face changes, but they were willing to adapt to those changes. Also, the children in the workshop showed an interest towards fantasy and superpowers. Practitioners in the interviews also mentioned the importance of using characters for the children, and moreover this

Table 2. Children participants in the workshop

Participant	Gender	Age
C1	Male	8
C2	Male	11

is supported by the literature: Weisberg et al. 2015 proved that stories with anthropomorphic animals and events, that cannot occur in reality, encourage greater learning than realistic stories. Characters or players was also mentioned in the interviews since this can motivate the children to use the application. Therefore, the researchers decided to include a fictional character in the app.

The literature review and pre-design studies resulted in a list of requirements for the user interface design of the application. Nielsen's 10 Usability Heuristics (Nielsen, 1994) and autism-specific guidelines for user interface design (Bartoli et al, 2014; Pavlov, 2014) helped add requirements to ensure that the app has good usability - both in general and for autistic users. For example, one of the autism-specific guidelines recommend the use of visual cues to improve reading comprehension, and a simple design with contrast between background and font, few and clear elements on screen, and simple graphics (Pavlov, 2014). Nielsen's 10 Usability Heuristics also suggest that the interfaces should be consistent, use real world conventions that are familiar to the users and allow the user to freely perform, undo and exit actions.

Overall, the most important requirements for the app were:

1. Having two distinct interfaces: one of practitioners and one of children.
2. Allowing practitioners to create/edit/delete Social Stories™, Schedules and coping strategies.
3. Allowing children to view the Social Stories™, Schedules and coping strategies which had been created by practitioners.
4. Providing simple templates for filling information by practitioners.
5. Providing examples of Social Stories™, Schedules and coping strategies for the practitioner.
6. Including a fictional character, a pet.
7. Allowing the users to add photographs and images
8. Preventing children from making changes to the application

Low-fidelity Prototype Design

Using the list of requirements, the researchers designed a low-fidelity prototype using the Figma design tool (Figma, 2019). The child interface opens with the Menu screen which contains four buttons which, when clicked, take the child to either to the Schedules screen (black arrow, Figure 2), the Social Stories screen (green arrow, Figure 2), the coping strategies screen (pink arrow, Figure 2) or the Pet screen (brown arrow, Figure 2). In the Schedules screen ('My Schedules'), users can choose either the 'Day Schedule' option or the 'Task Schedule' option. The 'Day Schedule' presents the schedule of the day where the activities are divided into Morning, Noon and Evening (according to the moment of the day). The 'Task Schedule' shows smaller task schedules such as school activities or morning routine. There, the child can mark each task as 'Done' (tick icon). The Social Stories screen ('My Stories') presents the stories about changes which the children can read. The coping strategies screen ('My Toolkit') presents

Figure 2. The child's interface to the ChangeIt app

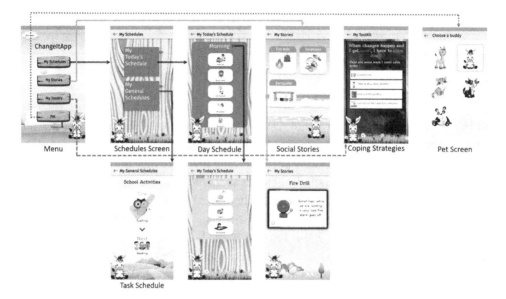

all the calming activities that the child use to overcome a stressful situation. The Pet screen presents a list of options where the child can select their favourite pet.

Clicking on the 'Edit mode' button from the Menu Screen (left top corner) leads to the practitioner interface (Figure 3). To create a new task schedule, the practitioner has to add tasks and create a new Social Story™. Icons are provided in each screen to add, save, and delete elements. An element can be edited by clicking on it.

For the first round of evaluation of this low-fidelity prototype, the researchers invited three TD children (Table 3), with the aim of gathering their perspectives on the prototype's usability and suitability for helping children cope with changes. Two of the children worked together, and the third individually. A task-based evaluation, followed by a post-task semi-structured interview, was employed. In the end, the children were asked to evaluate the application using a Likert scale question. The qualitative data gathered from the studies was analysed using Thematic Analysis, following a top-down approach (Braun & Clarke, 2006).

The workshop with the TD children showed that the application was very attractive to the children and all of them started interacting with it immediately, with no need of instructions. The average overall

Figure 3. The practitioner's interface to the ChangeIt app

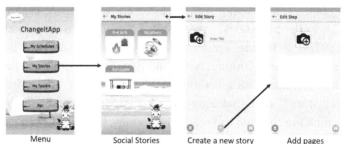

Table 3. Children participants in the evaluation workshop

Participant	Gender	Age
C1	Male	10
C2	Male	11

rating of the application was 4.7 out of 5. None of them found a notable difficulty in use. Of interest was the fact that all of them completed all the tasks very quickly. The fictional character, the pet, was also considered their favourite feature and C2 mentioned, referring to children in general:

Not only they see a happy, friendly pet but they are able to choose them. I think it's what would make them much happier.

Although they were very excited with the existence of a pet in the application, the children desired a greater interaction with the pet and C2 suggested that the pet should receive an accessory as a reward when they complete an exercise, and C3 suggested that the pet should encourage the children if they get stuck. Another suggestion was also to include a game in the end, such as a quiz. Also, during the workshop, the researchers noted that the children tried to click on features that are not clickable.

For the second round of evaluation, the researchers invited experts on HCI/ASD, to gather their feedback on the app's usability and its suitability for the target population and for helping children with ASD cope with changes. The experts were asked to individually participate to Cooperative Evaluation (Dix et al., 2004) followed by an online questionnaire with Likert scale questions. The questionnaire involved questions regarding the usability, suitability of the ChangeIt app for the target population and the overall experience with the app. The qualitative data gathered from the studies was analysed using Thematic Analysis (Braun & Clarke, 2006), following a top-down approach.

All the experts were very positive about the application and based on the online questionnaire the average overall rating of the application was 4 out of 5. In terms of suitability, all the experts agreed that the prototype is suitable for autistic children and may help them cope with changes. E1 stated that

Table 4. Expert participants in the evaluation

Expert	Position/Occupation	Areas of expertise
E1	Researcher in HCI	Experience in HCI and ASD, developing technologies for children with ASD
E2	Researcher in HCI	Experience in HCI and ASD, developing technologies for children with ASD
E3	Master's in Design Informatics	Experience in HCI and ASD, developing technologies for children with ASD
E4	Researcher in HCI	Experience in HCI and ASD
E5	Researcher in HCI and assistive technologies	Experience in HCI and ASD, developing technologies for children with ASD
E6	PhD in Usable Security	Experience in HCI and ASD
E7	Researcher in HCI	Experience in HCI and ASD

he could not find something wrong with the application but just areas for improvement. Also, 4 out of 7 experts suggested that a reward system should be implemented in order to increase children's motivation. E3 suggested that the pet can narrate the story, give encouraging comments or get rewards. E3 stated:

Why do we need a pet? What does it do? I would like something with the pet, giving carrots maybe.

Also, 2 out of 7 experts suggested that the practitioners should be able to upload a picture of the pet.

A lot of feedback was received about the Schedules screen and subscreens. Two experts (out of 7) mentioned that there are too many steps until you reach the 'Day Schedule' and the 'Task Schedule' screens. E4 added that the day schedule is too limited and should be changed into a week or month one.

In terms of usability, the average rating by the experts was 4.14 out 5 and the results helped identify some issues, such as misleading elements of the design and inconsistencies. For example, there were some inconsistencies between buttons and the font size was small in some cases, identified by 4 out of 7 experts. Furthermore, the experts tried to click on features that are not clickable. E2 also mentioned that there should be appropriate messages when adding/deleting/modifying elements. An important usability issue was the fact that changing modes was done by clicking one button without anything indicating that the mode was changed. E5 mentioned that children could easily enter into practitioner's interface without realizing it and make changes there.

The prototype was refined based on the evaluation results from both children and experts. The most important suggestions that were identified after analysing the data were the following:

- Adding a reward system for the pet in order to increase motivation. (4 out of 7 experts, 3 out of 3 children)
- Adding appropriate messages when adding, deleting or modifying a feature (1 out of 7 experts).
- Modifying the background colour when entering the practitioners-only interface. (3 out of 7 experts).
- Changing the day schedule into a weekly or monthly schedule (3 out of 7 experts)

A series of usability issues were fixed, such as removing elevation from buttons (5 out 7 expert, 3 out of 3 children) that are not clickable, adding both back and next buttons (4 out of 7 experts), and increasing font size (2 out of 7 experts).

High-Fidelity Prototype Implementation

A high-fidelity prototype was developed using Android Studio (2019). The child interface (see Figure 4) opens with the Menu screen with the same options as was shown in low-fidelity prototype. This time, the 'My Schedule' option directs the users to the Day Schedule screen by default. There, by clicking on the 'My Task Schedules' button, the users are directed to the Task Schedules screen and by choosing a specific task schedule they can complete it, by marking the subtasks as 'Done.' In this high-fidelity implementation, the task is marked as completed by checking the checkbox next to each task. Each coping strategy is now presented without the outer boarding since that misled the users to think that each coping strategy is clickable. In each section, after completing a series of tasks, the child is presented with the Rewards screen in which they can choose a reward for their pet.

Figure 4. The child interface to the ChangeIt app

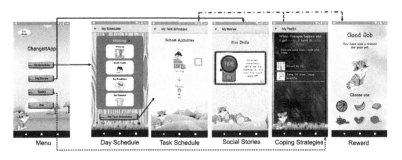

Clicking on the 'Edit mode' button from the Menu Screen leads to the practitioner interface (Figure 5). Once the practitioner enters the 'Edit Mode', the background becomes a plain colour in order to indicate that the mode is changed. The steps are the same as in the low-fidelity prototype - to create a new task schedule, the practitioner has to add tasks, and to create a new Social Story™, the practitioner has to add pages. Icons are provided in each screen to add, save, or delete elements. An element can be edited by clicking on it.

Evaluation

In the evaluation stage for the high-fidelity prototype, the researchers first conducted a study with students and staff from the University of Edinburgh, with the aim of assessing the app's general usability. In the evaluation, 28 people participated. Their details are presented in Table 5.

The researchers first asked university students and staff to freely interact with the app and fill in a small online questionnaire consisting of a combination of Likert scale questions and optional open-ended questions. At the same time, they were able to express any comments and raise questions. The data was analysed using Descriptive Statistics and Thematic Analysis (Braun & Clarke, 2006). The majority of the participants (25 out of 28) agreed that the app is 'Easy' (rating 4/5) or 'Very Easy' (rating 5/5) to use, as shown in Figure 6. Only one participant rated the application as 'Not Easy' (rating 2/5), but suggested that larger icons and a 'Help' section would make it easier in use. The rest of participants (2 out of 28) rated the application as 'Neither easy, nor difficult' (rating 3/5). Also, most of the participants (23 out

Figure 5. The practitioner interface to the ChangeIt app

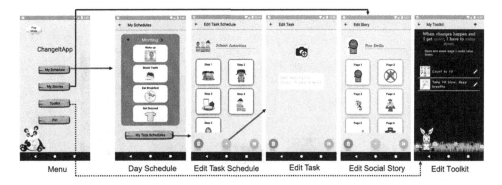

of 28) marked the application as 'Suitable' (rating 4/5) or 'Very Suitable' (rating 5/5) for 6-11-year-old children as shown in Figure 7. The rest (5 out of 28) marked the application as 'Neither suitable nor unsuitable' (rating 3/5) or 'Unsuitable' (rating 2/5).

Table 5. Participants in the feedback survey

	Age				Gender			Experience With HCI		
	<24	**24-44**	**>44**		**Male**	**Female**		**None**	**Some**	**Expert**
No. of participants	22	3	3	No. of participants	19	9	No. of participants	15	11	2

Figure 6. Perceived App Ease

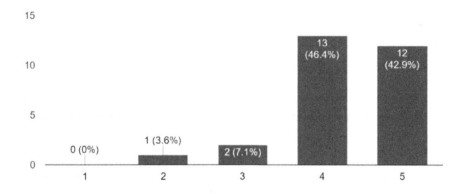

How easy was the application to use?
28 responses

Figure 7. Perceived App Suitability

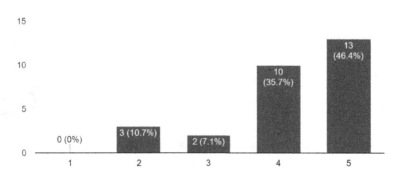

How suitable is the application for the target population (children between 6-11 years old)?
28 responses

Figure 8. Overall Rank

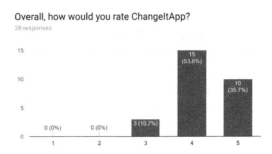

The app was rated overall as 'Very Good' (rating 4/5) or 'Excellent' (rating 5/5) with only 3 people rating it as 'Good' rating (3/5) as shown in Figure 8. A member of staff with experience with HCI stated that the ChangeIt app is a brilliant idea and she suggested that it should be tested further and released to the market.

The researchers then conducted a study with 5 TD children (3 out of 5 having also participated to the low-fidelity prototype evaluation). Children's details are presented in Table 6. The aims of the study were to assess the suitability of ChangeIt app, determine whether the app's activities are fun and enjoyable, and evaluate the children's perceptions of its usability.

The study consisted of a combination of task-based evaluation and free exploration followed by a post-task semi-structured interview. Children were involved individually or in pairs. The qualitative data was analysed using Thematic Analysis (Braun & Clarke, 2006). All of the children found the ChangeIt app very easy to use and perceived its activities as being fun. The majority (4 out of 5) of the children rated the app as 'Excellent' (rating 5/5) or 'Very Good' (rating 4/5). Only one child rated the application as 'Good' (rating 3/5) and he mentioned that he does not need such an application because he does not need to see his schedule on an app or read stories. However, the other 4 children commented that they would use ChangeIt app to check their daily schedule. Also, the children were able to interact with the app without any difficulties and they tried all the functionalities very quickly without any instruction. 4 out of 5 children commented that there is nothing that they did not like about the application and C4 remarked:

Nothing really. There is nothing I would take away from it, just more things to add.

Table 6. Children's details

Participant	Gender	Age
C1	Male	7
C2	Male	9
C3	Male	10
C4	Male	11
C5	Male	8

During the low-fidelity prototype evaluation, the experts had considered all the methods used as suitable for helping children with autism cope with changes. From the perspective of children, however, the coping strategies screen might not be appropriate. In particular, one child (C2) did not like the calming activities and he remarked:

If you look at a screen when you are upset, it doesn't help you. If I scream out, I just put my hand over my mouth and just do.

C5 also stated:

Honestly, I think of what I want and that is what calms me down...I want a cat so I might think about a cat or me getting a cat...One of the things could be a picture of a cat down here (as a coping strategy).

All the children agreed that they liked the idea of having a pet included in the app and 3 out of 5 mentioned that it is their favourite feature. All the children commented that a larger variety of pets would be better and each one proposed different types of animals such as horse, red panda, penguin, dog, bird, crocodile, hamster, hippo. C3 added that the parents should be able to edit the pet options by uploading photographs. Specifically, he stated that if a child has a real pet, it might be preferable to upload the picture of that pet.

The children were excited when they reached the 'Reward Interface', but they expected the reward system to be more elaborated. For example, C3 remarked:

What do these (rewards) do though? Yes, it is a reward but what happens if you get a reward? Maybe, it should be more interactive. I've seen on some other websites you get something for your pet and if it is food, they eat it and then they stop moving.

C5 stated that:

Maybe next time you look at your pet, it could be (the reward) next to it.

C3 also suggested that the pet could talk and guide the child to complete the schedules, read the story or calm them down when they get upset. C1 and C2 also suggested that they would like to have a game including the pet and that they would like the pet to ñy, die and then come back to life. The reward system is essential when developing applications for this purpose and for the specific target group and therefore more research should be done in order to develop a high-level reward system. That is similar with results in a prior study (Constantin et al., 2017), where the children suggested they prefer an incremental reward to reflect their achievements.

C3 and C4 suggested that the application should have a more advanced functionality for distinguishing the two modes rather than just a change in background. Specifically, they suggested a 4-digit pin that the practitioner has to enter in order to prevent children from entering into the 'Edit Mode'.

Finally, the researchers conducted a study with 6 experts on HCI/ASD as shown on Table 7, with the aim of evaluating the app's suitability and the experts' perceptions of its usability. All of the participants had also participated in previous studies and therefore they were familiar with the research and ChangeIt app.

Table 7. Experts' details

Experts	Position/Occupation	Areas of expertise
E1	Researcher	Experience in HCI and ASD, developing technologies for children with ASC
E2	PhD in Usable Security	Experience in HCI and ASD
E3	Master's in design informatics	Experience in HCI and ASD
E4	Researcher	Experience in HCI
E5	Researcher	Experience in HCI and ASD
E6	Researcher, Senior Laboratory Manager, School of Informatics	Experience in HCI and ASD

The evaluation followed the same procedure and analysis as the one in the low-fidelity prototype evaluation. The study consisted of a combination of Cooperative Evaluation (Dix et al. 2004) followed by a small online questionnaire. The questionnaire contained a combination of Likert scale questions and open ended-questions, and it was split into 3 sections: evaluation of children's screens ('Play Mode'), evaluation of practitioners' screens ('Edit Mode') and overall evaluation. The data was analysed using Thematic Analysis (Braun & Clarke, 2006) and Descriptive Statistics.

All experts rated ChangeIt as 'Very Good' (rating 4/5) or 'Excellent' (rating 5/5) (Figure 12) and the application received positive comments.

All the experts found the ChangeIt app easy to use and suitable for the target population. E1 remarked:

I think it is really easy to use...but I think there are some little things that can be added and enhance the usability of the app, overall. But I don't think it is difficult at all, it's not.

Based on the online questionnaire, all the experts rated the application as either 'Easy' (rating 4/5) or 'Very Easy' (rating 5/5) as shown in Figure 9. By observing the experts, it was obvious that they could easily interact with the app and complete all the tasks without difficulty.

They also found the methods used in the app effective for helping children with autism cope with changes. Most of the experts (4 out of 6) ranked ChangIt as 'Very Suitable' (rating 5/5) with one expert evaluating the methods as 'Suitable' (Figure 10). E3 also commented:

I think they [Social Stories™] are really good for children with autism. Stories are a big thing for children with autism and being able to edit the stories and customize them based on different situations is really good...So having these stories where the parent can edit them to reflect exactly the situation they are going through is really good and very suitable for this population.

However, 3 out of the 6 experts expressed some doubts with regards to the appropriateness of coping strategies. E4 remarked:

When they are upset, the children will not really go and look at something to calm them down.

Also, E3 and E5 had some concerns in regard to the coping strategies but both of them commented that more functionality is needed. E5 commented: I think it can help, but it needs more than advice. On

Figure 9. Perceived App Ease

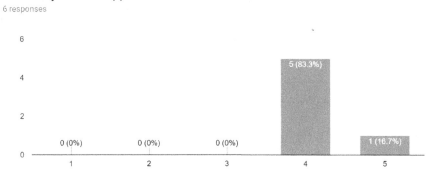

Figure 10. Perceived Methods Appropriateness

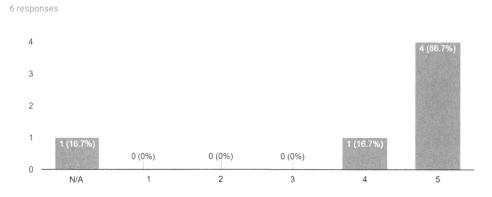

Figure 11. Perceived Suitability

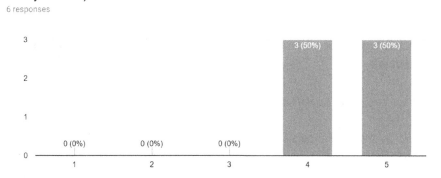

Figure 12. Overall Experience

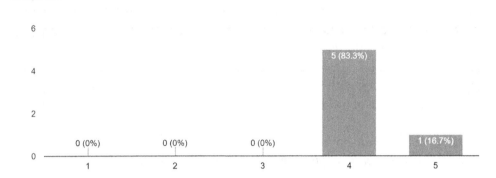

Overall, how would you rate ChangeltApp?
6 responses

the other hand, E2 mentioned: I think you have to train them to go and grab this toolkit. I think this is a great way for them, to remind them what they could do if they get upset.

Regarding the suitability of the application for children (aged 6-11) with autism, all the experts considered the application 'Suitable' or 'Very Suitable' (Figure 11). All the screens received a high overall rating between 3-4 out of 5 (Figure 13). The Menu screen was the most favourably seen, while the Rewards screen was the least favourably seen. Specifically, E3 mentioned:

I really like the screens and their design...I think it's what you typically see for this age group. It just needs a bit of more engagement in terms of games and animation.

Figure 13. Interfaces' Rating

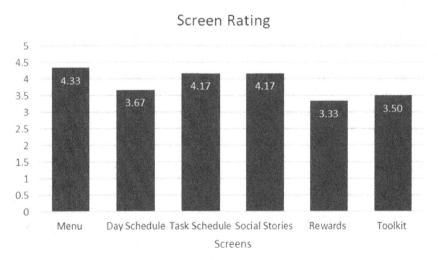

Screen Rating

FUTURE RESEARCH DIRECTIONS

Based on the results of the evaluation studies, the tool provides the base of a fully functioning application that can be fun, enjoyable, easy to use and able to help children with autism cope with changes. In order to achieve this, new features and functionality can be added. The most important suggestions that were identified after analysing the data of the studies were:

- **Adding more interaction with the pet and a high-level reward system** to increase motivation (4 out of 6 experts, 5 out of 5 children). E2 stated:

I wonder, the things that I gave to my pet, are they like saved somewhere?...So I think it is a good thing to have that interaction to make sure that my pet got it or find it somewhere, like how many things I collected.

The researchers consider that this requires more research with regard to children preferences. The reward system could contain several games or even be edited by the practitioner.

- **Adding interaction when clicking on the coping strategies:** This was the suggestion mentioned by most of the experts (5 out of 6). All of them tried to click on the coping strategies and they realised that it does not have any functionality. E3 remarked

So I might know that the autistic child has a particular video on YouTube that he really likes that I know that calms him down so I can have that in or maybe he likes a particular show or a joke that always gets him to laugh and then I can just add those things myself and allow him to pick which one he feels at that time he needs. So, the ability to add pictures or videos that can be recorded simply from the phone itself would be a super good feature to have.

E5 also explained:

It [the Coping Strategies screen] doesn't say much. So maybe if you could click and say a bit more... Maybe you need to include some audio, maybe an option is to listen to a song he likes or pictures or videos of their favourite cartoons.

- **Changing the day schedule to a calendar one,** to prepare children for changes in advance (1 out of 6 experts).
- **Making the app more customizable** by allowing practitioners to upload images of pets, videos or music (3 out of 6 experts), choose interactions for the pet as rewards (1 child, 1 expert), choose the colour scheme (1 out of 6 experts), as well as provide text-to-speech functionality (1 out of 6 experts). E1 commented:

I think if the child has a pet, they can put their own picture or something like that. I think given more customization it's always a good thing.

- **Adding more functionality on the screens with Visual Schedules** (2 out of 6 experts)

The screens containing Visual Schedules received a lot of feedback in both the Low-Fidelity prototype evaluation and High-Fidelity prototype evaluation. They were also the screens that were changed the most during the High-Fidelity prototype implementation. In the final evaluation, E3 suggested that the day schedule tasks should be linked to the 'Task Schedule' interfaces. Specifically, E3 mentioned that when a child clicks on a task on the day schedule, for example 'Prepare meal', he/she should be directed to a 'task schedule' where he/she can see the subtasks for preparing the meal. E2 also suggested that the day schedule should be synchronised with the current time and automatically alternate between Morning, Noon, Evening. Another suggestion was to freely create new periods of the day rather than being limited to just Morning, Noon and Evening. For example, E2 would like to be able to add 'School Time' as a separate category in between 'Morning' and 'Noon'.

- **Adding a password** to distinguish the 'Edit Mode' and 'Play mode', to prevent children from changing the mode (3 out of 6 experts, 1 out of 5 children). E2 remarked that changing the background when entering 'Edit Mode' is not enough since children can easily enter and modify the application. Instead, a password could be more effective.

E4 also recommended to **connect the application with a web server** (1 out of 6 experts) instead of storing data locally, so that the practitioner can modify the child's application from another device. In the school environment this can be very helpful since the practitioners will have to modify the ChangeIt app for multiple children and it will be very difficult to access each device individually.

- **Sorting mechanism or search bar** for stories and schedules (2 out of 6 experts) as it will be difficult to find a specific story/schedule if they increase in number. E6 proposed that they can be organised based on the day of the week and grouped into folders.

E3 and E5 suggested that **a small description or title identifying each page and task** should be added (2 out of 6 experts) since currently both of them are distinguished by the same numbers, i.e. step 1, 2, ..., page 1, 2, ... E5, mentioned that is very difficult to identify a specific story or a schedule by only its picture and its number. Instead, E5 suggested that a small phrase, such as the first line of the page or the first name of the first task should be enough.

Allowing the practitioners to easily **modify the sequence** of tasks, pages and coping strategies. (4 out 6 experts). E2, E3, E4 and E5 commented that the application lacks this functionality and it is something that it must be added in the future. E5 suggested that using drag and drop, the users should be able to change the sequence of tasks, pages and coping strategies.

- **Animating the Social Stories™** in order to be more realistic (1 out of 6 experts, 2 out of 5 children). C3 recommended that the pet could talk and guide the child to complete the story or calm them down when they get upset.

Because the application provides the ability to create Social Stories™, which are not only used for helping children with autism cope with changes, the researchers would like to use the ChangeIt app in more areas related to children with autism. The application is customisable based on each child's needs, therefore the users can add features that are not restricted by context.

In this project the researchers involved only TD children that acted as proxies for children with autism, along with HCI/ASD experts, and practitioners. This is because the researchers considered that involving children with autism in such preliminary stages should be avoided due to the stress that such evaluation might cause them. Instead, the approach taken helps discover major usability problems and integrate new suggestions before going to ASD children. After the usability problems are fixed and the suggestions resulted from the initial studies are integrated, the system should be further explored with children with autism. Previous studies also suggest that it is important to involve TD children when designing technologies for children with disabilities (Frauenberger et al., 2012).

CONCLUSION

This chapter presented a preliminary investigation of how technology can be best designed to help children with ASD cope with changes, which resulted in the development of an Android app called ChangeIt. The app was designed and evaluated by involving HCI/ASD experts, practitioners, TD children and general users, following a UCD framework. The results from its evaluation suggested that ChangeIt has potential for helping children with autism cope with changes, it is easy to use, fun and engaging. Furthermore, the evaluation led to a series of suggestions that will be considered for improving the ChangeIt app in the future.

Nevertheless, any conclusions should be taken with caution. Although the participation of TD children in the development of technology for children with disabilities is useful and important (Grynszpan et. al, 2014), involving children with ASD and a larger sample size would give clearer outcomes. Therefore, after getting these initial promising results, the next step is to extend the studies by including children with ASD, as well as more ASD practitioners, from schools and organisations for children with ASD from across Edinburgh.

ACKNOWLEDGMENT

The researchers would like to thank all of the children, experts, parents, and students and staff who were involved at various stages of this research. The information they provided was invaluable. This research received no specific grant from any funding agency in the public, commercial, or not-for-profit sectors.

REFERENCES

American Psychiatric Association (APA). (2013). *Diagnostic and statistical manual of mental disorders (DSM-5)*. American Psychiatric Pub.

Banda, D. R., Grimmett, E., & Hart, S. L. (2009). Activity schedules: Helping students with autism spectrum disorders in general education classrooms manage transition issues. *Teaching Exceptional Children, 41*(4), 16–21. doi:10.1177/004005990904100402

Bartoli, L., Garzotto, F., Gelsomini, M., Oliveto, L., & Valoriani, M. 2014, June. Designing and evaluating touchless playful interaction for ASD children. In *Proceedings of the Interaction design and children 2014* (pp. 17-26). ACM. 10.1145/2593968.2593976

Bellini, S. (2004). Social skills deficits and anxiety in high-functioning adolescents with autism spectrum disorders. *Focus on Autism and Other Developmental Disabilities*, *19*(2), 78–86. doi:10.1177/10883576040190020201

Braun, V., & Clarke, V. (2006). Using thematic analysis in psychology. *Qualitative Research in Psychology*, *3*(2), 77–101. doi:10.1191/1478088706qp063oa

Constantin, A. 2015. *Supporting practitioners in social story interventions: the ISISS Authoring Tool* [PhD dissertation]. University of Edinburgh.

Constantin, A., Johnson, H., Smith, E., Lengyel, D., & Brosnan, M. (2017). Designing computer-based rewards with and for children with Autism Spectrum Disorder and/or Intellectual Disability. *Computers in Human Behavior*, *75*, 404–414. doi:10.1016/j.chb.2017.05.030

Cramer, M., Hirano, S. H., Tentori, M., Yeganyan, M. T., & Hayes, G. R. (2011, May). Classroom-based assistive technology: collective use of interactive visual schedules by students with autism. In CHI (pp. 1-10). Academic Press. doi:10.1145/1978942.1978944

Dettmer, S., Simpson, R. L., Myles, B. S., & Ganz, J. B. (2000). The use of visual supports to facilitate transitions of students with autism. *Focus on Autism and Other Developmental Disabilities*, *15*(3), 163–169. doi:10.1177/108835760001500307

Dix, A., Finlay, J., Abowd, G., & Beale, R. (2004). Evaluation techniques. *Human-Computer Interaction*.

Farrugia, S., & Hudson, J. L. (2006). Anxiety in adolescents with Asperger syndrome: Negative thoughts, behavioral problems, and life interference. *Focus on Autism and Other Developmental Disabilities*, *21*(1), 25–35. doi:10.1177/10883576060210010401

Figma. (2019). Figma: the collaborative interface design tool. Retrieved from https://www.figma.com/

Frauenberger, C., Good, J., & Alcorn, A. 2012, June. Challenges, opportunities and future perspectives in including children with disabilities in the design of interactive technology. In *Proceedings of the 11th International Conference on Interaction Design and Children* (pp. 367-370). ACM. 10.1145/2307096.2307171

Gray, C. (2019). Social Stories. Retrieved from https://carolgraysocialstories.com/social-stories/what-is-it/

Grynszpan, O., Weiss, P. L., Perez-Diaz, F., & Gal, E. (2014). Innovative technology-based interventions for autism spectrum disorders: A meta-analysis. *Autism*, *18*(4), 346–361. doi:10.1177/1362361313476767 PMID:24092843

Hourcade, J. P., Bullock-Rest, N. E., & Hansen, T. E. (2012). Multitouch tablet applications and activities to enhance the social skills of children with autism spectrum disorders. *Personal and Ubiquitous Computing*, *16*(2), 157–168. doi:10.100700779-011-0383-3

Huitt, W. and Hummel, J., 2003. Piaget's theory of cognitive development. *Educational psychology interactive*, *3*(2), 1-5.

ITASD. (2014). *Innovative Technology for Autism Spectrum Disorders*. Digital Solutions for Autism.

Kanner, L. (1943). Autistic disturbances of affective content. *Nervous Child, 2*, 217–250.

Knapp, M., Romeo, R., & Beecham, J. (2009). Economic cost of autism in the UK. *Autism, 13*(3), 317–336. doi:10.1177/1362361309104246 PMID:19369391

Mesibov, G. B., Shea, V., & Schopler, E. (2005). *The TEACCH approach to autism spectrum disorders*. Springer Science & Business Media.

Mesibov, G. B., Shea, V., & Schopler, E. (2005). *The TEACCH approach to autism spectrum disorders*. Springer Science & Business Media.

Morin, K. L., Ganz, J. B., Gregori, E. V., Foster, M. J., Gerow, S. L., Genç-Tosun, D., & Hong, E. R. (2018). A systematic quality review of high-tech AAC interventions as an evidence-based practice. *AAC, 34*(2), 104–117. PMID:29697288

Nielsen, J. (1994, June). *Heuristic evaluation in usability inspection methods*. John Wiley & Sons, Inc..

Norman, D. A., & Draper, S. W. (1986). *User centered system design: New perspectives on HCI*. CRC Press. doi:10.1201/b15703

Parsons, S., Guldberg, K., MacLeod, A., Jones, G., Prunty, A., & Balfe, T. (2009). *International Review of the Literature of Evidence of Best Practice Provision in the Education of Persons with Autistic Spectrum Disorders*. Ireland: National Council for Special Education.

Pavlov, N. (2014). User interface for people with ASD. *Journal of Software Engineering and Applications, 7*(02), 128. doi:10.4236/jsea.2014.72014

Schopler, E. & Mesibov, G.B. (2013). *Learning and cognition in autism*. Springer Science & Business Media.

Spence, S. J., Sharifi, P., & Wiznitzer, M. (2004, September). Autism spectrum disorder: Screening, diagnosis, and medical evaluation. []. WB Saunders.]. *Seminars in Pediatric Neurology, 11*(3), 186–195.

Android Studio. (2019). Android Studio [System Software]. Retrieved from https://developer.android.com/studio/

Thiemann, K. S., & Goldstein, H. (2001). Social Stories, written text cues, and video feedback: Effects on social communication of children with autism. *Journal of Applied Behavior Analysis, 34*(4), 425–446. doi:10.1901/jaba.2001.34-425 PMID:11800183

Turner, M. (1999). Annotation: Repetitive behaviour in autism: A review of psychological research. *Journal of Child Psychology and Psychiatry, and Allied Disciplines, 40*(6), 839–849. doi:10.1111/1469-7610.00502 PMID:10509879

Vernhet, C., Dellapiazza, F., Blanc, N., Cousson-Gélie, F., Miot, S., Roeyers, H., & Baghdadli, A. (2018). Coping strategies of parents of children with autism spectrum disorder: A systematic review. *European Child & Adolescent Psychiatry*, 1–12. PMID:29915911

Weisberg, D. S., Ilgaz, H., Hirsh-Pasek, K., Golinkoff, R., Nicolopoulou, A., & Dickinson, D. K. (2015). Shovels and swords: How realistic and fantastical themes affect children's world learning. *Cognitive Development*, *35*, 1–14. doi:10.1016/j.cogdev.2014.11.001

ADDITIONAL READING

Attwood, T., Evans, C. R., & Lesko, A. (2014). Been there. Done that. Try this! An Aspie's guide to life on Earth.

Crutchfield, S. A., Mason, R. A., Chambers, A., Wills, H. P., & Mason, B. A. (2015). Use of a self-monitoring application to reduce stereotypic behavior in adolescents with autism: A preliminary investigation of I-Connect. *Journal of Autism and Developmental Disorders*, *45*(5), 1146–1155. doi:10.100710803-014-2272-x PMID:25326255

Heasley, S. (2013). Few young adults with autism living independently. *Palaestra*, *27*(4), 50–51.

Johnson, C. P., & Myers, S. M. (2007). Identification and evaluation of children with autism spectrum disorders. *Pediatrics*, *120*(5), 1183–1215. doi:10.1542/peds.2007-2361 PMID:17967920

Lindgren, S., & Doobay, A. (2011). *Evidence-based interventions for autism spectrum disorders*. Iowa: The University of Iowa.

Temple, G. (2006). *Thinking in Pictures and Other Reports from My Life with Autism*. New York: Vintage.

Thiemann, K. S., & Goldstein, H. (2001). Social stories, written text cues, and video feedback: Effects on social communication of children with autism. *Journal of Applied Behavior Analysis*, *34*(4), 425–446. doi:10.1901/jaba.2001.34-425 PMID:11800183

Wang, H., & Sun, C. T. (2011, September). Game reward systems: Gaming experiences and social meanings. In *Proceedings of the DiGRA Conference* (*Vol. 114*). Academic Press.

KEY TERMS AND DEFINITIONS

Autism Spectrum Disorder (ASD): A lifelong neurodevelopmental disorder characterized by deficits in social interaction and communication combined with repetitive patterns of behaviour and interests, including resistance to change.

Social Stories: A primary intervention for children with autism firstly introduced by Carol Gray. They represent small stories that describe certain situations, events or activities based on 10 criteria.

Software Prototyping: Software development activity involving the building of prototypes (incomplete versions of the software to be developed), which can be evaluated with users, checked for conformance with requirements and used to decide on the accuracy of the initial project plans.

Thematic Analysis: Qualitative analysis approach usually applied to text, which involves identifying, analysing and discussing themes in the data.

User-Centered Design (UCD): Framework in which the users are involved throughout the design process via a variety of research and design techniques, with the aim to create usable and accessible software that meets their needs.

Visual Activity Schedules: Graphically represented sequences of events which can prepare an individual for one or more future activities or their steps.

Section 2
Engagement, Immersion, and Agency

Chapter 5
Creativity and Digital Games:
A Study of Developing Creativity Through Digital Games

Werner Walder Marin
Mackenzie Presbyterian University, Brazil

Pollyana Notargiacomo
Mackenzie Presbyterian University, Brazil

ABSTRACT

In the last decades the interest in creativity has grown. One of the questions that has risen from this interest is whether it is possible to aid the development of creativity. This chapter reviews a study on the possibility of developing a digital game with this. The game Luovus was created, utilizing previous research on the subject of creativity and digital games as learning aids. The game has been tested with a group of users and seems to be an effect on the player's self-perceived creative capabilities and society's impact on their creativity. This chapter will also cover studies and past experiments on the subject and how they can be of interest to future experiments.

INTRODUCTION

Although creativity began to be studied in the early 40s by Maslow (1943), among others, increasing importance is being given to this topic, not only to its consequences to individual life but also to the possible benefits that creativity might bring to society as a whole (Alencar, Fleith, & Bruno-Faria, 2010). As interest in this topic grew, one of the questions studied throughout the years is how to exercise and/or develop the creative thought.

It seems, therefore, that the interest of psychology in creativity is relatively recent (Alencar, Fleith, & Bruno-Faria, 2010). This interest occurs more intensely from 1950, thanks to various factors such as the influence of the humanist movement. Rogers (1959) and Maslow (1959) both draw attention to mental health as a source of creative impulses. They also point out the human potential for self-realization and explain conditions that ease the expression of creativity. Rogers and Maslow conclude that creativity is

DOI: 10.4018/978-1-7998-2637-8.ch005

the result of a mutually beneficial interaction between an individual and the environment in which this individual is inserted. Rogers also defends that autonomy and protection from excessive social control are fundamental for a creative activity.

According to Alencar et al. (2010) the idea of developing creative competencies is not yet a topic in which consensus has been reached. That said, it is already legitimized by studies that have shown positive results with programs that attempt to develop said creative competencies. Therefore, it is possible to theorize that any and every person has a creative potential that can be systematically explored and developed (Runco, 2014). There are currently multiple strategies that aim at training the creative thought, from programs, to software to digital games (Runco & Jaeger, 2012).

Azevedo et al. (2017) conducted a study on the Future Problem Solving Program International. Developed with the objective of training the creative thoughts of children and teenagers, the FPSPI is a program that has been applied for decades and in various countries. This program came to be in the United States and has spread to other countries including, but not limited to, Australia, England, Singapore, etc. Every year an international competition takes place, in which children and teenagers from all around the world present projects developed with the aid of the program's methodology. In the experiment conducted by Azevedo et al. (2017) a group of teenagers showed significant positive results to being submitted to this program.

Based on this scenario, it seems that the interest in understanding creativity has consistently grown in the last decades. This brings forth the question of the possibility of aiding the development of creative thought. This study is concerned with investigating the possibility of developing a digital game capable of such. For this the game *Luovus* was created, based on past research on creativity and digital games as learning tools. The game was tested on a group of users and although the results are not enough to come to a conclusive answer to the main question proposed by this study, there seems to be an effect on the player's self-evaluation of their own creative capabilities and society's impact on their creativity.

Other studies and experiments that are similar or relevant to this topic will also be analyzed. Many of them are important to comprehend the relationship of the various factors involved in the exercise of creative thought, such as positive psychology and mental state of flow.

BACKGROUND

Creativity: Definition and Involved Variables

Creativity can be defined as an interaction between a person and the environment this person is inserted in, this being a beneficial interaction. This interaction needs autonomy, and also needs to be shielded from excessive social control to be effective. Some aspects commonly associated with creativity are strategies, decision making, thought managing, learning style, personality traits, motivation, aspects of cognitive abilities, etc. Creativity is a psychosocial phenomenon, which is born both from an individual's characteristics and the social environment in which this individual exists (Alencar, Fleith, & Bruno-Faria, 2010). In other words, creativity is a result both from the individual as well as the environment.

Creativity can be divided in two types. These two types are individual creativity and team creativity. These two types of creativity function in different ways, as are the variables that influence their manifestation. Each type has its advantages, but also its disadvantages. Individual creativity flourishes more easily in isolated tasks, while team creativity is believed to flourish more easily in tasks where there is a stronger interdependency between the tasks of each member of the team. Therefore, in the model proposed by Wang (2013), individual autonomy promotes the feeling of propriety of the task at hand, which in turn promotes motivation. Motivation mediates the positive relationship between individual autonomy and individual creativity. The autonomy of an individual or of a team is one of the variables that may affect the capacity to find creative solutions studied by Wang. The other variable is the interdependence of the tasks a team is responsible for.

One factor that influences the creative thought is psychological well-being. De Rooij et al. (2015) found a connection between satisfaction and the capacity to produce creative ideas. Another factor that influences the creative thought is the way in which a person receives feedback on their work. Qiong, Wee, and Li remark that past studies focused on the negative aspects of psychological stress caused by work, but that a reduced number of studies were conducted on the positive aspects of psychological stress, one of which, they say, is the likelihood to come to a creative solution thanks to continuing to visualize the problem outside of work (Li, Qiong, & Wee, 2014).

If on the one hand an individual may come to more creative ideas for focusing on the task for longer periods of time, on the other hand there is the possibility that a longer session of creative thought may lead to cognitive exhaustion and, thus, subpar results (Coppi, 2015).

Coppi (2015) noted that there was a problem in the initially proposed duration of her experiment. Having a duration superior to two hours, the attention span of the children participating in the experiment may have been negatively affected, which consequently affected the post test. No signs were found that the children's capacity to produce creative ideas was affected, only their capacity to focus on a single task.

In regards to group creativity, it manifests more frequently in tasks where there is a stronger interdependence between the tasks of each member of the team. In the model proposed by Wang (2013), when a task is approached by a team, in the case the interdependence of the responsibilities of each member of the team is high, the team's total creativity is approximately the sum of the individual creativity of each member of the team. On the other hand, if the interdependence between the responsibilities of each member is low or the individual autonomy of each member is high, it may lead to conflicts between the members of the team, which has a negative impact on the team's creativity.

High interdependence and high team autonomy promote the exchange of ideas, discussions of strategies and viewpoints, feedback exchange, integration among tasks, as well as interpersonal interactions, communication and cooperation (Wang, 2013). Alternatively, when interdependence is low, the lack of internal communication in the team and the low coordination may lead to a decrease of motivation, which has a negative impact on the team's creativity.

Wang also says that when individual autonomy is high, each member of the team may choose how to accomplish their own tasks without having to consider the others. This may lead to an increase in intrinsic motivation, through an increased feeling of propriety and authorship over the task and responsibility over the outcome. This feeling is considered key to leading to creative thinking. In a scenario in which task interdependence is low, this arrangement will not lead to conflicts in the team and the total creativity may be calculated as the sum of each member's individual creativity. But if it is not the case, and task interdependence is high, the high individual autonomy may cause each member to act in a way that, although beneficial to themselves, is not beneficial to the rest of the team. I addition to that, it may be the case that each member's intrinsic motivation is incompatible with each other. The necessary coordination for a team to be productive is compromised, which also affects the team's capacity to act and implement creative solutions.

Relationship Between Positive Psychology and Creativity

A psychologically healthy person is in a position where they may find it easier to express their creativity and originality. An important step to prepare oneself to a task that requires creative thinking is to care for one's well-being.

In their study, De Rooij, Corr, and Jones (2015), conducted a study in which they developed a system that would evaluate the originality of ideas. Then participants were asked to present ideas and the system would evaluate those ideas. The evaluations were manipulated, though, so that while some evaluations would be legitimate, some would be either more favorable or less favorable than they should be. This was done to measure the impact that feedback can have on the ability of the participants to conceive creative ideas.

De Rooij et al. (2015) analyzed the influence that the positive or negative emotions caused by the feedback had on the participants and found a significant positive correlation between satisfaction and originality. In other words, when the participants received a positive evaluation, they had a higher probability of conceiving creative ideas in subsequent stages of the experiment. Participants that received neutral evaluations had a smaller probability of conceiving creative ideas in subsequent stages of the experiment. Participants that received negative evaluations had the smallest probability of conceiving creative ideas in subsequent stages of the experiment.

De Rooij et al. defend that this correlation can only be explained by the feelings of satisfaction and frustration caused in the participants by the feedback, since there was no observed difference in the performance of participants that had their evaluations manipulated and the participants that did not have their evaluations manipulated.

It is important to note that the system was developed taking into consideration that an exaggeratedly positive feedback could be detected as insincere or irrelevant by being disconnected from reality by the participants, and would therefore be counterproductive to their study. It is also important to note that De Rooij et al. (2015) admit the possibility that is not the positive feelings of satisfaction that promote originality, but negative feelings of frustration that inhibit creative thought, although the fact that participants who received positive evaluations were more productive than participants who received neutral evaluations might indicate this is not the case.

Creativity Under Stress

One of the positive effects of stress, say Qiong, Wee, and Li (2014), is to increase the duration of the creative thinking process a worker dedicates to a task. They propose that when a worker becomes stressed by a task, they think about it even out of the workplace. Therefore, the solution this worker finds for this task has the potential to be even more creative than it would be if this worker thought about this task only during work hours. This effect becomes even more intense proportionally to the control the worker has over this task (Li, Qiong, & Wee, 2014).

Qiong et al. (2014) call this stress a cognitive irritation. They analyzed the relationship between the control a worker has over a task and their creativity, mediated by this cognitive irritation. While they observe there are negative aspects to this cognitive irritation, such as potential health problems, depression and conflicts in the family environment, the authors argue that the positive aspects are mostly ignored. When workers possess high autonomy and control over their tasks, they also suffer with the stress of the responsibility over these tasks. In the scenario that the worker feels as if they are not progressing in finding a solution for this task, they may continue to simulate the process of solving this task in their mind. For instance, a factory worker tasked with increasing productivity in their production line that is struggling to complete such task may continue to visualize their daily tasks at work and try to find a way to increase productivity. When the worker enters this state of cognitive irritation, they continue to think about their task even outside the workplace. Since they spend longer thinking about the task, they have a higher probability of developing and elaborating creative ideas and strategies, and therefore has a higher probability of generating creative ideas. On the other hand, with no cognitive irritation the worker may still think creatively about their task, but will limit these creative thinking sessions to the workplace.

Also, positive stress can contribute even in areas such as entrepreneurship, as there is enthusiasm and positive experiences associated with situations that cause reflective practices, work organization, mental preparation and recovery, as well as joy appreciation and positive pressure encouragement (Berg, Dutton, & Wrzesniewski, 2013); elements that can also integrate creative processes.

Types and Effects of Feedback on Creative Work

In the office environment, workers that receive feedback on their work from a superior show a positive growth of their creative thinking capabilities (Amabile & Gryskiewicz, 1987).

Zhou et al. (2013) theorize that this growth depends a great deal in the worker's habit to self-monitor. A worker that self-monitors themselves is more likely to adapt to their context. Therefore, this worker will react to their social environment in an active manner. According to Zhou et al., this may lead the worker to having a more constructive reaction to their superior's feedback.

Even if a superior supply their subordinates with feedback, the relationship between those subordinate's feedback and their creativity is mediated by the self-monitoring habit of each one of these subordinates, in such a way that different workers will be affected differently by the feedback given by the same superior. Zhou et al. note that the feedback also has an effect on the worker's creativity by means of aiding these workers at becoming better at their tasks. In other words, the feedback will make the workers better at performing their tasks, which will increase their interest in the task. This interest, in turn, will incentivize the worker's to take risks and experiment with new approaches, which are key behaviours in finding creative solutions.

In their study, Zhou et al. observed that people who possess the habit of self-monitoring are more sensitive to social and environmental signs, which in turn gives them better chances at adapting their behaviour to the context they are currently inserted into. This way, these people react in a much more active and agile way, which leads them to having a more positive response to feedback. People who do not have the habit of self-monitoring, however, tend to not catch these social and environmental signs, therefore they are not capable to react as well to them and can only have a passive reaction to feedback. They are not capable to alter their behaviour in an active way (Gangestad & Snyder, 2000).

The Effects of Too Many or Too Few Restrictions

The restrictions imposed on a person when attempting to find a solution to a given task may impact that person's capacity to find a creative solution for said task. Moffat and Shabalina (2016) conducted an experiment and arrived at the conclusion that none, too many or too strong restrictions may impact negatively a person's capacity to reach a creative solution, but a moderate amount of restrictions may in turn have a positive effect. On the one hand, restrictions suppress creativity. On the other hand, they force the person to focus their creativity. In other words, a balance in restrictions forces a non-conventional solution without also restricting too much the possibilities of how to solve the task.

In an experiment conducted by Yokochi and Okada (2015), an artist was asked to complete a painting incorporating line that were previously painted on the canvas by the researchers. After the experiment, the artist stated that the resulting paintings were more creative than his usual paintings, which were painted without any form of restriction.

Too much freedom of choice, it seems, makes the creative process harder, as with the lack of any restriction or condition there are possibilities and options that must be considered. While this factor becomes less impactful as experience is acquired, as it permits more familiarity and comfort with the number of choices, less experienced people may find it easier to arrive at creative solutions if they must act under some restrictions (Chua, & Iyengar, 2008).

In their study, Moffat et al. (2016) asked a group of students to participate in some creative exercises. These exercises consisted of ideating short digital games. These games were then evaluated by their colleagues participating in the experiment. Many games were designed in different stages of the experiment. In the first stage the games were designed with no restrictions. In the second stage some restrictions were imposed on the students. In the third stage were imposed even harsher restrictions than in the previous stage.

When the students were interviewed after the experiment, it was put forward the opinion that the restrictions limited the students' creativity, but that it also forced their focus to be trained on specific areas. That means some restrictions may have a positive impact, while other restrictions may have a negative impact. Indeed, the results of the evaluations of the games designed in the experiment indicate that the evaluations for games designed with no restrictions were consistent, while the evaluations for games with some or many restrictions showed higher variation, with some ideas receiving positive and negative evaluations simultaneously.

Relevant Works

The first step in this research was to find tools and strategies to develop a person's creativity. Some experiments of interest to this research were found, including workplace activities (Wang, 2013) and pedagogical exercises with children (Coppi, 2015).

Buzady (2017) studied the serious game FLIGBY as a tool to develop leadership skills using the mental state of flow. Buzady describe the benefits of the flow state in a serious game, such as strong engagement and a feeling of satisfaction. The usefulness of the feeling of satisfaction has been previously discussed by De Rooij et al. (2015). In Buzady's study it is possible to see potential in serious games as tools to train soft skills.

The experiment conducted by Azevedo et al. (2017) with the *Future Problem Solving Program International* had positive results. All the competencies showed a significant increase in the experimental group. The prospect of developing a game that can aid the development of creativity applying the principles of the FPSPI is promising.

While there is no conclusive evidence that it is possible to develop a game that develops a player's creativity, it is possible to develop a game that aims to do so, with past experiments showing promising results, such as Coppi (2015) and Buzady (2017).

There is reason to believe that the player's age has an impact on the final experience. The study conducted by Vella et al. (2013) with people ranging from 12 to 52 years of age found a positive relationship between age and the player's well-being. The higher their age, the stronger their feelings of well-being. In other words, the same game will have different effects on two players of different ages (Vella, Johnson, & Hides, 2013). Therefore, it is unlikely to develop a game that has equally satisfying results across all ages. It might be more effective to develop a game with a specific demographic in mind.

The study conducted by Vella et al. (2013) had three primary objectives: investigate whether there was any difference in the creativity levels of students in distinct stages of high school, the generalization or specification of creativity in relationship to different school subjects and to what extent creativity is related to performance. For the purpose of this research, the most relevant is the first objective.

Analyzing the results of their study, Vella et al. (2013) concluded that students at the end of high school exhibited the highest capacity to express creative thoughts. Vella et al. call attention to the competencies of producing ideas, producing original ideas and producing abstract ideas that give new meaning to known ideas. In other words, the further a student's education, the higher their creative capacities.

It is not clear, however, if this positive relationship between formal education and creative capability happens thanks to psychological and intellectual maturation reached naturally through the aging process of a child. It is possible this ease at expressing creative thought is a consequence either of intellectual maturity or of formal education, potentially both. It is also not clear if, in case this is caused by formal education, this formal education must also attempt to intentionally exercise the child's creativity. It is possible that merely by acquiring general knowledge the child also acquires better tools with which to express their creativity.

Vella et al. (2013) argue that the found data does not allow to confidently say the causal influence of these variables, but that studies of children with no formal education of the same age range may come to shed light on the relationship between education, age and creativity. That said, Vella et al. (2013) state that the data is in accord with most studies on the subject, which also point to a positive relationship between the capacity to think creatively and the end of adolescence (Lau & Cheung, 2010; Torrance, 1979).

Measuring Creativity

In the search for a reliable method to measure creativity, some tests were developed. The most famous among them are probably the *Torrance Tests of Creative Thinking*, in which was later based the *Abbreviated Torrance Test for Adults*, a reduced version focused on adults. The TTCT scores individuals on the attributes of Fluency, Originality, Elaboration and, at later versions of the test, Abstractness of Titles and Resistance to Premature Closure. Earlier versions of the test also evaluated Flexibility, but Torrance removed it from later versions as he believed it overlapped with Fluency. Also evaluated are the criterions of emotional expressiveness, storytelling articulateness, movement or action, expressiveness of titles, synthesis of incomplete figures, synthesis of lines or circles, unusual visualization, internal visualization, extending or breaking boundaries, humor, richness of imagery, colorfulness of imagery and fantasy. The TTCT are widely trusted and frequently referred to in studies about the measurement of creativity (Cramond, Matthews-Morgan, & Bandalos, 2005).

Torrance concluded that the *Torrance Tests of Creative Thinking* do not cover all dimensions of creativity and suggested that a second form of measurement should also be used to reach more reliable results (Treffinger, 1985). However, The TTCT are a good measuring tool, not only to detect particularly creative individuals, but also to discover and encourage creative thinking in the populace in general (Kim, 2006). In addition to this, the TTCT are still some of the most used tests in the field of creativity. The reasons for using it are as relevant today as they were in 1966: promoting the comprehension of the human mind, aiding the development of individual instruction, provide information for psychotherapeutic programs, understand the efficacy of different educational materials and reveal potentials that might otherwise go unnoticed (Cramond, Matthews-morgan, & Bandalos, 2005).

Another creativity test to be considered is the *Abedi Test for Creativity*. Developed by Ahmadi (2011). In contrast to the previously mentioned TTCT and ATTA, the ATC is a self-evaluative test. In this case it is possible to gain some understanding of how a person perceives their own creative capabilities, in such a way that the TTCT and the ATC may be used for distinct reasons. The questionnaire consists of 60 questions divided between expansiveness, originality, fluency and flexibility.

Last to be covered in this research is the test for creativity developed by Alencar et al. (2010). Just as the ATC, this test is self-evaluative. The relevance for this research is primarily the language in which it was developed. The game developed in this research will be played by native portuguese speakers, the language in which the test developed by Alencar et al. was originally conceived.

Experiments on the Development of Creativity

Azevedo et al. (2017) conducted a study to test the possibility of developing creative thought in adolescents, applying the *Future Problem Solving Program International* methodology, which was in turn developed based in the *Creative Problem Solving* methodology, the latter being developed by the likes of Isaksen, Dorval and Treffinger (2011). The FPSPI methodology proposes six stages of problem resolution, starting with the definition of the problem to be approached to the communication of the solution in such a way that it is accepted. This methodology assumes that for any problem there is always at least one solution, the question being finding and applying this solution.

The six stages of the FPSPI are, in order, defining a generic problem, selecting the problem to be tackled, producing decision criteria, evaluating the proposed solutions and finally implementing the selected solution.

At the end of the program, which lasts one school year, Azevedo et al. noted that the results indicate that the program had a positive effect on its participants. All the competencies practiced and evaluated in the FPSPI program showed significant growth in the experimental group, even in competencies in which this group already had above average scores.

An experiment conducted by Buzady (2017) concerned itself with studying the relevance of the mental state of flow, a concept of the field of Positive Psychology. For such, the serious game FLIGBY was used, a simulation game aimed towards teaching and training on how to manage and lead people based on the principles of "flow-based leadership". Buzady did not focus on evaluating the efficiency of a framework in particular, neither did the research had the objective of arriving at new numerical findings. Instead, Buzady was mainly concerned in presenting a case study as inspiration for possible future works in this field of psychology.

The state of flow is reached when there is a balance between two states extreme to each other: the state of anxiety and the state of boredom. The state of anxiety is reached when the level of skill required to perform a task is significantly higher than the level of skill a person possesses. The state of boredom, on the other hand, is reached when the level of skill a person possesses is significantly higher than the level of skill required to perform a task. The state of flow can be reached from either extreme. When in a state of anxiety, a person begins to develop their skills and acquire the knowledge necessary to perform the task, eventually migrating to the state of flow. Alternatively, a person in a state of boredom will feel compelled to seek tasks that challenge them and that demand new skills and knowledge, which will lead them to a situation in which they can reach the state of flow.

This mental state has received the name of "flow" because individuals that experience this state commonly describe it as a state in which their energy flows freely and in which their consciousness is carried by the task at hand (Csikszentmihalyi, 1975).

Another proposal, by Coppi (2015), resulted in the development of the game "Over the Gate". This game had as a premise to train the creativity of children by means of games and storytelling through digital media. In her article, Coppi not only describes the development of the game but also explains the pilot study conducted on top of this game.

"Over the Gate" is presented in the format of an electronic book, with story accompanied by illustrations and composed of verbal and visual games based on different aspects of creativity, such as originality, flexibility, fluency, etc. Some of the challenges presented to the players are riddles in which the player must find more than one answer, complete unfinished drawings, manipulate geometric shapes so as to form figures, choose different titles for stories, complete unfinished poems and solve logical challenges with rules similar to chess. Afterwards the player is told a story that illustrates the importance of creativity.

Based on this study it is possible to see potential in the use of digital games as a tool to develop creativity. Coppi concludes that some changes should be implemented in the game to reach better results, suggesting a deeper reading of the literature to better understand the required changes. These alterations show themselves to be necessary thanks to a possible problem that may be identified with the duration of the game, which is longer than two hours, negatively affecting the player's attention span as they are children. This negative impact may have affected the post test results. Coppi also proposes changes to the user interface, a reduction of the duration of the story told to the player and the introduction of a scoring system.

METHODOLOGY

To test the hypothesis proposed in this research, a game called *Luovus* was developed. This name was chosen for the similarity with the words *luovuus*, which means "creativity", and the word "love" in English, as a reminder of a positive feeling. While the literature indicates the potentially positive effect of positive feelings on creativity (De Rooij, Corr, & Jones, 2015), this benefit was not considered when choosing the title for the game. It is merely an artistic choice.

The game *Luovus* was developed in the JavaScript programming language, using the PixiJS graphical engine. This combination was chosen for its ease of universal access, seeing as a web-based page is easier to access than an application programmed for a specific operating system. Modules are attached to the main .html page that may be activated or deactivated as needed. Each module corresponds to a questionnaire, a game scene or a game screen. The modules are managed by an engine programmed specifically for *Luovus*, also in JavaScript, called *Vorhees* (Figure 1). This engine is tasked with initializing PixiJS and deciding which modules to activate and deactivate based on a state diagram.

When a scene module is loaded, Vorhees loads a .json file corresponding to the correct scene, containing information such as character art, dialogue and background graphics. Vorhees interprets this information and, in tandem with PixiJS, draws the scene on screen. Vorhees then receives and interprets the player's input and reacts accordingly.

Figure 1. Vorhees' state diagram
Source: (Marin & Notargiacomo, 2019)

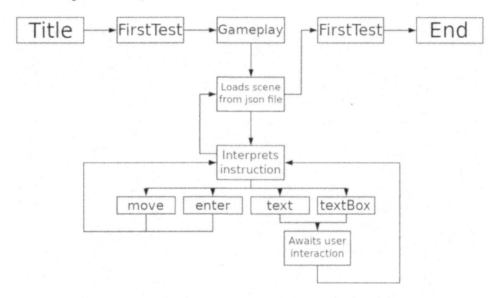

The results of the questionnaires answered by the players are each saved in a different *.json* file. These files do not contain any information that may compromise the privacy and anonymity of the players. Each file is identified by a randomly generated identification number.

Upon accessing the game by means of a chosen we browser, the user is presented the title screen, which contains the options "start" and "about." When the player selects the "start" option they are asked to complete the self-evaluative questionnaire for creativity created by Alencar et al. (2010) (Figure 2).

This specific creativity test was chosen for having been originally conceived in the portuguese language. This experiment was conducted with native portuguese speaking participants and keeping the test in its original language guarantees its integrity. The questionnaire consists of 66 questions in the format "I would be more creative if..." followed by a statement. For example, "I would be more creative if I were less shy to expose my ideas". For each statement the player must choose if they "completely disagree", "somewhat disagree ", is "uncertain", "somewhat agree" or "completely agree." The results are analyzed in a Likert scale. This initial questionnaire is used to evaluate the player's perception of their own creativity before their interaction with the game. The results of this questionnaire will posteriorly be compared to the results of the questionnaire completed by the player at the end of the game. This way, it is possible to examine the impact that the game had on the player and how their perception of their own creativity was affected after playing the game.

After completing the questionnaire, the player is presented to the game through a story.

This experiment counted on 15 participants. Of these 15 participants, 8 were female and 7 were male. The youngest participant was 20 years old and the oldest participant was 25 years old. The average of the ages of all participants is 22 years of age. Each player undertook the questionnaire twice. The questionnaire was identical to all players, consisting of the same 66 questions in the "I would be more creative if..." format with 5 replies on the Likert scale that were consisted throughout the questionnaire.

Figure 2. Translated questionnaire used in the game
Source: (Marin & Notargiacomo, 2019)

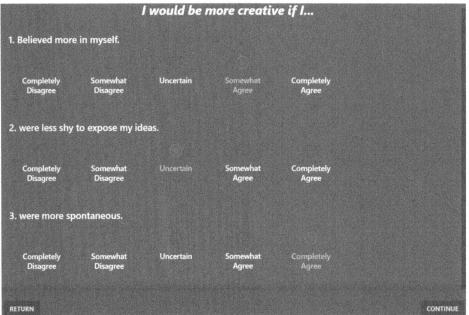

RESULTS AND ANALYSIS

Based on the developed computational application described in the methodology, the game *Luovus,* tests were conducted with real users. The players were asked to play the game, which included answering the two questionnaires, and then answer a few informal questions. Upon starting the game, the player is introduced to the *Artist*, a character that will serve as a guide and companion to the player throughout the game. The artist also serves as an interpreter to the player, as the player takes control of a silent character. Throughout the game the player will also meet other characters. In each interaction with one of these characters the player will be presented with challenges, that they must find a solution to in order to progress (Figure 3). The solutions presented by the player will be integrated into the game and commented on by other characters so that the player will have the opportunity to see that the solutions they present are being acknowledged by the game.

Throughout the game the player will meet new characters with whom they must interact. Each interaction affects the events of the story in a perceptible way. At the end, the artist will show the player the story they wrote. This story incorporates elements of the interactions between the player and the world. This approach is based on the structure of the game in which the player will meet characters that need assistance with a problem. Therefore, it is asked of the player that they propose a solution to this problem. The player receives a suggestion of what kind of solution they should propose, but the player has complete freedom to propose any solution they like. An example of a problem the player will be faced with is assisting a local bar owner with attracting clients to their establishment. This approach was chosen based on the study by Moffat and Shabalina (2016), and takes into consideration their findings and that and that a balance of some restrictions should be aimed for, as too many restrictions would suppress the players creativity, but too few restrictions may leave the player feeling confused and unsure

Figure 3. Translated scene from the game in which the player is presented with a challenge
Source: (Marin & Notargiacomo, 2019)

of how to proceed. The character's reactions to the solutions presented by the player seek to be fun and gratifying, without being exaggeratedly congratulatory. While generating positive feelings of satisfaction on the player has a positive impact on their capacity to express their creativity, this effect would be loss if the player felt a disconnection between their performance and the feedback given by the game (De Rooij, Corr, & Jones, 2015).

Since the solutions presented by the player, by means of their interactions with other characters, have an impact on the story and are discussed by other characters, at the end of the game the *Artist* character uses the player's suggestions as inspiration to write his story. This story is shown to the player and is altered to include the player interactions. For instance, at some point in the game the player is asked for a suggestion of which material to use to build a certain object. In the artist's story some object will be a reference to the material chosen by the player. The art style and direction of the game were chosen to be unobtrusive and simple, while also being fantastic, as to invite the player to think beyond the realm of the obvious.

It should also be noted that the challenges in the game were designed in such a way as not to limit the options of what the player can do, but also suggest a guide as to how to come to a solution. Based on the study by Moffat et al. (2016), an effort was made towards neither restricting too much the player's creative freedom, nor leave the solution so open that the player may feel lost or confused about how to progress (Figure 4). A high number of restrictions or restrictions that are too strict might impede the player from feeling they have autonomy to find their own solution, which according to Wang (2013) would have a negative impact on the player's motivation, which would, in turn, impact negatively the player's ability to find creative solutions to the challenges presented by the game. On the other hand, none or few restrictions could leave the player confused and without an idea of how deeply they can explore the game mechanics.

Figure 4. Translated scene from the game in which the player is asked for input
Source: (Marin & Notargiacomo, 2019)

The game was limited to three scenarios to avoid eroding the player's motivation. As this study depends on the post test results, it was deemed important to avoid having the player reach the end of the game feeling uninterested or cognitively exhausted, as this could affect the post test (Coppi, 2015).

Finally, the story presented by the artist at the end of the game is a way to show the player a different way that their solutions could be interpreted, and possibly incentivize reflection about how their input could have been interpreted had they come up with different solutions to the challenges presented by the game, as self evaluation is a catalyst for self development (Zhou & Li, 2013). A non intentional benefit was observed in the story presented to the player by the artist at the end of the game: it promoted discussion among the participants, as they compared their resulting stories and discussed the effects of each one's solutions.

At the end of the game the player is once again taken to the questionnaire taken at the start of the game. The purpose of this post test is to examine how the game influenced the player, specifically how their perception of their capacity to think creatively was altered. This second test allowed an analysis of a player's total variation, as well as the variation in the score for each question among all players.

The test for creativity implemented in the game Luovus was the one developed by Alencar et al. (2010). As the experiment was conducted with people whose primary and possibly only language is Portuguese, this test was chosen over the ATC. A self-evaluative test was chosen for the opportunity it grants to incentivize the player to reflect on their own creativity and to understand how each participant sees their own capacity to find creative solutions for a given task. A self-evaluative test was chosen to promote the practice of self-monitoring during the game on the player. As noted by Zhou et al. (2013), self-monitoring is a useful practice when attempting to train creative thought.

When analysing the results of the experiment, it is possible to observe that not significant variation was found on the player's perception of their own creativity on the post-test in comparison to the pre

Figure 5. Creativity score variation for users between pretest and post-test
Source: (Marin & Notargiacomo, 2019)

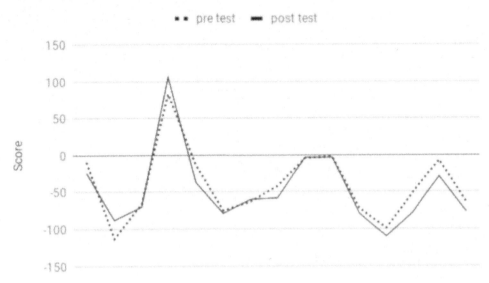

test. The average variation on player score is -6 on a scale of -132 to 132 (Figure 5). This slight negative variation may have been caused by cognitive exhaustion on the players' side.

The individual variation on the answers for each specific question was also analyzed (Figure 6). In other words, an analysis of the variation for the score of each question for all players. In this analysis it is possible to see which questions had the greatest variation between the pretest and post-test.

The variation for most questions was of 5 points or less, not presenting a significant variation. That said, some questions did present a more significant variation. The highest variation for a specific question found was of 10 points. The questions with variations considered significant were questions 9, 10, 30, 41, 43, 48, 53, 60 and 66 (Table 1).

Figure 6. Average score variation for each question between pretest and post-test
Source: (Marin & Notargiacomo, 2019)

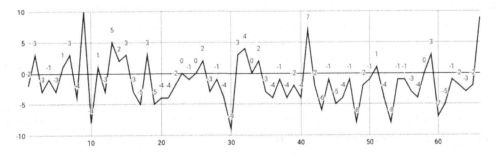

Table 1. Questions with most significative score variation

Question	"I would be more creative if..."	Variation
9	"I had more initiative"	10
10	"I weren't afraid to contradict people"	-8
30	"I weren't afraid to be misunderstood"	-9
41	"I had more resources to put my ideas into practice"	7
43	"I hadn't been suppressed by my teachers"	-6
48	"there was more cooperation between people"	-8
53	"people valued new ideas more"	-8
60	"I had a stronger sense of humor"	-7
66	"I had more knowledge"	9

Source: (Marin & Notargiacomo, 2019)

CONCLUSION AND FUTURE WORKS

This experiment was proposed with the idea of testing the possibility of developing a game that could aid the player in training their creativity, based on past experiments. While the results were not conclusive, they indicate a promising possibility that it is possible to have at least some impact on a person's creativity by means of a digital game, be it in the form of exercising their creative capabilities or promoting self-monitoring and reflection on their own creativity.

Analysing the results of the experiment it is not possible to state that the game did actually impact the player's self-perceived creativity. The slight negative variation found on the average score of all players might be explained by the self-evaluative nature of the test chosen for this experiment. It is possible that the players evaluated themselves more strictly after playing the game.

After the game the players were asked about their experience with Luovus. 11 of the participants said they found the game "fun", "interesting" or "cool". This means that over two thirds of the 15 participants reported having a positive experience with the game. On the other hand, 5 of the participants also said they found the game too short or expressed a desire that the game be longer. This means their experience may have been cut short while they were in the *flow* state of mind. A longer game might have been more successful in giving players ampler opportunities to exercise their creativity without becoming exhausting.

Also worth noting is that 7 of the participants complained about the extension of the creativity test chosen for this experiment, arguing that the high number of questions (66 questions to be exact) and taking the test twice was tiring. This number represents almost half of participants, so this factor should not be ignored. This problem points back to the problem found by Coppi (2015) in her experiment, in which the duration of the experiment may have negatively affected the post test results because of the cognitive exhaustion it may have caused on the players. This is another possible explanation for the negative average score variation found in this experiment. This effect might be mitigated by employing a shorter questionnaire or by integrating the test in the game in a way that is nearly or completely imperceptible to the player.

Roughly speaking the score variation for each player did not present a significant variation. That said, some questions presented higher average variations and are therefore worthy of deeper analysis. These questions had variations higher than 5 points, whether negative or positive. Analysing the questions with positive variations it is possible to theorize that the game made the players more confident in their capacity to express creative thoughts without the need of external material or intellectual resources. Questions such as "I would be more creative if I had more initiative" and "I would be more creative if I had more knowledge" had a notably positive variation, which may indicate that the experience of practicing their creativity led the players to feel more secure in their capacity to be creative without the need of external aid. On the other hand, analysing the questions that presented a negative variation it seems the players may have become less secure in their ideas being socially accepted. The analysis of questions such as "I would be more creative if I weren't afraid of being misunderstood" and "I would be more creative if there were higher cooperation between people" had a notably negative variation. This may be a sign that that, after playing the game, players became more critical of the impact that society and their environment had in the development of their creativity.

This hypothesis may be further explored in future experiments. Future studies may also reach more enlightening results by employing other tests for creativity, especially if tests that are not self-evaluative are also employed. The *Torrance Tests of Creative Thinking are suggested*, in conjunction with another test, as suggested by Torrance (Treffinger, 1985). Future investigations may benefit from a larger number of participants in future experiments, as this may function as a proof of concept of the game developed. Another technology that may be used in future experiments is telemetry, as a way to use data mining and neural networks to verify the formation of clumps that might allow a better understanding of how different player profiles interact with the game

REFERENCES

Ahmadi, G. A., Abdolmaleki, S., & Khoshbakht, M. (2011). Effect of computer-based training to increase creativity and achievement science, students in fourth grade of elementary. *Procedia Computer Science*, *3*, 1551–1554. doi:10.1016/j.procs.2011.01.047

Alencar, E. M. L. S., Fleith, D. S., & Bruno-Faria, M. F. (2010). A medida da criatividade: Teoria e prática. *The Art of Medication*.

Amabile, T. M., & Gryskiewicz, S. S. (1987). *Creativity in the R&D laboratory*. Center for Creative Leadership.

Azevedo, I., Morais, M. D. F., & Martins, F. (2017). Educação para a criatividade em adolescentes: Uma experiência com future problem solving program international. *Revista Electrónica Iberoamericana sobre Calidad, Eficacia y Cambio en Educación*, 75–87.

Berg, J. M., Dutton, J. E., & Wrzesniewski, A. (2013). Job crafting and meaningful work. In B. J. Dik, Z. S. Byrne, & M. F. Steger (Eds.), *Purpose and meaning in the workplace* (pp. 81–104). Washington, DC: American Psychological Association. doi:10.1037/14183-005

Buzady, Z. (2017). Flow, leadership and serious games – a pedagogical perspective. *World Journal of Science, Technology and Sustainable Development*, 14(2-3), 204-217.

Chua, R. Y.-J., & Iyengar, S. S. (2008). Creativity as a matter of choice: Prior experience and task instruction as boundary conditions for the positive effect of choice on creativity. *The Journal of Creative Behavior*, *42*(3), 164–180. doi:10.1002/j.2162-6057.2008.tb01293.x

Coppi, A. E. (2015). Fostering creativity through games and digital storytelling. In *Proceedings of the International Conference on Interactive Technologies and Games* (pp. 17-21). Academic Press. 10.1109/iTAG.2015.12

Cramond, B., Matthews-Morgan, J., Bandalos, D., & Zuo, L. (2005). A report on the 40-year follow-up of the torrance tests of creative chinking: Alive and well in the new millennium. *Gifted Child Quarterly*, *49*(4), 283–291. doi:10.1177/001698620504900402

Csikszentmihalyi, M. (1975). *Beyond boredom and anxiety: Experiencing flow in work and play*. Jossey-Bass.

De Rooij, A., Corr, P. J., & Jones, S. (2015). Emotion and creativity: Hacking into cognitive appraisal processes to augment creative ideation. In *Proceedings of the 2015 ACM SIGCHI Conference on Creativity and Cognition* (pp. 265-274). ACM. 10.1145/2757226.2757227

Gangestad, S. W., & Snyder, M. (2000). Self-monitoring: Appraisal and reappraisal. *Psychological Bulletin*, *126*(4), 530–555. doi:10.1037/0033-2909.126.4.530 PMID:10900995

Isaksen, S. G., Dorval, K. B., & Treffinger, D. J. (2011). *Creative approaches to problem solving: A framework for change. Sage.*

Kim, K. H. (2006). Can we trust creativity tests? A review of the Torrance tests of creative thinking (TTCT). *Creativity Research Journal*, *18*(1), 3–14. doi:10.120715326934crj1801_2

Lau, S., & Cheung, P. C. (2010). Developmental trends of creativity: What twists of turn do boys and girls take at different grades? *Creativity Research Journal*, *22*(3), 329–336. doi:10.1080/10400419.2010.503543

Li, Z., Qiong, B., & Wee, S. (2014). Impact of job control on employee creativity: The moderating effect of cognitive irritation. In *Proceedings of the 21th International Conference on Management Science & Engineering* (pp. 873-878). Academic Press.

Marin, W. W., & Notargiacomo, P. (2019). Study of development of creativity through digital games. In *Proceedings of the IADIS International Conference Game and Entertainment Technologies 2019* (pp. 391-395). Academic Press. 10.33965/g2019_201906C055

Maslow, A. H. (1943). A theory of human motivation. *Psychological Review*, *50*(4), 370–396. doi:10.1037/h0054346

Maslow, A. H. (1959). Creativity in self-actualizing people. In H. H. Anderson (Ed.), *Creativity and its cultivation* (pp. 83–95). New York: Harper & Row.

Moffat, D. C., & Shabalina, O. (2016). Student creativity exercises in designing serious games. In *Proceedings of the European Conference on Games Based Learning* (pp. 470-478). Academic Press.

Rogers, C. R. (1959). Toward a theory of creativity. In H. H. Anderson (Ed.), *Creativity and its cultivation* (pp. 69–82). New York: Harper & Row.

Runco, M., & Jager, G. (2012). The standard definition of creativity. *Creativity Research Journal*, *24*(1), 92–96. doi:10.1080/10400419.2012.650092

Runco, M. A. (2004). Creativity. *Annual Review of Psychology*, *55*(1), 657–687. doi:10.1146/annurev.psych.55.090902.141502 PMID:14744230

Torrance, E. (1979). Unique needs of the creative child and adult. In A. Passow (Ed.), The gifted and the talented: Their education and development (pp. 352-371). National Society for the Study of Education.

Treffinger, D. J. (1985). Review of the torrance tests of creative thinking. In J. V. Mitchell Jr., (Ed.), *The ninth mental measurements yearbook* (pp. 1632–1634). Lincoln: University of Nebraska, Buros Institute of Mental Measurements.

Vella, K., Johnson, D., & Hides, L. (2013). Positively playful: When videogames lead to player wellbeing. *Proceedings of the Gamification*, 99–102.

Wang, K. (2013). The effect of autonomy on team creativity and the moderating variables. In *Proceedings of PICMET '13: Technology Management for Emerging Technologies* (pp. 1156-1160). Academic Press.

Yokochi, S., & Okada, T. (2005). Creative cognitive process of art making: A field study of a traditional Chinese ink painter. *Creativity Research Journal*, *17*(2-3), 241–255. doi:10.1080/10400419.2005.9651482

Zhou, M.-J., & Li, S.-K. (2013). Can supervisor feedback always promote creativity? The moderating role of employee self-monitoring. In *Proceedings of the 6th International Conference on Information Management, Innovation Management and Industrial Engineering* (pp. 510-512). Academic Press. 10.1109/ICIII.2013.6703200

KEY TERMS AND DEFINITIONS

Autonomy: The social freedom to act as desired, without the need to follow orders or be watched.

Feedback: Constructive criticism received on a performed task or solution

Flow: The mental state achieved with the balance of the mental states of anxiety and boredom in which a person may be best suited to perform a task.

JavaScript: A programming language often employed in the development of web based applications.

Motivation: The intrinsic desire to perform a task or find a solution.

Restriction: A condition or limit imposed on the performance of a task or on possible solutions to a problem.

Solution: One of possibly many answers to a problem proposed to a person or group, be it in the form of an idea or a process.

Task: An activity or process to be executed by a person or group.

Well-Being: A positive emotion, achieved when a person has or is feeling satisfied.

Chapter 6
A Study to Further Understand the Link Between Immersion and Flow

Ehm Kannegieser
Fraunhofer IOSB, Germany

Daniel Atorf
Fraunhofer IOSB, Germany

ABSTRACT

Flow and immersion are states of extreme concentration on an activity. For serious games, that is games, which focus on achieving learning effects in players, high flow and immersion during gameplay can help to improve these learning effects. Both flow and immersion are currently only measured using questionnaires, which is both delayed and subjective. This work introduces a study, which aims to further the understanding of how flow and immersion are linked and to ease future work towards a new measurement method using physiological data.

INTRODUCTION

The design of Serious Games still presents an active field of research. Especially important are techniques to increase the learning rate of these games. Previous studies find in their research that high focus helps to transmit learning material through Serious Games (Deci and Ryan, 1985; Krapp, 2009). Two terms used to measure high focus are Flow and Immersion. These terms describe states of great focus on an activity or game. They are currently measured using questionnaires (Nordin, Denisova, and Cairns, 2014), which have a range of problems. A participant cannot fill out a questionnaire without interrupting the concentration state, meaning there must be a delay when gathering data. Additionally, questionnaires are inherently subjective, adding additional bias to the measured results. The solution to this problem would be to measure changes in the player's body and derive Flow and Immersion from that. This work in progress tries to present a step towards this solution. In order to better understand how Flow and Im-

DOI: 10.4018/978-1-7998-2637-8.ch006

mersion interact, a combined model is established. Afterwards, based on previous work (Atorf et al., 2016; Kannegieser et al., 2018), a study is presented, which attempts to validate the model and link it with physiological measurements taken from players.

BACKGROUND

Flow was first described by Csikszentmihalyi as the state of the optimal experience of an activity (Csikszentmihalyi, 1991). When entering a state of Flow, even taxing activities like work no longer feel taxing, but rather feel enjoyable. However, the Flow state cannot be achieved for every activity. Csikszentmihalyi bases Flow on the model of extrinsic and intrinsic motivation. Only intrinsically motivated actions, which are not motivated by external factors, can reach the Flow state. Flow is reachable when the challenge presented by such an intrinsically motivated action is balanced with the skill of the person performing the task. All this makes Flow an interesting point of research concerning games, as playing games usually is intrinsically motivated. Flow is mapped to games in the GameFlow questionnaire (Sweetser et al., 2005).

There exist two concurrent definitions of Immersion (Zhang et al., 2017). The first definition is called presence-based Immersion and refers to the feeling of being physically present in a virtual location. The second definition is known as engagement-based Immersion. It defines Immersion based on the strength of a player's interaction with the game. The model given by Cairns et al. in their series of papers (Cairns et al., 2006; Jenett et al., 2008), defines Immersion as a hierarchical structure, with different barriers of entry. The lowest level, Engagement, is reached by interacting with the game and spending time with it. Engrossment is reached by becoming emotionally involved with the game. During this state, feelings of temporal and spatial dissociation are starting to appear. The final state, Total Immersion, is reached by players having their feelings completely focused on the game. Cheng et al. improve upon this hierarchical model by adding dimensions to the three levels of the hierarchy (Cheng et al., 2015). The Engagement level is split into the three dimensions: Attraction, Time Investment and Usability. The second level, Engrossment, is split into Emotional Attachment, which refers to attachment to the game itself, and Decreased Perceptions. Finally, Total Immersion is defined by the terms Presence and Empathy.

Flow and Immersion share many similarities (see Table 1). Both have similar effects, such as decreased perceptions of both time and the environment, and refer to a state of focus. Georgiou and Kyza even take the empathy dimension in the immersion model by Cheng et al. and replace it with Flow (Georgiou and Kyza, 2017). There are two main differences between the two: First, Flow does not define an emotional component, while Immersion is focused heavily on the emotional attachment of players to the game. Second, while Flow refers to a final state of complete concentration, Immersion refers to a range of experiences, ranging from minimal engagement to complete focus on the game. This is reflected in how those two psychological states are described in their introduction. Csikszentmihalyi describes Flow as the "optimal experience of an activity", while Cairns et al. describe Immersion as the "sub-optimal experience of an activity".

Table 1. Key similarities in flow and immersion definitions

Flow	Immersion
Task	The Game
Concentration	Cognitive Involvement
Skill / Challenge – Balance	Challenge
Sense of Control	Control
Clear Goals	Emotional Involvement
Immediate Feedback	
Reduced Sense of Self and of Time	Real-World Dissociation

Validation of the combined Model of Immersion and Flow

Model

The combined model (Kannegieser et al., 2018) used in the study is based on the Flow model presented by Csikszentmihalyi (Csikszentmihalyi, 1991) and the Immersion model by Cheng et al. (Cheng et al., 2015), which itself is a refinement of the hierarchical model presented by Cairns et al.

Flow, as the optimal experience of an action, is considered as the highest point in the Immersion hierarchy, which implies that Total Immersion and Flow are regularly experienced together. Figure 1 presents the Immersion hierarchy (see Figure 2) imposed on top of the three-channel model by Csikszentmihalyi. As Immersion grows the possibility to reach the Flow state increases. It must be noted that the diagram is only meant to be a qualitative visualization, as Immersion is not dependent on the challenge/skill balance.

Figure 1. Hierarchical Immersion model on top of the three-channel Flow model by Csikszentmihalyi source: (Kannegieser et al., 2018).

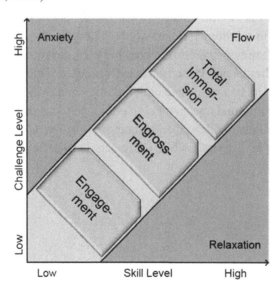

116

Figure 2. Levels of the Immersion model by Cairns et al., with dimensions for each level by Cheng et al. source: (Cairns et al., 2006; Cheng et al., 2015).

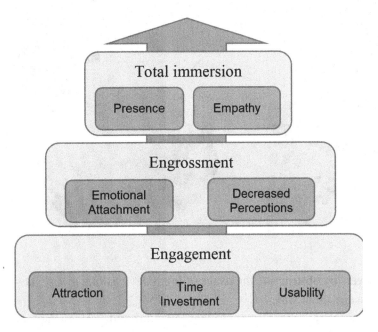

Experiment

The study was designed to both gather data to link physiological measurements with Flow and Immersion, as well as validate the combined Flow/Immersion model presented. Over 40 participants took part in the study. Participants were self-selected and not characterized into separate groups. Game choice was free. This method was chosen to help observe higher levels of Immersion and Flow. The study was split into three phases:

Setup Phase

During the Setup Phase, paperwork was signed, electrodes were set up, sensors were calibrated (see Figure 3) and a game was selected and installed. Free choice of game makes finding links between physiological measurements harder, but was chosen to help participants reach the Flow state more easily.

Gaming Phase

During the Gaming Phase, participants played the chosen game for 30 minutes, while physiological measurements, video and audio recordings were taken. 30 minutes of gameplay are deemed long enough, as the match duration of e.g. Overwatch is between ten to twenty minutes, allowing for at least two matches to being played. Similar (Portal) or shorter (Angry Birds) level durations apply to the other game titles used in the study, allowing the player to immerse into even more levels of the chosen game. The measurements used in this study were chosen due to being non-intrusive and not hindering

Figure 3. Experiment setup, Source: 2018 Ehm Kannegieser

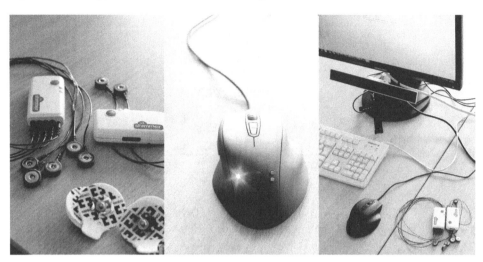

the immersion of players by obstructing the usage of input devices like mouse, keyboard or gamepad or causing discomfort in any other way.

Galvanic skin response, Electrocardiography, gaze tracking and web cam footage for emotion analysis were used: for every second of the video, a cropped image of the participant's face is generated. This cropped image is scaled to 256 × 256 and used as input for a pre-trained Convolutional Neural Network that recognizes emotions in cropped face images (Levi and Hassner, 2015) as shown in Figure 4. As the web cam footage features players frontally, this CNN delivers good results for the data presented. The output of the net are probabilities for the seven states anger, disgust, fear, happiness, neutral, sadness and surprise.

A facial EMG would be more precise for analyzing displayed emotions, however, placing electrodes on the face of the player would probably distract from the gameplay experience and make it harder to reach the flow state. For the same reasons, EEG measurement was not chosen for the study.

Figure 4. Cropped Image of participant's face as input for emotion recognition by a CNN

Figure 5. Phases and activities of the experiment

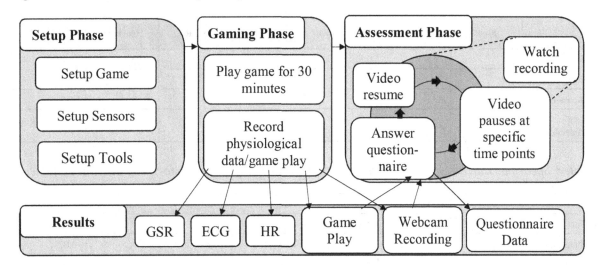

Assessment Phase

After the Gaming Phase has concluded, participants enter the Assessment Phase and watch their previous gaming session, while answering questionnaires about Immersion and Flow periodically. This setup was chosen to get more exact results and because it does not interrupt the Flow experience. Three questionnaires were used during the study:

The first questionnaire used is the Immersion questionnaire described by Cheng et al (Cheng et al., 2015). As the questionnaire was too long to be measured multiple times without worsening the results, it was split into an Immersive Tendency questionnaire asked at the beginning of playback and an iterative questionnaire asked every three minutes during playback. For Flow, the Flow Short Scale questionnaire by Rheinberg et al. was used (Rheinberg et al., 2003). It was originally designed for being used multiple times in a row, making it perfect for this iterative approach. During playback, it is asked every six minutes. The final questionnaire used is the Game Experience Questionnaire (IJsselsteijn, de Kort and Poels, 2013). It measures a more general set of questions and is used once after playback is over. Figure 5 shows the three phases of the experiment as well as the activities of each phase.

Model Analysis Results

The first step of the analysis is to check for correlations between Flow and Immersion. The results from both the Flow and Immersion questionnaires do not follow a normal distribution. For that reason, Spearman correlation was chosen. The correlation analysis found a strong correlation between all three levels of Immersion and Flow. The strongest correlation was found between Engagement and Flow (R = 0.69, p = 8.536e-30), which makes sense, knowing that Flow encompasses all features making up Engagement. The second strongest correlation exists between Total Immersion and Flow (R = 0.652, p = 1.91e-25). This is caused by the fact that players who played games without clear avatars, such as strategy games, found it difficult to emphasize with their avatar in the game, leading to reduced Total Immersion. The least correlated level of the three is Engrossment (R = 0.56, p = 1.829e-18), which can

Table 2. Spearman rho correlation coefficients for flow/immersion and physiological measurements

	Flow	Engagement	Engrossment	Total Immersion	GSR	Heartrate	Rest points / min
Flow	1	0.69	0.57	0.65	-0.02	-0.03	-0.07
Engagement	0.69	1	0.45	0.58	0.01	-0.08	-0.02
Engrossment	0.57	0.45	1	0.62	-0.04	-0.09	0.05
Total Immersion	0.65	0.58	0.62	1	-0.15	0	0.06

Table 3. Spearman rho correlation coefficients for flow/immersion and emotional recognition measurements

	Anger	Disgust	Fear	Happiness	Neutrality	Sadness	Surprise
Flow	0.11	-0.04	-0.04	-0.13	0.02	0.15	-0.13
Engagement	0.04	0.06	-0.14	-0.01	0.06	0.17	-0.07
Engrossment	-0.01	-0.07	-0.01	-0.06	0.05	0.10	-0.06
Total Immersion	0.08	-0.05	-0.02	0.01	-0.04	0.13	-0.13

be explained as Engrossment puts strong emphasis on emotional attachment of the player to the game, something Flow does not elicit. All three show strong correlation to Flow, meaning the relation between these two psychological states is likely.

Physiological Analysis Results

Direct correlation between normalized physiological data and answers of the Flow/Immersion questionnaires show no meaningful correlation (see Table 2). This means a more advanced method has to be employed. The first advanced method tried was using expert rules and fuzzy logic to create rules and activation methods based on an approach used by Goshvarpour et al. (Goshvarpour et al., 2017). Using this approach did not lead to meaningful results either, as it was difficult to create useful rules from the raw data and direct correlation results between physiological measurements and Flow/Immersion.

Emotion Detection Analysis Results

Direct correlation between normalized emotional data and answers of the Flow/Immersion questionnaires show very little meaningful correlation (see Table 3). The weakness of this approach is that only emotions clearly displayed on the face of the participant can be elicited with great confidence. High-framerate-video (HFV) capable cameras, Facial EMG and questionnaires might be employed in future experiments, to improve data quality - although EMG is considered more intrusive than video-based emotion detection.

CONCLUSION

With this work in progress, an attempt was made to link physiological or emotional reactions in players to the states of Flow and Immersion. Furthermore, a second aim was to get a clearer understanding of how Flow and Immersion are linked, and present a unified model. In order to reach these goals, a study was performed and the results evaluated.

As far as the link between Immersion and Flow is concerned, the results back up the model presented. The data shows strong correlation between high Flow and high Immersion for all three Immersion levels, which would imply Flow to be situated at the highest point of the Immersion hierarchy, along with total Immersion.

Results are less clear for the link between physiological or emotional measurements and the Flow/ Immersion model. Direct correlation did not find any connection between the recorded data. This also made creating an advanced rule-based system difficult to achieve. Future research will be aimed at further analyzing the connection between physiological measurements and Flow with advanced techniques enriched by additional (e.g. micro expressions recorded via electromyography (EMG) or high framerate video (HFV), brain activity (EEG)) or more solid sensor measurements (e.g. eyetracking).

REFERENCES

Atorf, D., Hensler, L., & Kannegieser, E. (2016). Towards a concept on measuring the Flow state during gameplay of serious games. In Proceedings of the European Conference on Games Based Learning (ECGBL) (pp. 955–959). Academic Press. Retrieved from http://publica.fraunhofer.de/documents/N-438328.html

Cairns, P., Cox, A., Berthouze, N., Jennett, C., & Dhoparee, S. (2006). Quantifying the experience of immersion in games. In *Proceedings of the Cognitive Science of Games and Gameplay workshop at Cognitive Science*. Academic Press.

Cheng, M.-T., She, H.-C., & Annetta, L. (2015). Game Immersion Experience: Its Hierarchical Structure and Impact on Game-based Science Learning. *Journal of Computer Assisted Learning*, *31*(3), 232–253. doi:10.1111/jcal.12066

Csikszentmihalyi, M. (1991). *Flow: The Psychology of Optimal Experience*. New York, NY: Harper Perennial.

Deci, E., & Ryan, R. (1985). *Intrinsic Motivation and Self-Determination in Human Behavior*. New York, NY: Plenum Press; doi:10.1007/978-1-4899-2271-7.

Georgiou, Y., & Kyza, E. A. (2017). The development and validation of the ARI questionnaire: An instrument for measuring immersion in location-based augmented reality settings. *International Journal of Human-Computer Studies*, *98*, 24–37. doi:10.1016/j.ijhcs.2016.09.014

Goshvarpour, A., Abbasi, A., & Goshvarpour, A. (2017). An accurate emotion recognition system using ECG and GSR signals and matching pursuit method. *Biomedical Journal*, *40*(6), 355–368. doi:10.1016/j.bj.2017.11.001

Ijsselsteijn, W., van den Hoogen, W., Klimmt, C., De Kort, Y., Lindley, C., Mathiak, K., . . . Vorderer, P. (2008). Measuring the experience of digital game enjoyment. In Proceedings of Measuring Behavior 2008, 6th International Conference on Methods and Techniques in Behavioral Research (pp. 88–89). Academic Press.

Jennett, C., Cox, A. L., Cairns, P., Dhoparee, S., Epps, A., Tijs, T., & Walton, A. (2008). Measuring and defining the experience of immersion in games. *International Journal of Human-Computer Studies*, *66*(9), 641–661. doi:10.1016/j.ijhcs.2008.04.004

Kannegieser, E., Atorf, D., & Meier, J. (2018). In: Surveying games with a combined model of Immersion and Flow. In Proceedings of the International Conferences on Interfaces and Human Computer Interaction 2018, Game and Entertainment Technologies 2018 and Computer Graphics, Visualization, Computer Vision and Image Processing 2018 (pp. 353-356). Academic Press.

Krapp, A., Schiefele, U., & Schreyer, I. (2009). Metaanalyse des Zusammenhangs von Interesse und schulischer Leistung. *Zeitschrift für Entwicklungspsychologie und Pädagogische Psychologie*, *25*, 120–148.

Levi, G., & Hassner, T. (2015). Emotion Recognition in the Wild via Convolutional Neural Networks and Mapped Binary Patterns. In Proceedings of the 2015 ACM on International Conference on Multimodal Interaction ICMI '15 (pp. 503–510). ACM. doi:10.1145/2818346.2830587

Nordin, A. I., Denisova, A., & Cairns, P. (2014). Too Many Questionnaires: Measuring Player Experience Whilst Playing Digital Games. In *Proceedings of the Seventh York Doctoral Symposium on Computer Science and Electronics*. Academic Press.

Rheinberg, F., Vollmeyer, R., & Engeser, S. (2003). Die Erfassung des Flow-Erlebens. In *Diagnostik von Motivation und Selbstkonzept* (pp. 261–279). Göttingen: Hogrefe.

Sweetser, P., & Wyeth, P. (2005). GameFlow: A Model for Evaluating Player Enjoyment in Games. *Computers in Entertainment*, *3*(3). doi:10.1145/1077246.1077253

Zhang, Z., Perkis, A., & Arndt, S. (2017). Spatial immersion versus emotional immersion, which is more immersive? In *Proceedings of the Ninth International Conference on Quality of Multimedia Experience* (pp. 1–6). Academic Press; doi:10.1109/QoMEX.2017.7965655.

Chapter 7
Measuring and Comparing Immersion in Digital Media Multitasking

Hao Wang
Department of Computer Science, National Chiao Tung University, Taiwan

Chien-Wen Ou Yang
iD https://orcid.org/0000-0002-9261-133X
Department of Computer Science, National Chiao Tung University, Taiwan

Chun-Tsai Sun
Department of Computer Science, National Chiao Tung University, Taiwan

ABSTRACT

In terms of digital media usage, immersion refers to user involvement in and focus on a single activity. However, the commonality of multi-tasking raises questions regarding whether one could enjoy immersion when using more than one media at the same time. Self-report questionnaires and eye trackers were used to measure the immersive experiences while playing video games and watching a television program at the same time. While we found evidence of immersion across the two activities while multitasking, some immersion dimensions were significantly weaker. However, we also noted that immersion experiences from multiple media might be cumulative. A possible explanation for our results is that the act of switching between two media compensated for any down time, users could abandon a less attractive medium and switch to the other, resulting in an impression of continuous immersion in the overall multitasking experience. On the other hand, keeping active awareness of other media beyond the current focus might be a primary cause of immersion degradation.

DOI: 10.4018/978-1-7998-2637-8.ch007

INTRODUCTION

Of the many definitions of immersion found in the literature, one of the most cited is from Murray's work (1997): "The sensation of being surrounded by a completely other reality, as different as water is from air, that takes over all of our attention, our whole perceptual apparatus ... In a participatory medium, immersion implies learning to swim, to do the things that the new environment makes possible." However, many other researchers have come up with their own definitions. For example, in the field of virtual reality (where immersion is considered an important characteristic), Coomans and Timmermans (1997) describe immersion as "a feeling of being deeply engaged" to the degree that virtual reality is accepted as actual reality. McMahan (2003) describes it as the feeling of being "caught up" in a virtual world. Bailenson, Blascovich, and Guadagno (2008) define it in terms of how closely participants interact with a virtual world, and Witmar and Singer (1998) describe it as a "feeling of presence" in a virtual environment. Slater, Usoh, and Steed (1994) offer a similar definition for the concept of presence—that is, the feeling of being in a digital 3D virtual environment that users can interact with. However, Slater (1999) later described immersion and presence as separate factors—the first an objective description of an environment, the second a subjective user experience.

Digital game researchers and designers have long acknowledged the importance of immersion (Brown and Cairns, 2004). Jennett, Cox, and Cairns (2008) note that immersion in the form of "drawing people in" is an important factor in game design. When proposing their SCI (sensory, challenge-based, imaginative) model for analyzing video game immersion experiences, Ermi and Mäyrä (2005) defined the target concept as "becoming physically or virtually a part of the experience itself." According to their model, sensory sources include "close-to-real" video and audio effects involving factors such as screen size/resolution, virtual reality (VR), and sound quality. However, most researchers agree that while such technological features can help increase immersion, they are not required (McMahan, 2003). The SCI model addresses player feelings when overcoming game challenges, especially their enjoyment of narratives, their commitment to and empathy for story characters, and their perceptions of "game atmosphere" (Brown and Cairns, 2004). McMahan (2003) also posits that immersion sources can be either diegetic or non-diegetic. The first involves narrative elements such as story and atmosphere, the second involves active play—that is, a "player's love of the game and the strategy that goes into it" (p. 68).

Jennett, Cox, Cairns, Dhoparee, Epps, Tijs et al. (2008) used questionnaires to measure and quantify immersion, and then performed exploratory analysis to decompose the immersion concept into five dimensions: cognitive involvement, emotional involvement, challenge, real world dissociation, and control. Some dimensions correspond to the SCI model—that is, they both involve challenge and cognitive involvement (with a sufficiently strong challenge requiring an investment in cognitive effort); emotional involvement is similar to imaginative source; and real-world dissociation is somewhat similar to the SCI sensory source idea. Jennett et al. also found that individuals often need to consciously "re-engage with the real world" after being immersed in an activity. This observation offers another opportunity for researchers to objectively measure immersion by recording the time required for study participants to complete certain tasks after a gaming session, and then comparing task completion times—the greater the time requirement, the greater the level of immersion in the preceding game activity.

The literature contains many conscious attempts to create or trigger immersion. McMahan (2003) has proposed three design rules based on the relationship between players and their environments: meet player expectations (e.g., use dragons instead of aliens and UFOs in games that have medieval settings), give players a sense of control over game environments, and ensure consistency in game mechanisms and rules. She notes that while game worlds have very different "natural laws" from the physical world, interested players eventually learn and adapt to them, and changing them can interrupt immersive experiences.

Brown and Cairns (2008) created three low-to-high immersion categories based on extent of involvement: engagement, engrossment, and total immersion. Entering the engagement level entails establishing game preference and a willingness to play. To entice players to invest the necessary time and energy to sustain interest, game designers must facilitate achievable learning curves and provide proper control interfaces to make barriers seem less challenging. Entering the engrossment level involves player emotion, with designers organizing game elements in ways that make players "feel moved" to the point that they have less awareness of their surroundings and selves. Brown and Cairns define total immersion in terms of presence—that is, players feel that they are "in the game," and that game content is all that matters in the moment. In addition to feeling empathy for the characters they control, immersed players focus all sensory attention on "atmosphere," meaning a game's visual, audio, and emotional content. Two game genres and designs that are thought to be better at creating empathy and atmosphere are first-person shooter (FPS) and role-playing games (RPGs), although any well-designed game can lower atmosphere-related barriers. According to Brown and Cairns, it is important to note that ultimate levels of immersion are fleeting experiences that are seldom achieved.

To date, most studies and experiments on various aspects of immersion have focused on situations in which only one type of media is being used. However, we now live in a period where it is very common for individuals to divide their attention between two or more information sources, sometimes involving more than one outlet of the same media type. Results from a digital consumer survey conducted by the Nielsen Corporation (2014) indicate that 84% of all smart phone/tablet users in their sample used their devices while watching television. It is also increasingly common for game players to watch television or monitor other players' live shows on Twitch or YouTube while playing their own games.

Understanding the potential for immersion among individuals who divide their attention between two or more media is the primary motivation for the present study. Toward that goal, the authors established four research questions involving two groups of study participants—a multitasking experimental group, and a control group focused on one video or one game:

1. Were immersion levels among participants in the multitasking group lower than immersion levels in control group participants?
2. How do study participants divide their attention between more than one type of media? Do multitasking participants use media in different ways compared to single-task participants?
3. What is the relationship between overall immersion level and immersion levels for each of the two activities? Is the overall immersion level for a single activity close to the average for both, or are immersive experiences cumulative?
4. Are multitasking participants concurrently immersed in both media, or do they tend to be immersed in only one at a time?

BACKGROUND

Definitions

Researchers in at least two topic areas have applied the immersion concept in their studies. In virtual reality research, Slater, Linakis, Usoh and Kooper (1996) used immersion in an effort to establish objective descriptions of virtual environment characteristics. Slater (1999) later suggested that immersion can be used to assess virtual environment systems—for instance, larger screen size is thought to be more conducive to higher levels of immersion. While they acknowledge a link between virtual system characteristics and immersion, Childs (2010) and Onyesolu (2009) argue that such systems only have the potential to provide immersive experiences, and that large numbers of users are still not guaranteed to experience immersion. Bredl, Groß, Hünniger and Fleischer (2012) described immersion as the feeling of being part of a virtual environment with which they directly interact, oftentimes with an intensity that exceeds that found in their real-world interactions. Weibel, Wissmath and Mast (2010), who also describe immersion as a subjective experience, found correlations between immersion tendencies and openness to experience, neuroticism, and extraversion—three of the Big 5 personality traits (Goldberg, 1990).

Researchers in the second topic area, digital games, often analyze immersion as a natural part of the gaming experience. Carr (2006) has proposed two immersion categories: as a perceptual phenomenon, which emphasizes the way that the human sensory apparatus is occupied by a stimulus or experience; or as a psychological phenomenon, which emphasizes the idea that imaginative play encourages extreme player focus and absorption. Breda (2008) emphasizes emotion when describing immersion as the feeling of connection to a game, especially when deep emotional experiences are involved. As part of their effort to clarify different types of game immersion, Johnson and Wiles (2003) define immersion as deep and effortless involvement in a game, and use the term "engagement" to describe effortful and concentrated play.

Similar Concepts

Two concepts closely linked with immersion are Flow (Csikszentmihalyi, 1990) and presence (McMahan, 2003; IJsselsteijn, de Ridder, Freeman and Avons, 2000; Lee, 2004; Lessiter, Freeman, Keogh and Davidoff, 2001; Schubert, Friedmann and Regenbrecht, 2001). In some studies, the terms are used interchangeably (see, for example, the discussion of 3D gaming in McMahan's (2003) work). While presence is attracting research attention in light of VR technology development, similar to immersion it remains a vague concept with no universally accepted definition, and with different criteria for measuring it (Zahorik and Jenison, 1998). A general definition is the feeling of being in a mediated environment while it is being used (Cairns, Cox, Berthouze, Jennett and Dhoparee, 2006; Mania and Chalmers, 2001; Mikropoulos and Strouboulis, 2004; Ryan, Rigby and Przybylski, 2006; Tamborini and Skalski, 2006). In other words, presence occurs when individuals acknowledge being occupied with a created stimulus. Slater and Usoh (1994) described presence as the degree to which people believe that an environment is real and can be interacted with naturally. Taking social interaction into consideration, Lombard and Ditton (1997) discuss two kinds of presence: spatial and social, with spatial presence entailing a sense of realism in a virtual environment plus a feeling of psychological/perceptual immersion—what they describe as "being teleported to an environment." Biocca, Harms and Burgoon (2003) use the term social presence to describe a sense of social interaction in a virtual environment, supported by factors such as the richness of the interaction, a sense of being a social actor, and the perception of other agents in the same environment as social actors. Lee (2004) lists three kinds of divided gaming presence in digital games as physical, social, and self. When describing physical presence as the perception that virtual objects are as real as objects in the physical world, Lee notes that many players only show interest in games that provide experiences that are "more than virtual." He describes self-presence as the belief among players that they are the avatars they control—a state that can only be achieved when players achieve a strong sense of empathy for their avatars.

There are important distinctions to note between immersion and presence. "Immersed" game players feel separated from the real world, but their degree of presence depends on their perceptions that game objects, environment, atmosphere, and other aspects are real. When positing that immersion leads to stronger presence, Witmar and Singer (1998) describe immersion as the degree to which participants are continuously occupied by a stimulus, and presence as one of several results of the process. Jennett, Cox and Cairns (2008) describe gaming presence as immediate but gaming immersion as gradual, perhaps because immersion involves additional factors, with some requiring more time for development. Other researchers have noted that it is not necessary for immersion and presence to exist concurrently, and cite as examples those times when players perform repetitive and boring tasks within vivid virtual environments—presence may be strong, but immersion is likely to be low (McMahan, 2003). In contrast, games such as Tetris that are played on handheld devices can be immersive, but without strong feelings of presence. Note Cox, Cairns, Shah and Carroll's (2012) observation that immersion can still be present even when game play involves small screens and simple graphics, with challenge level the most important determining factor.

Csikszentmihalyi (1990) uses the term "flow" to describe optimal experiences when engaging in activities. During interviews with experts in various fields such as chess, the arts, sports, and music, he discovered that they all viewed their activities as intrinsically rewarding. While engaged, they described themselves as concentrated and free of unrelated thoughts, but with senses of fulfillment and accomplishment. He summarized optimal experience properties as the existence of conditions for flow to occur (e.g., clear goals, immediate feedback, balance between challenge and skill), plus specific characteristics such as high degree of concentration, sense of control, and the merging of action and awareness, as well as flow-related consequences such as loss of self-consciousness, distorted sense of time, and autotelic activity (see also (Novak, Hoffman and Yung, 2000)). Csikszentmihalyi used his data to propose the three-channel flow model shown in Figure 1 to describe changes in mind status among flow, anxiety, and boredom, all of them affected by the balance between challenge and skill. According to flow theory, positive experiences emerge from a balance between the level of challenge of the activity and the skill level of the person doing it. When skill exceeds challenge, the person may feel bored; when challenge exceeds skill, the person may feel frustrated.

Csikszentmihalyi's model has been used to analyze gaming experiences, Internet usage, virtual environments, and extreme sports activities, among many other high-interest scenarios (Chen, Wigand and Nilan, 1999; Gaggioli, Bassi and Fave, 2003; Rettie, 2001). Sweetser and Wyeth (2005) used it to create a model they call GameFlow that integrates flow and immersion with game design principles. Immersion and flow share at least three similarities: loss of awareness of surroundings during an activity, distorted sense of time, and dissociation with the real world; differences between the two are often found in games lacking clear goals or immediate feedback mechanisms. Brown and Cairns (2004) and Cox et al. (2012) have observed that game players can still feel immersed when they fail, but are unlikely to achieve a sense of flow—evidence of challenge level exceeding skill level. As stated in the Introduction

Figure 1. The three channel flow

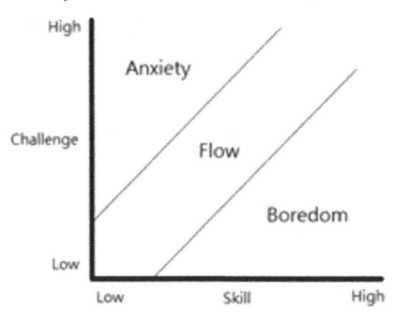

section of this paper, Brown and Cairns describe "total immersion" flow experiences as fleeting rather than enduring. Short-versus-long duration appears to be an important distinction between immersion and flow, therefore the two concepts should not be used interchangeably.

Game Design and Immersion

A number of researchers have looked at various ways to increase player sense of immersion in digital games. Hou, Nam, Peng and Lee (2012) and Thompson, Nordin and Cairns (2012) both found a positive correlation between screen size and a player's immersion experience. Sanders and Cairns (2010) and Zhang and Fu (2015) found that background music can increase or decrease immersion depending on player tastes and gaming level; they also observed that music affected time perception in their study participants. When studying the effects of similarities in appearance between players and their avatars, Hooi and Cho (2012) found that similar appearances resulted in higher levels of homophily in a group of Second Life players, which in turn positively affected self-awareness and immersion. Zhang, Perkis and Arndt (2017) compared the effectiveness from several immersion factors to different aspects of immersion experiences. In a study of how game difficulty affects immersion, Qin, Rau and Salvendy (2010) found that moderate increases in difficulty at the beginning and in the middle stages of a game, plus a decrease in difficulty near the game end, was the best combination for increasing immersion levels. Cox et al. (2012) found that the relationship between a player's self-assessment of skill and difficulty levels affected sense of immersion. Surprisingly, those who viewed themselves as game experts tended to experience less immersion when facing difficult challenges because of their strong focus on problem-solving, while those who viewed themselves as having poor gaming skills experienced a stronger sense of immersion when they failed, possibly because they did not feel nervous or frustrated. Connor, Greig, and Kruse (2017) studied whether procedural content generation (PCG) would negatively affect player immersion and found no significant differences in their experiment. This result shows the potential of PCG application in making games in that it can produce 'good enough' contents in terms of immersion.

Measures

Researchers have used both subjective and objective methods to measure immersion experiences. Subjective methods include self-report questionnaires, interviews, and researcher observations (Slater, 1999; Brown and Cairns, 2004; Csikszentmihalyi, 1990; Sweetser and Wyeth, 2005; Hamari, Shernoff, Rowe, Coller, Asbell-Clarke and Edwards, 2016; Richardson, 1999). Johnson, Gardner, and Perry (2018) compared two popular questionnaires and suggested to combine them depending on use cases. These methods have some well-studied limitations—for example, some respondents find it difficult to answer abstract questions that are commonly found in immersion research (e.g., "Do you feel surrounded by another reality?") A second challenge is the ephemeral nature of deep immersion, making it difficult for study participants to be aware of, remember, and report their immersion experiences at the end of game-playing sessions.

Objective data collection in immersion studies often entails physiological signal methods that are common to psychophysiological research (Nacke and Lindley, 2009). Commonly measured factors include heartbeat rate, perspiration, pupil dilation, electrodermal response, and electromyography. These and other signals indicate levels of arousal, emotional valence, attention, and cognitive workload (Fairclough, 2009; Kivikangas, Chanel, Cowley, Ekman, Salminen, Järvelä and Ravaja, 2011; Lum, Greatbatch, Waldfogle and Benedict, 2018). Objective methods also have shortcomings for gaming experience research, the most important being the complexity and lack of stability in the relationship between physiological signals and psychological phenomena. For instance, higher skin conductance levels can be triggered by both anxiety and excitement, and physiological responses to certain events can vary from person to person or from event to event. Second, immersion in gaming differs from immersion while reading or watching movies/television, and research results from one activity are often not applicable to others. Third, poorly defined cognitive processes in gaming make it difficult to interpret physiological signals. Fourth, since gaming is a voluntary activity, the experimental setting must be carefully designed so that players feel relaxed and able to enjoy themselves.

To overcome the disadvantages of individual methods, researchers suggest using several methods at the same time to increase analytical effectiveness (IJsselsteijn et al., 2000; Nacke and Lindley, 2009). Thus, Jennett et al. (2008) used both subjective (self-report questionnaire) and objective methods (task completion time and eye movement data) to measure immersion. Eye movement has been used to study how people look at pictures, watch videos (Duchowski, 2003; Hadizadeh, Enriquez and Bajić, 2012), and access websites (Silva and Cox, 2006; Velásquez, 2013). A number of researchers have commented on the drawbacks of eye-tracker methods and data in terms of rapidly changing game screens and individual differences in eye movement patterns (Almeida, Veloso, Roque and Mealha, 2011; El-Nasr and Yan, 2006). However, other researchers have reported success in using eye movement data to provide clues about immersion. For instance, Jennett et al. (2008) found negative correlations between self-reported immersion and both blinking frequency and total eye movement trajectory, as well as a positive correlation between average fixation time and self-reported immersion. In this chapter, the authors collected eye movement and pupil dilation and correlated to them to immersion questionnaire results in the experiment to see whether they can reflect subjective immersion. The authors hope that the results can help about measuring immersion in complex environment, such as multiple stimuli, where questionnaires are more difficult to use.

METHOD

Participants

Campus-based electronic bulletin board systems were used to recruit study participants from two universities. The final sample consisted of 38 males and 34 females between the ages of 18 and 38 (mean 23.2). Self-reported years of gaming experience ranged from 0 to 32 (mean 8.6). Self-reported average duration of individual gaming sessions was 1.69 hours (SD=1.14). Three groups were established from the initial sample, one labeled "multitasking" (30 individuals), one "video-only" (21), and one "game-only" (21). To develop the questionnaire for the formal experiment, the authors recruited 61 additional participants prior to the formal experiment via the same BBS (37 male, 24 female, age range of 19 to 30, 23.5 year mean). Gaming histories and average playing time data were not collected for these individuals.

Game and Video Selections

The authors designed the experiment to study a specific multitasking situation: playing a digital game and watching a video at the same time. This decision was made according to a prior survey: 15 males and 10 females between the age from 19 to 28 were asked to report their most frequent digital media multitasking scenario. 60% of the participants (10 males, 5 females) reported that the most frequent scenario is watching video (TV/live streaming/movie) and gaming. To accommodate the desire to record eye movement, both media were presented on the same computer display, despite that most participants (11 males, 8 females) reported that one of the device is mobile when multitasking. For selecting specific video and game, several factors dictated the decision. First, the game had to be suitable for multitasking; the authors rejected real time strategy and multiplayer online battle arena games due to the demands they make for continuous player attention. Puzzle games were considered suitable depending on the level of difficulty in problem solving. The same motivation guided the video selection—watchers had to be able to avert their eyes occasionally and catch up with the video storyline when they returned, therefore programs with intricate plots and exceptionally fast pacing were rejected. FEZ (a casual platformer game that allows for relaxed exploration) and The Mythbusters (a long-running TV program requiring less continuous attention, but with a key question saved for the end) fit the criteria. FEZ has another advantage: it has rather low-flashy graphical presentation, which reduces disturbance to pupil size measurement.

Questionnaires

The game and video immersion-measuring questionnaires used in this study were largely based on the work of Jennett et al. (2008) and Sweetser and Wyeth (2005) plus two additional dimensions: "merging of action and awareness" and "loss of self-consciousness" (Csikszentmihalyi, 1990; Fang, Zhang and Chan, 2013). The first questionnaire version consisted of eight dimensions, each one containing 2 to 7 items designed to collect data on basic attention, temporal dissociation, transport (i.e., inducing a feeling of being transported from the real world), loss of self-consciousness, merging of action and awareness, emotional involvement, challenge, and enjoyment. The five video dimensions were basic attention, temporal dissociation, transport, emotional involvement, and enjoyment. To assess the questionnaires, the 61 additional participants were requested to play FEZ while watching The Mythbusters and to fill out their questionnaires immediately afterwards. Results from an item analysis were used to eliminate some questions, and an exploratory factor analysis was used to identify immersion dimensions. Additional analyses were performed to identify and delete insufficiently discriminative items. Using the game immersion questionnaire as an example, the authors calculated a satisfactory Cronbach's α of 0.908, therefore this index was not used to delete question items. To check item discrimination, lower group below 27% and upper group above 73% are used in the calculation. Independent t-test data were used to remove items with t values of 3.0 or less. To confirm that questions accurately described their targeted dimensions, the authors calculated Pearson correlation coefficients between question scores and total dimension scores, and removed items with correlation coefficients below .4. Last, the authors calculated communality and factor loading values for each item, and removed those with values at or below .2 and .45, respectively.

Next, the authors conducted an exploratory factor analysis to define a new set of dimensions for the small questionnaire item set, using the Kaiser-Meyer-Olkin (KMO) measure of sampling adequacy and Bartlett's sphericity test to determine the suitability of questions for factor analysis. The KMO value of .733 and sphericity value of 987.9 ($p<.001$) indicated that the questions were suitable. The actual factor analysis consisted of principal axis factoring with direct oblimin for none-orthogonal rotation, considering the likelihood of correlations between factors. An Eigenvalue threshold >1.000 and scree plots were used to extract seven factors during the first round (62.9% proportion of variance explained). According to the results, the seventh factor contained two questions, with one having a .543 loading in the fourth factor, indicating a correlation between the question and the fourth factor. After removing the second question and repeating the exploratory analysis, the authors extracted six factors and calculated a new explained proportion of variance of 60.9%. The .914 Cronbach's α value for the game immersion questionnaire shown in Table 1 (see Appendix) indicated good internal consistency (5 of 6 factors had Cronbach's α values $>.700$, the other an α of .657). Final factor loadings for all questions were $>.400$.

The authors identified six factors according to the question items they contained: (a) transport, meaning feelings of disconnection with the real world and of being surrounded by a virtual world; (b) enjoyment, or having fun and interest in the activity; (c) cognitive involvement, with a strong focus on thinking and processing in-game information; (d) emotional involvement, including empathy for game characters, anticipation about how a plot will unfold, and emotional changes tied to the game; (e) loss of self-consciousness, such as lower levels of self-awareness and interest in the real-world environment; and (f) merging of action and awareness so that in-game actions feel spontaneous and natural. In light of the study goals, the authors added a simple statement to measure the participants' sense of immersion: "I felt deeply immersed in the game." This item could be used to check whether questionnaire responses actually reflected the participants' feelings. For the multitasking group, the question "I felt deeply immersed during the activity just completed" was used to measure overall feelings of immersion rather than immersion in either the game or video alone.

The same item and exploratory factor analysis processes were followed for the video immersion questionnaire used in the formal experiment (Cronbach's α .893, proportion of variance explained 56.8%, all question item factor loadings $>.400$) (Table 1 in Appendix). The four extracted factors were labeled according to their associated question items: (a) cognitive involvement, with its focus on thinking and processing information presented in the video; (b) emotional involvement and enjoyment, tied to the content that made the video interesting or that triggered an emotional reaction; (c) loss of self-consciousness,

Figure 2. Experiment environment

indicating lowered self-awareness of or interest in real world surroundings; and (d) transport, meaning feelings of disconnection from the real world accompanied by a sense of presence in the TV program.

Members of the multitasking group were requested to complete two additional questionnaires, one designed to measure their feelings about multitasking, the other a list of open questions for collecting data on their feelings about the experimental setting. These questionnaires are presented in Tables 1 and 2(see Appendix).

Apparatus

Details regarding the experimental setting are shown in Figures 2 and 3. A 24-inch LCD display was used to present the dual media content. Eye tracking was performed with a SR Research EyeLink 1000 (1 kHz sample rate). The infrared eye-tracking camera was placed in front of the screen so that the participants' heads could move freely within a limited range. The screen on the right side of the main display presented information for monitoring the eye-tracker to ensure that it was collecting useable data. A video camera recorded participant images.

Procedure

After explaining the experimental process, participants were asked to sit in front of the display and to adjust their positions to match the requirements of the eye tracker, mostly chair height and keyboard/mouse position. Eye tracker calibration required approximately 5 minutes per participant. Next, game-only and

Figure 3. Multitasking setting screenshot

multitasking group participants were asked to read and respond to the game tutorial to become familiar with game controls. At this time the video-only group members were told that the television program was an education-entertainment type. After a final check of the eye-tracking apparatus, participants were told to start playing and watching; each session lasted for 22 minutes. The researchers did not interact with the participants during the session. After each session, participants were asked to fill out their questionnaires and to take part in a brief interview to collect additional data on their feelings and experiences.

Eye Movement Data Processing

Eye movement data analysis required definitions for three areas of interest (AOI): the game, the main video area, and the video subtitle area. The authors then used the following features to summarize eye movement data: (a) total length of time that each participant's line of sight fell within an AOI, including fixation and saccades (eye movements across a field without focusing on an object); (b) fixation count, meaning the number of times participants "looked at" a certain AOI; (c) fixation duration, or total length of time spent gazing at an AOI; (d) average fixation duration, calculated as fixation duration divided by fixation count; (e) in-out count, meaning the number of times a participant's eye fixation position moved away from an AOI but returned later; (f) total saccade count; (g) total number of blinks during a session; and (h) average pupil dilation while gazing at an AOI.

RESULTS

Immersion Score Comparison

T-tests were performed to determine whether self-reported immersion levels among multitasking group participants were lower than those for the single task groups, as the authors predicted. As shown in

Table 5. Game immersion score comparison between multitasking and game-only groups

Factor	Game-only		Multitasking		t-value	p-value
	M	SD	M	SD		
Game Instinctive Feeling	7.33	1.24	6.40	1.48	2.3700*	.022
Game Cognitive Involvement	8.71	.56	7.00	1.98	4.4860***	.000
Game Emotional Involvement	20.29	4.16	17.30	4.55	2.3880*	.021
Game Transport	17.90	4.81	14.43	4.56	2.6170*	.012
Game Loss of Self-consciousness	14.29	2.43	10.80	3.08	4.3250***	.000
Game Merging of Action and Awareness	10.14	2.56	10.33	2.72	-.2520	.802
Game Enjoyment	24.57	3.92	20.77	4.60	3.0850**	.003
Game Total Immersion Score	95.90	14.61	80.63	15.51	3.5430**	.001

*p < .05, **p < .01, ***p < .001

Table 5, both instinctive feelings (i.e., responses to the item, "I felt deeply immersed in the game") and overall game immersion scores from the questionnaire were significantly lower for the multitasking group compared to the game-only group ($\alpha = 0.05$)—in other words, a decrease in immersion while multitasking. For individual dimensions, the authors found that with the exception of "merging of action and awareness," all other values were significantly lower in the multitasking group. The largest score differences were for "loss of self-consciousness" (17.4% lower) and "cognitive involvement" (17.1% lower). Significantly lower levels of enjoyment were also noted. The video-related data shown in Table 6 indicate significantly lower instinctive feeling and total questionnaire scores for the multitasking group, with "cognitive involvement" and "transport" having the most significant differences compared to the video-only group (35.8% and 16.6% lower, respectively).

Instinctive Feelings of Immersion

Instinctive feelings of immersion were measured according to the statement, "I felt deeply immersed during the activity just completed." The authors looked for correlations between response scores for this question and total scores from the multi-dimensional immersion questionnaire to determine if the

Table 6. Video immersion score comparison between multitasking and video-only groups

Factor	Video-only		Multitasking		t-value	p-value
	M	SD	M	SD		
Video Instinctive Feeling	7.19	1.63	4.67	2.20	4.4590***	.000
Video Cognitive Involvement	12.48	1.97	7.10	2.51	8.2040***	.000
Video Emotional Involvement and Enjoyment	23.00	4.49	19.43	6.05	2.2920*	.026
Video Loss of Self-consciousness	13.43	2.99	12.70	2.39	.9640	.340
Video Transport	16.90	4.45	12.77	3.95	3.4940**	.001
Video Total Immersion Score	65.81	11.63	52.00	12.24	4.0450***	.000

*p < .05, **p < .01, ***p < .001

questionnaire accurately measured instinctive feelings about immersion. For the single task groups, Pearson correlation coefficients for the instinctive feeling and total questionnaire scores were .715 for the game-only group and .869 for the video-only group. Among the multitasking study participants, the Pearson correlation coefficients between instinctive feeling and total questionnaire scores were .782 and .863 for the game and video, respectively. These results indicate a high correlation between the instinctive feeling and total questionnaire scores, suggesting that instinctive feeling can serve as an indicator of overall immersion.

Although game and video immersion scores were lower for the multitasking group, the overall instinctive feeling score for the multitasking group was higher (4.04) than those for both single task groups (game=3.67, video=3.60), indicating that immersion values from multiple sources can be summed to some extent, and suggesting that individuals can have strong immersive experiences when multitasking using digital media, even though the degree of immersion from each source is reduced.

Eye Movement and Immersion

AOI time distribution data are shown at Table 7. For multitasking group participants, proportions of time spent in each AOI were .80 for game, .07 for video_main, and .13 for video_subtitle—that is, study participants tended to spend more time playing the game than watching the video. For the video-only group, time proportions were .56 for video_main and .44 for video_subtitle. According to these data, multitasking group participants spent more time reading subtitles than watching the characters in the video—opposite of the video-only group. A likely explanation is that the multitasking participants needed a more efficient method for collecting and processing information.

Comparisons of eye movement data among multitasking and single-task groups are shown in Tables 8 (game) and 9 (video). A comparison between the game-only and multitasking groups indicates that a significant difference was only noted for total number of saccades, likely due to the act of switching between two windows. Although the multitasking group immersion score was lower, no significant difference between the two groups was noted for average fixation time, which conflicts with Jennett et al.'s (2008) finding of a positive correlation between immersion level and fixation time. According to a comparison between the video-only and multitasking groups, total number of blinks was significantly lower for the multitasking group, suggesting greater interest among those study participants who divided their time between the video and the game. Average AOI video_main fixation time was longer for the

Table 7. Focus time distribution in percentage

AOI	M	SD
Multitasking AOI_Game	.80	.13
Multitasking AOI_Video	.19	.13
Multitasking AOI_Video_Main	.07	.05
Multitasking AOI_Video_Subtitle	.13	.10
Video-only AOI_Video	.99	.01
Video-only AOI_Video_Main	.56	.11
Video-only AOI_Video_Subtitle	.44	.11

Table 8. Eye movement feature comparison between multitasking and game-only groups

Factor	Game-only		Multitasking		t-value	p-value
	M	SD	M	SD		
Total Number of Saccades	3011.39	454.54	3451.60	439.30	-3.0340**	.004
Total Number of Blinks	451.39	298.94	356.65	286.50	.9970	.325
Average Fixation Time (AOI_Game)	401.93	79.08	386.47	44.98	.7500	.458
Average Pupil Size (AOI_Game)	1408.06	1377.78	1432.88	1366.85	-.0560	.956

*p < .05, **p < .01, ***p < .001

Table 9. Eye movement feature comparison between multitasking and video-only groups

Factor	Video-only		Multitasking		t-value	p-value
	M	SD	M	SD		
Total Number of Saccades	3785.24	605.53	3451.60	439.30	1.938	.061
Total Number of Blinks	780.12	710.52	356.65	286.50	2.303*	.032
Average Fixation Time AOI_Video	299.78	69.18	225.27	45.61	3.795***	.001
Average Fixation Time AOI (Video_Main)	378.99	111.32	256.20	78.64	3.919***	.000
Average Fixation Time (AOI_Video_Subtitle)	236.49	47.23	213.55	36.30	1.669	.104
Average Pupil Size (AOI_Video)	1475.25	1429.61	1444.63	1446.30	.065	.949
Average Pupil Size (AOI_Video_Main)	1479.08	1431.68	1486.72	1447.17	-.016	.987
Average Pupil Size (AOI_Video_Subtitle)	1467.37	1424.16	1425.26	1439.33	.089	.929

*p < .05, **p < .01, ***p < .001

video-only group, suggesting that those participants exerted greater effort processing video content compared to multitasking group members, who relied more on subtitles and who paid less attention to other aspects of the video.

Task Immersion Distribution

Among multitasking group participants, individuals in the "high game immersion" category had total game immersion scores in the highest 27% of the sample, while those in the "low game immersion" group had scores in the lowest 27%. Next, the authors looked for differences in how participants in the two groups experienced the video and in their eye movement patterns. As shown in Table 10, significantly lower video immersion dimension scores were found for the high game immersion group. Further, eye movement data indicate that individuals in the high game immersion group spent much less time paying attention to the video compared to study participants in the low game immersion group (9.5% versus 30% of total time spent, respectively), underscoring the idea that immersion requires a time investment. No significant differences were noted between the two groups for other eye movement features such as average fixation time or blink frequency. The data for "high video immersion" versus "low video im-

Table 10. Video immersion comparison between high game immersion and low game immersion participants in the multitasking group

Factor	High game immersion		Low game immersion		t-value	p-value
	M	SD	M	SD		
Game Total Immersion Score	99.22	7.36	62.13	7.90	10.022***	.000
Video Cognitive Involvement	5.89	1.90	8.88	3.10	-2.432*	.028
Video Emotional Involvement and Enjoyment	15.67	5.94	22.50	5.18	-2.512*	.024
Video Loss of Self-consciousness	13.44	1.13	12.00	2.62	1.509	.152
Video Transport	10.33	3.54	14.63	3.66	-2.457*	.027
Video Total Immersion Score	45.33	10.86	58.00	12.01	-2.284*	.037

*p < .05, **p < .01, ***p < .001

Table 11. Game immersion comparison between high video immersion and low video immersion participants in the multitasking group

Factor	High video immersion		Low video immersion		t-value	p-value
	M	SD	M	SD		
Video Total Immersion Score	66.50	6.76	38.30	5.85	9.489***	.000
Game Cognitive Involvement	4.88	1.89	8.20	1.23	-4.520***	.000
Game Emotional Involvement	15.25	5.44	19.70	3.37	-2.133*	.049
Game Transport	11.63	4.24	14.90	4.33	-1.609	.127
Game Loss of Self-consciousness	8.63	3.66	11.90	3.00	-2.089*	.053
Game Merging of Action and Awareness	9.88	3.80	9.80	2.74	.049	.962
Game Enjoyment	17.00	4.38	22.00	4.22	-2.459*	.026
Game Total Immersion Score	67.25	13.35	86.50	14.51	-2.896*	.011

*p < .05, **p < .01, ***p < .001

mersion" participants shown in Table 11 also confirm the idea that immersion requires time investment, and that it is difficult to achieve high levels of immersion in two or more concurrent activities.

DISCUSSION

According to the comparisons of immersion scores, the biggest drops in game immersion in the multitasking group were in the dimensions of loss of self-consciousness, cognitive involvement, and enjoyment. A possible explanation for the loss of self-consciousness finding is increased awareness of the actual environment when switching between tasks—that is, cognizance of the need to maintain awareness of both tasks. This might also explain the sharp decline in the video-watching transport dimension for the multitasking group participants. Lower cognitive involvement may be due to the need for participants to exert cognitive effort on a second task. Possible reasons for the drop in enjoyment include the power of distraction or reductions in playing time and content interaction. A possible explanation for the lack of any decrease in the merging of action and awareness dimensions may be that FEZ does not require intense concentration, therefore game play was not strongly affected by interruptions. This characteristic may be viewed as positive by anyone wanting games that are suitable for multitasking.

Regarding eye movement data, no significant difference in average fixation time was observed between the multitasking group (lower game immersion score) and the game-only group, which conflicts with Jennett et al.'s (2008) finding of a positive correlation between average fixation time and immersion level. The authors can think of two possible explanations: a less complex experimental setting in Jennett et al.'s study, or the stronger instinctive feeling of overall immersion within the multitasking group (see section 4.2). However, this finding is difficult to analyze because of the combination of lower game immersion and higher instinctive immersion scores.

Study participants were asked to divide their attention between one game and one television program. Different results in terms of attention distribution patterns would have been likely had the choices been between two games, two programs, or one game and one conversation. The eye-tracking data indicate that the large majority of participants considered game playing as their primary task (average 80% of focus) and the video as secondary. According to the participant interviews, this combination is very common. Other researchers may be interested in using other media combinations to test the hypothesis that multitasking using two or more digital media is always more immersive than focusing on one. The authors are to deny this possibility, since immersion factors such as atmosphere are not likely to be sustained when switching between the two—for example, if two videos are involved, watchers are likely to make a decision to focus more on one than the other, depending on the content.

There are at least four conditions that determine immersion levels in multitasking individuals:

1. As Brown and Cairns (2004) point out, a minimum requirement for immersion is interest—that is, the ability to keep enjoying an activity or the content of a program while tuning in and out. For some games and videos, key factors such as sense of game control and feelings about a story line in a film are strongly affected by shifts in attention, thereby affecting immersion.
2. Both Ermi and Mäyrä (2005) and McMahan (2003) have observed that a consistent atmosphere is required for emotion to be affected by media. Immersion is more likely when two or more media have similar themes—for example, two comedy or two horror films. The reduced potential for immersion when one of each kind is being viewed is associated with the finding that in most situations, multitasking individuals deal with one primary task rather than give equal attention to two or more. They are likely to be emotionally affected by the primary media, and to simply absorb "necessary information" from the other. In such cases, a difference in atmosphere between two films may not hinder immersion, since viewers will only respond to the content of one.
3. Immersion sources are affected by multitasking to different extents. Using Ermi and Mäyrä's (2005) SCI model as an example, it appears that sensory sources—displays and sound—are affected more strongly by multitasking settings than by challenge sources due to video and audio device limitations. On the other hand, it is still possible for game challenges to be immersive in distractive environments, likely because challenge-triggered immersion is quicker to develop and less affected by the actual environment (Cox et al., 2012).
4. Different dimensions are also affected to different extents. The evidence suggests that of the six dimensions mentioned in this paper, it is harder for feelings of transport and loss of self-consciousness to emerge during multitasking. Both are associated with "forgetting about the real world," but the need to switch between media in a multitasking situation requires a return to the real world. Since feelings of being transported are so closely tied to feelings that emerge from virtual worlds,

switching between more than one medium is likely to interfere with developing and maintaining such kinds of feelings.

CONCLUSION

In this paper the authors compared levels and qualities of immersion in single-tasking and multitasking scenarios involving a game (FEZ) and a popular television program (The Mythbusters). Both self-report questionnaires and eye tracking data were used to measure immersion. The authors found that immersion levels among the multitasking study participants were significantly lower in most dimensions, especially in dimensions associated with feelings of separation from the real world and level of concentration. The authors also found that even though most aspects of immersion in two or more kinds of media were negatively affected in the multitasking setting, instinctive feelings of overall immersion were higher in the multitasking group. The authors interpret this finding as meaning that a cumulative sense of immersion can emerge from multiple media, depending on certain conditions. The eye-tracking data indicate that multitasking participants spent more time than the video-only group participants reading video subtitles. This difference likely affected immersion levels, both actual and potential, while watching the video.

The authors acknowledge that the experiments were limited in terms of material and apparatus, and that results would likely have been different had the authors used other games or videos. For example, if the authors chose online chess as the game, participants may have spent more time focusing on the video while their opponents considered their next moves. Factor analysis results for immersion dimensions may have differed because chess matches do not involve storylines or action beyond moving pieces on a board. Another study shortcoming is the use of a single computer display containing more than one task, since most multitasking involves multiple devices and screens. Future researchers will want to design their experiments so that they involve multiple kinds of user experiences involving a range of environments and materials.

REFRENCES

Almeida, S., Veloso, A., Roque, L., & Mealha, Ó. (2011). The Eyes and Games: A Survey of Visual Attention and Eye Tracking Input in Video Games. In *Proceedings of SBGames*. Academic Press.

Bailenson, J. N., Blascovich, J., & Guadagno, R. E. (2008). Self-Representations in Immersive Virtual Environments. *Journal of Applied Social Psychology*, *38*(11), 2673–2690. doi:10.1111/j.1559-1816.2008.00409.x

Biocca, F., Harms, C., & Burgoon, J. K. (2003). Toward a more robust theory and measure of social presence: Review and suggested criteria. *Presence*, *12*(5), 456–480. doi:10.1162/105474603322761270

Breda, L. (2008). Invisible Walls. Game Career Guide. Retrieved from http://www.gamecareerguide.com/features/593/invisible_.php

Bredl, K., Groß, A., Hünniger, J., & Fleischer, J. (2012). The Avatar as a Knowledge Worker? How Immersive 3D Virtual Environments May Foster Knowledge Acquisition. *Electronic Journal of Knowledge Management*, *10*(1).

Brown, E., & Cairns, P. (2004, April). A grounded investigation of game immersion. In CHI'04 extended abstracts on Human factors in computing systems (pp. 1297-1300). Academic Press.

Cairns, P., Cox, A. L., Berthouze, N., Jennett, C., & Dhoparee, S. (2006). Quantifying the experience of immersion in games. In *CogSci 2006 Workshop: Cognitive Science of Games and Gameplay*. Academic Press.

Carr, D. (2006). Games and narrative. In D. Carr, D. Buckingham, A. Burn, & G. Schott (Eds.), *Computer games: Text, narrative and play* (pp. 30–44). Cambridge, UK: Polity Press.

Chen, H., Wigand, R. T., & Nilan, M. S. (1999). Optimal experience of web activities. *Computers in Human Behavior*, *15*(5), 585–608. doi:10.1016/S0747-5632(99)00038-2

Childs, M. (2010). Learners' experience of presence in Virtual Worlds [doctoral dissertation]. University of Warwick. Retreived from http://wrap.warwick.ac.uk/4516/1/WRAP_THESIS_Childs_2010.pdf

Connor, A. M., Greig, T. J., & Kruse, J. (2017). Evaluating the impact of procedurally generated content on game immersion. *The Computer Games Journal*, *6*(4), 209–225. doi:10.100740869-017-0043-6

Coomans, M. K. D., & Timmermans, H. J. (1997). Towards a taxonomy of virtual reality user interfaces. In *Proceedings of the IEEE Conference on Information Visualization* (pp. 279-284). IEEE Press. 10.1109/IV.1997.626531

Cox, A. L., Cairns, P., Shah, P., & Carroll, M. (2012). Not doing but thinking: the role of challenge in the gaming experience. In *Proceedings of the SIGCHI Conference on Human Factors in Computing Systems* (pp. 79-88). Academic Pres. 10.1145/2207676.2207689

Csikszentmihalyi, M. (1990). *Flow: the psychology of optimal experience*. New York, NY: Harper & Row.

Duchowski, A. T. (2003). *Eye Tracking Methodology: Theory and Practice*. Secaucus, NJ: Springer. doi:10.1007/978-1-4471-3750-4

El-Nasr, M. S., & Yan, S. (2006). Visual attention in 3D video games. In *Proceedings of ACM SIGCHI international conference on Advances in computer entertainment technology*. ACM Press.

Ermi, L., & Mäyrä, F. (2005). Fundamental Components of the Gameplay Experience: Analysing Immersion. In S. D. Castell & J. Jenson (Eds.), *Worlds in play: Int. perspectives on digital games research* (Vol. 37). Bern, Switzerland: Peter Lang.

Fairclough, S. H. (2009). Fundamentals of physiological computing. *Interacting with Computers*, *21*(1), 133–145. doi:10.1016/j.intcom.2008.10.011

Fang, X., Zhang, J., & Chan, S. S. (2013). Development of an Instrument for Studying Flow in Computer Game Play. *International Journal of Human-Computer Interaction*, *29*(7), 456–470. doi:10.1080/1044 7318.2012.715991

Gaggioli, A., Bassi, M., & Fave, A. (2003). Quality of experience in virtual environments. In G. Riva, F. Davide, W.A. Jsselsteijn (Eds.), Being There: Concepts, effects and measurement of user presence in synthetic environments (pp. 122-136). Ios Press.

Goldberg, L. R. (1990). An alternative description of personality: The big-five factor structure. *Journal of Personality and Social Psychology, 59*(6), 1216–1229. doi:10.1037/0022-3514.59.6.1216 PMID:2283588

Hadizadeh, H., Enriquez, M. J., & Bajić, I. V. (2012). Eye-tracking database for a set of standard video sequences. *IEEE Transactions on Image Processing, 21*(2), 898–903. doi:10.1109/TIP.2011.2165292 PMID:21859619

Hamari, J., Shernoff, D. J., Rowe, E., Coller, B., Asbell-Clarke, J., & Edwards, T. (2016). Challenging games help students learn: An empirical study on engagement, flow and immersion in game-based learning. *Computers in Human Behavior, 54*, 170–179. doi:10.1016/j.chb.2015.07.045

Hooi, R., & Cho, H. (2012). Being immersed: avatar similarity and self-awareness. In *Proceedings of the 24th Australian Computer-Human Interaction Conference* (pp. 232-240). Academic Press.

Hou, J., Nam, Y., Peng, W., & Lee, K. M. (2012). Effects of screen size, viewing angle, and players' immersion tendencies on game experience. *Computers in Human Behavior, 28*(2), 617–623. doi:10.1016/j.chb.2011.11.007

IJsselsteijn, W. A., de Ridder, H., Freeman, J., & Avons, S. E. (2000). Presence: Concept, determinants, and measurement. In *Human vision and electronic imaging V* (Vol. 3959, pp. 520-529). International Society for Optics and Photonics. doi:10.1117/12.387188

Jennett, C., Cox, A. L., & Cairns, P. (2008). Being in the game. In S. Gunzel, M. Liebe, & D. Mersch (Eds.), *Proceedings of the Philosophy of Computer Games* (pp. 210-227). Academic Pres.

Jennett, C., Cox, A. L., Cairns, P., Dhoparee, S., Epps, A., Tijs, T., & Walton, A. (2008). Measuring and defining the experience of immersion in games. *International Journal of Human-Computer Studies, 66*(9), 641–661. doi:10.1016/j.ijhcs.2008.04.004

Johnson, D., Gardner, M. J., & Perry, R. (2018). Validation of two game experience scales: The player experience of need satisfaction (PENS) and game experience questionnaire (GEQ). *International Journal of Human-Computer Studies, 118*, 38–46. doi:10.1016/j.ijhcs.2018.05.003

Johnson, D., & Wiles, J. (2003). Effective affective user interface design in games. *Ergonomics, 46*(13-14), 1332–1345. doi:10.1080/00140130310001610865 PMID:14612323

Kivikangas, J. M., Chanel, G., Cowley, B., Ekman, I., Salminen, M., Järvelä, S., & Ravaja, N. (2011). A review of the use of psychophysiological methods in game research. *Journal of Gaming & Virtual Worlds, 3*(3), 181–199. doi:10.1386/jgvw.3.3.181_1

Lee, K. M. (2004). Presence, explicated. *Communication Theory, 14*(1), 27–50. doi:10.1111/j.1468-2885.2004.tb00302.x

Lessiter, J., Freeman, J., Keogh, E., & Davidoff, J. (2001). A cross-media presence questionnaire: The ITC-Sense of Presence Inventory. *Presence, 10*(3), 282–297. doi:10.1162/105474601300343612

Lombard, M., & Ditton, T. (1997). At the Heart of It All: The Concept of Presence. *Journal of Computer-Mediated Communication, 3*(2), 0. doi:10.1111/j.1083-6101.1997.tb00072.x

Lum, H. C., Greatbatch, R., Waldfogle, G., & Benedict, J. (2018). How Immersion, Presence, Emotion, & Workload Differ in Virtual Reality and Traditional Game Mediums. *Proceedings of the Human Factors and Ergonomics Society Annual Meeting*, *62*(1), 1474–1478. doi:10.1177/1541931218621334

Mania, K., & Chalmers, A. (2001). The effects of levels of immersion on memory and presence in virtual environments: A reality centered approach. *Cyberpsychology & Behavior*, *4*(2), 247–264. doi:10.1089/109493101300117938 PMID:11710251

McMahan, A. (2003). Immersion, engagement and presence. In M. J. P. Wolf & B. Perron (Eds.), *The video game theory reader* (pp. 67–86). Psychology Press.

Mikropoulos, T. A., & Strouboulis, V. (2004). Factors that influence presence in educational virtual environments. *Cyberpsychology & Behavior*, *7*(5), 582–591. doi:10.1089/cpb.2004.7.582 PMID:15667053

Murray, J. H. (1997). *Hamlet on the Holodeck: The Future of Narrative in Cyberspace*. Cambridge, MA: MIT Press.

Nacke, L. E., & Lindley, C. A. (2010). Affective ludology, flow and immersion in a first-person shooter: Measurement of player experience.

Nielsen Corporation. (2014). The Digital Consumer. Retrieved from http://www.nielsen.com/content/dam/corporate/us/en/reports-downloads/2014%20Reports/the-digital-consumer-report-feb-2014.pdf

Novak, T. P., Hoffman, D. L., & Yung, Y. F. (2000). Measuring the flow construct in online environments: A structural modeling approach. *Marketing Science*, *19*(1), 22–42. doi:10.1287/mksc.19.1.22.15184

Onyesolu, M. (2009). Virtual reality laboratories: An ideal solution to the problems facing laboratory setup and management. In *Proc. of the World Congress on Engineering and computer science*. Academic Press.

Qin, H., Rau, P.-L. P., & Salvendy, G. (2010). Effects of different scenarios of game difficulty on player immersion. *Interacting with Computers*, *22*(3), 230–239. doi:10.1016/j.intcom.2009.12.004

Raptis, G. E., Fidas, C., & Avouris, N. (2018). Effects of mixed-reality on players' behaviour and immersion in a cultural tourism game: A cognitive processing perspective. *International Journal of Human-Computer Studies*, *114*, 69–79. doi:10.1016/j.ijhcs.2018.02.003

Rettie, R. (2001). An exploration of flow during Internet use. *Internet Research*, *11*(2), 103–113. doi:10.1108/10662240110695070

Richardson, A. (1999). Subjective experience: Its conceptual status, method of investigation, and psychological significance. *The Journal of Psychology*, *133*(5), 469–485. doi:10.1080/00223989909599756

Ryan, R. M., Rigby, C. S., & Przybylski, A. (2006). The motivational pull of video games: A self-determination theory approach. *Motivation and Emotion*, *30*(4), 344–360. doi:10.100711031-006-9051-8

Sanders, T., & Cairns, P. (2010). Time perception, immersion and music in videogames. In *Proceedings of the 24th BCS Interaction Specialist Group Conference* (pp. 160-167). Academic Press. 10.14236/ewic/HCI2010.21

Schubert, T., Friedmann, F., & Regenbrecht, H. (2001). The experience of presence: Factor analytic insights. *Presence*, *10*(3), 266–281. doi:10.1162/105474601300343603

Silva, M., & Cox, A. L. (2006). What have eye movements told us so far, and what is next? In *Proceedings of 28th Annual Meeting of the Cognitive Science Society*. Academic Press.

Slater, M. (1999). Measuring presence: A response to the Witmer and Singer presence questionnaire. *Presence, 8*(5), 560–565. doi:10.1162/105474699566477

Slater, M., Linakis, V., Usoh, M., & Kooper, R. (1996). Immersion, presence, and performance in virtual environments: An experiment with tri-dimensional chess. In *ACM virtual reality software and technology* (pp. 163–172). ACM. doi:10.1145/3304181.3304216

Slater, M. & Usoh, M. (1994). Body centred interaction in immersive virtual environments. *Artificial life and virtual reality, 1*, 125-148.

Slater, M., Usoh, M., & Steed, A. (1994). Depth of presence in virtual environments. *Presence, 3*(2), 130–144. doi:10.1162/pres.1994.3.2.130

Sweetser, P., & Wyeth, P. (2005). GameFlow: a model for evaluating player enjoyment in games. *Computers in Entertainment, 3*(3).

Tamborini, R., & Skalski, P. (2006). The role of presence in the experience of electronic games. In *Playing video games: Motives, responses, and consequences* (pp. 225-240). Academic Press.

Thompson, M., Nordin, A. I., & Cairns, P. (2012). Effect of touch-screen size on game immersion. In *Proceedings of the 26th Annual BCS Interaction Specialist Group Conference on People and Computers*. Academic Press. 10.14236/ewic/HCI2012.38

Velásquez, J. D. (2013). Combining eye-tracking technologies with web usage mining for identifying Website Keyobjects. *Engineering Applications of Artificial Intelligence, 26*(5), 1469–1478. doi:10.1016/j.engappai.2013.01.003

Weibel, D., Wissmath, B., & Mast, F. W. (2010). Immersion in mediated environments: The role of personality traits. *Cyberpsychology, Behavior, and Social Networking, 13*(3), 251–256. doi:10.1089/cyber.2009.0171 PMID:20557243

Witmer, B. G., & Singer, M. J. (1998). Measuring presence in virtual environments: A presence questionnaire. *Presence (Cambridge, Mass.), 7*(3), 225–240. doi:10.1162/105474698565686

Zahorik, P., & Jenison, R. L. (1998). Presence as being-in-the-world. *Presence, 7*(1), 78–89. doi:10.1162/105474698565541

Zhang, C., Perkis, A., & Arndt, S. 2017. Spatial immersion versus emotional immersion, which is more immersive? In *Proceedings of the 2017 Ninth International Conference on Quality of Multimedia Experience (QoMEX)* (pp. 1-6). Academic Press. 10.1109/QoMEX.2017.7965655

Zhang, J., & Fu, X. (2015). The influence of background music of video games on immersion. *Journal of Psychology & Psychotherapy, 5*(4).

APPENDIX: QUESTIONNAIRES

Table 1. Video immersion questionnaire content

Number	Factor	Statement
Q01	cognitive involvement	The game grabbed most of my attention.
Q02	cognitive involvement	I focused intensely on the game.
Q03	emotional involvement	I felt that I experienced the story, instead of only playing a game.
Q04	emotional involvement	The game affected my emotions.
Q05	emotional involvement	I would have liked to talk with the in-game characters if it were possible.
Q06	emotional involvement	I enjoyed the game visuals.
Q07	emotional involvement	I felt disappointed when the experiment ended and I could not continue playing.
Q08	emotional involvement	I felt that the in-game characters and I were adventuring partners.
Q09	transport	I was not aware that I was physically in the real world while I was playing the game.
Q10	transport	I felt that I was directly part of the game, not acting indirectly via a computer screen.
Q11	transport	I felt that I left the real world while I was playing the game.
Q12	transport	I felt more connected to the game than to the real world.
Q13	transport	I felt that I was actually in the world created by the game.
Q14	transport	While I was playing, I did not think about myself. My thinking was all about the game.
Q15	loss of self-consciousness	While I was playing the game, I was aware of the real-world environment.
Q16	loss of self-consciousness	I noticed things happening in the real world while I was playing the game.
Q17	loss of self-consciousness	I thought about stopping and looking around to see if there was anything interesting happening in the real world.
Q18	loss of self-consciousness	I often forgot about myself while I was playing the game.
Q19	merging of action and awareness	I could perform game actions without thinking.
Q20	merging of action and awareness	I was so involved in the game that I was unaware of the keyboard and mouse I was using.
Q21	merging of action and awareness	I often had to stop playing in order to think about how to play.
Q22	merging of action and awareness	The game character acted exactly as I wanted.
Q23	enjoyment	Trivial everyday thoughts did not come to mind while I was playing the game.
Q24	enjoyment	I was interested in seeing what was going to happen next.
Q25	enjoyment	The game was challenging to me.
Q26	enjoyment	While I was playing, I wanted to continue playing for a long time.
Q27	enjoyment	I enjoyed the gaming sessions.
Q28	enjoyment	I want to play the game again if I have the chance.
Q29	instinctive feeling	I felt deeply immersed in the game.

Table 2. Game immersion questionnaire content

Number	Factor	Statement
Q01	cognitive involvement	The video grabbed most of my attention.
Q02	cognitive involvement	I focused intensely on the video.
Q03	cognitive involvement	I tried to focus on the video.
Q04	emotional involvement and enjoyment	The video affected my emotions.
Q05	emotional involvement and enjoyment	I was interested in seeing what was going to happen next in the video.
Q06	emotional involvement and enjoyment	I wanted to join the people in the video if it were possible.
Q07	emotional involvement and enjoyment	I enjoyed the video session.
Q08	emotional involvement and enjoyment	I felt disappointed when the video ended.
Q09	emotional involvement and enjoyment	I wanted to watch similar TV programs.
Q10	loss of self-consciousness	Trivial everyday thoughts did not come to mind while I was watching the video.
Q11	loss of self-consciousness	I was aware of my surroundings while watching the video.
Q12	loss of self-consciousness	I felt like looking around while watching the video.
Q13	loss of self-consciousness	I felt released from stress while watching the video.
Q14	transport	I felt that time passed faster than normal while I was watching the video.
Q15	transport	I felt disconnected from the real world while watching the video.
Q16	transport	The stimulus I felt from the video was stronger than the stimulus I felt from the real world.
Q17	transport	I felt that I was a participant in the activities of the people in the video.
Q18	transport	I felt that time stopped while I was watching the video.
Q19	instinctive feeling	I felt deeply immersed in the video.

Table 3. Video immersion questionnaire content.

Number	Statement
Q01	It would have been more enjoyable if I had only played the game without watching a video at the same time.
Q02	It would have been more enjoyable if I had only watched the video without playing a game at the same time.
Q03	While I was playing the game, I did not think about the video.
Q04	While I was watching the video, I did not think about the game.
Q05	While I was playing the game, I often tried to stop and pay attention to the video.
Q06	While I was watching the video, I often tried to stop and pay attention to the game.
Q07	I spent more time than expected on the game.
Q08	I spent more time than expected on the video.
Q09	While I was playing the game, the video did not attract my attention.
Q10	While I was watching the video, the game did not attract my attention.
Q11	While playing the game, I occasionally tried to look at the video.
Q12	While watching the video, I occasionally tried to play the game.
Q13	I felt deeply immersed during the activity just completed.

Table 4. Game-video multitasking questionnaire content.

Number	Question
Q01	What did you think about the video while you were playing the game?
Q02	What did you think about the game while you were watching the video?
Q03	When did you switch your focus from the game to the video?
Q04	When did you switch your focus from the video to the game?
Q05	When you switched your focus from the game to the video, what did you think, or how did you feel, about the video that you were returning to?
Q06	When you switched your focus from the video to the game, what did you think, or how did you feel, about the game that you were returning to?
Q07	How did you feel about doing both activities at the same time?

Chapter 8
Play Teaches Learning?
A Pilot Study on How Gaming Experience Influences New Game Learning

Hao Wang
Department of Computer Science, National Chiao Tung University, Taiwan

Wen-Wen Chen
Department of Computer Science, National Chiao Tung University, Taiwan

Chun-Tsai Sun
Department of Computer Science, National Chiao Tung University, Taiwan

ABSTRACT

To provide ideal learning environments for a wider audience, game designers must understand differences in how experienced and less experienced players learn new games. Using a sample of players with different experience levels, our goal is to understand learning processes for a simple real-time strategy game. Data from observations, post-game interviews, and eye movement recordings indicate that the majority of study participants relied on a trial-and-error approach, with more experienced gamers using a structured mental model involving feedback and expectations about making progress. Specifically, experienced gamers in the sample tended to use a top-down learning style emphasizing connections between goals and available actions, and to focus on the functions of game objects. There are also interfaces in which all experience levels of participants share the same opinion. For example, alarming voices/sound effects can catch their attention and be helpful while pop-ups are largely annoying.

INTRODUCTION

Digital games are increasingly being used for non-play purposes such as education (Mitchell and Savill-Smith, 2004; Prensky, 2007; van Eck, 2006; Perez-Colado, Alonso-Fernandez, Freire, Martinez-Ortiz, and Fernandez-Manjon, 2018), health care (Bandura, 2004; Basak et al., 2008; Bavelier et al., 2012; et al., 1997; Primack et al., 2012), and communication (Bogost, 2007; Flanagan, 2009). Digital game

DOI: 10.4018/978-1-7998-2637-8.ch008

playing is believed to exert positive influences in terms of spatial cognition (Feng et al., 2007; Green and Bavelier, 2003; Greenfield, 2009; Subrahmanyam and Greenfield, 1994), social skills (Steinkuehler and Williams, 2006; Taylor, 2006), and cooperative learning (Gee, 2007), among other abilities. Greenfield et al. (1994) are among many researchers asserting that the ability to understand graphically presented information during gaming experiences benefits reading skills for objects such as charts.

Despite the large body of research on the positive learning aspects of playing digital games, few efforts have been made to understand the processes involved in learning a new game. For commercial game designers it is important to understand how individuals in specifically targeted populations learn to play their products to provide pleasant learning experiences. Without such experiences, players may quickly move on to other games that offer faster and more pleasing results. Further, in game-based learning (GBL) and health care environments, it is important to ensure that the interests of users are quickly captured and held. Such efforts require an understanding of player learning style, with prior experience possibly influencing how players learn in other environments. If gaming does in fact exert an effect on player learning models, understanding the underlying mechanisms may support the design of more suitable curriculums, especially for students with considerable gaming experience. In this chapter the authors address two issues—learning behavior and the use of game information interfaces (i.e., interfaces that provide alerts and text regarding game rules)—to determine how gaming experiences affect learning behaviors, and how players use interfaces to learn. The authors invited study participants to learn a game they had never played before, and gathered data on their learning techniques (especially those associated with in-game information) by conducting post-game interviews and recording eye movements with an eye tracker.

BACKGROUND

Learning How to Play

In their study of children's game play behavior, Blumberg and Sokol (2004) found that most players use internal reliance strategies such as repetitive practice and trial-and-error. They reported that this was especially true for the older children in their sample (fifth graders compared to second graders), with no differences between genders. In a study of how players use a puzzle game interface, Sancar et al. (2007) also reported trial-and-error as the most basic game-learning pattern, again with no significant gender-based differences. Hamlen (2011) analyzed how players use various strategies to advance in different game genres, and concluded that trial-and-error is often used in action-oriented games, while imagination is preferred in adventure games. Blumberg and Randall (2013) analyzed young teenagers' game-related problem-solving processes and found that boys were more likely to evaluate various aspects of games, while girls were more likely to talk about their personal strategies. They did not find any significant differences between self-described frequent and non-frequent players.

While these and other researchers have addressed differences between male and female players and among various age groups in terms of learning processes, they have not proposed any theories describing differences in learning models between experienced and inexperienced players—the motivation for this chapter. The authors used the idea of concept maps to analyze structural aspects of learning processes, an approach that has been used to improve many types of learning (including game-based learning) via knowledge organization (Coller and Scott, 2009; Hwang et al., 2013; Novak et al., 1983). However, instead of having study participants physically organize and produce concept maps, the authors simply let them play, and used post-game interview and eye gaze data to determine how they learned game concepts. The authors created an original real time strategy (RTS) game for this experiment based on the suitability of RTS games for detailed analyses.

Eye Tracking in Gaming Research

Much of today's eye movement research is based on Just and Carpenter's (1980) eye-mind hypothesis, which asserts that cognitive processes such as information processing and attention can be measured and understood by tracking the gazes of individuals. In this manner researchers may be able to access cognitive clues that study participants are not aware of. Further, objective eye gaze data can complement or be compared to subjective data collected via interviews, and to support or challenge interview results. Eye tracking has been extensively used to study reading (Rayner, 1998; Reichle et al., 2003), multimedia learning (Hyönä, 2010; Mayer, 2010), and visual searches involving pictures and physical environments (Najemnik and Geisler, 2005; Rayner, 2009). In gaming research, they have been used as input devices so that players can interact with a game by simply moving their eyes, or as measuring devices to study attention, strategy, interest, and related topics (Almeida et al., 2011; Isokoski et al., 2009). In research involving non-electronic games, eye-tracking devices are best known for studying cognitive processes in chess—for example, Reingold and Charness's (2005) finding that expert players are more skilled at identifying and concentrating on the most critical parts of the board during individual games. The main motivations for using an eye tracker were to (a) identify which aspects of the introduced game attracted the greatest attention, and (b) determine how players integrated visual (text and image) information (Mayer, 2005; Rayner, 2009).

Learning Affordance

Gibson (1977) coined the term "affordance" to describe an environment's functionality and usability with respect to a specific actor. For example, the ability to open and walk through a door is considered an example of human affordance. The concept is widely used and emphasized in the field of design: the perceived affordance of an item must be close to its actual affordance so as to avoid confusing a user (Norman, 1988, 1999). Perceived affordance is affected by an actor's past experiences—for instance, a computer programmer is likely to use a palm-sized object with buttons next to a keyboard as a mouse, but someone with no computer or mouse experience is unlikely to perceive the object the same way. Affordance associated with ICT tool interfaces exerts strong impacts on user experience and learning behaviors. Based on their analysis of the components of a 3-D environment used as a learning resource, Dalgarno and Lee (2010) proposed a design framework for digital educational environments aimed at facilitating learning. Clark et al. (2009) looked at how social site interfaces create affordance for both formal and informal learning. When learning a new game, experienced and inexperienced players are likely to have different perceived affordances, and interfaces should be designed accordingly. Companies are wise to consider players' past gaming experiences when designing new games, and to pay close attention to creating interfaces that provide good learning affordance.

Teaching in Games

In the game industry, it is common to teach game mechanics through level design instead of giving instructions. It is widely believed that players will have more fun and feel they are getting better when they discover rules and solutions by themselves. Take Thorson's presentation (Thorson, 2017) about Celeste in the game developer's conference (GDC) for example, the designers just put new mechanics in levels and let players die (many times) figuring it out, and really put the mechanics as part of the challenge combination in the next levels. This kind of arrangement is similar to starting with trial-and-error and advancing to strategic planning. Taylor proposed level design principles (Taylor, 2013), in which constant teaching is one of them: the whole game as a large tutorial where players always learn and play, followed by challenge and surprise. He suggested to create confusion and let the players resolve the confusion: the designers should put a reasonable size 'gap' for players to jump over or fill in, not too large or too small, to avoid frustration or boredom. This idea is close to one of the conditions for optimal experience, balance of challenge and skill, in the theory of Flow. Taylor also suggests using level design to let players discover the gap by themselves and make choices, which provides deeper experiences both in learning and narration. Hayashida, from Nintendo, talked about his level design principle similar to 4-panel comics (Nutt, 2012). The player is first introduced with a core concept, then given a slightly higher challenge. After that, a surprise shows in order to make players reflect what they have learned, and then a final challenge is posted like a final exam. Although the lessons learned in games might not be directly usable in physical world, game designers are aware of the potentials. Critical thinking, optimization, and cooperation are some of the skills that may be brought out of games (Barr, 2019).

METHOD

The Game

The authors used a self-made RTS game for the experiments because RTS is considered a mainstream game genre with clearly defined structural concepts to be learned. In addition, some currently popular genres such as MOBA are evolved from RTS, and there are some seemingly common but different rules and contexts between them. We would also like to observe how learning behavior and perceived affordance of players who are experienced with these games are affected by the knowledge transfer. Although RTS is considered complex in terms of strategy, the game concepts can be summarized as follows:

1. Players are initially given several worker units and a command center that can produce additional worker units.
2. Worker units visit resource locations and deliver collected resources to a command center.
3. The purpose of producing additional worker units is to collect resources more quickly. However, worker unit production also consumes resources.
4. Resource-consuming worker units can also be used to construct buildings for military purposes.
5. Military buildings can be used to produce military units, a task that also consumes resources.
6. Military units can be used to destroy enemy units and buildings—two tasks that are considered ultimate game goals.

The authors analyzed progress in terms of how, as well as how quickly, study participants learned each game concept. Since the majority of players failed to progress to those activities within the allotted time, the last two game characteristics were not included in the final analysis.

To keep mechanics as simple as possible, the authors used the game making tool (known as map editor) that accompanies the mainstream RTS game Starcraft 2 to create an original RTS game. The game is supposed to contain all the 6 essential concepts mentioned above, with minimal details that are irrelevant to the research purpose of this chapter. Hence, the game features only one type of military unit and one type of military building, whereas a typical RTS game may have dozens of each. Upgrades of technologies, which provides more kinds of (and/or more powerful) military units for playing, is also absent in this game. At the beginning of the game, there is one command center and 5 workers on the screen, which can be controlled by the participant. There is also an enemy (computer controlled) at the other side of the map, which is supposed to be defeated by the participant. In this experiment, it will not attack the participant's units/buildings actively to avoid pressure. The participants are not informed about the existence of enemy, functions of buildings and units, and the goal of the game. In the scope of this chapter, the authors want to observe how participants with different gaming experiences start to play and understand the game mechanics and goals: collecting resources, produce military buildings/units, find enemy, defeat enemy, etc.

To analyze eye gaze data, multiple areas of interest (AOI) are sometimes assigned to different parts of content material based on research objectives. In reading studies, each word is considered a single AOI, since individual words must be distinguished from each other. In studies where the primary goal is to measure time spent gazing at the specific content of photographs and other kinds of images, AOIs can be limited to the content and not the accompanying text. Thus, advertising firms and researchers may assign AOIs to individual parts of advertisements such as the product being promoted or a celebrity holding the product, and compare fixation times between the two in order to evaluate ad effectiveness (Pieters, 2008).

A screenshot showing the main screen interface and AOI assignments is presented as Figure 1. The AOIs include worker units that are used to harvest resources for delivery to a command center and to construct buildings; a command center that produces worker units and receives resources; resource-containing mines; resource stock and a way to indicate accumulated quantities; mini-maps showing the general game environment; portrait and basic descriptions of selected objects that do not include object function; buttons to trigger actions by selected objects; and instructions for each action button to help players learn the purpose of each object.

The first three AOIs adjust when players move worker units or focus on different locations. The last five AOI positions are fixed. The current focus position is indicated as a quadrilateral on a mini map.

Gaming Experience Level

A primary study goal is to determine differences in new game learning behaviors among players with various gaming experience levels. The authors created three categories:

"RTS players" who describe themselves as having played games two or more times per week on average for three years or more, and who are therefore very familiar with real time strategy games;

"Experienced players" who describe themselves as having played games two or more times per week on average for three years or more, but who have never played RTS games; and

Figure 1. Game interface and AOI assignments.

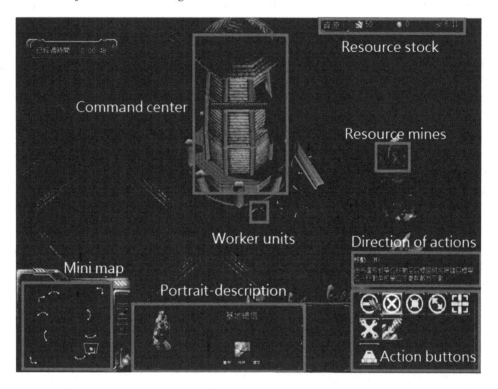

"Inexperienced players" who describe themselves as playing games less than one time per month on average.

The authors focused on differences in learning processes between experienced and inexperienced players, based on the assertion that they reflect how gaming experience influences the learning of new games. For experienced RTS players, recognizing that a new game is an RTS game is sufficient for their needs, and not much new learning is required. The authors therefore studied recognition processes rather than learning processes for the RTS player group.

Participants

Study participants were recruited through the Internet bulletin board system of a public university located in north-central Taiwan. Based on self-reports of gaming experiences, the final sample of 30 participants (22 male, 8 female) included 7 RTS players (6 male, 1 female), 14 experienced players (10 male, 4 female), and 9 inexperienced players (6 male, 3 female). Ages ranged from 18 to 26.

Eye-Tracker

Eye movement data were collected using a SR Research EyeLink 1000 tracker at a sampling rate of 1000 Hz. To reduce distractions while playing, the authors used a model with a forehead patch rather than a bracket requiring a fixed head position. Recording software was used to record data for each game for use during post-game interviews.

Figure 2. E*xperiment setting*

Procedure

Each session began with eye tracker calibration to ensure precision, followed by a five-minute casual game session for adjusting environmental settings and a ten-minute formal RTS game session. After the casual game session, participants were asked if they felt comfortable with the devices and environment. Readjustments of monitor position and chair height were made at this time. The game objective was simply stated as "defeat the enemy." No other information was given and no questions were allowed, thus ensuring that the participants learned the game concept and rules on their own. Eye movement, mouse input, and keyboard input were recorded with the eye tracker software and saved using gameplay video recording software.

Interviews were conducted immediately following each play session. Participants were viewing game videos as a memory aid while describing their thoughts during gameplay. The method is a variation of think-aloud: the participants watched their gameplay video and report what they thought while they played. The video can be paused while the participant was remembering and talking so that they can do the tasks without time pressure. Interviews lasted between 30 and 60 minutes in order to elicit as much detail as possible about the learning processes that were used. In addition to recording participants' active report, the interviewers also used semi-structured questions to collect data necessary for current research purposes: "What were you trying to do at this moment?", "What were you thinking when you saw this happening?", "Did you think something should happen next?", and "Why were you interested in this object at this moment?". The questions were prepared before the experiment and were mostly asked when the interviewers saw participants' behavior change or upon game events happening when reviewing the gameplay video.

Player comments and researcher observations were transcribed and coded according to five themes: aimless move, expectation, exploration, goal-achieving, and rule-discovery. Transcripts were separately

Figure 3. Eye tracker monitoring screen

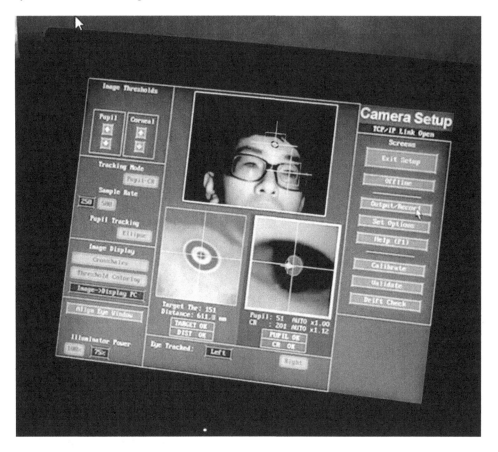

read by two researchers (92% inter-rater agreement). Examples of player comments in various theme categories include "I'm just moving this around" (aimless move); "Those crystal-like things should be valuable" and "there should be enemies somewhere" (expectation); "I'm trying to see more about the game" and "I am going to find if there is anything interesting on the map" (exploration); "I produce troops to win games" and "I think I should do this to win games" (goal-achieving); and "I found that this unit can collect crystals" and "now I know that crystals are necessary" (rule-discovery).

RESULTS

Interview Analyses

The authors will present the results in three stages corresponding to the above-described RTS game learning checkpoints:

Stage 1: Initial screen browsing. Due to the large number of visual elements on each screen, the authors looked at how players first observed the game screen, and whether they focused on certain objects or quickly browsed all objects. The authors found that all of the participants quickly focused on worker objects after noticing them, and then immediately tried to manipulate them with the computer mouse.

Table 1. **T**hree highest average AOI fixation count percentages during the 0-20 second game play time segment

Group	AOI	%	AOI	%	AOI	%
RTS players	Worker units	34	Portrait-description	9	Mini map	7
Experienced players	Worker units	32	Action buttons	10	Direction of action	10
Inexperienced players	Worker units	40	Portrait-description	10	Resource stock	9

None of them read directions or tried any other screen objects at the start. As shown in Table 1, the largest fixation count involving worker unit AOIs for all three player groups occurred during the first 20 seconds. This is consistent with previous video game research findings indicating that most people learn through trial and error rather than systematic reading or observing.

The authors believe that there are two possible explanations for the findings. First, worker objects were placed around the screen center and therefore easily noticed. Second, they generally looked "playable"—that is, the perceived affordance of their human-like appearances gave the impression that the objects were meant to be moved and used. To further compare the perceived affordance from unit looking and environmental information (map layout), the authors purposefully designed worker objects to carry swords to give them a military rather than resource-collector appearance. The authors wanted to see how RTS players would assume when they see military-looking units standing in resource-collector position. The result is that RTS players made inferences based on environmental information rather than graphical clues, and identified the game as an RTS game by acknowledging a building-like structure surrounded by objects that might be considered valuable at the screen center—two characteristics typical of RTS settings (Fig. 4). From this they apparently inferred that the human-like objects must be workers that could be used to collect resources (another typical RTS feature), and therefore did not bother to take a closer look at unit appearance.

The authors also tried to see how experienced players' perceived affordance are affected by their past gaming knowledge. The authors added three roads connecting the upper left and bottom right corners of the map. The two corners represent command center starting locations for the player and AI opponent. When attacking, players could only move their armies along three roads. This feature was taken from DotA games—a genre derived from RTS, but one that has some RPG features. Players use RTS-like maps, but they can only control one developable character at a time rather than an entire army. As planned, participants who described themselves as familiar with DotA but not with RTS games started to play the new game using DotA techniques until their expectations were no longer met. RTS players who stated that they were also familiar with DotA games were not misled due to the strong environmental features of a central building and surrounding units.

Stage 2: Resource collection. The behaviors of experienced and inexperienced players diverged during this stage. All of the experienced players moved worker objects so as to explore maps until their expectations regarding progress were satisfied—that is, when they felt a lack of potential for something new to happen, raising the possibility that they were playing incorrectly. At this point they started reading the directions on worker unit actions and discovered the capability of those units to collect resources. Upon this discovery, all of the experienced players assigned all of the worker units to collect resources, regard-

Figure 4. Contextual information and purposefully misleading information (i.e., worker units carrying swords, which makes them look like fighting characters)

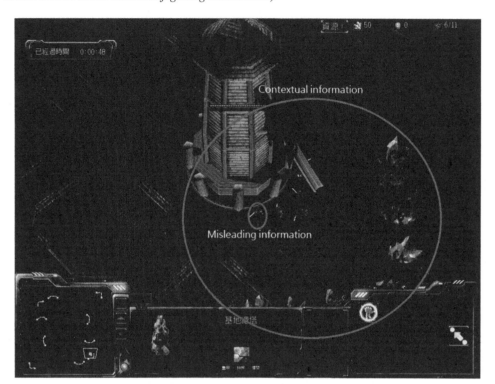

less of whether or not they understood the purposes of those resources. During post-game interviews these players described their expectations that everything in a game should be meaningful, therefore they collected as many resources as possible because they were confident that the resources would be useful at a later time.

The authors observed two types of learning patterns among the inexperienced players during this stage. One type turned to the written directions after playing with worker units for a short while, and then tried actions one-by-one. These were the only players in the entire sample to quickly rely on written directions. During interviews they described themselves as trying to learn the game and to make progress as quickly as possible. Another type completely ignored the written instructions and instead moved the worker units around the screen until the end of the play session. During interviews they described themselves as bored due to the lack of any on-screen action, but unconcerned by the thought that they might be playing incorrectly. Unlike their experienced counterparts, they described themselves as having no expectations about progress and feedback.

Another difference between the inexperienced and experienced players was that those in the first group only assigned all of their worker units to the task of resource collection once they discovered this capability. During interviews, all of them stated that they did not see the necessity of collecting resources during play sessions—unlike more experienced players, they did not have (or simply ignored) the concept that all game objects and actions must be useful and necessary to achieve game goals.

Stage 3: Discover worker unit construction powers and resource usage. The experienced players quickly discovered the ability of worker units to construct objects after looking at the written directions, but only when they felt that they were progressing in the right direction and had sufficient time to read those directions. In most cases they described themselves as believing that things were going well once they had assigned all of their worker units to collect resources, and when resources were flowing into their stocks—in other words, when all of their worker units were optimized. Among the inexperienced players, only those who systematically read the written directions discovered the construction function, and then only after trying the "move action" button located to the left of the resource-collection button.

As stated above, these inexperienced players simply read the directions and tried actions one-by-one without a sense of goal-oriented purpose. Further, both experienced and inexperienced players discovered that resources were required when they tried the construction action and received the warning message "not enough resources"—an example of trial-and-error discovery. The message also served as strong motivation for inexperienced players to assign all of their worker units to resource collection, perhaps because it clarified how resources were to be used. Experienced players were more likely to react once they were clear about the precise amount of resources required for a specific construction purpose. The authors noted that their gazes were more likely to move between their resource stocks and the construction action button as soon as they had gathered sufficient resource amounts—another example of behavior optimization. Inexperienced players (even those describing themselves as trying to progress quickly) did not exhibit similar behavior.

Learning Model Flowcharts

As shown in Figure 5, experienced players who tried to identify the game genre generally failed to do so due to their lack of RTS gameplay experience. Instead, they tried to construct a play model and to execute actions based on their experience playing RPG, DotA, or other game genres. Inexperienced players started out by browsing the screen and focusing on worker units because of the perceived affordance, and then started experimenting with worker unit actions, with some players reading directions and trying action buttons one-by-one, and others moving worker units around without any guidance.

The authors found that the main difference between experienced and inexperienced players was their expectations regarding progress and feedback. The observed actions of experienced players suggest that they quickly constructed mental models using past gaming encounters that could be applied to new ones, even in an unfamiliar game genres. Their expectations regarding progress and feedback encouraged them to refer to written directions much more quickly than some of the inexperienced players in the sample, who had no such models to rely on. However, other inexperienced players who acknowledged their lack of expertise were as likely as the experienced players to consult the written game instructions. The authors believe that this tendency to systematically read directions so as to learn complex game mechanics more quickly and thoroughly put them at an advantage over experienced players, who were only likely to read directions when they felt stuck.

The above-described differences partly explain the top-down versus bottom-up characteristic observed in the learning styles of the study participants. According to the eye-tracking data, when experienced goal achievement-oriented players read game directions, they compared several actions to determine which one was best to try first. In contrast, inexperienced players appeared to view the game either as a toy to mindlessly play with or to be mastered through the use of written directions. Whereas experienced players maintained and updated a mental model of relationships between actions and goals (a top-down learning approach), inexperienced players apparently did not acknowledge or did not care about connections between goals and available actions. Instead, their approach was similar to someone

Figure 5. TS game learning flowcharts.

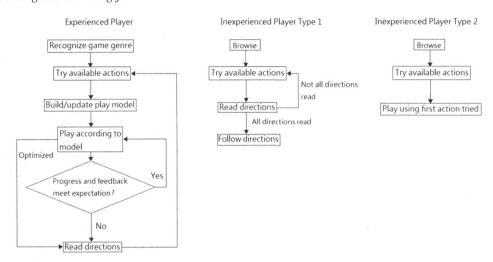

reading instructions to operate a machine without knowing (or even wondering) what the machine is for—a bottom-up approach.

Data-Driven Analysis

The authors used eye movement data to address learning characteristics that the participants did not report during their interviews, and to search for numerical evidence supporting the interview data. The authors used two indexes for this task: average fixation count for each AOI, and the number of transitions between specific AOIs. The average fixation count data revealed the overall AOI attention distribution, which is analyzed temporally. As shown in Table 2, both experienced and inexperienced players primarily focused on worker units during the first 20 seconds of each session, which is consistent with the interview data. Further, the experienced players spent more time than the inexperienced players focusing on other game objects. After the first 20 seconds, the percentage of experienced player fixation on worker units decreased by 46.8% (from 32% to 17% of total fixation) between the 60- and 120-second time points. For the inexperienced players the decrease was only 27.5% (from 40% to 29% of total fixation). Again, this result was consistent with the interview-based data.

Our index of the average number of transitions between AOIs is analogous to the regression behavior mentioned in reading eye movement research. Regression—defined in reading studies as the movement of a reader's attention to words that have already been read one time—is believed to reflect the extent to which readers are aware of the relationships among reading content AOIs. The concept has been used with different types of content. Mason et al. (2013) use the term "integrative transition" to describe how many times a reader moves between text and pictures, based on their goal of quantifying the process of efficiently integrating words and graphic information in science texts. In this chapter, transitions were assumed to indicate the degree to which players had learned or were checking relationships between two AOIs.

According to the RTS game concept list, resources are clearly at the center of concept learning. Players must quickly learn how to use worker units to collect resources, how to use those resources in construction, and how to monitor their stocks and manage resource inflow and outflow. The authors therefore

Table 2. Average fixation count percentages on worker unit AOIs during different time segments

Group	0-20 seconds	20-60 seconds	60-120 seconds
RTS players	34%	20%	16%
Experienced players	32%	23%	17%
Inexperienced players	40%	26%	29%

focused on transitions between the resource stock AOI and related AOIs in the resource collection system, including the command center, worker units, resource mines, and action buttons. The authors found that experienced players had significantly higher counts for all transitions connected to their resource stocks (Table 3), suggesting that they were building mental models of the resource collection system. Their counts were even higher than those for RTS players, perhaps because they felt a need to confirm their newly formed assumptions about how the system worked. Since RTS players were already familiar with similar game systems, their lower transition numbers suggest greater reliance on their mental model when focusing on gameplay. Inexperienced players had the smallest transition counts involving the resource collection system, suggesting the absence of both a model and model construction capability.

The visual presentation of transition counts in Figure 6 provides additional information for exploration. The width of each edge reflects the number of transitions between the AOIs denoted by the two vertices. A comparison of transition counts during the first 20 seconds shows that the experienced players had the highest percentage of transitions between the direction and action button AOIs (12.9% of all transitions), compared to only 4.8% for inexperienced players. According to the gameplay recordings, there was a significant difference between experienced and inexperienced players in terms of eye movement patterns when reading the written directions for actions, with the former making more transitions between the direction and action button AOIs due to their interest in finding worthwhile actions. The inexperienced players had the highest percentage of transitions between worker units and the portrait-description AOI (15.2% of all transitions compared to 7.1% for the experienced players). Gameplay video recording data indicate that some of the inexperienced players were curious about the nature of worker units, therefore they repeatedly checked the portrait-description AOI. Apparently none of the experienced players felt that the portrait-description was relevant to their learning, preferring instead to focus solely on worker unit actions at the beginning of their game sessions. During post-game interviews, several of the experienced players asserted that at first glance, the portrait-description did not have any great importance in terms of functionality.

Table 3. Average numbers of fixation transitions between resource stock (RS) AOIs and related AOIs

Group	RS <-> command center	RS <-> Action buttons	RS <-> Worker units	RS <-> Resource mines
RTS players	4.14	2.43	4.00	3.00
Experienced players	6.07	5.07	11.78	3.42
Inexperienced players	0.77	0.55	1.44	0.55

Figure 6. Average numbers of gaze shifts between AOIs during the first 20 seconds of play

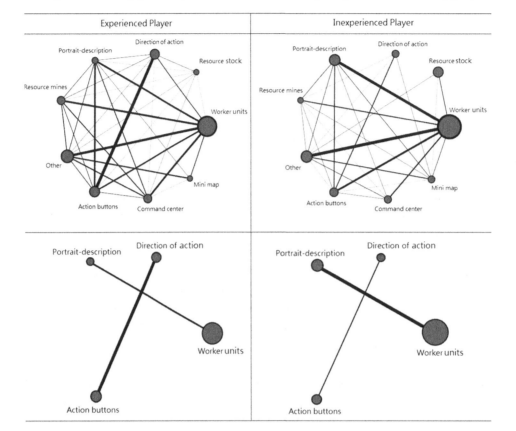

Broader line width means higher transition counts between corresponding AOIs. Significantly different transition counts are graphically indicated in the bottom row. Two primary differences were identified via a mix of gameplay video recordings and interview content.

Information Interface Usage

The information interface used in this study included directions that the participants could read (short game manual) and pop-up hints when the game system detected actions that players should learn immediately. Both features are similar to those found in mainstream commercial RTS games. The authors found that the interface was not the first choice of player attention—that is, it did not have sufficient perceived affordance to distract players from other objects that they thought were worth exploring. During interviews the participants told us that they chose objects that looked movable and life-like, and that they were not interested in things that they viewed as being uncontrollable. For players who were very familiar with a certain game genre, the contextual information they found supported their immediate assumption that the worker units around the command center were resource collectors, even though they carried swords rather than pickaxes. They made their decisions based on their quick recognition of a familiar object placement pattern. Further, regardless of experience level, most players stated that they perceived the resource mines as having high value because of their appearances as crystal-like objects.

The authors believe this is an example of good affordance design that speeds up the learning process via the efficient use of physical world experiences.

Regarding the written directions, the experienced players almost never read them spontaneously, but only when they felt stuck, or when they believed that they had exhausted all required actions in a situation and felt safe to engage in some exploratory actions. Some of the inexperienced players frequently read directions at the beginning of a session, while others spent their time experimenting with no clear focus because they lacked expectations concerning progress and feedback. The authors view this as evidence of a need for designers to clearly indicate which objects and game concepts require learning at the beginning, otherwise a significant number of first-time players may lose interest if they fail to perceive anything worthwhile taking place.

Regarding the pop-up hints, the authors programmed the system to present a pop-up message when players failed to collect any resources within the first five minutes of play. However, the authors found that the messages did not work as intended, with neither experienced nor inexperienced players reading them immediately. During interviews, many participants stated that they did not think it would be helpful to read the pop-ups right away, and that stopping their current actions to attend to "another stimulus" was annoying. This feedback suggests that the pop-up hint mechanism, though widely used, is not appropriately integrated into game systems—that is, it lacks good affordance. This issue is important for GBL designers because some kind of mechanism is required to highlight content that should be learned by new players right away. Sun et al. (2011) also point out that pop-up hints are generally unwelcomed by players, and that optional demonstration hints are more attractive to them.

DISCUSSION AND CONCLUSION

The goal of this chapter was to use interview-based and data-driven approaches to clarify how learning behavior is affected by gaming experience. The authors noted several significant differences between players with a great deal of experience and those without, and suggest that of these, the most important are expectations concerning feedback and progress—factors that may be generalizable to classrooms, skill training programs, software applications, and other learning situations. This assertion is consistent with previous descriptions of players being accustomed to receiving feedback and quick rewards in both digital game and physical worlds (Koepp et al., 1998; Reeves and Read, 2009). Further, today's students have very different expectations and motivations compared to those of past generations, and those different needs may be addressed, at least in part, by video games and other IT tools (Gee, 2007; McGonigal, 2011; Prensky, 2007). Future researchers may be interested in studying whether gaming experiences can increase student preferences for tangible progress and timely feedback. If so, efforts should be made to study the effects of game playing on factors tied to adult education—including open learning attitude and social participation, both of which have been described as having correlations with gaming activity (Flanagan, 2009; McGonigal, 2011; Tan, Goh, Ang and Huan, 2016).

Another important finding is that participants with more gaming experience favored a top-down learning style, while inexperienced players favored a bottom-up style. There are two possible explanations. First, most games have goals that players try to achieve, which encourages them to create mental models (Gee, 2007). Second, the "active processing assumption" associated with multimedia learning states that individuals actively engage in cognitive activity leading to coherent mental connections with past experiences (Mayer, 2005). Accordingly, experienced players may actively process a new game in a manner that fits with a familiar goal-achieving model. This preference may be tied to another observation: experienced players tend to be functionalists who care more about what in-game objects can do rather than text descriptions or external appearances. In other words, experienced players automatically try to understand relationships between available actions and game goals rather than learn game features in terms of their most basic elements. To transfer such a characteristic to classrooms, teachers need to clearly state the purposes of lessons in order to attract and maintain student interest—an important top-down instructional tactic.

The authors also looked at how and when players used the game information interface, and found that they tended to completely ignore it at the start of a playing session in favor of experimenting with worker objects—that is, the participants avoided systematic tasks such as reading directions until it was absolutely necessary. Though commercial and educational game designers appear to already understand this preference, there are still problems with specific interface features such as pop-up hints. The data indicate that affordance is an important factor in terms of intuitive learning, and that game designers need to acknowledge how players prefer contextual information to appearances when learning a new game. In game design, creating a sense of affordance requires taking advantage of players' physical world experiences to create interest and to support expectations; this is especially true for inexperienced gamers. Other researchers who have described affordance as central to digital learning include Dalgarno and Lee (2010) and McLoughlin and Lee (2007). Of course, most players can eventually learn a game if they stick to the task long enough. However, in light of the exceptionally large number of games and software applications in the market, users are increasingly likely to quickly abandon one game or application and try another if they are dissatisfied with the learning experience. Successful GBL game designers are acutely aware of the need to make games fun and to remove the sense of "work" and "forced effort"—factors that have great potential to reduce learning motivation (Charsky and Ressler, 2011; Prensky, 2007).

The authors acknowledge two study limitations, the first being the small number of participants and their narrow demographics. The authors identified two learning models among the nine inexperienced players; additional models and useful data might be found in an extended study entailing a larger number and broader range of players—for example, experienced players who have not played for an extended period of time. Further, assuming the potential value of this kind of research in educational settings, an important task is to determine whether the findings on different learning models in experienced/inexperienced players (e.g., top-down/bottom-up preference) are also true for young teenage learners. A second limitation is the sole use of a real time strategy game. The proposed learning model may not be suitable for certain game genres, especially basic games such as the original Tetris, in which the rule-learning stage tends to be extremely short. The authors believe the proposed learning model is more suitable for games with complex rules.

GBL is applied on education and schooling in several ways, including but not limited to: using game-like elements to motivate learners; using game content to teach certain subjects such as history and arithmetic; and using game design process to teach teamwork and inspire creativity (Nadolny, Nation and Fox, 2019; Meriläinen, 2019; Viswanathan and Radhakrishnan, 2018; Zin, Jaafar and Yue, 2009). Among them, teaching a certain subject is the most direct application for schooling, because of examinations. However, it is also quite limited: not all subjects are suitable for learning through game contents and teachers might feel this method inefficient. Also, from the students' point of view, they are told to play a game. It can be difficult to make sure they are motivated intrinsically, which is one of the most essential factors of GBL. Thus, teachers may choose using game-like elements such as reward systems (points, ranking, etc.) and narrative structures (missions, stories, etc.) in school. The findings of this chapter about gamers' expectations and top-down learning style raised a question: would young gamers bring the mental models to schools? The authors believe it is possible, especially when GBL is used in school. If it is true, GBL must be designed so that students feel the materials being useful for goal achieving, otherwise they will be confused or reluctant to learn because everything in game should be useful in some way. Teacher might also try a top-down arrangement of materials, in which goals and clues about what to learn to achieve it are given. Then let students decide what to learn by themselves, instead of teaching on schedule. The freedom of making choices can also enhance autonomy, and may increase overall motivation. Level design principles used in game industry provide valuable insight to GBL in school, too. For instance, introducing one mechanics at a time helps students learn the concept easier before taking higher challenge. Gradually increased challenge level can be used to avoid frustration and increase feeling of achievement. Surprise students with some confusing problems at right timing can make deeper understanding and a stronger impression of the subjects taught. These are only a few possibilities; it is worth exploring and experimenting further by teachers.

For game developers, transfer of knowledge from other games can be misleading and better be avoided sometimes. For example, in Crusader Kings 2 (Paradox Interactive, 2012), there are complex rules and they are introduced by manual: players must read through it. One rule, which is very different from most military strategy games (ex. Total War series by Creative Assembly and Three Kingdom Romance series by Koei) is that players cannot wage wars as they pleased. However, for players experienced with military strategy games, they are very likely to bring their knowledge and expectations because the environment (a map of ancient Europe and several control panels on screen) is very similar to military strategy games. This may make experienced players more confused and frustrated than inexperienced players if they skip the manual due to their experiences. Another idea is that for games with obscure goals, designers should foster both top-down and bottom-up learning. Some games, like Celeste, have simple goals and mechanics: just move the character from left/down to right/up of the map. Designers of these games are now using top-down style to teach players: proposing challenges and let players learn the mechanics to overcome them. However, it is hard to do so in games like Civilization series where players define their own goals and paths to success are more complicated. The way Civilization 6 (Firaxis Games, 2016) does the teaching is that it provides a step-by-step tutorial which is bottom-up and suitable for inexperienced gamers. On the other hand, the game also provides interfaces containing information and instructions to support top-down learning. For example, if a player decide to accumulate certain resources, he or she can move the mouse cursor to the resource icon and get advice. The authors of this chapter think that the teaching interface in the game is well designed, while teaching in Crusader Kings 2 can be more friendly by better fostering top-down learning. In some games, such as exergames like Wii Fit (Nintendo, 2007) and RingFit Adventure (Nintendo, 2019), players' play is the ultimate goal. This situation is similar to many GBL cases where the ultimate goal is learners' mastery over what they do in the games (make plans, doing arithmetic, driving, etc). Designers of such GBL materials might learn the design principles from these games to keep motivation of players (Macvean and Robertson, 2013; Staiano and Calvert, 2011).

REFRENCES

Almeida, S., Veloso, A., Roque, L., & Mealha, Ó. (2011). The Eyes and Games: A Survey of Visual Attention and Eye Tracking Input in Video Games. In *Proceedings of SBGames 2011*. Academic Press.

Bandura, A. (2004). Health promotion by social cognitive means. *Health Education & Behavior, 31*(2), 143–164. doi:10.1177/1090198104263660 PMID:15090118

Barr, M. (2019). How commercial video games are designed to develop players' skills. Gamasutra. Retrieved from https://www.gamasutra.com/blogs/MatthewBarr/20191021/352546/How_commercial_video_games_are_designed_to_develop_players_skills.php

Basak, C., Boot, W. R., Voss, M. W., & Kramer, A. F. (2008). Can training in a real-time strategy video game attenuate cognitive decline in older adults? *Psychology and Aging, 23*(4), 765–777. doi:10.1037/a0013494 PMID:19140648

Bavelier, D., Green, C. S., Pouget, A., & Schrater, P. (2012). Brain plasticity through the life span: Learning to learn and action video games. *Annual Review of Neuroscience, 35*(1), 391–416. doi:10.1146/annurev-neuro-060909-152832 PMID:22715883

Blumberg, F. C., & Randall, J. D. (2013). What do children and adolescents say they do during video game play? *Journal of Applied Developmental Psychology, 34*(2), 82–88. doi:10.1016/j.appdev.2012.11.004

Blumberg, F. C., & Sokol, L. M. (2004). Boys' and girls' use of cognitive strategy when learning to play video games. *The Journal of General Psychology, 131*(2), 151–158. doi:10.3200/GENP.131.2.151-158 PMID:15088867

Bogost, I. (2007). *Persuasive games: The expressive power of videogames.* MIT Press.

Brown, S., Lieberman, D. A., Gemeny, B., Fan, Y., Wilson, D., & Pasta, D. (1997). Educational video game for juvenile diabetes: Results of a controlled trial. *Informatics for Health & Social Care, 22*(1), 77–89. PMID:9183781

Charsky, D., & Ressler, W. (2011). Games are made for fun: Lessons on the effects of concept maps in the classroom use of computer games. *Computers & Education, 56*(3), 604–615. doi:10.1016/j.compedu.2010.10.001

Clark, W., Logan, K., Luckin, R., Mee, A., & Oliver, M. (2009). Beyond Web 2.0: Mapping the technology landscapes of young learners. *Journal of Computer Assisted Learning, 25*(1), 56–69. doi:10.1111/j.1365-2729.2008.00305.x

Coller, B. D., & Scott, M. J. (2009). Effectiveness of using a video game to teach a course in mechanical engineering. *Computers & Education, 53*(3), 900–912. doi:10.1016/j.compedu.2009.05.012

Dalgarno, B., & Lee, M. J. (2010). What are the learning affordances of 3-D virtual environments? *British Journal of Educational Technology, 41*(1), 10–32. doi:10.1111/j.1467-8535.2009.01038.x

Feng, J., Spence, I., & Pratt, J. (2007). Playing an action video game reduces gender differences in spatial cognition. *Psychological Science, 18*(10), 850–855. doi:10.1111/j.1467-9280.2007.01990.x PMID:17894600

Firaxis Games. (2016). Civilization 6.

Flanagan, M. (2009). *Critical play: radical game design.* The MIT Press. doi:10.7551/mitpress/7678.001.0001

Gee, J. P. (2007). *What Video Games Have to Teach Us about Learning and Literacy* (2nd ed.). Palgrave Macmillan.

Gibson, J. (1977). The concept of affordances. In *Perceiving, acting, and knowing* (pp. 67-82). Academic Press.

Green, C. S., & Bavelier, D. (2003). Action video game modifies visual selective attention. *Nature*, *423*(6939), 534–537. doi:10.1038/nature01647 PMID:12774121

Greenfield, P. M. (2009). Technology and informal education: What is taught, what is learned. *Science*, *323*(5910), 69–71. doi:10.1126cience.1167190 PMID:19119220

Greenfield, P. M., Camaioni, L., Ercolani, P., Weiss, L., Lauber, B. A., & Perucchini, P. (1994). Cognitive socialization by computer games in two cultures: Inductive discovery or mastery of an iconic code? *Journal of Applied Developmental Psychology*, *15*(1), 59–85. doi:10.1016/0193-3973(94)90006-X

Hamlen, K. R. (2011). Children's choices and strategies in video games. *Computers in Human Behavior*, *27*(1), 532–539. doi:10.1016/j.chb.2010.10.001

Hwang, G.-J., Yang, L.-H., & Wang, S.-Y. (2013). A Concept Map-Embedded Educational Computer Game for Improving Students' Learning Performance in Natural Science Courses. *Computers & Education*, *69*, 121–130. doi:10.1016/j.compedu.2013.07.008

Hyönä, J. (2010). The use of eye movements in the study of multimedia learning. *Learning and Instruction*, *20*(2), 172–176. doi:10.1016/j.learninstruc.2009.02.013

Isokoski, P., Joos, M., Spakov, O., & Martin, B. (2009). Gaze controlled games. *Universal Access in the Information Society*, *8*(4), 323–337. doi:10.100710209-009-0146-3

Just, M. A., & Carpenter, P. A. (1980). A theory of reading: From eye fixations to comprehension. *Psychological Review*, *87*(4), 329–354. doi:10.1037/0033-295X.87.4.329 PMID:7413885

Koepp, M. J., Gunn, R. N., Lawrence, A. D., Cunningham, V. J., Dagher, A., Jones, T., ... Grasby, P. M. (1998). Evidence for striatal dopamine release during a video game. *Nature*, *393*(6682), 266–268. doi:10.1038/30498 PMID:9607763

Koivisto, J., Malik, A., Gurkan, B., & Hamari, J. (2019). Getting Healthy by Catching Them All: A Study on the Relationship between Player Orientations and Perceived Health Benefits in an Augmented Reality Game. In *Proceedings of the 52nd Hawaii International Conference on System Sciences*. Academic Press. 10.24251/HICSS.2019.216

Macvean, A., & Robertson, J. (2013). Understanding exergame users' physical activity, motivation and behavior over time. In *Proceedings of the SIGCHI Conference on Human Factors in Computing Systems* (pp. 1251-1260). ACM. 10.1145/2470654.2466163

Mason, L., Tornatora, M. C., & Pluchino, P. (2013). Do fourth graders integrate text and picture in processing and learning from an illustrated science text? Evidence from eye-movement patterns. *Computers & Education*, *60*(1), 95–109. doi:10.1016/j.compedu.2012.07.011

Mayer, R. E. (2005). Cognitive theory of multimedia learning. In The Cambridge handbook of multimedia learning (pp. 31-48). Academic Press. doi:10.1017/CBO9780511816819.004

Mayer, R. E. (2010). Unique contributions of eye-tracking research to the study of learning with graphics. *Learning and Instruction*, *20*(2), 167–171. doi:10.1016/j.learninstruc.2009.02.012

McGonigal, J. (2011). Reality is broken: Why games make us better and how they can change the world. Penguin. com.

McLoughlin, C., & Lee, M. J. (2007). Social software and participatory learning: Pedagogical choices with technology affordances in the Web 2.0 era. *Paper presented at the ICT: Providing choices for learners and learning*. Academic Press.

Meriläinen, M. (2019). First-Timer Learning Experiences in Global Game Jam. *International Journal of Game-Based Learning*, *9*(1), 30–41. doi:10.4018/IJGBL.2019010103

Mitchell, A., & Savill-Smith, C. (2004). The use of computer and video games for learning: A review of the literature. Retrieved from https://dera.ioe.ac.uk/5270/7/041529_Redacted.pdf

Nadolny, L., Nation, J., & Fox, J. (2019). Supporting Motivation and Effort Persistence in an Online Financial Literacy Course Through Game-Based Learning. *International Journal of Game-Based Learning*, *9*(3), 38–52. doi:10.4018/IJGBL.2019070103

Najemnik, J., & Geisler, W. S. (2005). Optimal eye movement strategies in visual search. *Nature*, *434*(7031), 387–391. doi:10.1038/nature03390 PMID:15772663

Nintendo. (2007). Wii Fit.

Nintendo. (2019). RingFit Adventure.

Norman, D. (1988). The Design of Everyday Things. In *The psychology of everyday things*. New York: Basic Books.

Norman, D. (1999). Affordance, conventions, and design. *Interaction*, *6*(3), 38–43. doi:10.1145/301153.301168

Novak, J. D., Bob Gowin, D., & Johansen, G. T. (1983). The use of concept mapping and knowledge vee mapping with junior high school science students. *Science Education*, *67*(5), 625–645. doi:10.1002ce.3730670511

Nutt, C. (2012). The Structure of Fun: Learning from Super Mario 3D Land's Director." Gamasutra. Retrieved from https://www.gamasutra.com/view/feature/168460/the_structure_of_fun_learning_.php

Paradox Interactive, 2012. Crusader Kings 2.

Perez-Colado, I., Alonso-Fernandez, C., Freire, M., Martinez-Ortiz, I., & Fernandez-Manjon, B. (2018). Game learning analytics is not informagic! In *Proceedings of the 2018 IEEE Global Engineering Education Conference (EDUCON)* (pp. 1729-1737). IEEE Press. 10.1109/EDUCON.2018.8363443

Pieters, R. (2008). A review of eye-tracking research in marketing. *Review of marketing research*, *4*, 123-147.

Prensky, M. (2007). *Digital game-based learning*. St. Paul, MN: Paragon House.

Primack, B. A., Carroll, M. V., McNamara, M., Klem, M. L., King, B., Rich, M., ... Nayak, S. (2012). Role of video games in improving health-related outcomes: A systematic review. *American Journal of Preventive Medicine, 42*(6), 630–638. doi:10.1016/j.amepre.2012.02.023 PMID:22608382

Rayner, K. (1998). Eye movements in reading and information processing: 20 years of research. *Psychological Bulletin, 124*(3), 372–422. doi:10.1037/0033-2909.124.3.372 PMID:9849112

Rayner, K. (2009). Eye movements and attention in reading, scene perception, and visual search. *Quarterly Journal of Experimental Psychology, 62*(8), 1457–1506. doi:10.1080/17470210902816461 PMID:19449261

Reeves, B., & Read, J. L. (2009). *Total Engagement: How Games and Virtual Worlds to Change the Way People Work and Businesses Compete*. Harvard Business Press.

Reichle, E. D., Rayner, K., & Pollatsek, A. (2003). The EZ Reader model of eye-movement control in reading: Comparisons to other models. *Behavioral and Brain Sciences, 26*(4), 445–476. doi:10.1017/S0140525X03000104 PMID:15067951

Reingold, E. M., & Charness, N. (2005). Perception in chess: Evidence from eye movements. In *Cognitive processes in eye guidance* (pp. 325–354). Oxford University Press. doi:10.1093/acprof:oso/9780198566816.003.0014

Sancar, H., Karakus, T., & Cagiltay, K. (2007). Learning a New Game: Usability, Gender and Education. *Paper presented at the Young researchers furthering development of TEL research in Central and Eastern Europe*. Academic Press.

Staiano, A. E., & Calvert, S. L. (2011). Exergames for physical education courses: Physical, social, and cognitive benefits. *Child Development Perspectives, 5*(2), 93–98. doi:10.1111/j.1750-8606.2011.00162.x PMID:22563349

Steinkuehler, C. A., & Williams, D. (2006). Where everybody knows your (screen) name: Online games as "third places." *Journal of Computer-Mediated Communication, 11*(4), 885–909. doi:10.1111/j.1083-6101.2006.00300.x

Subrahmanyam, K., & Greenfield, P. M. (1994). Effect of video game practice on spatial skills in girls and boys. *Journal of Applied Developmental Psychology, 15*(1), 13–32. doi:10.1016/0193-3973(94)90004-3

Sun, C. T., Wang, D. Y., & Chan, H. L. (2011). How digital scaffolds in games direct problem-solving behaviors. *Computers & Education, 57*(3), 2118–2125. doi:10.1016/j.compedu.2011.05.022

Tan, J. L., Goh, D. H. L., Ang, R. P., & Huan, V. S. (2016). Learning efficacy and user acceptance of a game-based social skills learning environment. *International journal of child-computer interaction, 9*, 1-19.

Taylor, D. (2013). Ten Principles for Good Level Design. Presentation in GDC 2013 [YouTube video]. Retrieved from https://www.youtube.com/watch?v=iNEe3KhMvXM

Taylor, T. L. (2006). *Play between worlds*. MIT Press. doi:10.7551/mitpress/5418.001.0001

Thorson, M. (2017). Level Design Workshop: Designing Celeste. Presentation in GDC 2017 [YouTube video]. Retrieved from https://www.youtube.com/watch?v=4RlpMhBKNr0

Van Eck, R. (2007). Building artificially intelligent learning games. In Games and simulations in online learning: Research and development frameworks (pp. 271-307). Academic Press. doi:10.4018/978-1-59904-304-3.ch014

Viswanathan, S., & Radhakrishnan, B. (2018). A Novel 'Game Design' Methodology for STEM Program. *International Journal of Game-Based Learning*, 8(4), 1–17. doi:10.4018/IJGBL.2018100101

Wang, H., & Sun, C. T. (2011). Game reward Systems: gaming experiences and social meanings. In DiGRA 2011. Academic Press.

Zin, N. A. M., Jaafar, A., & Yue, W. S. (2009). Digital game-based learning (DGBL) model and development methodology for teaching history. *WSEAS Transactions on Computers*, 8(2), 322–333.

Chapter 9
Affective Computing in E–Learning Modules:
Comparative Analysis With Two Activities

Mahima Maharjan
University of Tasmania, Australia

Soonja Yeom
https://orcid.org/0000-0002-5843-101X
University of Tasmania, Australia

Soo-Hyung Kim
Chonnam National University, South Korea

Si Fan
https://orcid.org/0000-0003-1572-3677
University of Tasmania, Australia

ABSTRACT

This article presents a study on emotions of students and their reactions towards learning and watching video clips with different personality traits, with the help of existing facial expression analyzing applications. To demonstrate this, the user's expressions are recorded as video while watching the movie trailer and doing the quiz. The results obtained are studied to find which emotion is most prevalent among the users in different situations. This study shows that students experience seemingly different emotions during the activity. This study explores the use of affective computing for further comprehension of student emotion in learning environments. While previous studies show that there is a positive correlation between emotion and academics, the current study demonstrated the existence of the inverse relation between them. In addition, the study of the facial analysis of movie trailer confirmed that different people have different ways of expressing the feeling. Results of the study will help to further clarify connection between various personality traits and emotions.

DOI: 10.4018/978-1-7998-2637-8.ch009

INTRODUCTION

Biological actions like facial expressions, body gestures, gaze movement can be used to extract emotional contents from human beings. The process of detection and recognition of these actions is an essential aspect of affective computing and artificial intelligence. Getting a machine to recognize the human actions is demanding and is an active field of research. There are many scenarios where a researcher can be motivated in this emerging field. For instance, the ability to sense whether a student is feeling nervous, confused or happy; analyze witnesses' expressions by lawyers and numerous examples exist in our daily activities (Pantic & Rothkrantz, 2003). Among the two approaches of affective computing, which are audio-based approach and video-based approach, this study focuses on video-based techniques which examine and categorize facial expressions to gather information of emotion with the aid of different facial expression recognition applications.

Affective issues in learning technologies are concerned with emotional areas such as inspiration, attitudes, and feelings (Jones & Issroff, 2004). It is the study of Human-Computer Interaction to diagnose and measure the emotion (Lin, Wu and Hsueh, 2014). Emotion is one of the most researched topics in the study of psychology (Cho & Heron, 2015; Plutchik, 2001). Plutchik (2001) notes that over 90 definitions of emotion have been proposed since the 20th century; emotion is expressed in the form of anger, despair, joy, and grief. Learning strategies like critical thinking (Cho & Heron, 2015), and effort contributed less in explaining students' achievement compared to motivation and emotions related to it. Therefore, more motivational and emotional supports are necessary to enhance the student's success. Moreover, affective states play a significant role in the daily activities of humans, including tasks performed in front of the computer (Jones & Issroff, 2005). An objective study of emotion itself is a challenging task as several emotions could be experienced at the same time (Plutchik, 2001). Emotion can be treated as on or off switch for learning (Vail, 1994). Positive/negative emotional states increase/decrease intellectual energies and capacities. Having to attend the time-limited quiz where there is continuous tension of ongoing time and memory, can impede students' performance increasing anxiety (Jones & Issroff, 2005).

The limbic system, also known as the emotional brain, is one part of the three-way view of the human brain interprets the emotional value of incoming stimuli and decides if they are neutral, good or deadly; controls the ability to learn, memory and make novel connections (LeDoux, 2003). The active states of different parts of the brain give different facial expressions. For example, anger results from activation of some parts of the brain that help to react with more speed and strength while overpowering prudent things replacing cautiousness with aggressiveness and compassion with resentment. Emotional expressions are states that define different ways of thinking. Furthermore, facial signs are perceived differently than non-facial signs such as audio for the same emotions (Ekman & Friesen, 2003).

Robinson (2008) categorizes interest, curiosity, surprise, joy, and love as positive emotions; while panic, aversion or disgust, fear, anger, anxiety, sorrow, and frustration are considered as negative emotions. Positive states like happiness cause positive impacts on learning while negative states like anger and sadness generate negative effects. The theoretical assumption of the control-value theory suggests that negative emotions can produce a positive outcome (Pekrun, 2006). To the contrary, "learning by positive reinforcement" does account for how people learn.

The relationship between emotional intelligence (EI) and academic performance (AP) of the students shows a substantial positive association between them. EI is the ability to perceive and express emotion. It is used to facilitate thoughts, understand and reason with emotion. The technologies which recognize, and express emotional states are leading to the development of different algorithms which can provide an artificial environment to explore human nature further, control cognition, attention, and action. Until now, to enable computers to adapt the human behavior has been the main goal rather than the way round (Minsky, 2007).

The analysis of quiz attended video is a fertile base for further studies on affective interaction. Having to attend the time limit quiz where there is continuous tension of ongoing time and memory, can impede students' performance increasing anxiety (Jones & Issroff, 2005). The issue on the agenda is whether we can detect more accurately what a person is experiencing and feeling during the activities. The hint that facial expression may provide an idea of this readily arises, but the expressions that are being displayed cannot be taken as the sole factor of the mental state. To make an association of outer expression and the inner state is no minor task. We, therefore, commenced research in which we looked for answers to the following question: what kind of facial expressions induce on the faces of participants during the interaction with different facial expression recognition applications and how are different moods related to them. We collected video material from students attending the quiz and watching the movie trailer and analysed it is using the available applications.

There have been only limited studies about an affective and emotional outcome associated learning. Most of the studies only focused on positive emotions such as happy portraying positive outcome or success in the overall grade (Macfadden et al., 2005; Fitriani, Apriliaswati & Rosnija, 2017); yet the evidence of negative emotion producing success is somewhat limited. In the present study, we would like to investigate the correlation between negative emotions and positive outcome.

BACKGROUND

Emotion Categorization

Emotions originate from people's experiences. People experience the joy of winning a lottery, sadness of breakups, anxiety due to deadlines, the fright of exams, Astonishment of new ideas and disgusted by cacophonies. They are felt in the form of anger, sadness, joy, fright, astonishment, and disgust. These experiences are consequent in subsequent behavior, thoughts, and decisions. Barrett (2006) argues that there are separate mechanisms for different emotions felt in our daily lives. Studies often conclude that emotions trigger facial expressions and have different procedures for different kinds of emotions or facial expressions. The experience of facial expression results with conceptualization of an ongoing emotion. For instance, when anger procedure is triggered, anger emotion is felt and becomes visible as facial expression. A person contracts the muscles in between the eyebrows, and it is recognized that the person is feeling angry.

In the study of psychological studies, there are several notable examples where psychologists have categorized the types of emotions experienced by human beings. Barrett (2006) define emotion as entities where it is triggered by external agents and influence people's activities, opinions, and behavior. Emotions are associated with corresponding response patterns. Several proposals and theories have been made for emotion categorization into groups. Psychologist Paul Eckman categorized basic emotion into 6 types which were identified as happiness, sadness, fear, anger, surprise, and disgust. Facial expressions are signaled by different muscle, eye and lip movements (Ekman & Friesen, 2003). Positive facial expressions are indicated by Eyes Opening wide with raising the eyebrows which are represented as comprehensible. Negative emotions are conveyed by contracting eyes and eyebrows raised high, enlarged eyes, curling lips, which represent the student's incomprehension and confused state (Sathik & Jonathan, 2013).

Faces contain details about the identity, mood and mind state which are the mechanisms governing the emotions and the most expressive way humans portray emotions is through facial expressions (Sathik & Jonathan 2013). Facial Action Coding System (FACS) (Ekman & Friesen, 2003) which is a system of facial action analysis determines the facial muscular movement based on a set of 46 facial Action Units (AUs) was also proposed. FACS is a system to describe visually noticeable facial movements. It breaks down the expressions of humans into components of movements of muscles which are called Action Units (AUs). It has been established as the automated system which detects faces from the images or videos and draws facial geometrical features. It can also be coded manually by deconstructing the facial features into corresponding AUs. In terms of FACS, AUs are contraction and relaxation of facial muscles. These AUs are automatically related to the contraction of a specific set of facial muscles. For instance, AU0 represents a neutral face, AU1 represents inner brow raiser and so on. Six basic emotions: happy, sad, angry, surprised, scared, disgusted, plus neutral are a combination of one or many AUs. FACS intensities are represented by letters A–E (described as maximum, severe or extreme, marked or pronounced, slight and trace, respectively), with A being minimal and E as maximal intensity to the action unit number. Later Ekman with other psychologists revised the six basic emotions, including a range of positive as well as negative emotions which may or may not be encoded in the facial action units (Ekman, 1992). In addition to the six basic emotions, it included amusement, excitement, contempt, relief, guilt, satisfaction, pride, shame, embarrassment and excitement.

Similarly, Plutchik (2001) put forward a wheel of emotion that mentioned emotion is a combination of different feelings analogous to colors which are combined to create different shades. A wheel of emotion consisted of eight emotions which are namely, joy, anticipation, trust, anger, fear, disgust, surprise and sadness. The author further categorized the eight emotion into primary, secondary and tertiary dyads. According to the researcher, the basic emotion is the building blocks for expressing emotions. For instance, love, a primary dyad is the combination of joy and trust; a secondary dyad is an envy which is the combination of sadness and anger; and shame, a tertiary dyad is the combination of fear and disgust. Also, a different combination of emotions exists for other human feelings like optimism, hope, friendliness, delight and so on. They influence cognitive states in humans, which include processes like learning, memory, intellect, perception and solving of problems which are crucial for academics. Vuilleumier (2005) say that emotion affects the attention, Phelps (2004) argue that emotion affects learning and memory and Jung et al. (2014) claim that emotion affects the reasoning of students in the academic setting.

Emotion facilitates in ciphering and retrieval of information. Different emotions are associated with different settings of academics, for instance, examinations, deadlines, assignments can be linked with various emotions such as boredom, anxiety, confusion, interest and so on. Some of the common emotions during the learning process are a delight, hope, pride, satisfaction, anger, shame, frustration and boredom. Positive emotions like to enjoy, hope associate motivation, effort and learning strategies (Pekrun et al., 2011). Positive affect also increases motivation in learners (Goleman, 2006). Negative emotions impact students' performance, such as inactive behavior, less concentration, motivation and confidence (Fitriani, Apriliaswati & Rosnija, 2017). Emotions upset mental life and those who have negative emotions like anxiety, annoyance, and depression are not capable of learning (Goleman, 2006).

In contrast to conventional classrooms, where lecturers, for the most part, give direction and structure (both verbal and non-verbal direction), students should exercise self-administrative ability to achieve their learning objectives in today's context (Artino, 2010). For example, a person may feel worried or anxiety due to threat of encounter. Failure leads people to convey negative emotions which as a result outcomes low self-esteem (Schunk, 1996). Self-confidence is a factor in learning and helps to show more perseverance when problems arise. Some researchers also claim that joy and anxiety experienced by the students depend on individual goals (Goleman, 2006). If the goal of the student is achieving high marks and if the goal is approaching, the student might feel positive emotions like joy; whereas if the students are not satisfied, the student might experience negative emotions like anxiety (Pekrun, 2006). Another research claims that success instigates positive emotions while failure promotes negative emotions (Weiner, 1985). Negative states like confusion could prove beneficial because of increased attention on learning activities which consequently gives higher performances (D'mello et al., 2014). Moreover, negative emotion like anxiety is induced if a student expects failure in the quiz or examination, whereas no anxiety will occur if the student does not care about it or does not expect failure. Furthermore, Stress which is also a negative state of emotion is considered to encourage or inhibit the learning process (Vogel & Schwabe, 2016). The surprise is a strange situation which refers to inconsistency among prior and new information (Sathik & Jonathan, 2013). While negative emotions are associated with low performance; there is limited research on negative emotions portraying positive outcome. The need for a more precise understanding of the relation between facial emotion and learning outcome is being driven today by technologies being built to interact with learners.

In the similar fashion, Lazarus (1994) extended Ekman's six basic emotions into fifteen emotions: shape, aesthetic experience, compassion, relief, compassion, pride, depression, love, envy, jealousy, gratitude, hope, guilt, sadness, fright, and anger. The author says that emotion expressed by people is the reflection of physical and social issues the person is going through. Anger, envy, and jealousy are categorized as nasty emotions which create interpersonal and social problems; anxiety, fright, guilt, and shame are characterized as existential emotions which are concerned with the senses that underlie our lives; relief, hope, sadness, and depression are emotions triggered by adverse life circumstances which come from negative situations; happiness, pride, and love are the emotions triggered by positive life conditions which reveal an optimistic and inspiring side of lives; gratitude, compassion, and aesthetic experiences are the empathetic emotions which are experienced when a person receives altruistic gift and compassion of others emotion.

A more recent study done by Cowen and Keltner (2017) suggests that there are twenty-seven discrete emotions rather than only six basic emotions. The author explains that emotions do not occur in isolation, rather they occur as a gradient of emotions which are inter-related. The emotional studies prior to this stated that emotion state occurs in segregation from one another. twenty-seven emotions are namely, admiration, adoration, aesthetic appreciation, amusement, anger, anxiety, awe, awkwardness, boredom, calmness, confusion, craving, disgust, empathic pain, entrancement, excitement, fear, horror, interest, joy, nostalgia, relief, romance, sadness, satisfaction, sexual desire, surprise.

Models for Emotion Recognition

The technologies which recognize, and express emotional states are leading to the development of different algorithms which can provide an artificial environment to explore human nature further, control cognition, attention and action. Until now, to enable computers to adapt the human behavior has been the main goal rather than the way round (Minsky, 2007). However, an increasing number of researchers are paying attention to the recognition of facial expressions. The main motive of these kinds of researches is to automatically, consistently, efficaciously use the information for facial expression recognition.

The Affective recognition system mainly uses two steps to measure the emotion: a collection of data from the emotion and prediction of emotional state based on existing models and stored databases (Jaques et al., 2011). Several models exist for the analysis of the emotional state, for instance, a categorical model explains the cognitive process that induces emotion from the already existing categories of emotions. There exists another type of model which refers to a dimensional model where the emotion is considered as the combination of arousal learning and valence/effect. Pekrun (2006) used the model to review the control value theory. The spiral and the circumplex model are also popular. Most of the studies use these models with the Facial Action Coding System (FACS) (Ekman, 1992), Ortony, Clore and Collins Structure of emotions (OCC) (Ortony, Clore & Collins, 1988).

The working of these recognition systems primarily depends on the facial expression feature. Therefore, feature extraction is vital to the expression recognition process. The facial feature is not always adequate; they can be high or low most of the times. The problems during the facial expression examination include detection of a face in images or sequences, extraction of facial expression data and the classification of expressions identified (Pantic & Rothkrantz, 2000). In such cases, machine learning algorithms are used to work as intended and yield true results. Ou (2012) used K-Nearest Neighbour (KNN) to classify extracted facial feature into facial expression emotions. In this model, the feature extraction is done with Principal Component Analysis (PCA). However, this model had some deficits, such as the base locations in the human face are narrow. Clarizia with colleagues adopted the sentiment analysis methodology for the recognition of mood during the learning process using Latent Dirichlet Allocation (LDA) as the Sentiment Grabber (Clarizia et al. 2018).

Several studies have been published for face recognition on the basis of image intensities. Elastic Bunch Graph Matching method proposed by Okada et al. (1998) and Latent Dirichlet Allocation method proposed by Zhao et al. (1999) works best for small images. The recognition of faces from a sequence of the video has been a challenging task till date, as the quality of the video could hinder the performance of facial expression recognition. Michel & Kaliouby (2003) used Support Vector Machines (SVM) to classify the facial features and evaluated the method in different scenarios with the accuracy of approximately 60%. Duc, Huu and Tan (2009) categorized facial features into 4 basic expressions which are angry, happy, normal and surprise using Active Appearance Model (AAM) combined with neural network and PCA. Shan, Gong & McOwan (2009) proposed a study of facial expressions based on Local Binary Pattern (LBP) features. LBP features have a high tolerance against light changes in the environment and simplicity in computation. The authors used SVM and LDA to perform expression recognition. The mean recognition rate of this method on different datasets is 79.28%, which is better than that of the genetic algorithm: 72.64%.

There are studies which not only detects objects from stationary images, but also the sequence of images. Viola and Jones (2001) used the AdaBoost algorithm for face detection over images with multiple scales which was 15 times faster than any other approaches at those times. This algorithm also detected pedestrians walking in the road which is a technique for feature selection. Similarly, Kapoor, Qi and Picard (2003) used PCA to extract eye and eyebrow regions and SVM to classify these features. The algorithm developed could recognize very fast-moving image sequences with the accuracy of approximately 70%. Bartlett et al. (2003) used a combination of AdaBoost and SVM classifier for grouping the facial expression into six basic facial expressions of Ekman including the neutral expression. The system developed by Kapoor, Qi and Picard (2003) and Bartlett et al. (2003) used the Cohn-Kanade facial database to test the recognition (Kanade, Cohn & Tian, 2000). To extract image motion blobs from the image sequences, Essa and Pentland (1997) performed the combination of spatial and temporal filtering and thresholding. The presence of facial expressions is detected using eigenfaces method with PCA. However, they are not resilient to variation in illumination. and his colleagues proposed a Local Directional Pattern (LDP) which considers the illumination problem of previous studies and analyses the image on the basis of the pixel; this method increased the accuracy of facial expression recognition to approximately 96% (Uddin et al. 2017). Among the classifiers and extraction techniques discussed above, SVM had the highest facial expression recognition accuracy of 99% which identifies several expressions: happy, sad, surprise, fear, neutral, angry and disgust (Revina & Emmanuel, 2018).

The recognition system developed is integrated into a mobile platform, robots, animators, and various other applications like FaceReader, video games and many more. There are also various technologies in the form of Software Development Kits (SDKs) such as Affectiva SDK (McDuff et al., 2016), opensource tool such as Openface (Baltrušaitis et al., 2016) which is a realtime facial behavior analysis system and software like Noldus facereader (Lewinski, den Uyl & Butler, 2014), a facial coding software which provides a consistent indicator for basic emotions with FACS coding.

Facial Emotions and Personality Traits

Developing techniques for analysis of expressions are crucial for more effective human and computer interaction (Cohen et al., 2003). Although there is amassing evidence that the experience of emotion triggers facial emotions, it remains unclear whether different people have different mechanisms or procedures for anger, joy, fear, and so on. Moreover, people tend to represent false expressions as they might be hiding their true emotions. Some claim that facial expressions are unnatural and might not represent the true intention of psychological signals attained from electroencephalogram (ECG), electromyogram (EMG), electrocardiogram (ECG) (Littlewort et al., 2009; Hill & Craig, 2002).

An individual's ways of expressing emotions in the form of facial expressions largely depend on their individuality, such as introverted or extroverted. The same facial expression is not identical for two individual personalities but can be varied according to the personality attributes (Chin et al., 2009). The authors of the study of brain-computer interface conclude that extroverted traits are more conspicuous than those of introverted personalities. It determines that facial expression in extroverted people is more distinct from one another.

According to the social-functional approach, emotion is a central motivating and organizational force which is a base for personality. Emotions are the grounds which organize people's cognitive and processes and direct interactions in society (Barrett, 2006). Fox (2002) say that individual cognitive power, behavior and interpersonal styles which define personality traits appear early in the development process as a human being. Neuroticism, a personality trait where a person experience emotion like anxiety, fear envy, jealousy, depression, and loneliness are related to negative affect and Extraversion, a personality trait where a person is social, outgoing, enjoy with people relate to positive affect (Watson & Clark, 1992). Fox (2002) says that even though anxiety is a response to a threatening event, people tend to experience different levels of anxiety and have the facial expression of both anger and fear. The role of the amygdala, the specific part of the brain, plays a critical role in processing facial expressions (Calder, Ewbank & Passamonti, 2011). The expressions of fear, anger, and sadness showed no relationship with the nature of people from the analysis of amygdala response; however, the people's response to facial expressions of happiness relative to a neutral expression showed significant correlations with the extroversion. In addition, Wiggins, Trapnell, and Phillips (1988) point out that a competitive person would be dominant and shy people tend to have a high affiliation. Wiggins with his colleagues proposed an "interpersonal circumplex", emotional expressions carry individual information about the personal traits. Likewise, Schaefer and Plutchik (1966) also claim that emotional experience resembles individual dominant and affiliative traits. Nevertheless, in the field of human-computer interaction, the relationship between the interpersonal traits and expressions has received relatively little attention.

The need for more a precise understanding of the relation between facial emotion and learning outcome is being driven today by technologies being built to interact with learners.

In this research, four different applications are investigated for the analysis of the student's emotions which are explained below.

OpenFace: It is intended for computer vision and machine learning researchers, affective computing community and people interested in building interactive applications. In this application, facial behavior is composed of facial landmark detection, head pose estimation, facial AU recognition, and eye-gaze estimation (Baltrusaitis, Robinson & Morency, 2016).

Noldus Facereader: It has an accuracy rate of 88% (Lewinski, Den Uyl & Butler, 2014); allows evaluation of expressions quantitatively. Viola Jones cascaded algorithm with a deep facial classification for finding the position of the face in an image. Active Appearance Model (AAM) is used to synthesize an artificial model. The expressions are represented as the scale between 0 and 1. The trained artificial neural network is used to classify six basic or universal emotions (Ekman & Friesen, 2003). Facereader can analyze 20 AUs and 3 affective attitudes (interest, boredom, and confusion).

Face Plus Plus: It only supports an image. The application analyzes and identifies the emotion of detected faces and provides simple and powerful APIs and SDKs to add onto a deep learning-based image analysis recognition technology (Faceplusplus.com, 2019).

Affectiva: It uses cross-platform real-time multi-phase expression recognition toolkit, for research in Emotion AI. Affectiva detects 14 facial actions and 7 different emotional states and has an accuracy of 84.27% and tested for robust databases (Magdin & Prinkler, 2018)

Based on the empirical findings from Face reader, our approach is to experiment and get results from various technologies dealing with facial emotions to better comprehend the emotions in learning.

Motivation

This paper studies the gap between students' learning and their related emotions. Faces broadcast information about not only emotion but also mood, attitude, character, intelligence, attractiveness, age, sex, race and so on (Ekman & Friesen, 2003). Emotion messages conveyed by facial signals is the primary focus of this study. As mentioned earlier, emotions refer to feelings such as fear, anger, happiness, surprise, confusion, etc.; when these feelings occur, they are visible in the face in the form of facial muscle contraction. Thus, emotion can be judged from facial signals (Ekman & Friesen, 2003). The main significance of this study is to determine if there are differences in expressing the emotions according to their traits, though the same circumstances (quiz and movie trailer) are provided and to what degree do facial emotions predict student accomplishment. This paper would help Human Computer Interaction (HCI), Artificial Intelligence (AI) and affective studies understand and respond to the information provided by the face.

Methodology

This section describes the data collection and cleaning to achieve noise-free results. Informed consent was obtained from all the participants for data collection and storage. In this research, the data are collected in the form of video for quiz activity and the movie trailer (Jumanji: Welcome to the jungle), which is then analyzed with the help of application described in background section. Depending upon the applications, expressions and their understandings may vary. Facereader is a commercially trusted and reliable indicator of facial expressions of basic emotions in terms of factors like facial expressions, facial states, AUs, affective attitudes, heart rate and many more with the accuracy of 89% with various databases like Warsaw Set of Emotional Facial Expression Pictures (WSEFEP) and Amsterdam Dynamic Facial Expression Set (ADFES) (Lewinski, den Uyl & Butler, 2014). Thus, more analysis is done from Facereader and most of the results are focused based on Facereader. Facial expressions can be universal or culture-specific. Paul Ekman's six basic facial expressions, including the neutral expression, is used in the paper as it is the pioneering research on the emotion recognition and is the de facto for the emotion categorization (Ekman, 1979). Countless other studies support this categorization and findings which are now considered universal. After the analysis, the result of the relationship between emotion and student learning is discussed. Computer-oriented activities generally generate neutral expressions; hence, to study sparse human emotion, the movie trailer is used. Since movie trailer is comprised of different scenes (action, humor, sad, surprise, fear and so on), we used movie trailer data to study different emotions. Students who are enrolled in one of the master units are requested to participate in the study by recording their faces during the activities. The participation is voluntary and could be withdrawn anytime without an explanation. Among the participated students, 33% of the participants were male and 67% female participated in the research. The participants were mainly international students; China, Hong Kong, Korea, and Nepal, aged between 20-30 years. Only those who were enrolled for the summer course are included in the analysis. The university cloud storage is used to store the video recordings from the participants, expression, affective intensity and AUs are recorded during the evaluation. The result obtained from applications is discontinuous; so, it has been resampled to make it continuous. The result of the analysis is then compared with the participant's grade of the quiz as well as overall performance in the unit.

Experiment and Results

The experiment is performed based on the video sample recorded as mentioned in methodology section. The analysis is broken into three sections: expression, affective attitude, and AU intensity analysis.

Expression Intensity Analysis

The same dataset is used for all the application as mentioned in background section to analyze and compare the effect of participants basic emotions towards the quiz and a movie trailer.

Facereader Results

As the facial expression plays a substantial role in understanding the human nature with a different emotion varied by personality traits, this section compares different facial expressions produced during the academic quiz performance and watching the same movie trailer. The results of seven participants studied is illustrated in Figure 1 depicts an occurrence of different facial expressions. The observation studied for each participant is labelled as obs* in the tables. It is seen that there is a significant effect of neutral and sad emotion for all the participants during the quiz. The effect of surprise and disgust expression is negligible in all the participants. While the neutral expression is dominant in most of the participants, sad emotion is elevated for participant 1 (0.419523) compared to other participants. Among the seven participants, angry emotion for two participants is also preeminent (0.137894 and 0.127455). The amount of scared expression (0.09344) is also recorded high for one of the participants. The difference between the scores of those participants is statistically significant. This suggests that different people have divergent ways of perceiving situations.

These emotion of sad, angry and scared indicates that the participant might have faced difficult questions or unseen questions which participants found tough to answer. Because of the difficult questions, the participants' angry and sad emotions are caused (Macfadden et al., 2005). As stated by Vogel and Schwabe (2016), negative emotional states like stress represented by sad and angry facial expressions bring a positive learning process and memory as well. The stress-induced increment in processing and encoding of learning materials inside the brain results in better performance of memory. Several types of research have been done to investigate it, for instance, in the study seminal findings of rodents, it was concluded that the effects of stress can extend memory retrieval and recall (Schwabe & Wolf, 2014). It was also shown that more robust memory is created which are less vulnerable to false information are learned during stressful situations (Hoscheidt et al., 2014). The neutral emotion could be because the participants are thought to emote to computers and are aware of the video being recorded and therefore, the notable facial emotions are rarely shown. Thus, emotions like fear and surprise are kept away from computers. Ambivalent could be assumed as an impact of happiness, wellbeing, and satisfaction. The result of neutral facial expression could infer the ambivalent state (Pekrun, 2006). Techno-phobic people could also experience anger, fear towards computers (Lisetti & Schiano, 2000). The surprise is a strange situation which refers to inconsistency among prior and new information (Sathik & Jonathan, 2013). Thus, surprise emotion could be because of difficulties or never seen questions at the beginning of the video which is observed in some of the participants. It could also imply that the participant is amazed by the result.

Next, the participants were given to watch the same movie trailer, which was expected to stimulate amusement. The same movie trailer was given to watch so that diverse participants' expressions could be analyzed for the same scenario. As seen in Figure 1 and Table 2, different people had a different way of expressing their emotion. Two of the participants had an almost neutral response to the movie trailer (Observation 2 and Observation 4), as they might have already seen the video clip. Even though the movie clip was intended to cause happy and excite emotions, only three participants expressed happy emotion and only one participant expressed surprise emotion. The movie trailer also had some fright scenes; therefore, the effect of scared disgust emotion is also not negligible, though it is seen in trace amounts in all the participants. Overall, the participant experienced different positive emotions: surprised and happy as well as negative emotions: sad, disgusted and neutral as seen in Figure 1, Table 1 and Table 2.

Face Plus Plus Results

The result obtained from Face Plus Plus insinuates that neutral is the dominant expression for most of the participants (Figure 2 (a)) which resemble the result given by the Facereader. Negative emotions

Figure 1 Emotions expressed in Facereader for quiz and movie trailer

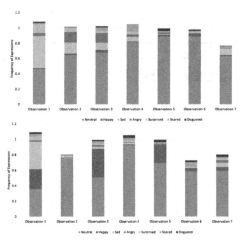

like sadness or anger are prominent in the quiz similar to the result demonstrated in Figure 1, Table 1 and Table 2. Surprise and happy emotion were also seen in some of the participants while most of the participant lacked it.

Table 1. The average score of emotions experienced by Participants during the quiz

	Obs* 1	Obs* 2	Obs* 3	Obs* 4	Obs* 5	Obs* 6	Obs* 7
Neutral	**0.460142**	0.64401	0.675114	0.814685	0.888051	0.885765	0.630617
Happy	0.015147	0.019329	0.036834	0.009262	0.022468	**0.044648**	0.01313
Sad	**0.419523**	0.146618	0.093611	0.060222	0.010500	0.012904	0.085547
Angry	0.040258	**0.137894**	**0.127455**	0.031612	0.022523	0.002928	**0.013527**
Surprised	0.112018	0.047512	0.026278	0.035347	0.0081060	0.001795	0.009835
Scared	0.016089	0.013441	0.046764	**0.09344**	0.0064675	0.012146	0.004928
Disgusted	0.018552	0.006866	0.017373	0.003685	0.0356229	0.018881	0.008384

Table 2. The average score of emotions experienced by Participants during the movie trailer

	Obs* 1	Obs* 2	Obs* 3	Obs* 4	Obs* 5	Obs* 6	Obs* 7
Neutral	0.354262	**0.765769**	0.508787	**0.92506**	0.696066	0.585765	0.593454
Happy	0.263191	0.000843	0.368104	0.009117	0.243504	0.044648	0.047314
Sad	**0.352398**	0.025631	**0.02977**	0.024121	0.007798	0.022904	0.059656
Angry	0.01889	0.010061	0.022267	0.007667	0.008488	0.007927	0.032407
Surprised	0.047041	0.001565	0.013861	0.017265	0.00581	0.006535	0.020653
Scared	0.034302	0.001846	0.032907	0.034811	0.001654	0.03755	0.019629
Disgusted	0.022994	0.000622	0.016405	0.035987	0.032141	0.02365	0.031368

Figure 2 Realtime facial emotion detected by Face Plus Plus

Affectiva Results

The result obtained as demonstrated in Figure 3 and Figure 4 indicates that disgust expression is also prominent over other expressions in addition to neutral, which is quite different from the other two applications. It is seen from the figures that although they have 100% of happy expression recorded, the way of expressing is different, for instance, teeth are visible in figure 3 while it is not visible in figure 4 The other notable emotions are fear and sadness which, however, matches the result from the Facereader and Face Plus Plus results. The possible reason for the variant result could be because of the sensitivity of the mobile phone camera and distance between the camera and data. The result obtained which are disgust, fear and anger could be compared to neutral expressions (Sprengelmeyer et al., 1998).

Affective Attitude Intensity Analysis

Affective attitudes are complex emotional states that differ from basic emotions (Ekman & Friesen, 2003). Affective attitudes are associated with a mixture of AUs activations over time. By examining the participants' responses, a clear distinction of affective intensities like confusion, boredom, and interest is found. Interest is induced from the occurrence of a new incident, intricate and unacquainted and as logical (Silvia 2009). The research also points out that interest is related to physiological activation, behavioral exploration, and novelty. As mentioned in introduction and background, emotions such as confusion represent the positive impact on learning because of increased focus (D'mello et al., 2014). Learning comes from confusion, problems, taking risks and discomfort. Learners need to cope with uncertainty which results in negative emotions. Nevertheless, confusion is somewhat made for concentration, worry, and skepticism (Rozen & Cohen, 2003). In this study, the level of confusion, as well as the interest, is observed high in the quiz for four of the participants, while the rest of the participants had a significant effect of boredom as seen in Figure 5 and Table 3. Regarding the movie trailer, boredom is more prevalent for four of the participants as shown in Figure 5. The effect of confusion was prominent for one of the participants by a score of approximately 0.39. Although the video was intended to cause

Figure 3 Expressions in Affectiva identified as joy   *Figure 4 Expressions in Affectiva identified as fear*

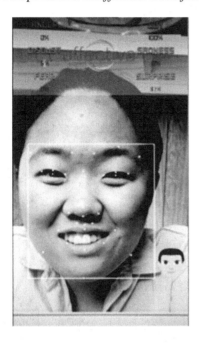   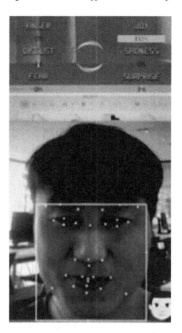

interest, there was a presence of more boredom and confusion with a trace amount of interest to the majority of participants which can be seen in Table 4.

Action Unit Intensity Analysis

Results from two applications: Openface and Facereader suggest that AU for inner brow raiser are high compared to other AUs. In addition to inner brow, outer brow raiser is also prevalent in Facereader. The action of opening the eyes wider and lifting the eyebrows bears positive emotions; whereas, negative emotions are represented by the shrinking eyes with lowering eyebrows and wrinkles on the forehead. The raised eyebrows enlarged eyes and curled lips convey negative emotions (Sathik & Jonathan, 2013). These negative emotions are indications of incomprehension and confusion. In this study, lip corner depressor and chin raiser were also detected, in addition to the eyebrow's movement, which are indications of negative emotions. The AUs (X-axis) and frequencies of five intensities (Y-axis) of AUs of Facereader are shown in Figure 6.

DISCUSSION

The present study investigated the emotions in two activities: learning and watching the movie trailer of students. The primary focus of the study was to discuss the relation between emotion and various activities. The study also found that people reacted differently to the same situation. When the same movie trailer was given to watch to the participants, each of the individuals had disparate emotions expressed. In spite of the fact that the movie trailer was intended to cause happy and surprising emotion, the effect of sadness and disgusted was also noteworthy. As stated by Fox (2002), Wiggins, Trapnell and Phillps

Figure 5 Affective attitudes expressed in Facereader for quiz and movie trailer

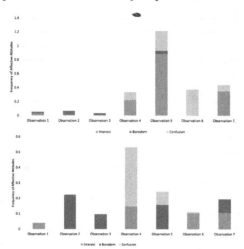

Table 3. The average score of affective attitudes experienced by Participants during the quiz

	Obs*1	Obs* 2	Obs* 3	Obs* 4	Obs* 5	Obs* 6	Obs* 7
Interest	0.030804	0.014294	0.000689	0.223207	**0.885765**	0.004919	**0.35236**
Boredom	0.0244827	0.053182	0.036834	0	0.044648	0	0
Confusion	1.5E-06	0.000689	0	**0.117677**	**0.288904**	**0.375277**	0.092447

Table 4. The average score of affective attitudes experienced by Participants during the movie trailer

	Obs* 1	Obs* 2	Obs* 3	Obs* 4	Obs* 5	Obs* 6	Obs* 7
Interest	0.0414714	0.001175	0.00161	0.147298	0	0.104161	0.107578
Boredom	0	**0.222834**	0.095938	4.98E-05	0.157356	0	0.088138
Confusion	0	8.2E-05	0	0.386008	0.088004	0.008554	0.000173

Figure 6 Notable AUs during the quiz by Facereader

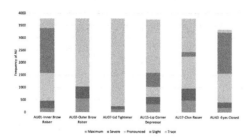

(1988), there is a crucial role of personality traits and way of expressing the emotion. As we noted in the introduction that emotions such as confusion represent the positive impact on learning as a result of increased focus (D'Mello et al., 2014). By collating the result of facial expressions and written responses, it was found that learning process brought negative emotions like neutral, sad and angry. 100% of the participants' outcome was Neutral, 71% was sad, 42% angry, 29% surprised and disgusted, 14% scared and happy. Regarding participants' emotional responses in the movie trailer, we found that participants showed a trace amount of exaggerated facial expressions like anger, surprise, and disgust. The more prominent emotion was neutral. 100% of the participants' movie trailer expression outcome neutral, 71% happy, 42% scared, 29% sad, 14% surprised and disgusted and 0% anger. From the above observation, it is seen that there is a significant effect of participants' neutral, sad and angry emotion throughout the academic learning. The neutral emotion could be because the participant was aware of the video being recorded and therefore the notable facial emotions are rarely shown. As Pekrun (2006) said ambivalent could be assumed as an impact of happiness, wellbeing, and satisfaction, the result of Neutral facial expression could infer the ambivalent state. The second-highest score of sad during the quiz indicated that participant might have faced difficult questions or unseen questions which they found tough to answer. As a result of difficult questions, the participants' consequence of angry emotion which is 42% is caused. Angry is one of the prominent emotional responses to stressors and concentration (Rozin & Cohen, 2003). According to the authors, concentration, worry, stress involves the same movement of facial muscles, such as narrow eyes, bringing together or lowering of eyebrows. Fear and disgust are other notable ones. Similarly, it was confirmed that the lowering of eyebrows (AU4) was more linked to negative emotions like frustration, confusion, and stress, which is also the facial movement linked to anger emotion (Grafsgaard et al., 2013) (Ekman & Friesen, 2003). Here, the magnitude of eyebrows lowering was found to have a positive correlation with the learning. It is observed that there is a substantial effect on participants' neutral, happy, and scared emotion during the movie trailer.

The finding of our study, yet unanticipated is that facial expressions did not correspond to the result mentioned by the participant. This suggests that facial expressions may not be a clear indicator of the emotions as mentioned by (Ekman, 1979). In most of the emotion literature, affective attitudes like confusion, boredom and interested are not included. Still, in our study, it is seen as one of the factors affecting the learning process. The result from the study suggests that, in the context of learning, a higher level of confusion; which may result in frustration may actually produce positive outcomes. Yet, the paper does not encourage negative emotions while in the learning process. Nevertheless, the paper confirms negative emotions like confusion and worry produce a positive outcome in academics.

The facial actions reported as the most common in confusion involve the eyes and eyebrows: narrowing of the eyes, lowering and bringing together of the eyebrows. These actions, often characteristic of frowns, are seen in several facial expressions. These situations may be related to confusion (Ekman & Friesen, 2003). Results from the facial expression study of the movie trailer support the theory of positive emotions such as happiness is directly proportional to the outcome. Positive emotions strengthen inspiration while negative can be disadvantageous to the learning process. Finally, boredom is also prevalently seen in the movie trailer. As the previous researches regarding the boredom emotion say that boredom is induced from the absence of positive and negative emotions (Ekman & Friesen, 2003), the result achieved from the analysis may be because of an already watched movie trailer.

CONCLUSION AND FUTURE WORK

As mentioned in background section, many kinds of research have been done to understand the emotional expressions conveyed by learners. In this research paper, the results of different facial expression recognition applications are studied by recording video of participant's facial expression performing quiz activity and watching a movie trailer. The result shows a variant neutral, sad, surprise and disgust emotions during the quiz. Negative emotions like anger, sadness and affective states like confusion have extensive consequences on students' learning the process. The outcome from the study of the movie trailer is more of a positive facial expression like happy and surprise. The outcome studied are compared to the self-reports and grades of the participants. These reports accompanied the plausible emotions generated by the studied applications. The result of our study might be helpful to enhance the learning setting by comprehending how students react to the learning environment.

To explore the reliability of the different applications used during the analysis, the outcome of the analysis was compared to the final grade and response given by the participants. Among the applications used, the analysis from the Facereader had higher accuracy compared to other applications. The results from other applications were not in resemblance to the actual outcome and the response provided by the student. For instance, Affectiva detected disgust emotion during happy situations in the movie trailer. Regarding the other two applications: Openface and faceplusplus, the former could only analyse AUs and was not able to convert to the respective facial emotions while the later displayed only the results of basic emotions without the underlying facial encoding system. Hence, the results from facereader were more reliable and accurate on the basis of factual data and working.

The personal attributes and personality of the individuals across the time are not studied. It is assumed that the students who studied the unit with a positive attitude likely maintained a high score. The variety of emotions is slightly biased because students are pre-informed about the quiz and the movie trailer is old, so they might have already watched that video. It is also reasonable that the graduate students are already motivated to study as participants are at a higher level of studies.

Future work will focus on developing optimal and efficient emotion recognition in the learning environment with the aid of facial expression. This analysis of emotional states can be used as feedback for the improvement of teaching strategy for the enhancement of the rate of learning. The database for the categorization and classification of different affective states of students in the learning process could be created for the better comprehension of student learning. As the number of participants was low in the research, more participants will be researched in the future. Undeniably, there has been plenty of studies in neuroscience and psychology about the significance of emotional intelligence in rational decision making, performance and adaptation; the aim would be to better comprehend human emotions by building tools with increased awareness of the users' expressions and mental states which would support psychologists to understand more complex processes of human systems with different ethnicity, gender, and ages. In the field of human-computer interaction, the relationship between the interpersonal traits and expressions has received relatively little attention. The goal would be to investigate how people react to different emotions according to their personal traits that might impact how people interact with facial cues. Most of the studies claim that there is a universal facial expression for emotions, very few studies have findings state that facial expressions are not the same for all people (Ekman, 1989). The future work would also be to recognize the facial expression of emotion same for different types of people. Besides, as most of the facial expressions are brief, they are missed by observers as well as computers. These micro-expressions usually reveal the real emotions a person is trying to conceal, such as delight, hope, pride, satisfaction, anger, shame, frustration, and boredom. Automatic recognition procedures need to be studied further.

ACKNOWLEDGMENT

The research involving human subjects were approved by the Social Science Human Research Ethics Committee (HREC) Tasmania Network (reference H0016953). This research was supported by the Basic Science Research Program through the National Research Foundation of Korea (NRF) funded by the Ministry of Education (NRF-2017R1A4A1015559).

REFERENCES

Artino, A. R. Jr. (2010). Online or face-to-face learning? Exploring the personal factors that predict students' choice of instructional format. *The Internet and Higher Education, 13*(4), 272–276. doi:10.1016/j.iheduc.2010.07.005

Baltrušaitis, T., Robinson, P., & Morency, L. P. (2016, March). Openface: an open source facial behavior analysis toolkit. In *Proceedings of the 2016 IEEE Winter Conference on Applications of Computer Vision (WACV)* (pp. 1-10). IEEE. 10.1109/WACV.2016.7477553

Barrett, L. F. (2006). Solving the emotion paradox: Categorization and the experience of emotion. *Personality and Social Psychology Review, 10*(1), 20–46. doi:10.120715327957pspr1001_2 PMID:16430327

Bartlett, M. S., Littlewort, G., Fasel, I., & Movellan, J. R. (2003, June). Real Time Face Detection and Facial Expression Recognition: Development and Applications to Human Computer Interaction. In *Proceedings of the 2003 Conference on computer vision and pattern recognition workshop* (Vol. 5, pp. 53-53). IEEE. 10.1109/CVPRW.2003.10057

Calder, A. J., Ewbank, M., & Passamonti, L. (2011). Personality influences the neural responses to viewing facial expressions of emotion. *Philosophical Transactions of the Royal Society of London. Series B, Biological Sciences, 366*(1571), 1684–1701. doi:10.1098/rstb.2010.0362 PMID:21536554

Chin, S., Lee, C. Y., & Lee, J. (2009). Personal Style and non-negative matrix factorization based exagerative expressions of face. *dimensions, 9*, 10.

Cho, M. H., & Heron, M. L. (2015). Self-regulated learning: The role of motivation, emotion, and use of learning strategies in students' learning experiences in a self-paced online mathematics course. *Distance Education, 36*(1), 80–99. doi:10.1080/01587919.2015.1019963

Clarizia, F., Colace, F., De Santo, M., Lombardi, M., Pascale, F., & Pietrosanto, A. (2018, January). E-learning and sentiment analysis: a case study. In *Proceedings of the 6th International Conference on Information and Education Technology* (pp. 111-118). ACM. 10.1145/3178158.3178181

Cohen, I., Sebe, N., Garg, A., Chen, L. S., & Huang, T. S. (2003). Facial expression recognition from video sequences: Temporal and static modeling. *Computer Vision and Image Understanding, 91*(1-2), 160–187. doi:10.1016/S1077-3142(03)00081-X

Cowen, A. S., & Keltner, D. (2017). Self-report captures 27 distinct categories of emotion bridged by continuous gradients. *Proceedings of the National Academy of Sciences of the United States of America, 114*(38), E7900–E7909. doi:10.1073/pnas.1702247114 PMID:28874542

D'Mello, S., Lehman, B., Pekrun, R., & Graesser, A. (2014). Confusion can be beneficial for learning. *Learning and Instruction, 29*, 153–170. doi:10.1016/j.learninstruc.2012.05.003

Duc, T. N., Huu, T. N., & Tan, L. N. (2009). *Facial Expression Recognition Using AAM Algorithm.* Vietnam: Ho Chi Minh University of Technology.

Ekman, P. (1989). The argument and evidence about universals in facial expressions. In Handbook of social psychophysiology (pp. 143-164). Academic Press.

Ekman, P. (1992). An argument for basic emotions. *Cognition and Emotion, 6*(3-4), 169–200. doi:10.1080/02699939208411068

Ekman, P., & Friesen, W. V. (2003). *Unmasking the face: A guide to recognizing emotions from facial clues.* Ishk.

Essa, I. A., & Pentland, A. P. (1997). Coding, analysis, interpretation, and recognition of facial expressions. *IEEE Transactions on Pattern Analysis and Machine Intelligence, 19*(7), 757–763. doi:10.1109/34.598232

Faceplusplus.com. (2019). *Face++ - Face++ AI Open Platform.* Retrieved from https://www.faceplusplus.com

Fitriani, I., Apriliaswati, R., & Rosnija, E. (2017). Analysis of EFL students' negative emotions towards english learning process in smpn 23 pontianak. *Jurnal Pendidikan dan Pembelajaran, 6*(6).

Fox, E. (2002). Processing emotional facial expressions: The role of anxiety and awareness. *Cognitive, Affective & Behavioral Neuroscience, 2*(1), 52–63. doi:10.3758/CABN.2.1.52 PMID:12452584

Goleman, D. (2006). The socially intelligent. *Educational Leadership, 64*(1), 76–81.

Grafsgaard, J., Wiggins, J. B., Boyer, K. E., Wiebe, E. N., & Lester, J. (2013, July). Automatically recognizing facial expression: Predicting engagement and frustration. In Educational Data Mining 2013. Academic Press.

Hill, M. L., & Craig, K. D. (2002). Detecting deception in pain expressions: The structure of genuine and deceptive facial displays. *Pain, 98*(1-2), 135–144. doi:10.1016/S0304-3959(02)00037-4 PMID:12098625

Hoscheidt, S. M., LaBar, K. S., Ryan, L., Jacobs, W. J., & Nadel, L. (2014). Encoding negative events under stress: High subjective arousal is related to accurate emotional memory despite misinformation exposure. *Neurobiology of Learning and Memory, 112*, 237–247. doi:10.1016/j.nlm.2013.09.008 PMID:24055594

Jaques, P. A., Vicari, R., Pesty, S., & Martin, J. C. (2011, October). Evaluating a cognitive-based affective student model. In *Proceedings of the International Conference on Affective Computing and Intelligent Interaction* (pp. 599-608). Springer. 10.1007/978-3-642-24600-5_63

Jones, A., & Issroff, K. (2005). Learning technologies: Affective and social issues in computer-supported collaborative learning. *Computers & Education, 44*(4), 395–408. doi:10.1016/j.compedu.2004.04.004

Jung, N., Wranke, C., Hamburger, K., & Knauff, M. (2014). How emotions affect logical reasoning: Evidence from experiments with mood-manipulated participants, spider phobics, and people with exam anxiety. *Frontiers in Psychology*, *5*, 570. doi:10.3389/fpsyg.2014.00570 PMID:24959160

Kanade, T., Cohn, J. F., & Tian, Y. (2000, March). Comprehensive database for facial expression analysis. In *Proceedings of the Fourth IEEE International Conference on Automatic Face and Gesture Recognition* (pp. 46-53). IEEE. 10.1109/AFGR.2000.840611

Kapoor, A., Qi, Y., & Picard, R. W. (2003, October). Fully automatic upper facial action recognition. In *Proceedings of the 2003 IEEE International SOI Conference* (pp. 195-202). IEEE. 10.1109/AMFG.2003.1240843

Lazarus, R. S., & Lazarus, B. N. (1994). *Passion and reason: Making sense of our emotions*. USA: Oxford University Press.

LeDoux, J. (2003). The emotional brain, fear, and the amygdala. *Cellular and Molecular Neurobiology*, *23*(4-5), 727–738. doi:10.1023/A:1025048802629 PMID:14514027

Lewinski, P., den Uyl, T. M., & Butler, C. (2014). Automated facial coding: Validation of basic emotions and FACS AUs in FaceReader. *Journal of Neuroscience, Psychology, and Economics*, *7*(4), 227–236. doi:10.1037/npe0000028

Lin, H. C. K., Wu, C. H., & Hsueh, Y. P. (2014). The influence of using affective tutoring system in accounting remedial instruction on learning performance and usability. *Computers in Human Behavior*, *41*, 514–522. doi:10.1016/j.chb.2014.09.052

Lisetti, C. L., & Schiano, D. J. (2000). Automatic facial expression interpretation: Where human-computer interaction, artificial intelligence and cognitive science intersect. *Pragmatics & Cognition*, *8*(1), 185–235. doi:10.1075/pc.8.1.09lis

Littlewort, G. C., Bartlett, M. S., & Lee, K. (2009). Automatic coding of facial expressions displayed during posed and genuine pain. *Image and Vision Computing*, *27*(12), 1797–1803. doi:10.1016/j.imavis.2008.12.010

MacFadden, R. J., Moore, B., & Herie, M. (Eds.). (2005). *Web-based education in the human services: Models, methods, and best practices* (Vol. 23). Psychology Press.

Magdin, M., & Prikler, F. (2018). Real time facial expression recognition using webcam and SDK affectiva. *IJIMAI*, *5*(1), 7–15. doi:10.9781/ijimai.2017.11.002

McDuff, D., Mahmoud, A., Mavadati, M., Amr, M., Turcot, J., & Kaliouby, R. E. (2016, May). AFFDEX SDK: a cross-platform real-time multi-face expression recognition toolkit. In *Proceedings of the 2016 CHI conference extended abstracts on human factors in computing systems* (pp. 3723-3726). ACM. 10.1145/2851581.2890247

Michel, P., & El Kaliouby, R. (2003, November). Real time facial expression recognition in video using support vector machines. In *Proceedings of the 5th international conference on Multimodal interfaces* (pp. 258-264). ACM. 10.1145/958432.958479

Minsky, M. (2007). *The emotion machine: Commonsense thinking, artificial intelligence, and the future of the human mind*. Simon and Schuster.

Okada, K., Steffens, J., Maurer, T., Hong, H., Elagin, E., Neven, H., & von der Malsburg, C. (1998). The Bochum/USC face recognition system and how it fared in the FERET phase III test. In *Face Recognition* (pp. 186–205). Berlin: Springer. doi:10.1007/978-3-642-72201-1_10

Ortony, A., Clore, G. L., & Collins, A. (1988). *The cognitive structure of emotions*. Cambridge Uni. doi:10.1017/CBO9780511571299

Ou, J. (2012). Classification Algorithms Research on Facial Expression Recognition. *Physics Procedia*, *25*, 1241–1244. doi:10.1016/j.phpro.2012.03.227

Pantic, M., & Rothkrantz, L. J. (2000). Automatic analysis of facial expressions: The state of the art. *IEEE Transactions on Pattern Analysis and Machine Intelligence*, *22*(12), 1424–1445. doi:10.1109/34.895976

Pantic, M., & Rothkrantz, L. J. (2003). Toward an affect-sensitive multimodal human-computer interaction. *Proceedings of the IEEE*, *91*(9), 1370–1390. doi:10.1109/JPROC.2003.817122

Pekrun, R. (2006). The control-value theory of achievement emotions: Assumptions, corollaries, and implications for educational research and practice. *Educational Psychology Review*, *18*(4), 315–341. doi:10.100710648-006-9029-9

Pekrun, R., Goetz, T., Frenzel, A. C., Barchfeld, P., & Perry, R. P. (2011). Measuring emotions in students' learning and performance: The Achievement Emotions Questionnaire (AEQ). *Contemporary Educational Psychology*, *36*(1), 36–48. doi:10.1016/j.cedpsych.2010.10.002

Phelps, E. A. (2004). Human emotion and memory: Interactions of the amygdala and hippocampal complex. *Current Opinion in Neurobiology*, *14*(2), 198–202. doi:10.1016/j.conb.2004.03.015 PMID:15082325

Plutchik, R. (2001). The nature of emotions: Human emotions have deep evolutionary roots, a fact that may explain their complexity and provide tools for clinical practice. *American Scientist*, *89*(4), 344–350. doi:10.1511/2001.4.344

Revina, I. M., & Emmanuel, W. S. (2018). A survey on human face expression recognition techniques. *Journal of King Saud University-Computer and Information Sciences*.

Robinson, D. L. (2008). Brain function, emotional experience and personality. *Netherlands Journal of Psychology*, *64*(4), 152–168. doi:10.1007/BF03076418

Rozin, P., & Cohen, A. B. (2003). High frequency of facial expressions corresponding to confusion, concentration, and worry in an analysis of naturally occurring facial expressions of Americans. *Emotion (Washington, D.C.)*, *3*(1), 68–75. doi:10.1037/1528-3542.3.1.68 PMID:12899317

Sathik, M., & Jonathan, S. G. (2013). Effect of facial expressions on student's comprehension recognition in virtual educational environments. *SpringerPlus*, *2*(1), 455. doi:10.1186/2193-1801-2-455 PMID:24130957

Schaefer, E. S., & Plutchik, R. (1966). Interrelationships of emotions, traits, and diagnostic constructs. *Psychological Reports*, *18*(2), 399–410. doi:10.2466/pr0.1966.18.2.399

Schunk, D. H. (1996). Attributions and the Development of Self-Regulatory Competence.

Schwabe, L., & Wolf, O. T. (2014). Timing matters: Temporal dynamics of stress effects on memory retrieval. *Cognitive, Affective & Behavioral Neuroscience, 14*(3), 1041–1048. doi:10.375813415-014-0256-0 PMID:24492994

Shan, C., Gong, S., & McOwan, P. W. (2009). Facial expression recognition based on local binary patterns: A comprehensive study. *Image and Vision Computing, 27*(6), 803–816. doi:10.1016/j.imavis.2008.08.005

Silvia, P. J. (2009). Looking past pleasure: Anger, confusion, disgust, pride, surprise, and other unusual aesthetic emotions. *Psychology of Aesthetics, Creativity, and the Arts, 3*(1), 48–51. doi:10.1037/a0014632

Sprengelmeyer, R., Rausch, M., Eysel, U. T., & Przuntek, H. (1998). Neural structures associated with recognition of facial expressions of basic emotions. *Proceedings of the Royal Society of London. Series B, Biological Sciences, 265*(1409), 1927–1931. doi:10.1098/rspb.1998.0522 PMID:9821359

Uddin, M. Z., Hassan, M. M., Almogren, A., Zuair, M., Fortino, G., & Torresen, J. (2017). A facial expression recognition system using robust face features from depth videos and deep learning. *Computers & Electrical Engineering, 63*, 114–125. doi:10.1016/j.compeleceng.2017.04.019

Vail, P. L. (1994). *Emotion: The on/off switch for learning.* Modern Learning Press.

Viola, P., & Jones, M. (2001). Robust real-time object detection. *International journal of computer vision, 4*(34-47), 4.

Vogel, S., & Schwabe, L. (2016). Learning and memory under stress: implications for the classroom. *NPJ Science of Learning, 1*, 16011.

Vuilleumier, P. (2005). How brains beware: Neural mechanisms of emotional attention. *Trends in Cognitive Sciences, 9*(12), 585–594. doi:10.1016/j.tics.2005.10.011 PMID:16289871

Watson, D., & Clark, L. A. (1992). On traits and temperament: General and specific factors of emotional experience and their relation to the five-factor model. *Journal of Personality, 60*(2), 441–476. doi:10.1111/j.1467-6494.1992.tb00980.x PMID:1635050

Weiner, B. (1985). An attributional theory of achievement motivation and emotion. *Psychological Review, 92*(4), 548–573. doi:10.1037/0033-295X.92.4.548 PMID:3903815

Wiggins, J. S., Trapnell, P., & Phillips, N. (1988). Psychometric and geometric characteristics of the Revised Interpersonal Adjective Scales (IAS-R). *Multivariate Behavioral Research, 23*(4), 517–530. doi:10.120715327906mbr2304_8 PMID:26761163

Zhao, W., Chellappa, R., & Phillips, P. J. (1999). *Subspace linear discriminant analysis for face recognition.* Computer Vision Laboratory, Center for Automation Research, University of Maryland.

Chapter 10
The Fallacies of MDA for Novice Designers:
Overusing Mechanics and Underusing Aesthetics

Kenneth Chen

Drexel University, USA

ABSTRACT

Ever since MDA was publicized by Hunicke, Leblanc, and Zubek in 2004, it has become a building block for game developers and scholars. However, it has also incited several misconceptions that have spread among students and the gaming community. For example, players have overused the term "mechanics," to the point that it is virtually meaningless. On the other side, the terms "dynamics" and "aesthetics" have been comparatively neglected, despite their value. Building upon our experiences of teaching an undergraduate game design course, we argue that these misconceptions stem from the ways that consumers have misinterpreted the MDA framework. Game educators are not necessarily working with experienced designers: they are working with students who are often more passionate about playing games than making them. Thus, game educators need to target this misconception in order to shed light on preconceived biases.

INTRODUCTION

With the rise of game development as a viable career choice, more and more students are entering game design programs for higher education. Decades ago, potential designers were seen as solitary tinkerers, but now, they are players who feel inspired by games and have paths to turn that inspiration into production. However, this introduces a new problem: these players often develop misconceptions about game design based on their experiences from consuming games rather than creating them. On the academic level, instructors need to be aware of these misconceptions and specifically target them.

DOI: 10.4018/978-1-7998-2637-8.ch010

The misconception I want to discuss is the concept of mechanics. This word was popularized by Hunicke et al. in a 2004 workshop paper at GDC, along with dynamics and aesthetics in their foundational MDA model (Hunicke, Leblanc, Zubek, 2004). MDA argues that game design can be understood as the connections among mechanics (data, formulas, rules), dynamics (behaviors, interactions, decisions), and aesthetics (emotions, reactions, feelings). Since its inception, MDA has been appropriated by players and morphed into an amalgamation of different definitions. In its current state, the word "mechanics" is nearly meaningless, and has lost all of its insight into the MDA framework. Despite this, the word is still extremely common not only among players, but also among students who are relying on their previous experience as players.

For instructors in game development, it is not sufficient to teach students how to make games. They also need to unteach students how they thought games were supposed to be made. Many of the students who are entering university-level game design programs are primarily inspired by playing games rather than making games. Even though MDA was originally developed as a means to bridge this divide, I argue that it has unintentionally yet ironically widened it. However, if we become more aware of the problem, we can take steps to fix the situation.

Game Design and MDA

The field of game design, as a specific area of discipline within the larger context of game development, has faced misunderstandings and misinterpretations throughout its history. In the formative days of video games as an industry, there was no distinct role for a "designer." Often, there was only one programmer building everything, from graphics to rulesets. As productions grew larger, those programmers began to work with dedicated artists. Design became an explicit role with the rise of adventure games, where design overlapped with narrative in puzzles and dialogue (Williams, 2017).

Even today, "game design" is often used as a nebulous concept. For example, Drexel University's undergraduate game curriculum is called "Game Design and Production." However, this name is inaccurate, because the curriculum has historically not taught game design. It has focused on art production such as 3D modeling and animations which are then imported into games. In the past, the curriculum was accurately called "Game Art and Production," but it was renamed to "Game Design and Production" with very little change in the actual curriculum. There is still so much confusion among the terms "game design," "game development," and "game programming." In classes, students still struggle to even define a "game" in the first place, unaware that such arguments have already been explored (Juul, 2003) (Aarseth, 2015). Students are often surprised at how difficult game design can be when they first start plumbing its depths, which is why Jesse Schell quickly reassures readers to have the confidence to say "I am a game designer" in his textbook "The Art of Game Design" (Schell, 2008).

Game designers themselves seem to find difficulty in defining their role. Loosely, a game designer creates an experience for the player, but the precise manner in which this is achieved seems to be a black box. Daniel Cook likened this to the process of alchemy: experimenting wildly with different potions and brews, relying on mysticism and voodoo rather than logical scientific rigor (Cook, 2007).

The game design community has informally rallied around the "door problem" as an example of how game design differs from and interacts with other aspects of development (England, 2014). A game designer decides what a door does: how it opens, what the player does, when certain events associated with the door are triggered, and so on. This gives a concrete example of game design in practice, which the field sorely lacks.

Game design is naturally difficult to perceive. In various design-oriented communities, there is an informal mantra that "good design is invisible." Don Norman's seminal book, "The Design of Everyday Things," opens with this concept on its very first page (Norman, 2013):

"Good design is actually a lot harder to notice than poor design, in part because good designs fit our needs so well that the design is invisible, serving us without drawing attention to itself. Bad design, on the other hand, screams out its inadequacies, making itself very noticeable."

People who want to learn game design often end up fixating on bad design, simply because that is what they can actually observe. This has led to the mythos of the "idea guy," a person whose job is to think of ideas for games. For students and prospective designers, games seem filled with problems that could be solved if only there was someone who could think of an idea to fix those problems. "Idea guys" have become so prevalent that the game design industry treats the term as a pejorative descriptor, since the stereotype underplays the amount of effort that game design requires (Mullich, 2015).

The MDA model was created in order to relieve these tensions. Robin Hunicke, Mark LeBlanc, and Robert Zubek wrote the original whitepaper to clarify the process of game design for a whole range of audiences: not only other designers but also academics, researchers, and consumers. In particular, the paper focuses on the ways in which programming intersects with game design, especially with AI programming. An AI is driven by mechanics (code) in order to achieve certain dynamics (actions) which in turn are decided by the target aesthetics (experiences). When one part of the chain is changed, a ripple distorts everything else around it.

Since then, MDA has been widely integrated into the communities surrounding game design, to the point where it is almost regarded as an undisputed fact. It is used in textbooks (Kim, 2015), research foundations (Suh, Wagner, Liu, 2015), and exercises for workshops and game jams (Buttfield-Addison, Manning, Nugent, 2016). Although this paper's goal is to refute MDA, the framework is also an important milestone. MDA's history, popularity, and transformation can give us a greater understanding of not only game design itself, but also the way in which game design is understood outside of its field.

The Gap Between Definitions

The primary word to be discussed is "mechanics." Although the word "mechanics" is only one out of three words in the MDA framework, it has been disproportionately misused. Hunicke et al. defined mechanics as "the particular components of the game, at the level of data representation and algorithms." Modern discourse seems to have left this definition in the past, replacing it with personal interpretations, or worse, nothing.

Player/Consumer Definitions

Some of the more experienced and established members of the industry and academic communities might not be familiar with the ways in which the gaming community has twisted the word "mechanics." Although there isn't exactly a true dictionary definition, players have generally taken the term to mean something along the lines of the expression of skillful play through controlled intentional inputs. This is often paired with a positive connotation.

In some online gaming communities, mechanics are considered as an element of skill, separated from tactics or communication or foresight. Thus, mechanics in this sense become more closely related to reflexes or precision in timing and aiming. This approach to mechanics becomes especially prevalent in eSports communities which toe the line between consumers and creators. For example, in the game *League of Legends*, official casters and commentators discuss the teams and players in the eSports scene, and they will often invoke the term "mechanics" as a positively connoted quality. The following quote refers to a professional player nicknamed Goldenglue, written by an eSports journalist (Lam, 2018).

Goldenglue isn't some kind of prodigy. Neither are you or me. He doesn't have godly mechanics, and he's not likely to ever be a superstar. But what he did do was go to Korea on his own and play 400 games of Solo Queue. What he did do was keep his head down and grind out all of his opportunities even as the community wrote him off as deadweight. - Kien Lam

In this usage, we see that the word "mechanics" is no longer being used as a tool to analyze game design, but rather as a tool to analyze player performance in games. This is not intrinsically problematic: words and meanings naturally change over time. The problem occurs when people take their new definitions and try to use them in their previous contexts. For example, the following quote refers to a player's reaction to the boss monster Kushala Daora in *Monster Hunter World*, from the wiki page:

Technically among the worst designed enemies in the history of video games. Design and execution-wise obviously. Really*****ty and meaningless enemy design; sloppy hitboxes and stagger. This is how you literally ruin a mechanical game and turn it into a cheese/equipment fest. - Anonymous

This quote from a gaming wiki forum illustrates a different, but related use of "mechanics" than the one seen before in the player analysis. Here, the word is used to attempt to describe a fault in the game's design. The concepts of hitbox and stagger call back to the idea of mechanical skill where the player must accurately aim their attacks and time their dodges. We can reinterpret this passage to mean that the stifling of player skill is an indication of poor design. And yet, that is false, because the stifling of player skill is an important part of a game designer's toolbox. Perhaps the designer has decided that this is the point at which players should stop trying to muscle their way through a fight with quick reflexes, but rather take a more deliberate and methodical approach.

Clearly, the player is just frustrated and most likely not actually trying to conduct an insightful design analysis. This is just an exaggerated example of the overreaching mentality that I want to expose. When students emphasize the importance of mechanics as a skill, they fail to recognize the larger design implications behind these decisions. Even though both players and designers are saying "mechanics," they are not communicating the same meaning. If this anonymous player were a college-bound game design major, we as educators cannot teach them the formal definition of a mechanic until we first address their misconception of that definition.

Industry/Academic Definitions

Unfortunately, that may be slightly difficult because the industry has also wavered on the definition of mechanics for quite some time. This reflects a similar struggle across the gaming industry to create standardized terms for discussing design. Greg Costikyan wrote "I Have No Words & I Must Design" in 1999 (Costikyan, 1999), and in some respects we haven't evolved far since then.

"Mechanics" is just another term which has been caught in this crossfire. Some designers have circled around the concept of mechanics, such as the term "ludemes" which also refers to elements of gameplay (Parlett, 2007). Others have simply taken the word itself and ascribed their own meaning to it. Daniel Cook, whose article "The Chemistry of Game Design" was briefly discussed above, used the term mechanics to denote chunks of learned knowledge over the course of a game experience (Cook, 2007).

Mike Stout, formerly from Insomniac Games, wrote "Evaluating Game Mechanics For Depth" which formalizes the player/consumer definitions seen above, with a focus on player skill (Stout, 2010).

When I say 'game mechanic' I'm referring to any major chunk of gameplay in a video game. Using the classic The Legend of Zelda: A Link to the Past as an example, here are a batch of game mechanics: sword combat, block pushing, boomerang throwing, swimming, button-based puzzles, hazard-avoidance, use of specific weapons, etc... - Mike Stout

These are not truly mechanics in Hunicke et al.'s original sense of the term, but are instead extensions of the player's interpretation of mechanics as expressions of skill. This might be the definition that a designer would use if they wanted to answer the question, "How do we improve the Kushala Daora boss fight in *Monster Hunter World*?" However, Hunicke et al.'s use of the word would ask the question, "Should we improve the Kushala Daora boss fight in the first place? Certainly, it may be frustrating, but could that lead to the final experience that we want to create?"

We can see an especially odd use of this term in Martin Sahlin's GDC 2017 talk *"Unravel - Using Empathy as a Game Mechanic"* (Sahlin, 2017):

Unravel turned empathy into a game mechanic. I wanted players to fall in love... Then break their hearts! Then we make it all worth it. - Martin Sahlin

While these are certainly interesting and valuable goals for a game designer, the use of the word "mechanic" just invites even more confusion. Moreover, this is a point at which the term "aesthetics" from the original framework would have been perfectly appropriate. It is doubtful that Sahlin was unaware of the MDA framework. The word "mechanic" just communicated the point better, because the word has expanded to mean practically any part of a game.

When Sahlin uses the term "mechanics" instead of the more appropriate term "aesthetics," he reflects a similar shift in public perception. People are putting less emphasis on dynamics/aesthetics and more emphasis on mechanics, and then expanding the definition of mechanics to include dynamics/aesthetics. The whole purpose of MDA was to separate these three concepts so that designers could intelligently discuss how they interacted with each other. But the direction of modern discourse seems to indicate the opposite effect. If Greg Costikyan had no words to design with, we may end up with only one, which isn't a much better situation.

MISCONCEPTIONS AND MISTAKES

Although MDA is a victim of misinterpretation, I argue that it is also a perpetrator. I do not attack developers/academics/players for misinterpreting MDA out of faith in the framework. Rather, I believe that MDA cannot be treated as a truth of game design, and that we need to consider it along with other approaches. However, we cannot teach students how to deconstruct MDA if they did not understand MDA in the first place.

One of MDA's arguments is that designers experience games from mechanics to dynamics to aesthetics, whereas players experience games from aesthetics to dynamics to mechanics. The terms of mechanics, dynamics, and aesthetics are insightful and valuable. However, I believe that the illustrated progression from one to the next is not only false, but also a reason why the words have become so severely misinterpreted.

Players who want to talk about games in a more intelligent manner will try to use more advanced language, which from this perspective, is the word "mechanics." Anonymous could have written "Kushala

Daora beat me and I felt weak and helpless" and that would be an illustration of game aesthetics, but that's not how humans express frustration. Likewise, designers who want to appeal to players will use the same language that they use, as seen in Sahlin's GDC talk about empathy as a game mechanic.

We have ended up in a situation where we use the word "mechanics" far too often, and the word "aesthetics" far too rarely. It doesn't help that the word "aesthetic" is already commonly used to refer to artistic quality, which causes people to think that "game aesthetics" means "game art." In game design, aesthetics are one of the most important parts, and that we must not neglect the value of this term.

Players: From Mechanics to Aesthetics

Hunicke et al. state that "From the player's perspective, aesthetics set the tone, which is born out in observable dynamics and eventually, operable mechanics."

On the contrary, players need to first learn the mechanics and then the dynamics in order to properly appreciate the aesthetics. For example, let us examine chess. The mechanics of chess cover the core rules and the movement for each piece. The dynamics of chess illustrate different strategies, openings, counterattacks, sieges, and all the other types of events that can happen during play. The aesthetics represent the final experience: not only the joy of winning or the sadness of defeat, but also the cleverness of a tricky move, or the bravery of a reckless assault, or the desperation of an unlikely plan.

But when a player first sits down at the chess board, they cannot experience these emotions directly. They cannot be told to feel clever, or brave, or desperate, or joyful or sad. Those emotions need to be earned through gameplay. If the player does not know the rules, then they are not responsible for their actions. And if they are not responsible for their actions, they will not have an emotional attachment. Imagine a player who loses because they do not know the rules. Such a player will not feel disappointed: they will only feel bored. Thus, it makes more sense to say that players experience games from mechanics to dynamics to aesthetics: the complete opposite of what Hunicke et al. described.

The original players-from-aesthetics-to-mechanics position can be understood as a product of its time. MDA was first publicized in 2004, around the period of the ludology vs narratology debate (Aarseth, 2012). This was a period when mainstream AAA games operated primarily through cutscenes, and the indie market with more experimental narrative formats was still growing. Cutscenes can be interpreted as a shortcut to aesthetics which bypasses mechanics and dynamics (Klevjer, 2002). If the player watches enough cutscenes of their character being powerful, eventually they will feel powerful too despite never touching a button. In this context, it is understandable that Hunicke et al. said that aesthetics set the tone.

But today, long after ludology vs narratology, the field of game development has generally settled into the agreement that players are an important part of their own experience. We are seeing more and more games, AAA games even, which are breaking away from the strict cutscene-gameplay-cutscene-gameplay rhythm. Clint Hocking's work on ludonarrative dissonance (Hocking, 2007) has illustrated the importance of guiding players through mechanics to dynamics to aesthetics, rather than just forcing an aesthetic directly. The IMP framework (Elson, Breuer, Ivory, Quandt, 2014) is better suited to understand how cutscenes and other external forces influence the experience outside of the MDA loop.

Designers: From Aesthetics to Mechanics

Hunicke et al. state that "From the designer's perspective, the mechanics give rise to dynamic system behavior, which in turn leads to particular aesthetic experiences."

This progression from mechanics to dynamics to aesthetics can also be seen as a product of its time, although the argument is weaker. Modern approaches to game design have shown the importance of working backwards from a strong aesthetic goal. Matt Thorson, creator of *Towerfall* and *Celeste* described his process in a GDC talk in 2018 (Thorson, 2018). He starts with the experience that he wants players to have and then iterates his levels until they properly evoke the intended reaction. Each mechanic in *Celeste* such as dashing or climbing up walls is reverse derived from the final aesthetic experience.

However, this was a popular view even around the 2004 period. Tracy Fullerton's book "Game Design Workshop" quickly emphasizes that the first thing a designer should do is set "player experience goals": the type of experience that players will have during the game, or in other words, aesthetics (Fullerton, 2004). This is mirrored in Jesse Schell's "The Art of Game Design," where the very second chapter is titled "The Designer Creates An Experience" (Schell, 2008). Even outside of games, we can see the same kind of division between aesthetics/experiences and mechanics/handicraft in Scott McCloud's "Understanding Comics", where out of six steps, the idea is first and the form is second (McCloud, 1993). All of these established works of knowledge focus on the designer's ability to conceptualize a central vision and lay out the path carefully and deliberately.

Hunicke et al.'s argument, that designers start with mechanics which lead to dynamics which lead to aesthetics, seems haphazard in comparison. Is the designer supposed to throw together a bunch of mechanics with no plan or direction and just hope that it ends up being fun? There are several prominent modern designers who are exploring that exact question. Frank Lantz casts doubt on "the iconic image of the designer - smart, confident, sophisticated, stylish, informed" in his post "Against Design", and argues that perhaps we should say that games are discovered or composed rather than designed (Lantz, 2015).

This perspective exists because it is built on top of the previous one. There cannot be an "Against Design" if there is not a "Design" in the first place. Once we realize the limits of our ability to build aesthetics, we can come back to the mechanics-first approach. But starting with mechanics from the very beginning is hardly designing: it is only throwing a game together and hoping it sticks (Pulsipher, 2016).

Naturally, every game production has a different process: some start with aesthetics, some start with mechanics, some with a different approach altogether. However, when Hunicke et al. propose that designers start with mechanics, they don't acknowledge this full range of possibilities. They would not have been able to do so in a short workshop paper, but unfortunately that short workshop paper seems to have developed more traction than expected.

PEDAGOGICAL PROBLEMS

Through these twists and turns, this focus on mechanics has led to several subtle mindsets around game design which are harmful to the learning process. These are only a few mindsets that I have identified, and they are caused by a multitude of factors, not just MDA. However, we can see their effects propagating throughout the game design community, even into academia.

Lack of Resonance

From a philosophical perspective, artwork mirrors design in the way that it focuses on delivering a core experience. This is echoed in fields from poetry (Poe, 1846) to novels (Forster, 1985) to games, as discussed previously. When prospective designers focus on mechanics rather than aesthetics, they lose sight of this goal, causing their works to suffer from a lack of resonance.

We can see an explicit example of this effect in the *Super Mario Maker* games, which allow players to create 2D sidescrolling levels using characters, obstacles, and environments from the *Mario* series. These games are spaces for players to apply their knowledge of game design and create new, interesting levels using the same tools that Nintendo's designers use. However, *Super Mario Maker* games are infamous for being filled with low-quality levels (Thomson, 2015). In this case, quality does not refer to the overall level of production and polish, but rather the degree to which the design resonates with the player experience.

There are many forms of low-quality design. Some authors will create levels that are empty except for rows of coins that spell out their name. Others will create "automatic levels" which are elaborate Rube Goldberg machines that propel Mario to the finish through no player input whatsoever. Although these levels can become popular through spectacle and complexity, they are still a far cry from the types of experiences that made the mainline *Mario* games famous. These types of levels exist to make the designer feel clever about themselves, rather than the player.

Kaizo-style levels are a form of low-quality design that represents the problems of a lack of resonance, and the mechanics-first perspective. These levels are characterized by absurd difficulty, with hidden traps and unexpected deaths which are intended to frustrate the player (Newman, 2018). It is no wonder that Kaizo-style design doesn't exist in professional game design, and that it emerged from ROM hacking and pranks played on friends. Fullerton describes the role of a game designer as "an advocate for the player," (Fullerton, 2004) which is practically the complete opposite of a Kaizo-style level.

For this discussion, it is important to note that Kaizo-style levels are built using an extremely wide array of available mechanics. The solution typically involves some kind of unexpected interaction, including glitches, which involves multiple different mechanics. Since these interactions are so obscure, these levels are extremely difficult not only to beat, but to figure out how to beat.

This style of design is nearly the complete opposite of Nintendo's style, where each level revolves around the exploration of a small set of mechanics, gradually building up on top of each other to form a smooth difficulty curve. In an interview, the director Koichi Hayashida explained how he used four-panel comic structures as an inspiration for *Super Mario 3D Land* levels (Nutt, 2012). Each level introduces a new mechanic, ramps up the difficulty slightly, adds an unexpected twist, then finishes with a display of mastery. Even though Hayashida named this specific structure, other game designers have been using similar models of progression across all sorts of genres or styles.

There is a reasonable argument that a person who creates Kaizo-style levels is not practicing game design. While it is certainly better to create Kaizo-style levels than to create nothing at all, the mechanics-driven approach leads to a dead end because of a lack of resonance. Outside of *Super Mario Maker*, this same sentiment can be seen in the myth of the game design document, where aspiring designers believe that if they can fill out a form describing all of the aspects of their game, then they will be well on their way towards a finished product. Jesse Schell explicitly attacks this mentality (2008), arguing that design is a continuous process and must remain fluid. A list of mechanics neglects the aesthetic vision, and adhering to such a document can be dangerous.

Trophy Productions

I use the term "trophy productions" to temporarily discuss the production of games (or other forms of entertainment) where the process of creation is treated with greater regard than the actual result. This leads to a project which is seen much like a trophy: interesting to look at and discuss from a distance, but not necessarily usable as a tangible product.

This problem has plagued the field of interactive emergent narrative, which is an academic discipline which seeks to use games to create stories alongside the player rather than thrusting the player into a prewritten story. Interactive emergent narratives rely heavily on AI, not only for depicting individual characters but also for acting in a managerial/directorial role. These interactions closely follow the path which is charted in the MDA paper's treatment of AI: a designer cannot actually cause an AI to execute any specific behavior, but must work on the level of code and rules.

Ryan, Mateas, and Wardrip-Fruin feared that the field was judging its successes by the craftsmanship of successful simulations, rather than the interactive experience of a human player (Ryan et al, 2015). As a concrete example, we can see this situation in *Façade*, one of the earliest successes of interactive emergent narrative (Mateas & Stern, 2005). *Façade* is a game in which the player is a dinner guest at a dysfunctional couple's apartment, and may intervene as much or as little as they wish in order to defuse a routine argument. The simulation is built in order to dynamically follow dramatic narrative structures, pulling the player into new story beats.

Technically, *Façade* fulfills the fantasy of interactive emergent narrative, which is why we still consider it to be the foremost example of the field even despite its age. However, the original authors quickly realized that the actual experience of playing *Façade* was far different from what they intended. Players should have felt like a heartbroken friend, sad to see a couple breaking apart in front of them and desperate to repair their relationship. If the player places themselves in such a role, they can experience *Façade* in its fully realized glory.

But most players did not do this (El-Nasr, Milam, Maygoli, 2013). They struggled to figure out the system, or they treated the conversation like a puzzle game, or they pushed the boundaries of absurdist humor. In the end, *Façade* is more of a beneficial project for the field rather than an enjoyable playable product.

Although *Façade* does not map neatly into the MDA framework, it represents a high-level focus on systems over experiences. Coming back to game design education, we can see a similar focus. Students may build a game not for the sake of producing a good experience, but rather just to demonstrate that they are capable of working with the technology. While this is a good way to show skills in programming or art, design is naturally difficult to perceive, as discussed in a previous section.

Overemphasis on Skill

Game scholars have dedicated great amounts of research to identifying types of fun, and Lazzaro's eight kinds of fun are even a central part of the original MDA paper. However, the current consumer dialogue around game mechanics places a greater focus on fun through skillful play, even if it comes at the cost of fun through other means. While fun from skillful play is a useful tool in a designer's kit, it is only one aspect of games, and a designer must be able to wield many.

We can observe a prominent and recent example of this in the *Fortnite: Battle Royale* community. *Fortnite: BR* is a multiplayer shooter game where players collect resources such as ammunition or crafting components, which let them fight more effectively. Some time after the game's launch, the developers added "siphon," a mechanic which automatically transfers a player's materials to their killer if they are defeated. This can be said to have led to the dynamic of snowballing, where stronger players are able to maintain their lead by continuing to kill, rather than having to stop and lose time to collect resources after every skirmish. The aesthetic is that better players (those who are better at the "mechanics" of aiming, shooting, and building) can enjoy rapid sequences of action, whereas worse players spend comparatively long periods of time on resource gathering.

Siphon was removed from the game later, which caused a public opinion backlash in the *Fortnite: BR* community (spread across Twitter, Reddit, and other forums). Experienced players enjoyed siphon because it rewarded them for skillful play, whereas inexperienced players typically didn't self-select themselves into these communities in the first place. This is exemplified in a tweet by Daequan Loco, a professional *Fortnite: BR* player under the Team Solo Mid organization (Loco, 2019):

One day game developers will realize that you can't protect noobs from getting bopped. You add ranked, people will smurf. You separate casual and ranked, ppl will just go bot farm in casuals. You try to change game mechanics to save them, you ruin your game. History doesn't lie! - Daequan Loco

Daequan speaks with slang, which I will explain briefly. "Noobs" is a short way to say "newbies," which in turn is a short way to say "new player." This comes with a connotation of low skill, so "noobs" has actually evolved to be an insult rather than an objective statement: even highly experienced players can be called noobs if they make a blunder. "Bopped" refers to being defeated, especially in a humiliating one-sided manner. A player who is "smurfing" has manipulated the system in order to play against opponents at a lower skill level, which often results in a one-sided victory, or in other terms, a Smurf bopping noob. The terms "ranked," "casual," and "bot farm" are not as closely related to the topic at hand.

This example demonstrates a player/consumer attempting to make statements from a designer/creator perspective, but using the term "game mechanics" in the wrong context. On a pedantic level, the designers of *Fortnite: BR* were not necessarily trying to change game mechanics: they were trying to change the game aesthetics of the strong trampling the weak, which resulted in a need to change game dynamics, which resulted in a need to change game mechanics. Although this is only a minor misunderstanding, it indicates a misguided focus.

However, putting that aside, this tweet is still problematic because it is blatantly incorrect that "protecting noobs from getting bopped" will "ruin your game." Game designers devote great amounts of effort into ensuring that the path of mastery follows a smooth curve. This is the core concept of psychological flow (Chen, 2006) and the reason why learning is fun (Koster, 2003). Players are supposed to get better over time, the challenge is supposed to match their skill level, if it's too hard they experience anxiety, if it's too easy they experience boredom. The player has used the concept of mechanics in terms of skill in order to discuss the concept of mechanics in terms of design. Since these two concepts are different, the player fails to realize some of the most basic principles of game design.

There are plenty of historical examples of games that have found success by "protecting noobs from getting bopped." Virtually every game that has a reasonably-designed difficulty curve can be argued to have used such an approach. *Fortnite: BR* itself has not been ruined in the months since removing siphon. Many multiplayer games develop advanced matchmaking algorithms to keep new players separated from experienced ones (Menke, 2017). In player-vs-player modes for the *Gears of War* games, new players are given a damage boost to put them on the same level as more experienced ones, and combat is fast enough that people typically don't notice (Scheurle, 2018). By formal and informal standards, none of these games can be said to have been ruined by introducing an easing curve for new players.

A new player may be unskilled, but they still deserve to have fun and enjoy the game's experience. Professional players like Daequan are primarily concerned with winning, and winning is often conflated with entertainment. Skill and entertainment do not need to be linearly related, and entertainment is not a zero-sum resource. But if we swap the words around, skill and winning are linearly related, and winning is a zero-sum resource. The fallacy is that winning and entertainment should be treated as separate concepts, but the word "mechanics" is not sufficient by itself to reveal those differences.

PEDAGOGICAL SOLUTIONS

As teachers, being aware of the problem is the first step towards fixing it. MDA has spread various misconceptions about game design, whether through unfortunate misinterpretations or faulty logic in the paper itself. Instead of teaching MDA as an unquestioned part of a course syllabus, we can use it as a stepping stone to illustrate the divide between players and designers.

Reinforcing MDA Through Programming

Game design curriculums often neglect the importance of code, such as how Drexel renamed the Game Art major to Game Design. Full Sail University also keeps game art and game design closely related. However, MDA shows us a different perspective, because in the strictest sense, mechanics are code. When a designer is able to program, they are able to see the ramifications of decisions that they never would have considered. A single change in a mechanic can cause a butterfly effect to drastically change the player's experience.

For example, imagine that a student is designing some kind of card game, along the lines of *Hearthstone* or *Magic: The Gathering*. These types of games are filled with specific rules and orders to resolve certain interactions. One card may say "at the beginning of your next turn, gain five health" and the enemy may play a card that says, "at the beginning of your opponent's next turn, they lose five health." Which card resolves first, and why? If the player in question has less than five health at the time, this could be a win-or-lose situation.

Either way could completely change a player's tactics, which would in turn change that player's emotional experience. If the designer was not experienced in programming, they might not have realized that this was a decision between mechanics. They might have written these card effects in a document and handed it off to their programmer, who doesn't realize the ramifications of prioritizing one over the other. A designer with no programming knowledge does not recognize the choice, and a programmer with no design knowledge does not care about the choice. This is why MDA was originally written with a specific focus on AI developers coming from a programming background.

Other companies are already moving in directions that integrate game design and programming. Riot Games, creator of *League of Legends*, develops champions with teams called DNA (design, narrative, art) where the designer fulfills the roles of a programmer (Riot, 2017). Brian Schwab also argues for a greater degree of interaction between designers and programmers, and suggests the creation of a "technical designer" role to properly bridge the gap (Schwab, 2014). Colleges and universities can keep up by putting prospective game designers through a deeper programming background, with emphasis on interactivity through quick projects like game jams.

Emphasizing Emerging Gameplay/Design

An instructor could also explore the design-oriented questions from section 4.2 and present both perspectives: aesthetics-first, or mechanics-first. The mechanics-first approach could be discussed using the term "emergence," which has unique implications from a programming background. Emergence in programming refers to the ability for a system to create unintended behaviors based on a core set of rules. Conway's Game of Life is an iconic example of emergence (Gardner, 1970), but in video games specifically we can see the same patterns in *Middle Earth: Shadow of War*'s Nemesis System (Hoge, 2018).

Players often discuss emergent gameplay in titles like *Deus Ex* which allow them to make a wide variety of decisions. However, just like how emergent gameplay exists based on the rules of the game, we could also create emergent game design based on the rules of the class. Once students become familiar with programming, they can start to experiment with emergent game design. This could possibly be some kind of form of Exquisite Corpse, or perhaps some kind of platformer where every student is given a base template and an assignment to create some kind of obstacle. Then, the students experiment with various combinations of each other's obstacles to create levels in a collaborative manner. An exercise like this could highlight the importance of a guiding vision and its double-edged blade: on one hand it creates more cohesion, but on the other hand, sometimes some reckless experimentation will reveal a fun combination that no one would have thought to design intentionally.

Alternatives to MDA

Finally, MDA is not the only framework for understanding games. I briefly discussed Elson's IMP framework, but it is more about constructing social relationships rather than game design specifically. One exercise could ask students to develop their own synonyms for MDA to avoid the loaded definitions of "mechanics" and "aesthetics". A professor at SAE Institute renamed it to "elements, behaviors, experiences" in order to help their students understand the framework better.

One notable alternative to MDA is SSM, developed by Thomas Grip of Frictional Games (Grip, 2017). SSM stands for system, story, and mental model. The system encompasses mechanics and dynamics for gameplay, and the story encompasses the same for narrative (a mechanical in narrative is like a character, whereas a dynamic in narrative is a relationship between characters). However, the most important part is the mental model, which is a concept borrowed from psychology. Mental models represent the ways in which people make sense of the world around them and develop their own logic for why things happen. It is like the experience of an aesthetic, but it leans more heavily towards the player's perception rather than the game's actual rules. A mental model can be different from reality, and it is especially important for a game designer to recognize this and use it to their advantage.

The story is that Thomas Grip discovered this effect while working on *Amnesia: The Dark Descent*. When he was working on the sanity system, he tried various game mechanics in order to create specific dynamics, but the gameplay was either easily manipulated or unnoticeable. Eventually, he just removed all challenge from the sanity system and left it only as a visual effect. However, players did not realize this and played through the game believing that sanity would affect them, which pushed them towards interesting gameplay without having an actual mechanic driving this process. Mental models can describe behaviors that couldn't be described by the MDA framework.

CONCLUSION

MDA has been one of the most prominent game frameworks in not only industry and academia, but also player communities. We need to properly assess the impact of MDA in order to teach the next generation of game designers how to use it more effectively. In programming, we call this effect a "tech debt," when a whole system is built on top of a piece of outdated legacy code. Removing or refactoring that code could end up sending the whole system crashing down, but then you would be able to rebuild it stronger than before. The burden of handling this tech debt should fall to university teachers, who are in the best position to pinpoint this problem and turn it into a learning opportunity. MDA should be taught as one type of approach, rather than as an incontrovertible truth. Educators can use other models such as SSM (Grip, 2017) or DDE (Walk, 2017) as juxtapositions to better understand MDA and its relation to game design.

This research received no specific grant from any funding agency in the public, commercial, or not-for-profit sectors.

REFERENCES

Aarseth, E. (2012, May). A narrative theory of games. In *Proceedings of the International Conference on the Foundations of Digital Games* (pp. 129-133). ACM.

Aarseth, E., & Calleja, G. (2015, June). The Word Game: The ontology of an undefinable object. In FDG.

Buttfield-Addison, P., Manning, J., & Nugent, T. (2016, March). A better recipe for game jams: using the Mechanics Dynamics Aesthetics framework for planning. In *Proceedings of the International Conference on Game Jams, Hackathons, and Game Creation Events* (pp. 30-33). ACM. 10.1145/2897167.2897183

Chen, J. (2006). *Flow in games* (Doctoral dissertation, University of Southern California).

Cook, D. (2007). *The chemistry of game design*. Gamasutra. Retrieved from https://www.gamasutra.com/view/feature/129948/the_chemistry_of_game_design.php

Costikyan, G. (2005). I Have No Words & I Must Design. *The game design reader: A rules of play anthology*, 24.

El-Nasr, M. S., Milam, D., & Maygoli, T. (2013). Experiencing interactive narrative: A qualitative analysis of Façade. *Entertainment Computing*, 4(1), 39–52. doi:10.1016/j.entcom.2012.09.004

Elson, M., Breuer, J., Ivory, J. D., & Quandt, T. (2014). More than stories with buttons: Narrative, mechanics, and context as determinants of player experience in digital games. *Journal of Communication*, 64(3), 521–542. doi:10.1111/jcom.12096

England, L. (2014). *The door problem*. Retrieved from http://www.lizengland.com/blog/2014/04/the-door-problem/

Forster, E. M. (1985). *Aspects of the Novel* (Vol. 19). Houghton Mifflin Harcourt.

Fullerton, T. (2018). *Game design workshop: a playcentric approach to creating innovative games*. AK Peters/CRC Press.

Gardener, M. (1970). MATHEMATICAL GAMES: The fantastic combinations of John Conway's new solitaire game" life. *Scientific American*, *223*, 120–123. doi:10.1038cientificamerican1070-120

Grip, T. (2017). *The SSM framework of game design*. Frictional Games. Retrieved from https://frictionalgames.blogspot.com/2017/05/the-ssm-framework-of-game-design.html

Hocking, C. (2007). *Ludonarrative dissonance in Bioshock*. Typepad. Retrieved from https://clicknothing.typepad.com/click_nothing/2007/10/ludonarrative-d.html

Hoge, C. (2018). *Helping players hate (or love) their nemesis* [YouTube Video]. Retrieved from https://www.youtube.com/watch?v=p3ShGfJkLcU

Hunicke, R., LeBlanc, M., & Zubek, R. (2004, July). MDA: A formal approach to game design and game research. In *Proceedings of the AAAI Workshop on Challenges in Game AI* (Vol. 4, No. 1, p. 1722).

Juul, J. (2018). The game, the player, the world: Looking for a heart of gameness. *PLURAIS-Revista Multidisciplinar, 1*(2).

Kim, B. (2015). *Understanding gamification*. ALA TechSource.

Klevjer, R. (2002, June). In Defense of Cutscenes. In *CGDC Conf*. Academic Press.

Koster, R. (2003). *Theory of fun for game design*. O'Reilly Media, Inc.

Lam, K. (2018). *Vault boy's emergence: Goldenblue's big break*. League of Legends. Retrieved from https://nexus.leagueoflegends.com/en-us/2018/09/vault-boys-emergence-goldenglues-big-break/

Lantz, F. (2015). *Against design*. Game Design Advance. Retrieved from http://gamedesignadvance.com/?p=2930cpage=1

Mateas, M., & Stern, A. (2005, June). *Structuring Content in the Façade Interactive Drama Architecture*. AIIDE.

McCloud, S. (1993). *Understanding comics: the invisible art*. Tundra Publishing.

Menke, J. (2017). *Skill, Matchmaking, and Ranking Systems Design* [YouTube video]. Retrieved from https://www.youtube.com/watch?v=-pglxege-gU

Mullich, D. (2015). *Sorry, there is no "idea guy" position in the game industry*. Retrieved from https://davidmullich.com/2015/11/23/sorry-there-is-no-idea-guy-position-in-the-game-industry/

Newman, J. (2018). Kaizo Mario Maker: ROM hacking, abusive game design and Nintendo's Super Mario Maker. *Convergence*, *24*(4), 339–356. doi:10.1177/1354856516677540

Norman, D. (2013). *The design of everyday things: revised and expanded edition*. Basic Books.

Nutt, C., & Hayashida, K. (2012). The structure of fun: learning from Super Mario 3D Land's director. *Gamasutra*. Retrieved from http://www.gamasutra.com/view/feature/168460/the_structure_of_fun_learning_.php

Parlett, D. (2017). What's a ludeme? Game & Puzzle Design, 2(2), 81.

Poe, E. A. (1846). The philosophy of composition.

Pulsipher, L. (2016). *Are you designing a game, or throwing one together? You can't design a game as though you were playing a video game.* Gamasutra. Retrieved from https://www.gamasutra.com/blogs/ LewisPulsipher/20161214/287544/Are_you_designing_a_game_or_throwing_one_together_You_cant_ design_a_game_as_though_you_were_playing_a_video_game.php

Riot Games. (2017). *Creative collaboration: making League of Legends champions* [YouTube video]. Retrieved from https://www.youtube.com/watch?v=j-k3TbFwMgI

Ryan, J. O., Mateas, M., & Wardrip-Fruin, N. (2015, November). Open design challenges for interactive emergent narrative. In *Proceedings of the International Conference on Interactive Digital Storytelling* (pp. 14-26). Springer. 10.1007/978-3-319-27036-4_2

Sahlin, M. (2017). *Unravel - using empathy as a game mechanic.* GDC Vault. Retrieved from https:// www.gdcvault.com/play/1024661/-Unravel-Using-Empathy-as

Schell, J. (2008). *The art of game design: A book of lenses.* CRC Press. doi:10.1201/9780080919171

Scheurle, J. (2018). *Good game design is like a magic trick* [YouTube video]. Retrieved from https:// www.youtube.com/watch?v=2YdJa7v99wM

Schwab, B. (2014). *Designers are from Saturn, programmers are from Uranus* [YouTube video]. Retrieved from https://www.youtube.com/watch?v=6b-o_-Xb50E

Suh, A., Wagner, C., & Liu, L. (2015, January). The effects of game dynamics on user engagement in gamified systems. In *Proceedings of the 2015 48th Hawaii International Conference on System Sciences* (pp. 672-681). IEEE. 10.1109/HICSS.2015.87

Thomsen, M. (2015). Super Mario Maker is an engine for circulating horrible new Mario levels. *The Washington Post.*

Thorson, M. (2018). *Level design workshop: Designing Celeste* [YouTube video]. Retrieved from https:// www.youtube.com/watch?v=4RlpMhBKNr0

TSM_Daequan. (2019, March 29). One day game developers will realize that you can't protect noobs from getting bopped. You add ranked, people will smurf. You separate casual and ranked, ppl will just go bot farm in casuals. You try to change game mechanics to save them, you ruin your game. 🐧♂️History doesn't lie! [Tweet]. Retrieved from https://twitter.com/tsm_daequan/status/1111744197294346240?lang=en

Walk, W., Görlich, D., & Barrett, M. (2017). Design, Dynamics, Experience (DDE): an advancement of the MDA framework for game design. In *Game Dynamics* (pp. 27–45). Cham: Springer. doi:10.1007/978- 3-319-53088-8_3

Williams, A. (2017). *History of digital games: Developments in art, design and interaction.* Routledge. doi:10.1201/9781315715377

ADDITIONAL READING

De Koven, B. (2013). *The well-played game: A player's philosophy*. MIT Press. doi:10.7551/mitpress/9722.001.0001

Juul, J. (2011). *Half-real: Video games between real rules and fictional worlds*. MIT Press.

Sellers, M. (2017). *Advanced Game Design: A Systems Approach*. Addison-Wesley Professional.

Sylvester, T. (2013). *Designing games: A guide to engineering experiences*. O'Reilly Media, Inc.

KEY TERMS AND DEFINITIONS

AI: Artificial intelligence, a system which makes decisions independently based on its directed goals. Game AIs can focus on problem solving or user experience: in chess, a problem-solving AI will find the most optimal move, whereas a user experience AI will make moves that are fun and interesting to play against.

Aesthetics: The experiences and emotions which emerge out of dynamics.

Dynamics: The behaviors and tactics which emerge out of mechanics.

Emergence: The capacity for a system to produce outputs which were unexpected by the original designers.

Game Design: The process of ensuring that a game has a unified core theme, reinforces that theme throughout the act of playing, and delivers that theme intact to the player.

Game Development: The process of creating a game, including design, art, programming, and production, but typically not including marketing, PR, and manufacturing.

Fun: The subjective experience of enjoyment, often redefined by each individual designer. Notably, Raph Koster defines fun as learning, and the MDA paper introduces a taxonomy (including but not limited to sensation, fantasy, narrative, challenge, fellowship, discovery, expression, submission).

Mechanics: The rules and pieces of a game.

Chapter 11
Model–Based Interview Method Selection Approach in Participatory Design

Arsineh Boodaghian Asl
https://orcid.org/0000-0002-1985-3690
Karlstad University, Sweden

Michel Gokan Khan
Karlstad University, Sweden

ABSTRACT

Participatory design is a technique which is being used by system designers to involve the end users and product owners throughout the design process. Even though utilizing this approach brings customers to the design process, implementing it requires a budget, a place, time, and other resources. This chapter demonstrates a model-based approach to facilitate the selection of interviews for each design phase such as listing elements for the interface, choosing location for components, making decision for the general look of the component, finally making the component interactable. Interface designers can use the model to choose different type of interview method for different design phases such as interface components, sketching, lo-fi prototyping and hi-fi prototyping, according to their resources. The research focus is on four different participatory design interview method, which are GUI-ii face-to-face, GUI-ii screen-sharing, GUI-ii Ozlab, and traditional face-to-face interview.

INTRODUCTION

A user-friendly designed interface is essential for engaging more users to use applications and software, especially if there are various applications serving the same goal. Most people interact with different applications in their daily life, and it is a reasonable assumption that they prefer the applications which are easiest to interact with. Therefore, having a graphical user interface to satisfy users' needs is a requirement. One of the critical aspects of designing interfaces is to find out what are the most vital end-users'

DOI: 10.4018/978-1-7998-2637-8.ch011

needs and their knowledge of using a system. There are multiple cases where it is essential to gather information from the end-user during the designing process. To obtain information from the end-users, as co-designers in a co-design environment, designers combine participatory design techniques (Simonsen and Robertson, 2013; Spinuzzi, 2005) with interview methods. The process includes involving the users or owners of the products in some or all phases of the design.

There are different participatory design interview methods, one of the most basic ones is the traditional face-to-face interview, where the designer meets the co-designer in person, and use paper and pencil to gather information according to the design phase prerequisites. This interview method is not the most efficient way to have everything on paper, it may slow down the process of gathering information, mislead the test participant or even make them tired (Heintz et al., 2015). There are other interview methods developed such as think-aloud (Nielsen et al., 2002), post-task, and survey-based (Baauw et al., 2004) interviews. In this chapter some more recent interview methods are presented, and they are analyzed and compared with each other and with traditional Face-to-Face interview, to demonstrate why choosing the most efficient interview method is beneficial in participatory design.

GUI interaction interviews (GUI-ii) (Pettersson et al., 2017) is a new interview method where interviewees are creating user interfaces and interact with them. It is interesting to evaluate its benefits under different conditions, to find out its limitations, advantages, and disadvantages. There are various approaches for using the GUI-ii interview method, such as face-to-face interview, interviewing via screen-sharing and interviewing using the *Ozlab* web application (Pettersson and Siponen, 2002; Pettersson and Wik, 2015) which provides Wizard-of-Oz (Steinfeld et al., 2009) (Schlögl et al., 2015) functionalities to enhance the interactive experience (Pettersson et al., 2018).

Majority of designers go through different interview methods to get the necessary information from the users according to their needs, whether it is remote, face-to-face or combination of interview methods. Nonetheless, wrong selection of interview method may lead to inaccurate data collection, and eventually designers will encounter with an ineffective and impractical user interface, or an unfinishable product.

To assist designers choosing the most efficient interview method for each or every design phase of participatory design procedure, a mathematical model has been developed. This model will help and facilitate designers to list their parameters such as resources, design phases and interview methods and determine how to continue with test participants. This chapter provides a model-based approach for designers to improve their collaboration with end users by utilizing resources, phases and interview methods as input parameters. The output parameter returns different values for each interview method, the highest value determines if the interview method is suitable for the design phase.

BACKGROUND

Related Works

In this section, some of the research works which has been conducted previously, will be briefly described. These researches are related to participatory design techniques, interview methods, and their analysis criteria in the field of human-computer interaction. There are researchers who perform an empirical study on interview methods which are slightly different from the ones covered in this chapter. Their research was mostly focused on gathering information before starting the design phase (i.e. listing necessary requirements), the information gathering phase (i.e. who are the end users), or after finishing the design (i.e. usability test), in the usability test phase. None of them, in fact, cover the importance of choosing a suitable interview method in a co-design environment, specifically from the human-computer interaction (HCI) perspective. Furthermore, so far there is no mathematical model designed to facilitate the utility of interview method and highlight the significant importance of each method from the model perspective.

Dimond et al. (2012) did a comparison test on instant messaging, e-mail and phone interviewing, to be able to find out that different methods have different effects; the authors had used two parameters for analyzing the result: first word count and secondly the quality code. They did not take the difficulty level of using the method into consideration, which can affect the willingness to provide information, and thus on the quality of the test. In this chapter willingness to provide information is an important factor and is one of the test parameters. Therefore, its impacts are also discussed and presented.

Baauw and Markopoulous (2004) research focus was to run and analyze a usability test on children. The Results showed that girls tend to communicate more and ask question while encountering problems during the usability test comparing to boys. However, all the children in this research were used for usability testing, and they were not involved to be co-designers in any design phase.

Brush et al. (2004) also conducted a similar comparison analysis. The authors listed five different issues of usability testing and they did a survey on users who participated to remote and local tests and asked about their difficulties during the test. Moreover, they also recorded participants' voices and their interaction with the screen co-design sessions. Even though the tools and techniques of their tests are very useful, the test was concentrated on the usability test and not on participatory design.

In another empirical study by Gratch et al. (2014), four different interview methods, namely face-to-face, teleconference, Wizard-of-Oz, and automated character (Ellie, a virtual animated character), has been compared and discussed. At the first two interview methods, the conductor was a human being, on the third and fourth interview methods the interviewer was Ellie. However, the goal of the research was not related to the participatory design field and not even to usability testing and it focused on supporting psychological conditions.

The previously mentioned GUI-ii method has been developed by Pettersson, Wik and Andersson in a study called "GUI interactive interviews in the Evolving Map of Design Research" (Pettersson et al., 2018). The research focused on studying on how the GUI-ii method and the use of Wizard of Oz tools can benefit the designers while interacting with co-designer. The method can also help the test participants to feel comfortable in giving feedback during the interview sessions.

Clemensen et al. (2007) applied participatory design technique in their research by focusing on developing digital health and computer technology. The authors focused on overviewing the technique history and evaluated the test outcome and the challenges they encountered while using the technique. Therefore, use of the mathematical model developed in this chapter could assist in choosing the best approach of utilizing the participatory design technique.

Interview Methods and Design Phases in Participatory Design Technique

The procedure of designing an interface for the end users tend to becoming more and more complicated through simplification, one might say. Supporting applications and software come in large numbers. At any rate, designers cannot recognize what kind of interface is suitable for end users without involving prospective users in design phases. An interview method is natural option to collect feedbacks. Interview methods also manage and guide the design sessions if chosen correctly. Time constraints, financial limitations, available equipment and resources may affect the design procedure. As discussed in previous section, other authors focused on comparing two or more interview methods. However, new interview methods need equipment and it might be harder to choose among the alternatives. Therefore, the attempt is to design a generic model to calculate and select the "best" interview method.

Interview Methods

Interacting with the test participant, who referred to as co-designer, is the most important part of the participatory design technique, therefore interview methods are used. During each design phase, choosing the most efficient interview method is an important decision that should be made by the test leader, who referred to as designer, or a committee who are responsible for the design resources. The designer is also responsible of preparing the requirements and questionnaire for the design sessions. There are three different types of questionnaire for the interview (Preece et al., 2015). The first type is the structured questionnaires. In this type the list is restricted to the questions previously created and should not be changed or edited during the real design process. The second type is the unstructured questionnaire, where only very few questions will be generated before the design session, the rest of the questions will be generated during the interview according to the last feedback collected from the co-designer. And finally, the last type is the semi-structured questionnaire, which is a combination of structured and unstructured questionnaires (Wethington et al., 2015).

Unstructured questionnaire has been proven (Zhang et al., 2016) very effective while interacting with co-designers, since the questions arise according to co-designer's creativity and feedbacks. If designers are interested in measuring to what extent the co-designer is contributing, then it is arguable that an unstructured approach should be used not the level out effects from different interview techniques, and also not to hamper the contribution from the co-designer (participative design should honestly seek to involve the co-designer in the design process why it appears to us to be wrong to structure the discussion beforehand).

Below is listed the four interview methods evaluated in this chapter:

- **GUI-ii Face-to-Face**: In this method, both the designer and the co-designer share one computer screen in a face-to-face manner. The computer accessories such as keyboard and mouse are mainly accessible by the co-designer to be able to interact with the design application, which provides for a freedom of creativity. Designers mainly observe the screen and the co-designer, and meanwhile asks relevant questions, i.e. "What are the advantages of having the component in the top-corner?", This way co-designers may elaborate more ideas about the choices.
- **GUI-ii Screen-Sharing**: In this method, the designer and co-designer conduct the interview remotely via a telecommunication application (such as Skype) and the co-designer can only see a shared screen with the designer, without being able to interact with it. The designer applies the necessary changes according to the co-designer's feedbacks. After each feedback the designer asks the second question according to the unstructured questionnaire and relevant to the previously given feedback.
- **GUI-ii Ozlab**: Ozlab's primary use is to perform usability test (Pettersson, 2002) (Nilsson et al., 2006). Ozlab has different view panels for the designer, co-designer and non-interacting beholders. In the first view panel, which is called "Test Leader", the designers can add, remove, and edit scenes and GUI elements, and it also allows co-designers to freely move GUI elements and the designer can track their mouse movements. Second view panel, which is called "Test Participant",

is for the co-designers in order to interact with the system; and the last panel, which is called "Test Viewer(s)", is for possible remote spectators, just in case another person is going to do the analysis, who would like to monitor the test but not to interact with the test participant. GUI-ii with Ozlab was conceived as a method to facilitate remote co-designing and an audio channel has also been used to supplement the GUI channel provided by Ozlab (Pettersson et al., 2018). Here, instead usability lab is used. The lab has to be facilitated with at least two computers, one for the designer and another one for the co-designer, with a microphone and speaker, where the designer can communicate with the co-designer. The co-design session starts by pressing the "start session" button from the designer side and finishes by "stop session" button. The lab may also be facilitated with a dark glassed wall, for the purpose of observing co-designer's behavior.

- **Traditional Face-to-Face**: In this method, the designers and co-designer work together face-to-face, but instead of using software and computers, they utilize paper and pencil. Even though this method is traditional but still in use widely by designers, especially in the first and second design phase. In this method, the co-designer is the main person writing and drawing on the paper, and the designer just cooperates with the co-designer as a secondary designer.

Note that the first three methods for arranging the discussion during co-design sessions are the combination of the GUI interaction interview method and other interview methods.

Design Phases

In order to design user interfaces, designers divide the complete design procedure into different phases. Generally, interface designers may choose to fulfill some of the phases. However, this chapter divides the design into four main phases during a participatory design cycle. The goal is to evaluate these design phases values in the mathematical model.

1. **Listing Interface Components Phase:** In this phase, the user interface designer prepares a list of interface components to present it to the co-designers such as video panel, comment placeholder, menu, notepad and etc. The session begins by an unstructured questionnaire. Then, the co-designer is asked to edit, delete, combine or add components if necessary. Generally, this phase is done only by designers, without involving the end users, if designers already know what components are necessary.

2. **Sketching:** This is the phase where the designer and co-designer roughly estimate the overall look of the user interface using sketching (Rettig, 1994). The designer presents the co-designer with the result of the design's first phase and asks him/her to review the components list and decide the location and the size of each component on the user interface.

3. **Lo-Fi Prototyping:** This is the third and the most used phase by designers. Lo-Fi prototyping phase delivers almost a finished interface but not an interactable interface. Most of the time designers involve co-designers only in this phase and then send the designed interface to software programmers to develop it further. In this phase the co-designer's task is to follow the previous phase's sketch and to replace components with satisfactory GUI elements such as buttons, textboxes, menus, etc. (Rettig, 1994).

4. **Hi-Fi Prototyping:** This is the last phase of the design. In this phase co-designer chose a convenient way to interact with GUI elements (i.e. if it is best to open a menu by hovering the mouse over an

element or click to open that specific element). In this phase, the interface will look presentable and interactable. The result will be also used for usability testing before sending it for further development (Rettig, 1994).

METHODOLOGY USED TO EVALUATE THE INTERVIEW METHODS

This section describes what parameters were observed in order to compare the four methods. It also describes how the parameters for the resulting model was conceived. Furthermore, it describes all relevant details pertaining to the test of the different methods, such as participants, the test design, and scenario presented to the participants.

Test Parameter

To analyze the interview methods in each design phase, some aspects which are influential when choosing the most suitable interview method should be considered. These data may differ from one design group to another i.e. one designer group may have access to rooms and labs freely and another group may not have. Here, the list of test parameters used during the participatory design test are presented.

- **Duration Per Component**: It is important for designers to know how long an interview method is taking. In some design phases, a short and quick interview method may not extract enough information, as it takes time for the co-designers to feel comfortable and also learn the test scenario to give feedback for each component. On the contrary, in some other phases, it can be cumbersome to use long interview methods, as the co-designer can get exhausted and may start to give insufficient feedback at the end of the session. The reason for considering duration of co-design session according to the number of components instead of total duration, is that co-designers list different components at the beginning of the design phase, and dependent on the number of components and the co-designers added list, the total duration of co-design sessions may vary. So, for the purpose of accurately compare interview methods from the time perspective, it is necessary to compare the session duration based on the number of components that has been listed at the beginning of design phase.
- **Willingness to Provide Information**: The lead designer asks the co-designers to step-by-step elaborate the reason behind their choices of the component. For this purpose, think-aloud method has been used; however, it is not convenient for the co-designer to constantly be reminded to think aloud while co-designing, as it may put the co-designer in an awkward and uncomfortable situation. By comparing this parameter, the study show which interview method can make the co-designer to speak more willingly. The lead designer also analyzed each of the video recordings from all sessions and counted the number of words that the co-designer spoke out regarding each component. Additionally, the co-designer may always speak about the component during the co-design session, unless having difficulties using the design tools. The test also did not count co-designers' interjections.
- **Difficulty**: In some interview methods, it can take some time for the co-designer to learn and understand how to interact with the co-designing environment such as the room or equipment, or the related software while co-designing, specifically if the software has a lot of functionality.

Sometimes this may cause negative effect on the co-designer's willingness to provide information. While the co-designer might need enough time to learn about the co-designing environment and related software in use, s/he should not go into details while doing a sketch for the first time. This can slow down the co-design session and may cause longer duration and eventually the co-designer may get tired or even unresponsive. This will be measured by the amount of time the co-designer learns how to interact with the environment and asks questions regarding their problems with the interview tools.

- **Cost**: No matter how easy and straightforward an interview method can be, there are always limitations of budget for running different interview methods. Things such as computers, software license, renting a lab, and even participants expenses are costly. In some cases, the product owner provides the facilities to designers or the company the designers work for, however there are general costs that designers need to consider such as inviting participants to join as a co-designer. Therefore, most of the times designers cover the expenses for them such as transportation.

Take into consideration that some of the test parameters defined here may be applicable in the case of using participatory design technique. For other types of user-centred design such as usability testing, different evaluation parameters need to be considered. Moreover, designers may edit the parameter set and use other parameters relevant to their requirements.

Model Parameter

The goal of developing a model is to simplify the process of analyzing and evaluating a method or technique before applying it in a real test or system. Each model can have multiple   input and output parameters. For the purpose of developing the mathematical model, first, the input parameters are defined according to the number of applicable design phases, interview methods, and the test parameters. The indexing in each parameter set is necessary to make a reference while applying it to the model equation. The sets below can be edited and enhance for further uses.

- P = {Listing-Components, Sketching, Lo-Fi-Prototyping, Hi-Fi-Prototyping}: P notation indicates the set of phases used for calculating the most efficient interview method. If *Pi =2,* sketching will be used for the estimation. The order in this set is important to complete the design procedure. That means designers may utilize only some of the design phases, however the design phases must be followed in order.
- M = {GUI-ii Face-to-Face, GUI-ii Screen Sharing, GUI-ii Ozlab at Lab, Traditional Face-to-Face}: M notation stands for methods of interview. Take into consideration that the set size can be changed or substituted by other interaction methods.
- X = {Duration Per Component, Willingness to Provide Information, Difficulty, Cost}: X represents the test parameters. This set includes the parameters which have been used to evaluate the participatory design test. More analysis parameters can be added to the list.

Software and Tools

For the purpose of applying these interview methods in some of the mentioned design phases, *Pencil* and *Sketch* desktop applications has been used, which are both designing tools with GUI elements available for quick interface designing, corresponding to the design phase. Some of the software can have multiple functionalities that may not be necessary for all the design phases. Therefore, it is important to mention for the co-designers which functionalities they need to know and work with. Also, *Skype* has been used as a messaging application for internet-based remote interview methods since it has a screen-sharing feature and all the co-designers are familiar how to use it. In case of GUI-ii Ozlab interview method, *Ozlab* application has been used, which is a tool developed at Karlstad University. Eventually, the data was collected by analyzing videos recorded in each session and the co-designer's interaction with the screen using *Screenflow* software.

Test Participants

For the mathematical calculations demonstrated in this chapter, there were in total four subjects selected from the participant registered for a test presented in (Boodaghian Asl et al., 2019). All the test participants (co-designers) were university students from various study fields between the age range of 20 to 40, six of them were males and two of them were females. None of the participants had previously been in any participatory design situation and were not familiar with the Sketch and Pencil desktop applications or Ozlab web application. Throughout the experiment, test participants will be referred as co-designers.

Test Leader

The test leader is responsible for preparing the unstructured questionnaire, orientation script, non-disclosure agreement (Rubin and Chisnell, 2008) and observation. He/she is also responsible for analyzing test results, and act as the Wizard-of-Oz in GUI-ii Ozlab interview method. Throughout this experiment, main test leader will be referred as the designer.

Participatory Design Test

The first criteria to conduct the participatory design test is to select co-designers who are not familiar with the interview methods and never been in any participatory design test before, to improve the data accuracy. The second criteria for participant selection was that the co-designers should be already familiar with the test scenario when participating in second, third and fourth design phases. Therefore, a 4*4 within-subject design experiment method has been applied on selecting the co-designers, with counterbalancing order (see Table 1). It is an approach to iterate the test subjects into all phases of design without repeating the same interview method on co-designers. The counterbalancing order spares the lead designers time on finding more co-designers and furthermore the co-designers will have the knowledge of the test scenario when participating to the next design phase.

In Table 1, the first row represents interview methods, and the first column represents design phases. All the test subjects who are the co-designers, went through all the phases of design one by one. However, in each design phase the co-designer were interviewed by different methods and no one has repeated the same phase by the same interview method. On the other hand, they received the results from the same interview method. So that co-designers did not work on their own results from the previous design phase.

The reason for choosing within-subject design method is that the co-designer is already familiar with the previous design phase results and will be able to continue the test using other interview methods in the

Table 1. 2*2 with-in subject design with counterbalancing order

Participatory Design Phases	GUI-ii Face-to-Face	GUI-ii Screen Sharing	GUI-ii Ozlab at Lab	Traditional Face-to-Face
Listing Interface Components	1st Subject	2nd Subject	3rd Subject	4th Subject
Sketching	4th Subject	1st Subject	2nd Subject	3rd Subject
Lo-Fi Prototyping	3rd Subject	4th Subject	1st Subject	2nd Subject
Hi-Fi Prototyping	2nd Subject	3rd Subject	4th Subject	1st Subject

next design phase. The main purpose here is to demonstrate how the mathematical model works, therefore four test subjects, as demonstrated in Table 1, were considered sufficient to extract the necessary data.

For the purpose of reducing the mistakes in real participatory design test and increase the accuracy, a pilot test (Rubin and Chisnell, 2008) has been performed with three participants. As a result, first, some changes have been applied to the unstructured questionnaire, secondly, to keep the test simple for the co-designers, the *Sketch* application has been used for having limited interface component, which makes it easy to learn and use for co-designers.

Boodaghian Asl's and Gokan Khan's (2019) research also explicitly discussed and graphically presented, that co-design sessions which take shorter than one hour may not have gathered enough data from the co-designers, and on the contrary co-design sessions which take longer than one hour may cause disinterest and be tiresome.

Test Scenario

In order to run the participatory design test, a test scenario was designed to be performed. The test target was to design online synchronous learning system user interface from the students' perspective, using participatory design technique, where the teacher and students meet online at the same time. The purpose of choosing the following scenario is that, firstly, it is easy to understand by a majority of end users and proceed with the design without having lots of trouble, and secondly, the scenario has a wide range of end users to collaborate as a co-designer. Though, the goal of the research study is to test the interview methods and not the user interface. Same test scenario was used for pilot test but with different participants which all of the participants were male students. The goal of the pilot test was to make sure there were no malfunctions running the real test.

Measurement and Analysis

To do the measurement and analysis, the values of each test parameter which were gathered from the participatory design test were presented in numerical form. Each test parameter represents different range of values. Duration per component range is [0.1,350], which is the length of the recorded video, willingness to provide information range is [0,900], which was measured by the number of the words the participant shared ideas and suggestions, difficulty range is [0,10], which has been measured by number of the times the participants struggled to use the software, and the cost range is [500$,15000$], which has been calculated separately by summing up the transportation, equipment and time expenditure.

Table 2. Test results from listing interface components phase

Listing Interface Components Phase	GUI-ii Face-to-Face	GUI-ii Screen Sharing	GUI-ii Ozlab at Lab	Traditional Face-to-Face
Duration Per Component (seconds)	43.71	56.25	74.25	163.63
Willingness to Provide Information	200	600	900	400
Difficulty	30	30	30	30
Cost	2000	3000	15000	500

After completing all the design phases with each test participant, the numerical data has been normalized. The normalization purpose was to scale the numerical data in a range of 0 to 1. Then the data has been used to calculate the most efficient interview method depending on designers' resources.

Result

An empirical study which has been conducted by Boodaghian Asl et al. the goal was to perform a scale-based empirical data research analysis and compare the results by using graphs and tables, where results were divided into separate value ranges and presented in the following scales: very low, low, below average, average, above average, high and very high. However, in this chapter the purpose is to present a mathematical model-based approach to calculate the most efficient interview method in each design phase. Therefore, first the numerical values which are enhanced from the participatory design test are presented in tables, and later the normalized values are calculated and then the normalized values are used to evaluate the most efficient interview method.

Numerical Data Tables

Tables 2, 3, 4 and 5 show the results gathered from the test. The first row in these tables are the interview methods and the first column to the left are the test parameters.

In the first phase (see Table 3), considering both duration per component and willingness to provide information, the GUI-ii face-to-face has the lowest outcome as the co-designers always has the false impression the designer fully understands the steps taken while looking at the same screen, therefore, it is not easy for co-designers to constantly remember to think aloud.

Regarding *cost*, GUI-ii Ozlab at Usability Lab is the most expensive one, as it requires to rent/own a lab with sophisticated with facilities such as dark glassed wall, at least 2 computers, microphones and speakers. But if designers have access to such facilities, then GUI-ii Ozlab is very advantageous for both designers and co-designers

In the sketching phase (Table 3), once again GUI-ii Ozlab at Usability Lab has the most satisfactory results by merging both duration per component and willingness to provide information. There is also a huge variation for the difficulty parameter; especially on GUI-ii face-to-face: it was twice as difficult as GUI-ii screen-sharing even though the designer is close by the co-designer during the face-to-face interview, the co-designer is supposed to interact with the system alone and requires some basic understanding about the *Pencil* desktop application.

Table 3. Test results from sketching phase

Sketching Phase	GUI-ii Face-to-Face	GUI-ii Screen Sharing	GUI-ii Ozlab at Lab	Traditional Face-to-Face
Duration Per Component (seconds)	128.57	74.25	74.25	189.81
Willingness to Provide Information	200	600	900 .	400
Difficulty	240	120	30	30
Cost	3500	3000	15000	500

One of the advantages of using GUI-ii Ozlab web application is that it is not possible to have margins for the components on the sketching phase, which helps the designers and developers to cover the empty spaces on the web by resizing existing components. However, on the other hand, the empty spaces may be misleading and therefore cause misunderstanding while proceeding with the next design phase.

Table 4 with data from Lo-Fi prototyping differs from the other tables presented. First, the GUI-ii Ozlab method is not applicable on this phase, which is an advantage as it has interactive GUI elements which are easy to rearrange, which helps the designers to combine both Lo-Fi and Hi-Fi prototypes, and instead of doing the design in four different phases, it can be done in three design phases, by avoiding Lo-Fi prototyping phase. However, if a designer is going to use an interview method other than GUI-ii Ozlab for Lo-Fi prototyping phase, it is better to use GUI-ii screen-sharing as it consumes less time and promotes higher *willingness to provide information* for co-designers. The only disadvantage is that GUI-ii screen-sharing is twice as difficult as GUI-ii face-to-face (Table 4) which has totally the opposite value, by comparing to sketching phase (Table 5). In the sketching phase the co-designer only needs to show the location and the size for different components, but for Lo-Fi the co-designer needs to access different GUI elements in the software, which forces them to spend more time on learning during the test.

In the Hi-Fi prototyping phase (the last phase) (Table 5) the GUI-ii screen-sharing interview method is exceptionally difficult as the co-designer cannot interact with the software her/himself, and s/he can only see the shared screen via *Skype*. Also, the co-designers need to learn and remember the GUI elements location in the design application in order to ask the designer to add it to the screen, it takes longer to accomplish the test than using the GUI-ii Ozlab. Furthermore, co-designers are not initially designers; thus, remembering design terminologies and using the application can be very challenging while struggling to be effective.

Table 4. Test results from Lo-Fi prototyping phase

Lo-Fi Prototyping Phase	GUI-ii Face-to-Face	GUI-ii Screen Sharing	GUI-ii Ozlab at Lab	Traditional Face-to-Face
Duration Per Component (seconds)	257.14	112.5	N/A	189.81
Willingness to Provide Information	200	600	N/A	400
Difficulty	120	240	N/A	30
Cost	3500	3000	N/A	500

Table 5. Test results from Hi-Fi prototyping phase

Hi-Fi Prototyping Phase	GUI-ii Face-to-Face	GUI-ii Screen Sharing	GUI-ii Ozlab at Lab	Traditional Face-to-Face
Duration Per Component (seconds)	300.8	299.25	112.5	327.27
Willingness to Provide Information	200	600	900	400
Difficulty	500	750	30	300
Cost	3500	3000	15000	500

Designing the Mathematical Model

In this section, a mathematical model is presented to find the most efficient interview method which is suitable for a specific design phase. As previously mentioned in the background section, there are three model parameters, namely, the design phases, the interview methods and the test parameters. Here, the procedure of how the model was designed is covered step by step.

Since the outcomes from tables 3, 4, 5 and 6 are not in the range of 0 to 1, it is necessary to normalize the values and be able to use them later in the equation. Normalization equation (1) helps so that all the values enhanced from the experiment, be in one range. It makes the data comparison much easier.

$$EV_{\text{Normalized}}\left(P_i, M_j, X_k\right) = \frac{EV\left(P_i, M_j, X_k\right) - \mu_{EV(P_i, X_k)}}{Max_{EV(P_i)} - Min_{EV(P_i)}}. \tag{1}$$

As Eq 1 elaborates, the model takes the three paramers P for Phase, M for method of interview, and X for experimental test parameter, as input variables. The i, j and k are the index numbers in the parameter lists. EV stands for "experimental value", and μ is the average number of each phase's experimental test parameters. If the experimental value function inputs are $EV(P_2, M_4, X_3)$ then the focus is on the sketching design phase, traditional face-to-face interview and difficulty as a test parameter.

$$Weight\left(P_i, X_k\right) \subseteq [0,1], s.t\, \exists i \in P_i, \sum_{l=1}^{d} Weight\left(P_i, X_l\right) = 1 \tag{2}$$

Each test component has been given a value to define its importance for each phase. The sum of the weights for each design phase should be equal to 1. Therefore, according to Eq 1, if and only if, the weight of a test parameter in each design phase which is in a range of 0 to 1, such that every phase belongs to the list of P, the sum of the weights should be equal to 1.

$$InterviewEfficiency\left(P_i, M_j\right) = \sum_{l=1}^{d}\left(ExperimentValue\left(P_i, M_j, X_l\right) * Weight\left(P_i, X_l\right)\right) \tag{3}$$

Therefore, the outcome for the interview efficiency equation (Eq. 3) can be calculated by the sum of multiplying the weight of each test parameter to the experiment value enhanced from Eq. 4.

Table 6. Phase weights for each test parameter

Weights	P=1	P=2	P=3	P=4
X=1	0.25	0.25	0.25	0.25
X=2	0.25	0.20	0.20	0.20
X=3	0.25	0.10	0.10	0.10
X=4	0.25	0.45	0.45	0.45
Total	1.00	1.00	1.00	1.00

Table 7. Normalized parameters for listing interface component phase

P=1	M=1	M=2	M=3	M=4
X=1	0.339790448	0.235258285	0.085160819	-0.660209552
X=2	-0.464285714	0.107142857	0.535714286	-0.178571429
X=3	0	0	0	0
X=4	0.215517241	0.1465517241	-0.681034483	0.318965517

Table 8. Normalized parameters for sketching phase

P=2	M=1	M=2	M=3	M=4
X=1	-0,102528445	0.367509482	0.367509482	-0.632490518
X=2	-0.464285714	0.107142857	0.535714286	-0178571429
X=3	-0.642857143	-0.07428571	0.357142857	0.357142857
X=4	0.137931034	0.172413793	-0.655172414	0.344827586

$$BestEfficiency\left(P_i\right) = Max\left(\{\text{InterviewEfficiency}(P_i, M_1), \ldots, \text{InterviewEfficiency}\left(P_i, M_m\right)\}\right)$$

(4)

And eventually, the most efficient interview method in each phase can be obtained by Eq 4. The equation finds the highest value of different interview methodology in one design phase by returning the maximum number as a result.

Finding and Analyzing Most Efficient Interview Method

The weights (Table 6) for each test parameter are used to calculate the interview efficiency. The total weights in each phase (column) should be equal to 1.00. These weights help the interface designers indicate the importance of each parameter for each design phase to choose the most efficient interview method. If designers have more than four test parameters, then the total weight for all test parameter should be equal to 1. Table 6 has been developed by the lead designers. Designers evaluate and rank the importance of each test parameter. If the importance is equal, then the values can be equal too (i.e. table column 2). Table 7, 8, 9 and 10 represents the normalized (Eq. 1) experiment values collected during the participatory design study.

Table 9. Normalized parameters for Lo-Fi prototyping phase

P=3	M=1	M=2	M=3	M=4
X=1	-0.488484848	0.511515152	N/A	-0.023030303
X=2	-0.5	0.5	N/A	0
X=3	0.047619048	-0.523809524	N/A	-0.476190476
X=4	-0.388888889	-0.222222222	N/A	0.611111111

Table 10. Normalized parameters for Hi-Fi prototyping phase

P=4	M=1	M=2	M=3	M=5
X=1	-0.190374134	-0.182891154	0.686632644	-0.313367356
X=2	0.464285714	-0.107142857	-0.535714286	0.178571429
X=3	-.145833333	-0.493055556	0.506944444	0.13194444
X=4	0.137931034	0.172413793	-0.655172414	0.344827586

Eventually, Table 11 represents the interview efficiency and the best efficiency of the interview methods. The efficiency value is calculated by using Eq. 3, and the best efficiency is selected by substituting the efficiency values in Eq. 4 to enhance the greatest interview efficiency value in each phase.

The Table 11 is very self-explanatory. in the first and third participatory design phase, the GUI-ii Screen Sharing has the highest efficiency. One of the reasons is that *listing interface components* is comparingly a straightforward phase to follow for co-designers, therefore complicating it by using other tools and software that the co-designers are not familiar with, may confuse them at the beginning of the design. In the third phase, the GUI-ii Ozlab method is not advisable, due to high fidelity and inter-actable interface components, instead, the GUI-ii Screen Sharing has been selected as the best efficient interview method. On the other hand, it is very useful for designers to merge the third and fourth phases during the participatory design technique and finish the designing in three phases. It is also very crucial to have a simple interview method in the first design phase. It will help the co-designer to concentrate on the design topic rather than on how to use a design software. More complicated interview methods, which involve lots of learning can be utilized in the third and the fourth phases. Eventually, data from the fourth phase shows that GUI-ii Face-to-Face is the most efficient method. However, by neglecting the high cost of using Ozlab application at Usability Lab (in interview efficiency values column), the method has the potential of being very valuable if used remotely.

Finally, in case designers do not have enough resources to use the best efficient interview method, then the focus of choosing another interview method should be on the positive values from the model outcome. From the Table 11, the traditional face-to-face interview has negative value in each participatory design phase. In all four phases, there is a wide gap of value differences among traditional face-to-face and other interview methods, especially in the third and fourth design phases. This validate a claim that the most technically sophisticated interview methods can facilitate the procedure of involving participatory design technique in developing interfaces.

In this chapter, the mathematical model proved that GUI-ii Ozlab is a suitable interview method for most of the phases, however costly, therefore it is advisable to use GUI-ii Screen Sharing interview

Table 11. Interview efficiency and best efficiency

Design Phase Index	Interview Method Index	Interview Efficiency Values	Best Efficiency of Interview methods
1	1	0.022755494	
1	2	0.122238216	GUI-ii Screen Sharing
1	3	-0.015039845	
1	4	-0.129953866	
2	1	-0.349339008	
2	2	0.143047321	
2	3	0.338860129	GUI-ii Ozlab at Lab
2	4	-0.132568442	
3	1	-0.376486291	
3	2	0.225894661	GUI-ii Screen Sharing
3	3	N/A	
3	4	0.150591631	
4	1	0.145961475	GUI-ii Face-to-Face
4	2	-0.175306806	
4	3	0.062886951	
4	4	-003354162	

method if the design phase is not very important or GUI-ii Ozlab interview method is not applicable such as in Lo-Fi prototyping phase, which can have useful results also.

CONCLUSION

When involving users in interface design procedure, there are parameters that lead designers need to take into consideration such factors as users' background and knowledge, collaboration aptness and design tools, expenses and other factors. For this chapter were selected some of the main factors and presented a mathematical model-based approach to help designers choose the most relevant interview method for participatory design technique.

It is possible to apply various interview methods for each design phase. Designers do not necessarily require following one interview method throughout all design phases. Therefore, the focus was to develop a generic mathematical model to give the flexibility of combing these methods. The mathematical model demonstrated in this chapter can be extended to cover other types of work.

In this chapter the model focus is on participatory design development. The test parameters used for the model evaluation generated by focusing on the requirements needed from co-designers and is vital for the designers' team resources such as *cost*. By neglecting some test parameters, the model may return totally different values, for instance, if the weight value for *cost* becomes 1 it alters the weight values for other test parameters.

Finally, for the future work, the model can be revised to be applicable for usability testing phase also. For that matter, the model should accept different set of input parameters such as duration of finding a component in interface, struggling count, confusion in component functionality, gestures and interjections. The usability testing can also be divided into different phases such as observing and interviewing phases and applied in to the revised model.

ACKNOWLEDGMENT

We would like to thank professor John Sören Pettersson for letting us use the Usability Lab at the Karlstad University to run the test and to take the time guiding, helping and reviewing this chapter.

REFERENCES

Baauw, E., & Markopoulous, P. (2004). A comparison of think-aloud and post-task interview for usability testing with children. In Proceeding of the 2004 Conference on Interaction Design and Children Building a Community IDC '04 (pp. 115–116). ACM Press. 10.1145/1017833.1017848

Boodaghian Asl, A., & Gokan Khan, M. (2019). An empirical study on GUI-ii interview methods in participatory design. In *Proceeding of the 13th International Conference on Interfaces and Human Computer Interaction*. Academic Press.

Brush, A. J. B., Ames, M., & Davis, J. (2004). A comparison of synchronous remote and local usability studies for an expert interface. In *Extended Abstracts of the 2004 Conference on Human Factors and Computing Systems CHI '04*. ACM Press. 10.1145/985921.986018

Clemensen, J., Larsen, S. B., Kyng, M., & Kirkevold, M. (2007). Participatory design in health sciences: Using cooperative experimental methods in developing health services and computer technology. *Qualitative Health Research*, *17*, 122–130. PMID:17170250

Dimond, J. P., Fiesler, C., DiSalvo, B., Pelc, J., & Bruckman, A. S. (2012). Qualitative data collection technologies: a comparison of instant messaging, email, and phone. In *Proceedings of the 17th ACM International Conference on Supporting Group Work - GROUP '12*. ACM Press. 10.1145/2389176.2389218

Gratch, J., Artstein, R., Lucas, G., Stratou, G., Scherer, S., Nazarian, A., . . . Morency, L.-P. (2014). The distress analysis interview corpus of human and computer interviews. In *Proceedings of the Ninth International Conference on Language Resources and Evaluation (LREC-2014)*. European Language Resources Association (ELRA).

Heintz, M., Law, E. L. C., & Soleimani, S. (2015, September). Paper or pixel? comparing paper-and tool-based participatory design approaches. In *IFIP Conference on Human-Computer Interaction* (pp. 501-517). Springer.

Nielsen, J., Clemmensen, T., & Yssing, C. (2002). Getting access to what goes on in people's heads?: reflections on the think-aloud technique. In *Proceedings of the Second Nordic Conference on Human-Computer Interaction NordiCHI '02*. ACM Press.

Nilsson, J. & Siponen, J. (2006). Challenging the HCI Concept of Fidelity by Positioning. Ozlab Prototypes.

Pettersson, J. S. (2002). Visualising interactive graphics design for testing with users. *Digital Creativity*, *13*(3), 144–156. doi:10.1076/digc.13.3.144.7341

Pettersson, J. S., & Siponen, J. (2002). Ozlab: a simple demonstration tool for prototyping interactivity. In *Proceedings of the Second Nordic Conference on Human-Computer Interaction NordiCHI '02*. ACM Press. 10.1145/572020.572071

Pettersson, J. S., & Wik, M. (2015). The longevity of general purpose Wizard-of-Oz tools. In B. Ploderer, M. Carter, & M. Gibbs et al. (Eds.), *Proceedings of the Annual Meeting of the Australian Special Interest Group for Computer Human Interaction (OzCHI '15)* (pp. 422-426). ACM. 10.1145/2838739.2838825

Pettersson, J. S., Wik, M., & Andersson, H. (2017). Wizards of Oz in the Evolving Map of Design Research – Trying to Frame GUI Interaction Interviews Supporting Development of Interactive Systems in Interactive Sessions. In *Information Systems Development: Advances in Methods, Tools and Management (ISD2017 Proceedings)*. Academic Press..

Pettersson, J. S., Wik, M., & Andersson, H. (2018). GUI interaction interviews in the evolving map of design research. In N. Paspallis, M. Raspopoulos, C. Barry, M. Lang, H. Linger, & C. Schneider (Eds.), *Advances in Information Systems Development* (pp. 149–167). Cham: Springer International Publishing. doi:10.1007/978-3-319-74817-7_10

Preece, J., Rogers, Y., & Sharp, H. (2015). Interaction design: beyond human-computer interaction (4th ed.). Wiley.

Rettig, M. (1994). Prototyping for tiny fingers. *Communications of the ACM*, *37*, 21–27.

Rubin, J. Z., & Chisnell, D. (2008). *Handbook of usability testing: how to plan, design, and conduct effective tests, 2*. Indianapolis, Ind.: Wiley.

Schlögl, S., Doherty, G., & Luz, S. (2015). Wizard of Oz experimentation for language technology applications: Challenges and tools. *Interacting with Computers*, *27*(6), 592–615.

Simonsen, J., & Robertson, T. (Eds.). (2013). *Routledge international handbook of participatory design, Routledge international handbooks*. London: Routledge.

Spinuzzi, C. (2005). The Methodology of Participatory Design. *Open Journal of Nursing*, *52*, 163–174.

Steinfeld, A., Jenkins, O. C., & Scassellati, B. (2009). The oz of wizard: simulating the human for interaction research. In *Proceedings of the 4th ACM/IEEE International Conference on Human Robot Interaction - HRI '09*. ACM Press. 10.1145/1514095.1514115

Wethington, E., & McDarby, M. L. (2015). Interview methods (structured, semistructured, unstructured). In *The Encyclopedia of Adulthood and Aging*. Academic Press.

Zhang, Y. M., & Wildemuth, B. (2016). *Unstructured Interviews* (M. Wildemuth, Ed., 2nd ed.). Barbara.

KEY TERMS AND DEFINITIONS

GUI-ii: Graphical User Interface Interaction Interview.

Hi-Fi Prototyping: High Fidelity Prototyping.

Lo-Fi Prototyping: Low Fidelity Prototyping.

Ozlab: A web application developed by Karlstad University for mainly running usability tests.

Chapter 12
Femininities and Technologies:
Gender Identities and Relations in Video Games

Mariana Michels Fontoura
Federal University of Technology - Paraná (UTFPR), Brazil

Marília Abrahão Amaral
Federal University of Technology - Paraná (UTFPR), Brazil

ABSTRACT

The role of gender in the design of technologies has been a topic of growing importance in fields such as interaction design, HCI, and games. Understanding that technology development and usage practices emerge within the cultural processes, the authors propose in this chapter a discussion about the notions of traditional femininity, its relation to video games, as well as new approaches to female representation. It is also assessed the cultural understanding of gender, sex, and sexuality, as well as how these notions may influence the players experience. The issues discussed and briefly analyzed here point to a production and regulation of gender by technologies such as video games. Therefore, the goal is to assess how gender notions and relations influence the design and use of games in terms of visuals, narrative and sociability.

INTRODUCTION

This chapter starts with the premise that technology development and its usage practices emerge within social and cultural processes. That means that technology's historical heritage and the developers' context influence its processes and products (Bardzell, 2010). Video games, as technological artifacts, are equally affected by the social, historical and cultural dynamics. The role of gender in designing technologies has been a topic of growing importance in fields such as Interaction design and HCI (Bardzell, 2010; Breslin & Wadhwa, 2014), and Games (Shaw, 2014; Cassel & Jenkins, 2000; Rodrigues, 2014; Goulart & Nardi, 2017). Most discussions involving female representation or femininity in video games approach visual and narrative aspects. Those are important pillars to understand representation, and in addition to these

DOI: 10.4018/978-1-7998-2637-8.ch012

topics, the approach regarding the interaction between players, and how gender notions and relations shape the sociability between players is proposed here.

Therefore, in this chapter, the goal is to analyze the influence of gender norms and relations related to femininity in the development and use of video games. It starts with an explanation of essential terms to ground the theoretical discussion around gender relations in video games, and later a brief analysis about female representation and player's experiences. In the brief analysis, the authors first focus on the representation of three characters from the game "Overwatch." Later, a few players' shared experiences, concerning gender and game discussions, are also briefly analyzed, taking into account the notion of rape culture and the power relations that structure gender relations in society. This analysis took into consideration: visual aspects, narrative and sociability, in order to cover both the designer/project and the player/usage realms. The visual and narrative factors are considered relevant because they take part in the development and design of games. The sociability factor is relevant because it focuses on how players act upon gender in video games. Without further ado, in this chapter, the intention is to discuss how gender norms, identities and relations shape the design of video games, as well as the ways the notion of femininity can be reinforced or subverted by its use.

Important Concepts and Definitions

In this chapter, gender is approached by denying the ideas that men and women are essentially and naturally different. The authors understand that this vision would reinforce stereotypes, and would rely on the notion that the body is a mirror to an inner biological feminine/masculine essence. This approach would be reductive, seeking to explain subjects as automatic results of inner impulses (Weeks, 2001). We argue that gender is constructed, and therefore it doesn't represent a biological given essence of bodies. According to Weeks (2001), in the last two centuries, "sex" has acquired a meaning based on anatomic differences between the female and the male body, that is, what biologically divides people into women and men. Our approach draws on the notion introduced by Simone de Beauvoir, that "one is not born a woman, but rather, becomes a woman" (De Beauvoir, 1989), which distinguishes sex (as a biological, or anatomical feature of a body) and the notions expected and built under it (namely gender). Even though sex is understood as describing anatomic features of the body, the meanings that are associated to them belong to the social and historical realms (Weeks, 2001). Breslin and Wadhwa (2014b), based on Beauvoir's notion describe the following definitions: 1) sex, as a biological sexual identity assigned to one at birth; and 2) gender, as the behaviors, values, and other attributes associated to a given sex, which are learned throughout life. Breslin and Wadhwa (2014b) point out that this implies that being female and being a woman do not mean the same thing, and these categories are not necessarily associated.

With this approach to gender as socially constructed, we intend to deviate from universal notions of "men" and "women" and understand that people are able to belong to these categories or not. Still, as Breslin and Wadhwa (2014b) point out, it is important to acknowledge that in many cultures around the world there are societal norms and habits that associate femininity and being female. The notion of what it means to be a woman in a given society is influenced by what is socially and culturally constructed as appropriate to that gender. In the construction of your own gender identity these factors are relevant, both to be denied or identify with.

According to Weeks (2001), the Victorian age was a period that sexual conservatism towards women was growing strong. In a time when venereal diseases were a huge threat to people's lives, women's sexuality was constantly controlled and regulated instead of men's. This contradictory moral sense intended to keep a "pure" status related to women's sexuality, at the same time that prostitution was abundant. Later, in the 1940s a preoccupation with birth control arose, as well as a notion of roles appropriate to men and women in the context of family. In the 70s and 80s, sexuality started to be considered a political matter, with the New Right pointing the "decline of the family", feminism and the new homosexual movements as potential symbols for the national decline (Weeks, 2001, p.54). In that matter, both women and homosexuals fighting for their rights faced a political criticism towards their identities and the way they should or should not live the possibilities of their bodies.

Sousa (2017) points out that in contemporary societies women are socialized into a culture that teaches them how to live in their bodies and sexuality, as part of a rape culture. According to Sousa, rape culture is "the set of symbolic violence that enable the legitimation, tolerance and encouragement of sexual violation" [1] (Sousa, 2017, p. 13). In this sense, women are taught what to wear, how to behave in public spaces, not to walk late at night without the company of a trusted man, and are seen as partially responsible for the acts of other towards their sexual integrity, based on how they "respect" these prescriptions. That same culture encourages men to live their sexualities, while repressing women's. This notion is contradicting and it grounds rape culture, since heteronormative societies encourage relations between men and women (and condemn those who do not conform to this norm), at the same time that women should keep their "pure" status related to sexuality, and man should experiment their sexualities with women. A solution to this paradox has been the social distinction of women into two groups, the ones that are appropriate for marriage (those who keep this "pure" status) and those who are not, and are considered "deviated", inappropriate for long term relationships (Sousa, 2017). This distinction is highly dangerous for women because it separates them into two groups, one that is "respectable" and one that is not, allowing a variety of violence based in this perception. These notions also influence how women are represented in cultural media, and how women's sexuality is socially perceived.

Weeks (2001) points out that over the past two centuries different fields (e.g. psychology, medicine, school…) have been looking for ways to regulate people's body activities. One of them is the representation of heterosexuality as an inevitable and natural identity, which Weeks (2001) highlights as one of the ways that power is grounded in modern society. Louro (2001) points out that the production of heterosexuality comes with the denial of homosexuality, working as a way of defining and also maintaining a hierarchy between these identities. The normalization of heterosexuality presumes a complementarity between the two sexes and that this identity is natural and desirable, a notion that is socially and culturally constructed and therefore cannot be natural in that sense. But according to this logic, every sexual identity that does not conform to heterosexuality is pointed as a deviation from the norm, and tends to be marginalized. In terms of game culture, representation and socialization matters can be related to how players act and react regarding to gender and sexuality. Femininities are often associated to women in general and homosexual men through stereotypical elements and representations in various mediums. Video games are also influenced by these gender notions, and therefore represent a relevant subject for cultural studies and gender studies in general.

Besides the notion of gender, in order to theoretically ground the discussion, there is another relevant concept to our analysis. Inspired in the work of Michel Foucault, De Lauretis (1987, p. 38) developed the concept of "technology of gender", which means "the techniques and discursive strategies by which gender is constructed." Rodrigues (2017) provides us the understanding that these techniques and discourses are embedded in video games. Based on De Lauretis' concept, Rodrigues (2017) suggests that gender relations are constructed by these gender technologies, therefore creating and reaffirming subject positions. The work of Wajcman (2004, p. 7) presents the notion of technology as a sociotechnical product, that is, "shaped in social relations that use and produce it." Wajcman explains the mutually shaping relationship between gender and technology, comprehending that technology is not only a consequence, but also a source of gender relations.

Based on these concepts, like Rodrigues (2017), we intend to analyze games as technologies of gender that reaffirm notions of femininity and masculinity and produce gender identities. We also highlight the role of institutionalized discourses in the construction of gender, once they have reached the digital space within technologies such as video games.

CULTURAL PROCESSES IN TECHNOLOGIES, GENDER AND SEXUALITY

Technology Fields Through the Lens of Gender

Technology development and its usage practices emerge within social and cultural processes. That statement leads to the conclusion that values and societal norms may influence the design of technologies. Games, as interactive technologies, have a natural connection to the HCI area. Human interactions (player-player) and human-computer interactions (player-video game) can be mediated by video games. Gender relations can be seen in both these cases, such as a player interacting with gender representation through visual and narrative content in a game, or how players' interaction and socialization are influenced by gender notions in online environments. The way cultural notions and practices (such as rape culture and gender stereotypes) influence how technologies are designed is a relevant topic in the HCI field and in Game Studies, requiring attention and criticism over the developer's practices.

A few authors have been discussing gender perspectives in the HCI field. The work of Bardzell (2010), for instance, discusses the integration of feminism to the practice and research of interaction design. The author proposes a dialogue between these two fields that could aid in the development of new approaches and methods in HCI. Bardzell (2010) understands that gender relations and identities shape the use and the design of interactive technologies. Video games, as interactive technologies, also embedded notions of gender, both in the design and use of such artifacts.

Another reference in the HCI area are the works of Breslin and Wadhwa (2014), that also emphasize the role of gender in the design and use of technologies. They argue that the problematics of ignoring gender in the design of technologies are that the artifacts being developed will implicitly embed scripts about play and usage behavior based on the developer's experiences. Since the majority of developers, in the United States and Europe for instance, are white, middle class males, it often leads to hindrances on women's use (Breslin & Wadhwa, 2014b). That means that even when developers do not explicitly approach gender as a category of matter in the project, it will be embed implicitly, since their notion of "user" is gendered. On the other hand, when focusing on gender differences, the project tends to reinforce stereotypes tied to ideas of essential and natural differences between women and men, and how their use of technological artifacts differs based on that (Breslin & Wadhwa, 2014a). A balance between these two approaches could provide more gender inclusive interactive technologies, paying attention to the contextual differences of use without homogenizing women's or men's use.

A tendency in the 90's that continues till the present is the design of games oriented to the female audience based on elements culturally comprehended as feminine: the pink games (Goulart, 2012). These games are an example of designing technology for women, and they often reaffirm stereotypes tied to the feminine culture, such as fashion, beauty care and motherhood (Rodrigues & Merkle, 2017).

According to Rodrigues and Merkle (2017), based on Warren's (2015) work, the separation of games by gender originates from the toys' marketing logic. The authors point out that this reiterates not only gender stereotypes, but also expectations based on notions of femininity and masculinity. While "girl games" represent stereotyped notions of femininity, relating women to passive and permissive roles, the categorization of "boy games" present themselves problematic as well, maintaining boys tied to themes culturally comprehended as masculine, such as competitiveness, war, violence and roles related to domination (Rodrigues & Merkle, 2017). The hierarchy between games understood as belonging to a male culture or a female culture becomes clear.

The argument used to justify the development of pink games is the notion that it represents girls' tastes, and for that reason it is consequently profitable (Rodrigues 2017). Such excuse not only shows the traditional notion of femininity incorporated in the digital realm, but also reinforces values and expectations over the female players. That doesn't mean that women won't or shouldn't play and enjoy these games. What is argued in this chapter is that their use of technology should not be limited by gender roles, neither by notions of traditional femininity (Breslin & Wadhwa, 2014b). There should be space for multiple femininities.

Technology is often portrayed as part of a masculine culture. As Wajcman (2004, p. 15) points out, "schooling, youth cultures, the family and the mass media all transmit meanings and values that identify masculinity with machines and technological competence". She describes this as the sex-stereotyping of technology, and argues that it portrays the field as appropriate to men, creating a hindrance for women that want to "enter" technology fields. To enter that world, women must forsake their femininity, in order to belong. This chapter argues that this happens not only in technological work fields, but also with technological products, such as video games. This also traces a territory where men and women can/ should enact their masculinity or femininity, as well as when they are able to do that freely.

Just like women have to forsake their femininity in order to enter technological fields (Wajcman, 2004), men are also tied to gender norms that encourage them to forsake their masculinity to enter in fields associated to feminine culture, such as fashion design for instance. Besides this, fields associated to masculinity tend to be valued in culture, and those related to femininity remain less valued. Therefore, the gender transgressions previously discussed (e.g. women working in tech fields) are part of a power structure, and negotiate differently with societal values when they come "from above" in this established gender hierarchy or vice-versa.

Gender and Sexuality Notions

The behavior and attitudes towards the body and sexuality can only be understood in its historical context, paying attention to power relations that shape what is considered normal and abnormal, or acceptable and inacceptable in a given place, time and culture (Weeks, 2001). In this chapter, the authors believe that the same can be affirmed about gender, and the notions associated with it. Gender notions varies cross-culturally, and for that reason there is not a universal model of femininity or masculinity (Breslin & Wadhwa, 2014b). Also, notions of what is "natural" or not are constructed in cultural processes, which means that the notion of natural "gender" identities are also being constructed in the cultural dynamics (Louro, 2001). The cultural context influences the gender identities, notions of femininity/masculinity, and behaviors that are enacted.

Weeks' (2001) essay also draws attention to the meaning that modern societies have given to the body and sexuality, and how the latter is a social and historical construct. These meanings associated to the body and its sexual possibilities are an important part of a person's identity, relating to how she/he signifies them, and how it is socially perceived. Louro (2001) points out that sexuality is learned and built throughout life, meaning that it is not only a matter of personal realm, it is also social and political. The construction of sexuality involves rituals, languages, fantasies, representations amongst others, and it is immersed in cultural processes.

According to Weeks (2001), sexuality is related not only to the physical body, but with ideologies and beliefs regarding it. Louro (2001) affirms that the bodies are both signified by the cultural processes and modified by it. Based on Michel Foucault's notion of biopower, Weeks (2001) points out that the way homosexuality is portrayed, how people are specified into such characteristics and how subject positions are constructed in relation to these sexual activities is a historical process. This historical process involves discourses about sexuality and the ways particular sexual behaviors are encouraged and valued, as a prescription to how a person should experience sex and the body itself.

As well as gender, sexuality is shaped in social relations and it is produced within the culture. In the 19th century, the sexology field constructed the notion of normal/natural masculinity and femininity as distinct characteristics of men and women, and cataloged sexual practices into normal or abnormal (Weeks, 2001). Sexology literature was part of a bigger cultural process that worked to institutionalize heterosexuality and specific gendered behaviors as desirable to people, as well as the practices that should be avoided. This aided the production of a hierarchy between gender identities (since some values and behaviors are considered appropriate to a specific gender, and not to the other), and the construction of notions that distinguishes normal and abnormal subjects towards gender identities, based on how the person is (or is not) conforming to gender norms. While some values and roles are expected of men, others are expected of women, delimiting how a subject should enact his/her gender in society.

In addition, the oppositional binary categories are relevant to understand how the hierarchy of power is grounded, since one is defined by its relation to the norm (Rodrigues, 2014). Femininity is constructed as the opposition to masculinity, so masculinity is taken as the norm, and femininity is a deviation from that same norm. In video games, this becomes clear when opening a character selection screen and the default characters is male, or that masculinity sometimes is depicted as neutral (such as the representation of Pacman) and the "feminine" version (Ms. Pacman) is a variant from the masculine. These examples have different perceptions and consequences than, for instance, women's hyper sexualization, but still they can be understood as "smaller" gender technologies working to maintain and construct gender itself. From the smallest to the biggest problematics in the representation of femininity in video games, they are all established in power relations, and require a reflexive perception by developers, designers and academics of game studies.

Identities and Video Games

A common distinction in videogame culture is the so called "reality realm" and the "game realm", as if these spaces where completely separate and unconnected. The distinction between these two require cautious, since as a methodological resource it may be useful to separate the digital space from the space outside the game, but the edges between these categories may be blurry when it comes to identities and social relations. According to Goulart (2017) the distinction between the in-game space and reality maintains the notion that social and political matters have no place in games, which privilege the identities that are already represented and established in the video game culture (such as the cis-gender, white, male player). This comes from the notion that games have no political content, and the "game realm" should not be influenced by political and social demands from the "reality realm", otherwise it would ruin the entertainment experience of the player.

But identities in video game appear to have a meaning to the gaming experience, and groups have spoken up for their place in these communities. An example of this is the Proudmoore Pride, a pride parade organized by LGBT players in the World of Warcraft game since 2006 (Goulart, 2012). That is, the gamer's sexuality influences his/her interaction with the medium, to the point where players may organize themselves to promote events that represent their own identities. Other examples are the documentaries GTFO (Sun-Higginson, 2015) and Donzela em Defesa (Américo, Nogueira, & Ferrarini, 2017) that approach women's experiences in video games, how they relate (or not) to the representations available and deal with the harassment directed towards them in the online environment. As shown in these documentaries, people may choose not to play a game based on how they feel about some characters' representation. An argument defended by the researcher and designer Nathalie Down, in Donzela em Defesa, is that hypersexual representations should not be the only representation available; there should be more options for women in games (Américo, Nogueira, & Ferrarini, 2017). Fortim and Monteiro (2013) point out that the way female characters are depicted in games make it hard for women to identify with them, representing more an appealing gaze for heterosexual men than an actual depiction of women.

Even though it is relevant to focus on representation, it could be shallow to analyze women's gamming experiences based only in how they are depicted by the developers. Women's experiences with games are also influences by how they engage with the gamming community and how they are treated in these spaces (described as the socialization aspect in this chapter). It may not be possible to separate women's reaction to hypersexual representations and the harassment directed towards them in gamming environments, because all those elements compose their experiences in gaming, and may influence how they interact (or not) with games.

The problematic involving video games and identities is the notion that the representation topics which matter to the demands of the groups who are already established in the game culture are not seen as political (e.g. the representation of heterosexual men), but those related to other identities are pointed as political and tend to receive a lot of criticism (e.g. the diverse representation of women and LGBTQI+[2]).

Representations may produce social effects. The normalization of a particular identity is one example of that. There may be various representations available, but sometimes one in particular gains visibility and transforms from one of the possible representations, to the only one socially desirable (Louro 2001). This grounds the power relation among representations, and the one taken as the norm starts to be seen not as one of the possibilities, but a reality that should be followed. The process of normalization has many sources, and may happen in several layers of a person's life, from schooling to media representation. In this matter, Louro (2001) emphasizes how the school is a place in which gender identities are reinforced and the body is disciplined. In her work, Louro shares experiences on how docility, obedience and other behaviors culturally comprehended as appropriate to girls were taught to her in school, as well as how other gender and sexuality notions where reinforced.

In media representation, games can exemplify how gender notions are reinforced, and which identities are perceived as the norm. How some groups are commonly misrepresented in video games can be violent, and can become both recurrent and the norm. Gender and sexuality representation in games are relevant to understand which groups are being privileged, how this constructs the notion of who belongs to the gaming community and how this influences the interaction with these identities within the community.

FEMININITIES IN VIDEO GAMES

Gender values and norms are usually tied to the constructed cultural notions of femininity and masculinity in a given society. Femininities are often considered less valuable in tech fields, moreover because the field itself is perceived as part of a masculine culture. But games, as technological devices that are influenced by this very culture, are affected by the notions of femininity and masculinity, meaning that identities and representations in video games are involved in a net of cultural values associated to gender. The way this is translated into visual language, narrative aspects of stories and sociability between players is approached in this section. It is relevant to understand that the way gender is represented in video games is not a mirror of how it is perceived in society, it also works actively to construct the notion of gender. The representations and gender are in a mutually shaping relationship, and when video games portray these notions they work as technologies of gender, reproducing and producing gender notions.

This section structure is divided into three parts. The first part is about the visual aspects of gender representation in video games, focusing on character design and its stereotypes. According to Flick (2009) visual content such as films and photos are not only data but instruments of knowledge. A case study described in Flick's (2009) book points to the use of visual material, as complementary documentation to the textual form, on analyzing culture and practices. This means that the visual content, as much as the literature, is relevant to this discussion. Besides this, video games visual representation contains social reflections and experiences, which are relevant to this paper.

The second part is dedicated to the narrative content regarding femininity and gender norms, highlighting plot stereotypes associated to female representation and femininity in general. In the third and last part of this section we assess a few gaming informal documentation practices in a brief analysis on how gender roles and relations influences communication among players.

Visual Aspects

The visual aspects of femininity are often portrayed as stereotypical elements; the color pink, ribbons, make-up and high heels, for instance. Rodrigues (2014) explains that character design can be a device to reinforce gender stereotypes, pointing out that not only the female representation, but the femininity itself is sexually objectified. These representations are related to societal values and expectations over gender and sexuality. The work of Romanus (2012) discusses the representations of femininities and masculinities in video games. According to Romanus (2012), just like in advertising, the creation and design of characters in video games presupposes a male spectator. Romanus (2012), points out that the way femininities are understood in the popular culture is influenced by the invention and popularization of the computer and the internet, originating images of "digital" women and men. In her essay, Romanus (2012), analyses graphic representations of characters in video games, such as Metroid, Tomb Raider and Devil May Cry. The importance of these analyses is that stereotypes are taken as a place for resistance and questioning of these cultural representations. For that, the available social and cultural representations must be considered for subjects to identify with, always remembering that these are embedded with values and societal norms.

Other aspects of representation that composes the traditional stereotypes of femininities are audio features (e.g. female character's fighting cries in games such as Street Fighter, which the sounds could also fit in sexual contexts) and the movement animation of female characters in games (e.g. how in several games women's walking animation can be compared to a runway walk, and their standing poses show delicacy even in war-oriented scenarios and narratives (Américo, Nogueira, & Ferrarini, 2017; Sarkeesian, 2016).

Rodrigues and Merkle (2017) discuss in their essay the customization tools for characters in video games. The tools are seen as technologies of gender, offering in a scale of masculinities and femininities the ways one can be a man or a woman, producing notions of viable subjects/bodies. According to Rodrigues and Merkle (2017) gender notions are constructed based on the biological sex, and the parameters for customizations of physical attributes and clothing are tied to it, having particular anatomic features.

Video games have shown, throughout the years, a wide range of visual styles for characters, from the abstract designs to the most realistic aesthetics. Hamm (2010) points out that male characters in video games present a large range of body types and facial features, while female characters present a lack of diversity. Rodrigues (2014) points to the same problem when analyzing women's representation in the League of Legends game. According to her, one of the differences between the representation of male and female characters is the objectification. While male characters' sexualization is represented as empowering (related to strength, power and control), women character' sexualization is related to a notion of being "available" to the player's gaze. This provides an understanding on how sexuality is portrayed when associated to masculinity or femininity, how these differs in terms of objectification, and who is the expected player, that is, the one who enjoys or (seeks to) identify with these characters' representation.

Even though women are represented in games, these representations are not diverse. Hamm (2010) points out that the game "Team Fortress 2", by Valve Corporation, is a good example of variety in character designs. The author, based on the character's silhouettes, affirms that their design is diverse, presenting different weights, heights and body shapes. What Hamm intends by drawing attention to their silhouettes is to criticize the homogeny in the design of female characters, suggesting that they can be as diverse as the male characters represented in Team Fortress 2.

The lack of diversity in representing female bodies tends to show only one way of being woman, and which is usually hypersexualized and conforming to the societal standards of female beauty (young, thin…). The hyper-sexualization of female characters is tied to the presumption that gamers are heterosexual males, and for that reason the design is targeted at them. This also works as a mechanism to avoid the homoerotic gaze of male characters, by only sexualizing the female characters (Rodrigues & Merkle, 2017). The many ways to be a man or a woman are always socially suggested, announced, promoted, besides being regulated, condemned and denied (Louro, 2001). The recurrent eroticized representation of the female characters regulates both genders by constantly representing the imagery of a specific type of desirable woman (large breasts, thin waist, submissive, hero's prize to be won, etc.), as well as the player's expected sexuality (one who is supposed to be interested in these representations).

A relevant topic towards visual aspects is when femininity is depicted in non-female characters. One example of this is the character Sylvando from Dragon Quest XI, that besides being a man is associated to stereotypical elements of femininity (Fontoura et. al., 2019). His association with the feminine culture is related to imagery culturally related to homosexual men that portrays them by similar stereotypes as women's. Again, the problematic around this topic is related to gender and sexuality prescriptions in representing homosexual men only by one perspective, as if it was a homogenous identity.

Narrative

Femininity is misrepresented in the visual content of games, as argued in the previous section, but the way in which it is explored in the narrative content tends to be less evident. While visual content is more explicit on representation, narrative content is presented through various means, such as in values and ideas within the game's plot.

Cerdera and Lima's (2016) work focuses on video games and education, and the authors emphasize that games can produce narratives related to gender, race and sexuality. These narratives work as cultural artifacts that are able to teach particular cultural curricula, such as consumption patterns or even violence (directed to specific identities, usually not white, not male and not heterosexual). In this matter, ways by which gender, race and sexuality are represented can reinforce how players see groups that are historically marginalized both in media representation and in technology's history, as well as how to relate and interact with them. While game producers/developers/designers continue to construct narratives that associate femininity with less valued practices towards technology, people whose identity relate to femininity may struggle.

Also, the presence of stereotypes appears not only in the graphic part of the games, but can also be present in the characters' plots, the game's universe and other types of narrative content. With this in mind, this section focus on femininity and women's representation, narrative stereotypes and a few examples of them in games.

Damsel in Distress

The role of the damsel in distress can be seen in several prominent franchises, such as Mario, The Legend of Zelda, Dragon Quest, amongst others. Anita Sarkeesian (2013) in her web series "Tropes vs Women" presents several aspects of female disempowerment stemming from this stereotype. According to Sarkeesian (2013), "as a trope the damsel in distress is a plot device in which a female character is placed in a perilous situation from which she cannot escape on her own and must be rescued by a male character, usually providing a core incentive or motivation for the protagonist's quest" [3]. Sarkeesian (2013) analyses the damsel through the subject/object dichotomy, understanding that while subjects act, the objects are acted upon. In the damsel trope, the protagonists are the subjects, and this role is associated to men, while the damsels are the objects, often associated to women. The latter is most often reduced to "a prize to be won, a treasure to be found or a goal to be achieved" (Sarkeesian, 2013).

The damsel role traces expectations and regulations about femininity and gender roles. The mechanism of the damsel trope reaffirms a culture of submission and dependency of the feminine over the masculine (Rodrigues, 2014), representing the feminine culture as lacking of agency. Rodrigues (2014) points out that this stereotype also works as a device to produce ideas of feminine fragility and inexperience, reinforcing a devaluation of femininity. Arantes (2016) discusses the universalization of gender categories (man and woman), pointing out that gender institutes a hierarchical role, which reinforces inequality amongst the notions of femininity and masculinity. Once gender notions reach the "digital realm", they influence not only the technological production, but the very participation in this field is tied to the hierarchical gender relations.

Although the trope of the Damsel in Distress is more evident in women's representations, this trope can also be observed in games that present other types of female characters, such as anthropomorphic animals (like in Starfox Adventures and Sonic CD) (Sarkeesian, 2014).

Character's Plot

Productions involving female characters are commonly criticized because of the undeveloped backgrounds and plots, which maintain the representation of them as young, attractive, a sidekick or the hero's prize. Hamm's (2010) analysis of the game "Gears of War" points the very same problem. While the male characters are huge and represented with "battle-scarred forms", Lieutenant Anya Stroud, the only female character in the game, seems to be a lot younger than the male characters, besides having a flawless appearance. According to Hamm (2010) "her personality is calm, her background is undeveloped and she seems very detached from the game, as if she were included only to represent a pretty face."

Even though Hamm's analysis was written in 2010, it remains a common current topic. Lima (2018), for instance, discusses gender representation in crowdfunded games. His analysis starts with the hypothesis that independent game producers that rely on crowdfunding have the potential to be more diverse on gender representations than the big names in the game industry. At the end of his analysis, the conclusion pointed to an opposite direction. According to Lima (2018), even though independent developers relaying on crowdfunding campaigns have more creative freedom, new constrains arise for them by the backers as they participate on the creation process. Lima points out that the backers' control extends through all phases (early campaign to post-campaign), restraining the final product to what these players demand. Therefore, not only the AAA games, but as well as independent productions are still below expectations on female representation (Lima, 2018).

Despite this little diverse scenario, there have been some changes. A few games have been moving towards subverting these femininity stereotypes and the lack of female protagonism, featuring stories and plots as well developed as the male characters' have been for years. Blizzard Entertainment's first-person shooter game, Overwatch, is a strong example of that. The game explores multiple platforms to construct its stories and backgrounds, even outside the game itself. Extra content can be accessed through their official website, containing comics, informative pages on each character and cinematic videos. Overwatch stands out because of the diversity represented amongst the female characters, in both visual and narrative aspects, deviating from the traditional notions of femininity. In this paper, three characters were selected to exemplify this, and also for a brief analysis.

Ana Amari, character represented in figure 1, is one of the founding members of Overwatch. She is an Egyptian ex-commander and snipper, considered to be the world's best. What stands out in Ana's story is her age and her high ranking in the hierarchy at Overwatch organization. She remained active until the age of 50, when she got seriously injured in battle, even losing her right eye. Ana represents an elderly woman (now at her sixties) that has severe war injuries and scars, elements that contrasts the notion of flawless beauty commonly depicted in female characters, and the age limit for female characters to remain active in stories.

Aleksandra Zaryanova, also known as Zarya, is represented in figure 2. According to Overwatch's official website, she is "one of the world's strongest women, a celebrated athlete who sacrificed personal glory to protect her family, friends, and country in a time of war" ("Zarya", n.d.). Zarya is a 28-year-old Russian soldier whose goal is to help her people recover from post-war destruction, related to the conflicts that have taken place in the game's universe. The first deviation from the traditional femininity lies in the identification of the character with bodybuilding, in addition to a war-oriented narrative. Her story also influences the character's design, resulting in battle-scarred muscles and scars.

The third character is Tracer, whose full name is Lena Oxton. This character stresses differently the notions of gender and sexuality. First of all, she is a core character, appearing on both the cover of the

Figure 1. Comic's art of Ana Amari (Robinson & Bengal, 2016)

physical edition of the game and the banner for digital purchase. Since Tracer is one of the most popular characters, it caused great controversy when the Christmas comic "Reflections" came out in December of 2016, and Tracer was shown kissing her girlfriend.

Some players responses to that were quite problematic, such as posted in the Blizzard's online forum by the player "IgorJCorrea": "in fact the problem is to meet her as a normal/regular girl, and after almost a year 'out of nowhere' a lesbian kiss scene shows up."[4] ("Não deveria, pelo menos aqui", 2016). By that reaction, and others presented by players in the official forum, when sexuality is not explicitly shown, the character is considered heterosexual. That is to say, when no sexuality is represented, the character is associated to the normative sexuality.

According to this perspective, normal/regular girls are heterosexual, and Tracer, when not conforming to gender/sexuality norms, is pointed as abnormal. That leads us to think that the traditional notion of femininity does not include lesbian women. Therefore, gender regulation itself will also take into account other factors such as sexuality.

The strategies briefly discussed in this section are examples of how a designer may engage with more diverse representations regarding gender. Femininity representation does not require a character to be fragile or sexualized. A character does not need to be depicted in stereotypical ways to be perceived as female. Some strategies that can be replicated based in these examples are: femininity does not have to be associated with fragility, meaning that characters in this scope can be strong and have visual and narrative aspects that represent that; there should be a diversity in ages, not only young females should be active in stories; and sexuality notions may influence the design, so trying to deviate from the heterosexual norm and represent various sexual identities, allowing other players to feel represented.

Figure 2. Comic's art of Zarya (Robinson, Sellner, & Niemczyk, 2017)

Figure 3. Comic's art of Tracer and Emily (Chu & Montlló, 2016)

Sociability

As video games become more and more popular, it is important to understand the ways in which communication and socialization between players have a meaning to the gaming experience. In the 1990s and 2000s, game magazines were a very popular way of sharing passwords, tutorials and even tips on how to surpass challenging parts of a game. At that time, this was not only a popular way to access game content, but also a player's experience. Later, another common practice arose from the gaming community, as players started to share content in websites, allowing other players to comment and respond. It is interesting to note that people consume games in different ways, and looking at forms of documentation reveals diverse appropriations of these technologies, as well as unexpected uses. Speedruns are a kind of appropriation practice, that consist in beating a game in the shortest amount of time possible. There are a lot of categories of speedruns, such as completing the game with a 100% "save" (that is, accomplishing everything that is expected in the game, for instance: collecting all the coins, beating all the bosses, etc.), or even by using glitches to beat the game. Summoning Salt is a Youtuber who documents iconic speedruns on vintage consoles, such as Super Nintendo, and Nintendo64. In one of his videos, he explains how the documentation of time records were (and are) done (Choco Mountain, 2018). It started with players contacting each other via email, later becoming more accessible to others by posts on websites, till the uploading or streaming of videos, which is now a popular and more trusted way of sharing time records. Summoning Salt's documentaries are a strong example of how the gaming community can appropriate different ways of playing and even organize itself to document its achievements.

New technologies are being developed, and in many cases the exchange of information between players has been facilitated, meaning that there are many ways that one can socialize and communicate with other players in the gaming community (e.g. voice chats, forums, video recording, streaming live for an audience). Even though new tools are being developed and may allow new kinds of socialization practices to occur, the way players interact is influenced by the culture outside this environment, such as the way gender and sexuality are portrayed and valued in society generally. Some experiences involving interactions among players will be highlighted in this topic. The first is a video shared by Glisa, an Overwatch player (Sexist Throwers, 2017). Glisa recorded 16 minutes of harassment during a competitive match of the game. In the beginning of the match, Glisa started to be harassed without even contacting her teammates though the voice chat. This means the only representation of femininity associated to her was the character she chose, called Mercy. The provocations directed at Glisa at first concerned her character, like the phrases "I like how Mercy is trying to heal me because she wants me", or about her beauty, as in "Mercy, cure me. I will not call you ugly again. Just kidding, you're probably ugly."[5] After Glisa contacted her team on the voice chat, the offenses changed from a figurative aggression, towards the feminine (that is, the female character), to the player. The offenses documented by Glisa had contents such as: condemning her for being a woman and playing the game, blaming her for the team's failure and associating her with domestic housework spaces (such as the laundry room and kitchen). What draws our attention to this video is how the harassment started with the character, and not with the female player, meaning that in order to experience such harassments one can be associated with femininity symbolically, not necessarily required being a female.

The second example takes place in the role-play servers of World of Warcraft, a game also developed by Blizzard Entertainment. The tavern known as the "Goldshire Inn" has become a meeting point for players who enjoy erotic role-play, i.e. performing characters for erotic purposes. A problem pointed out in an interview conducted by Motherboard with players (Schott, 2017), was the rape fantasies that some players are performing towards female characters. This is an example of how rape and sexual violence against women are normalized in popular culture, as a part of the rape culture. Sousa (2017) points out that rape is one of the most widespread forms of gender violence, and it is usually directed towards women. According to her, the rape culture teaches men to seize every sexual opportunity they get, at the same time that woman's sexuality is repressed. The sexist speeches spread in society's culture and socialization reinforces male's sexual power and women's passiveness. These ideas also encourage men to use this power and dominance towards women and other man who don't identify or reproduce masculinity and males' virility stereotypes, behaviors that some men choose to engage with.

The example of players performing rape fantasies towards female characters is part of a rape culture already structured in society, and how this reached the digital realm in game. In this example, the role-play is performed through the character's actions and the messages sent through the game's chat system, which means that similar to the case of Glisa, described previously, violence is associated with a female figure without necessarily having an identification of the player with it. It is important to highlight that even though there is no need to be a woman to experience these harassments, when one experiences this, it is very meaningful, since women already experience this type of violence outside the online environment.

This final paragraph approaches the production of online content by people who subvert patterns of femininity and masculinity. The first example is the Brazilian drag queen Samira Close, who streams games like *Fortnite, Grand Theft Auto, Overwatch* and *League of Legends*. The character is performed by a homosexual man named Wenner Pereira, who has a strong relationship with the LGBTQ community and related subjects. Samira is highlighted in this section for playing a female role through drag, in the online game environment. That is, in an environment understood as masculine. Other subversive streamers also considered relevant are: Anaxisde, a woman who has sought to work as an eSports commentator; and Mandy Candy, a transgender woman who is a game streamer. What is interesting is how these diverse manifestations of gender have gained space in the context of games through tools for transmitting and publishing videos.

CONCLUSION

The issues discussed throughout this essay point to a production and regulation of gender by technologies such as video games. In this chapter, the authors proposed an analysis of how femininities are portrayed in video games, and the way players' interaction may be influenced by gender notions and relations. It is important to understand that the cultural and social context, outside the digital environment, influence the production of games, bring into these fanciful universes various gender regulations. It is also emphasized that the consumption and appropriations made by players are quite relevant to understand how femininities and masculinities can be incorporated into the project by the developers, but also can be subverted in the use, and vice versa. Transgressions towards gender and sexuality norms can be political in that sense, aiding in the process of creating "gender" possibilities that are broad and less prescriptive. Representation in video games is both influenced by how gender is perceived in society, and how it produces gender notions through them, exemplifying how these technologies of gender work. The players' shared experiences about rape role-play performances in World of Warcraft shows that the rape culture has reached the digital spaces of games. As Sousa (2017) points out, it is necessary to do research on how violence is normalized by cultural productions. It is also relevant to promote a reflexive perception over the femininity portrayal in video games, and how men are encouraged to interact with it in particular ways. Therefore, this chapter sought to discuss these matters in the context of video games.

When working as a game developer, the practice of assuming the audience is masculine and heterosexual shapes production, not only in the implicit narratives, but in the design itself. Since representations in games are influenced by cultural dynamics outside the digital realm, the hyper sexualization and the representation of women as prizes to the male protagonist can reinforce a culture that men have the right to a women's body as they please, contributing to the rape culture.

There are many ways to escape from the scope of traditional femininity in video games (usually represented as fragile and sexualized) and present it in a more multiple and diverse way. Allowing characters to be more open to what is understood as feminine and masculine (e.g. less gender restrictive parameters for representing characters) can aid in the process of not producing only one possible form of male/female subject. Promoting positive values linked to femininity can also challenge this hierarchical relation that makes femininity little explored and valued in video games.

It is suggested at the end of this essay that if it is possible to think of fanciful universes in games, with mystical creatures, superpowers, etc. it is also possible to detach itself from the traditional stereotypes of femininity and masculinity, and be more creative in the ways of representing these universes.

FUTURE RESEARCH DIRECTIONS

The issues approached in this chapter are related to visual, narrative and sociability factors in video games, through the lens of gender. The scope of this work only addressed notions of femininities, but future researches could focus on masculinities, or the relation between both. An approach to gender that considers other identities beyond the binary separation of men and women could be another path for research. Also, even though sexuality is briefly explored in this chapter, it deserves more attention, and could be a topic for further discussions. Another direction for researchers could be the focus in other aspects of a person's identity, such as race, class, age, and how they interact with the player's experiences. At last, as new technologies are being developed, other aspects can become a subject of matter in game analysis (beyond visual, narrative and sociability), but in the preset time the recommended topics of research about gender relations in video games could be: the analysis of other aspects of games that could reproduce gender relations (game mechanics, rules, gaming systems…), new ways people are interacting with games (streaming devices, virtual reality environments and Esports) and the pervasiveness of virtual game environments in people's lives.

ACKNOWLEDGMENT

This chapter is only viable because of the work of Letícia Rodrigues. Her work is responsible for putting Teresa de Lauretis' perspective in game analysis and discussions in Brazil, which provided us with the possibility to analyze games as technologies of gender. We owe her a special thanks. This study was partially financed by the Coordenação de Aperfeiçoamento de Pessoal de Nível Superior – Brasil (CAPES) – Finance Code 001.

REFERENCES

Américo, M., Nogueira, H., & Ferrarini, M. (Directors). (2017). *Donzela em Defesa* [YouTube video. Retrieved from https://youtu.be/Tw2yBuYuseI

Arantes, M. L. P. (2016). *Sexismo nos Campos de Justiça: O Posicionamento de Marca Interferindo na Jogabilidade de League of Legends.* Undergraduate dissertation, Federal University of Paraná, Curitiba, Brazil. Retrieved from http://hdl.handle.net/1884/45179

Bardzell, S. (2010). Feminist HCI: Taking Stock and Outlining an Agenda for Design. In *Proceedings of the SIGCHI Conference on Human Factors in Computing Systems (CHI '10).* ACM. 10.1145/1753326.1753521

Breslin, S., & Wadhwa, B. (2014a). EnGendering Interaction Design. In *Proceedings of the 3rd International Conference on User Science and Engineering (i-USEr).* IEEE.

Breslin, S., & Wadhwa, B. (2014b). Exploring Nuanced Gender Perspectives Within the HCI Community. In *Proceedings of the India HCI 2014 Conference on Human Computer Interaction (IndiaHCI '14).* ACM. 10.1145/2676702.2676709

Cassell, J., & Jenkins, H. (Eds.). (2000). *From Barbie to Mortal Kombat: gender and computer games.* Cambridge, MA: The MIT Press.

Cerdera, C. P., & Lima, M. R. O. (2016). Estereótipos de gênero em video games: diálogos sobre sexismo, homofobia e outras formas de opressão na escola. In *Proceedings of SBGames 2016.* SBC.

Chu, M., & Montlló, M. (2016) *Reflections.* Retrieved from https://static.playoverwatch.com/media/comics/10/pt-br/comic-overwatch-reflections.pdf

De Beauvoir, S. (1989). *The Second Sex.* New York, NY: Vintage Books.

De Lauretis, T. (1987). *Technologies of Gender: Essays on Theory, Film, and Fiction.* Indianapolis, IN: Indiana University Press. doi:10.1007/978-1-349-19737-8

Flick, U. (2009). *Introdução à pesquisa qualitativa.* Porto Alegre, Brazil: Artmed.

Fontoura, M. M., Rodrigues, L., Leite, P. S., Amaral, M. A., Almeida, L. D. A., & Merkle, L. E. (2019). Relações de gênero em mecânicas de jogos. In *Proceedings of SBGames 2019.* SBC.

Fortim, I., & Monteiro, L. F. (2013). Choose your character: Mulheres e Personagens femininos nos videogames. In *Proceedings of SBGames 2013.* SBC.

Goulart, L., & Nardi, H. (2017). GAMERGATE: Digital games culture and male gamer identity. *Revista Mídia e Cotidiano, 11*(3), 250–268.

Goulart, L. A. (2012). *Proudmoore pride: Potencialidades da cultura de jogo digital e identidade política de gênero/sexualidade* [Master's thesis]. Federal University of Rio Grande do Sul, Porto Alegre, Brazil. Retrieved from https://lume.ufrgs.br/handle/10183/66649

Goulart, L. A. (2017). Jogos vivos para pessoas vivas: Composições queer-contrapúblicas nas culturas de jogo digital [Doctoral dissertation]. Federal University of Rio Grande do Sul, Porto Alegre, Brazil. Retrieved from https://lume.ufrgs.br/handle/10183/165868

Hamm, S. (2010, May 20). *The Aesthetics of Unique Video Game Characters*. Game Career Guide. Retrieved from http://gamecareerguide.com/features/854/the_aesthetics_of_unique_video_.php?page=1

Lima, L. A. B. 2018. The struggles of diversity in gaming: an analysis of gender representation in crowdfunded games. In *Proceedings of SBGames 2018*. SBC.

Louro, G. L. (2001). Pedagogias da Sexualidade. In G. L. Louro (Ed.), *O corpo educado: pedagogias da sexualidade* (pp. 7–34). Belo Horizonte, Brazil: Editora Autêntica.

Mountain, C. (2018, June 3). The History of Mario Kart 64's Most Infamous Track. [Video file] Retrieved from https://www.youtube.com/watch?v=Y99Wj-NStok&ab_channel=SummoningSalt

Não deveria, pelo menos aqui. (2016, December 22). Message posted to https://us.battle.net/forums/pt/overwatch/topic/20752537624

Robinson, A., Sellner, J., & Niemczyk, K. (2017) *Searching*. Retrieved from https://static.playoverwatch.com/media/comics/15/pt-br/comic-overwatch-searching.pdf

Robinson, A., & Bengal. (2016) *Legacy*. Retrieved from https://static.playoverwatch.com/media/comics/7/pt-br/comic-overwatch-legacy.pdf

Rodrigues, L. (2014). *Um Estudo em Representações Gráficas nos Jogos Eletrônicos na Perspectiva de Gênero: Os Tipos de Feminilidade em League of Legends*. Undergraduate dissertation, Federal University of Technology, Curitiba, Brazil. Retrieved from http://repositorio.roca.utfpr.edu.br/jspui/handle/1/6778

Rodrigues, L. (2017). Questões de Gênero em Jogos Digitais: uma coleção de recursos educacionais abertos de apoio à mobilização [Master's thesis]. Federal University of Technology – Paraná, Curitiba, Brazil. Retrieved from http://repositorio.utfpr.edu.br/jspui/handle/1/2839

Rodrigues, L., & Merkle, L. E. (2017). Technologies of Gender in the construction of Digital Games character bodies. In *Proceedings of Seminário Internacional Fazendo Gênero 11 & 13th Women's Worlds Congress*, Florianópolis, Brazil. Retrieved from http://www.wwc2017.eventos.dype.com.br/site/anaiscomplementares

Romanus, J. S. (2012). *Gênero em Jogo: Um olhar sobre personagens e as representações de tipos de feminilidades e masculinidades nos games de ação contemporâneos*. Undergraduate dissertation, Federal University of Technology, Curitiba, Brazil. Retrieved from http://repositorio.roca.utfpr.edu.br/jspui/handle/1/2994

Sarkeesian, A. (2013, March 7) Feminist Frequency. Damsel in Distress (Part 1) Tropes vs Women [Video log]. Feminist Frequency. Retrieved from http://www.feministfrequency.com/2013/03/damsel-in-distress-part-1/

Sarkeesian, A. (2016, March 31) Feminist Frequency. Body Language & The Male Gaze - Tropes vs Women in Video Games [Video log]. Feminist Frequency. Retrieved from https://feministfrequency.com/video/body-language-the-male-gaze/

Schott, D. (2017, September 25). 'World of Warcraft' Has a Rape Problem. *Motherboard*. Retrieved from https://motherboard.vice.com/en_us/article/mb7b9q/world-of-warcraft-has-a-rape-problem?utm_source=mbtwitter

Sexist Throwers in Competitive Overwatch [YouTube video]. (2017, February 3). Retrieved from https://youtu.be/9f4dW1YpuoA

Shaw, A. (2014). *Gaming at the edge: sexuality and gender at the margins of gamer culture*. Minneapolis, MN: University of Minnesota Press.

Sousa, R. F. (2017). Cultura do estupro: Prática e incitação à violência sexual contra mulheres. In *Revista. Estudos Feministas*, *25*(1), 9–29. doi:10.1590/1806-9584.2017v25n1p9

Sun-Higginson, S. (Producer/Director). (2015). GTFO: The Movie [Motion picture]. Retrieved from https://www.amazon.com/GT FO-Movie-Patrick-Klepek/dp/B00ZFDNGA8)

Wajcman, J. (2004). *TechnoFeminism*. Cambridge, England: Polity Press.

Warren, J. (2015, Oct 20). Why Do "Girl Games" Matter? [YouTube video]. Retrieved from https://youtu.be/4GKZ-u0cJsI

Weeks, J. (2001). O corpo e a sexualidade. In G. L. Louro (Ed.), *O corpo educado: pedagogias da sexualidade* (pp. 35–82). Belo Horizonte, Brazil: Autêntica Editora.

Zarya. (n.d.). Play Overwatch. Retrieved from https://playoverwatch.com/pt-br/heroes/zarya/

ADDITIONAL READING

Bardzell, S., & Bardzell, J. (2011) Towards a feminist HCI methodology: social science, feminism, and HCI. In *Proceedings of the SIGCHI Conference on Human Factors in Computing Systems (CHI'11)*. ACM. 10.1145/1978942.1979041

Bowey, J. T., Depping, A. E., & Mandryk, R. L. (2017) Don't Talk Dirty to Me: How Sexist Beliefs Affect Experience in Sexist Games. In *Proceedings of the 2017 CHI Conference on Human Factors in Computing Systems (CHI'17)*. ACM 10.1145/3025453.3025563

Bragança, L. C., Mota, R. R., & Fantini, E. P. C. (2016). Twine Game Narrative and discussion about LGBTQ representation. In *Proceedings of SBGames 2016*. SBC.

Erete, S., Israni, A., & Dillahunt, T. (2018, May/June). An Intersectional Approach to Designing in the Margins. *Interaction*, *25*(3), 66–69. doi:10.1145/3194349

Fristoe, T., Denner, J., MacLaurin, M., Mateas, M., & Wardrip-Fruins, N. (2011). Say it with systems: expanding Kodu's expressive power through gender-inclusive mechanics. In *Proceedings of the 6th International Conference on Foundations of Digital Games (FDG'11)*. ACM. 10.1145/2159365.2159396

Goulart, L. A., & Nardi, H. C. (2017). A Morte dos Video games: Comunidade queer e ironia em Quing's Quest IV: The Death of Video games. In *Proceedings of I Workshop Culturas, Alteridades e Participações em IHC: Navegando ondas em movimento (CAPAihc 2017)*. SBC.

Massanari, A. (2017). #Gamergate and The Fappening: How Reddit's algorithm, governance, and culture support toxic technocultures. *New Media & Society*, *19*(3), 329–346. doi:10.1177/1461444815608807

Shaw, A. (2012). Do you identify as a gamer? Gender, race, sexuality, and gamer identity. *New Media & Society*, *14*(1), 28–44. doi:10.1177/1461444811410394

KEY TERMS AND DEFINITIONS

Femininity: Gender notions associated to the feminine culture, and socially suggested as appropriate to women

Gender: Behaviors, values, clothing, and other social and cultural attributes that are portrayed and perceived as appropriate to a particular sex.

Masculinity: Gender notions associated to the masculine culture, and socially suggested as appropriate to men

Narrative: The backgrounds and plots that ground a game's story; aspects of a game that transmit a story to the player.

Visual Aspects: The elements of a game that are perceived through vision

Sex: Biological feature of a body that incur in a person being female, male or intersex.

Sexuality: The ways a person experiences its body in terms of sexual orientation, identity and desire.

Sociability: The social aspect of a game; how players interact in a given game.

Video game: Play activity, mediated by a computer, in the context of a pretended reality that the participants choose to engage with, seeking to fulfill a goal in accordance with the established rules.

ENDNOTES

[1] Translation of the original in Portuguese: "(...) é denominado cultura do estupro o conjunto de violências simbólicas que viabilizam a legitimação, a tolerância e o estímulo à violação sexual" (Sousa, 2017, p.13).

[2] Abbreviation of: lesbian, gay, bisexual, transgender, queer, intersex and more.

[3] Transcription of 3'10'' to 3'39'' from the episode 1, Tropes vs Women: Damsel in Distress (Sarkeesian, 2013).

[4] Translation of the original in Portuguese: "na real o problema é você conhecer ela como uma menina normal e depois de quase um ano 'do nada' aparecer uma cena de beijo lésbico..." ("Não deveria, pelo menos aqui", 2016).

[5] Transcript dialogues from 0'21'' to 0'38'' ("Sexist Throwers", 2017).

Chapter 13
A Study of Using VR Game in Teaching Tajweed for Teenagers

Haya Hasan AlKhatib
Prince Sultan University, Saudi Arabia

Evi Indriasari Mansor
https://orcid.org/0000-0002-5749-5142
Prince Sultan University, Saudi Arabia

Zainab Alsamel
Prince Sultan University, Saudi Arabia

Joud Allam AlBarazi
Prince Sultan University, Saudi Arabia

ABSTRACT

This research aims to study the use of VR games to entertain players while teaching and improving the knowledge of Quran Tajweed for teenagers. Tajweed is an Islamic science that studies the correct recitation of the letters and words in the Qur'an. Teenagers between the ages of thirteen to eighteen were chosen for this research because it has been proven that learning at an early age ensures long-lasting knowledge, and in addition, teenagers are more capable of controlling and modifying their pronunciation. As teenagers nowadays are exposed to a variety of game technologies and their expectations and satisfaction levels are particularly high, a 3D VR game was introduced as an attractive modern solution. Viewed on HTC Vive, a 3D VR game prototype consisting of two levels was developed and evaluated by 20 teenage participants. The evaluation session resulted in a positive outcome with a few suggestions for future modifications.

DOI: 10.4018/978-1-7998-2637-8.ch013

INTRODUCTION

The game development world has expanded greatly during the last few decades and has covered a wide variety of areas. Entertaining is indeed one of the most important values that are provided through games. However, spending too much time playing games that reward the player nothing but entertainment leaves a negative impact on the player's mental health. Since this attitude is noticed to be common among teenagers, adding some learning outcome to the games would help in enriching the player's knowledge and hence, making a better use of his time.

The content of the produced game was chosen to be the science of Tajweed. Tajweed is an Islamic science that is related to the Glorious Qur'an. It is defined as "articulating every letter from its articulation point and giving the letter its rights and dues of characteristics." In other words, it is a betterment of the pronunciation of Arabic letters when reciting Qur'an. Following are some key points about Tajweed and its importance that motivated the authors to target it. First of all, Qur'an is the holy book for Muslims and it contains the words of Allah which were revealed to Prophet Muhammad peace be upon him (PBUH). It is the primary source for the Muslims' faith and practice. Due to that, it is very important to prevent it from being altered or read mistakenly. After the spread of Islam, Arabs were mixing with non-Arab and the Arab tongue was vulnerable to becoming corrupted with this intermixing. Therefore, the rules of Tajweed were put to guard and preserve the Qur'an from being distorted, and to ensure that it is being read exactly as it was revealed to Prophet Muhammad PBUH. Not following these rules may lead to changes in the meaning which is not acceptable. In fact, every Muslim has to recite Qur'an at least while praying (which is done 5 times per day). In addition, there are plenty of verses that state the importance of reciting Qur'an properly (i.e. with Tajweed) and the great reward that people get when they do so. Because of the previously mentioned points, many people have the willingness to learn it. However, some of them get discouraged because of the difficulties that are faced while learning it. Being more specific, not only must a Tajweed learner know the articulation points of the letters and their characteristics, but he also must understand what rules change in the letters due to the order of letters.

To give an example, the letter "ن" pronounced as "Noon" (similar to 'N' in English) is read differently depending on the situation. In the general case, the "ن" / "Noon" letter is pronounced normally, but in some cases, the letter is pronounced differently. More specifically, when it's followed with a specific set of letters, it becomes hidden and its articulation point changes to near the articulation point of the letter that is following it (this rule is known as Ikhfaa إخفاء). In addition, if the "ن" / "Noon" is followed with another set of letters, it becomes merged into the letter immediately following it and its articulation point changes to the articulation point of the letter it is merged with (this rule is known as Idgham إدغام). The above overview aims to give the reader a better understanding of the nature of this science and to elaborate on the reasons that encouraged the authors of this research to target this tough and critical science through this game.

The existing applications that are based on Tajweed hold no appeal towards teenagers because they are found to be purely educational. Others may include some gaming, but they are usually of a low quality and don't provide the user with the desired level of interactivity. In general, they are not as attractive as other popular games are. This reduces their popularity among youths. Therefore, *Qee* - a Virtual Reality (VR) in 3D environment game is proposed to serve as a solution. *Qee* is an Arabic word that means the imperative verb of protection. This name conveys the main task in the game which requires the user to protect himself from the devil. This is done through achieving several tasks in each level (explained in detail throughout the chapter).

BACKGROUND

The topic of this chapter can be viewed as a combination of two research areas: e-learning and gaming. The e-learning systems have caught the interests of the researchers many years ago. Some efforts in this area target VR in specific. Mantovani (2001) in her paper discussed the use of VR technology in the learning process as a mode of experiential learning for the students. This mode ensures a high level of interaction between the students and the learning content which raise the students' motivation and interest making the learning process more effective. Dede, Salzman, & Loftin (1996) suggested that learning through VR technology has many added features more than other learning media. These features are as follows: immersion where the player has comprehensive and realistic experience, telepresence which allow geographically separated learners to join same learning environment, player's motivation to interact with the immersive environments, enhancing the meaningfulness of data and providing qualitative insights. Winn (1993) conducted a research at the Human Interface Technology Laboratory at the University of Washington argued that learning through VR would be the best way for learning stating that immersion in a virtual world allows students to construct knowledge from direct experience and to learn while they are situated in the context. Moreover, the psychological processes the student has while constructing knowledge in VR experience and in the real world are the same.

Proceeding to the e-learning for teaching Tajweed, there are quite a lot of papers considering this topic. However, very few of them address this issue by providing a solution in the gaming field, which is in most cases not as entertaining as the proposed game in this chapter. Several papers worked on speech recognition to correct recitation. Many of them relied on Mel-Frequency Cepstral Coefficient (MFCC) algorithm for feature extraction and Hidden Markov Models (HMM) for classification. Ahsiah, Noor, & Idris (2013) suggested an e-learning technique that applies speech recognition mechanisms to figure out the mistakes made by the students through comparing them with a database of recitations recorded for experienced teachers. This approach applies MFCC and HMM algorithms. Another study that uses these two algorithms was done by Yousfi, Zeki, & Haji (2017). They used natural language processing to extract and correct a specific rule of Tajweed named Iqlab. In this paper ASR speech recognition system is used to identify the spoken versus. The proposed system is capable of pointing out the mismatch in this rule with an accuracy of 70% obtained for words that were included in the training database of famous reciters and 40% for new words that classifiers was not trained on.

Another educational tool is provided by Ibrahim, Idris, Razak, & Abdul Rahman (2013) and it also uses MFCC and HMM. This system is a Quranic verse recitation recognition system with a function that checks for the rules of Tajweed. It was tested on Surah AlFatiha. The resulted recognition rate is 91.95% (ayates) and 86.41% (phonemes). One more purely educational solution is proposed by Marlina et al. (2018). This study is more focused on a specific and basic rule of Tajweed which is called Makhraj. Makhraj is the rule that specifies how each letter is correctly pronounced by identifying the speech organ that produces it. Kapi, Osman, Ramli, and Taib (2017) developed an e-learning application that focuses on teaching the surah of Yassin. A combination of audio, video and animation was implemented in the application. The application focuses on the mistakes of the previous students who have taken the course in the traditional way. By testing the application on 51 students, it was found that the application helps in reducing the number of mistakes made by the students, the instructional time and supports self-studying. A new mechanism that is focused on practically improving the recitation is proposed by Altalmas et al. (2017). This technique uses lips tracking identification methods to extract the correct way of pronouncing the letters from video records for professional reciters. Then the extracted lips movements and final shapes are used to check the recitation of novice readers and figure out their mistakes. It also gives suggestions for improving the recitation.

Furthermore, a study done by Alfaries, Albahlal, Almazrua, and Almazrua (2013) applies natural language processing techniques in order to extract the Tajweed rules from the Qur'an text and annotate them. In this study, GATE environment was used to develop an application that processes and annotates the text. The followed approach uses two tokenizers (word and letter tokenize) then applies Java Annotation Patterns Engine (JAPE) for annotating the rules. Precision and recall metrics were used to evaluate the application with a 100% result for both metrics. Learning Tajweed is also supported through the proposed online portal for all sciences related to Qur'an. This portal is suggested by Adhoni, AlHamad, Siddiqi, and El Mortaji (2013) and it is made accessible through different devices. A friendly mobile app is also developed. Ragheb and Mahmoud (2013) have studied the effectiveness of one of the major computer software in this area which is The Hafs Tajweed Teacher Software. The software was tested on 200 users in four countries. The experiment proved the important role of Hafs software in accelerating the learning process especially for beginners.

Moreover, researchers have also used deep learning techniques to enhance the solutions provided for teaching tajweed. Al-Ayyoub, Damer, & Hmeidi (2018) proposed an approach that uses Convolutional Deep Belief Network (CDBN) which improved the accuracy of the classification to 97.7%. Support Vector Machine classifier was used to classify the features extracted from thousands of records for reciters from both genders. Moving to the work that integrates some entertaining methods, Tajweed Race Online Game Via Facebook Platform developed by Nordin, Rahman, Abd Rawi, & Yusof (2013), introduced an enthusiastic multiplayer game prototype for children in age range of seven to twelve years old. Its aim is to enrich and assess children's knowledge of Tajweed. It contains highly attractive factors. Children can communicate and at the same time play and compete with their friends. The winner is identified using a specific formula that calculates time, speed and player's correct answers. All these factors energize the game players to participate and consequently learn more about Tajweed rules. An interactive game was proposed by Noor, Yussof, Yusoff, & Ismail (2018) but has not yet been implemented. This game also includes the use of AR. The approach was designed and developed using an instructional design model (ADDIE) with five basic stages: Analysis, Design, Development, Implementation and Evaluation. Learners can scan a marker in an AR book which leads them to different challenges, videos, animations that explain and examine the learners' knowledge. A suggested approach by Basuhail (2013) takes into consideration instructors who don't have good IT skills. In his chapter, Basuhail, provides a workable model that is simple and straightforward for implementing learning objects. The approach circulates through several steps: planning, interface, visuals, multimedia, texting, formatting, animation, integration and testing. Based on a chosen topic, the instructor can add the suitable buttons, animations, windows and play with many other options to produce an effective teaching object that can be used separately or integrated in an e-learning environment. Most importantly, it satisfies each student's preferable style of learning. For example, the student can listen to a sound of specific letter pronunciation, read its description or see a picture that visualizes the actual positioning of the internal organs with the pronunciation of that letter.

As noticed, the uniqueness of this research comes from the high level of attractiveness and entertainment accompanied by the educational value. The following sections are organized as follows: the first section explains the methodology in detail covering the brain storming session, the device used to play the game, the game story, game design and game development as subsections. The next section is about the user study including subsections about the participants and testing settings. The third section displays the results of the study. The following section discusses the participants' answers and results. Then the future plans are stated. Finally, the conclusion section sums up the chapter.

DESIGNING QEE VR GAME

Brainstorming Session

The first step was conducting a brainstorming session to get the teenagers' preferences (ages 13-18) and consider them in the game design and development. The session contained verbal discussions, written surveys and an activity that encourages the participants to come up with a basic design for a new game. The participants' requirements were mostly focused on a good graphic design quality, immersive music and sound effects, and the use of modern technologies such as AR and VR. Based on these results a basic design was proposed.

Technology and Hardware

This section states the technology used in the project, its significance in the future of HCI and the criteria considered to select the hardware. Tracking the innovative HCI progress that is provided by Hasan and Yu (2015), it can be clearly seen that the evolution of technological devices has a rapid movement that is greatly impacting human computer interaction. It started with cell phones to make voice calls and developed to include smartphones with high resolution cameras, touch screens, global positioning system and many more features that continuously aim to provide the user with an easier and more immersive and realistic experience. With less clicks, drags and drops and more of the human real-life movements such as holding, blinking, walking and jumping, VR devices bring the user experience to a higher level of interactivity and allows users to enjoy a very engaging experience. This makes it a great potential for technological investments in a smart-technology demanding society. Integrating this technology within the newly built solutions helps reinforcing the innovation and creativity in the digital media world. To keep up with this technological evolution, ensure the entertainment factor is emphasized, and based on the results of the brainstorming session, the choice of VR was an excellent option to consider.

Moreover, there is some evidence that VR contributes in increasing the effectiveness of the learning process and raising the students' motivation. According to Mantovani (2001), what makes VR a good choice for learning is that it enables the users to build knowledge by directly interacting with it rather than perceiving it from an instructor or a text. Mantovani also mentions some benefits from the use of VR such as experiential and active rather than passive learning, visualization, and motivation enhancement. After some investigations, the decision was made to employ these unique and effective features of VR in this game.

In order to select the best VR device to work on, a product comparison was done to check what options there are in the market, what features each one has and their prices. After all, HTC Vive was found to be ideal for this case (VIVE™|VIVE Virtual Reality System, n.d.). The HTC Vive set is a wearable immersive interaction device which allows the player to interact with the game via a special headset, two hand controllers and two base stations (Figure 1). This ensures a fully immersive experience with a variety of actions to apply (through the controllers). In addition, its price is considered affordable which

Figure 1. HTC Vive device
Source: (Vive, n.d.)

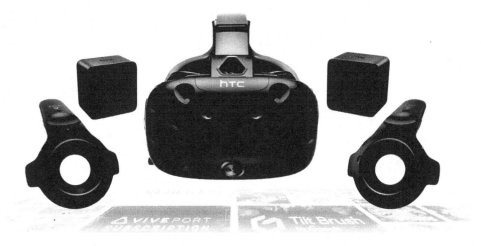

Figure 2. (a) Devil character; (b) Collectable object - the Qee game logo

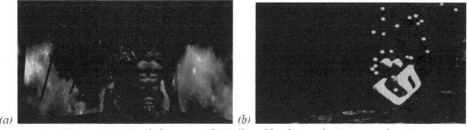

(a)   (b)

Figure 2. (a) Devil character; (b) Collectable object - the Qee game logo

allows for a wider spread among people. The main downside of this device is the technical issues that the users face while setting it up and the time consumed to get it ready.

Game Story

The basic task of the game is for the player to protect himself from the devil (Figure 2a). To do so, the player has to collect an object by the end of each level. This object is symbolized in the *Qee* game logo (will be referred to as Q Symbol) (Figure 2b). The only way to be able to collect this object is to succeed in each level's challenge. Once all levels are passed successfully, the devil dies and the player gets his freedom. To better explain the implicit meanings behind the game story, in the following are some insights: (a) The questions examine the player's knowledge of Tajweed; (b) The obstacles represent the difficulties that people face while learning Tajweed and the devil in this game symbolizes the player's lack of knowledge; and (c) His fear to start learning and improve. To further clarify the progress of the game, a flowchart is shown in Figure 3. The game starts with a video that explains the main idea of the game to the player. Then, the instructions of the first level are given. After that the first level starts. Once the player solves the challenge and gets the Q Symbol, the level ends and the instructions of the

Figure 3. Sample of game flowchart (Level 1)

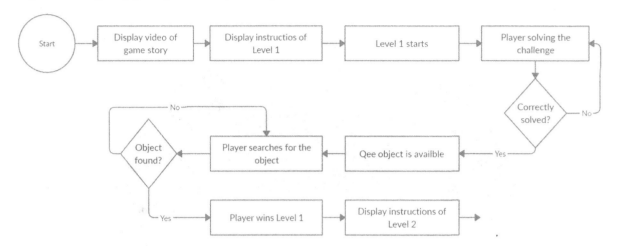

next level are displayed. The flowchart is limited to one level only as the same process is repeated in level 2 with different challenges.

Game Design

When describing a good and fun game, in his book "Theory of Fun for Game Design" Koster (2014) focuses on understanding patterns. This can be achieved by the iteration through the player's interactions and the feedback, which helps the player develop a mental model of the game. This loop can be seen clearly in *Qee* game through the general flowchart (Figure 3). The game responds to each interaction from the player, usually through a message on the screen or by altering a score counter. The game mechanics are designed in a way that makes the game engaging and retains a level of excitement and eagerness to proceed. An example of this is that the *Q* symbol is not enabled for the player until he solves the challenge. Further, a scoring system is provided to keep the player updated on how far he is from the goal. All these factors combine to produce an interactive and informative gameplay.

The design of each level started with rough storyboards and sketches that only showed the basic features of the level. Later, these sketches were modified and finally implemented using Unity engine. The game was designed in two levels: (a) The Desert; and (b) The Cave. The details of each level are described as below:

Level 1 - The Desert

Environment and challenge: This level takes place in a desert setting with palm trees scattered randomly. Furthermore, the level's area is wide and includes a lot of props that play a big role in attracting the player and keeping him excited to discover more. For instance, there are houses, trees, camels and shops that have a very realistic appearance especially through the VR view (Figure 4a). In this level there are six valid collectables (Figure 4b) which are Arabic letters that constitute together the correct answer of the following question: *What are the correct letters of Izhar* (a very well-known rule in Tajweed)? *Find them scattered in this level.* This question is displayed on the screen once the level starts to assist the player.

Figure 4. (a) Level 1- Desert setting; (b) Collectable objects

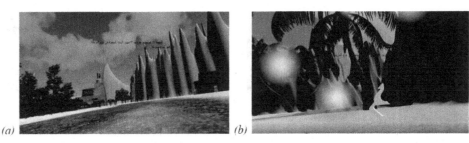

(a) (b)

Figure 4. (a) Level 1- Desert setting; (b) Collectable objects

Obstacles and rewards: This challenge is meant to be an easy one as a start. Therefore, no wrong letters were added. In order to help the player, some sparkles were added to each letter so that the player can easily find them. In addition, the level contains a maze that leads to the Q Symbol. The maze gate is locked until the player gets all the letters. Once he does so, the player can enter the maze. The player has to select one of three routes, of which only one is correct. If he does not go through it, he will be in a loop and get back to the beginning of the maze. The player wins the level when he manages to find the Q Symbol inside the maze.

Audio and sound effects: Audio and sound effects play an important role in making the player's experience more immersive. Therefore, the sounds in each level are chosen to support the level's theme. For example, in this level a wind sound is used. In addition, a check sound effect plays when the player collects a letter.

Instructions scene: In this scene, the player's movement is disabled. He can only have a 360 view to check all the instructions that are displayed around him. Models of the controllers are added to explain how each button can be used for the next level. In addition, the devil and the Q Symbol are displayed to remind the player about his task. This scene is displayed twice (before each level) each time with different instructions.

Level 2 - The Cave

Environment and Challenge: This level was designed by combining the rocks in different models to form a cave environment. It has a scary theme and a higher level of difficulty. The player goes through several paths and comes across many catchy and scary props. For example, there are some glowy stones (Figure 5) and cracked bridges. Moreover, several lighting objects were added to lighten the cave. In this level, the player has to answer two questions, each with three options. The possible answers are 3D Arabic letters that can be picked up using the controllers. Each question asks the player to collect the right letter for a specific Tajweed rule (Figure 5).

Obstacles and Rewards: The player faces many obstacles while searching for the questions to answer them and win the level. The environment contains some creepy monsters and some tough roads which makes the walking and searching through the level challenging for the player (Figure 5). To reward the player for his right answers, there is a counter displayed named "Score". The score's initial value is zero. If the player picks the right letter, his score increases by one. Besides that, there is another counter named

Figure 5. Level 2 – Cave setting End of the game scene

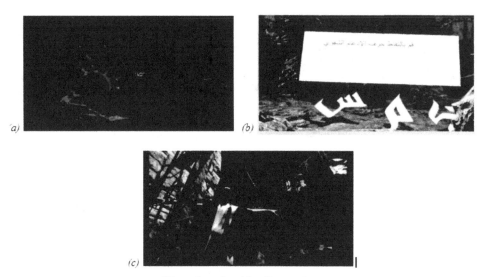

Figure 5a-c. Level 2 – Cave setting

"Power" that is decreased by one when choosing a wrong answer. The initial value for this counter is two. If the power reaches zero, the player loses and the level is automatically restarted. Once the player answers the two questions correctly, he will be able to collect the Q Symbol which will be available somewhere in the level's environment. By collecting it, the player wins this level and the game ends with a final scene (Figure 6).

Audio and sound effects: A scary background music is set to be playing with the loop option checked so that it keeps playing while the level is in progress.

The ending scene is played when the player wins the game. This scene is composed of the defeated devil lying on the ground with fires all around him (Figure 6). The fire effect was done using a special type of particle systems. An audio of the devil screaming is added to the scene.

Game Development

This game was developed using Unity software accompanied by Visual Studio for the code. Blender was used for creating 3D models. The game was mainly developed in two stages: building the environment, and writing the required code according to the player's movement and tasks.

Unity allows the user to come up with a variety of very creative environments. Raising terrains, adding textures, creating particle systems and many other techniques are some of the very powerful design options provided by Unity and applied in this game. Another feature, which is used in the desert level and the instructions scene, is creating skyboxes. Skyboxes are themes for the surrounding world of the player which are used to give a texture behind all other objects, representing a sky or any other space. Some assets are imported from Unity Asset Store as well (Unity Asset Store - The Best Assets for Game Making, n.d.). These assets are ready made objects that can either be downloaded for free or bought.

In order to set up the camera view, an asset named SteamVR is downloaded and imported to the project. After that, the main camera is deleted and replaced with the cameraRig (imported from the

Figure 6. End of game scene

SteamVR asset). The cameraRig is given a RigidBody which makes its motion follow the unity physics engine. A box collider is added to the camera as well. The next step is writing the scripts. Throughout the game, the following functionalities are implemented:

- **Walking:** The forward movement is attached to the touchpad of the controllers while the direction is decided through the camera head (the player's head direction). In the second level (Cave level), jumping is applied by letting the movement on the y-axis correspond to the camera head direction.
- **Collecting by Colliding With an Object:** This method is used in the first level. The isTrigger option is enabled on each collectable (i.e. letter) so that once the camera's collider (the player) collides with the letter, the score increases and the letter disappears.
- **Laser Pointer:** To start each level the player uses the laser pointer to refer to the "Play" button and uses the controller's trigger to click it.
- **Grabbing:** The player in the second level answers by touching the letter with the controller then pressing the trigger to hold it. A common tag was given to the correct letters and another one for the wrong ones. Once the letter is in hand, its tag is checked. If it is correct, the score increases; else, the power decreases.

Moreover, some important settings needed to be modified for the Vive to work properly such as freezing rotation, adding colliders, and checking the gravity option to let the objects behave as if they are in the real world.

USER STUDY

The testing was conducted to evaluate the efficiency of the game and get user feedback for improvement suggestions. Two questions were proposed:

Figure 7. Answering result to question: How often do you play computer games?

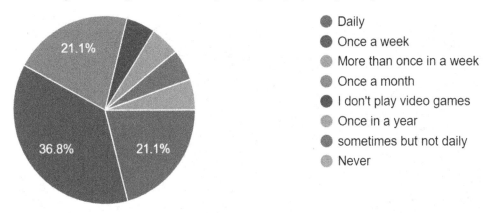

Daily
Once a week
More than once in a week
Once a month
I don't play video games
Once in a year
sometimes but not daily
Never

- Is the game entertaining enough to attract teenagers?
- Is it helpful in improving the player's knowledge of Tajweed?

To answer these questions the testers' interactions were carefully monitored during the testing session. In addition, a post-testing survey was given to the players to get their neutral opinion and suggestions.

Participants and Setting

The game was evaluated with 20 female participants of ages between 13 and 18, with 59% and 41% percentages for middle and high school respectively. Only female students were recruited in this study due to the gender segregation system at school in Saudi Arabia. Therefore, since all the team members of this research are female, the research team had no access to the male section at the period of the user study. The sample was chosen randomly to cover a diversity of technical backgrounds. A pre-testing survey was conducted to collect demographic information about the players and their backgrounds. The survey shows that 58% of the participants have a previous experience with a VR device. The percentage of using computer games varied between daily, weekly and monthly, with (once a week) option being the most significant (Figure 7). In terms of the Tajweed knowledge background, only 15% of them did not have any previous experience in learning Tajweed. Most of those who have learned Tajweed previously were taught by a teacher. Some of them used other methods such as books, mobile app. Most of the players were familiar with at least two of the Tajweed lessons covered by the game challenges.

Since the target audience of this study is teenagers, the testing was decided to be done in Alfahd private school, Riyadh, KSA, that has students from grade seven to twelve in one campus. The VR device was set up in a room with enough space for the players to move freely while playing (Figure 8). Since some people face motion sickness while using virtual reality technology, a chair was provided if this case was encountered. The laptop, the information sheet, consent form and all the required materials were arranged on a desk beside the device set up. Mobile phones were used for the online survey.

Figure 8. Evaluation setting

Procedure

The testing session lasted for about 15-20 minutes for each player. After introducing the project and the team to the testers, they went one by one through the following steps:

1. Reading information sheet and signing the consent form
2. Completing the pre-testing survey
3. Playing the game
4. Completing the post-testing survey

All participants were notified about the probability of getting dizzy and were requested to note it immediately if it happened. After that, the participant was given the controllers and helped to wear the headset and adjust its size. Then the game was started. Some players managed to win the first level and move to the second one while others only tested the first level.

RESULTS

The results were obtained by analyzing the post-testing survey answers and monitoring the players' reactions and attitudes while playing. The survey questions covered three areas: playing experience, game interface and game content. All players tried out level 1 whereas only 42% of them tested level 2.

Figure 9. Answering result to question: To what extent did you enjoy playing the game, rather than something you were just doing?

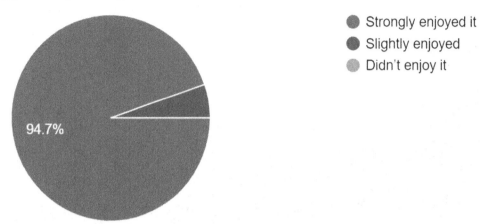

Figure 10. Answering result to question: To what extent you enjoy the graphics and the imagery?

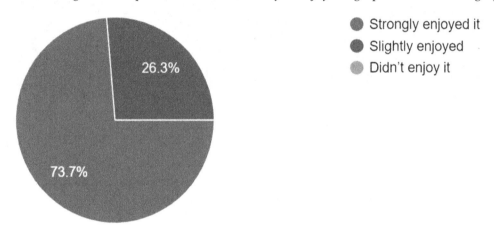

Based on the players' answers in the playing experience section, 94.7% of the players strongly enjoyed playing the game (Figure 9), 52% of them found it challenging and 100% showed their interest to try it again. When asked to measure the difficulty of each level, most of the testers rated level one as easy, considering its collecting method (i.e. collect by colliding) the most comfortable one. The reason for that is that the player's attention is focused only on walking by touching the controller's forward button. On the other hand, answering with the controller (laser and picking) requires more effort from the player to manage using both controllers, one for walking and the other for answering. Therefore, most players who tried level 2 rated it as medium or hard.

To evaluate the game interface, questions were asked about the creativity and quality of the graphics. As shown in Figure 10, 73.7% of the participants strongly enjoyed the design of the environment. However, it was a common note among testers that the clarity of the displayed texts needs to be increased.

For the last examined area, the game's content, all participants replied positively to the question that asks about their familiarity of Tajweed. However, not all of them managed to answer all the questions.

Figure 11. Answering result to question: Did you find the game helpful to support your knowledge of Tajweed?

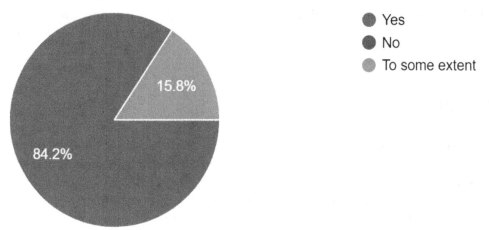

This ensures the role of the game in refreshing and enhancing the players' knowledge of Tajweed. Furthermore, 84.2% of the participants agreed that the game helps supporting their knowledge (Figure 11).

DISCUSSION

Going back to the main proposed questions: "Is the game entertaining enough to attract teenagers?" and "Is it helpful in improving the player's knowledge of Tajweed?" and taking the players' feedback into account, many outcomes can be derived. First of all, the testing has proved that the game has an appealing design, and a novel and unique playing technique that catches the player's attention. The immersive experience provided by the game comes from the combination of the realistic environment (Figure 4a) with some fantastic characters (Figure 2a) and props (Figure 5a & c). Secondly, the questions added a sense of challenge and aided in reviewing some Tajweed information, which fulfills the game's purpose.

Beside these remarkable findings, some modifications were extracted from the players' reactions and recommendations. From the user experience perspective, the instructions of using the controllers have to be stated more clearly, especially for those who have not tried a VR device previously. In addition, the font's size and resolution must be increased. Talking about the development aspect, level two has some gaps where the player falls down unexpectedly. These comments will be taken into consideration in future improvements.

FUTURE WORK

By providing a unique solution that covers a rarely targeted content with most advanced technologies, this project aims to contribute to the development and advancement of the future of HCI. Powered by the authors' ambitions to further enrich this area with effective and innovative solutions, a future plan is set to enhance the product and reach a larger audience. To do so, the game will be modified to be compatible with other devices. Applying this will help avoid the complexity of the HTC Vive set up and increase the game's popularity. Based on the testers' feedback, their interaction with the game and the survey's results, the authors believe that developing new levels would make the game more fruitful and enjoyable. Therefore, innovative ideas for the challenges and the environments are being looked for. In addition, the testers' suggestions will be taken into consideration to enhance their experience and increase their satisfaction level.

CONCLUSION

This chapter provides a unique addition to the game development world. At the same time, it supplies the educational sector with a non-traditional learning method. Proceeding from the teenagers' attitude of spending too much time playing computer games and the importance of learning in this age, the idea of developing an entertaining game that at the same time participates in teaching an important science was introduced. Noticing the teenagers' need for a variety of educational resources and ways in Tajweed science resulted in choosing this science for the game content. Tajweed is a science that teaches the correct pronunciation of letters and words in reciting Qur'an. A VR 3D design was chosen for the game to be attractive and satisfying enough for today's teenagers. The testers showed their excitement and enthusiasm towards the game's environment and challenges. The future work will focus on expanding this game to have more levels and challenges. Furthermore, we plan to test the game with teenage male participants.

ACKNOWLEDGEMENT

This work was supported by the Human Computer Interaction Research Group; Prince Sultan University; Riyadh; Saudi Arabia [RG-CCIS-2017-06-01]. Many thanks are also due to Alfahad Private School for giving us the permission to do the testing in its campus. Lastly, a big gratitude is expressed to the authors' families for their permanent support. Indeed, none of this would be possible without them.

REFERENCES

Adhoni, Z. A., AlHamad, H., Siddiqi, A. A., & El Mortaji, L. (2013). Towards a Comprehensive Online Portal and Mobile Friendly Qur'an Application. In *Proceedings of the 2013 Taibah University International Conference on Advances in Information technology for the Holy Quran and Its Sciences* (pp. 138-143). IEEE. 10.1109/NOORIC.2013.38

Ahsiah, I., Noor, N. M., & Idris, M. Y. I. (2013). Tajweed Checking System to Support Recitation. In *Proceedings of the 2013 International Conference on Advanced Computer Science and Information Systems* (pp. 189-193). IEEE.

Al-Ayyoub, M., Damer, N. A. M., & Hmeidi, I. (2018). Using Deep Learning for Automatically Determining Correct Application of Basic Quranic Recitation Rules. *The International Arab Journal of Information Technology, 15*(3A), 620–625.

Alfaries, A., Albahlal, M., Almazrua, M., & Almazrua, A. (2013). A Rule Based Annotation System to Extract Tajweed Rules from Quran. In *Proceedings of the 2013 Taibah University International Conference on Advances in Information technology for the Holy Quran and Its Sciences* (pp. 281-286). IEEE. 10.1109/NOORIC.2013.63

Altalmas, T. M., Jamil, M. A., Ahmad, S., Sediono, W., Salami, M. J. E., Hassan, S. S., & Embong, A. H. (2017). Lips Tracking Identification of a Correct Pronunciation of Quranic Alphabets for Tajweed Teaching and Learning. *IIUM Engineering Journal*, *18*(1), 177–191. doi:10.31436/iiumej.v18i1.646

Basuhail, A. A. (2013). A Model for Implementing E-Teaching Objects for the Holy Quran and Related Sciences Using Animations. In *Proceedings of the 2013 Taibah University International Conference on Advances in Information technology for the Holy Quran and Its Sciences* (pp. 83-88). IEEE. 10.1109/NOORIC.2013.28

Czerepinski, K. C. (2000). *Tajweed rules of the Quran = Aḥkām tajwīd al-Qurʾān*. Jeddah: Dar Al-Khair Islamic Books Publisher.

Dede, C. J., Salzman, M., & Loftin, R. B. (1996). The development of a virtual world for learning newtonian mechanics. In P. Brusilovsky, P. Kommers, & N. Streitz (Eds.), *Multimedia, Hypermedia, and Virtual Reality Models, Systems, and Applications. MHVR 1996* (pp. 87–106). Springer. doi:10.1007/3-540-61282-3_10

Hasan, M. S., & Yu, H. (2017). Innovative developments in HCI and future trends. *International Journal of Automation and Computing*, *14*(1), 10–20. doi:10.100711633-016-1039-6

Ibrahim, N. J., Idris, M. Y. I., Razak, Z., & Abdul Rahman, N. N. (2013). Automated Tajweed Checking Rules Engine for Quranic Learning. *Multicultural Education & Technology Journal*, *7*(4), 275–287. doi:10.1108/METJ-03-2013-0012

Kapi, A. Y., Osman, N., Ramli, R. Z. & Taib, J. M. (2017). Multimedia Education Tools for Effective Teaching and Learning. *Journal of Telecommunication, Electronic and Computer Engineering, 9*(2-8), 143-146.

Koster, R. (2014). *A theory of fun for game design. Sebastopol*. Cali: OReilly Media.

Mantovani, F. (2001). VR Learning: Potential and Challenges for the Use of 3D Environments in Education and Training. In G. Riva & C. Galimberti (Eds.), *Towards cyberpsychology: Mind, cognition, and society in the Internet Age* (pp. 207–225). Amsterdam: IOS Press.

Marlina, L., Wardoyo, C., Sanjaya, W. S. M., Anggraeni, D., Dewi, S. F., Roziqin, A., & Maryanti, S. (2018). Makhraj Recognition of Hijaiyah Letter for Children Based on Mel-Frequency Cepstrum Coefficients (MFCC) and Support Vector Machines (SVM) Method. In *Proceedings of the 2018 International Conference on Information and Communications Technology* (pp. 935-940). IEEE. 10.1109/ICOIACT.2018.8350684

Noor, M. N., Yussof, R. L., Yusoff, F. H., & Ismail, M. (2018). Gamification and Augmented Reality Utilization for Islamic Content Learning: The Design and Development of Tajweed Learning. In N. Abdullah, W. Wan Adnan, & M. Foth (Eds.), *User Science and Engineering. i-USEr 2018. Communications in Computer and Information Science* (pp. 163–174). Singapore: Springer.

Ragheb, A., & Mahmoud, A. (2013). The Role of e-Learning Software in Teaching Quran Recitation. In *Proceedings of the 2013 Taibah University International Conference on Advances in Information technology for the Holy Quran and Its Sciences* (pp. 429-440). IEEE.

Saany, S. I., Nordin, M., Rahman, A., Abd Rawi, N., & Yusof, A. I. (2013). Tajweed Race Online Game via Facebook Platform. In *Proceedings of 2013 Taibah University International Conference on Advances /in Information Technology for the Holy Quran and Its Sciences*. IEEE.

Unity Asset Store - The Best Assets for Game Making. (n.d.). Retrieved from https://assetstore.unity.com/

Vive [Digital image]. (n.d.). Retrieved from https://www.vive.com/media/filer_public/b1/5f/b15f1847-5e1a-4b35-8afe-dca0aa08f35a/vive-pdp-ce-ksp-family-2.png

VIVE. (n.d.). VIVE Virtual Reality System. Retrieved from https://www.vive.com/us/product/vive-virtual-reality-system/

Winn, W. (1993). *A conceptual basis for educational applications of virtual reality*. University of Washington.

Yousfi, B., Zeki, A. M., & Haji, A. (2017). Isolated Iqlab Checking Rules Based on Speech Recognition System. In *Proceedings of the 2017 8th International Conference on Information Technology* (pp. 619-624). IEEE. 10.1109/ICITECH.2017.8080068

Section 3
Technical Advances

Chapter 14
3D Single Image Face Reconstruction Approaches With Deep Neural Networks

Hafiz Muhammad Umair Munir

Department of Mechanical Engineering, Tokai University, Japan & Department of Mechatronics Engineering, National University of Sciences and Technology, Islamabad, Pakistan

Waqar S. Qureshi

Department of Mechatronics Engineering, National University of Sciences and Technology, Islamabad, Pakistan & Robot Design and Development Lab, NUST College of Electrical and Mechanical Engineering, Rawalpindi, Pakistan

ABSTRACT

3D facial reconstruction is an emerging and interesting application in the field of computer graphics and computer vision. It is difficult and challenging to reconstruct the 3D facial model from a single photo because of arbitrary poses, non-uniform illumination, expressions, and occlusions. Detailed 3D facial models are difficult to reconstruct because every algorithm has some limitations related to profile view, fine detail, accuracy, and speed. The major problem is to develop 3D face with texture of large poses, wild faces, large training data, and occluded faces. Mostly algorithms use convolution neural networks and deep learning frameworks to create facial model. 3D face reconstruction algorithms used for application such as 3D printing, 3D VR games and facial recognition. Different issues, problems and their proposed solutions are discussed. Different facial dataset and facial 3DMM used for 3D face reconstructing from a single photo are explained. The recent state of art 3D facial reconstruction and 3D face learning methods developed in 2019 is briefly explained.

INTRODUCTION

Mostly algorithms for 3D facial shape is used only for small poses, medium poses, and uniform illumination but challenge comes when there is profile view and occluded view. Current algorithms and system are using multiple images as an input and getting more fine details as compared to using single image

DOI: 10.4018/978-1-7998-2637-8.ch014

as an input. The computational cost of multi-view algorithm is always high. Constructing the 3D facial model from a single photo is still a problem and researchers are going to solve that problem. Existing algorithms of facial reconstruction are designed that are based on variety of models such as landmark-based face model and 3D Morphable Models (3DMM). This paper focuses on 3D facial reconstruction from single image using deep neural network architecture. Single photo face reconstruction is rarely employed by modern face recognition systems. 3DMM is the most popular method for reconstructing the full 3D facial model from a single photo. CNN has applications in the field of image classification, object detection and extract meaningful information from photos. Currently, there are four popular 3D facial deformation models which are publicly available. Bolkart et al. (Brunton, 2014) developed the first 3D face model that has neutral different subjects, Imperial College LSFM (Booth, 2018) built the large-scale face model built by, which contains faces of different races and ages. The BFM (Paysan, 2009) model proposed by the University of Basel. University of Surrey, UK (Huber, 2016) developed the multi-resolution 3D face model. There are following 3D facial reconstruction techniques where 3D Morphable Models created from High-quality Scans. 1) Monocular 3D Reconstruction. 2) 3D Reconstruction via Photo-collections. 3) Multi-frame 3D Reconstruction.

CNN-based methods (Jourabloo, Liu, 2016) (Zhu, 2016) (Liu, 2016) (Liu, 2017) (Tran, 2017) (Tran, 2018) are expensive because they need a lot of training data with labeled the 3D faces which is very expensive to collect, They generally lacking in face appearance, expression, occlusions and environment conditions, and limiting the generalization performance of resulted 3D estimated facial models. Some recently algorithms used to reconstruct the 3D facial model by bypass the 3DMM coefficient. They use image to image (Feng, 2018) and image to volume (Jackson, 2017) strategy but they are lack in ground truths. The proposed algorithms (Richardson, 2016) (Richardson, 2017) reconstructed the 3D facial model with using CNN cascaded structure that consume too much time because of their CNN has multi stages. These methods (Dou, 2017) (Tan, 2017) (Jourabloo, Liu, 2015), used the holistic approach to regress the 3DMM parameters. Jackson et al. (Jackson, 2017) proposed an algorithm that is used to reconstruct the 3D face model by mapping the image pixels to a voxel representation. This method does not need a 3DMM but needs a complex structure takes a lot of time to get voxel information. Feng et al. (Feng, 2018) trained the image to image CNN approach that stored the 3D model into UV position map and reconstruct the 3D facial from a single image. 3D facial reconstruction from a photo collection (Kemelmacher-Shlizerman, 2013)(Liang, 2016)(Suwajanakorn, 2014) does not 3DMM face models.

The earliest approaches is utilized the reference 3D faces (Hassner, Basri, 2006) (Hassner, Basri, 2013) to adjust the shape estimated for an input face image. These old methods are emphasized on robustness rather than fine details. Later methods are designed to construct the 3D face model by detection of facial landmarks (Jourabloo, Liu, 2016) (Zhu, 2016) and these algorithms give importance to accuracy regarding detection of landmarks. The 3DMM fitting methods are widely used which is originally proposed by Blanz and Vetter (Blanz, Vetter, 1999). Shape from shading techniques (Kemelmacher-Shlizerman, Basri, 2011) (Li, 2014) showed accurate and detailed 3D face reconstruction. Now a day deep neural networks (Jackson, 2017) (Tran, 2017) (Tran, 2018) are used for the estimation of 3D face shape with unconstrained images. These deep 3D face estimation methods are still challenging and focus on speed, accuracy and low computational cost. Nikolai et al. (Nikolai, 2018) proposed mobile-net based 3D facial reconstruction which is fast. Coarse-to-fine method is used to reconstruct a high-quality 3D facial model from a single photo (Jiang, 2018) but whole face is reconstructed during reconstruction. Self-supervised bootstrap method (Xing, 2018) and model free approach (Feng, 2018) is new technique for 3D face reconstruction. Different types of old and new techniques are explained for 3D facial reconstruction from single image and later on description is focused on the single photo 3D facial reconstruction by deep neural networks.

BACKGROUND

Optimization Techniques

Mostly recently face model is based on 3DMM that is proposed by Blanz and vetter in 1999 (Blanz, Vetter, 1999), and then some advancement comes such as model proposed by (Gerig, 2018) and (Li, 2017). The method (Kemelmacher-Shlizerman, Seitz, 2011) has used multi image shading for reconstruction of 3D model by the multiple images with different shapes and poses. The proposed approach in (Thies, 2016) has produced exact results on different video sequences that are recorded from a single camera. Many developed methods crop an input image for reconstruction of 3D face model because developed face model is suitable on that cropped region of image. These all methods can get best results in terms of accuracy and robustness but they are computationally expensive and consume too much time also. The researchers have developed and used various techniques which are briefly discussed below.

3D Supervision Learning

The methods that are using deep learning architecture are more convenient than traditional methods (Tran, 2018) (Zhu, 2016) (Kim, 2018) (Jackson, 2017). Tran et al. (Tran, 2017) is proposed the approach which estimates parameters 3DMM of a face model with a deep neural network. This method has used different images of same person and extracts the 3DMM by using 2D landmarks. The proposed approach by Feng et al. (Feng, 2018) is used to reconstruct the 3D face model by using UV position map and render the dense correspondence to the appropriate position of each point on UV space. All the previously mentioned methods have 3D supervision technique like volumetric representation, fitting of a 3DMM, and UV maps. These all methods have limitation of the accuracy of fitting process and lack of ground truth information.

Weak 3D Supervision Learning

Lambertian rendering is used in the method that is proposed by Sengupta et al. (Sengupta, 2018). It is using a mixture of synthetically rendered images and real images. The method is based upon the cropped facial images and cannot produce the animated face model. The proposed end-to-end learning approach by Genova et al. (Genova, 2018) using a rendering process that is differentiable. Synthetic data and its corresponding 3D parameters are used in the training process of this method. Nonlinear 3DMM model in a weakly supervised fashion with 3D data is learned by Tran and Liu (Tran, 2018).

Without 3D Supervision Learning

MoFA (Tewari, 2017) has limitation with cropping and severe expressions and output results are looking good but not a wanted 3D face model. The pros and cons of this method is that it is faster than the optimization approaches (Tewari, 2018) and do not produce the accurate results because 3D model is approximate. The method is reconstructed the 3D facial model without 3D supervision.

3DMM MODELS

Recently 3D facial reconstruction methods based on 3DMMs and are appropriate for wild images (Booth, 2016) (Booth, 2017) (Booth, 2018). 3D face modeling is now fast and accurate and is very useful for 3D face reconstruction (Blanz, Vetter, 1999) (Gerig, 2018) (Paysan, 2009) and face recognition (Liu, 2018) (Taigman, 2014), as well as computer graphics applications. Gerig et al. (Gerig, 2018) update a new BFM 2017 with an expressive model. FaceWarehouse (Cao, 2014) is a popular multi-linear 3D face model. The recent FLAME model (Li, 2017) contains head rotation models. Deep models have successfully been recovers 3D face shape from RGB images (Dou, 2017) (Ranjan, 2018)(Tewari, 2017) (Tran, 2017)(Zhu, 2016) or depth images (Abrevaya, 2018). There are two major types of 3DMMs are briefly explained.

Linear 3DMMs

For the past two decades, in many approaches (Blanz, Vetter, 1999) (Blanz, Vetter, 2003) (Romdhani, 2003), principal component analysis (PCA) was used in building statistical 3D shape models. Recently, PCA is used for building large-scale statistical models of the 3D facial geometry (Booth, 2016) and head (Dai, 2017). Decouple of the facial identity from expression is very convenient for generating and representing faces. Hence, statistical blend shape models using PCA were introduced that is used for only the expression variations. For describing the texture variations, the original 3DMM (Blanz, Vetter, 1999) also used a PCA 3DMM model. Describing the texture variation in the wild setting is limited.

Non-Linear 3DMMs

The methods (Tran, 2018) (Tran, 2019) (Tewari, 2018) were introduced nonlinear 3DMMs for learning in the past few years. These 3DMMs are used DCNNs and considered as decoders that use DCNNs. However, the method (Tewari, 2018) combined a linear 3DMM and decoder with fully connected layers and used a self-supervision for reconstructing arbitrary images. Similarly, the proposed methods in (Tran, 2018) (Tran, 2019) decoded the facial shape and facial texture by using either UV map or fully connected layers to define the nonlinear 3DMM decoders. Moreover, these methods used deep neural networks with a huge number of coefficients. Therefore, the non-Euclidean facial mesh domain should be built because decoders are using convolutions directly. Geometric Deep Learning (Bronstein, 2017) is the field of deep learning on non-Euclidean domains.

DATASETS FOR EVALUATION

There are different databases for evaluation of 3D facial reconstruction from a single image, but some is explained.

AFLW and AFLW-LFPA

AFLW (Kostinger, 2011) comprises of 21,080 wild images with profile view with yaw angle from -90o to 90o. Every image in this dataset is labeled with 21 landmarks that are visible. The dataset is very appropriate for analysis of 3D facial reconstruction across large poses. This database has large amount images regarding expressions, illuminations and poses.

AFLW-LFPA (Jeni, 2016) is the constructed for poses and images are extracted from AFLW database. It contains 1,299 test images and every image is labeled with 34 facial landmarks.

AFLW2000-3D

This database (Zhu, 2016) has 2000 samples that are extracted from AFLW database. Every face has 3D ground truth faces and 68 3D facial landmarks. This database plays an important in the analysis of 3D facial reconstruction.

LS3D-W and 300W-LP

LS3D-W (Bulat, 2017), a large facial 2D image dataset containing about 200K unconstrained face images in the wild was used for bootstrapping. The dataset 300W-LP (Zhu, 2016) dataset contains more than 60K face images with marked 3DMM coefficients.

The NoW Dataset

The NoW dataset (Not quite in-the-Wild) (Sanyalhas, 2019) hundred high quality images and ground truth 3D head scan with high resolution. When it is compared with (Tran, 2018) (Tran, 2017) (Feng, 2018) that are trained with 3D supervision. The NoW dataset is addresses the problems of extreme large poses, facial expressions, and different kinds of occlusions. It has 2054 images captured by iPhone X and 3D head scan as well for every subject. The database contains 620 neutral images, 675 expression images, 528 occlusion images and 231 selfie images.

MICC and D3DFACS Dataset

This database (Bagdanov, 2017) is recorded in three different environments and contains 53 videos with corresponding scanned model with ground truth. Each video has different resolution. The D3DFACS dataset (Li, 2017) is trained a 3800 human heads scans and used linear shape space with neck, eyeball, pose, expressions and jaws. The pose and expression are learned from 4D sequences of face. It is publicly feely available.

CHALLENGES OF 3D FACIAL RECONSTRUCTION

There are many challenges that are occurring now a day in 3D face reconstruction methods. Some challenges are explained here. Firstly, commonly landmark-based face model is used but this method is not suitable for profile views because appearance of face dramatically changes from frontal view to profile view. Secondly, in large poses landmark labeling is extremely challenging task that invisible landmarks have to be guessed. Thirdly, 3D estimates of wild facial faces are unstable and change for different photos while the last one is need of robustness, large data and detailed 3D facial reconstruction. Firstly, different algorithms are described which are used to reconstruct the 3D facial model from single photo using deep convolution neural network (CNN) and 3DMM and their comparison too. Pros and cons are explained briefly. Secondly, explained the selected different features for analyzing these algorithms. Finally, experimental setup and results based upon qualitative and quantitative analysis of 3D facial reconstruction methods are described. The different algorithms that have been deployed for solving the above challenges are as follows:

1. 3D dense face alignment (3DDFA).
2. Regressing robust and discriminative (RRD).
3. Volumetric regression network (VRN).
4. 3D detailed reconstruction (3DDR).
5. Position map regression network (PRN)
6. RingNet Architecture
7. 2D-assisted self-supervised learning (2DASL)
8. Weakly Supervised Learning
9. Pose invariant face reconstruction (PIFR)
10. Self-Supervised Bootstrap Method
11. Coloured Mesh Decoding (CMD)
12. Diverse Raw Scan Data
13. Landmark Updating, Inverse rendered and Model Free Approach
14. Face Model Learning (FML)
15. Towards High-fidelity

METHODS

This section describes the different methods which are designed for 3D facial reconstruction from an input single photo. The state of art approaches is described which is used to solved the problem regarding labeled landmarks, huge amount of training data in the wild setting images, facial occlusions, facial large poses and profile view, illumination and lightening, facial expressions, facial hair and albedo.

3D Dense Face Alignment (3DDFA) and Regressing Robust and Discriminative (RRD)

3DDFA (Zhu, 2016) is used to fit the face model to the image via convolution neural network with project normalized coordinate code (PNCC). This algorithm is solved the first challenge that is listed above. An evaluation is conducted on 300W, AFLW and construction of AFLW200-3D database. This algorithm estimates the 3D facial reconstruction and facial alignment across large poses by using convolution neural network and landmarks. The input is the $100 \times 100 \times 3$ color image stacked by PNCC and the architecture consists of four convolution layers. Framework of face profiling is used to creating the large poses from medium poses to solve the second challenge.

When applied the single view 3D face reconstruction on wild facial faces, their 3D estimates are either unstable and change for different facial poses. So, Tran et al. (Tran, 2017) proposed to solve the problem described in third challenge. This algorithm has tested on LFW, YTF and IJB-A while best for face recognition in case of wild faces. This algorithm estimates the 3D facial shape and texture directly from an unconstrained 2D face image. For a given input image, it produces a standard .ply file of the face shape and texture. ResNet-101 or Caffe deep network is used for regressing 3DMM shape and texture parameters under Linux.

Volumetric Regression Network (VRN) and 3D Detailed Reconstruction (3DDR)

Jackson et al. proposed method (Jackson, 2017) approaches the problem of reconstruction regarding segmentation. This algorithm specially estimates large pose 3D facial reconstruction using simple CNN architecture bypassing the training and testing of 3DMM. This method also performs direct regression of a volumetric representation of the 3D facial geometry from single input photo. The images are unconstrained and downloaded from websites that including arbitrary facial poses, expression and occlusion. Evaluation of this method is conducted on three different databases, namely AFLW2000-3D, BU-4DFE, and Florence. This method is developed under Linux and Torch 7 deep neural network framework is used. This architecture does not need accurate alignment but performs direct regression of a volumetric representation.

Tran et al. proposed method (Tran, 2018) has ability to reconstruct the 3D facial model in detail under extreme conditions such as wearing glasses, hide by hairs etc. The algorithm is motivated by old age computer graphic concept named bump mapping (Blinn, 1978) that is used to separate the global shape from local details (wrinkles etc.). It naturally creates plausible details and better capability to produce the 3D facial with good texture model for out of plane rotations and occluded facial regions. The references set of this algorithm consists of 12K unoccluded face images that are selected from the VGG and CASIA sets. The recent method of Sela et al. (Sela, 2017) close to this method that produces good detailed results when face become unoccluded but fails completely on occluded faces because of weak regularization. This algorithm estimates a coarse 3D face shape which acts as a foundation and then separately layer this foundation with details represented by a bump map. This method is developed under Linux and Pytorch deep neural network framework is utilized.

Position Map Regression Network (PRN)

This method (Feng, 2018) uses a concept of UV position map that is used to records the 3D facial model of a complete face in UV space and train a CNN to regress 3D shape from a single photo. It has runtime to reconstruct the 3D model just in 9.8ms which is faster than other methods. The PRN architecture transfers the RGB input image into position map image and UV coordinates based on 3DMM. Its CNN architecture is designed to learn the mapping from unconstrained RGB image to its 3D model. The algorithm has tested on AFLW2000-3D, AFLW-LFPA and Florence datasets. It takes less than 10ms to reconstruct a 3D facial model (shown in Fig. 4). In some cases, non-visible areas of faces are is distorted because of self-occlusion. This method has relatively small errors and becomes more stable when compared to 3DDFA and VRN-Guided. It has also high performance than VRN-Guided (Jackson, 2017) on the Florence dataset. This method is developed under Linux and Tensor flow deep neural network framework is utilized.

RingNet

The best approach (Sanyal, 2019) among all the approaches that are used to reconstruct the 3D face model with full face, head with neck from a single face image. This algorithm has solved the problem of large training data for wild images. It has many applications in augmented reality and virtual reality games. FLAME (Li, 2017) model is used instead of 3D Morphable Models (3DMM's) that is used for achieving the invariance to expression by representing the face. Not quite in-the-wild (NoW) dataset is developed that is more complex than other dataset but it is with high resolution ground truth 3D head scans and high-quality images of 100. The approach is focuses on the shortage of training data and 2D facial features is automatically extracted from the OpenPose library (Simon, 2017). The method is trained on a wild images and lot of other images which regresses the 3D face model from image pixels directly without supervised training data. During it also consider robustness to illumination, camera noise, occlusion and facial hair. The images with these conditions lack the 3D data with ground truth. The RingNet architecture takes a lot of images of same person during training but single image is needed at a run time for 3D facial reconstruction because the change occurs in poses, lighting and expressions but not in face shape. RingNet has more accuracy than all other methods that is based upon 3D supervision and Images are taken from (Cao, 2018).

2D-Assisted Self-Supervised Learning (2DASL)

A novel 2D-assisted self-supervised learning (2DASL) (Tu, 2019) method is solved the problem of lacking 3D annotations training data in the wild setting for improving the learning of 3D facial model and training of 3D facial model as well. This method proposed the four new self-supervision schemes. The first one is cycle-consistency that is used to predict 2D landmark and second one is self-critic that is used to produce better 3D face model. The third one is self-mapping process that is basically based on the prediction of 3D landmark and 2D landmark. The last one is self-prediction consistency landmarks of 3D model and 2D image. 2DASL method renders more higher-quality 3D face models without any additional 3D annotations by using these four self-supervision approaches. The reconstructed face model of this approach comprises of Basel Face Model (BFM) (Paysan, 2009) and Face Warehouse dataset (Cao, 2014). BFM is used for face shape parameters and face Warehouse for face expression parameters.

Weakly-Supervised Learning

The proposed 3D facial reconstruction method (Deng, 2019) is given solution to deep neural networks where required huge volume of facial images with 3D ground truth. The method utilized the weakly supervised learning for reconstruction 3D face model, but it does not need a 3D ground truth. The weakly supervised approach considers both perception level and low-level information for supervision. The approach is accurate, fast, and robust to facial poses and occlusions. The method trained the 3D face model from different images in an unsupervised manner. The skin color algorithm is proposed by this method that is based on photometric error that robust the 3D facial reconstruction with beard and heavy makeup. The accuracy of this method is better than other methods (Sela, 2017) (Feng, 2018) (Tran, 2017).

Pose Invariant Face Reconstruction (PIFR)

The proposed Pose invariant face reconstruction (PIFR) (Jiang, 2018) algorithm reconstructed the 3D facial reconstruction from a single image across large poses. The method is based on 3D Morphable Model (3DMM) and produce accurate results under the extreme facial poses. At first stage, the generation of frontal image by normalizing the image. At the second stage, the weighted sum of the 3D coefficient of the two images. 2D facial data is easy to obtain but 3D facial data is difficult to obtain with high precision and high resolution. The landmark points are occluded when reconstructed the 3D facial model across large poses. This method uses the HPEN (Zhu, 2015) and Poisson Image Editing (Perez, 2003) for normalizing the facial image and recovering the occluded area in the profile view.

Self-Supervised Bootstrap Method

This method (Xing, 2019) is improved 3D facial reconstruction from single image. The proposed self-supervised bootstrap approach comprises of four steps. The first one is existing model, the second one is application of rigid-body transformations, third one is rendering, and the fourth one is bootstrap fine-tuning. The self-supervised bootstrap technique is applied to the volumetric regression network (VRN) method (Jackson, 2017) for fine tuning of 3D facial reconstruction.

Landmark Updating, Inverse Rendered and Model Free Approach

Landmark updating technique (Liu, 2019) is reconstructed the 3D facial model from a single photo by using landmark updating technique. The method uses BFM (Paysan, 2009) and face++. 3DMM data is extracted by using BFM and landmarks are extracted by using face++.

The inverse rendered approach (Guo, 2018) provided a large number of photo-realistic face images with different attributes for 3D facial reconstruction. Face inverse rendering is the process of regresses, albedo, illumination, face geometry, camera parameters and facial pose. This inverse rendering consists of three levels. The first one is fitting of parametric face, refinement of geometry and last one is blending of albedo.

The proposed model-free approach (Feng, 2018) is used for reconstructing 3D facial model from light field images using deep convolution neural network named FaceLFnet. It does not base on landmark detection or fitting of model and it is robust to facial poses, lightning, and expressions. The FaceLFnet is used to learn 3D face curves by epipolar plane images (EPIs). This method also created face image dataset that is based upon light field.

Coloured Mesh Decoding (CMD)

The proposed method (Zhou, 2019) is used the direct mesh convolutions and on non-linear 3DMMs for 3D facial reconstruction in the wild photos. The 3D dense face is decoded by learning joint texture and shape auto-encoders that is used for training light weight model. Coloured Mesh Decoding (CMD) has speed of over 2500 FPS in the wild setting. Mesh convolutions have low computational complexity and few parameters. The CMD approach decodes both face texture and faces shape with model size of 17MB and estimate the 3D shape over 300 FPS for the whole system. First time, this method qualitatively

Figure 1. 3D Model of 3DDFA

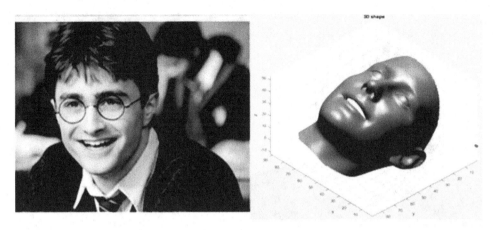

compared with five recent 3D facial reconstruction methods, the Sela et al. (Sela, 2017), MoFA (Tewari, 2017), and VRN (Jackson, 2017).

Diverse Raw Scan Data

The proposed innovative approach (Liu, 2019) is used to learn jointly a facial model from a multiple set of raw 3D scan databases and establishes dense correspondence among all scans with weakly supervised learning approach. This method learned an expressive, preserve high resolution detailed 3D scans and fast facial model. The PointNet framework is used for converting point clouds to facial identity and features of expression, from which 3D facial shapes are reconstructed.

Face Model Learning (FML)

This approach (Tewari, 2019) is solved the two ill posed problem. The first one is regarding parameters of 3D facial geometry based on monocular camera. The other one is depth ambiguity including face expressions, albedo, profile view and lightening. The proposed method is used the self-supervised training of a deep neural framework that is based upon multi-frame video. The method is used for 3D facial reconstruction and multi frame learning of a facial model. The proposed model is based upon huge number of wild setting internet videos (Chung, 2018) and trained from scratch without ground truth.

Towards High-Fidelity

This method (Tran, 2019) proposed the high-fidelity 3D facial reconstruction. High fidelity face models are needed to represent facial images in high level of details. The proposed approach reconstructed 3D facial model by strong regularizations and detailed albedo and shape. This novel method enables learning of albedo and shape with proper regularization and uses local global based architecture.

Figure 2. 3D Model of RRD

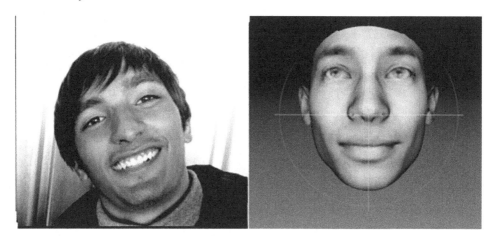

EXPERIMENTAL ANALYSIS

Qualitative Analysis

All the algorithms are state of the art on reconstruction of 3D face model by using deep neural network that are described above. Qualitative and quantitative analysis is explained for generation of 3D facial model of different algorithms. 3DDFA method is the first algorithm which is used to reconstruct the 3D face model from single image using cascaded CNN. This algorithm has solved the problem of invisible landmarks in large poses and face alignment across large poses as well. The areas around mouth and nose are more sensitive while texture of 3D face shape is not so good. This method takes less than a minute to build one 3D solid facial model with pose and slightly texture to small extent. The qualitative result of this algorithm is shown in the Fig. 1.

The RRD method is accurate, fast and robust that is used for estimating the parameters of 3DMM face shape from an input image using a deep CNN architecture. The areas around nose and mouth have very low errors and texture of 3D facial model is better than 3DDFA algorithm. This method is robust to recognize faces in the wild setting. This method takes less than 1 minute to build a 3D facial model with texture and slightly pose to some extent. It is failed in some cases when reconstructing the facial model such as beard hairs or facial hairs. This method is faster to predict the 3DMM parameters than 3DDFA and qualitative results are shown in the Fig. 2.

The VRN approach works with unconstrained facial images of different poses, occlusions and facial expressions downloaded from the websites and reconstruct 3D face shape from single image. This CNN architecture for 3D segmentation is based on hourglass network (Newell, 2016). The volumetric architecture consists of two hourglasses modules. The limitation is that it reconstructs the unwanted part of image also. The qualitative results are shown in the Fig. 3.

The 3DDR method is complex than others but more efficient and robustness for 3D facial reconstruction from single photo by using deep neural frameworks with wild setting while using bump mapping concept and mid-level details. You can see the wrinkles and expression in every facial model as in the facial image while result seems good. It takes 50s per image producing 3D facial model and producing beautiful texture as compared to other methods. This algorithm is better for 3D printing faces, visual

Figure 3. 3D Model of VRN

Figure 4. 3D Model of 3DDR

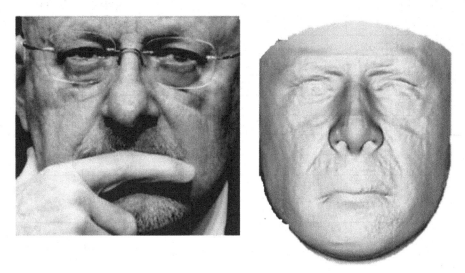

speech recognition and facial recognition, facial augmented reality and virtual reality. The qualitative results are shown in the Fig. 4.

The PRN is best to reconstruct the 3D model of face and it takes 9.8ms per image producing 3D facial model while using the concept of UV mapping but producing beautiful texture as well poses as compared to other methods. The qualitative results are shown in Fig. 5.

Quantitative Analysis

The comparison of different methods on Feng et al. benchmark and NoW dataset (Sanyal, 2019) is shown in the Table 1, Table 2 and Table 3 and gets the numerical values from the respective research papers. The RingNet network has better results than other methods.

Figure 5. 3D Model of PRN

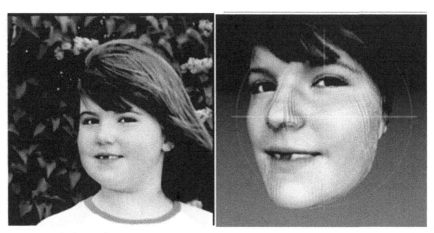

Table 1. Comparison of algorithms

Algorithms	3DDFA	VRN	RRD	PRN	3DDR
3D Morphable Model (3DMM)	Yes	Yes	Yes	Yes	Yes
Convolution neural Network (CNN) Architecture	Yes	Yes	Yes	Yes	Yes
Deep Neural Framework	No	Torch 7	Caffe	Tensor Flow	Pytorch
Operating System	Windows	Linux	Linux	Linux	Linux
Graphic Processing Unit (GPU)	No	Yes	Yes	Yes	Yes
Robustness	Low	Medium	Fast	Fast	Fast
Complexity	Low	Medium	Medium	High	High
Runtime	75.7ms	69ms	88ms	9.8ms	50s

Table 2. Quantitative Analysis on the NoW dataset (Sanyal, 2019) face challenge.

Method	Median (mm)	Mean (mm)	Standard Deviation (mm)
3DDR (Tran, 2018)	1.83	2.33	2.05
PRN (Feng, 2018)	1.51	1.99	1.90
FLAME-neutral (Li, 2017)	1.24	1.57	1.34
RingNet (Sanyal, 2019)	1.23	1.55	1.32

Table 3. Quantitative Analysis on Feng et al. (Feng, 2018) benchmark

Method	Median (mm)		Mean (mm)		Standard Deviation (mm)	
	LQ	HQ	LQ	HQ	LQ	HQ
PRN	1.79	1.60	2.38	2.06	2.19	1.79
RRD	2.40	2.37	3.49	3.58	6.15	6.75
3DDR	1.88	1.85	2.32	2.29	1.89	1.88
RingNet	1.63	1.58	2.08	2.02	1.79	1.69

CONCLUSION

The state of art methods regarding detailed 3D facial reconstruction from single image using deep neural network are explained. The recent approaches play an important in the field of computer vision community, graphics and deep learning field. Many previous ill-posed problems have been solved by these state-of-the-art methods. Different deformation models, 3D face model learning techniques and 3D facial reconstruction has been explained. NoW face databases is covering the head, face, eyeball and neck. This dataset is very useful for the 3D single photo facial analysis. 3D face model learning from diverse raw scan data plays an important in future 3D face reconstruction algorithm. Some algorithms produce better result across large poses, some better for robustness regarding texture parameter, some for occlusions and utmost conditions. Benefits and proposed solution of different problems is described. The performance of all the deep networks is used for different purposes such as facial expressions, occluded images and wild photos are discussed. Future work may include the application of these state-of-the-art algorithms in 3D facial printing and virtual reality games. Anyone can use different kinds of faces in a virtual environment and feel like a real-world environment. 3D facial reconstruction plays a vital role in entertainment industry as well. Reviewing the state-of-the-art methods in 3D hair reconstruction from a single photo is needed. There is requirement of developing a method and application as well for the reconstruction of 3D facial shape with hairs from single image by using deep neural networks.

REFERENCES

Abrevaya, V. F., Wuhrer, S., & Boyer, E. (2018, March). Multilinear autoencoder for 3d face model learning. In *Proceedings of the 2018 IEEE Winter Conference on Applications of Computer Vision (WACV)* (pp. 1-9). IEEE. doi:10.1109/WACV.2018.00007

Bagdanov, A. D., Del Bimbo, A., & Masi, I. (2011, December). The florence 2d/3d hybrid face dataset. In *Proceedings of the 2011 joint ACM workshop on Human gesture and behavior understanding* (pp. 79-80). ACM.

Bas, A., Smith, W. A., Bolkart, T., & Wuhrer, S. (2016, November). Fitting a 3D morphable model to edges: A comparison between hard and soft correspondences. In *Proceedings of the Asian Conference on Computer Vision* (pp. 377-391). Springer.

Blanz, V., & Vetter, T. (1999). A morphable model for the synthesis of 3D faces. In *Proceedings of the 26th annual conference on Computer graphics and interactive techniques*, pages 187– 194, 1999. 10.1145/311535.311556

Blanz, V., & Vetter, T. (2003). Face recognition based on fitting a 3d morphable model. *IEEE Transactions on Pattern Analysis and Machine Intelligence*, 25(9), 1063–1074.

Blinn, F. J. (1978). Simulation of wrinkled faces. In *Proceedings of the ACM SIGGRAPH Conf. Comput. Graphics*, 12(3), 286-292.

Booth, J., Antonakos, E., Ploumpis, S., Trigeorgis, G., Panagakis, Y., & Zafeiriou, S. (2017, July). 3D face morphable models" In-The-Wild". In *Proceedings of the 2017 IEEE Conference on Computer Vision and Pattern Recognition (CVPR)* (pp. 5464-5473). IEEE. doi:10.1109/CVPR.2017.580

Booth, J., Roussos, A., Ponniah, A., Dunaway, D., & Zafeiriou, S. (2018). Large scale 3d morphable models. *International Journal of Computer Vision, 126*(2-4), 233–254. doi:10.100711263-017-1009-7

Booth, J., Roussos, A., Zafeiriou, S., Ponniah, A., & Dunaway, D. (2016). A 3d morphable model learnt from 10,000 faces. In *Proceedings of the IEEE Conference on Computer Vision and Pattern Recognition* (pp. 5543-5552). IEEE Press.

Bronstein, M. M., Bruna, J., LeCun, Y., Szlam, A., & Vandergheynst, P. (2017). Geometric deep learning: Going beyond Euclidean data. *IEEE Signal Processing Magazine, 34*(4), 18–42.

Brunton, A., Salazar, A., Bolkart, T., & Wuhrer, S. (2014). Review of statistical shape spaces for 3D data with comparative analysis for human faces. *Computer Vision and Image Understanding, 128*, 1–17.

Bulat, A., & Tzimiropoulos, G. (2017). How far are we from solving the 2d & 3d face alignment problem? (and a dataset of 230,000 3d facial landmarks). In *Proceedings of the International Conference on Computer Vision (ICCV)*. Academic Press. 10.1109/ICCV.2017.116

Cao, Q., Shen, L., Xie, W., Parkhi, O. M., & Zisserman, A. (2018, May). Vggface2: A dataset for recognising faces across pose and age. In *Proceedings of the 2018 13th IEEE International Conference on Automatic Face & Gesture Recognition* (FG 2018) (pp. 67-74). IEEE. 10.1109/FG.2018.00020

Cheng, S., Kotsia, I., Pantic, M., & Zafeiriou, S. (2018). 4dfab: A large scale 4d database for facial expression analysis and biometric applications. In *Proceedings of the IEEE conference on computer vision and pattern recognition* (pp. 5117-5126). IEEE Press.

Chinaev, N. (2018). MobileFace: 3D face reconstruction with efficient CNN regression.

Chung, J. S., Nagrani, A., & Zisserman, A. (2018). Voxceleb2: Deep speaker recognition.

Dai, H., Pears, N., Smith, W. A., & Duncan, C. (2017). A 3d morphable model of craniofacial shape and texture variation. In *Proceedings of the IEEE International Conference on Computer Vision* (pp. 3085–3093). IEEE Press; . doi:10.1109/ICCV.2017.335

Deng, Y., Yang, J., Xu, S., Chen, D., Jia, Y., & Tong, X. (2019). Accurate 3d face reconstruction with weakly-supervised learning: From single image to image set. In *Proceedings of the IEEE Conference on Computer Vision and Pattern Recognition Workshops*. IEEE Press.

Dou, P., Shah, S. K., & Kakadiaris, I. A. (2017). End-to-end 3D face reconstruction with deep neural networks. In *Proceedings of the IEEE Conference on Computer Vision and Pattern Recognition* (pp. 5908-5917). IEEE Press.

Dou, P., Shah, S. K., & Kakadiaris, I. A. (2017). End-to-end 3D face reconstruction with deep neural networks. In *Proceedings of the IEEE Conference on Computer Vision and Pattern Recognition* (pp. 5908-5917). IEEE Press.

Cao, C., Weng, Y., Zhou, S., Tong, Y., & Zhou, K. (2014). Facewarehouse: A 3d facial expression database for visual computing. *T-VCG, 20*(3), 413–425. PMID:24434222

Feng, Y., Wu, F., Shao, X., Wang, Y., & Zhou, X. (2018). Joint 3d face reconstruction and dense alignment with position map regression network. In *Proceedings of the European Conference on Computer Vision (ECCV)* (pp. 534-551). Academic Press.

Feng, M., Zulqarnain Gilani, S., Wang, Y., & Mian, A. (2018). 3D face reconstruction from light field images: A model free approach. In *Proceedings of the European Conf. Comput. Vision.* Academic Press. 10.1007/978-3-030-01249-6_31

Genova, K., Cole, F., Maschinot, A., Sarna, A., Vlasic, D., & Freeman, W. T. (2018). Unsupervised training for 3d morphable model regression. In *Proceedings of the IEEE Conference on Computer Vision and Pattern Recognition* (pp. 8377-8386). IEEE Press.

Gerig, T., Morel-Forster, A., Blumer, C., Egger, B., Luthi, M., Schönborn, S., & Vetter, T. (2018, May). Morphable face models-an open framework. In *Proceedings of the 2018 13th IEEE International Conference on Automatic Face & Gesture Recognition (FG 2018)* (pp. 75-82). IEEE.

Gerig, T., Morel-Forster, A., Blumer, C., Egger, B., Luthi, M., Schönborn, S., & Vetter, T. (2018, May). Morphable face models-an open framework. In *Proceedings of the 2018 13th IEEE International Conference on Automatic Face & Gesture Recognition (FG 2018)* (pp. 75-82). IEEE. doi:10.1109/FG.2018.00021

Guo, Y., Cai, J., Jiang, B., & Zheng, J. (2018). Cnn-based real-time dense face reconstruction with inverse-rendered photo-realistic face images. *IEEE Transactions on Pattern Analysis and Machine Intelligence, 41*(6), 1294–1307.

Hassner, T., & Basri, R. (2006). Example based 3D reconstruction from single images. In *Proceedings of the Conf. Comput. Vision Pattern Recognition (CVPR) Workshops.* Academic Press. 10.1109/CVPRW.2006.76

Hassner, T., & Basri, R. (2013). Single view depth estimation from examples.

Huber, P., Hu, G., Tena, R., Mortazavian, P., Koppen, P., Christmas, W. J., ... & Kittler, J. (2016, February). A multiresolution 3d morphable face model and fitting framework. In *Proceedings of the 11th International Joint Conference on Computer Vision, Imaging and Computer Graphics Theory and Applications.* Academic Press. 10.5220/0005669500790086

Jackson, A. S., Bulat, A., Argyriou, V., & Tzimiropoulos, G. (2017). Large pose 3D face reconstruction from a single image via direct volumetric CNN regression. In *Proceedings of the IEEE International Conference on Computer Vision* (pp. 1031–1039). IEEE Press; . doi:10.1109/ICCV.2017.117

Jeni, L. A., Tulyakov, S., Yin, L., Sebe, N., & Cohn, J. F. (2016, October). The first 3d face alignment in the wild (3dfaw) challenge. In *Proceedings of the European Conference on Computer Vision* (pp. 511–520). Springer; . doi:10.1007/978-3-319-48881-3_35

Jiang, L., Wu, X., & Kittler, J. (2018). Pose-Invariant 3D Face Reconstruction.

Jiang, L., Zhang, J., Deng, B., Li, H., & Liu, L.(2018). 3D face reconstruction with geometry details from a single image.

Jourabloo, A., & Liu, X. (2015). Pose-invariant 3D face alignment. In *Proceedings of the IEEE International Conference on Computer Vision* (pp. 3694-3702). IEEE Press.

Jourabloo, A., & Liu, X. (2016). Large-pose face alignment via CNN-based dense 3D model fitting. In *Proceedings of the IEEE conference on computer vision and pattern recognition* (pp. 4188-4196). IEEE Press.

Kemelmacher-Shlizerman, I. (2013). Internet based morphable model. In *Proceedings of the IEEE international conference on computer vision* (pp. 3256-3263). IEEE Press.

Kemelmacher-Shlizerman, I., & Basri, R. (2011). 3D face reconstruction from a single image using a single reference face shape. *Trans. Pattern Anal. Mach. Intell.*, *33*(2), 394–405. doi:10.1109/TPAMI.2010.63 PMID:21193812

Kemelmacher-Shlizerman, I., & Seitz, S. M. (2011, November). Face reconstruction in the wild. In *Proceedings of the 2011 International Conference on Computer Vision* (pp. 1746-1753). IEEE.

Kim, H., Zollhöfer, M., Tewari, A., Thies, J., Richardt, C., & Theobalt, C. (2018). Inversefacenet: Deep monocular inverse face rendering. In Proceedings of the IEEE Conference on Computer Vision and Pattern Recognition (pp. 4625-4634). doi:10.1109/ICCV.2011.6126439

Koestinger, M., Wohlhart, P., Roth, P. M., & Bischof, H. (2011, November). Annotated facial landmarks in the wild: A large-scale, real-world database for facial landmark localization. In *Proceedings of the 2011 IEEE international conference on computer vision workshops (ICCV workshops)* (pp. 2144-2151). IEEE. 10.1109/ICCVW.2011.6130513

Li, C., Zhou, K., & Lin, S. (2014). Intrinsic face image decomposition with human face priors. In *Proceedings of the European Conf. Comput. Vision* (pp. 218-233). Springer. 10.1007/978-3-319-10602-1_15

Li, T., Bolkart, T., Black, M. J., Li, H., & Romero, J. (2017). Learning a model of facial shape and expression from 4D scans. *ACM Transactions on Graphics*, *36*(6), 194. doi:10.1145/3130800.3130813

Li, T., Bolkart, T., Black, M. J., Li, H., & Romero, J. (2017). Learning a model of facial shape and expression from 4D scans. *TOG*, *36*(6), 194. doi:10.1145/3130800.3130813

Liang, S., Shapiro, L. G., & Kemelmacher-Shlizerman, I. (2016, October). Head reconstruction from internet photos. In *Proceedings of the European Conference on Computer Vision* (pp. 360-374). Springer.

Liu, F., Tran, L., & Liu, X. (2019). 3D Face Modeling from Diverse Raw Scan Data. In *Proceedings of the IEEE International Conference on Computer Vision* (pp. 9408-9418). IEEE Press.

Liu, F., Zeng, D., Zhao, Q., & Liu, X. (2016, October). Joint face alignment and 3d face reconstruction. In *Proceedings of the European Conference on Computer Vision* (pp. 545–560). Springer; . doi:10.1007/978-3-319-46454-1_33

Liu, F., Zhu, R., Zeng, D., Zhao, Q., & Liu, X. (2018). Disentangling features in 3D face shapes for joint face reconstruction and recognition. In *Proceedings of the IEEE conference on computer vision and pattern recognition* (pp. 5216–5225). IEEE Press; . doi:10.1109/CVPR.2018.00547

Liu, P., Yu, Y., Zhou, Y., & Du, S. (2019, March). Single view 3d face reconstruction with landmark updating. In *Proceedings of the 2019 IEEE Conference on Multimedia Information Processing and Retrieval (MIPR)* (pp. 403-408). IEEE. doi:10.1109/MIPR.2019.00082

Liu, Y., Jourabloo, A., Ren, W., & Liu, X. (2017). Dense face alignment. In *Proceedings of the IEEE International Conference on Computer Vision Workshops* (pp. 1619-1628). IEEE Press.

Mahmood, F., Munir, U., Mehmood, F., & Iqbal, J. (2018, April). 3D shape recovery from image focus using gray level co-occurrence matrix. In *Proceedings of the Tenth International Conference on Machine Vision (ICMV 2017)*. International Society for Optics and Photonics.

Munir, H. M. U., & Qureshi, W. S. (2019). Towards 3D Facial Reconstruction using Deep Neural Networks. In *Proceedings of the 13th International Conference on Computer Graphics, Visualization, Computer Vision and Image Processing (CGVCVIP)*. Academic Press.

Newell, A. (2016). Stacked hourglass networks for human pose estimation. In *Proceedings of the European Conf. Comput. Vision*. Academic Press. 10.1007/978-3-319-46484-8_29

Paysan, P., Knothe, R., Amberg, B., Romdhani, S., & Vetter, T. (2009, September). A 3D face model for pose and illumination invariant face recognition. In *Proceedings of the 2009 Sixth IEEE International Conference on Advanced Video and Signal Based Surveillance* (pp. 296-301). IEEE. doi:10.1109/AVSS.2009.58

Pérez, P., Gangnet, M., & Blake, A. (2003). Poisson image editing. In ACM SIGGRAPH 2003 Papers (pp. 313-318). ACM Press.

Ranjan, A., Bolkart, T., Sanyal, S., & Black, M. J. (2018). Generating 3D faces using convolutional mesh autoencoders. In *Proceedings of the European Conference on Computer Vision (ECCV)* (pp. 704-720). Academic Press.

Richardson, E., Sela, M., & Kimmel, R. (2016, October). 3D face reconstruction by learning from synthetic data. In *Proceedings of the 2016 Fourth International Conference on 3D Vision (3DV)* (pp. 460-469). IEEE.

Richardson, E., Sela, M., & Kimmel, R. (2016, October). 3D face reconstruction by learning from synthetic data. In *Proceedings of the 2016 Fourth International Conference on 3D Vision (3DV)* (pp. 460-469). IEEE. doi:10.1109/CVPR.2017.589

Romdhani, S., & Vetter, T. (2003). Efficient, robust and accurate fitting of a 3d morphable model. In *Proceedings Ninth IEEE International Conference on Computer Vision*. IEEE Press; . doi:10.1109/ICCV.2003.1238314

Sanyal, S., Bolkart, T., Feng, H., & Black, M. J. (2019). Learning to regress 3D face shape and expression from an image without 3D supervision. In *Proceedings of the IEEE Conference on Computer Vision and Pattern Recognition* (pp. 7763-7772). IEEE Press.

Sela, M., Richardson, E., & Kimmel, R. (2017). Unrestricted facial geometry reconstruction using image-to-image translation. In *Proceedings of the IEEE International Conference on Computer Vision* (pp. 1576-1585). IEEE Press. 10.1109/ICCV.2017.175

Sengupta, S., Kanazawa, A., Castillo, C. D., & Jacobs, D. W. (2018). SfSNet: Learning Shape, Reflectance and Illuminance of Facesin the Wild'. In *Proceedings of the IEEE Conference on Computer Vision and Pattern Recognition* (pp. 6296-6305). IEEE Press.

Simon, T., Joo, H., Matthews, I., & Sheikh, Y. (2017). Hand keypoint detection in single images using multiview bootstrapping. In Proceedings of the IEEE conference on Computer Vision and Pattern Recognition (pp. 1145-1153). IEEE Press. doi:10.1109/CVPR.2017.494

Suwajanakorn, S., Kemelmacher-Shlizerman, I., & Seitz, S. M. (2014, September). Total moving face reconstruction. In *Proceedings of the European Conference on Computer Vision* (pp. 796-812). Springer.

Taigman, Y., Yang, M., Ranzato, M. A., & Wolf, L. (2014). Deepface: Closing the gap to human-level performance in face verification. In *Proceedings of the IEEE conference on computer vision and pattern recognition* (pp. 1701-1708). IEEE Press.

Tewari, A., Bernard, F., Garrido, P., Bharaj, G., Elgharib, M., Seidel, H. P., ... Theobalt, C. (2019). Fml: Face model learning from videos. In *Proceedings of the IEEE Conference on Computer Vision and Pattern Recognition* (pp. 10812-10822). IEEE Press.

Tewari, A., Zollhöfer, M., Garrido, P., Bernard, F., Kim, H., Pérez, P., & Theobalt, C. (2018). Self-supervised multi-level face model learning for monocular reconstruction at over 250 hz. In *Proceedings of the IEEE Conference on Computer Vision and Pattern Recognition* (pp. 2549–2559). IEEE Press; . doi:10.1109/CVPR.2018.00270

Tewari, A., Zollhofer, M., Kim, H., Garrido, P., Bernard, F., Perez, P., & Theobalt, C. (2017). Mofa: Model-based deep convolutional face autoencoder for unsupervised monocular reconstruction. In *Proceedings of the IEEE International Conference on Computer Vision Workshops* (pp. 1274-1283). IEEE Press.

Thies, J., Zollhofer, M., Stamminger, M., Theobalt, C., & Nießner, M. (2016). Face2face: Real-time face capture and reenactment of RGB videos. In *Proceedings of the IEEE conference on computer vision and pattern recognition* (pp. 2387-2395).

Tran, A. T., Hassner, T., Masi, I., Paz, E., Nirkin, Y., & Medioni, G. G. (2018, June). Extreme 3D Face Reconstruction: Seeing Through Occlusions. In CVPR (pp. 3935-3944). Academic Press.

Tran, L., Liu, F., & Liu, X. (2019). Towards high-fidelity nonlinear 3D face morphable model. In *Proceedings of the IEEE Conference on Computer Vision and Pattern Recognition* (pp. 1126-1135). IEEE Press.

Tran, L., & Liu, X. (2018). Nonlinear 3d face morphable model. In *Proceedings of the IEEE conference on computer vision and pattern recognition* (pp. 7346-7355). IEEE Press.

Tran, L., & Liu, X. (2019). On learning 3d face morphable model from in-the-wild images. *IEEE Transactions on Pattern Analysis and Machine Intelligence*.

Tu, X., Zhao, J., Jiang, Z., Luo, Y., Xie, M., Zhao, Y., ... Feng, J. (2019). Joint 3D Face Reconstruction and Dense Face Alignment from A Single [-Assisted Self-Supervised Learning.]. *Image, §§§*, 2D.

Tuan Tran, A., Hassner, T., Masi, I., & Medioni, G. (2017). Regressing robust and discriminative 3D morphable models with a very deep neural network. In *Proceedings of the IEEE conference on computer vision and pattern recognition* (pp. 5163–5172). IEEE Press; . doi:10.1109/CVPR.2017.163

Xing, Y. (2018). A self-supervised bootstrap method for single-image 3D face reconstruction.

Zhou, Y., Deng, J., Kotsia, I., & Zafeiriou, S. (2019). Dense 3d face decoding over 2500fps: Joint texture & shape convolutional mesh decoders. In *Proceedings of the IEEE Conference on Computer Vision and Pattern Recognition* (pp. 1097-1106). IEEE Press.

Zhu, X., Lei, Z., Liu, X., Shi, H., & Li, S. Z. (2016). Face alignment across large poses: A 3d solution. In *Proceedings of the IEEE conference on computer vision and pattern recognition* (pp. 146-155). IEEE Press.

Zhu, X., Lei, Z., Yan, J., Yi, D., & Li, S. Z. (2015). High-fidelity pose and expression normalization for face recognition in the wild. In *Proceedings of the IEEE Conference on Computer Vision and Pattern Recognition* (pp. 787-796). IEEE Press.

Zollhöfer, M., Thies, J., Garrido, P., Bradley, D., Beeler, T., Pérez, P., ... & Theobalt, C. (2018). State of the art on monocular 3D face reconstruction, tracking, and applications. *Computer Graphics Forum*, *37*(2), 523–550.

Chapter 15
Visualization and Minima Finding of Multidimensional Hypersurface

Eugene Vladimirovich Popov

https://orcid.org/0000-0002-3058-2369

Nizhegorodsky State Architecture and Civil Engineering University, Russia

Anatoliy Aleksandrovich Batiukov

Nizhegorodsky State Architectural and Civil Engineering University, Russia

Natalja Vogt

Lomonosov Moscow State University, Russia

Tatyana Petrovna Popova

https://orcid.org/0000-0002-1351-222X

National Research University Higher School of Economics, Russia

Jürgen Vogt

University of Ulm, Germany

ABSTRACT

Analysis of multidimensional function properties is required for industrial applications. The solution of its problems is a challenge in economics, sociology, chemistry, biology, biochemistry, and other sciences. For example, the study of the potential energy surface (PES) of a free molecule is of fundamental importance in structural chemistry because it is necessary to determine the stable conformations of a molecule and the ways of interconversion between them. However, if the PES is a function of more than three rotational coordinates, the costs of its quantum-chemical calculation rapidly increases and the problem of its graphical visualization can be hardly solved for a large number of variables. This work describes how a specially developed multidimensional interpolation procedure can contribute to solve these problems. To visualize a five dimensional (5D) hypersurface, the authors applied a special coordinate system.

DOI: 10.4018/978-1-7998-2637-8.ch015

INTRODUCTION

Multidimensional data visualization as a special type of information visualization has been the subject of active research with numerous applications in a wide range of fields – from natural sciences and engineering design to industrial and financial markets in which the correlation between many attributes is of vital interest. Together with the gigantic increase of volumes of data in the world the possibility of gaining inexhaustible sources of information is growing too, enabling human knowledge to expand. However, extracting the meaningful information is a complex task when great amounts of data are presented in a plain text or in a traditional tabular form. Effective graphical presentation of data, therefore, is popular due to the fact that a person mainly gets information through visual perception. Visualization of information is the use of computer interactive visual representations of abstract and non-physical data to enhance human cognition. It aims to help users to swiftly discover and explore what is expected, as well as detect the unexpected in order to gain insight into the data. Multidimensional data are formed from a set of properties that possess a high dimension and often correlate with each other. In this sense the use of the terms multidimensional and multivariate is often ambiguous. Strictly speaking, multidimensional usually refers to a number of independent dimensions, while multivariate refers to a number of dependent variables (Bergeron et al., 1994). Hoffman considers multidimensional multivariate visualization to be a more suitable term (Hoffman et al., 2001). However, multivariate data have a high dimensionality and can be considered multidimensional because the relationships between attributes are usually not known in advance. The multidimensional will be therefore implied below in usage. Multidimensional data are analyzed by researchers, engineers, manufacturers, financial managers and various types of analysts in all aspects. Thus, multi-factor data visualization is motivated by many situations when they try to get a comprehensive understanding of data distributions and examine the relationships between different data attributes. Such a powerful visual display tool is needed to facilitate users to the identification, location, distinction, categorization, clustering, ranking, comparing or matching of base data (Wehrend et al., 1990).

For instance, in structural chemistry, one of the actual problems is determination of the energetically favorable stable conformations of a molecule (conformers) corresponding to minima (global and local) on the potential energy surface (PES) and prediction of the interconversion barriers between the conformers corresponding to local maxima, where PES is considered as a function of coordinates describing internal rotation of molecular fragments. Quantum chemical methods have become a useful tool for computations of molecular structure and, thus, for predictions of chemical properties of compounds and reaction mechanisms. It has become an alternative way to study materials before running the actual experiments that can be too difficult, too expensive or even not possible.

There are several computer software packages used in computational chemistry, such as GAUSSIAN, GAMESS, MOLPRO, SPARTAN, CFOUR, etc. The widely used program GAUSSIAN (Frisch, 2003 and the following updates) considered by most scholars to be the "industry standard" is supplemented by the visualization tool (GAUSSVIEW) which allows the graphical presentation of obtained results. In general, visualization of the PES is usually limited by two variables (3D PES). The visualization of four-dimensional and more complex hypersurfaces is still a challenge for structural chemists. Therefore, there is a need to create a reliable and affordable processor for visualization and minima finding of complex hypersurfaces. In the present work, the authors used the output of the GAUSSIAN program package.

DISPLAYING MULTIDIMENSIONAL ENERGY SURFACE

The multidimensional hypersurface processor should perform two main functions, namely: determining all the minima of the tabulated PES computed by quantum-chemical methods and visualization of these minima. The main requirements for visualization are the clarity of the function and its behavior in the considered range, the ability to display all the function minima found in its area, and the ability to observe the function model from any viewpoint. In practice, the maximum size of the hypersurface is limited to four variables (5D hypersurface). The calculations of tabulated multidimensional function is usually associated with extremely high costs. Therefore, it is usually made on a sparse grid. Moreover, the multidimensional tables are extremely difficult to analyze in terms of finding energy minima. The only way to improve the calculation reliability without increasing the calculation time is to condense the grid at the post-processing stage. To condense the source network means using multidimensional data interpolation. However, it should be marked that interpolation leads to the appearance of new grid points at which the function values are approximate and should be further verified by computational or experimental methods.

The authors have developed a hypersurface processor that allows the scientists to visualize and find the minima of the 3D, 4D and 5D hypersurfaces.

Generally, visualization of the three-dimensional surface is carried out by NURBS approximation and is not labour-consuming. NURBS curves and surfaces are widely used in many Computer Aided Design (CAD) applications for representing the form of cars, aircraft, ships, shoes and numerous other items with sculptured features (Rogers, 2001). They are parametrically defined polynomial entities, thus well suited for software implementation, whilst their rational nature provides additional degrees of freedom compared to their non-rational counterparts. This enables them to exactly reproduce sphere, conic and other special surfaces. NURBS have remained a very popular representation for curves and surfaces in CAD software. Many factors may have contributed to their success including their versatility, thereby allowing CAD models to be transferred between different systems easily. Studies on other spline forms have been published subsequently, but none have surpassed NURBS in terms of their universal support, despite any advantages they may offer (see Figure 1).

To visualize 4D function the authors apply volumetric modeling methods to represent solid shapes rather than surfaces. Doing so enables richer simulation, both for dynamics and for illumination in the presence of translucency. The volumetric models are represented by voxels as described, for example, by James Foley (Foley et al., 1990). The division of area of function definition naturally lends itself to a regular grid, making for straightforward representations, and is also easy to build a hierarchy form. This representation is known as a voxel model. In volumetric modeling an object is represented as a collection of voxels in 3D arrangement which may be regular or irregular. Cubic voxels inside a uniform grid aligned with the coordinate axes is the simplest and commonly used representation. It is very common for fluid flow simulation and medical or geoscientific imaging, where the underlying source data are often captured on a regular grid. A much more complex problem is to visualize 5D hypersurface.

There are a large number of methods of visual representation for multidimensional data described by scholars. Keim and Kriegel (1996), (Keim, 1997) divided them into six classes, namely geometric, pictogram, pixel-oriented, hierarchical, graphical and hybrid methods. The authors will accept this taxonomy and adapt it to multivariate data visualization methods, which are divided into four broad categories in accordance with the general approaches used to generate the resulting visualizations (de Oliveira, 2003): geometric projection, pixel-oriented methods, hierarchical display and iconography. Geometric projec-

Figure 1. NURBS representation of 3D energy hypersurface

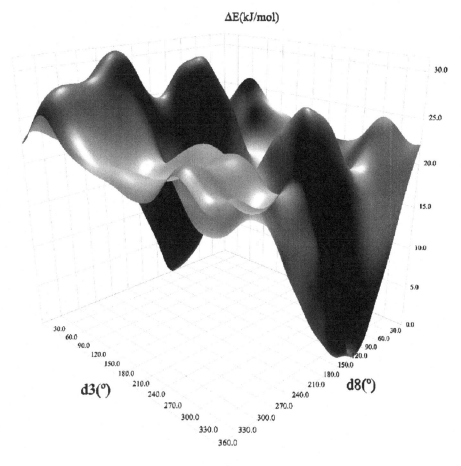

ΔE(kJ/mol)

tion techniques are aimed at finding informative projections and transformations of multidimensional datasets (Keim, Kriegel, 1996). It may map the attributes to a typical Cartesian plane like scatterplot, or which is more innovative, to an arbitrary space such as parallel coordinates. Scatterplot is used for bivariate discrete data in which two attributes are projected along the x-y axes of the Cartesian coordinates. One can easily observe patterns in the relationships between pairs of attributes, but there may be important patterns in higher dimensions which are barely recognized in it. Another method is based on the principle of prosection. The term prosection was first introduced by Furnas and Buja (Furnas at al, 1994); Tweedie and Spence (Tweedie et al., 1998) later extended it to prosection matrix which supports a higher dimensionality. In the simplest sense, prosection is the orthogonal projections where the data items (of different colors) lie in the selected multidimensional range (Keim, 1997). Like the scatterplot and prosection matrix, Hyper Slice (Wijk et al., 1993) has a matrix graphics representing a scalar function of the variables (Wong et al., 1997). This method targets at continuous scalar functions rather than discrete data. The most significant improvement over scatterplot is the interactive data navigation around a user-defined focal point (Wong et al., 1997). The Hyper Slice was later enhanced (Wong et al., 1996) and it incorporates the concept of display resolution supported by space projection, together with the concept of data resolution provided by wavelets to form a powerful multiresolution visualization system. Often, when analyzing multidimensional data, dimensionality reduction (DR) techniques are displayed

Figure 2. Hypersurface minima representation by Lumigraph

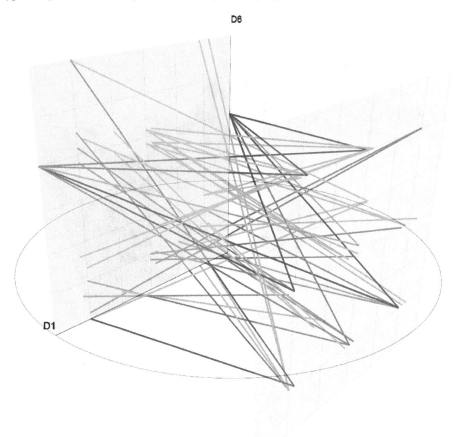

in the form of 2D or 3D scatterplots that project the multidimensional points onto a lower-dimensional visual space (Etemadpour et al., 2016).

One can also reconstruct 5D hypersurface to 4D hypersurface with energy level represented by color and apply the model called Lumigraph. The usual two-plane parameterized light field (2PP) extended with object geometry for the reconstruction process was published by Görtler (1996) who coined the term Lumigraph. The term Lumigraph is applied usually to stress the fact that proxy geometry is required and used for light field reconstruction. Basically, it is a subset of the complete plenoptic function that describes the flow of light in all positions and in all directions. The two-plane setup is a global parameterization and it describes a ray in space with the intersection points on two parallel planes. Each intersection point is 2D and this leads to four sampling parameters. In our case this kind of ray can be considered as 4D point. The color of the point, considered as an additional parameter, transforms this point into 5D point (Figure 2). The listing of the procedure createLumiGraph written in Java 3D one can find in Appendix 1.

Though such representation is very simple and convenient it is not clear for perception. Therefore, the authors had to abandon it further. Alternatively, they applied a special coordinate system (see Figure 3) which includes four independent variables. Such coordinate system makes point A in Figure 3 a five-

Figure 3. Special coordinate system to display 5D hypersurface (Four arguments + color)

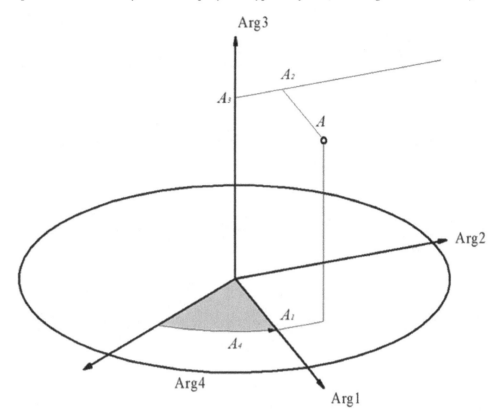

dimensional point including its color. To visualize 5D hypersurface the authors introduced a set of 5D elementary hyper volumes (tetraxels) (Vogt, 2009) corresponding to 5D points.

An example of this type of visualization is presented in Figure 4, where low energy values for the calculated function are covered in blue. Green areas correspond to high energy values.

FINDING ENTIRE MINIMA ON THE MULTIDIMENSIONAL HYPERSURFACE

The stable conformations of a molecule are defined by the minima on PES. Mathematically, the problem of finding the function minima is related to finding such points of it in which the first partial derivatives of functions go to zero, and the second partial derivatives are nonnegative at the same time.

This issue requires finding such point x that the scalar function $f(x_1, x_2, x_3 \ldots x_n)$ takes a value that is lower than at any neighboring point. For smooth functions, the gradient $g = \tilde{N}f$ vanishes at the minimum. This problem is also known in mathematics as optimization problem which is a famous field of science, engineering and technology. When solving the so called optimization problem, it is necessary to calculate the global extremum (or its good approximation) of a function with multiple variables. The variables which define the optimized function can be continuous or discrete and, additionally, they often have to satisfy certain constraints. Problems of NP-hard complexity class which include optimization problems, are very difficult to solve. Therefore, traditional descent optimization algorithms are not suitable for their

Figure 4. Render of 5D energy hypersurface

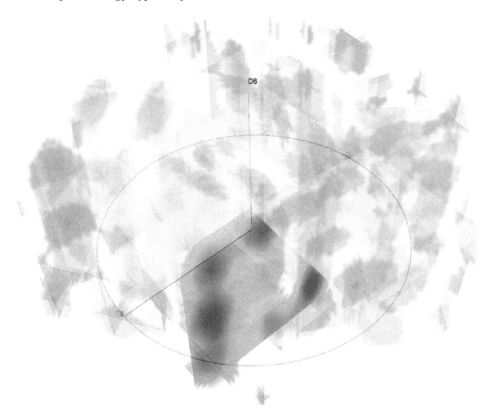

solution due to the local nature of the processed information (Zhigljavsky, 1991). In recent decades a lot of new algorithms for Global optimization problem solution have appeared (Tunchan, 2010). This has led to success in a wide class of problem solution in different areas, such as, for example, computational chemistry and biology, computer science, economics, engineering design and others. But in general, there are no efficient methods available to minimize n-dimensional functions. The algorithms come from the initial assumption using a search algorithm that tries to move in an oblique direction. Algorithms using a gradient function minimize the one-dimensional line along this direction until the lowest point with a suitable tolerance is found. Then, the search direction is updated according to local information about the function and its derivatives, and the whole process is repeated until a true n-dimensional minimum is found. Algorithms that do not require a function gradient use a different approach. That is, the Nelder-Mead Simplex algorithm supports n + 1 test parameter vectors as vertices of an n-dimensional simplex. The algorithm tries to correct the worst vertex of the simplex at each iteration using geometric transformations. Iterations continue until the total size of the simplex is sufficiently reduced. The problem seems to be very challenging for non-smooth or discrete functions. Actually, computational chemistry packages produce molecular energy values in the form of a large multidimensional table, depending on 2, 3, 4 or more variables, which correspond to a number of molecule variables. In this case, tabulated hypersurface has no analytic expression, which seriously complicates the search for its minima. In addition, the time for calculating energy critically depends on a number of variables, as well as on the calculation step for each given variable. With a larger number of variables and more condensed step, the

Figure 5. The scheme of minima finding. a) 3D case; b) 3D + color = 4D; c) 4D + color = 5D

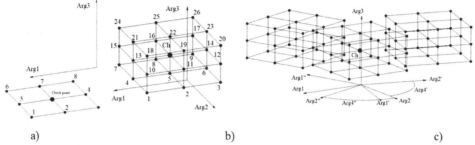

a)   b)   c)

calculation time can take up to several months of continuous calculation on super computing platforms. Thus it complicates obtaining PES minima landscape with an acceptable reliability.

To solve this problem the approach for PES local minima finding has been developed. It contains two stages:

1. To improve the minima finding one should replace the initial multidimensional function defined as a regular grid of calculated points by a more condensed regular grid. The function values at the nodes of the condensed grid are calculated by multidimensional spline interpolation. Multidimensional or, strictly speaking, multivariate interpolation is particularly applied in geostatistics, where it is used to create a digital elevation model from a set of points on the Earth's surface (for example, spot heights in a topographic survey or depths in a hydrographic survey). There are several approaches to multidimensional interpolation. In the described version of the hypersurface processor, the authors apply a poly cubic spline interpolation procedure developed by Flanagan M. (2014) that allows interpolating the values of a function specified in a table of any dimension. In the mathematical numerical analysis, spline interpolation is a form of interpolation where the interpolant is a special type of piecewise polynomial called 'spline'. This procedure contains a method for performing a multidimensional cubic spline interpolation, i.e. an interpolation within n-dimensional arrays of data points, $y = f(x_1, x_2, x_3 \ldots x_n)$, using natural cubic splines and where n may take any integer value. The data is represented in the tabulated form for the arrays $x_1, x_2, x_3 \ldots x_n$ and for $y = f(x_1, x_2, x_3 \ldots x_n)$. The dimension of arrays x_i and steps of their subdivision may be different. The interpolation procedure is recursive.

2. The next stage is a consistent comparison of the function values at each grid node with the function values at the neighboring nodes surrounding it. If this value is the smallest one, then one can consider this value as a local minimum. The number of neighboring nodes depends on the dimension of the problem being solved. In 3D case, such nodes are 8, in 4D case there are 26 nodes, in 5D case such nodes are 80 (see Figure 5). To make the minima more precise the grid should be condensed as much as possible. This approach enables the energy function minima to be found at a sufficient reliability level, even if the calculation is relatively rough. Unlike the classical optimization solution, this approach allows finding both global minimum and local minima very quickly (within several minutes). However, it should be stated that grid condensation does not actually improve the accuracy of the original solution. This may cause the appearance of some dummy minima that really do not exist, at the same time some real minima can be lost. Therefore, the entire minima

Figure 6. Part of 5D PES with the first 11 minima

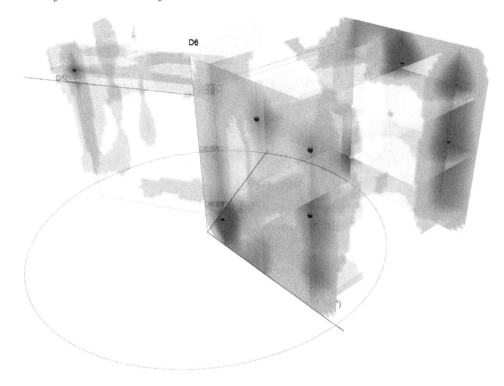

should be confirmed by proper experiment. Figure 6 shows the first 11 found minima together with a 5D hypersurface.

MULTIDIMENSIONAL HYPERSURFACE PROCESSOR

While selecting a programming tool for further development several platforms of comparative advantages and disadvantages were analyzed and the Java language (Niemeyer, 2013) together with its Java 3D extension (Selman, 2003) appeared to be the most suitable tools. The Internet technologies and the Java language in particular have brought about a fundamental change in the way that applications are designed and deployed. Java's "write once, run anywhere" model has lessened the complexity and cost normally associated with producing software on multiple distinct hardware platforms. With Java, the browser paradigm has evolved as a compelling way to produce applications for the Internet and the corporate intranet. As new classes of applications emerge for the Web environment, there is an increasing pressure for full multimedia capabilities to become seamlessly integrated into the browser paradigm. Application developers are demanding a smaller number of high-level interfaces to work with, but users prefer a seamless environment which is easy to operate and maintain. In addition to software innovations, ASIC (application specific integrated circuit) technology and high levels of integration have made accelerated 3D visualization-capable and multimedia-capable hardware affordable. High end graphics features, previously available on specialized graphics workstations only, are now at any user's disposal on low-cost platforms, making them adaptable for new kinds of applications. Besides, the 3D hypersurface processor in the application form can be provided with aesthetically well-presented user-friendly interface. Java 3D API (Application Programming Interface) is known as an interface for writing programs to display and interact with 3D geometry models. Java 3D is a standard extension to Java 2 JDK (Selman, 2003). The API provides a collection of high-level tools for creating and manipulating 3D geometry and for nice rendering. Java 3D is an addition to Java for displaying three-dimensional graphics. As a matter of point, programs written in Java 3D can be run on several different types of computer and other gadjets. In its turn, the Java 3D class library provides a simpler interface than most other graphics libraries, but has enough capabilities to produce good games and animation. Thus, Java 3D is built on existing technology such as DirectX and OpenGL. So, the programs do not run as slowly as one might expect. Also, Java 3D can incorporate objects created by 3D modeling packages like AutoCAD, SolidWorks, CATIA, TrueSpace etc. In addition, it can support VRML and many other models (Hopkins, 2007).

It is worth mentioning that all the calculations were obtained by a number of program modules. Some of the most important procedures should be specially described. The multidimensional 4D interpolation procedure is carried out by the program module saveGlobeMatrix. This procedure tries to open on the outer file where a new global matrix is to be written. If there is no such file to open, the procedure interpolates input data to a new density and saves it to a new created file. If such file exists, it means that it has been already created and there is no need to interpolate input data. In Appendix 2 one may find the listing of the procedure. The input data to the procedure x_v, y_v, z_v, p_v - are the arrays of grid nodal arguments; globe – the matrix of nodal function values; density – the desirable new grid density; grid4D – new matrix of nodal function values and cords – new nodal arguments of condensed matrix. The main objective of this procedure is to restructure the input data for the multidimensional interpolation.

During the process of finding minima the hypersurface processor analyses a number of variables and chooses an appropriate procedure to find minima. There are three types of such functions in the current version of the hypersurface processor, namely, for variables 2, 3 and 4. The listing of one of them named find4DMinima is represented in Appendix 3. This function requires 4D volumetric raster in the table form of studied function values that are calculated by poly spline interpolation. All found minima are sorted by function BubbleSortMin based on bubble sorting algorithm of data in ascending order of energy value. The procedure for minima finding in the case of 3D and 5D is constructed according to a similar principle.

The key function of rendering a hypersurface with minima uses a triple of mutually perpendicular planes, passing through each minimum. In this case, the color legend is constructed in such a way that the minimum energy in the considered range corresponds to the deep blue color, which, passing through shades of green-blue, turns into deep green as the energy level increases. Parts of the surface in the transition zones are conditionally depicted as transparent. This allows displaying the areas of all extrema more clearly. Besides, the procedure has the ability to display both a single minimum and the desired group of minima. The output of this procedure is shown in Figures 4 and 6. The text of the Java3D procedure createTripleofQuadroLayers that implements the rendering function is shown in Appendix 4.

The hypersurface processor is equipped with a set of functions that allows control of the modes of minima finding and their visualization (see Table 1).

While processing a multidimensional data table, the software produces a large number of calculations. At the same time the hypersurface processor writes the main part of intermediate data to a file. This file has PLO extension and is placed in the same folder as the original data. In this case, the name of the file coincides with the name of the file with the original data. This means that if a calculation with a

Table 1. The list of tools of the hypersurface processor

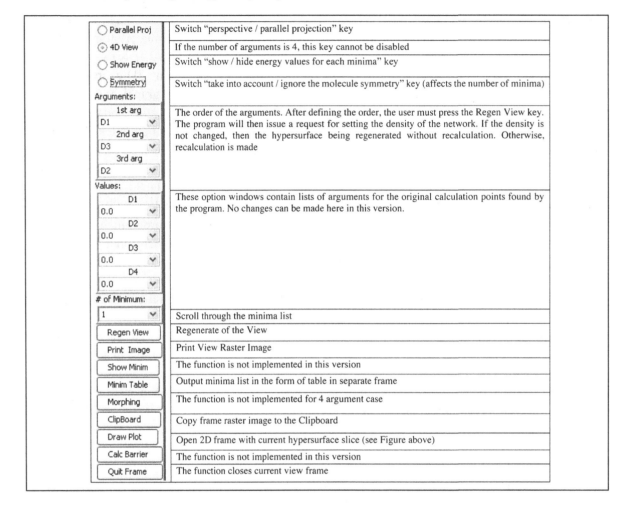

○ Parallel Proj	Switch "perspective / parallel projection" key
◉ 4D View	If the number of arguments is 4, this key cannot be disabled
○ Show Energy	Switch "show / hide energy values for each minima" key
○ Symmetry	Switch "take into account / ignore the molecule symmetry" key (affects the number of minima)
Arguments: 1st arg D1 ⌄ 2nd arg D3 ⌄ 3rd arg D2 ⌄	The order of the arguments. After defining the order, the user must press the Regen View key. The program will then issue a request for setting the density of the network. If the density is not changed, then the hypersurface being regenerated without recalculation. Otherwise, recalculation is made
Values: D1 0.0 ⌄ D2 0.0 ⌄ D3 0.0 ⌄ D4 0.0 ⌄	These option windows contain lists of arguments for the original calculation points found by the program. No changes can be made here in this version.
# of Minimum: 1 ⌄	Scroll through the minima list
Regen View	Regenerate of the View
Print Image	Print View Raster Image
Show Minim	The function is not implemented in this version
Minim Table	Output minima list in the form of table in separate frame
Morphing	The function is not implemented for 4 argument case
ClipBoard	Copy frame raster image to the Clipboard
Draw Plot	Open 2D frame with current hypersurface slice (see Figure above)
Calc Barrier	The function is not implemented in this version
Quit Frame	The function closes current view frame

certain density of the table has already been done, then, setting the same density (when the hypersurface processor restarts with the same source data) computer time is saved significantly due to the reading of the previously performed calculations.

EXAMPLE OF SCIENTIFIC APPLICATION

By means of the hypersurface processor developed on Java3D basis the authors analysed the PESs of molecules with very complex conformational landscape. Several molecules of biological importance, such as glyceraldehyde and fumaric acid with four axes of internal rotations and succinic acid with even five ones, were systematically investigated by experimental and quantum-chemical methods (Vogt et al., 2007 – 2011). The developed post-processor was benchmarked by the results of these studies and applied for finding the minima on the PES of glyceraldehyde (Vogt et al., 2009). The PES of glyceraldehyde was calculated as a function of four torsion angles with their alternate variation from 0° to 360° with steps of 60° (i.e., in the 2401 points) at simultaneous optimization of the remaining geometrical parameters

Figure 7. PES cross-sections indicating the energy minima corresponding to two lowest-energy conformers (1 and 2) of glyceraldehyde

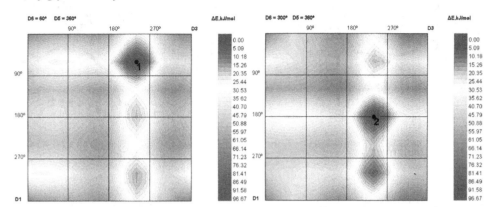

(bond lengths and bond angles) by means of the GAUSSIAN program package (at the B3LYP/6-31G(d) level of theory). The tabulated hypersurface (5D PES) taken from the output of these computations was treated by the post-processor in the following way. The intermediate energy values were estimated by polyspline interpolation. The 4D points of the geometrical space with the lower energy values in comparison with their direct neighbors were identified as local minima. For the presentation of the 5D PES, the 4D geometrical coordinate system was modeled by the 3D system rotating about the vertical axis along the fourth coordinate with identification of relative energy level in a different colors (see Figure 3). Thus, the energy surface as a function of 4D space variables is a 5D data set. Finaly, 36 minima were found to be present on the PES of glyceraldehyde. The cross-sections of PES shown in Figure 6 indicate the positions of the energy minima corresponding to the most stable conformers of the studied molecule (see Figure 7).

For example, Figure 8 shows the structures of the first lowest energy conformers (I-IV) of glyceraldehyde predicted by quantum chemical calculations (Vogt, 2009). The first conformer corresponds to global minima, whereas three further conformers correspond to the three lowest energy local minima. The minima of PES calculated at the density functional level of theory were found by means of the approach described in this chapter. The existence of conformer I was confirmed by gas-phase electron diffraction experiment. Visualization of molecular structures was carried out by means of the program developed by the authors.

FURTHER RESEARCH

This study was a good basis for creating software for analysis of multidimensional hypersurfaces of various nature. At the same time, when analyzing hypersurface, it is often necessary to find the shortest paths between its two or more minima. Usually the problem of finding such a path is important in structural chemistry for determining the ways of transforming one conformer into another separated by an energetic barrier. This issue is directly related to geodetic lines finding of the hypersurface. These lines usually generate directions on the surface, being one of the ways to parameterize it. A geodetic line can be found by minimizing the curve length equation using the calculus of variations. This has some minor

Figure 8. The structures of the first lowest energy conformers of glyceraldehyde

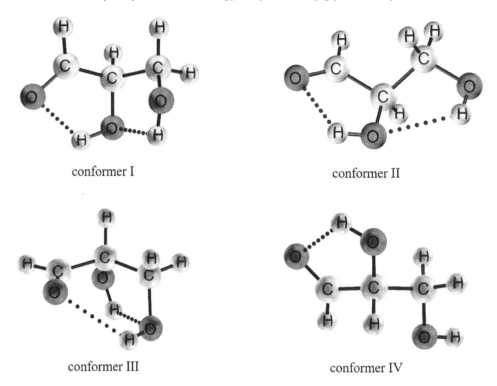

conformer I   conformer II

conformer III   conformer IV

technical problems, for there are different methods to parameterize the shortest paths. The shortest path between two points on the *plane* is a straight line, by analogy, the shortest path between two points on the *surface* passes along a geodetic line. In many existing techniques of generalization, one of the most useful methods is searching for analytical solution of the Euler equation (Euler, 1728). A geodetic can be represented by a solution of an ordinary second-order differential equation

$$u''v' - v''u' + Av' - Bu' = 0 \qquad (1)$$

where

(u,v) – parametric coordinate of a surface point;

$$\left.\begin{array}{l} u = u(t) \\ v = v(t) \end{array}\right\} , \text{ - a curve equation near a given point.}$$

In most cases analytical solution of equation (1) (Nathaphon et al., 2010) is impossible due to the lack of analytical descriptions of the surface (Popov, 2002, 2014). This is especially true for multidimensional hypersurfaces represented in the form of a multidimensional table.

Actually, the approach to the minima finding described in this work can be very useful in the shortest paths tracing along a hypersurface. The way to solve this problem may lie in finding the so-called saddle point closest to a certain minimum, which is a point where two paths cross, i.e. the shortest path between two neighboring minima and the path between two banks of the valley tracing along the upper edge of the pass between the minima. Therefore, the saddle point is the maximum point on the pass between two local minima. The Gauss curvature at this point is negative. There can be several neighboring saddle points around a certain minimum. Nevertheless, the saddle point with the lowest function value is the most preferable one for the intermolecular interconversion. Thus, finding the path crossing such saddle point is a very important topic in structural chemistry.

The developed approaches are also planned to apply to studying the pseudo-symmetry of biological objects. To quantify the pseudo-symmetry of biological objects one can propose the convolution of functions, which is widely used in various fields of physics and mathematics. Convolution can be interpreted as a scalar product of functions forming an infinite-dimensional space of vectors. In order to search for symmetry operators, a list of typical symmetry elements containing inversion center, rotational axes of various orders, symmetry planes, etc. is included. In addition, each typical symmetry element has a certain direction corresponding to the local maxima of such convolution. The approaches described in this article are very promising for the solution of this problem.

CONCLUSION

The processor developed on Java3D basis is aimed at processing the multidimensional hypersurface. In this work it was applied to analize PES, for instance, calculated by quantum-chemical methods by means of GAUSSIAN program. A poly cubic spline interpolation procedure developed by Flanagan is used for interpolation of the function values specified in a table of any dimension. The processor can be applied for a systematic analysis of multidimensional potential energy surfaces and for finding their minima. The solution of this problem is very important, for example, for the study of biomolecules with a complex conformational landscape. The grid condensation technology significantly improves the reliability of the PES minima finding. However, it should be noted that grid condensation does not actually improve the accuracy of the original solution. This may cause the appearance of some dummy minima that do not really exist, at the same time some real minima can be mislaid. The selection of programming tools is carried out by comparative analysis of pros and cons of computer languages, and the Java language together with its Java 3D extension are found to be the most suitable in our case. The developed processor has a very attractive visualization platform that allows the user to analyze the complete hypersurface. In addition, it seems promising to use the processor for solving other problems, for example, for searching the lowest-energy path between the local minima of multidimensional hypersurface, or for finding the ways of the interconversion between the conformers of molecules. This can be a purpose for further research.

ACKNOWLEDGMENT

This research was supported by the Dr. B. Mez-Starck Foundation (Germany).

REFERENCES

Bergeron, R. D., Cody, W., Hibbard, W., Kao, D. T., Miceli, K. D., Treinish, L. A., & Walther, S. (1994). Database Issues for Data Visualization: Developing a Data Model. In *Proceedings of the IEEE Visualization '93 Workshop on Database Issues for Data Visualization*. Springer-Verlag. 10.1007/BFb0021141

Chan, W. W. Y. (2006). A Survey on Multivariate Data Visualization. In Encyclopedia of Environmetrics. Academic Press.

Foley, J. D., Van, F. D., Van Dam, A., Feiner, S. K., Hughes, J. F., Angel, E., & Hughes, J. (1990). Computer Graphics: Principles and Practice (2nd ed.). Addison-Wesley.

Cura, T. (2010). A Random Search to Finding the Global Minimum, Int. *J. Contemp. Math. Sciences*, 5(4), 179–190.

de Oliveira, M. C. F., & Levkowitz, H. (2003). From Visual Data Exploration to Visual Data Mining: A Survey. *IEEE Transactions on Visualization and Computer Graphics*, 9(3), 378–394. doi:10.1109/TVCG.2003.1207445

Dorofeeva, O. V., Vogt, N., Vogt, J., Popik, M. V., Rykov, A. N., & Vilkov, L. V. (2007). Molecular Structure and Conformational Composition of 1,3-Dihydroxyacetone Studied by Combined Analysis of Gas-Phase Electron Diffraction Data, Rotational Constants, and Results of Theoretical Calculations: Ideal Gas Thermodynamic Properties of 1,3-Dihydroxyacetone. The Journal of Physical Chemistry A, 111(28), 6434–6442.

Etemadpour, R., Linsen, L., Paiva, J. G., Crick, C., & Forbes, A. G. (2015, March). Choosing visualization techniques for multidimensional data projection tasks: A guideline with examples. In Proceedings of the International joint conference on computer vision, imaging and computer graphics (pp. 166-186). Springer.

EulerL. (1728). Concerning The Shortest Line on Any Surface by which any two Points can be joined together.

Flanagan, M.T. (2014). *Java Scientific Library*. Retrieved from http://www.ee.ucl.ac.uk/~mflanaga/java/index.html

Frisch, M. J., Trucks, G. W., Schlegel, H. B., Scuseria, G. E., Robb, M. A., Cheeseman, J. R., Montgomery Jr, J. A., ... Iyengar, S. S. (2003). GAUSSIAN 03, Revision E.01. Pittsburgh, PA: Gaussian, Inc.

Furnas, G. W., & Buja, A. (1994). Prosection Views: Dimensional Inference through Sections and Projections. *Journal of Computational and Graphical Statistics*, 3(4), 323–353.

Gortler, S. J., Grzeszczuk, R., Szeliski, R., & Cohen, M. F. (1996, August). The lumigraph. In Proceedings of the 23rd annual conference on Computer graphics and interactive techniques (pp. 43-54). Academic Press.

Greg, H. (2007). *The Joy of Java 3D*. Java3D. Retrieved from http://www.java3d.org/introduction.html

Hoffman, P. E., & Grinstein, G. G. (2001). *A Survey of Visualizations for High-Dimensional Data Mining. In Information Visualization in Data Mining and Knowledge Discovery* (pp. 47–82). Morgan Kaufmann Publishers.

Keim, D. A. (1997). Visual Techniques for Exploring Databases. In *Proceedings of the 3rd International Conference on Knowledge Discovery and Data Mining Tutorial*. Academic Press.

Keim, D. A., & Kriegel, H.-P. (1996). Visualization Techniques for Mining Large Databases: A Comparison. *IEEE Transactions on Knowledge and Data Engineering, 8*(6), 923–938. doi:10.1109/69.553159

Niemeyer, P., & Knudsen, J. (2013). Learning Java (4th ed.). O'Reilly Media, Inc.

Popov, E. V. (2002).Geometric Approach to Chebyshev Net Generation Along an Arbitrary Surface Represented by NURBS. In *Proceedings of the 12th Int. Conference on Computer Graphics & Vision GRAPHICON'2002*. Academic Press.

Popov, E. V., Popova, T. P., & Rotkov, S. I. (2014). *The Shortest Path Finding between two Points on a Polyhedral Surface. In WSCG 2014 Communication Papers Proceedings* (pp. 1–11). Academic Press..

Rogers, D. F. (2001).*An introduction to NURBS: with historical perspective.* Morgan Kaufmann Publishers.

Selman, D. (2003). *Java3D Programming*. Austin, TX: Manning Publications Co.

Squire, R. (1997). *Fundamentals of Radiology* (5th ed.). Harvard, UniversityPress.

Tweedie, L., & Spence, R. (1998). The Prosection Matrix: A Tool to Support the Interactive Exploration of Statistical Models and Data. *Computational Statistics, 13*, 65–76.

vanWijk, J. J., & vanLiere, R. (1994). Hyperslice visualization of scalar functions of many variables. *Proceedings of the 4th IEEE Conference on Visualization '93* (pp. 119-125). IEEE Press.

Vogt, N., Abaev, M. A., & Karasev, N. M. (2011). Molecular structure and stabilities of fumaric acid conformers: Gas phase electron diffraction (GED) and quantum-chemical studies. Journal of Molecular Structure, 987(1-3), 199-205.

Vogt, N., Abaev, M. A., Rykov, A. N., & Shishkov, I. F. (2011). Determination of molecular structure of succinic acid in a very complex conformational landscape: Gas-phase electron diffraction (GED) and ab initio studies. Journal of Molecular Structure, 996(1-3), 120-127.

Vogt, N., Atavin, E. G., Rykov, A. N., Popov, E. V., & Vilkov, L. V. (2009). Equilibrium structure and relative stability of glyceraldehyde conformers: Gas-phase electron diffraction (GED) and quantum-chemical studies. Journal of Molecular Structure, 936(1-3), 125-131.

Wehrend, S., & Lewis, C. (1990). A Problem-Oriented Classification of Visualization Techniques, In *Proceedings of the 1st IEEE Conference on Visualization* (pp. 139-143). IEEE Press. 10.1109/VISUAL.1990.146375

Wong, P. C., & Bergeron, R. D. (1997). *30 Years of Multidimensional Multivariate Visualization. In Scientific Visualization Overviews, Methodologies, and Techniques* (pp. 3–33). IEEE Computer Society Press.

Wong, P. C., Crabb, A. H., & Bergeron, R. D. (1996). Dual Multiresolution HyperSlice for Multivariate Data Visualization. In *Proceedings of IEEE Symposium on Information Visualization '96* (pp. 74-75). IEEE Press. 10.1109/INFVIS.1996.559224

Zhigljavsky, A. A. (1991). *Theory of Global Random Search*. Kluwer Academic. doi:10.1007/978-94-011-3436-1

KEY TERMS AND DEFINITIONS

Hypersurface: It is a generalization of the surface concept for the space with more than two dimensions.

Lumigraph: It is a subset of the complete plenoptic function that describes the flow of light in all positions and in all directions.

Multidimensional: The term multidimensional usually refers to the number of independent dimensions, while multivariate refers to the number of dependent variables.

Multidimensional Interpolation: Interpolation of the function defined by more than 3D table.

NP-Hard Complexity: The term from computational complexity theory. NP (nondeterministic polynomial time) is a complexity class used to classify the solution of a problem.

NURBS: Non-Uniform Rational B-Splines. It is a mathematical model commonly used in computer graphics for generating and representing curves and surfaces.

PES: Potential energy surface. It is (relative) potential energy of a molecule defined as a function of some geometrical variables describing internal rotation of molecular fragments.

APPENDIX 1

Listing of Procedure createLumiGraph

```
//============================================================================
        public BranchGroup createLumiGraph() {
                BranchGroup objSp = new BranchGroup();
                objSp.setCapability(TransformGroup.ALLOW_TRANSFORM_WRITE);
                objSp.setCapability(TransformGroup.ALLOW_TRANSFORM_READ);
                objSp.setCapability(BranchGroup.ALLOW_CHILDREN_EXTEND);
                objSp.setCapability(BranchGroup.ALLOW_DETACH);
                Color3f color2 = new Color3f(0.75f, 0.75f, 0.75f);
                Color3f color = new Color3f(0.0f, 0.0f, 0.0f);
TransformGroup spinTg1 = new TransformGroup();
                Appearance appearplane = new Appearance();
                PolygonAttributes apop =
 new PolygonAttributes(PolygonAttributes.POLYGON_FILL,
                                                PolygonAttributes.CULL_
NONE,0.0f);
        Material mp = new Material(color2, color2, color2, color2, 1000.0f);
                ColoringAttributes colorAttrp = new ColoringAttributes();
                TransparencyAttributes tranAttrp = new TransparencyAttrib-
utes();

                tranAttrp.setTransparencyMode(TransparencyAttributes.NICEST);
                tranAttrp.setTransparency(0.75F);
                 colorAttrp.setColor(color2);
                appearplane.setTransparencyAttributes(tranAttrp);
                appearplane.setColoringAttributes(colorAttrp);
                appearplane.setPolygonAttributes(apop);
                appearplane.setMaterial(mp);
                Plane plan_1 = new Plane(new Point3d(0.0, 0.0, 0.0),
                                new Point3d(1.0, 0.0, 0.0),
                                        new Point3d(1.0, 0.0, 1.0),
                                        new Point3d(0.0, 0.0, 1.0), appear-
plane);
                Plane plan_2 = new Plane(new Point3d(0.0, 1.0, 0.0),
                                        new Point3d(1.0, 1.0, 0.0),
                                        new Point3d(1.0, 1.0, 1.0),
                                        new Point3d(0.0, 1.0, 1.0), appear-
plane);
                spinTg1.addChild(plan_1);
                spinTg1.addChild(plan_2);
                objSp.addChild(spinTg1);
```

```
                int fancy = 6;
                BranchGroup edgeTG = new BranchGroup();
                for (int m = 0; m < fancy; m++) {
                        LineAttributes lineattr =
new LineAttributes(0.0005f, LineAttributes.PATTERN_SOLID, true);
                        LineArray axisX =
new LineArray(2,LineArray.COORDINATES|LineArray.COLOR_3);
                        LineArray axisY =
new LineArray(2,LineArray.COORDINATES|LineArray.COLOR_3);
                        LineArray axisXX =
new LineArray(2,LineArray.COORDINATES|LineArray.COLOR_3);
                        LineArray axisYY =
new LineArray(2,LineArray.COORDINATES|LineArray.COLOR_3);
                        edgeTG.setCapability(TransformGroup.ALLOW_TRANSFORM_
WRITE);
                        edgeTG.setCapability(TransformGroup.ALLOW_TRANSFORM_
READ);
                        edgeTG.setCapability(BranchGroup.ALLOW_CHILDREN_EX-
TEND);
                        edgeTG.setCapability(BranchGroup.ALLOW_DETACH);
                        ColoringAttributes colorAttr = new ColoringAttrib-
utes();
                        Material mat = new Material(color, color, color, col-
or, 1000.0f);
                        mat.setLightingEnable(true);
                        colorAttr.setColor(color);
                        Appearance appear = new Appearance();
                        appear.setColoringAttributes(colorAttr);
                        appear.setLineAttributes(lineattr);
                        appear.setMaterial(mat);

                        axisX.setCapability(GeometryArray.ALLOW_COORDINATE_
WRITE);
                        axisX.setCapability(GeometryArray.ALLOW_COORDINATE_
READ);
                        axisX.setCapability(GeometryArray.ALLOW_COLOR_WRITE);
                        axisX.setCapability(GeometryArray.ALLOW_COLOR_READ);
                        axisX.setCoordinate(0, new Point3f(0.0f, 0.0f,
0.0f + (1f/(float)fancy)*(float)m));
                        axisX.setCoordinate(1, new Point3f(1.0f, 0.0f,
0.0f + (1f/(float)fancy)*(float)m));
                        axisX.setColor(0,color);
                        axisX.setColor(1,color);
```

```
                        Shape3D axeslineX = new Shape3D(axisX);
                        axeslineX.setAppearance(appear);
                        edgeTG.addChild(axeslineX);

                        axisY.setCapability(GeometryArray.ALLOW_COORDINATE_
WRITE);
                        axisY.setCapability(GeometryArray.ALLOW_COORDINATE_
READ);
                        axisY.setCapability(GeometryArray.ALLOW_COLOR_WRITE);
                        axisY.setCapability(GeometryArray.ALLOW_COLOR_READ);
                        axisY.setCoordinate(0, new Point3f(0.0f + (1f/
(float)fancy)*(float)m, 0.0f, 0.0f));
                        axisY.setCoordinate(1, new Point3f(0.0f + (1f/
(float)fancy)*(float)m, 0.0f, 1.0f));
                        axisY.setColor(0,color);
                        axisY.setColor(1,color);
                        Shape3D axeslineY = new Shape3D(axisY);
                        axeslineY.setAppearance(appear);
                        edgeTG.addChild(axeslineY);
                        axisXX.setCapability(GeometryArray.ALLOW_COORDINATE_
WRITE);
                        axisXX.setCapability(GeometryArray.ALLOW_COORDINATE_
READ);
                        axisXX.setCapability(GeometryArray.ALLOW_COLOR_WRITE);
                        axisXX.setCapability(GeometryArray.ALLOW_COLOR_READ);
                        axisXX.setCoordinate(0, new Point3f(0.0f, 1.0f, 0.0f
+ (1f/
(float)fancy)*(float)m));
                        axisXX.setCoordinate(1, new Point3f(1.0f, 1.0f, 0.0f
+ (1f/
(float)fancy)*(float)m));
                        axisXX.setColor(0,color);
                        axisXX.setColor(1,color);
                        Shape3D axeslineXX = new Shape3D(axisXX);
                        axeslineXX.setAppearance(appear);
                        edgeTG.addChild(axeslineXX);

                        axisYY.setCapability(GeometryArray.ALLOW_COORDINATE_
WRITE);
                        axisYY.setCapability(GeometryArray.ALLOW_COORDINATE_
READ);
                        axisYY.setCapability(GeometryArray.ALLOW_COLOR_WRITE);
                        axisYY.setCapability(GeometryArray.ALLOW_COLOR_READ);
```

```
                        axisYY.setCoordinate(0, new Point3f(0.0f + (1f/
(float)fancy)*(float)m, 1.0f, 0.0f));
                        axisYY.setCoordinate(1, new Point3f(0.0f + (1f/
(float)fancy)*(float)m, 1.0f, 1.0f));
                        axisYY.setColor(0,color);
                        axisYY.setColor(1,color);
                        Shape3D axeslineYY = new Shape3D(axisYY);
                        axeslineYY.setAppearance(appear);
                        edgeTG.addChild(axeslineYY);
                }
                edgeTG.addChild(createMinsForLumiGraph());
                objSp.addChild(edgeTG);
                return objSp;
        }


//===========================================================================
```

APPENDIX 2

Listing of Procedure Saveglobematrix

```
//===============================================================
        public void saveGlobeMatrix(File infFile, double[] x_v, double[] y_v,
double[] z_v,
                                                                          dou-
ble[] p_v){
           try {
                   System.out.println(" FileBase doesn't exist== ");
                   OutputStream is = new FileOutputStream(infFile);
                   String str = String.valueOf(den)+"\n";
                   byte buf0 [] = str.getBytes();
                   is.write(buf0);
                   grid4D = new double [den+1][den+1][den+1][den+1];
                   coords = new Point4f[den+1][den+1][den+1][den+1];
                   for(int i=0; i<=den; i++){
                   double xx1 = x_v[0]+(x_v[x_v.length-1]-x_v[0])*(double)i/(dou-
ble)den;
           for(int j=0; j<=den; j++){
                   double xx2 = y_v[0]+(y_v[y_v.length-1]-y_v[0])*(double)j/(dou-
ble)den;
                   for(int k=0; k<=den; k++){
                        double xx3 = z_v[0]+(z_v[z_v.length-1]-
```

```
z_v[0])*(double)k/(double)den;
                        String subst = "";
                        for(int l=0; l<=den; l++){
                        double xx4 = p_v[0]+(p_v[p_v.length-1]-
p_v[0])*(double)l/(double)den;
                        grid4D[i][j][k][l] = quadro.interpolate(xx1, xx2,
xx3, xx4);

                        coords[i][j][k][l] =
                                new Point4f((float)xx1, (float)xx2, (float)
xx3, (float)xx4);

                        subst = subst + " " + String.
valueOf(grid4D[i][j][k][l])+
                                                " " + String.valueOf(xx1)+
                                                " " + String.valueOf(xx2)+
                                                " " + String.valueOf(xx3)+
                                                " " + String.valueOf(xx4);
                                }
                        subst = subst + "\n";
                        byte buf1 [] = subst.getBytes();
                        is.write(buf1);
                        }
                }
            }
            is.close();
            for(int i=0; i<4; i++) gridqueue[i] = i;
        }
        catch(IOException ee) {}
    }
//================================================================
```

APPENDIX 3

Listing of Procedure find4DMinima

```
//================================================================
    private void find4DMinima (int raster) {
        int layers = raster;
        int around = 26;
        VertexScanner scan = new VertexScanner ();
        Point4f [] coor = new Point4f[around];
        scan.create3DGrid(nurbs_s, raster);
```

```
for (int k = 0;k < layers;k++){
        float w = (float) k/(float)raster;
        float wm = (float) (k-1)/(float)raster;
        float wp = (float) (k+1)/(float)raster;
        if (k == 0) wm = (float)(raster-1)/(float)raster;
        for (int j = 0;j < raster;j++){
        int v = j;
        int vm = j-1;
        int vp = j+1;
        if (j == 0) vm = raster-1;
        for (int ii = 0;ii < raster;ii++){
                Point4f poin = new Point4f(0.0f, 0.0f, 0.0f, 0.0f);
                int u = ii;
                int um = ii-1;
                int up = ii+1;
                if (ii == 0) um = raster-1;
                        poin = scan.getSplineValue4Dfast (nurbs_s,
u, v, w);

                        coor[0] = scan.getSplineValue4Dfast
(nurbs_s, u, v, wm);

                        coor[1] = scan.getSplineValue4Dfast
(nurbs_s, um, vm, wm);

                        coor[2] = scan.getSplineValue4Dfast
(nurbs_s, u, vm, wm);

                        coor[3] = scan.getSplineValue4Dfast
(nurbs_s, up, vm, wm);

                        coor[4] = scan.getSplineValue4Dfast
(nurbs_s, um, v, wm);

                        coor[5] = scan.getSplineValue4Dfast
(nurbs_s, up, v, wm);

                        coor[6] = scan.getSplineValue4Dfast
(nurbs_s, um, vp, wm);

                        coor[7] = scan.getSplineValue4Dfast
(nurbs_s, u, vp, wm);

                        coor[8] = scan.getSplineValue4Dfast
(nurbs_s, up, vp, wm);

                        coor[9] = scan.getSplineValue4Dfast
(nurbs_s, um, vm, w);

                        coor[10] = scan.getSplineValue4Dfast
(nurbs_s, u, vm, w);

                        coor[11] = scan.getSplineValue4Dfast
(nurbs_s, up, vm, w);

                        coor[12] = scan.getSplineValue4Dfast
```

```
(nurbs_s, um, v, w);
                                    coor[13] = scan.getSplineValue4Dfast
(nurbs_s, up, v, w);
                                    coor[14] = scan.getSplineValue4Dfast
(nurbs_s, um, vp, w);
                                    coor[15] = scan.getSplineValue4Dfast
(nurbs_s, u, vp, w);
                                    coor[16] = scan.getSplineValue4Dfast
(nurbs_s, up, vp, w);
                                     coor[17] = scan.getSplineValue4Dfast
(nurbs_s, u, v, wp);
                                    coor[18] = scan.getSplineValue4Dfast
(nurbs_s, um, vm, wp);
                                    coor[19] = scan.getSplineValue4Dfast
(nurbs_s, u, vm, wp);
                                    coor[20] = scan.getSplineValue4Dfast
(nurbs_s, up, vm, wp);
                                    coor[21] = scan.getSplineValue4Dfast
(nurbs_s, um, v, wp);
                                    coor[22] = scan.getSplineValue4Dfast
(nurbs_s, up, v, wp);
                                    coor[23] = scan.getSplineValue4Dfast
(nurbs_s, um, vp, wp);
                                    coor[24] = scan.getSplineValue4Dfast
(nurbs_s, u, vp, wp);
                                    coor[25] = scan.getSplineValue4Dfast
(nurbs_s, up, vp, wp);
                        boolean is = true;
                        for (int m = 0;m < around;m++)
                        if (poin.z > coor[m].z) is = false;
                        if (is) {
                                    float mini[] = new float[6];
                                    mini[0] = poin.z;
                                    mini[1] = poin.x * scale_a;
                                    mini[2] = poin.y * scale_a;
                                    mini[3] = poin.w * scale_a;
                                    mini[4] = p0;
                                    mini[5] = (float)k;
                                    if (MinPoint.size() == 0)
MinPoint.addElement(mini);

                                    else {
                                    boolean no = true;
                                    Point3f p_2 = new
```

```
Point3f(mini[1],
mini[2], mini[3]);

size(); kk++){


get(kk);

Point3f(min[1],min[2],min[3]);

scale_a;

1.5f*(float)Math.hypot(Math.hypot(1.0/
(double)raster,1.0/
(double)raster),1.0/
(double)raster);

epsn) {


(mini[0] + min[0])/2.0f;

(mini[1] + min[1])/2.0f;

(mini[2] + min[2])/2.0f;

(mini[3] + min[3])/2.0f;

(mini[4] + min[4])/2.0f;

0.0f;

set(kk,mini);


addElement(mini);
                                    }
                            }
                    }
                }
            }
                BubbleSortMin();
```

```
for (int kk=0; kk<MinPoint.

float min[] = new float[6];
min = (float[])MinPoint.

Point3f p_1 = new

dist = p_2.distance(p_1)/

float epsn =



                        if (dist <=

                        no = false;
                        mini[0] =

                        mini[1] =

                        mini[2] =

                        mini[3] =

                        mini[4] =

                        mini[5] =

                        MinPoint.

                        }
                }
        if (no)        MinPoint.
```

```
        }
//================================================================
```

APPENDIX 4

Listing of Procedure createTripleofQuadroLayers

```
//================================================================
private void createTripleofQuadroLayers (TransformGroup objTmp, int number,
boolean is) {
        int u = 0, v = 0, w = 0, p = 0;
        float point[] = new float[6];
        Point3f verts[] = new Point3f[grid_4D_raster*grid_4D_raster*4];
        Color4f objCol [] = new Color4f[grid_4D_raster*grid_4D_raster*4];

        point = (float[])MinPoint.get(number);
        u = (int)((point[1] * grid_4D_raster)/scale_a);
        v = (int)((point[2] * grid_4D_raster)/scale_a);
        w = (int)((point[3] * grid_4D_raster)/scale_a);
        p = (int)((point[4] * grid_4D_raster)/scale_a);
        float ppp = point[0];
        Matrix4f poin;

        for (int l=0; l<3; l++) {
                Point4f gridp[][] = new Point4f[grid_4D_raster+1][grid_4D_ras-
ter+1];
                for (int i=0; i<=grid_4D_raster; i++) {
                for (int j = 0;j <= grid_4D_raster;j++){
                switch (l) {
                case 0:
                        poin = scanner.get4DGrid_flan(j, i, w, p);
                        gridp[j][i] = new Point4f(poin.m00,
poin.m01,
                                                          point[3]/scale_a,
                                                          poin.m10);
                        break;

                case 1:
                        poin = scanner.get4DGrid_flan(u, i, j, p);
                        gridp[j][i] = new Point4f(         point[1]/scale_a,
                                                          poin.m01,
                                                          poin.m02,
```

```
                                                    poin.m10);
                        break;

                case 2:
                        poin = scanner.get4DGrid_flan(j, v, i, p);
                        gridp[j][i] = new Point4f(        poin.m00,
point[2]/scale_a,
poin.m02,
poin.m10);
                        break;
                        }
                }
        }
    int count = 0;
    for (int i=0; i<grid_4D_raster; i++) {
for (int j = 0;j < grid_4D_raster;j++){
verts[count*4 ] = new Point3f(gridp[j ][i].x,gridp[j ][i].y,gridp[j ][i].z);
verts[count*4+1] = new Point3f(gridp[j+1][i].x,gridp[j+1][i].y,gridp[j+1]
[i].z);
verts[count*4+2] = new Point3f(gridp[j+1][i+1].x,gridp[j+1][i+1].y,gridp[j+1]
[i+1].z);
verts[count*4+3] = new Point3f(gridp[j ][i+1].x,gridp[j ][i+1].y,gridp[j ]
[i+1].z);
        float rc[] = new float[4];
        float gc[] = new float[4];
        float bc[] = new float[4];
        float wc[] = new float[4];
        float np[] = new float[4];
        np[0] = gridp[j ][i].w;
        np[1] = gridp[j+1][i].w;
        np[2] = gridp[j+1][i+1].w;
        np[3] = gridp[j ][i+1].w;
        float level = 0.3f;
        for (int k = 0;k < 4;k++){
                if(np[k] > level) {rc[k] = (np[k] - level)/level-1.0f;}
                else                    {rc[k] = 0.0f;}
                if(np[k] < level) {gc[k] = np[k]/level;}
                else                    {gc[k] = (1.0f - np[k])/level;}
                if(np[k] < level) {bc[k] = -np[k]/level+1.0f;}
                else                    {bc[k] = 0.0f;}
                wc[k] = 1.0f;
                wc[k] = 0.95f;
                if(np[k] < 0.1f+ppp&&np[k] >= ppp) {wc[k] = 1.0f - (np[k]-
```

```
ppp)/0.1f;}
                else {wc[k] = 0.0f;}
                    wc[k] = 0.5f - np[k]/2.0f;
                }
        objCol[count*4 ] = new Color4f(rc[0], gc[0], bc[0], wc[0]);
        objCol[count*4+1] = new Color4f(rc[1], gc[1], bc[1], wc[1]);
        objCol[count*4+2] = new Color4f(rc[2], gc[2], bc[2], wc[2]);
        objCol[count*4+3] = new Color4f(rc[3], gc[3], bc[3], wc[3]);
        count++;
                }
        }

        QuadArray slice = new QuadArray(grid_4D_raster*grid_4D_raster*4,
        QuadArray.COORDINATES | GeometryArray.COLOR_4);
        slice.setCoordinates(0, verts);
        slice.setColors(0, objCol);
Appearance surfaceApp = new Appearance();
        Material surfMat = new Material();
        surfMat.setLightingEnable(true);
        PolygonAttributes pa = new PolygonAttributes(PolygonAttributes.POLY-
GON_FILL
        PolygonAttributes.CULL_NONE,0.5f,false);//true);
        TransparencyAttributes tran = new TransparencyAttributes();
tran.setCapability(TransparencyAttributes.ALLOW_MODE_WRITE);
        tran.setCapability(TransparencyAttributes.ALLOW_MODE_READ);
        tran.setCapability(TransparencyAttributes.ALLOW_VALUE_READ);
        tran.setCapability(TransparencyAttributes.ALLOW_VALUE_WRITE);
        tran.setTransparencyMode(TransparencyAttributes.BLENDED);//NICEST);
        tran.setTransparency(0.0F);
        surfaceApp.setTransparencyAttributes(tran);
        surfaceApp.setPolygonAttributes(pa);
        surfaceApp.setMaterial(surfMat);
        Shape3D shape = new Shape3D(slice, surfaceApp);
        if (l==0)
        if(is)
        Cut_Layers.add(gridp);
        objTmp.addChild(shape);
        }
}
//==============================================================
```

Compilation of References

Aarseth, E., & Calleja, G. (2015, June). The Word Game: The ontology of an undefinable object. In FDG.

Aarseth, E. (2012, May). A narrative theory of games. In *Proceedings of the International Conference on the Foundations of Digital Games* (pp. 129-133). ACM.

ABNT (Associação Brasileiras de Normas Técnicas). (2004). *ABNT NBR 9050: Acessibilidade a edificações, mobiliário, espaços e equipamentos urbanos.*

Abran, A., Khelifi, A., Suryn, W., & Seffah, A. (2003). Usability meanings and interpretations in ISO standards. *Software Quality Journal, 11*(4), 325–338. doi:10.1023/A:1025869312943

Abrevaya, V. F., Wuhrer, S., & Boyer, E. (2018, March). Multilinear autoencoder for 3d face model learning. In *Proceedings of the 2018 IEEE Winter Conference on Applications of Computer Vision (WACV)* (pp. 1-9). IEEE. doi:10.1109/WACV.2018.00007

Abu Shawar, B. (2015). Evaluating Web Accessibility of Educational websites. *International Journal of Emerging Technologies in Learning, 10*(4), 4–10. doi:10.3991/ijet.v10i4.4518

Acessibilidade Brasil. (2017). *DaSilva - Avaliador de Acessibilidade para Websites.* Retrieved from http://www.dasilva.org.br

Acosta, T., Acosta-Vargas, P., & Luján-Mora, S. (2018, April). Accessibility of eGovernment Services in Latin America. In *Proceedings of the 2018 International Conference on eDemocracy & eGovernment (ICEDEG)* (pp. 67-74). IEEE. 10.1109/ICEDEG.2018.8372332

Acosta-Vargas, P., Luján-Mora, S., & Salvador-Ullauri, L. (2016). Evaluation of the Web accessibility of higher-education websites. In *Proceedings of 15th International Conference on Information Technology Based Higher Education and Training* (pp. 1-6). Academic Press. 10.1109/ITHET.2016.7760703

Acosta-Vargas, P., Acosta, T., & Luján-Mora, S. (2018). Challenges to assess accessibility in higher education websites: A comparative study of Latin America universities. *IEEE Access, 6,* 36500–36508. doi:10.1109/ACCESS.2018.2848978

Adhoni, Z. A., AlHamad, H., Siddiqi, A. A., & El Mortaji, L. (2013). Towards a Comprehensive Online Portal and Mobile Friendly Qur'an Application. In *Proceedings of the 2013 Taibah University International Conference on Advances in Information technology for the Holy Quran and Its Sciences* (pp. 138-143). IEEE. 10.1109/NOORIC.2013.38

Ahmadi, G. A., Abdolmaleki, S., & Khoshbakht, M. (2011). Effect of computer-based training to increase creativity and achievement science, students in fourth grade of elementary. *Procedia Computer Science, 3,* 1551–1554. doi:10.1016/j.procs.2011.01.047

Ahmi, A., & Mohamad, R. (2019). Bibliometric Analysis of Global Scientific Literature on Web Accessibility. *International Journal of Recent Technology and Engineering, 7*(6), 250–258.

Ahsiah, I., Noor, N. M., & Idris, M. Y. I. (2013). Tajweed Checking System to Support Recitation. In *Proceedings of the 2013 International Conference on Advanced Computer Science and Information Systems* (pp. 189-193). IEEE.

Aizpurua, A., Arrue, M., Vigo, M., & Abascal, J. (2009). Transition of accessibility evaluation tools to new standards. In *Proceedings of the 2009 International Cross-Disciplinary Conference on Web Accessibility* (W4A) (pp. 36-44). ACM. 10.1145/1535654.1535662

Al-Ayyoub, M., Damer, N. A. M., & Hmeidi, I. (2018). Using Deep Learning for Automatically Determining Correct Application of Basic Quranic Recitation Rules. *The International Arab Journal of Information Technology, 15*(3A), 620–625.

Alencar, E. M. L. S., Fleith, D. S., & Bruno-Faria, M. F. (2010). A medida da criatividade: Teoria e prática. *The Art of Medication.*

Alfaries, A., Albahlal, M., Almazrua, M., & Almazrua, A. (2013). A Rule Based Annotation System to Extract Tajweed Rules from Quran. In *Proceedings of the 2013 Taibah University International Conference on Advances in Information technology for the Holy Quran and Its Sciences* (pp. 281-286). IEEE. 10.1109/NOORIC.2013.63

Al-Khalifa, A. S., & Al-Khalifa, H. S. (2011). An educational tool for generating inaccessible page examples based on WCAG 2.0 failures. In *Proceedings of the International Cross-Disciplinary Conference on Web Accessibility* (p. 30). ACM. 10.1145/1969289.1969328

Al-Khalifa, H. S., Al-Kanhal, M., Al-Nafisah, H., Al-Soukaih, N., Al-Hussain, E., & Al-Onzi, M. (2011). A pilot study for evaluating Arabic websites using automated WCAG 2.0 evaluation tools. In *Proceedings of the 2011 International Conference on Innovations in Information Technology* (pp. 293-296). IEEE. 10.1109/INNOVATIONS.2011.5893835

Almeida, S., Veloso, A., Roque, L., & Mealha, Ó. (2011). The Eyes and Games: A Survey of Visual Attention and Eye Tracking Input in Video Games. In *Proceedings of SBGames 2011*. Academic Press.

Almeida, S., Veloso, A., Roque, L., & Mealha, Ó. (2011). The Eyes and Games: A Survey of Visual Attention and Eye Tracking Input in Video Games. In *Proceedings of SBGames*. Academic Press.

Alonso-Ríos, D., Vázquez-García, A., Mosqueira-Rey, E., & Moret-Bonillo, V. (2009). Usability: A critical analysis and a taxonomy. *International Journal of Human-Computer Interaction, 26*(1), 53–74. doi:10.1080/10447310903025552

Al-Soud, A. R., & Nakata, K. (2010). Evaluating e-government websites in Jordan: Accessibility, usability, transparency and responsiveness. In *Proceedings of the 2010 IEEE International Conference on Progress in Informatics and Computing* (Vol. 2, pp. 761-765). IEEE. 10.1109/PIC.2010.5688017

Altalmas, T. M., Jamil, M. A., Ahmad, S., Sediono, W., Salami, M. J. E., Hassan, S. S., & Embong, A. H. (2017). Lips Tracking Identification of a Correct Pronunciation of Quranic Alphabets for Tajweed Teaching and Learning. *IIUM Engineering Journal, 18*(1), 177–191. doi:10.31436/iiumej.v18i1.646

Amabile, T. M., & Gryskiewicz, S. S. (1987). *Creativity in the R&D laboratory*. Center for Creative Leadership.

American Psychiatric Association (APA). (2013). *Diagnostic and statistical manual of mental disorders (DSM-5)*. American Psychiatric Pub.

Américo, M., Nogueira, H., & Ferrarini, M. (Directors). (2017). *Donzela em Defesa* [YouTube video. Retrieved from https://youtu.be/Tw2yBuYuseI

Android Studio. (2019). Android Studio [System Software]. Retrieved from https://developer.android.com/studio/

Arantes, M. L. P. (2016). *Sexismo nos Campos de Justiça: O Posicionamento de Marca Interferindo na Jogabilidade de League of Legends.* Undergraduate dissertation, Federal University of Paraná, Curitiba, Brazil. Retrieved from http://hdl.handle.net/1884/45179

Arh, T., & Jerman-Blazic, B. (2007). Application of Multi-Attribute Decision Making Approach to Learning Management Systems Evaluation. *JCP, 2*(10), 28–37.

Artino, A. R. Jr. (2010). Online or face-to-face learning? Exploring the personal factors that predict students' choice of instructional format. *The Internet and Higher Education, 13*(4), 272–276. doi:10.1016/j.iheduc.2010.07.005

Atorf, D., Hensler, L., & Kannegieser, E. (2016). Towards a concept on measuring the Flow state during gameplay of serious games. In Proceedings of the European Conference on Games Based Learning (ECGBL) (pp. 955–959). Academic Press. Retrieved from http://publica.fraunhofer.de/documents/N-438328.html

Azevedo, I., Morais, M. D. F., & Martins, F. (2017). Educação para a criatividade em adolescentes: Uma experiência com future problem solving program international. *Revista Electrónica Iberoamericana sobre Calidad, Eficacia y Cambio en Educación,* 75–87.

Baauw, E., & Markopoulous, P. (2004). A comparison of think-aloud and post-task interview for usability testing with children. In Proceeding of the 2004 Conference on Interaction Design and Children Building a Community IDC '04 (pp. 115–116). ACM Press. 10.1145/1017833.1017848

Babbie, E. (1999). *The basics of social research.* New York, NY: Wadsworth.

Bach, C. F., Ferreira, S. B. L., Silveira, D. S., & Nunes, R. R. (2009). Diretrizes de acessibilidade: uma abordagem comparativa entre WCAG e e-MAG. *Revista Eletrônica de Sistemas de Informação, 8*(1).

Bagdanov, A. D., Del Bimbo, A., & Masi, I. (2011, December). The florence 2d/3d hybrid face dataset. In *Proceedings of the 2011 joint ACM workshop on Human gesture and behavior understanding* (pp. 79-80). ACM.

Bailenson, J. N., Blascovich, J., & Guadagno, R. E. (2008). Self-Representations in Immersive Virtual Environments. *Journal of Applied Social Psychology, 38*(11), 2673–2690. doi:10.1111/j.1559-1816.2008.00409.x

Bailey, C., & Pearson, E. (2010). An educational tool to support the accessibility evaluation process. In *Proceedings of the 2010 International Cross Disciplinary Conference on Web Accessibility (W4A)* (p. 12). ACM. 10.1145/1805986.1806003

Bailey, C., & Pearson, E. (2011). Development and trial of an educational tool to support the accessibility evaluation process. In *Proceedings of the International Cross-Disciplinary Conference on Web Accessibility* (p. 2). ACM. 10.1145/1969289.1969293

Baltrušaitis, T., Robinson, P., & Morency, L. P. (2016, March). Openface: an open source facial behavior analysis toolkit. In *Proceedings of the 2016 IEEE Winter Conference on Applications of Computer Vision (WACV)* (pp. 1-10). IEEE. 10.1109/WACV.2016.7477553

Banda, D. R., Grimmett, E., & Hart, S. L. (2009). Activity schedules: Helping students with autism spectrum disorders in general education classrooms manage transition issues. *Teaching Exceptional Children, 41*(4), 16–21. doi:10.1177/004005990904100402

Bandura, A. (2004). Health promotion by social cognitive means. *Health Education & Behavior, 31*(2), 143–164. doi:10.1177/1090198104263660 PMID:15090118

Bardzell, S. (2010). Feminist HCI: Taking Stock and Outlining an Agenda for Design. In *Proceedings of the SIGCHI Conference on Human Factors in Computing Systems (CHI '10).* ACM. 10.1145/1753326.1753521

Barr, M. (2019). How commercial video games are designed to develop players' skills. Gamasutra. Retrieved from https://www.gamasutra.com/blogs/MatthewBarr/20191021/352546/How_commercial_video_games_are_designed_to_develop_players_skills.php

Barrett, L. F. (2006). Solving the emotion paradox: Categorization and the experience of emotion. *Personality and Social Psychology Review, 10*(1), 20–46. doi:10.120715327957pspr1001_2 PMID:16430327

Bartlett, M. S., Littlewort, G., Fasel, I., & Movellan, J. R. (2003, June). Real Time Face Detection and Facial Expression Recognition: Development and Applications to Human Computer Interaction. In *Proceedings of the 2003 Conference on computer vision and pattern recognition workshop* (Vol. 5, pp. 53-53). IEEE. 10.1109/CVPRW.2003.10057

Bartoli, L., Garzotto, F., Gelsomini, M., Oliveto, L., & Valoriani, M. 2014, June. Designing and evaluating touchless playful interaction for ASD children. In *Proceedings of the Interaction design and children 2014* (pp. 17-26). ACM. 10.1145/2593968.2593976

Bas, A., Smith, W. A., Bolkart, T., & Wuhrer, S. (2016, November). Fitting a 3D morphable model to edges: A comparison between hard and soft correspondences. In *Proceedings of the Asian Conference on Computer Vision* (pp. 377-391). Springer.

Basak, C., Boot, W. R., Voss, M. W., & Kramer, A. F. (2008). Can training in a real-time strategy video game attenuate cognitive decline in older adults? *Psychology and Aging, 23*(4), 765–777. doi:10.1037/a0013494 PMID:19140648

Basuhail, A. A. (2013). A Model for Implementing E-Teaching Objects for the Holy Quran and Related Sciences Using Animations. In *Proceedings of the 2013 Taibah University International Conference on Advances in Information technology for the Holy Quran and Its Sciences* (pp. 83-88). IEEE. 10.1109/NOORIC.2013.28

Bavelier, D., Green, C. S., Pouget, A., & Schrater, P. (2012). Brain plasticity through the life span: Learning to learn and action video games. *Annual Review of Neuroscience, 35*(1), 391–416. doi:10.1146/annurev-neuro-060909-152832 PMID:22715883

Bellini, S. (2004). Social skills deficits and anxiety in high-functioning adolescents with autism spectrum disorders. *Focus on Autism and Other Developmental Disabilities, 19*(2), 78–86. doi:10.1177/10883576040190020201

Benyon, D. (2014). Designing interactive systems: A comprehensive guide to HCI, UX and interaction design.

Bergeron, R. D., Cody, W., Hibbard, W., Kao, D. T., Miceli, K. D., Treinish, L. A., & Walther, S. (1994). Database Issues for Data Visualization: Developing a Data Model. In *Proceedings of the IEEE Visualization '93 Workshop on Database Issues for Data Visualization*. Springer-Verlag. 10.1007/BFb0021141

Berg, J. M., Dutton, J. E., & Wrzesniewski, A. (2013). Job crafting and meaningful work. In B. J. Dik, Z. S. Byrne, & M. F. Steger (Eds.), *Purpose and meaning in the workplace* (pp. 81–104). Washington, DC: American Psychological Association. doi:10.1037/14183-005

Bevan, N. (1995). Usability is quality of use. *Advances in human factors ergonomics, 20,* 349-349.

Bevan, N., Carter, J., & Harker, S. (2015). ISO 9241-11 revised: What have we learnt about usability since 1998? In *Proceedings of the International Conference on Human-Computer Interaction* (pp. 143-151). Springer. 10.1007/978-3-319-20901-2_13

Biocca, F., Harms, C., & Burgoon, J. K. (2003). Toward a more robust theory and measure of social presence: Review and suggested criteria. *Presence, 12*(5), 456–480. doi:10.1162/105474603322761270

Blanz, V., & Vetter, T. (1999). A morphable model for the synthesis of 3D faces. In *Proceedings of the 26th annual conference on Computer graphics and interactive techniques*, pages 187– 194, 1999. 10.1145/311535.311556

Blanz, V., & Vetter, T. (2003). Face recognition based on fitting a 3d morphable model. *IEEE Transactions on Pattern Analysis and Machine Intelligence*, *25*(9), 1063–1074.

Blinn, F. J. (1978). Simulation of wrinkled faces. In *Proceedings of the ACM SIGGRAPH Conf. Comput. Graphics*, 12(3), 286-292.

Blumberg, F. C., & Randall, J. D. (2013). What do children and adolescents say they do during video game play? *Journal of Applied Developmental Psychology*, *34*(2), 82–88. doi:10.1016/j.appdev.2012.11.004

Blumberg, F. C., & Sokol, L. M. (2004). Boys' and girls' use of cognitive strategy when learning to play video games. *The Journal of General Psychology*, *131*(2), 151–158. doi:10.3200/GENP.131.2.151-158 PMID:15088867

Bogost, I. (2007). *Persuasive games: The expressive power of videogames*. MIT Press.

Boodaghian Asl, A., & Gokan Khan, M. (2019). An empirical study on GUI-ii interview methods in participatory design. In *Proceeding of the 13ᵗʰ International Conference on Interfaces and Human Computer Interaction*. Academic Press.

Booth, J., Antonakos, E., Ploumpis, S., Trigeorgis, G., Panagakis, Y., & Zafeiriou, S. (2017, July). 3D face morphable models" In-The-Wild". In *Proceedings of the 2017 IEEE Conference on Computer Vision and Pattern Recognition (CVPR)* (pp. 5464-5473). IEEE. doi:10.1109/CVPR.2017.580

Booth, J., Roussos, A., Ponniah, A., Dunaway, D., & Zafeiriou, S. (2018). Large scale 3d morphable models. *International Journal of Computer Vision*, *126*(2-4), 233–254. doi:10.100711263-017-1009-7

Booth, J., Roussos, A., Zafeiriou, S., Ponniah, A., & Dunaway, D. (2016). A 3d morphable model learnt from 10,000 faces. In *Proceedings of the IEEE Conference on Computer Vision and Pattern Recognition* (pp. 5543-5552). IEEE Press.

Botelho, L., & Porciúncula, K. (2018). Os desafios para a produção de indicadores sobre pessoa com deficiência - ontem, hoje e amanhã. [The challenges for producing indicators on people with disability - yesterday, today and tomorrow]. In Panorama nacional e internacional da produção de indicadores sociais: grupos populacionais específicos e uso do tempo [National and International Overview of Social Indicator Production: Specific Population Groups and Time Use]. IBGE, Brazilian Institute of Geography and Statistics. Retrieved from https://biblioteca.ibge.gov.br/visualizacao/livros/liv101562.pdf

Botelho, L., & Porciúncula, K. (2018). The challenges for producing indicators on people with disability: yesterday, today and tomorrow. In: *National and International Overview of Social Indicator Production: specific Population Groups and Time Use*. IBGE, Brazilian Institute of Geography and Statistics. Retrieved Sep 24, 2019, from https://biblioteca.ibge.gov.br/visualizacao/livros/liv101562.pdf

Bradbard, D. A., & Peters, C. (2010). Web accessibility theory and practice: An introduction for university faculty. *The Journal of Educators Online*, *7*(1), 1–46. doi:10.9743/JEO.2010.1.1

Braun, V., & Clarke, V. (2006). Using thematic analysis in psychology. *Qualitative Research in Psychology*, *3*(2), 77–101. doi:10.1191/1478088706qp063oa

Brazil (2018). IFFluminense Portal. Retrieved July 2, 2018, from http://portal1.iff.edu.br

Brazil. (1996). LDB Law of Directives and Bases of National Education, Brazil. Retrieved from www.planalto.gov.br/ccivil_03/LEIS/L9394.htm

Brazil. (2007). Brazilian Ordinance that institutionalizes the e-Government Accessibility Model eMAG within the scope of the Information and Computer Resource Management System – SISP, Brazil. Retrieved from http://www.normas.gov.br/materia/-/asset_publisher/NebW5rLVWyej/content/id/54991011

Brazil. (2009). Brazilian Decree that promulgates the International Convention on the Rights of Persons with Disabilities and its Optional Protocol, Brazil. Retrieved from http://www.planalto.gov.br/ccivil_03/_ato2007-2010/2009/decreto/d6949.htm

Brazil. (2014). eMAG - Accessibility Model in Electronic Government, Brazil. Retrieved from http://emag.governo-eletronico.gov.br

Brazil. (2015). Brazilian Law on the Inclusion of Persons with Disabilities (Statute of Persons with Disabilities), Brazil. Retrieved from http://www.planalto.gov.br/ccivil_03/_Ato2015-2018/2015/Lei/L13146.htm

Breda, L. (2008). Invisible Walls. Game Career Guide. Retrieved from http://www.gamecareerguide.com/features/593/invisible_.php

Bredl, K., Groß, A., Hünniger, J., & Fleischer, J. (2012). The Avatar as a Knowledge Worker? How Immersive 3D Virtual Environments May Foster Knowledge Acquisition. *Electronic Journal of Knowledge Management*, *10*(1).

Breslin, M. (2004). Data warehousing battle of the giants. *Business Intelligence Journal*, *7*, 6–20.

Breslin, S., & Wadhwa, B. (2014a). EnGendering Interaction Design. In *Proceedings of the 3rd International Conference on User Science and Engineering (i-USEr)*. IEEE.

Breslin, S., & Wadhwa, B. (2014b). Exploring Nuanced Gender Perspectives Within the HCI Community. In *Proceedings of the India HCI 2014 Conference on Human Computer Interaction (IndiaHCI '14)*. ACM. 10.1145/2676702.2676709

Brinck, T. Gergle D. & S. Wood, D. (2001). Usability for the Web: designing Web sites that work. Elsevier.

Bronstein, M. M., Bruna, J., LeCun, Y., Szlam, A., & Vandergheynst, P. (2017). Geometric deep learning: Going beyond Euclidean data. *IEEE Signal Processing Magazine*, *34*(4), 18–42.

Brown, E., & Cairns, P. (2004, April). A grounded investigation of game immersion. In CHI'04 extended abstracts on Human factors in computing systems (pp. 1297-1300). Academic Press.

Brown, S., Lieberman, D. A., Gemeny, B., Fan, Y., Wilson, D., & Pasta, D. (1997). Educational video game for juvenile diabetes: Results of a controlled trial. *Informatics for Health & Social Care*, *22*(1), 77–89. PMID:9183781

Brunton, A., Salazar, A., Bolkart, T., & Wuhrer, S. (2014). Review of statistical shape spaces for 3D data with comparative analysis for human faces. *Computer Vision and Image Understanding*, *128*, 1–17.

Brush, A. J. B., Ames, M., & Davis, J. (2004). A comparison of synchronous remote and local usability studies for an expert interface. In *Extended Abstracts of the 2004 Conference on Human Factors and Computing Systems CHI '04*. ACM Press. 10.1145/985921.986018

Bulat, A., & Tzimiropoulos, G. (2017). How far are we from solving the 2d & 3d face alignment problem? (and a dataset of 230,000 3d facial landmarks). In *Proceedings of the International Conference on Computer Vision (ICCV)*. Academic Press. 10.1109/ICCV.2017.116

Buttfield-Addison, P., Manning, J., & Nugent, T. (2016, March). A better recipe for game jams: using the Mechanics Dynamics Aesthetics framework for planning. In *Proceedings of the International Conference on Game Jams, Hackathons, and Game Creation Events* (pp. 30-33). ACM. 10.1145/2897167.2897183

Buzady, Z. (2017). Flow, leadership and serious games – a pedagogical perspective. *World Journal of Science, Technology and Sustainable Development*, *14*(2-3), 204-217.

Cairns, P., Cox, A. L., Berthouze, N., Jennett, C., & Dhoparee, S. (2006). Quantifying the experience of immersion in games. In *CogSci 2006 Workshop: Cognitive Science of Games and Gameplay*. Academic Press.

Cairns, P., Cox, A., Berthouze, N., Jennett, C., & Dhoparee, S. (2006). Quantifying the experience of immersion in games. In *Proceedings of the Cognitive Science of Games and Gameplay workshop at Cognitive Science*. Academic Press.

Calder, A. J., Ewbank, M., & Passamonti, L. (2011). Personality influences the neural responses to viewing facial expressions of emotion. *Philosophical Transactions of the Royal Society of London. Series B, Biological Sciences*, *366*(1571), 1684–1701. doi:10.1098/rstb.2010.0362 PMID:21536554

Cao, C., Weng, Y., Zhou, S., Tong, Y., & Zhou, K. (2014). Facewarehouse: A 3d facial expression database for visual computing. *T-VCG*, *20*(3), 413–425. PMID:24434222

Cao, Q., Shen, L., Xie, W., Parkhi, O. M., & Zisserman, A. (2018, May). Vggface2: A dataset for recognising faces across pose and age. In *Proceedings of the 2018 13th IEEE International Conference on Automatic Face & Gesture Recognition (FG 2018)* (pp. 67-74). IEEE. 10.1109/FG.2018.00020

Carneiro, G. de A. S., & Rocha, M. A. A. (2019). MIAV: an inclusive method for accessibility assessment by visually impaired people. In *Proceedings of International Conference Interfaces and Human Computer Interaction 2019 (part of MCCSIS 2019)* (pp. 57-64). Academic Press. 10.33965/ihci2019_201906L008

Carr, D. (2006). Games and narrative. In D. Carr, D. Buckingham, A. Burn, & G. Schott (Eds.), *Computer games: Text, narrative and play* (pp. 30–44). Cambridge, UK: Polity Press.

Carter, J., & Markel, M. (2001). Web accessibility for people with disabilities: An introduction for Web developers. *IEEE Transactions on Professional Communication*, *44*(4), 225–233. doi:10.1109/47.968105

Cassell, J., & Jenkins, H. (Eds.). (2000). *From Barbie to Mortal Kombat: gender and computer games*. Cambridge, MA: The MIT Press.

Casters, M., Bouman, R., & Van Dongen, J. (2010). *Pentaho Kettle solutions: building open source ETL solutions with Pentaho Data Integration*. John Wiley & Sons.

Cerdera, C. P., & Lima, M. R. O. (2016). Estereótipos de gênero em video games: diálogos sobre sexismo, homofobia e outras formas de opressão na escola. In *Proceedings of SBGames 2016*. SBC.

Chan, W. W. Y. (2006). A Survey on Multivariate Data Visualization. In Encyclopedia of Environmetrics. Academic Press.

Charsky, D., & Ressler, W. (2011). Games are made for fun: Lessons on the effects of concept maps in the classroom use of computer games. *Computers & Education*, *56*(3), 604–615. doi:10.1016/j.compedu.2010.10.001

Chen, J. (2006). *Flow in games* (Doctoral dissertation, University of Southern California).

Cheng, M.-T., She, H.-C., & Annetta, L. (2015). Game Immersion Experience: Its Hierarchical Structure and Impact on Game-based Science Learning. *Journal of Computer Assisted Learning*, *31*(3), 232–253. doi:10.1111/jcal.12066

Cheng, S., Kotsia, I., Pantic, M., & Zafeiriou, S. (2018). 4dfab: A large scale 4d database for facial expression analysis and biometric applications. In *Proceedings of the IEEE conference on computer vision and pattern recognition* (pp. 5117-5126). IEEE Press.

Chen, H., Wigand, R. T., & Nilan, M. S. (1999). Optimal experience of web activities. *Computers in Human Behavior*, *15*(5), 585–608. doi:10.1016/S0747-5632(99)00038-2

Childs, M. (2010). Learners' experience of presence in Virtual Worlds [doctoral dissertation]. University of Warwick. Retreived from http://wrap.warwick.ac.uk/4516/1/WRAP_THESIS_Childs_2010.pdf

Chin, S., Lee, C. Y., & Lee, J. (2009). Personal Style and non-negative matrix factorization based exaggerative expressions of face. *dimensions, 9*, 10.

Chinaev, N. (2018). MobileFace: 3D face reconstruction with efficient CNN regression.

Cho, M. H., & Heron, M. L. (2015). Self-regulated learning: The role of motivation, emotion, and use of learning strategies in students' learning experiences in a self-paced online mathematics course. *Distance Education*, *36*(1), 80–99. doi:10.1080/01587919.2015.1019963

Chowdhury, S., Landoni, M., & Gibb, F. (2006). Usability and impact of digital libraries: A review. *Online Information Review*, *30*(6), 656–680. doi:10.1108/14684520610716153

Chu, M., & Montlló, M. (2016) *Reflections*. Retrieved from https://static.playoverwatch.com/media/comics/10/pt-br/comic-overwatch-reflections.pdf

Chua, R. Y.-J., & Iyengar, S. S. (2008). Creativity as a matter of choice: Prior experience and task instruction as boundary conditions for the positive effect of choice on creativity. *The Journal of Creative Behavior*, *42*(3), 164–180. doi:10.1002/j.2162-6057.2008.tb01293.x

Chung, J. S., Nagrani, A., & Zisserman, A. (2018). Voxceleb2: Deep speaker recognition.

Clarizia, F., Colace, F., De Santo, M., Lombardi, M., Pascale, F., & Pietrosanto, A. (2018, January). E-learning and sentiment analysis: a case study. In *Proceedings of the 6th International Conference on Information and Education Technology* (pp. 111-118). ACM. 10.1145/3178158.3178181

Clark, W., Logan, K., Luckin, R., Mee, A., & Oliver, M. (2009). Beyond Web 2.0: Mapping the technology landscapes of young learners. *Journal of Computer Assisted Learning*, *25*(1), 56–69. doi:10.1111/j.1365-2729.2008.00305.x

Clemensen, J., Larsen, S. B., Kyng, M., & Kirkevold, M. (2007). Participatory design in health sciences: Using cooperative experimental methods in developing health services and computer technology. *Qualitative Health Research*, *17*, 122–130. PMID:17170250

Cohen, I., Sebe, N., Garg, A., Chen, L. S., & Huang, T. S. (2003). Facial expression recognition from video sequences: Temporal and static modeling. *Computer Vision and Image Understanding*, *91*(1-2), 160–187. doi:10.1016/S1077-3142(03)00081-X

Coller, B. D., & Scott, M. J. (2009). Effectiveness of using a video game to teach a course in mechanical engineering. *Computers & Education*, *53*(3), 900–912. doi:10.1016/j.compedu.2009.05.012

Connor, A. M., Greig, T. J., & Kruse, J. (2017). Evaluating the impact of procedurally generated content on game immersion. *The Computer Games Journal*, *6*(4), 209–225. doi:10.100740869-017-0043-6

Constantin, A. 2015. *Supporting practitioners in social story interventions: the ISISS Authoring Tool* [PhD dissertation]. University of Edinburgh.

Constantin, A., Johnson, H., Smith, E., Lengyel, D., & Brosnan, M. (2017). Designing computer-based rewards with and for children with Autism Spectrum Disorder and/or Intellectual Disability. *Computers in Human Behavior*, *75*, 404–414. doi:10.1016/j.chb.2017.05.030

Cook, D. (2007). *The chemistry of game design*. Gamasutra. Retrieved from https://www.gamasutra.com/view/feature/129948/the_chemistry_of_game_design.php

Coomans, M. K. D., & Timmermans, H. J. (1997). Towards a taxonomy of virtual reality user interfaces. In *Proceedings of the IEEE Conference on Information Visualization* (pp. 279-284). IEEE Press. 10.1109/IV.1997.626531

Coppi, A. E. (2015). Fostering creativity through games and digital storytelling. In *Proceedings of the International Conference on Interactive Technologies and Games* (pp. 17-21). Academic Press. 10.1109/iTAG.2015.12

Costikyan, G. (2005). I Have No Words & I Must Design. *The game design reader: A rules of play anthology*, 24.

Cowen, A. S., & Keltner, D. (2017). Self-report captures 27 distinct categories of emotion bridged by continuous gradients. *Proceedings of the National Academy of Sciences of the United States of America*, *114*(38), E7900–E7909. doi:10.1073/pnas.1702247114 PMID:28874542

Cox, A. L., Cairns, P., Shah, P., & Carroll, M. (2012). Not doing but thinking: the role of challenge in the gaming experience. In *Proceedings of the SIGCHI Conference on Human Factors in Computing Systems* (pp. 79-88). Academic Pres. 10.1145/2207676.2207689

Cramer, M., Hirano, S. H., Tentori, M., Yeganyan, M. T., & Hayes, G. R. (2011, May). Classroom-based assistive technology: collective use of interactive visual schedules by students with autism. In CHI (pp. 1-10). Academic Press. doi:10.1145/1978942.1978944

Cramond, B., Matthews-Morgan, J., Bandalos, D., & Zuo, L. (2005). A report on the 40-year follow-up of the torrance tests of creative chinking: Alive and well in the new millennium. *Gifted Child Quarterly*, *49*(4), 283–291. doi:10.1177/001698620504900402

Csikszentmihalyi, M. (1975). *Beyond boredom and anxiety: Experiencing flow in work and play*. Jossey-Bass.

Csikszentmihalyi, M. (1990). *Flow: the psychology of optimal experience*. New York, NY: Harper & Row.

Csikszentmihalyi, M. (1991). *Flow: The Psychology of Optimal Experience*. New York, NY: Harper Perennial.

Cunningham, K. (2012). *Accessibility Handbook: Making 508 Compliant Websites*. O'Reilly Media, Inc.

Cura, T. (2010). A Random Search to Finding the Global Minimum, Int. *J. Contemp. Math. Sciences*, *5*(4), 179–190.

Czerepinski, K. C. (2000). *Tajweed rules of the Quran = Aḥkām tajwīd al-Qur'ān*. Jeddah: Dar Al-Khair Islamic Books Publisher.

D'Mello, S., Lehman, B., Pekrun, R., & Graesser, A. (2014). Confusion can be beneficial for learning. *Learning and Instruction*, *29*, 153–170. doi:10.1016/j.learninstruc.2012.05.003

da Silva, A. B. P., da Silva, C. G., & Moraes, R. L. de O. (2019). On the Use of a Continuous Accessibility Assessment Process for Dealing with Website Evolution. In *Proceedings of International Conference Interfaces and Human Computer Interaction 2019 (part of MCCSIS 2019)* (pp. 57-64). Academic Press.

Dai, H., Pears, N., Smith, W. A., & Duncan, C. (2017). A 3d morphable model of craniofacial shape and texture variation. In *Proceedings of the IEEE International Conference on Computer Vision* (pp. 3085–3093). IEEE Press; . doi:10.1109/ICCV.2017.335

Dalgarno, B., & Lee, M. J. (2010). What are the learning affordances of 3-D virtual environments? *British Journal of Educational Technology*, *41*(1), 10–32. doi:10.1111/j.1467-8535.2009.01038.x

De Beauvoir, S. (1989). *The Second Sex*. New York, NY: Vintage Books.

De Lauretis, T. (1987). *Technologies of Gender: Essays on Theory, Film, and Fiction*. Indianapolis, IN: Indiana University Press. doi:10.1007/978-1-349-19737-8

de Oliveira, M. C. F., & Levkowitz, H. (2003). From Visual Data Exploration to Visual Data Mining: A Survey. *IEEE Transactions on Visualization and Computer Graphics*, *9*(3), 378–394. doi:10.1109/TVCG.2003.1207445

De Rooij, A., Corr, P. J., & Jones, S. (2015). Emotion and creativity: Hacking into cognitive appraisal processes to augment creative ideation. In *Proceedings of the 2015 ACM SIGCHI Conference on Creativity and Cognition* (pp. 265-274). ACM. 10.1145/2757226.2757227

de Santana, V. F., & de Paula, R. A. (2013, May). Web accessibility snapshot: an effort to reveal coding guidelines conformance. In *Proceedings of the 10th International Cross-Disciplinary Conference on Web Accessibility* (p. 2). ACM. 10.1145/2461121.2461144

Deci, E., & Ryan, R. (1985). *Intrinsic Motivation and Self-Determination in Human Behavior*. New York, NY: Plenum Press; doi:10.1007/978-1-4899-2271-7.

Dede, C. J., Salzman, M., & Loftin, R. B. (1996). The development of a virtual world for learning newtonian mechanics. In P. Brusilovsky, P. Kommers, & N. Streitz (Eds.), *Multimedia, Hypermedia, and Virtual Reality Models, Systems, and Applications. MHVR 1996* (pp. 87–106). Springer. doi:10.1007/3-540-61282-3_10

Deng, Y., Yang, J., Xu, S., Chen, D., Jia, Y., & Tong, X. (2019). Accurate 3d face reconstruction with weakly-supervised learning: From single image to image set. In *Proceedings of the IEEE Conference on Computer Vision and Pattern Recognition Workshops*. IEEE Press.

Dettmer, S., Simpson, R. L., Myles, B. S., & Ganz, J. B. (2000). The use of visual supports to facilitate transitions of students with autism. *Focus on Autism and Other Developmental Disabilities*, *15*(3), 163–169. doi:10.1177/108835760001500307

Dimond, J. P., Fiesler, C., DiSalvo, B., Pelc, J., & Bruckman, A. S. (2012). Qualitative data collection technologies: a comparison of instant messaging, email, and phone. In *Proceedings of the 17th ACM International Conference on Supporting Group Work - GROUP '12*. ACM Press. 10.1145/2389176.2389218

Dix, A., Finlay, J., Abowd, G., & Beale, R. (2004). Evaluation techniques. *Human-Computer Interaction*.

Djamasbi, S., Siegel, M., & Tullis, T. (2010). Generation Y, web design, and eye tracking. *International Journal of Human-Computer Studies*, *68*(5), 307–323. doi:10.1016/j.ijhcs.2009.12.006

Dorofeeva, O. V., Vogt, N., Vogt, J., Popik, M. V., Rykov, A. N., & Vilkov, L. V. (2007). Molecular Structure and Conformational Composition of 1,3-Dihydroxyacetone Studied by Combined Analysis of Gas-Phase Electron Diffraction Data, Rotational Constants, and Results of Theoretical Calculations: Ideal Gas Thermodynamic Properties of 1,3-Dihydroxyacetone. The Journal of Physical Chemistry A, 111(28), 6434–6442.

Dou, P., Shah, S. K., & Kakadiaris, I. A. (2017). End-to-end 3D face reconstruction with deep neural networks. In *Proceedings of the IEEE Conference on Computer Vision and Pattern Recognition* (pp. 5908-5917). IEEE Press.

Duchowski, A. T. (2003). *Eye Tracking Methodology: Theory and Practice*. Secaucus, NJ: Springer. doi:10.1007/978-1-4471-3750-4

Duc, T. N., Huu, T. N., & Tan, L. N. (2009). *Facial Expression Recognition Using AAM Algorithm*. Vietnam: Ho Chi Minh University of Technology.

Eklund, T., Tétard, F., Ståhl, P., Hirkman, P., & Back, B. (2008*)*. Usability evaluation of an XP product. In *Proceedings of the 19th Australasian Conference on Information Systems (ACIS)* (pp. 280-289). Academic Press.

Ekman, P. (1989). The argument and evidence about universals in facial expressions. In Handbook of social psychophysiology (pp. 143-164). Academic Press.

Ekman, P. (1992). An argument for basic emotions. *Cognition and Emotion*, *6*(3-4), 169–200. doi:10.1080/02699939208411068

Ekman, P., & Friesen, W. V. (2003). *Unmasking the face: A guide to recognizing emotions from facial clues*. Ishk.

El-Aleem, A. A., El-Wahed, W. F. A., Ismail, N. A., & Torkey, F. A. (2005). Efficiency Evaluation of E-Commerce Websites. In WEC (2) (pp. 20-23). Academic Press.

El-Nasr, M. S., Milam, D., & Maygoli, T. (2013). Experiencing interactive narrative: A qualitative analysis of Façade. *Entertainment Computing*, *4*(1), 39–52. doi:10.1016/j.entcom.2012.09.004

El-Nasr, M. S., & Yan, S. (2006). Visual attention in 3D video games. In *Proceedings of ACM SIGCHI international conference on Advances in computer entertainment technology*. ACM Press.

Elson, M., Breuer, J., Ivory, J. D., & Quandt, T. (2014). More than stories with buttons: Narrative, mechanics, and context as determinants of player experience in digital games. *Journal of Communication, 64*(3), 521–542. doi:10.1111/jcom.12096

England, L. (2014). *The door problem*. Retrieved from http://www.lizengland.com/blog/2014/04/the-door-problem/

Ermi, L., & Mäyrä, F. (2005). Fundamental Components of the Gameplay Experience: Analysing Immersion. In S. D. Castell & J. Jenson (Eds.), *Worlds in play: Int. perspectives on digital games research* (Vol. 37). Bern, Switzerland: Peter Lang.

Espadinha, C., Pereira, L. M., da Silva, F. M., & Lopes, F. M. (2011). Accessibility of Portuguese Public Universities' sites. *Disability and Rehabilitation*, *33*(6), 475–485. doi:10.3109/09638288.2010.498554 PMID:20594034

Essa, I. A., & Pentland, A. P. (1997). Coding, analysis, interpretation, and recognition of facial expressions. *IEEE Transactions on Pattern Analysis and Machine Intelligence*, *19*(7), 757–763. doi:10.1109/34.598232

Etemadpour, R., Linsen, L., Paiva, J. G., Crick, C., & Forbes, A. G. (2015, March). Choosing visualization techniques for multidimensional data projection tasks: A guideline with examples. In Proceedings of the International joint conference on computer vision, imaging and computer graphics (pp. 166-186). Springer.

EulerL. (1728). Concerning The Shortest Line on Any Surface by which any two Points can be joined together.

Faceplusplus.com. (2019). *Face++ - Face++ AI Open Platform*. Retrieved from https://www.faceplusplus.com

Fairclough, S. H. (2009). Fundamentals of physiological computing. *Interacting with Computers*, *21*(1), 133–145. doi:10.1016/j.intcom.2008.10.011

Fang, X., Zhang, J., & Chan, S. S. (2013). Development of an Instrument for Studying Flow in Computer Game Play. *International Journal of Human-Computer Interaction*, *29*(7), 456–470. doi:10.1080/10447318.2012.715991

Farrugia, S., & Hudson, J. L. (2006). Anxiety in adolescents with Asperger syndrome: Negative thoughts, behavioral problems, and life interference. *Focus on Autism and Other Developmental Disabilities*, *21*(1), 25–35. doi:10.1177/10883576060210010401

FCT, Foundation for Science and Technology. (2013). AccessMonitor. ACCESS Unit of FCT, I.P. Portugal. Retrieved from http://www.acessibilidade.gov.pt/accessmonitor

Feng, M., Zulqarnain Gilani, S., Wang, Y., & Mian, A. (2018). 3D face reconstruction from light field images: A model free approach. In *Proceedings of the European Conf. Comput. Vision*. Academic Press. 10.1007/978-3-030-01249-6_31

Feng, J., Spence, I., & Pratt, J. (2007). Playing an action video game reduces gender differences in spatial cognition. *Psychological Science*, *18*(10), 850–855. doi:10.1111/j.1467-9280.2007.01990.x PMID:17894600

Feng, Y., Wu, F., Shao, X., Wang, Y., & Zhou, X. (2018). Joint 3d face reconstruction and dense alignment with position map regression network. In *Proceedings of the European Conference on Computer Vision (ECCV)* (pp. 534-551). Academic Press.

Fernandez, A., Insfran, E., & Abrahão, S. (2011). Usability evaluation methods for the web: A systematic mapping study. *Information and Software Technology, 53*(8), 789–817. doi:10.1016/j.infsof.2011.02.007

Fernández, J. M., Roig, J., & Soler, V. (2010). Web Accessibility on Spanish Universities. In *Proceedings of 2nd International Conference on Evolving Internet* (pp. 215-219). IEEE.

Ferreira, S. B. L. (2007). E-acessibilidade: tornando visível o invisível. *Revista Morpheus – Estudos Interdisciplinares em Memória Social, 6*(10).

G. Fick, & R. H. Sprague (Eds.). (2013). Decision Support Systems: Issues and Challenges. In *Proceedings of an International Task Force Meeting* (Vol. 11). Elsevier.

Figma. (2019). Figma: the collaborative interface design tool. Retrieved from https://www.figma.com/

Firaxis Games. (2016). Civilization 6.

Fitriani, I., Apriliaswati, R., & Rosnija, E. (2017). Analysis of EFL students' negative emotions towards english learning process in smpn 23 pontianak. *Jurnal Pendidikan dan Pembelajaran, 6*(6).

Flanagan, M.T. (2014). *Java Scientific Library.* Retrieved from http://www.ee.ucl.ac.uk/~mflanaga/java/index.html

Flanagan, M. (2009). *Critical play: radical game design.* The MIT Press. doi:10.7551/mitpress/7678.001.0001

Flick, U. (2009). *Introdução à pesquisa qualitativa.* Porto Alegre, Brazil: Artmed.

Flor, C. S. (2012). Diagnóstico da acessibilidade dos principais museus virtuais disponíveis da internet [Master thesis]. Centro Tecnológico, Universidade Federal de Santa Catarina.

Foley, J. D., Van, F. D., Van Dam, A., Feiner, S. K., Hughes, J. F., Angel, E., & Hughes, J. (1990). Computer Graphics: Principles and Practice (2nd ed.). Addison-Wesley.

Fong, S., & Meng, H. S. (2009, November). A web-based performance monitoring system for e-government services. In *Proceedings of the 3rd International Conference on Theory and Practice of Electronic Governance* (pp. 74-82). ACM. 10.1145/1693042.1693058

Fontoura, M. M., Rodrigues, L., Leite, P. S., Amaral, M. A., Almeida, L. D. A., & Merkle, L. E. (2019). Relações de gênero em mecânicas de jogos. In *Proceedings of SBGames 2019.* SBC.

Forster, E. M. (1985). *Aspects of the Novel* (Vol. 19). Houghton Mifflin Harcourt.

Fortim, I., & Monteiro, L. F. (2013). Choose your character: Mulheres e Personagens femininos nos videogames. In *Proceedings of SBGames 2013.* SBC.

Fox, E. (2002). Processing emotional facial expressions: The role of anxiety and awareness. *Cognitive, Affective & Behavioral Neuroscience, 2*(1), 52–63. doi:10.3758/CABN.2.1.52 PMID:12452584

Frauenberger, C., Good, J., & Alcorn, A. 2012, June. Challenges, opportunities and future perspectives in including children with disabilities in the design of interactive technology. In *Proceedings of the 11th International Conference on Interaction Design and Children* (pp. 367-370). ACM. 10.1145/2307096.2307171

Freire, A. P., Bittar, T. J., & Fortes, R. P. (2008). An approach based on metrics for monitoring web accessibility in Brazilian municipalities web sites. In *Proceedings of the 2008 ACM Symposium on Applied Computing* (pp. 2421-2425). ACM. 10.1145/1363686.1364259

Freire, A. P., Russo, C. M., & Fortes, R. P. (2008). A survey on the accessibility awareness of people involved in web development projects in Brazil. In *Proceedings of the 2008 International Cross-disciplinary Conference on Web Accessibility (W4A)* (pp. 87-96). ACM. 10.1145/1368044.1368064

Frisch, M. J., Trucks, G. W., Schlegel, H. B., Scuseria, G. E., Robb, M. A., Cheeseman, J. R., Montgomery Jr, J. A., ... Iyengar, S. S. (2003). GAUSSIAN 03, Revision E.01. Pittsburgh, PA: Gaussian, Inc.

Fullerton, T. (2018). *Game design workshop: a playcentric approach to creating innovative games.* AK Peters/CRC Press.

Furnas, G. W., & Buja, A. (1994). Prosection Views: Dimensional Inference through Sections and Projections. *Journal of Computational and Graphical Statistics, 3*(4), 323–353.

Gaggioli, A., Bassi, M., & Fave, A. (2003). Quality of experience in virtual environments. In G. Riva, F. Davide, W.A. Jsselsteijn (Eds.), Being There: Concepts, effects and measurement of user presence in synthetic environments (pp. 122-136). Ios Press.

Gangestad, S. W., & Snyder, M. (2000). Self-monitoring: Appraisal and reappraisal. *Psychological Bulletin, 126*(4), 530–555. doi:10.1037/0033-2909.126.4.530 PMID:10900995

Gardener, M. (1970). MATHEMATICAL GAMES: The fantastic combinations of John Conway's new solitaire game" life. *Scientific American, 223,* 120–123. doi:10.1038cientificamerican1070-120

Gee, J. P. (2007). *What Video Games Have to Teach Us about Learning and Literacy* (2nd ed.). Palgrave Macmillan.

Genova, K., Cole, F., Maschinot, A., Sarna, A., Vlasic, D., & Freeman, W. T. (2018). Unsupervised training for 3d morphable model regression. In *Proceedings of the IEEE Conference on Computer Vision and Pattern Recognition* (pp. 8377-8386). IEEE Press.

Georgiou, Y., & Kyza, E. A. (2017). The development and validation of the ARI questionnaire: An instrument for measuring immersion in location-based augmented reality settings. *International Journal of Human-Computer Studies, 98,* 24–37. DOI:10.1016/j.ijhcs.2016.09.014

Gerig, T., Morel-Forster, A., Blumer, C., Egger, B., Luthi, M., Schönborn, S., & Vetter, T. (2018, May). Morphable face models-an open framework. In *Proceedings of the 2018 13th IEEE International Conference on Automatic Face & Gesture Recognition (FG 2018)* (pp. 75-82). IEEE. doi:10.1109/FG.2018.00021

Gerig, T., Morel-Forster, A., Blumer, C., Egger, B., Luthi, M., Schönborn, S., & Vetter, T. (2018, May). Morphable face models-an open framework. In *Proceedings of the 2018 13th IEEE International Conference on Automatic Face & Gesture Recognition (FG 2018)* (pp. 75-82). IEEE.

Ghazi, A. N., Petersen, K., Reddy, S. S. V. R., & Nekkanti, H. (2018). Survey Research in Software Engineering: Problems and Mitigation Strategies. *IEEE Access, 7,* 24703–24718. doi:10.1109/ACCESS.2018.2881041

Gibson, J. (1977). The concept of affordances. In *Perceiving, acting, and knowing* (pp. 67-82). Academic Press.

Goldberg, L. R. (1990). An alternative description of personality: The big-five factor structure. *Journal of Personality and Social Psychology, 59*(6), 1216–1229. doi:10.1037/0022-3514.59.6.1216 PMID:2283588

Goleman, D. (2006). The socially intelligent. *Educational Leadership, 64*(1), 76–81.

Golfarelli, M., & Rizzi, S. (2009). *Data warehouse design: Modern principles and methodologies.* New York: McGraw-Hill.

Golfarelli, M., Rizzi, S., & Proli, A. (2006). Designing what-if analysis: towards a methodology. In *Proceedings of the 9th ACM international workshop on Data warehousing and OLAP* (pp. 51-58). ACM. 10.1145/1183512.1183523

Gortler, S. J., Grzeszczuk, R., Szeliski, R., & Cohen, M. F. (1996, August). The lumigraph. In Proceedings of the 23rd annual conference on Computer graphics and interactive techniques (pp. 43-54). Academic Press.

Goshvarpour, A., Abbasi, A., & Goshvarpour, A. (2017). An accurate emotion recognition system using ECG and GSR signals and matching pursuit method. *Biomedical Journal*, *40*(6), 355–368. DOI:10.1016/j.bj.2017.11.001

Goulart, L. A. (2012). *Proudmoore pride: Potencialidades da cultura de jogo digital e identidade política de gênero/ sexualidade* [Master's thesis]. Federal University of Rio Grande do Sul, Porto Alegre, Brazil. Retrieved from https:// lume.ufrgs.br/handle/10183/66649

Goulart, L. A. (2017). Jogos vivos para pessoas vivas: Composições queer-contrapúblicas nas culturas de jogo digital [Doctoral dissertation]. Federal University of Rio Grande do Sul, Porto Alegre, Brazil. Retrieved from https://lume. ufrgs.br/handle/10183/165868

Goulart, L., & Nardi, H. (2017). GAMERGATE: Digital games culture and male gamer identity. *Revista Mídia e Cotidiano*, *11*(3), 250–268.

Grafsgaard, J., Wiggins, J. B., Boyer, K. E., Wiebe, E. N., & Lester, J. (2013, July). Automatically recognizing facial expression: Predicting engagement and frustration. In Educational Data Mining 2013. Academic Press.

Gratch, J., Artstein, R., Lucas, G., Stratou, G., Scherer, S., Nazarian, A., . . . Morency, L.-P. (2014). The distress analysis interview corpus of human and computer interviews. In *Proceedings of the Ninth International Conference on Language Resources and Evaluation (LREC-2014)*. European Language Resources Association (ELRA).

Gray, C. (2019). Social Stories. Retrieved from https://carolgraysocialstories.com/social-stories/what-is-it/

Green, C. S., & Bavelier, D. (2003). Action video game modifies visual selective attention. *Nature*, *423*(6939), 534–537. doi:10.1038/nature01647 PMID:12774121

Greenfield, P. M. (2009). Technology and informal education: What is taught, what is learned. *Science*, *323*(5910), 69–71. doi:10.1126cience.1167190 PMID:19119220

Greenfield, P. M., Camaioni, L., Ercolani, P., Weiss, L., Lauber, B. A., & Perucchini, P. (1994). Cognitive socialization by computer games in two cultures: Inductive discovery or mastery of an iconic code? *Journal of Applied Developmental Psychology*, *15*(1), 59–85. doi:10.1016/0193-3973(94)90006-X

Greg, H. (2007). *The Joy of Java 3D*. Java3D. Retrieved from http://www.java3d.org/introduction.html

Grip, T. (2017). *The SSM framework of game design*. Frictional Games. Retrieved from https://frictionalgames.blogspot. com/2017/05/the-ssm-framework-of-game-design.html

Grynszpan, O., Weiss, P. L., Perez-Diaz, F., & Gal, E. (2014). Innovative technology-based interventions for autism spectrum disorders: A meta-analysis. *Autism*, *18*(4), 346–361. doi:10.1177/1362361313476767 PMID:24092843

Guenther, K (2003). Assessing web site usability.

Guo, Y., Cai, J., Jiang, B., & Zheng, J. (2018). Cnn-based real-time dense face reconstruction with inverse-rendered photo-realistic face images. *IEEE Transactions on Pattern Analysis and Machine Intelligence*, *41*(6), 1294–1307.

Hadizadeh, H., Enriquez, M. J., & Bajić, I. V. (2012). Eye-tracking database for a set of standard video sequences. *IEEE Transactions on Image Processing*, *21*(2), 898–903. doi:10.1109/TIP.2011.2165292 PMID:21859619

Hamari, J., Shernoff, D. J., Rowe, E., Coller, B., Asbell-Clarke, J., & Edwards, T. (2016). Challenging games help students learn: An empirical study on engagement, flow and immersion in game-based learning. *Computers in Human Behavior*, *54*, 170–179. doi:10.1016/j.chb.2015.07.045

Hamlen, K. R. (2011). Children's choices and strategies in video games. *Computers in Human Behavior*, *27*(1), 532–539. doi:10.1016/j.chb.2010.10.001

Hamm, S. (2010, May 20). *The Aesthetics of Unique Video Game Characters*. Game Career Guide. Retrieved from http://gamecareerguide.com/features/854/the_aesthetics_of_unique_video_.php?page=1

Hasan, M. S., & Yu, H. (2017). Innovative developments in HCI and future trends. *International Journal of Automation and Computing*, *14*(1), 10–20. doi:10.100711633-016-1039-6

Hassner, T., & Basri, R. (2006). Example based 3D reconstruction from single images. In *Proceedings of the Conf. Comput. Vision Pattern Recognition (CVPR) Workshops*. Academic Press. 10.1109/CVPRW.2006.76

Hassner, T., & Basri, R. (2013). Single view depth estimation from examples.

Hearst, M., & Landay, J. (1999). Improving the Early Phases of Web Site Design via Informal Design Tools and Automated Usability Assessment.

Heintz, M., Law, E. L. C., & Soleimani, S. (2015, September). Paper or pixel? comparing paper-and tool-based participatory design approaches. In *IFIP Conference on Human-Computer Interaction* (pp. 501-517). Springer.

Hill, M. L., & Craig, K. D. (2002). Detecting deception in pain expressions: The structure of genuine and deceptive facial displays. *Pain*, *98*(1-2), 135–144. doi:10.1016/S0304-3959(02)00037-4 PMID:12098625

Hocking, C. (2007). *Ludonarrative dissonance in Bioshock*. Typepad. Retrieved from https://clicknothing.typepad.com/click_nothing/2007/10/ludonarrative-d.html

Hoffman, P. E., & Grinstein, G. G. (2001). *A Survey of Visualizations for High-Dimensional Data Mining. In Information Visualization in Data Mining and Knowledge Discovery* (pp. 47–82). Morgan Kaufmann Publishers.

Hoge, C. (2018). *Helping players hate (or love) their nemesis* [YouTube Video]. Retrieved from https://www.youtube.com/watch?v=p3ShGfJkLcU

Hooi, R., & Cho, H. (2012). Being immersed: avatar similarity and self-awareness. In *Proceedings of the 24th Australian Computer-Human Interaction Conference* (pp. 232-240). Academic Press.

Hoscheidt, S. M., LaBar, K. S., Ryan, L., Jacobs, W. J., & Nadel, L. (2014). Encoding negative events under stress: High subjective arousal is related to accurate emotional memory despite misinformation exposure. *Neurobiology of Learning and Memory*, *112*, 237–247. doi:10.1016/j.nlm.2013.09.008 PMID:24055594

Hou, J., Nam, Y., Peng, W., & Lee, K. M. (2012). Effects of screen size, viewing angle, and players' immersion tendencies on game experience. *Computers in Human Behavior*, *28*(2), 617–623. doi:10.1016/j.chb.2011.11.007

Hourcade, J. P., Bullock-Rest, N. E., & Hansen, T. E. (2012). Multitouch tablet applications and activities to enhance the social skills of children with autism spectrum disorders. *Personal and Ubiquitous Computing*, *16*(2), 157–168. doi:10.100700779-011-0383-3

Huber, P., Hu, G., Tena, R., Mortazavian, P., Koppen, P., Christmas, W. J., ... & Kittler, J. (2016, February). A multiresolution 3d morphable face model and fitting framework. In *Proceedings of the 11th International Joint Conference on Computer Vision, Imaging and Computer Graphics Theory and Applications*. Academic Press. 10.5220/0005669500790086

Huitt, W. and Hummel, J., 2003. Piaget's theory of cognitive development. *Educational psychology interactive*, *3*(2), 1-5.

Hunicke, R., LeBlanc, M., & Zubek, R. (2004, July). MDA: A formal approach to game design and game research. In *Proceedings of the AAAI Workshop on Challenges in Game AI* (Vol. 4, No. 1, p. 1722).

Hwang, G.-J., Yang, L.-H., & Wang, S.-Y. (2013). A Concept Map-Embedded Educational Computer Game for Improving Students' Learning Performance in Natural Science Courses. *Computers & Education, 69*, 121–130. doi:10.1016/j.compedu.2013.07.008

Hyönä, J. (2010). The use of eye movements in the study of multimedia learning. *Learning and Instruction, 20*(2), 172–176. doi:10.1016/j.learninstruc.2009.02.013

IBGE (Instituto Brasileiro de Geografia e Estatística). (2010). *CENSO 2010*. Retrieved from http://www.censo2010.ibge.gov.br

IBGE, Brazilian Institute of Geography and Statistics. (2015). National Health Survey (PNS) 2013: Life Cycles. Brazil and Major Regions. Retrieved from https://biblioteca.ibge.gov.br/visualizacao/livros/liv94522.pdf

Ibrahim, N. J., Idris, M. Y. I., Razak, Z., & Abdul Rahman, N. N. (2013). Automated Tajweed Checking Rules Engine for Quranic Learning. *Multicultural Education & Technology Journal, 7*(4), 275–287. doi:10.1108/METJ-03-2013-0012

Ijsselsteijn, W., van den Hoogen, W., Klimmt, C., De Kort, Y., Lindley, C., Mathiak, K., . . . Vorderer, P. (2008). Measuring the experience of digital game enjoyment. In Proceedings of Measuring Behavior 2008, 6th International Conference on Methods and Techniques in Behavioral Research (pp. 88–89). Academic Press.

IJsselsteijn, W. A., de Ridder, H., Freeman, J., & Avons, S. E. (2000). Presence: Concept, determinants, and measurement. In *Human vision and electronic imaging V* (Vol. 3959, pp. 520-529). International Society for Optics and Photonics. doi:10.1117/12.387188

Inclusive Design Institute. *AChecker*. Retrieved from https://achecker.ca/

Isaksen, S. G., Dorval, K. B., & Treffinger, D. J. (2011). *Creative approaches to problem solving: A framework for change. Sage.*

İşeri, E. İ., Uyar, K., & İlhan, Ü. (2017). The accessibility of Cyprus Islands' higher education institution websites. *Procedia Computer Science, 120*, 967–974. doi:10.1016/j.procs.2017.11.333

ISO. (2001). *Standard 9126: Software Engineering Product Quality*, parts 1, 2 and 3.

ISO. (2011). *IEC 25010: 2011. Systems and Software Engineering—Systems and Software Quality Requirements and Evaluation (SQuaRE)—System and Software Quality Models.*

ISO. (2016). *IEC 25066: 2016. Systems and software engineering — Systems and software Quality Requirements and Evaluation (SQuaRE) — Common Industry Format (CIF) for Usability — Evaluation Report.*

ISO/IEC (International Organization for Standardization). (1998). *Standard 9241: Ergonomic Requirements for Office Work with Visual Display Terminals (VDT)s, Part 11. Guidance on Usability*, Retrieved from https://www.iso.org/obp/ui/#iso:std:iso:9241:-11:ed-1:v1:en

ISO/IEC. (2011). ISO/IEC 25010:2011. Systems and software engineering — Systems and software Quality Requirements and Evaluation (SQuaRE) — System and software quality models.

ISO/IEC. (2012). ISO/IEC 40500:2012. Information technology - W3C Web Content Accessibility Guidelines (WCAG) 2.0.

Isokoski, P., Joos, M., Spakov, O., & Martin, B. (2009). Gaze controlled games. *Universal Access in the Information Society, 8*(4), 323–337. doi:10.100710209-009-0146-3

ITASD. (2014). *Innovative Technology for Autism Spectrum Disorders*. Digital Solutions for Autism.

Ivory, M., & Hearst, M. (n.d.). Comparing performance and usability evaluation: new methods for automated usability assessment.

Jackson, A. S., Bulat, A., Argyriou, V., & Tzimiropoulos, G. (2017). Large pose 3D face reconstruction from a single image via direct volumetric CNN regression. In *Proceedings of the IEEE International Conference on Computer Vision* (pp. 1031–1039). IEEE Press; . doi:10.1109/ICCV.2017.117

Jaques, P. A., Vicari, R., Pesty, S., & Martin, J. C. (2011, October). Evaluating a cognitive-based affective student model. In *Proceedings of the International Conference on Affective Computing and Intelligent Interaction* (pp. 599-608). Springer. 10.1007/978-3-642-24600-5_63

Jeng, J. (2005). What is usability in the context of the digital library and how can it be measured? *Information Technology and Libraries*, *24*(2), 3. doi:10.6017/ital.v24i2.3365

Jeng, J. (2006). Usability of the digital library: An evaluation model. *College & Research Libraries News*, *67*(2), 78.

Jeni, L. A., Tulyakov, S., Yin, L., Sebe, N., & Cohn, J. F. (2016, October). The first 3d face alignment in the wild (3dfaw) challenge. In *Proceedings of the European Conference on Computer Vision* (pp. 511–520). Springer; . doi:10.1007/978-3-319-48881-3_35

Jennett, C., Cox, A. L., & Cairns, P. (2008). Being in the game. In S. Gunzel, M. Liebe, & D. Mersch (Eds.), *Proceedings of the Philosophy of Computer Games* (pp. 210-227). Academic Pres.

Jennett, C., Cox, A. L., Cairns, P., Dhoparee, S., Epps, A., Tijs, T., & Walton, A. (2008). Measuring and defining the experience of immersion in games. *International Journal of Human-Computer Studies*, *66*(9), 641–661. DOI:10.1016/j.ijhcs.2008.04.004

Jiang, L., Wu, X., & Kittler, J. (2018). Pose-Invariant 3D Face Reconstruction.

Jiang, L., Zhang, J., Deng, B., Li, H., & Liu, L.(2018). 3D face reconstruction with geometry details from a single image.

Johnson, D., Gardner, M. J., & Perry, R. (2018). Validation of two game experience scales: The player experience of need satisfaction (PENS) and game experience questionnaire (GEQ). *International Journal of Human-Computer Studies*, *118*, 38–46. doi:10.1016/j.ijhcs.2018.05.003

Johnson, D., & Wiles, J. (2003). Effective affective user interface design in games. *Ergonomics*, *46*(13-14), 1332–1345. doi:10.1080/00140130310001610865 PMID:14612323

Jones, A., & Issroff, K. (2005). Learning technologies: Affective and social issues in computer-supported collaborative learning. *Computers & Education*, *44*(4), 395–408. doi:10.1016/j.compedu.2004.04.004

Joo, S. (2010). How are usability elements efficiency, effectiveness, and satisfaction correlated with each other in the context of digital libraries? *Proceedings of the American Society for Information Science and Technology*, *47*(1), 1–2. doi:10.1002/meet.14504701323

Joo, S., Lin, S., & Lu, K. (2011). A usability evaluation model for academic library websites: Efficiency, effectiveness and learnability. *Journal of Library and Information Studies*, *9*(2), 11–26.

Jourabloo, A., & Liu, X. (2015). Pose-invariant 3D face alignment. In *Proceedings of the IEEE International Conference on Computer Vision* (pp. 3694-3702). IEEE Press.

Jourabloo, A., & Liu, X. (2016). Large-pose face alignment via CNN-based dense 3D model fitting. In *Proceedings of the IEEE conference on computer vision and pattern recognition* (pp. 4188-4196). IEEE Press.

Jung, N., Wranke, C., Hamburger, K., & Knauff, M. (2014). How emotions affect logical reasoning: Evidence from experiments with mood-manipulated participants, spider phobics, and people with exam anxiety. *Frontiers in Psychology*, *5*, 570. doi:10.3389/fpsyg.2014.00570 PMID:24959160

Just, M. A., & Carpenter, P. A. (1980). A theory of reading: From eye fixations to comprehension. *Psychological Review*, *87*(4), 329–354. doi:10.1037/0033-295X.87.4.329 PMID:7413885

Juul, J. (2018). The game, the player, the world: Looking for a heart of gameness. *PLURAIS-Revista Multidisciplinar, 1*(2).

Kanade, T., Cohn, J. F., & Tian, Y. (2000, March). Comprehensive database for facial expression analysis. In *Proceedings of the Fourth IEEE International Conference on Automatic Face and Gesture Recognition* (pp. 46-53). IEEE. 10.1109/AFGR.2000.840611

Kane, S. K., Shulman, J. A., Shockley, T. J., & Ladner, R. E. (2007, May). A Web accessibility report card for top international university Web sites. In *Proceedings of the 2007 international cross-disciplinary conference on Web accessibility (W4A)* (pp. 148-156). ACM. 10.1145/1243441.1243472

Kannegieser, E., Atorf, D., & Meier, J. (2018). In: Surveying games with a combined model of Immersion and Flow. In Proceedings of the International Conferences on Interfaces and Human Computer Interaction 2018, Game and Entertainment Technologies 2018 and Computer Graphics, Visualization, Computer Vision and Image Processing 2018 (pp. 353-356). Academic Press.

Kanner, L. (1943). Autistic disturbances of affective content. *Nervous Child*, *2*, 217–250.

Kapi, A. Y., Osman, N., Ramli, R. Z. & Taib, J. M. (2017). Multimedia Education Tools for Effective Teaching and Learning. *Journal of Telecommunication, Electronic and Computer Engineering, 9*(2-8), 143-146.

Kapoor, A., Qi, Y., & Picard, R. W. (2003, October). Fully automatic upper facial action recognition. In *Proceedings of the 2003 IEEE International SOI Conference* (pp. 195-202). IEEE. 10.1109/AMFG.2003.1240843

Keim, D. A. (1997). Visual Techniques for Exploring Databases. In *Proceedings of the 3rd International Conference on Knowledge Discovery and Data Mining Tutorial*. Academic Press.

Keim, D. A., & Kriegel, H.-P. (1996). Visualization Techniques for Mining Large Databases: A Comparison. *IEEE Transactions on Knowledge and Data Engineering*, *8*(6), 923–938. doi:10.1109/69.553159

Kemelmacher-Shlizerman, I. (2013). Internet based morphable model. In *Proceedings of the IEEE international conference on computer vision* (pp. 3256-3263). IEEE Press.

Kemelmacher-Shlizerman, I., & Basri, R. (2011). 3D face reconstruction from a single image using a single reference face shape. *Trans. Pattern Anal. Mach. Intell.*, *33*(2), 394–405. doi:10.1109/TPAMI.2010.63 PMID:21193812

Kemelmacher-Shlizerman, I., & Seitz, S. M. (2011, November). Face reconstruction in the wild. In *Proceedings of the 2011 International Conference on Computer Vision* (pp. 1746-1753). IEEE.

Kim, H., Zollhöfer, M., Tewari, A., Thies, J., Richardt, C., & Theobalt, C. (2018). Inversefacenet: Deep monocular inverse face rendering. In Proceedings of the IEEE Conference on Computer Vision and Pattern Recognition (pp. 4625-4634). doi:10.1109/ICCV.2011.6126439

Kim, B. (2015). *Understanding gamification*. ALA TechSource.

Kimball, R. (1996). *The data warehouse toolkit: practical techniques for building dimensional data warehouses* (Vol. 1). New York: John Wiley & Sons.

Kim, K. H. (2006). Can we trust creativity tests? A review of the Torrance tests of creative thinking (TTCT). *Creativity Research Journal, 18*(1), 3–14. doi:10.120715326934crj1801_2

Kivikangas, J. M., Chanel, G., Cowley, B., Ekman, I., Salminen, M., Järvelä, S., & Ravaja, N. (2011). A review of the use of psychophysiological methods in game research. *Journal of Gaming & Virtual Worlds, 3*(3), 181–199. doi:10.1386/jgvw.3.3.181_1

Klevjer, R. (2002, June). In Defense of Cutscenes. In *CGDC Conf.* Academic Press.

Knapp, M., Romeo, R., & Beecham, J. (2009). Economic cost of autism in the UK. *Autism, 13*(3), 317–336. doi:10.1177/1362361309104246 PMID:19369391

Koepp, M. J., Gunn, R. N., Lawrence, A. D., Cunningham, V. J., Dagher, A., Jones, T., ... Grasby, P. M. (1998). Evidence for striatal dopamine release during a video game. *Nature, 393*(6682), 266–268. doi:10.1038/30498 PMID:9607763

Koestinger, M., Wohlhart, P., Roth, P. M., & Bischof, H. (2011, November). Annotated facial landmarks in the wild: A large-scale, real-world database for facial landmark localization. In *Proceedings of the 2011 IEEE international conference on computer vision workshops (ICCV workshops)* (pp. 2144-2151). IEEE. 10.1109/ICCVW.2011.6130513

Koivisto, J., Malik, A., Gurkan, B., & Hamari, J. (2019). Getting Healthy by Catching Them All: A Study on the Relationship between Player Orientations and Perceived Health Benefits in an Augmented Reality Game. In *Proceedings of the 52nd Hawaii International Conference on System Sciences.* Academic Press. 10.24251/HICSS.2019.216

Koster, R. (2003). *Theory of fun for game design.* O'Reilly Media, Inc.

Koster, R. (2014). *A theory of fun for game design. Sebastopol.* Cali: OReilly Media.

Kous, K., Pušnik, M., Heričko, M., & Polančič, G. (2018). Usability evaluation of a library website with different end user groups. *Journal of Librarianship and Information Science.*

Krapp, A., Schiefele, U., & Schreyer, I. (2009). Metaanalyse des Zusammenhangs von Interesse und schulischer Leistung. *Zeitschrift für Entwicklungspsychologie und Pädagogische Psychologie, 25,* 120–148.

Lam, K. (2018). *Vault boy's emergence: Goldenblue's big break.* League of Legends. Retrieved from https://nexus.leagueoflegends.com/en-us/2018/09/vault-boys-emergence-goldenglues-big-break/

Lantz, F. (2015). *Against design.* Game Design Advance. Retrieved from http://gamedesignadvance.com/?p=2930cpage=1

Lau, S., & Cheung, P. C. (2010). Developmental trends of creativity: What twists of turn do boys and girls take at different grades? *Creativity Research Journal, 22*(3), 329–336. doi:10.1080/10400419.2010.503543

Lazarus, R. S., & Lazarus, B. N. (1994). *Passion and reason: Making sense of our emotions.* USA: Oxford University Press.

LeDoux, J. (2003). The emotional brain, fear, and the amygdala. *Cellular and Molecular Neurobiology, 23*(4-5), 727–738. doi:10.1023/A:1025048802629 PMID:14514027

Lee, K. M. (2004). Presence, explicated. *Communication Theory, 14*(1), 27–50. doi:10.1111/j.1468-2885.2004.tb00302.x

Lee, Y., & Kozar, K. A. (2012). Understanding of Website Usability: Specifying and Measuring Constructs and Their Relationships. *Decision Support Systems, 52*(2), 450–463. doi:10.1016/j.dss.2011.10.004

Lessiter, J., Freeman, J., Keogh, E., & Davidoff, J. (2001). A cross-media presence questionnaire: The ITC-Sense of Presence Inventory. *Presence, 10*(3), 282–297. doi:10.1162/105474601300343612

Leveson, N. (2011). *Engineering a safer world: Systems thinking applied to safety.* MIT press.

Levi, G., & Hassner, T. (2015). Emotion Recognition in the Wild via Convolutional Neural Networks and Mapped Binary Patterns. In Proceedings of the 2015 ACM on International Conference on Multimodal Interaction ICMI '15 (pp. 503–510). ACM. doi:10.1145/2818346.2830587

Lewinski, P., den Uyl, T. M., & Butler, C. (2014). Automated facial coding: Validation of basic emotions and FACS AUs in FaceReader. *Journal of Neuroscience, Psychology, and Economics, 7*(4), 227–236. doi:10.1037/npe0000028

Li, C., Zhou, K., & Lin, S. (2014). Intrinsic face image decomposition with human face priors. In *Proceedings of the European Conf. Comput. Vision* (pp. 218-233). Springer. 10.1007/978-3-319-10602-1_15

Li, Z., Qiong, B., & Wee, S. (2014). Impact of job control on employee creativity: The moderating effect of cognitive irritation. In *Proceedings of the 21th International Conference on Management Science & Engineering* (pp. 873-878). Academic Press.

Liang, S., Shapiro, L. G., & Kemelmacher-Shlizerman, I. (2016, October). Head reconstruction from internet photos. In *Proceedings of the European Conference on Computer Vision* (pp. 360-374). Springer.

Lima, L. A. B. 2018. The struggles of diversity in gaming: an analysis of gender representation in crowdfunded games. In *Proceedings of SBGames 2018*. SBC.

Lin, H. C. K., Wu, C. H., & Hsueh, Y. P. (2014). The influence of using affective tutoring system in accounting remedial instruction on learning performance and usability. *Computers in Human Behavior, 41*, 514–522. doi:10.1016/j.chb.2014.09.052

Lisetti, C. L., & Schiano, D. J. (2000). Automatic facial expression interpretation: Where human-computer interaction, artificial intelligence and cognitive science intersect. *Pragmatics & Cognition, 8*(1), 185–235. doi:10.1075/pc.8.1.09lis

Li, T., Bolkart, T., Black, M. J., Li, H., & Romero, J. (2017). Learning a model of facial shape and expression from 4D scans. *ACM Transactions on Graphics, 36*(6), 194. doi:10.1145/3130800.3130813

Littlewort, G. C., Bartlett, M. S., & Lee, K. (2009). Automatic coding of facial expressions displayed during posed and genuine pain. *Image and Vision Computing, 27*(12), 1797–1803. doi:10.1016/j.imavis.2008.12.010

Liu, P., Yu, Y., Zhou, Y., & Du, S. (2019, March). Single view 3d face reconstruction with landmark updating. In *Proceedings of the 2019 IEEE Conference on Multimedia Information Processing and Retrieval (MIPR)* (pp. 403-408). IEEE. doi:10.1109/MIPR.2019.00082

Liu, F., Tran, L., & Liu, X. (2019). 3D Face Modeling from Diverse Raw Scan Data. In *Proceedings of the IEEE International Conference on Computer Vision* (pp. 9408-9418). IEEE Press.

Liu, F., Zeng, D., Zhao, Q., & Liu, X. (2016, October). Joint face alignment and 3d face reconstruction. In *Proceedings of the European Conference on Computer Vision* (pp. 545–560). Springer; . doi:10.1007/978-3-319-46454-1_33

Liu, F., Zhu, R., Zeng, D., Zhao, Q., & Liu, X. (2018). Disentangling features in 3D face shapes for joint face reconstruction and recognition. In *Proceedings of the IEEE conference on computer vision and pattern recognition* (pp. 5216–5225). IEEE Press; . doi:10.1109/CVPR.2018.00547

Liu, Y., Jourabloo, A., Ren, W., & Liu, X. (2017). Dense face alignment. In *Proceedings of the IEEE International Conference on Computer Vision Workshops* (pp. 1619-1628). IEEE Press.

Lombard, M., & Ditton, T. (1997). At the Heart of It All: The Concept of Presence. *Journal of Computer-Mediated Communication, 3*(2), 0. doi:10.1111/j.1083-6101.1997.tb00072.x

Lorenz, M., Rüßmann, M., Strack, R., Lueth, K. L., & Bolle, M. (2015). *Man and machine in industry 4.0: How will technology transform the industrial workforce through 2025. The Boston Consulting Group.*

Louro, G. L. (2001). Pedagogias da Sexualidade. In G. L. Louro (Ed.), *O corpo educado: pedagogias da sexualidade* (pp. 7–34). Belo Horizonte, Brazil: Editora Autêntica.

Luján-Mora, S., Navarrete, R., & Peñafiel, M. (2014, April). Egovernment and web accessibility in South America. In *Proceedings of the 2014 First International Conference on eDemocracy & eGovernment* (ICEDEG) (pp. 77-82). IEEE. 10.1109/ICEDEG.2014.6819953

Lum, H. C., Greatbatch, R., Waldfogle, G., & Benedict, J. (2018). How Immersion, Presence, Emotion, & Workload Differ in Virtual Reality and Traditional Game Mediums. *Proceedings of the Human Factors and Ergonomics Society Annual Meeting*, *62*(1), 1474–1478. doi:10.1177/1541931218621334

MacFadden, R. J., Moore, B., & Herie, M. (Eds.). (2005). *Web-based education in the human services: Models, methods, and best practices* (Vol. 23). Psychology Press.

Macvean, A., & Robertson, J. (2013). Understanding exergame users' physical activity, motivation and behavior over time. In *Proceedings of the SIGCHI Conference on Human Factors in Computing Systems* (pp. 1251-1260). ACM. 10.1145/2470654.2466163

Magdin, M., & Prikler, F. (2018). Real time facial expression recognition using webcam and SDK affectiva. *IJIMAI*, *5*(1), 7–15. doi:10.9781/ijimai.2017.11.002

Mahmood, F., Munir, U., Mehmood, F., & Iqbal, J. (2018, April). 3D shape recovery from image focus using gray level co-occurrence matrix. In *Proceedings of the Tenth International Conference on Machine Vision (ICMV 2017)*. International Society for Optics and Photonics.

Mania, K., & Chalmers, A. (2001). The effects of levels of immersion on memory and presence in virtual environments: A reality centered approach. *Cyberpsychology & Behavior*, *4*(2), 247–264. doi:10.1089/109493101300117938 PMID:11710251

Mantovani, F. (2001). VR Learning: Potential and Challenges for the Use of 3D Environments in Education and Training. In G. Riva & C. Galimberti (Eds.), *Towards cyberpsychology: Mind, cognition, and society in the Internet Age* (pp. 207–225). Amsterdam: IOS Press.

Marçal, B., Amante, M. J., Pinto, C., & Neto, L. (2015, December). Evaluation of the accessibility levels of the pages and bibliographic catalogs of the libraries of higher education institutions. In *Proceedings of the III International Conference for Inclusion (INCLUDiT)*. Academic Press.

Marin, W. W., & Notargiacomo, P. (2019). Study of development of creativity through digital games. In *Proceedings of the IADIS International Conference Game and Entertainment Technologies 2019* (pp. 391-395). Academic Press. 10.33965/g2019_201906C055

Marlina, L., Wardoyo, C., Sanjaya, W. S. M., Anggraeni, D., Dewi, S. F., Roziqin, A., & Maryanti, S. (2018). Makhraj Recognition of Hijaiyah Letter for Children Based on Mel-Frequency Cepstrum Coefficients (MFCC) and Support Vector Machines (SVM) Method. In *Proceedings of the 2018 International Conference on Information and Communications Technology* (pp. 935-940). IEEE. 10.1109/ICOIACT.2018.8350684

Maslow, A. H. (1943). A theory of human motivation. *Psychological Review*, *50*(4), 370–396. doi:10.1037/h0054346

Maslow, A. H. (1959). Creativity in self-actualizing people. In H. H. Anderson (Ed.), *Creativity and its cultivation* (pp. 83–95). New York: Harper & Row.

Mason, L., Tornatora, M. C., & Pluchino, P. (2013). Do fourth graders integrate text and picture in processing and learning from an illustrated science text? Evidence from eye-movement patterns. *Computers & Education, 60*(1), 95–109. doi:10.1016/j.compedu.2012.07.011

Mateas, M., & Stern, A. (2005, June). *Structuring Content in the Façade Interactive Drama Architecture.* AIIDE.

Matouk, K., & Owoc, M. L. (2012). A survey of data warehouse architectures—Preliminary results. In *Proceedings of the 2012 Federated Conference on Computer Science and Information Systems (FedCSIS)* (pp. 1121-1126). IEEE.

Mayer, R. E. (2005). Cognitive theory of multimedia learning. In The Cambridge handbook of multimedia learning (pp. 31-48). Academic Press. doi:10.1017/CBO9780511816819.004

Mayer, R. E. (2010). Unique contributions of eye-tracking research to the study of learning with graphics. *Learning and Instruction, 20*(2), 167–171. doi:10.1016/j.learninstruc.2009.02.012

Mazumder, F. K., & Das, U. K.Fourcan Karim Mazumder. (2014). Usability guidelines for usable user interface. *International Journal of Research in Engineering and Technology, 3*(9), 79–82. doi:10.15623/ijret.2014.0309011

McCloud, S. (1993). *Understanding comics: the invisible art.* Tundra Publishing.

McDuff, D., Mahmoud, A., Mavadati, M., Amr, M., Turcot, J., & Kaliouby, R. E. (2016, May). AFFDEX SDK: a cross-platform real-time multi-face expression recognition toolkit. In *Proceedings of the 2016 CHI conference extended abstracts on human factors in computing systems* (pp. 3723-3726). ACM. 10.1145/2851581.2890247

McGonigal, J. (2011). Reality is broken: Why games make us better and how they can change the world. Penguin. com.

McLoughlin, C., & Lee, M. J. (2007). Social software and participatory learning: Pedagogical choices with technology affordances in the Web 2.0 era. *Paper presented at the ICT: Providing choices for learners and learning.* Academic Press.

McMahan, A. (2003). Immersion, engagement and presence. In M. J. P. Wolf & B. Perron (Eds.), *The video game theory reader* (pp. 67–86). Psychology Press.

Medina, J. L., Cagnin, M. I., & Paiva, D. M. B. (2015). Investigating accessibility on web-based maps. *Applied Computing Review, 15*(2), 17–26. doi:10.1145/2815169.2815171

Menke, J. (2017). *Skill, Matchmaking, and Ranking Systems Design* [YouTube video]. Retrieved from https://www.youtube.com/watch?v=-pglxege-gU

Menzi-Çetin, N., Alemdağ, E., Tüzün, H., & Merve, Y. M. (2017). Evaluation of a university website's usability for visually impaired Students. *Universal Access in the Information Society, 16*(1), 151-160.

Menzi-Cetin, N., Alemdağ, E., Tüzün, H., & Yıldız, M. (2017). Evaluation of a university website's usability for visually impaired students. *Universal Access in the Information Society, 16*(1), 151–160. doi:10.100710209-015-0430-3

Meriläinen, M. (2019). First-Timer Learning Experiences in Global Game Jam. *International Journal of Game-Based Learning, 9*(1), 30–41. doi:10.4018/IJGBL.2019010103

Mesibov, G. B., Shea, V., & Schopler, E. (2005). *The TEACCH approach to autism spectrum disorders.* Springer Science & Business Media.

Michel, P., & El Kaliouby, R. (2003, November). Real time facial expression recognition in video using support vector machines. In *Proceedings of the 5th international conference on Multimodal interfaces* (pp. 258-264). ACM. 10.1145/958432.958479

Microsoft. (2019). *Microsoft Excel.* Retrieved from https://products.office.com/pt-pt/excel?rtc=1

Mikropoulos, T. A., & Strouboulis, V. (2004). Factors that influence presence in educational virtual environments. *Cyberpsychology & Behavior*, *7*(5), 582–591. doi:10.1089/cpb.2004.7.582 PMID:15667053

Minsky, M. (2007). *The emotion machine: Commonsense thinking, artificial intelligence, and the future of the human mind*. Simon and Schuster.

Mitchell, A., & Savill-Smith, C. (2004). The use of computer and video games for learning: A review of the literature. Retrieved from https://dera.ioe.ac.uk/5270/7/041529_Redacted.pdf

Moffat, D. C., & Shabalina, O. (2016). Student creativity exercises in designing serious games. In *Proceedings of the European Conference on Games Based Learning* (pp. 470-478). Academic Press.

Moodle. (2017). Moodle PTCE - Campus Campos Centro. Retrieved from http://ensino.centro.iff.edu.br/moodle/

Moreno, C. G. (2008). Web accessibility. In C. Calero, M. A. Moraga, & M. Piattini (Eds.), Handbook of Research on Web Information Systems Quality (pp. 163–180). Hershey, PA: IGI Global. doi:10.4018/978-1-59904-847-5.ch010

Morin, K. L., Ganz, J. B., Gregori, E. V., Foster, M. J., Gerow, S. L., Genç-Tosun, D., & Hong, E. R. (2018). A systematic quality review of high-tech AAC interventions as an evidence-based practice. *AAC*, *34*(2), 104–117. PMID:29697288

Mountain, C. (2018, June 3). The History of Mario Kart 64's Most Infamous Track. [Video file] Retrieved from https://www.youtube.com/watch?v=Y99Wj-NStok&ab_channel=SummoningSalt

Mullich, D. (2015). *Sorry, there is no "idea guy" position in the game industry*. Retrieved from https://davidmullich.com/2015/11/23/sorry-there-is-no-idea-guy-position-in-the-game-industry/

Munir, H. M. U., & Qureshi, W. S. (2019). Towards 3D Facial Reconstruction using Deep Neural Networks. In *Proceedings of the 13th International Conference on Computer Graphics, Visualization, Computer Vision and Image Processing (CGVCVIP)*. Academic Press.

Muntean, M. I., & Târnăveanu, D. (2012). *A Multidimensional View Proposal of the Data Collected Through a Questionnaire. Database Systems Journal*, *3*(4), 33–46.

Murray, J. H. (1997). *Hamlet on the Holodeck: The Future of Narrative in Cyberspace*. Cambridge, MA: MIT Press.

Mustafa, N., Labiche, Y., & Towey, D. (2019, July).Mitigating threats to validity in empirical software engineering: A traceability case study. In *Proceedings of the 2019 IEEE 43rd Annual Computer Software and Applications Conference (COMPSAC)* (Vol. 2, pp. 324-329). IEEE. 10.1109/COMPSAC.2019.10227

MySQL Workbench. (2019). *MySQL Workbench 8.0*. Retrieved from https://www.mysql.com/products/workbench/

MySQL. (2019). *MySQL 8.0 Community Edition*. Retrieved from https://www.mysql.com/

Nacke, L. E., & Lindley, C. A. (2010). Affective ludology, flow and immersion in a first-person shooter: Measurement of player experience.

Nadolny, L., Nation, J., & Fox, J. (2019). Supporting Motivation and Effort Persistence in an Online Financial Literacy Course Through Game-Based Learning. *International Journal of Game-Based Learning*, *9*(3), 38–52. doi:10.4018/IJGBL.2019070103

Najemnik, J., & Geisler, W. S. (2005). Optimal eye movement strategies in visual search. *Nature*, *434*(7031), 387–391. doi:10.1038/nature03390 PMID:15772663

Não deveria, pelo menos aqui. (2016, December 22). Message posted to https://us.battle.net/forums/pt/overwatch/topic/20752537624

Newell, A. (2016). Stacked hourglass networks for human pose estimation. In *Proceedings of the European Conf. Comput. Vision*. Academic Press. 10.1007/978-3-319-46484-8_29

Newman, J. (2018). Kaizo Mario Maker: ROM hacking, abusive game design and Nintendo's Super Mario Maker. *Convergence*, 24(4), 339–356. doi:10.1177/1354856516677540

Nielsen Corporation. (2014). The Digital Consumer. Retrieved from http://www.nielsen.com/content/dam/corporate/us/en/reports-downloads/2014%20Reports/the-digital-consumer-report-feb-2014.pdf

Nielsen, J. (1994, June). *Heuristic evaluation in usability inspection methods*. John Wiley & Sons, Inc..

Nielsen, J. (2003). Usability 101: Introduction to usability.

Nielsen, J., Clemmensen, T., & Yssing, C. (2002). Getting access to what goes on in people's heads?: reflections on the think-aloud technique. In *Proceedings of the Second Nordic Conference on Human-Computer Interaction NordiCHI '02*. ACM Press.

Nielsen, J. (1994). Usability inspection methods. In *Conference companion on Human factors in computing systems* (pp. 413–414). ACM.

Nielsen, J., & Landauer, T. (1993). A mathematical model of the finding of usability problems. In *Proceedings of the INTERACT'93 and CHI'93 conference on Human factors in computing systems* (pp. 206-213). ACM. 10.1145/169059.169166

Nielsen, J., & Loranger, H. (2006). *Prioritizing web usability*. Berkeley, CA: New Riders Press.

Niemeyer, P., & Knudsen, J. (2013). Learning Java (4th ed.). O'Reilly Media, Inc.

Nilsson, J. & Siponen, J. (2006). Challenging the HCI Concept of Fidelity by Positioning. Ozlab Prototypes.

Nintendo. (2007). Wii Fit.

Nintendo. (2019). RingFit Adventure.

Noor, M. N., Yussof, R. L., Yusoff, F. H., & Ismail, M. (2018). Gamification and Augmented Reality Utilization for Islamic Content Learning: The Design and Development of Tajweed Learning. In N. Abdullah, W. Wan Adnan, & M. Foth (Eds.), *User Science and Engineering. i-USEr 2018. Communications in Computer and Information Science* (pp. 163–174). Singapore: Springer.

Nordin, A. I., Denisova, A., & Cairns, P. (2014). Too Many Questionnaires: Measuring Player Experience Whilst Playing Digital Games. In *Proceedings of the Seventh York Doctoral Symposium on Computer Science and Electronics*. Academic Press.

Norman, D. (1988). The Design of Everyday Things. In *The psychology of everyday things*. New York: Basic Books.

Norman, D. (1999). Affordance, conventions, and design. *Interaction*, 6(3), 38–43. doi:10.1145/301153.301168

Norman, D. (2013). *The design of everyday things: revised and expanded edition*. Basic Books.

Norman, D. A., & Draper, S. W. (1986). *User centered system design: New perspectives on HCI*. CRC Press. doi:10.1201/b15703

Novak, J. D., Bob Gowin, D., & Johansen, G. T. (1983). The use of concept mapping and knowledge vee mapping with junior high school science students. *Science Education*, 67(5), 625–645. doi:10.1002ce.3730670511

Novak, T. P., Hoffman, D. L., & Yung, Y. F. (2000). Measuring the flow construct in online environments: A structural modeling approach. *Marketing Science*, 19(1), 22–42. doi:10.1287/mksc.19.1.22.15184

Nutt, C. (2012). The Structure of Fun: Learning from Super Mario 3D Land's Director." Gamasutra. Retrieved from https://www.gamasutra.com/view/feature/168460/the_structure_of_fun_learning_.php

Nutt, C., & Hayashida, K. (2012). The structure of fun: learning from Super Mario 3D Land's director. *Gamasutra*. Retrieved from **Error! Hyperlink reference not valid.**http://www.gamasutra.com/view/feature/168460/the_structure_of_fun_learning_.php

NV Access. (n.d.). About NVDA. Retrieved from https://www.nvaccess.org/

Okada, K., Steffens, J., Maurer, T., Hong, H., Elagin, E., Neven, H., & von der Malsburg, C. (1998). The Bochum/USC face recognition system and how it fared in the FERET phase III test. In *Face Recognition* (pp. 186–205). Berlin: Springer. doi:10.1007/978-3-642-72201-1_10

Okhovati, M., Karami, F., & Khajouei, R. (2017). Exploring the usability of the central library websites of medical sciences universities. *Journal of Librarianship and Information Science*, *49*(3), 246–255. doi:10.1177/0961000616650932

Oliveira, A., de Souza, E. M., & Eler, M. M. (2017, May). Accessibility model in electronic government: Evaluation of Brazilian web portals. In *Proceedings of the XIII Brazilian Symposium on Information Systems* (pp. 332-339). Academic Press. 10.5753bsi.2017.6060

Onyesolu, M. (2009). Virtual reality laboratories: An ideal solution to the problems facing laboratory setup and management. In *Proc. of the World Congress on Engineering and computer science*. Academic Press.

Ortony, A., Clore, G. L., & Collins, A. (1988). *The cognitive structure of emotions*. Cambridge Uni. doi:10.1017/CBO9780511571299

Ou, J. (2012). Classification Algorithms Research on Facial Expression Recognition. *Physics Procedia*, *25*, 1241–1244. doi:10.1016/j.phpro.2012.03.227

Pantic, M., & Rothkrantz, L. J. (2000). Automatic analysis of facial expressions: The state of the art. *IEEE Transactions on Pattern Analysis and Machine Intelligence*, *22*(12), 1424–1445. doi:10.1109/34.895976

Pantic, M., & Rothkrantz, L. J. (2003). Toward an affect-sensitive multimodal human-computer interaction. *Proceedings of the IEEE*, *91*(9), 1370–1390. doi:10.1109/JPROC.2003.817122

Paradox Interactive, 2012. Crusader Kings 2.

Parlett, D. (2017). What's a ludeme? Game & Puzzle Design, 2(2), 81.

Parsons, S., Guldberg, K., MacLeod, A., Jones, G., Prunty, A., & Balfe, T. (2009). *International Review of the Literature of Evidence of Best Practice Provision in the Education of Persons with Autistic Spectrum Disorders*. Ireland: National Council for Special Education.

Pavlov, N. (2014). User interface for people with ASD. *Journal of Software Engineering and Applications*, *7*(02), 128. doi:10.4236/jsea.2014.72014

Paysan, P., Knothe, R., Amberg, B., Romdhani, S., & Vetter, T. (2009, September). A 3D face model for pose and illumination invariant face recognition. In *Proceedings of the 2009 Sixth IEEE International Conference on Advanced Video and Signal Based Surveillance* (pp. 296-301). IEEE. doi:10.1109/AVSS.2009.58

Pekrun, R. (2006). The control-value theory of achievement emotions: Assumptions, corollaries, and implications for educational research and practice. *Educational Psychology Review*, *18*(4), 315–341. doi:10.100710648-006-9029-9

Pekrun, R., Goetz, T., Frenzel, A. C., Barchfeld, P., & Perry, R. P. (2011). Measuring emotions in students' learning and performance: The Achievement Emotions Questionnaire (AEQ). *Contemporary Educational Psychology, 36*(1), 36–48. doi:10.1016/j.cedpsych.2010.10.002

Pentaho (2019). *Data Integration – Kettle*. Hitachi Vantara Community. Retrieved from https://community.hitachivantara.com/docs/DOC-1009855-data-integration-kettle

Pereira, A. S., Machado, A. M. & Carneiro, T. C. J. (2013). Web Accessibility Evaluation on Brazilian Institutions in Higher Education. *Informacao & Sociedade - Estudos, 23*(3), 123-142.

Pérez, P., Gangnet, M., & Blake, A. (2003). Poisson image editing. In ACM SIGGRAPH 2003 Papers (pp. 313-318). ACM Press.

Perez-Colado, I., Alonso-Fernandez, C., Freire, M., Martinez-Ortiz, I., & Fernandez-Manjon, B. (2018). Game learning analytics is not informagic! In *Proceedings of the 2018 IEEE Global Engineering Education Conference (EDUCON)* (pp. 1729-1737). IEEE Press. 10.1109/EDUCON.2018.8363443

Pettersson, J. S., & Siponen, J. (2002). Ozlab: a simple demonstration tool for prototyping interactivity. In *Proceedings of the Second Nordic Conference on Human-Computer Interaction NordiCHI '02*. ACM Press. 10.1145/572020.572071

Pettersson, J. S., Wik, M., & Andersson, H. (2017). Wizards of Oz in the Evolving Map of Design Research – Trying to Frame GUI Interaction Interviews Supporting Development of Interactive Systems in Interactive Sessions. In *Information Systems Development: Advances in Methods, Tools and Management (ISD2017 Proceedings)*. Academic Press..

Pettersson, J. S. (2002). Visualising interactive graphics design for testing with users. *Digital Creativity, 13*(3), 144–156. doi:10.1076/digc.13.3.144.7341

Pettersson, J. S., & Wik, M. (2015). The longevity of general purpose Wizard-of-Oz tools. In B. Ploderer, M. Carter, & M. Gibbs et al. (Eds.), *Proceedings of the Annual Meeting of the Australian Special Interest Group for Computer Human Interaction (OzCHI '15)* (pp. 422-426). ACM. 10.1145/2838739.2838825

Pettersson, J. S., Wik, M., & Andersson, H. (2018). GUI interaction interviews in the evolving map of design research. In N. Paspallis, M. Raspopoulos, C. Barry, M. Lang, H. Linger, & C. Schneider (Eds.), *Advances in Information Systems Development* (pp. 149–167). Cham: Springer International Publishing. doi:10.1007/978-3-319-74817-7_10

Phelps, E. A. (2004). Human emotion and memory: Interactions of the amygdala and hippocampal complex. *Current Opinion in Neurobiology, 14*(2), 198–202. doi:10.1016/j.conb.2004.03.015 PMID:15082325

Pieters, R. (2008). A review of eye-tracking research in marketing. *Review of marketing research, 4*, 123-147.

Plutchik, R. (2001). The nature of emotions: Human emotions have deep evolutionary roots, a fact that may explain their complexity and provide tools for clinical practice. *American Scientist, 89*(4), 344–350. doi:10.1511/2001.4.344

Poe, E. A. (1846). The philosophy of composition.

Ponniah, P. (2011). *Data warehousing fundamentals for IT professionals*. John Wiley & Sons.

Popov, E. V. (2002).Geometric Approach to Chebyshev Net Generation Along an Arbitrary Surface Represented by NURBS. In *Proceedings of the 12th Int. Conference on Computer Graphics & Vision GRAPHICON'2002*. Academic Press.

Popov, E. V., Popova, T. P., & Rotkov, S. I. (2014). *The Shortest Path Finding between two Points on a Polyhedral Surface. In WSCG 2014 Communication Papers Proceedings* (pp. 1–11). Academic Press..

Preece, J., Rogers, Y., & Sharp, H. (2015). Interaction design: beyond human-computer interaction (4th ed.). Wiley.

Preece, J., Benyon, D., Davies, G., Keller, L., & Rogers, Y. (1993). *A guide to usability: Human factors in computing.* Reading, MA: Addison-Wesley.

Preece, J., Rogers, Y., Sharp, H., Benyon, D., Holland, S., & Carey, T. (1994). *Human-computer interaction.* Reading, MA: Addison-Wesley.

Prensky, M. (2007). *Digital game-based learning.* St. Paul, MN: Paragon House.

Primack, B. A., Carroll, M. V., McNamara, M., Klem, M. L., King, B., Rich, M., ... Nayak, S. (2012). Role of video games in improving health-related outcomes: A systematic review. *American Journal of Preventive Medicine, 42*(6), 630–638. doi:10.1016/j.amepre.2012.02.023 PMID:22608382

Pulsipher, L. (2016). *Are you designing a game, or throwing one together? You can't design a game as though you were playing a video game.* Gamasutra. Retrieved from https://www.gamasutra.com/blogs/LewisPulsipher/20161214/287544/Are_you_designing_a_game_or_throwing_one_together_You_cant_design_a_game_as_though_you_were_playing_a_video_game.php

Qin, H., Rau, P.-L. P., & Salvendy, G. (2010). Effects of different scenarios of game difficulty on player immersion. *Interacting with Computers, 22*(3), 230–239. doi:10.1016/j.intcom.2009.12.004

Qualidata. (2017). Welcome to Q-AcademicoWeb. Retrieved from https://academico.iff.edu.br

Quesenbery, W. (2001). What does usability mean: Looking beyond 'ease of use'. In *Proceedings of the 18th Annual Conference Society for Technical Communications.* Academic Press.

Quesenbery, W. (2003). Dimensions of usability: Opening the conversation, driving the process. In *Proceedings of the UPA 2003 Conference.* Academic Press.

Quesenbery, W. (2004). Balancing the 5Es: Usability. *Cutter IT Journal, 17*(2), 4–11.

Ragheb, A., & Mahmoud, A. (2013). The Role of e-Learning Software in Teaching Quran Recitation. In *Proceedings of the 2013 Taibah University International Conference on Advances in Information technology for the Holy Quran and Its Sciences* (pp. 429-440). IEEE.

Ranjan, A., Bolkart, T., Sanyal, S., & Black, M. J. (2018). Generating 3D faces using convolutional mesh autoencoders. In *Proceedings of the European Conference on Computer Vision (ECCV)* (pp. 704-720). Academic Press.

Raptis, G. E., Fidas, C., & Avouris, N. (2018). Effects of mixed-reality on players' behaviour and immersion in a cultural tourism game: A cognitive processing perspective. *International Journal of Human-Computer Studies, 114*, 69–79. doi:10.1016/j.ijhcs.2018.02.003

Rawat, D. B., Brecher, C., Song, H., & Jeschke, S. (2017). *Industrial Internet of Things: Cybermanufacturing Systems.* Springer.

Rayner, K. (1998). Eye movements in reading and information processing: 20 years of research. *Psychological Bulletin, 124*(3), 372–422. doi:10.1037/0033-2909.124.3.372 PMID:9849112

Rayner, K. (2009). Eye movements and attention in reading, scene perception, and visual search. *Quarterly Journal of Experimental Psychology, 62*(8), 1457–1506. doi:10.1080/17470210902816461 PMID:19449261

Reeves, B., & Read, J. L. (2009). *Total Engagement: How Games and Virtual Worlds to Change the Way People Work and Businesses Compete.* Harvard Business Press.

Reichle, E. D., Rayner, K., & Pollatsek, A. (2003). The EZ Reader model of eye-movement control in reading: Comparisons to other models. *Behavioral and Brain Sciences, 26*(4), 445–476. doi:10.1017/S0140525X03000104 PMID:15067951

Reingold, E. M., & Charness, N. (2005). Perception in chess: Evidence from eye movements. In *Cognitive processes in eye guidance* (pp. 325–354). Oxford University Press. doi:10.1093/acprof:oso/9780198566816.003.0014

Rettie, R. (2001). An exploration of flow during Internet use. *Internet Research, 11*(2), 103–113. doi:10.1108/10662240110695070

Rettig, M. (1994). Prototyping for tiny fingers. *Communications of the ACM, 37*, 21–27.

Revina, I. M., & Emmanuel, W. S. (2018). A survey on human face expression recognition techniques. *Journal of King Saud University-Computer and Information Sciences.*

Rheinberg, F., Vollmeyer, R., & Engeser, S. (2003). Die Erfassung des Flow-Erlebens. In *Diagnostik von Motivation und Selbstkonzept* (pp. 261–279). Göttingen: Hogrefe.

Richardson, E., Sela, M., & Kimmel, R. (2016, October). 3D face reconstruction by learning from synthetic data. In *Proceedings of the 2016 Fourth International Conference on 3D Vision (3DV)* (pp. 460-469). IEEE. doi:10.1109/CVPR.2017.589

Richardson, A. (1999). Subjective experience: Its conceptual status, method of investigation, and psychological significance. *The Journal of Psychology, 133*(5), 469–485. doi:10.1080/00223989909599756

Richardson, E., Sela, M., & Kimmel, R. (2016, October). 3D face reconstruction by learning from synthetic data. In *Proceedings of the 2016 Fourth International Conference on 3D Vision (3DV)* (pp. 460-469). IEEE.

Riot Games. (2017). *Creative collaboration: making League of Legends champions* [YouTube video]. Retrieved from https://www.youtube.com/watch?v=j-k3TbFwMgI

Robinson, A., & Bengal. (2016) *Legacy.* Retrieved from https://static.playoverwatch.com/media/comics/7/pt-br/comic-overwatch-legacy.pdf

Robinson, A., Sellner, J., & Niemczyk, K. (2017) *Searching.* Retrieved from https://static.playoverwatch.com/media/comics/15/pt-br/comic-overwatch-searching.pdf

Robinson, D. L. (2008). Brain function, emotional experience and personality. *Netherlands Journal of Psychology, 64*(4), 152–168. doi:10.1007/BF03076418

Rodrigues, L. (2014). *Um Estudo em Representações Gráficas nos Jogos Eletrônicos na Perspectiva de Gênero: Os Tipos de Feminilidade em League of Legends.* Undergraduate dissertation, Federal University of Technology, Curitiba, Brazil. Retrieved from http://repositorio.roca.utfpr.edu.br/jspui/handle/1/6778

Rodrigues, L. (2017). Questões de Gênero em Jogos Digitais: uma coleção de recursos educacionais abertos de apoio à mobilização [Master's thesis]. Federal University of Technology – Paraná, Curitiba, Brazil. Retrieved from http://repositorio.utfpr.edu.br/jspui/handle/1/2839

Rodrigues, L., & Merkle, L. E. (2017). Technologies of Gender in the construction of Digital Games character bodies. In *Proceedings of Seminário Internacional Fazendo Gênero 11 & 13th Women's Worlds Congress*, Florianópolis, Brazil. Retrieved from http://www.wwc2017.eventos. dype.com.br/site/anaiscomplementares

Rogers, C. R. (1959). Toward a theory of creativity. In H. H. Anderson (Ed.), *Creativity and its cultivation* (pp. 69–82). New York: Harper & Row.

Rogers, D. F. (2001). *An introduction to NURBS: with historical perspective.* Morgan Kaufmann Publishers.

Romanus, J. S. (2012). *Gênero em Jogo: Um olhar sobre personagens e as representações de tipos de feminilidades e masculinidades nos games de ação contemporâneos.* Undergraduate dissertation, Federal University of Technology, Curitiba, Brazil. Retrieved from http://repositorio.roca.utfpr.edu.br/jspui/handle/1/2994

Romdhani, S., & Vetter, T. (2003). Efficient, robust and accurate fitting of a 3d morphable model. In *Proceedings Ninth IEEE International Conference on Computer Vision.* IEEE Press; . doi:10.1109/ICCV.2003.1238314

Root, R. W., & Draper, S. (1983). Questionnaires as a software evaluation tool. In *Proceedings of the SIGCHI conference on Human Factors in Computing Systems* (pp. 83-87). ACM. 10.1145/800045.801586

Rozin, P., & Cohen, A. B. (2003). High frequency of facial expressions corresponding to confusion, concentration, and worry in an analysis of naturally occurring facial expressions of Americans. *Emotion (Washington, D.C.), 3*(1), 68–75. doi:10.1037/1528-3542.3.1.68 PMID:12899317

Rubin, J. Z., & Chisnell, D. (2008). *Handbook of usability testing: how to plan, design, and conduct effective tests, 2.* Indianapolis, Ind.: Wiley.

Rubinstein, R. Y., & Kroese, D. P. (2016). *Simulation and the Monte Carlo method* (Vol. 10). John Wiley & Sons. doi:10.1002/9781118631980

Runco, M. A. (2004). Creativity. *Annual Review of Psychology, 55*(1), 657–687. doi:10.1146/annurev.psych.55.090902.141502 PMID:14744230

Runco, M., & Jager, G. (2012). The standard definition of creativity. *Creativity Research Journal, 24*(1), 92–96. doi:10.1080/10400419.2012.650092

Rungta, N., Brat, G., Clancey, W. J., Linde, C., Raimondi, F., Seah, C., & Shafto, M. (2013). Aviation safety: modeling and analyzing complex interactions between humans and automated systems. In *Proceedings of the 3rd international conference on application and theory of automation in command and control systems* (pp. 27-37). ACM. 10.1145/2494493.2494498

Russom, P. (2011). Big data analytics. *TDWI best practices report, 19*(4), 1-34.

Ryan, J. O., Mateas, M., & Wardrip-Fruin, N. (2015, November). Open design challenges for interactive emergent narrative. In *Proceedings of the International Conference on Interactive Digital Storytelling* (pp. 14-26). Springer. 10.1007/978-3-319-27036-4_2

Ryan, R. M., Rigby, C. S., & Przybylski, A. (2006). The motivational pull of video games: A self-determination theory approach. *Motivation and Emotion, 30*(4), 344–360. doi:10.100711031-006-9051-8

Saany, S. I., Nordin, M., Rahman, A., Abd Rawi, N., & Yusof, A. I. (2013). Tajweed Race Online Game via Facebook Platform. In *Proceedings of 2013 Taibah University International Conference on Advances /in Information Technology for the Holy Quran and Its Sciences.* IEEE.

Sahlin, M. (2017). *Unravel - using empathy as a game mechanic.* GDC Vault. Retrieved from https://www.gdcvault.com/play/1024661/-Unravel-Using-Empathy-as

Sancar, H., Karakus, T., & Cagiltay, K. (2007). Learning a New Game: Usability, Gender and Education. *Paper presented at the Young researchers furthering development of TEL research in Central and Eastern Europe.* Academic Press.

Sanders, T., & Cairns, P. (2010). Time perception, immersion and music in videogames. In *Proceedings of the 24th BCS Interaction Specialist Group Conference* (pp. 160-167). Academic Press. 10.14236/ewic/HCI2010.21

Santos, R., & Bastos, G. *Clareou.* Retrieved from http://clareou.com/

Sanyal, S., Bolkart, T., Feng, H., & Black, M. J. (2019). Learning to regress 3D face shape and expression from an image without 3D supervision. In *Proceedings of the IEEE Conference on Computer Vision and Pattern Recognition* (pp. 7763-7772). IEEE Press.

Sarkeesian, A. (2013, March 7) Feminist Frequency. Damsel in Distress (Part 1) Tropes vs Women [Video log]. Feminist Frequency. Retrieved from http://www.feministfrequency.com/2013/03/damsel-in-distress-part-1/

Sarkeesian, A. (2016, March 31) Feminist Frequency. Body Language & The Male Gaze - Tropes vs Women in Video Games [Video log]. Feminist Frequency. Retrieved from https://feministfrequency.com/video/body-language-the-male-gaze/

Sartoretto, M., & Bersch, R. (2017). Assistive Technology and Education. Retrieved from http://www.assistiva.com.br/tassistiva.html

Sathik, M., & Jonathan, S. G. (2013). Effect of facial expressions on student's comprehension recognition in virtual educational environments. *SpringerPlus*, *2*(1), 455. doi:10.1186/2193-1801-2-455 PMID:24130957

Schaefer, E. S., & Plutchik, R. (1966). Interrelationships of emotions, traits, and diagnostic constructs. *Psychological Reports*, *18*(2), 399–410. doi:10.2466/pr0.1966.18.2.399

Schell, J. (2008). *The art of game design: A book of lenses.* CRC Press. doi:10.1201/9780080919171

Scheurle, J. (2018). *Good game design is like a magic trick* [YouTube video]. Retrieved from https://www.youtube.com/watch?v=2YdJa7v99wM

Schlögl, S., Doherty, G., & Luz, S. (2015). Wizard of Oz experimentation for language technology applications: Challenges and tools. *Interacting with Computers*, *27*(6), 592–615.

Schopler, E. & Mesibov, G.B. (2013). *Learning and cognition in autism.* Springer Science & Business Media.

Schott, D. (2017, September 25). 'World of Warcraft' Has a Rape Problem. *Motherboard*. Retrieved from https://motherboard.vice.com/en_us/article/mb7b9q/world-of-warcraft-has-a-rape-problem?utm_source=mbtwitter

Schubert, T., Friedmann, F., & Regenbrecht, H. (2001). The experience of presence: Factor analytic insights. *Presence*, *10*(3), 266–281. doi:10.1162/105474601300343603

Schunk, D. H. (1996). Attributions and the Development of Self-Regulatory Competence.

Schwab, B. (2014). *Designers are from Saturn, programmers are from Uranus* [YouTube video]. Retrieved from https://www.youtube.com/watch?v=6b-o_-Xb50E

Schwabe, L., & Wolf, O. T. (2014). Timing matters: Temporal dynamics of stress effects on memory retrieval. *Cognitive, Affective & Behavioral Neuroscience*, *14*(3), 1041–1048. doi:10.375813415-014-0256-0 PMID:24492994

Seffah, A., Donyaee, M., Kline, R. B., & Padda, H. K. (2006). Usability measurement and metrics: A consolidated model. *Software Quality Journal*, *14*(2), 159–178. doi:10.100711219-006-7600-8

Sela, M., Richardson, E., & Kimmel, R. (2017). Unrestricted facial geometry reconstruction using image-to-image translation. In *Proceedings of the IEEE International Conference on Computer Vision* (pp. 1576-1585). IEEE Press. 10.1109/ICCV.2017.175

Selman, D. (2003). *Java3D Programming.* Austin, TX: Manning Publications Co.

Sengupta, S., Kanazawa, A., Castillo, C. D., & Jacobs, D. W. (2018). SfSNet: Learning Shape, Reflectance and Illuminance of Facesin the Wild'. In *Proceedings of the IEEE Conference on Computer Vision and Pattern Recognition* (pp. 6296-6305). IEEE Press.

Sexist Throwers in Competitive Overwatch [YouTube video]. (2017, February 3). Retrieved from https://youtu.be/9f4dW1YpuoA

Shah, B. P., & Shakya, S. (2007, December). Evaluating the web accessibility of websites of the central government of Nepal. In *Proceedings of the 1st International Conference on Theory and Practice of Electronic Governance* (pp. 447-448). ACM. 10.1145/1328057.1328154

Shan, C., Gong, S., & McOwan, P. W. (2009). Facial expression recognition based on local binary patterns: A comprehensive study. *Image and Vision Computing*, *27*(6), 803–816. doi:10.1016/j.imavis.2008.08.005

Shaw, A. (2014). *Gaming at the edge: sexuality and gender at the margins of gamer culture*. Minneapolis, MN: University of Minnesota Press.

Silva, A. B. P., Silva, C. G., & Moraes, R. L. O. (2019). On the use of a continuous accessibility assessment process for dealing with website evolution. In *Proceedings of the International Conferences Interfaces and Human Computer Interaction 2019; Game and Entertainment Technologies 2019; and Computer Graphics, Visualization, Computer Vision and Image Processing 2019* (pp. 35-42). IADIS Press.

Silva, M., & Cox, A. L. (2006). What have eye movements told us so far, and what is next? In *Proceedings of 28th Annual Meeting of the Cognitive Science Society*. Academic Press.

Silvia, P. J. (2009). Looking past pleasure: Anger, confusion, disgust, pride, surprise, and other unusual aesthetic emotions. *Psychology of Aesthetics, Creativity, and the Arts*, *3*(1), 48–51. doi:10.1037/a0014632

Simon, T., Joo, H., Matthews, I., & Sheikh, Y. (2017). Hand keypoint detection in single images using multiview bootstrapping. In Proceedings of the IEEE conference on Computer Vision and Pattern Recognition (pp. 1145-1153). IEEE Press. doi:10.1109/CVPR.2017.494

Simonsen, J., & Robertson, T. (Eds.). (2013). *Routledge international handbook of participatory design, Routledge international handbooks*. London: Routledge.

Slater, M. & Usoh, M. (1994). Body centred interaction in immersive virtual environments. *Artificial life and virtual reality*, *1*, 125-148.

Slater, M. (1999). Measuring presence: A response to the Witmer and Singer presence questionnaire. *Presence*, *8*(5), 560–565. doi:10.1162/105474699566477

Slater, M., Linakis, V., Usoh, M., & Kooper, R. (1996). Immersion, presence, and performance in virtual environments: An experiment with tri-dimensional chess. In *ACM virtual reality software and technology* (pp. 163–172). ACM. doi:10.1145/3304181.3304216

Slater, M., Usoh, M., & Steed, A. (1994). Depth of presence in virtual environments. *Presence*, *3*(2), 130–144. doi:10.1162/pres.1994.3.2.130

Sousa, R. F. (2017). Cultura do estupro: Prática e incitação à violência sexual contra mulheres. In *Revista. Estudos Feministas*, *25*(1), 9–29. doi:10.1590/1806-9584.2017v25n1p9

Spence, S. J., Sharifi, P., & Wiznitzer, M. (2004, September). Autism spectrum disorder: Screening, diagnosis, and medical evaluation. [). WB Saunders.]. *Seminars in Pediatric Neurology*, *11*(3), 186–195.

Spinuzzi, C. (2005). The Methodology of Participatory Design. *Open Journal of Nursing*, *52*, 163–174.

Sprengelmeyer, R., Rausch, M., Eysel, U. T., & Przuntek, H. (1998). Neural structures associated with recognition of facial expressions of basic emotions. *Proceedings of the Royal Society of London. Series B, Biological Sciences, 265*(1409), 1927–1931. doi:10.1098/rspb.1998.0522 PMID:9821359

Squire, R. (1997). *Fundamentals of Radiology* (5th ed.). Harvard, UniversityPress.

Staiano, A. E., & Calvert, S. L. (2011). Exergames for physical education courses: Physical, social, and cognitive benefits. *Child Development Perspectives, 5*(2), 93–98. doi:10.1111/j.1750-8606.2011.00162.x PMID:22563349

Stair, R., & Reynolds, G. (2013). *Principles of information systems.* Cengage Learning.

Steinfeld, A., Jenkins, O. C., & Scassellati, B. (2009). The oz of wizard: simulating the human for interaction research. In *Proceedings of the 4th ACM/IEEE International Conference on Human Robot Interaction - HRI '09.* ACM Press. 10.1145/1514095.1514115

Steinkuehler, C. A., & Williams, D. (2006). Where everybody knows your (screen) name: Online games as "third places." *Journal of Computer-Mediated Communication, 11*(4), 885–909. doi:10.1111/j.1083-6101.2006.00300.x

Subrahmanyam, K., & Greenfield, P. M. (1994). Effect of video game practice on spatial skills in girls and boys. *Journal of Applied Developmental Psychology, 15*(1), 13–32. doi:10.1016/0193-3973(94)90004-3

Suh, A., Wagner, C., & Liu, L. (2015, January). The effects of game dynamics on user engagement in gamified systems. In *Proceedings of the 2015 48th Hawaii International Conference on System Sciences* (pp. 672-681). IEEE. 10.1109/HICSS.2015.87

Sun, C. T., Wang, D. Y., & Chan, H. L. (2011). How digital scaffolds in games direct problem-solving behaviors. *Computers & Education, 57*(3), 2118–2125. doi:10.1016/j.compedu.2011.05.022

Sun-Higginson, S. (Producer/Director). (2015). GTFO: The Movie [Motion picture]. Retrieved from https://www.amazon.com/GT FO-Movie-Patrick-Klepek/dp/B00ZFDNGA8)

Suwajanakorn, S., Kemelmacher-Shlizerman, I., & Seitz, S. M. (2014, September). Total moving face reconstruction. In *Proceedings of the European Conference on Computer Vision* (pp. 796-812). Springer.

Sweetser, P., & Wyeth, P. (2005). GameFlow: a model for evaluating player enjoyment in games. Computers in Entertainment, 3(3).

Sweetser, P., & Wyeth, P. (2005). GameFlow: A Model for Evaluating Player Enjoyment in Games. *Computers in Entertainment, 3*(3). DOI:10.1145/1077246.1077253

Taigman, Y., Yang, M., Ranzato, M. A., & Wolf, L. (2014). Deepface: Closing the gap to human-level performance in face verification. In *Proceedings of the IEEE conference on computer vision and pattern recognition* (pp. 1701-1708). IEEE Press.

Tamborini, R., & Skalski, P. (2006). The role of presence in the experience of electronic games. In Playing video games: Motives, responses, and consequences (pp. 225-240). Academic Press.

Tan, J. L., Goh, D. H. L., Ang, R. P., & Huan, V. S. (2016). Learning efficacy and user acceptance of a game-based social skills learning environment. *International journal of child-computer interaction, 9*, 1-19.

Tanaguru Project. (2017). *Tanaguru Monitor.* Retrieved from http://www.tanaguru.com/en/

Tanaka, E. H., & Da Rocha, H. V. (2011). Evaluation of web accessibility tools. In *Proceedings of the 10th Brazilian Symposium on Human Factors in Computing Systems and the 5th Latin American Conference on Human-Computer Interaction* (pp. 272-279). Brazilian Computer Society.

Tangarife, T., & Mont'Alvão, C. (2005, October). Estudo comparativo utilizando uma ferramenta de avaliação de acessibilidade para Web. In *Proceedings of the 2005 Latin American conference on Human-computer interaction* (pp. 313-318). ACM. 10.1145/1111360.1111394

Taylor, D. (2013). Ten Principles for Good Level Design. Presentation in GDC 2013 [YouTube video]. Retrieved from https://www.youtube.com/watch?v=iNEe3KhMvXM

Taylor, T. L. (2006). *Play between worlds*. MIT Press. doi:10.7551/mitpress/5418.001.0001

Tewari, A., Bernard, F., Garrido, P., Bharaj, G., Elgharib, M., Seidel, H. P., ... Theobalt, C. (2019). Fml: Face model learning from videos. In *Proceedings of the IEEE Conference on Computer Vision and Pattern Recognition* (pp. 10812-10822). IEEE Press.

Tewari, A., Zollhöfer, M., Garrido, P., Bernard, F., Kim, H., Pérez, P., & Theobalt, C. (2018). Self-supervised multi-level face model learning for monocular reconstruction at over 250 hz. In *Proceedings of the IEEE Conference on Computer Vision and Pattern Recognition* (pp. 2549–2559). IEEE Press; . doi:10.1109/CVPR.2018.00270

Tewari, A., Zollhofer, M., Kim, H., Garrido, P., Bernard, F., Perez, P., & Theobalt, C. (2017). Mofa: Model-based deep convolutional face autoencoder for unsupervised monocular reconstruction. In *Proceedings of the IEEE International Conference on Computer Vision Workshops* (pp. 1274-1283). IEEE Press.

Thiemann, K. S., & Goldstein, H. (2001). Social Stories, written text cues, and video feedback: Effects on social communication of children with autism. *Journal of Applied Behavior Analysis*, *34*(4), 425–446. doi:10.1901/jaba.2001.34-425 PMID:11800183

Thies, J., Zollhofer, M., Stamminger, M., Theobalt, C., & Nießner, M. (2016). Face2face: Real-time face capture and reenactment of RGB videos. In *Proceedings of the IEEE conference on computer vision and pattern recognition* (pp. 2387-2395).

Thompson, M., Nordin, A. I., & Cairns, P. (2012). Effect of touch-screen size on game immersion. In *Proceedings of the 26th Annual BCS Interaction Specialist Group Conference on People and Computers*. Academic Press. 10.14236/ewic/HCI2012.38

Thomsen, M. (2015). Super Mario Maker is an engine for circulating horrible new Mario levels. *The Washington Post*.

Thorson, M. (2017). Level Design Workshop: Designing Celeste. Presentation in GDC 2017 [YouTube video]. Retrieved from https://www.youtube.com/watch?v=4RlpMhBKNr0

Thorson, M. (2018). *Level design workshop: Designing Celeste* [YouTube video]. Retrieved from https://www.youtube.com/watch?v=4RlpMhBKNr0

Torrance, E. (1979). Unique needs of the creative child and adult. In A. Passow (Ed.), The gifted and the talented: Their education and development (pp. 352-371). National Society for the Study of Education.

Tran, A. T., Hassner, T., Masi, I., Paz, E., Nirkin, Y., & Medioni, G. G. (2018, June). Extreme 3D Face Reconstruction: Seeing Through Occlusions. In CVPR (pp. 3935-3944). Academic Press.

Tran, L., Liu, F., & Liu, X. (2019). Towards high-fidelity nonlinear 3D face morphable model. In *Proceedings of the IEEE Conference on Computer Vision and Pattern Recognition* (pp. 1126-1135). IEEE Press.

Tran, L., & Liu, X. (2018). Nonlinear 3d face morphable model. In *Proceedings of the IEEE conference on computer vision and pattern recognition* (pp. 7346-7355). IEEE Press.

Tran, L., & Liu, X. (2019). On learning 3d face morphable model from in-the-wild images. *IEEE Transactions on Pattern Analysis and Machine Intelligence*.

Treffinger, D. J. (1985). Review of the torrance tests of creative thinking. In J. V. Mitchell Jr., (Ed.), *The ninth mental measurements yearbook* (pp. 1632–1634). Lincoln: University of Nebraska, Buros Institute of Mental Measurements.

TSM_Daequan. (2019, March 29). One day game developers will realize that you can't protect noobs from getting bopped. You add ranked, people will smurf. You separate casual and ranked, ppl will just go bot farm in casuals. You try to change game mechanics to save them, you ruin your game. 🤖♂️History doesn't lie! [Tweet]. Retrieved from https://twitter.com/tsm_daequan/status/1111744197294346240?lang=en

Tuan Tran, A., Hassner, T., Masi, I., & Medioni, G. (2017). Regressing robust and discriminative 3D morphable models with a very deep neural network. In *Proceedings of the IEEE conference on computer vision and pattern recognition* (pp. 5163–5172). IEEE Press; . doi:10.1109/CVPR.2017.163

Turner, C. J., Hutabarat, W., Oyekan, J., & Tiwari, A. (2016). Discrete event simulation and virtual reality use in industry: New opportunities and future trends. *IEEE Transactions on Human-Machine Systems*, *46*(6), 882–894. doi:10.1109/THMS.2016.2596099

Turner, M. (1999). Annotation: Repetitive behaviour in autism: A review of psychological research. *Journal of Child Psychology and Psychiatry, and Allied Disciplines*, *40*(6), 839–849. doi:10.1111/1469-7610.00502 PMID:10509879

Tu, X., Zhao, J., Jiang, Z., Luo, Y., Xie, M., Zhao, Y., ... Feng, J. (2019). Joint 3D Face Reconstruction and Dense Face Alignment from A Single [-Assisted Self-Supervised Learning.]. *Image*, *§§§*, 2D.

Tweedie, L., & Spence, R. (1998). The Prosection Matrix: A Tool to Support the Interactive Exploration of Statistical Models and Data. *Computational Statistics*, *13*, 65–76.

Uddin, M. Z., Hassan, M. M., Almogren, A., Zuair, M., Fortino, G., & Torresen, J. (2017). A facial expression recognition system using robust face features from depth videos and deep learning. *Computers & Electrical Engineering*, *63*, 114–125. doi:10.1016/j.compeleceng.2017.04.019

United Nations, Department of Economic and Social Affairs, Population Division. (2019). World Population Prospects 2019: Ten Key Findings. Retrieved from https://population.un.org/wpp/Publications/Files/WPP2019_10KeyFindings.pdf

Unity Asset Store - The Best Assets for Game Making. (n.d.). Retrieved from https://assetstore.unity.com/

Vail, P. L. (1994). *Emotion: The on/off switch for learning*. Modern Learning Press.

VaMoLà Project. (2010). *VaMoLà Monitor*. Retrieved from http://sourceforge.net/projects/vamola-monitor/

Van Eck, R. (2007). Building artificially intelligent learning games. In Games and simulations in online learning: Research and development frameworks (pp. 271-307). Academic Press. doi:10.4018/978-1-59904-304-3.ch014

vanWijk, J. J., & vanLiere, R. (1994). Hyperslice visualization of scalar functions of many variables. *Proceedings of the 4th IEEE Conference on Visualization '93* (pp. 119-125). IEEE Press.

Velásquez, J. D. (2013). Combining eye-tracking technologies with web usage mining for identifying Website Keyobjects. *Engineering Applications of Artificial Intelligence*, *26*(5), 1469–1478. doi:10.1016/j.engappai.2013.01.003

Vella, K., Johnson, D., & Hides, L. (2013). Positively playful: When videogames lead to player wellbeing. *Proceedings of the Gamification*, 99–102.

Vernhet, C., Dellapiazza, F., Blanc, N., Cousson-Gélie, F., Miot, S., Roeyers, H., & Baghdadli, A. (2018). Coping strategies of parents of children with autism spectrum disorder: A systematic review. *European Child & Adolescent Psychiatry*, 1–12. PMID:29915911

Viola, P., & Jones, M. (2001). Robust real-time object detection. *International journal of computer vision, 4*(34-47), 4.

Viswanathan, S., & Radhakrishnan, B. (2018). A Novel 'Game Design' Methodology for STEM Program. *International Journal of Game-Based Learning, 8*(4), 1–17. doi:10.4018/IJGBL.2018100101

Vive [Digital image]. (n.d.). Retrieved from https://www.vive.com/media/filer_public/b1/5f/b15f1847-5e1a-4b35-8afe-dca0aa08f35a/vive-pdp-ce-ksp-family-2.png

VIVE. (n.d.). VIVE Virtual Reality System. Retrieved from https://www.vive.com/us/product/vive-virtual-reality-system/

Vogel, S., & Schwabe, L. (2016). Learning and memory under stress: implications for the classroom. *NPJ Science of Learning, 1*, 16011.

Vogt, N., Abaev, M. A., & Karasev, N. M. (2011). Molecular structure and stabilities of fumaric acid conformers: Gas phase electron diffraction (GED) and quantum-chemical studies. Journal of Molecular Structure, 987(1-3), 199-205.

Vogt, N., Abaev, M. A., Rykov, A. N., & Shishkov, I. F. (2011). Determination of molecular structure of succinic acid in a very complex conformational landscape: Gas-phase electron diffraction (GED) and ab initio studies. Journal of Molecular Structure, 996(1-3), 120-127.

Vogt, N., Atavin, E. G., Rykov, A. N., Popov, E. V., & Vilkov, L. V. (2009). Equilibrium structure and relative stability of glyceraldehyde conformers: Gas-phase electron diffraction (GED) and quantum-chemical studies. Journal of Molecular Structure, 936(1-3), 125-131.

VU., T.H., Tuan, D. T., & Phan, V. H. (2012). Checking and correcting the source code of web pages for accessibility. In *Proceedings of the 2012 IEEE RIVF International Conference on Computing & Communication Technologies, Research, Innovation, and Vision for the Future* (pp. 1-4). IEEE.

Vuilleumier, P. (2005). How brains beware: Neural mechanisms of emotional attention. *Trends in Cognitive Sciences, 9*(12), 585–594. doi:10.1016/j.tics.2005.10.011 PMID:16289871

W3C, World Wide Web Consortium. (2008). Web content accessibility guidelines (WCAG), version 2.0. Retrieved from https://www.w3.org/Translations/WCAG20-pt-PT

W3C, World Wide Web Consortium. (2016). Web Accessibility Evaluation Tools List. Retrieved from https://www.w3.org/WAI/ER/tools

W3C, World Wide Web Consortium. (2018). Web Content Accessibility Guidelines (WCAG) 2.1. Retrieved from https://www.w3.org/TR/WCAG21/

Wajcman, J. (2004). *TechnoFeminism*. Cambridge, England: Polity Press.

Walk, W., Görlich, D., & Barrett, M. (2017). Design, Dynamics, Experience (DDE): an advancement of the MDA framework for game design. In *Game Dynamics* (pp. 27–45). Cham: Springer. doi:10.1007/978-3-319-53088-8_3

Wang, H., & Sun, C. T. (2011). Game reward Systems: gaming experiences and social meanings. In DiGRA 2011. Academic Press.

Wang, K. (2013). The effect of autonomy on team creativity and the moderating variables. In *Proceedings of PICMET '13: Technology Management for Emerging Technologies* (pp. 1156-1160). Academic Press.

Warren, J. (2015, Oct 20). Why Do "Girl Games" Matter? [YouTube video]. Retrieved from https://youtu.be/4GKZ-u0cJsI

Watson, D., & Clark, L. A. (1992). On traits and temperament: General and specific factors of emotional experience and their relation to the five-factor model. *Journal of Personality*, *60*(2), 441–476. doi:10.1111/j.1467-6494.1992.tb00980.x PMID:1635050

Weeks, J. (2001). O corpo e a sexualidade. In G. L. Louro (Ed.), *O corpo educado: pedagogias da sexualidade* (pp. 35–82). Belo Horizonte, Brazil: Autêntica Editora.

Wehrend, S., & Lewis, C. (1990). A Problem-Oriented Classification of Visualization Techniques, In *Proceedings of the 1st IEEE Conference on Visualization* (pp. 139-143). IEEE Press. 10.1109/VISUAL.1990.146375

Weibel, D., Wissmath, B., & Mast, F. W. (2010). Immersion in mediated environments: The role of personality traits. *Cyberpsychology, Behavior, and Social Networking*, *13*(3), 251–256. doi:10.1089/cyber.2009.0171 PMID:20557243

Weiner, B. (1985). An attributional theory of achievement motivation and emotion. *Psychological Review*, *92*(4), 548–573. doi:10.1037/0033-295X.92.4.548 PMID:3903815

Weisberg, D. S., Ilgaz, H., Hirsh-Pasek, K., Golinkoff, R., Nicolopoulou, A., & Dickinson, D. K. (2015). Shovels and swords: How realistic and fantastical themes affect children's world learning. *Cognitive Development*, *35*, 1–14. doi:10.1016/j.cogdev.2014.11.001

Wethington, E., & McDarby, M. L. (2015). Interview methods (structured, semistructured, unstructured). In *The Encyclopedia of Adulthood and Aging*. Academic Press.

WHO, World Health Organization. (2018). Disability and health: Key facts. Retrieved from https://www.who.int/en/news-room/fact-sheets/detail/disability-and-health

Wiggins, J. S., Trapnell, P., & Phillips, N. (1988). Psychometric and geometric characteristics of the Revised Interpersonal Adjective Scales (IAS-R). *Multivariate Behavioral Research*, *23*(4), 517–530. doi:10.120715327906mbr2304_8 PMID:26761163

Williams, A. (2017). *History of digital games: Developments in art, design and interaction*. Routledge. doi:10.1201/9781315715377

Winn, W. (1993). *A conceptual basis for educational applications of virtual reality*. University of Washington.

Witmer, B. G., & Singer, M. J. (1998). Measuring presence in virtual environments: A presence questionnaire. *Presence (Cambridge, Mass.)*, *7*(3), 225–240. doi:10.1162/105474698565686

Wong, P. C., & Bergeron, R. D. (1997). *30 Years of Multidimensional Multivariate Visualization. In Scientific Visualization Overviews, Methodologies, and Techniques* (pp. 3–33). IEEE Computer Society Press.

Wong, P. C., Crabb, A. H., & Bergeron, R. D. (1996). Dual Multiresolution HyperSlice for Multivariate Data Visualization. In *Proceedings of IEEE Symposium on Information Visualization '96* (pp. 74-75). IEEE Press. 10.1109/INFVIS.1996.559224

World Wide Web Consortium. (1999). *Web content accessibility guidelines (WCAG) 1.0*. Retrieved from http://www.w3.org/TR/WCAG10/

World Wide Web Consortium. (2008). *Web content accessibility guidelines (WCAG) 2.0*. Retrieved from http://www.w3.org/TR/WCAG20/

World Wide Web Consortium. (2018). *Web content accessibility guidelines (WCAG) 2.1*. Retrieved from http://www.w3.org/TR/WCAG21/

Xie, H. (2006). Evaluation of digital libraries: Criteria and problems from users' perspectives. *Library & Information Science Research*, *28*(3), 433–452. doi:10.1016/j.lisr.2006.06.002

Xing, Y. (2018). A self-supervised bootstrap method for single-image 3D face reconstruction.

Xu, M., David, J. M., & Kim, S. H. (2018). The fourth industrial revolution: opportunities and challenges. *International journal of financial research*, *9*(2), 90-95.

Yokochi, S., & Okada, T. (2005). Creative cognitive process of art making: A field study of a traditional Chinese ink painter. *Creativity Research Journal*, *17*(2-3), 241–255. doi:10.1080/10400419.2005.9651482

Yousfi, B., Zeki, A. M., & Haji, A. (2017). Isolated Iqlab Checking Rules Based on Speech Recognition System. In *Proceedings of the 2017 8th International Conference on Information Technology* (pp. 619-624). IEEE. 10.1109/ICITECH.2017.8080068

Zahorik, P., & Jenison, R. L. (1998). Presence as being-in-the-world. *Presence*, *7*(1), 78–89. doi:10.1162/105474698565541

Zarya. (n.d.). Play Overwatch. Retrieved from https://playoverwatch.com/pt-br/heroes/zarya/

Zhang, C., Perkis, A., & Arndt, S. 2017. Spatial immersion versus emotional immersion, which is more immersive? In *Proceedings of the 2017 Ninth International Conference on Quality of Multimedia Experience (QoMEX)* (pp. 1-6). Academic Press. 10.1109/QoMEX.2017.7965655

Zhang, J., & Fu, X. (2015). The influence of background music of video games on immersion. *Journal of Psychology & Psychotherapy*, *5*(4).

Zhang, Y. M., & Wildemuth, B. (2016). *Unstructured Interviews* (M. Wildemuth, Ed., 2nd ed.). Barbara.

Zhang, Z., Perkis, A., & Arndt, S. (2017). Spatial immersion versus emotional immersion, which is more immersive? In *Proceedings of the Ninth International Conference on Quality of Multimedia Experience* (pp. 1–6). Academic Press; doi:10.1109/QoMEX.2017.7965655.

Zhao, W., Chellappa, R., & Phillips, P. J. (1999). *Subspace linear discriminant analysis for face recognition*. Computer Vision Laboratory, Center for Automation Research, University of Maryland.

Zhigljavsky, A. A. (1991). *Theory of Global Random Search*. Kluwer Academic. doi:10.1007/978-94-011-3436-1

Zhou, M.-J., & Li, S.-K. (2013). Can supervisor feedback always promote creativity? The moderating role of employee self-monitoring. In *Proceedings of the 6th International Conference on Information Management, Innovation Management and Industrial Engineering* (pp. 510-512). Academic Press. 10.1109/ICIII.2013.6703200

Zhou, Y., Deng, J., Kotsia, I., & Zafeiriou, S. (2019). Dense 3d face decoding over 2500fps: Joint texture & shape convolutional mesh decoders. In *Proceedings of the IEEE Conference on Computer Vision and Pattern Recognition* (pp. 1097-1106). IEEE Press.

Zhu, X., Lei, Z., Liu, X., Shi, H., & Li, S. Z. (2016). Face alignment across large poses: A 3d solution. In *Proceedings of the IEEE conference on computer vision and pattern recognition* (pp. 146-155). IEEE Press.

Zhu, X., Lei, Z., Yan, J., Yi, D., & Li, S. Z. (2015). High-fidelity pose and expression normalization for face recognition in the wild. In *Proceedings of the IEEE Conference on Computer Vision and Pattern Recognition* (pp. 787-796). IEEE Press.

Zin, N. A. M., Jaafar, A., & Yue, W. S. (2009). Digital game-based learning (DGBL) model and development methodology for teaching history. *WSEAS Transactions on Computers*, *8*(2), 322–333.

Zollhöfer, M., Thies, J., Garrido, P., Bradley, D., Beeler, T., Pérez, P., ... & Theobalt, C. (2018). State of the art on monocular 3D face reconstruction, tracking, and applications. *Computer Graphics Forum*, *37*(2), 523–550.

About the Contributors

Cristina Adriana Alexandru is a Research Associate and University Teacher in the University of Edinburgh School of Informatics, UK. She specialises in User-Centred Design and usability evaluation, with main application in healthcare. She also has a strong interest in designing tools for users with diverse and special needs. She leads the CISA HCI group.

Haya Al Khateeb is a Computer Science graduate from Prince Sultan University. Trained at King AbdulAziz City for Science and Technology (KACST) in the AI and Big Data center.

Daniel Atorf is a scientist at the Fraunhofer IOSB since 2004. Since then he has done research on the field of technology-based learning and developed several e-learning tools and applications. After graduating extra occupational studies on Educational Technology in 2010, he concentrated on game-based learning. He was the project manager and lead designer of the Serious Game "Lost Earth 2307". His current work focuses on the measurement of flow while playing games.

Anatoliy Aleksandrovich Batiukov is a postgraduate student of the Nizhegorodsky State Architectural & Civil Engineering University. He specializes in Computer Graphics, Programming and Scientific Visualization.

Orlando Belo is an Associate Professor, with habilitation, in the Department of Informatics at University of Minho, Portugal. He is a member of the Department of Informatics at University of Minho since 1986, and a member of the Algoritmi R&D Centre, at the same university, working in Business Intelligence and Business Analytics, with particular emphasis in areas involving databases, data warehousing systems, data analysis, and data visualization. During the last few years he was involved with several projects in the decision support systems area designing and implementing computational platforms for specific applications, such as fraud detection and control in telecommunication systems, data quality evaluation, and ETL systems for industrial data warehousing systems. He received a 5-year degree in Systems and Informatics Engineering in 1986, with his thesis "Provas de Aptidão Pedagógica e Capacidade Científica" (MSc equivalent) in 1991 in Expert Systems, finished its Ph.D. thesis in Multi-Agent System in 1998 in the Department of Informatics at University of Minho, and got his Habilitation in 2013 in Data Warehousing Systems. He published several scientific works, most of them in international conferences with peer reviewing, related to his main researching areas, with particular emphasis in business intelligence, business analytics, data warehousing systems, online analytical processing, and data mining applications.

Arsineh Boodaghian Asl was a research intern at Karlstad University in the field of Computer Science and was a research assistant at KTH. Received her master's degree from Stockholm University in the field of Computer and System Sciences, and her bachelor's degree from State Engineering University of Armenia in the field of Information System. She worked as a software developer in various IT companies for 8+ years. She is interested in research and development in the field of eHealth, simulation, augmented reality, virtual reality, game development, and human computer interaction.

Aline Bossi Pereira da Silva has a master's in Technology and Innovation, specialized in Teaching in Higher Education and Graduated in Systems Analysis and Information Technology.

Gabriel Carneiro holds a Bachelor in Information Systems from IFFluminense, a Brazilian VET school in upstate Rio, received in 2019.

Mariana Carvalho is a PhD student in the PhD Program in Informatics at the University of Minho. She graduated in Computer Science/Informatics and got a MSc degree in Informatics Engineering also at the University of Minho with a major in Decision Support Systems. Her MSc thesis was on Knowledge Discovery in Certification Systems in Portuguese Companies. She is a member of the R&D Centre ALGORITMI. Her main research areas are data mining, data warehousing systems, and OLAP.

Kenneth Chen is a doctoral student at Drexel University studying digital media. His work focuses on games education and interactive emergent narrative.

Wen-Wen Chen received a Master's degree from National Chiao Tung University, 2014. She is working as a data engineer in TSMC, Taiwan.

Aurora Constantin is a university teacher and postdoctoral researcher at the University of Edinburgh, School of Informatics, UK. Her research focuses on designing technology for individuals with Autism Spectrum Disorder (ASD), PD, User-Centred Design (UCD), and Action Research (AR) with various stakeholders. Currently, she is working on designing a tool to support children with ASD to express their creativity during PD. She leads the CISA HCI group.

Mariana Fontoura graduated in graphic design from The Federal University of Technology - Paraná. She is currently a graphic designer, researcher, and a member of the Gender and Games Study Group of the Federal University of Technology - Paraná. Her research interests are: HCI, video games, and the relationship between graphic design and gender.

Michel Gokan Khan received a M.S. degree in software engineering from Iran University of Science and Technology, Tehran, Iran, in 2016 and a B.S. degree in applied mathematics from Azad University, Tehran, Iran, in 2014. He is currently pursuing a Ph.D. degree in computer science at Karlstad University, Karlstad, Sweden. His main research interest includes network function virtualization, cloud-native applications, network optimization for telecom clouds, cloud computing, and applications of AI in distributed systems.

Celmar Guimarães da Silva is a Professor at the School of Technology at University of Campinas (Brazil) since 2008. Doctor in Computer Science (2006) and graduate in Computer Science (2001) at the Institute of Computing at University of Campinas. Has experience on information visualization and human-computer interaction.

Ehm Kannegieser works at Fraunhofer IOSB as a scientist since 2008. He focusses on serious games projects, physiology of Flow and Immersion, gamification techniques, and operation of technology assisted learning systems.

Evi Indriasari Mansor obtained her BSc. in IT from the Universiti Teknologi Petronas (UTP), Perak, Malaysia and MSc. degree in Multimedia Applications & Virtual Environment from the University of Sussex, UK. She was awarded a Ph.D. from the University of Manchester, UK for studies in multi-touch interactive tabletop for preschool children's play. Her work is interdisciplinary, combining research areas from human computer interaction (HCI), early childhood development, education and innovation & multimodal interactive technologies.

Werner W. Marin graduated in Computer Sciences (2018) by the Mackenzie Presbyterian University. His areas of research include creativity, education, serious games, and digital games.

Regina Moraes is an Associate Professor at the University of Campinas (UNICAMP), Brazil, where she has been involved in the research on dependable computing since 2002. She is currently the head of the Information Engineering and Systems Group of the UNICAMP. Her research interests include experimental dependability and security evaluation (including cloud environment and network), privacy solutions, fault injection and robustness testing. Regina Moraes has served on programme committees of Brazilian and Latino-American dependability conferences. She has participated in several national and international research projects including JiTClouds supported by RNP / CTIC, DEVASSES and EuBra-BigSea and ATMOSPHERE.

Hafiz Muhammad Munir has an undergraduate in electronic engineering from the University of Engineering and Technology, Taxila, Pakistan in 2015. I have studied mechatronics engineering from the National University of Sciences and Technology, Islamabad, Pakistan. I have received a master's degree in Mechanical Engineering from Tokai University, Japan in 2020. My research area includes computer vision, human friendly robot and Eye-tracking application.

Pollyana Notargiacomo graduated in pedagogy (1992) from the University of São Paulo, an institution where she also earned the title of Master (1999) and Doctor of Education (2003). In 2015, she obtained a postdoctoral degree in Electrical Engineering by Federal University of Uberlândia (UFU). She is currently a Professor at Mackenzie Presbyterian University, where she develops activities for research and teaching at the Computer Science College and Electrical Engineering and Computer Graduate Course. Among her areas of research, the following themes stand out: serious games, game culture studies, game design, game mechanics, narratology, instructional design, distance learning, podcasts, and social media.

Chien-Wen Ou-Yang received his master's degree in Department of Computer Science, National Chiao Tung University in 2015. He is working as a software engineer in Rayark.

Tatyana Petrovna Popova is an Associate Professor of the Department of Applied Linguistics and Foreign Languages at the National Research University Higher School of Economics (HSE) Nizhny Novgorod (current position). She has a degree of a Candidate of Pedagogical Sciences obtained in Lomonosov Moscow State University in 2000. Her research interests lie in the areas of Technology- based learning, Academic English, Methodology of Teaching foreign languages.

Maria Alcileia Rocha received a Computer Technologist's Degree from the IFFluminense and a Master's Degree in Production Engineering from the State University of North Fluminense (UENF) in 2005 and 2009 respectively. She is an IT teacher in IFFluminense, a Brazilian VET school in upstate Rio. Her research interests include software quality, web accessibility, and educational technologies.

Saulo Silva is a PhD candidate in the Informatics PhD Program at the University of Minho. He holds a Bachelor (BSc) degree in Informatics and a Master (MSc) degree in Sustainable Process Technologies (SPT), both from Federal Institute of Science and Technology of Goiás (IFG). His research interests are in the area of Human-Machine Interfaces (HMI) of Cyber-Physical Systems (CPS), with special interests in those with high-assurance needs, in which the combination of modelling and analysis of the Interactive Systems considering Human Factors and Software Engineering aspects might play an important role in the resulting Human Computer Interaction (HCI) process(es).

Chuen-Tsai Sun received a B.S. degree in electrical engineering from the National Taiwan University, Taiwan, in 1986. He received a Ph.D. degree in EECS from University of California, Berkeley, in 1992. He is now a Distinguished Professor in the Department of Computer Science, National Chiao Tung University. Since 2011, he has been the discipline coordinator of the digital learning discipline in the National Science Committee in Taiwan. He is the author of several books and more than 150 papers. His current research interests are about game-based learning, game AI, and culture issues of digital media.

Vivian Varnava received her bachelor's degree in Computer Science from the University of Edinburgh in 2019. During her final year, she worked on a research project about how technology can help children with autism cope with changes. She currently works as a software developer. Her research interests include mobile development and Human-Computer Interaction (HCI).

Eugene Vladimirovich Popov is a Professor (current position) of the Nizhegorodsky Architectural and Civil Engineering University. His Academic titles are Professor and Doctor of Science. His scientific interests are in the fields of Scientific Visualization, Descriptive Geometry, Computer Graphics, CAD/CAM/CAE and RP Technologies, Research in CALS-Technologies, Geometry &Computer Graphics. He is also teaching Engineering Geometry and Computer Graphics to undergraduates as well as postgraduates. His teaching experience includes supervision of Ph.D. students and Dip Engineers. Since 2017 he has been Chairman of the Academic Council of Nizhegorodsky Architectural and Civil Engineering University. He has published more than 100 scientific works.

Jürgen Vogt is the former director of the Section of Chemical Information Systems at the University of Ulm, Germany. The fields of his scientific interests are Physical Chemistry (especially the Structural Chemistry of isolated molecules) and Applied chemoinformatics (especially the development, upkeep, and maintenance of the molecular gas-phase documentation database called MOGADOC). He has written over 80 scientific publications; among them he has coauthored a handbook and a textbook in chemoinformatics as well as 20 handbooks on structural and spectroscopic properties of free polyatomic molecules.

Natalja Vogt is a Professor (current position), Doctor of Science at the Chemistry Department of Lomonosov Moscow State University (Russia) and a Senior Scientist at the Section of Chemical Information Systems of the University of Ulm (Germany). The fields of her scientific interests are Physical Chemistry (especially gas-phase electron diffraction and rotational spectroscopy) and chemoinformatics (mainly the development of the MOGADOC database with experimental gas-phase molecular structures). She has published about 110 papers in scientific journals. She is a coauthor of two textbooks and editor and/or coauthor of twelve monographs with the title "Structure Data of Free Polyatomic Molecules" (the last one was published by Springer Nature Switzerland in 2019).

Hao Wang received B.S. degrees in both computer science and management science from the National Chiao Tung University, Taiwan, 2005. He received a M.S. degree in complex adaptive systems from the Chalmers University of Technology, Sweden, in 2005. He is currently working towards a Ph.D. in computer science. His main research interests are game AI, player modeling, and learning in games.

Soonja Yeom is a lecturer in the School of Engineering and ICT, Faculty of Science, Engineering, and Technology. She teaches Secure web programming, dynamic web development, and data science of the Bachelor of ICT and Master of IT courses. Soonja was the Program Chair of the International Conference on Smart Media and Applications in 2016. Also, Soonja has been invited as a speaker at various workshops and conferences and an invited reviewer of a number of conference. Her main areas of research include technology-enhanced learning, human computer interface, affective computing, computer security, and Big Data analytics.

Index

Ensure Quality Research is Introduced to the Academic Community

Become an IGI Global Reviewer for Authored Book Projects

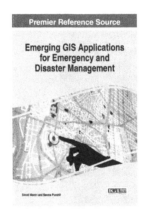
Premier Reference Source
Emerging GIS Applications for Emergency and Disaster Management

Premier Reference Source
Managerial Strategies and Green Solutions for Project Sustainability

Premier Reference Source
Comparative Approaches to Using R and Python for Statistical Data Analysis

Premier Reference Source
Solutions for High-Touch Communications in a High-Tech World

The overall success of an authored book project is dependent on quality and timely reviews.

In this competitive age of scholarly publishing, constructive and timely feedback significantly expedites the turnaround time of manuscripts from submission to acceptance, allowing the publication and discovery of forward-thinking research at a much more expeditious rate. Several IGI Global authored book projects are currently seeking highly-qualified experts in the field to fill vacancies on their respective editorial review boards:

Applications and Inquiries may be sent to:
development@igi-global.com

Applicants must have a doctorate (or an equivalent degree) as well as publishing and reviewing experience. Reviewers are asked to complete the open-ended evaluation questions with as much detail as possible in a timely, collegial, and constructive manner. All reviewers' tenures run for one-year terms on the editorial review boards and are expected to complete at least three reviews per term. Upon successful completion of this term, reviewers can be considered for an additional term.

If you have a colleague that may be interested in this opportunity,
we encourage you to share this information with them.

Printed in the United States
By Bookmasters